Historical Dictionary of
CHILE

Second Edition
revised, enlarged, and updated

by
SALVATORE BIZZARRO

Latin American Historical Dictionaries, No. 7

The Scarecrow Press, Inc.
Metuchen, N.J., & London
1987

Library of Congress Cataloging-in-Publication Data

Bizzarro, Salvatore.
    Historical dictionary of Chile.

    (Latin American historical dictionaries ; no. 7)
    Bibliography: p.
    1. Chile--Dictionaries and encyclopedias.
I. Title. II. Series.
F3054.B5 1987   983'.003'21   87-4681
ISBN 0-8108-1964-3

This book is dedicated to Salvador Allende, Carlos Prats, Orlando Letelier, José de Tohá, and the countless other Chileans who were killed or tortured without ever compromising their democratic ideals. This book is also dedicated to the Chilean men and women who are struggling against the military regime installed in their country on September 11, 1973. They deserve our solidarity and active support. ¡VIVA CHILE MIERDA!

CONTENTS

ACKNOWLEDGMENTS

Most of the research for the second edition of the <u>Historical Dictionary of Chile</u> was done in Santiago during the summer of 1975 and in Washington, D.C. since then, and was made possible by generous financial assistance from the Colorado College.

I should like to thank first of all the writers who have preceded me in the study of Chile, especially Lîa Cortés, Jordi Fuentes, Jaime Eyzaguirre, K. H. Silvert, Luîs Galdames, Eduardo Labarca Goddard, Jorge Palacios, Stefan de Wylder, Byron Milius, Carmen Castillo, Arturo and Samuel Valenzuela, Laurence Birns, Ernst Halperin, James Petras, Penny Lernoux, Sheila Cassidy, Carol Andreas, and so many others, from whose work I have gleaned countless details.

I am deeply grateful to my wife, Kathy Surman, for her invaluable and faultless help with statistical research; to my friend Carlo Castelli for allowing me to use the libraries of the World Bank and the International Monetary Fund, and for his advice in matters dealing with the economy; to my secretary Betty Welch for her typing and computer printing, but mostly for her patience; to Mary Lynn Sheetz for providing the expertise in her line drawings of Chilean maps and calligraphy that she brings to all her work; and to the Colorado College Reference Librarian, Robin Satterwhite, for her courteous assistance in finding obscure references.

The series editor, Laurence Hallewell, read and commented extensively on various drafts for the second edition, especially being helpful with materials dealing with the earlier periods of Chilean history. He is a critic in the best sense of the word and has strengthened the manuscript in numerous ways. In a manner of speaking, this is his book too.

Finally, a word of appreciation to my many Chilean friends who helped make the preparation of this book such a rich experience.

Salvatore Bizzarro

CHILE

EDITOR'S FOREWORD TO THE SECOND EDITION

The first edition of Professor Bizzarro's <u>Historical Dictionary of Chile</u> came out when Salvador Allende had recently embarked on what was proclaimed to be the peaceful, constitutional Chilean road to Socialism. After an early success, with rapidly rising living standards, he failed --or was not permitted to succeed, according to your point of view. Now, sixteen years later, we seem (hopefully?) to be approaching the end of a completely contrary experiment, which, in its time, also presented an equally dramatic (and equally short-lived) success story.

Sixteen years ago it was the common wisdom that Chile was the most stable, most democratic, most civilized country in South America, with the most impartial courts and police, and the least politicized armed forces. Now it is the common wisdom that Chile's history is one of continual political oscillation, with violent revolution--suppressed, narrowly averted, or triumphant--in 1810, 1814, 1817, 1829, 1851, 1859, 1891, 1924, 1927, 1931, 1932, 1937, 1939, 1969, 1973; to say nothing of wars, or rumors of wars, in 1819-22, 1836-39, 1843, 1865-66, 1877, 1879-83, 1896, 1914, 1945, 1982....

Chile has been an independent nation for only just over a century and a half, so perhaps a longer time-frame is needed before we can decide fairly which of these two gross generalizations comes nearer to the truth. One difficulty, perhaps, is that we are still suffering from what one might call the "Myth of the 19th-Century Norm": the belief that whatever characterized the pre-World War One <u>Belle Epoque</u> (and a few years on either side)--relative political, social and monetary stability, recognized rules of personal, institutional, and international conduct, fixed and respected frontiers, tolerance of alien beliefs, eternal material progress, and so on--is somehow part of the natural order of things, in Chile or elsewhere, and that everything else is a temporary and accidental aberration requiring explanation, when the converse is rather nearer the truth.

Now the whole world is living in what the old Chinese curse calls "interesting times." Chile has had the singular fate of having served as a living laboratory for the successive experiments of two completely opposed schools of socio-political theory. For this reason, the last sixteen years, however traumatic for the Chileans who have had to live through them, are of exceptional interest to the student of modern society and government.

In revising and enlarging this Historical Dictionary of Chile, Professor Bizzarro has accordingly paid particular attention to the 1970s and 1980s. Nevertheless, elaboration of the dictionary's treatment of the earlier periods of Chilean history has not been foregone. Notice has been taken of criticisms of the first edition, and the reader will find that this new version compares very favorably with its predecessor in its coverage of the pre-1970 years also.

The result should prove eminently useful to anyone needing information on any period and almost any aspect of this interesting, albeit in recent times singularly unfortunate, country.

Laurence Hallewell
Ohio State University

FOREWORD TO THE FIRST EDITION

Chile has been described as a "geographical extravaganza" by one of
its leading writers. Its northern section contains one of the most
absolute deserts in the world, while its southern extremity is one of
the wettest, windiest, and coldest areas in the Western Hemisphere.
The central heartland, the "Valley of Chile," has often been called
the "California of South America." Its mountainous backbone, snow
covered and earthquake prone, shares with Argentina several "Swit-
zerlands." Its banana shape, if placed on a map of North America,
would extend from Canada to Cuba, while if placed horizontally on
a map of the United States it would reach from New York City to
Los Angeles.

Historically, Chile may be as well described as a "political extravaganza." It has had some 60 political parties and scores of political factions and splinter groups ranging through every political
persuasion: Conservative, Liberal, Social, Christian Democrat, Communist, Marxist, and multiple combinations of these and others. In-
numerable cabinet changes, which give the impression of political
fickleness, have allowed politicians to express their individualism and
to let off political steam from the body politic. With all its numerous
large and small political disturbances, Chile has had only nine constitutions, and relative political stability has been the rule. One factor
contributing to this characteristic has been the largely European immigrants who have provided social leaven and a cultural stimulus
during more than a century. As the most militant country in South
America, Chile has made use of Germans to train the army and of
British to develop the navy. And to finance many national projects
and to improve life in general the government has encouraged Americans from the United States to develop its industry and promote its
prosperity. At present, however, national political, economic, and
social objectives are changing, as may be seen from this presentation.

Dr. Bizzarro, like other compilers of volumes in this series,
was given the assignment of selecting topics for inclusion which to
him seemed logical, comprehensive, and justifiable so that a well-
balanced guide to historical facts would result. Here as a result is
a concise and detailed historical dictionary showing a clear compre-
hension of the Chilean people and their problems.

The author's understanding of Latin people results in part

from the fact that he was born of Italian parents and lived in Italy for 16 years, after which he went to the United States and became a citizen. His B.A. degree, taken at Fordham University in Spanish, was followed by an M.A. and a Ph.D. (1965; 1969) at Stanford University where his dissertation on a Chilean topic was entitled, "Social and Political Themes in the Poetry of Pablo Neruda from 1936 to 1950." He acquired early teaching experience at Stanford and he is now Assistant Professor of Spanish and Latin American Studies at Colorado College, Colorado Springs.

In the course of his investigations and academic activities, Dr. Bizzarro has studied and carried on research at the Universidad Católica (1962-63) in Santiago, Chile, in Cuernavaca, Mexico, and in Brazil, and he has several times visited all South American countries except Paraguay. He has been assisted in his research by grants from Stanford, Colorado College, the Ford Foundation, the United States Department of State, and the Foundation on the Arts and Humanities. His writings have appeared in scholarly publications and in the Encyclopaedia Britannica. In his present position Dr. Bizzarro has helped to create a Latin American program and his is offering a course on "Brazil and Hispanic America since Independence." This volume, which is the culmination of his special interest in Chile, makes an important contribution to a better understanding of that country.

A. Curtis Wilgus (1897-1981)
Late Emeritus Director
School of Inter-American Studies
University of Florida

INTRODUCTION

The following pages aim to present a global view of the history and politics of Chile, emphasizing the contemporary period. As a subject of study, the Historical Dictionary of Chile possesses all the liabilities which a balanced sense of intellectual concern would persuade any writer to avoid. It is not always easy to deal at the same time with controversial historical figures, living persons, contending political forces, and, in recent years, a massive polarization and urbanization of the people. At that level, one tends to examine historical data in a sketchy way. And how much more vulnerable classifications in a dictionary become when they are meant to give a factual identification of important people and events in the stormy contemporary scene.

All this is by way of admitting openly that much of what will be included here is subject to any number of qualifications and additions. And yet Chile, a country known up to 1973 for its political stability in the mercurial world of Latin American politics, has received much commentary in the United States, but surprisingly little objective study. Hence, it seemed useful to publish an up-to-date dictionary which would analyze not only the past, but also contemporary events.

As in other volumes in this series, the arrangement is by the English alphabet (ch follows cg, ll follows lk, ñ is treated as n). The order is word-by-word (SALA Y GOMEZ precedes SALAS CORVALAN). Acronyms (abbreviations pronounced as words--e.g., ACHA, LAFTA) are filed as single words, but letter abbreviations (e.g., I.T.T.) will be found at the head of their respective initial letter sections. The abbreviations St. (for "Saint") and Mc (for "Mac") are filed as if spelled out. Initial articles are ignored, with the traditional exception of French surnames.

Hispanic personal names consist of three elements: the baptismal (one or more given names), the patronymic, and lastly the maternal (sometimes preceded by "y")--or--in the case of a married woman--the marital (preceded by "de"). It is always the patronymic (the father's surname) which determines the filing order, even for a married woman. Thus Salvador Allende Gossens will be found under "A," his wife, Hortensia Beatriz Bussy de Allende, under "B," and their daughter, Isabel Allende Bussy, under "A." Prefixes are ignored, so Alberto de Solar is under "S."

Internationally known events, places, persons, and institutions can generally be found under the name by which they are normally referred to in English (Charles V, Easter Island, Inquisition, Jesuits). For Chilean institutions, organizations, and places, the Spanish name has mostly been used (Unidad Popular, Universidad de Chile), but many exceptions have been made where it was thought the reader might be likely to know only the English form (Army, Civil War of 1891, Congress, Parliamentary Period). Cross-references from forms not chosen have been liberally provided. Inverted forms, for example, "Obras públicas, Ministerio de," and "Pacific, War of," have been adopted to avoid bulking entries under such generic terms as "Battle," "Treaty," "War," etc. There are also entries for Spanish words peculiar to Chile or which have special Chilean connotations (e.g., Inquilino).

An asterisk is used throughout the text with any word used as an entry heading. Thus a mention of "Lord *Cochrane" is indicative of the article on "Cochrane, Thomas, 10th earl of Dundonald." Where the name (of an event, institution, person, place, etc.) is in capitals (e.g., COCHRANE, Thomas) and preceded by "See" or "See also," or followed by "q.v.," this indicates that, unlike a term merely asterisked, the corresponding entry is directly related to the subject being sought or discussed.

Any user of this work is invited to consult the various subentries under CHILE first, which together provide an overview of the country itself, as well as of this book.

More than a dozen years have passed since the original manuscript was completed--a long time in the frenetic history of the Chilean nation. Because of the extraordinary changes that have taken place in Chile since 1972, preparing the second edition of the Historical Dictionary of Chile was almost like writing a new book (only portions of the first edition were basically the same). Like its predecessor, the new volume treats in a concise and careful manner major figures and political events, focusing especially on the contemporary period and, even more specifically, on events since the coup d'état of September 11, 1973. A complete bibliography, subdivided by topics, appears at the end of the book. Sources of information include scholarly journals and monographs, official reports of the Chilean government and international organizations, documents obtained from the United States Congress, foreign and domestic newspapers, numerous periodicals, current books on Chile, and interviews with Chileans living in exile.

LIST OF ILLUSTRATIONS

THE DICTIONARY

ABC TREATY. In April 1915, three South American nations, *Argentina, *Brazil, and Chile, signed a treaty to act as a block in inter-American relations. This alliance lasted until the era (1945-55) of dictator Juan Domingo Perón, when both Brazil and Chile rejected the domineering attitude of Argentina in guiding their international interests. Argentina, which by the end of the 19th-century was one of the most prosperous countries in Latin America, had created the block in order to offset the *United States' concept of being the only country in the Western Hemisphere with a "manifest destiny" policy. The most important function of the ABC countries was that of mediation in international disputes. As early as 1915, President Woodrow Wilson accepted their mediation in the dispute between Mexico and the United States. The ABC powers were also responsible for drafting the peace plans between *Bolivia and Paraguay during the costly Chaco War (1928-35). The peace conference was held in Buenos Aires on July 1, 1935. A settlement of the war was finally achieved three years later in the Argentine capital, with the ABC countries mediating the peace terms with the aid of *Peru and the United States.

ABRAZO DEL ESTRECHO ("The Embrace on the *Strait [of Magellan]"). In 1896, Chile and *Argentina were on the brink of war over interpretation of the *Boundary Treaty of 1881. Largely owing to the efforts of Chilean *archbishop Mariano *Casanova Casanova, the two governments agreed to negotiate, and agreement in principle over the points in dispute was reached in 1898. To celebrate this, presidents Federico *Errázuriz Echaurren of Chile and Julio Argentino Roca of Argentina (who had been directly involved in the negotiations) held a prearranged meeting by warship in the Strait of Magellan in 1899.

Further detailed negotiations followed, leading to a series of four treaties signed by foreign ministers José Vergara Donoso of Chile and José Antonio Terry of Argentina on May 28, 1902, and known as the PACTOS DE MAYO (q.v.).

ABTAO. Inconclusive Spanish naval victory on February 2, 1866, in the War of 1865-66 with *Spain.

ACADEMIA DE GUERRA. Chile's *Army Staff College was modeled on the Brazilian Escola Superior de Guerra (combined armed forces' staff college), which had been refounded in its present form in 1949, with the help of a United States mission, to fight international Communism on the declared premise that "we live in a climate of world-wide war that will decide the destiny of Western civilization." The Chilean Academia has been further developed since the *coup d'état of 1973, and it is currently directed by General César Raúl *Benavides Escovar, army representative on the governing *junta, 1981-85.

ACADEMIA DE GUERRA DE LA FUERZA AEREA (AGA). The *Air Force Staff College is, like the ACADEMIA DE GUERRA (q.v.), modeled on *Brazil's anti-Communist Escola Superior de Guerra. The AGA's ideology stems from the "science" of geopolitics--the inter-relationship of geography and politics. Most of its teaching staff have studied in Brazil or the United States.

ACADEMIA DE HUMANISMO CRISTIANO. The Christian Humanism Academy was founded by Raúl Cardinal *Silva Henríquez in the late 1970s as a fact-finding component of the *Vicariate of Solidarity. It was a research and teaching institution that upheld the tradition of scholarly research on social issues at a time when the Vicariate was having difficulties with the government of strongman President Augusto *Pinochet Ugarte.

ACADEMIA DE LA LENGUA. The purpose of this scholarly academy is to be the guardian of the Spanish language. There is an Academia de la Lengua in virtually every Spanish-speaking country. In Chile, Rodolfo Oroz Scheibe is the director of the Academia, which now has 21 honorary members.

ACADEMIA DE SAN LUIS. South America's first technical college was founded in 1797 by Manuel de *Salas Corvalán to teach mathematics, drawing, surveying, mining engineering, and modern languages. It was later incorporated into the *Instituto Nacional.

ACCION CATOLICA CHILENA. Since the mid-1920s the Roman Catholic *Church has sought to distance itself from partisan politics, ceasing to endorse specific political parties or permit individual clergy to join them. It has endeavored, however, to develop cadres of laity committed to the practical application of the Church's social teaching in the secular world. Existing movements of socially concerned Catholic laymen in Germany, Italy, France, and Belgium were officially endorsed by the Vatican in the 1920s under the name "Catholic Action," and similar bodies were later created elsewhere, but their precise political orientation varied. In *Spain, Portugal, *Argentina, and *Peru they supported corporative (fascist) solutions. In Western Europe and Venezuela they provided the bases of post-World War Two Christian Democracy.

Chilean Catholic Action was founded by archbishop José Horacio

*Campillo Infante in November 1931. Its membership was 45,761
in 1936, and 58,071 in 1945, and was overwhelmingly middle and
upper class. Its relationship with the *Falange Nacional was distant. In 1947 its national episcopal chaplain, bishop Augusto Sa-
linas, publicly rebuked the Falange for favoring diplomatic relations with the *U.S.S.R. and promoting Catholic participation in
Marxist-led *trade unions. In the 1950s it spawned a number of
specialized branches. Those promoting working class participa-
tion--Juventud Obrera Católica and *Acción Sindical Chilena
(ASICH)--had little success, but the two Catholic student movements, Acción Universitaria Católica (AUC), formed in 1955, and
Juventud Estudantil Católica (JEC), were Chile's only effective
non-Marxist national student organizations and produced many
future *Partido Demócrata Cristiano leaders.

ACCION CHILENA ANTICOMUNISTA (AChA). A reactionary military
institution formed in 1946 to protest the admission of three Communist Party (*Partido Comunista Chileno) members in the cabinet
of the then President (1946-52) Gabriel *González Videla. It was
presided over by Artero Olavarria Bravo, Minister of Agriculture
in the government (1938-41) of Pedro *Aguirre Cerda. AChA's
aim was to prevent a Communist take-over in Chile. As part of
Chile's *armed forces, AChA had seven regiments and was responsible for many public demonstrations until it achieved its
goal in 1948, when Gonzalez Videla outlawed the Communist Party.
During the Eduardo *Frei Montalva and Salvador *Allende Gossens governments, AChA remained active and engaged in some
extralegal activities to keep Chile safe from Communism. It remains operational under the *Pinochet Ugarte regime. On June
5, 1984, a bomb was found in the garden of the home of opposition Christian Democrat leader Gabriel *Valdés Subercaseaux.
The bomb was wrapped in anti-opposition leaflets signed by members of AChA.

ACCION CIVICA. See: CONFEDERACION REPUBLICANA DE ACCION
CIVICA.

ACCION NACIONAL. (1) A political party of the right, formed in
1935 and dissolved in 1937, when it fused with the *Unión Republicana. The Executive President of Acción Nacional was Eulogio
*Sánchez Erráruriz, who had also been the founder of the *Milicia
Republicana. The party's ideology was: to oppose all extremist
ideas; to oppose dictatorships; and to create a new political force
to give Chile a strong and effective government. Its objectives
included the establishment of liberty and justice for all men, the
protection of private property, and the formation of a corporative
state.
    (2) A resurgence of the old Acción Nacional. Reestablished
in November 1963, it lasted until March 1965. In the presidential
elections of 1964, Acción Nacional backed the candidacy of Jorge
*Prat Echaurren. In the congressional elections of 1965, the

party announced the senatorial candidacies of Prat Echaureen and Sergio Onofre *Jarpa Reyes, but neither won election. As a result, the party ceased to exist legally after the elections. Its members joined the newly formed *Partido Nacional, a coalition of three parties from the right and the Independents in June 1966.

ACCION POPULAR INDEPENDIENTE (API). A political party which is left-of-center but not Marxist, founded in 1969 to aid the presidential candidacy of social democrat Rafael *Tarud Siwady. In December 1969, API joined a coalition of leftist parties which backed the candidacy of Socialist Salvador *Allende Gossens (see: UNIDAD POPULAR). With the advent of the military *junta, the party was proscribed from engaging in any activities.

ACCION POPULAR UNITARIA. See: MOVIMIENTO DE ACCION POPULAR UNITARIA.

ACCION REPUBLICANA. Political party organized in 1937 by the merging of the *Acción Nacional with the *Unión Republicana. This fusion was possible because of the two parties' similar doctrines, which were reflected in their common aims: 1) to awaken a sense of responsibility in the electors; 2) to respect the political *constitution of 1925; 3) to preserve law and order, and oppose dictatorships; 4) to incorporate power in the political life of Chile; 5) to secure universal suffrage; 6) to repudiate the class struggle; and, 7) to secure equal employment opportunities for all Chileans. In March 1937, the new party elected two deputies to *Congress, one of whom, Benjamin *Claro Velasco, became President of Acción Republicana. The party organ was the newspaper La *Aurora. The party did not win representation in the congressional elections of 1939, and was dissolved.

ACCION REVOLUCIONARIA SOCIALISTA. A precursor of the Socialist Party of Chile (*Partido Socialista de Chile), founded in 1931 by Oscar Schnake Vergara, Eugenio González Rojas, Augusto Pinto, Julio E. Valiente, Gregorio Guerra, and Mario Inostrosa, most of whom dropped out of politics or left the country. The party's aim was to unify the Socialist groups in Chile, and on April 19, 1933, the Socialist Party (*Partido Socialista, eventually to become the Partido Socialista de Chile) was founded.

ACCION SINDICAL CHILENA (ASICH). A private institution founded in 1950 to educate and advise Catholic trade unionists. (See: ACCION CATOLICA CHILENA.)

ACEVEDO HERNANDEZ, Antonio (1886-1962). One of the most prolific Chilean writers, who knew how to remain faithful to the essence of his country and his people through his many works in theater, novels, and folklore. He wrote some 40 plays and novels, and more than 800 chronicles about Chilean folklore. Among his most successful plays we find El rancho, La sangre, El vino triste,

Almas perdidas; some of his more famous novels are Cabrerita, Arbol viejo, Caín, La guerra a muerte, and Aventuras del roto Juan García. In 1936 he was awarded the National Theater Prize.

ACHA. See: ACCION CHILENA ANTICOMUNISTA.

ACHARAN ARCE, Carlos. Elected representative of the Liberal Party (*Partido Liberal). From 1926 to 1930 he was a deputy from *Valdivia, La Unión and Villarica, and Río Bueno. From 1933 to 1953 he represented Valdivia, La Unión, and *Osorno in the *Congress. From 1953 to 1961 he was senator from the 9th District. In the Senate, Acharán Arce was the promotor of a university reform bill which created the *Universidad Austral in Valdivia. He was also responsible for bringing government funds to the flooded zone of Valdivia, badly damaged by the *earthquake of 1960 and by incessant rain.

ACOMODADO. A person who is well-off financially; wealthy or fond of comfort.

ACONCAGUA. Former province and present region of central Chile. The province in its original form was constituted by the law of August 1826 that made Chile a federal republic (see: FEDERALISM). In 1842 it lost the Department of Quillota to the newly formed province of *Valparaíso, and lost further territory to that province in 1864, reducing its area to 14,210 km^2 (5,486 square miles). Subsequent readjustments in the 20th century reduced the province's area to 9,873 km^2 (3,812 square miles). The provincial capital was *San Felipe. This largely agricultural province experienced little growth of population, which was 124,828 in 1865; 128,486 in 1907; 128,378 in 1952; 159,752 in 1972 (est.).

In the reorganization of 1974 (see: REGIONS AND ADMINISTRATIVE RESTRUCTURING), Aconcagua was the name given to Region V, which embraces the former provinces of Aconcagua and *Valparaíso, the Department of San Antonio (from the former province of *Santiago), plus the *Juan Fernández Islands and *Easter Island, giving it a combined area of 16,109 km^2 (6,220 square miles) and a total estimated population in 1982 of 1,264,061. The regional capital is Valparaíso.

ACONCAGUA, Mount. Mountain on the Argentine border. The peak, which is on the Argentine side, rises to 22,835 feet, the highest point in the *Andes.

ACUERDO NACIONAL (Acuerdo para la transición hacia la plena democracia). See: FRESNO LARRAIN, Juan Francisco.

AD-MAPU (Asociación gremial de pequeños agricultores y artesanos de Chile). See: MAPUCHES.

ADELANTADOS. Royal appointees authorized to stake their own
fortunes in the colonization of new lands. The term comes from
the Spanish verb adelantar ("to advance"), and describes all
the discoverers, colonizers, and conquerors who came to the New
World. The adelantados had a wide range of powers. They were
not only the military leaders of the expedition, but also the
governors and legislators of the territory discovered. They had
the right to apportion lands and Indians, and to oversee the
development of the new lands. After the conquest there was
a period of consolidation and settlement, and the office of adelantado began to disappear.

ADENA (Acuerdo Democrático Nacional). See: FRESNO LARRAIN,
Juan Francisco.

ADUANA DE IQUIQUE ("The custom house of Iquique"). *Iquique
is a city in northern Chile, but when Chileans refer to Aduana
de Iquique they are reminded of a bloody battle on February 16,
1891, during the CIVIL WAR OF 1891 (q.v.) between the troops
of President (1886-91) José Manuel *Balmaceda Fernández, who
tried to occupy the city, and its defenders, who had sided with
the army of the revolutionary *Congress. The battle was won by
the revolutionaries and was an important early victory in their
fight to overthrow Balmaceda and establish the *Parliamentary
regime.

AFRICAN SLAVERY. Slavery was never important in Chile, thanks to
the largely pastoral nature of the Chilean economy, the climate,
and, above all, the limited capital resources of Chilean farmers.
The largest influx took place in the 16th century, but its actual
size was never confirmed. Estimates of the slave population circa
1650 range from 5,000 to 20,000. When Chile's first *census was
held in 1770 (limited to the diocese of Santiago--or most of central
Chile), some 25,508 Blacks were counted. Their relative unimport-
ance to the economy allowed Chile to become the second country
of the Americas (after Haiti) to end Negro slavery. All future
offspring of slaves were declared free in 1811, and any newly
imported slaves were to become free after six months' residence.
In 1823 Ramón *Freire Serrano was able to secure the total abolition of slavery in Chile.
    The subsequent fate of the 4,000 freed slaves is puzzling.
Many of them joined José de *San Martín's Ejército de los *Andes,
reputed to have included 1,500 former slaves. San Martín's reference to his Blacks and mulattoes as "the best infantry soldier we
have" may have indicated a readiness to squander them wherever
the fighting was fiercest, but it does not explain why there
were allegedly only 100 Blacks left in Chile by 1827. It may be
that those of San Martín's Black troops remaining after the campaign in *Peru settled there.
    Miscegenation is the usually accepted explanation for the virtual
disappearance of the Chilean Blacks. There were 2,000 persons

(slave or free) of mixed blood by 1650, and 20,651 enumerated in the 1770 census. Nowadays the only obvious case of African descent in the Chilean population is a small settlement of Blacks at Azapatal in *Arica, territory acquired from Peru in 1879.

AFUERINO. A migrant farm worker. See also: INQUILINO, PEON.

AGRARIAN REFORM. Prior to the military *coup d'état of September 11, 1973, there were two analogous but different agrarian reforms in Chile, initiated in 1965 by the Christian Democrats and in 1970 by the Socialists. At the beginning of the Eduardo *Frei Montalva administration (1964-1970) a mere 730 estates controlled half of Chile's agricultural land--over 25 million acres. In contrast, 45,233 farms were of less than 2.5 acres (1 hectare), and 159,769 were of less than 25 acres (10 hectares); 1.5 percent of the land-owners owned more than 70 percent of the land. In the fertile Central Valley, 8 percent of the landowners controlled more than 80 percent of the land. Almost half of the rural population was deprived of land ownership and survived as permanent laborers on the large estates (*latifundia). When things got tough, the rural poor were jarred loose from the estates on which they worked and went to the cities to look for work, often finding none and thus becoming human cyphers in the urban slums (see: INTERNAL MIGRATION).

As the elections of 1964 approached, the urgency of land reform could no longer be denied. The Christian Democrats (*Partido Demócrata Cristiano) promised a reform that would have expropriated all large land holdings not under cultivation; it would have given land to 100,000 *campesino families, regrouping into *cooperatives those farmers with plots too small to be productive. The coalition of leftist parties grouped as the *Frente de Acción Popular (FRAP), on the other hand, insisted on collective owner-ship of the land. While the Christian Democrats wanted to apply the mechanics of promotion to increase production, such as price and tax incentives, before redistributing the land, the left be-lieved that it was necessary to first give the land to those who farmed it and then provide them with technical aid.

After the election of Frei, the agrarian reform initiated by the Christian Democrats fell far short of their goal of 100,000 new landowners; only 20,000 families in fact received land. Although agricultural production was on the increase (3 percent annually, as against 1.8 percent per annum increase over the previous 30 years), Chile was importing $100 million worth of food a year. The peasants began to organize into unions, and some of them, motivated by unkept promises and continued injustice in the countryside, began to seize untilled land (a custom that was to become widespread during the presidency of Salvador *Allende Gossens).

It was not however until the *Unidad Popular government (1970-73) that agrarian reform accelerated, under great pressure from organized campesino groups. Cooperative structures (*asen-

<u>tamientos</u>) were created to rationalize the use of land, bank credits, and modern equipment, with the active participation of the rural majority traditionally disfranchised from national political power. In the case of land seizure, the MIR (*Movimiento de Izquierda Revolucionaria) made it clear to Allende that they would support the <u>campesinos</u>. By the demise of the Allende government in 1973, there were no longer any estates with more than 200 acres of prime land; over 40 percent of arable land was in the hands of the <u>campesinos</u>, who were by then massively organized.

After the *coup d'état, the *junta's policies regarding land tenure were clearly aimed at reinstating the <u>status quo ante</u>. All expropriation was immediately halted. Some 30 percent of the land already appropriated under Allende was returned to its former owners. Another 30 percent was auctioned off to private buyers, 33 percent was parceled into plots to be paid for by the new owners over a number of years, and the remaining 7 percent became government owned. The distribution was determined by a military-appointed commission. Members of the dissolved cooperatives wanting land exceeded by far the number of parcels of land to be assigned. Under the "law of the market," only those with capital could become new landowners. Open competition without state intervention was looked upon as the best way to achieve maximum efficiency. The government did, however, allow the assigning of titles to about 45,000 agrarian reform beneficiaries. The Agrarian Reform Corporation (*CORA) was dismantled in 1978.

By 1977, following the free trade norms of the Milton Friedman school, the junta sought to throw local producers into competition with the international market, eliminating significant tariffs on agricultural imports. Domestic price supports were likewise virtually eliminated. All controls on food prices except milk were removed. Even bread was "liberated" in 1978, and within months its retail price had gone up by 83 percent.

In sharp contrast to the two previous agrarian reforms, the real beneficiaries of the new agrarian policies were the wealthy. By 1984 most of the rich Central Valley was owned by the same *latifundistas as of old. Today 5 percent of Chilean families own 35 percent of the agricultural land. Overwhelmingly, these large landowners specialize in producing crops for export. The total value of farm exports expanded from $26 million worth in 1973 to almost $200 million in 1978. But in 1977 Chile imported $323 million worth of food products, and $430 million worth a year later, in contrast to the $165 million worth imported during the first year of the Allende agrarian reform program.

The peasants who had received their *minifundias under the Frei and Allende reforms were soon searching for work, as they were unable to borrow money for their farms with interest rates under the junta of up to 60 percent per annum, compared to 12 percent under Allende. Besides these displaced farmers, there were at least another 300,000 <u>campesinos</u> and their families without

jobs as a result of the junta's having taken away their land.
The bulk of such rural poor has migrated to the cities to seek
*employment (see: INTERNAL MIGRATION). Most of them have
discovered the harsh reality that survival in the cities is even
harder than it was in the countryside.

See also: AGRICULTURE; CAJA DE LA COLONIZACION
AGRICOLA; CONSEJOS COMUNALES.

AGRICULTURA, Ministerio de. The Ministry of Agriculture was
created by Statute no. 3524 on August 5, 1930, when the Department of Agriculture was separated from the Ministry of Development (Ministerio de *Fomento). The Development Ministry had
existed only since 1927; before then there had been a Ministerio
de *Agricultura, Industria y Colonización. The functions of the
Ministry of Agriculture have been to coordinate the development
of agricultural products, *livestock, and forestry, and to implement the *agrarian reforms of 1962, 1965, and 1971. Branches
of the ministry have included the Corporación de Reforma Agraria
(*CORA)--dismantled in 1978--and the Instituto de Desarrollo
Agropecuario (*INDAP).

Agriculture ministers since the *coup d'état have been: Colonel
Sergio Crespo Monterio (September 1973); General Tucapel
Vallejos Reginalto (July 1974); General Mario Mackay Jarquemada
(mid-1976), Alfonso Márquez de la Plata (April 1978); José Luis
Toro Hevia (December 1980), Jorge Prado Aranguiz (April 1982).

AGRICULTURA, INDUSTRIA Y COLONIZACION, Ministerio de. The
ministry of Agriculture, Industry and Land Settlement was created
by Statute no. 43 on October 14, 1924, when the Ministry of
Industry and Development (Ministerio de *Industria, Obras Públicas
y Ferrocarriles) was divided into two ministries, the other being
the Ministry of Public Works (Ministerio de *Obras y Vías Públicas).
The Ministry of Agriculture, Industry and Land Settlement coordinated the development of the agricultural, mining, and manufacturing sectors of the economy, as well as forestry and fishing.
In 1927 it was dissolved and the Ministry of Development (Ministerio de *Fomento) was created in its place.

AGRICULTURE. In early colonial times Chile had a largely pastoral
economy (see: CATTLE). *Wheat growing for export to *Peru
began in the late 17th century. When the Californian gold rush
began in 1848, Chile was almost the only wheat growing area in
the entire Pacific basin, and a dynamic export trade in wheat
and other foodstuffs quickly developed. Exports to California
began to fall after 1855 as that state's own wheatfields came into
production, but by then a similar market had been created by
Australia's gold rush. Although this market in turn failed to
last (largely due to competition from Californian wheat growing,
which began to produce a surplus for export in the 1860s), Chile
found another market (by way of *Cape Horn) in the River Plate
countries and Brazil. Lower freight costs, both at sea, and over-

land to the ports as Chilean *railways were developed, helped
hold down the cost of Chilean wheat, and in the 1870s it was
being sent to Europe. From the 1880s, however, it was priced
off the world market by the growth of wheat production in North
America, Australia, Russia and, eventually, *Argentina. By 1898
it was necessary to introduce a tariff on imported flour just to
preserve the home market. Although Chile's competitors had the
advantage of enormous extensions of flat wheatland in the prairies,
steppes, and pampas, Chile's failure to mechanize was at least
as important. Even its flour mills, which had been technically
advanced in the 1850s, were allowed to become obsolete while
cultivation and cropping remained primitive: ox-ploughs, broad-
cast sowing, harvesting with sickles, and threshing by trampling
persisted into the 1930s. Profits from *nitrates and, later,
*copper, were ample to pay for imported food, and the low pur-
chasing power of the average Chilean gave farmers no incentive
to improve the quality of their products.

Besides technical backwardness, there is the persistance of
an almost colonial land-ownership pattern, with the attendant ills
of absentee landlordism, and of holdings that are excessively large
(*latifundia) or excessively small (*minifundia) and frequently of
a size inappropriate for the crop being cultivated. Barely half
the rural population own any land at all. (See: AGRARIAN RE-
FORM; INQUILINO; PEON).

The Central Valley in particular has excellent soil and climate,
and prior to 1940 Chile remained, on balance, a net exporter of
agricultural products. Leading crops include wheat, barley, rice,
potatoes, citrus fruits, and grapes (which make excellent *wine).
LIVESTOCK (q.v.) is mainly *cattle in the Central Valley, and
*sheep farming in the far south.

Since the early 1940s, however, food imports have come to
make up half the nation's import bill. In 1947 agriculture contributed 17 percent of the gross national product; by 1971 this
proportion had fallen to 9 percent. Such natural problems as
the serious droughts of 1961-62, 1964-65, 1968-69, and almost
every two or three years since then, have also affected production.
Nevertheless, the period of the Eduardo *Frei Montalva and
Salvador *Allende Gossens land reforms boosted production until
about 1971, when the rate of increase fell below that of the
natural growth of *population, due in large part to the destabilization of the countryside. Allende's policies stimulated consumer
demand, but many medium- and large-scale farmers "froze" their
output and refused to invest in their farms or even to cultivate
them at all. Rapid expropriation followed, coupled with increases
in the outright illegal land seizures that had begun shortly after
Allende's accession. The peasants who remained in the countryside to work on the large expropriated estates were free from
their bondage to the big landlords but became dependent on a far
more demagogic state bureaucracy, against which it was more
difficult to fight. Profit expectations among the *campesinos
were increased, and loans were given by the State Bank (Banco

del Estado de Chile) with few strings attached. But by the end
of 1972, the new agrarian reform centers (*asentamientos), far
from making profits, were deeper in debt to the bank. This,
in turn, led to large-scale black marketeering, in which many
*asentados participated by falsifying production data. Those
opposed to the government, particularly the big landlords, engaged
in outright sabotage, burning crops, slaughtering livestock, and
supplying only the *black market.

Sixteen years of military rule has not eliminated the backwardness in Chilean agriculture. The average annual increase in
output since 1973 has never exceeded 1.8 percent, and agriculture's share of the gross national product continues to fall--to
only 7.8 percent in 1985. Countless farmers have gone out of
business, unable to meet their financial obligations in the face
of interest rates of 60 percent per annum. Erosion of the agricultural labor force continues. In 1971 agriculture was employing
28 percent of the national workforce (compared with 1.9 percent
in the *United Kingdom and a Latin American average of 33 percent). By 1985 this proportion was down to 18 percent.

As a result the industry is stagnating, aggravating the balance-
of-trade situation. Many latifundistas prefer to grow grapes,
peaches, nectarines, plums, pears, and other fruit for export,
this being more profitable than the cultivation of such staples
as rice, beans, and grain for internal consumption, so making
Chile ever more dependent on the importation of foodstuffs.

AGUIRRE, Francisco de (1500?-1580). *Conquistador and founder of
  La *Serena. Born in Talavera, Spain, he came to the New World
  with Pizarro in 1536, accompanied Pedro de *Valdivia to Chile in
  1540, and became *alcalde mayor of *Santiago in 1541, 1545, and
  1549. In 1551 Valdivia made him lieutenant governor over northern
  Chile. In the 1560s, on an expedition to Tucumán, mutineers
  denounced him to the *Inquisition. This resulted in the loss of
  his governorship of the new province, a heavy fine, and five
  years' imprisonment. He died poor and lonely in La Serena.

AGUIRRE CERDA, Pedro (1879-1941). Lawyer, large landowner,
  leader of the Radical Party (*Partido Radical), Aguirre Cerda
  became President of Chile from 1938 to 1941, the year in which he
  died. He won the presidential elections with the help of the
  Popular Front (*Frente Popular), a Socialist-Communist-dominated
  coalition, defeating Gustavo *Ross Santa María, the candidate of
  the Right, by some 9,000 votes. A major *earthquake in January
  1939 slowed down the economic progress made under his administration and the one immediately previous. On assuming the
  presidency, Aguirre Cerda had pledged "to end conditions in
  which the Chilean masses lack food, culture, clothes and dwellings."
  But the earthquake brought about much ruin, from *Santiago to
  *Valdivia. More than 50,000 were killed, 60,000 were injured,
  and 750,000 were made homeless. The government, as a result,
  had to bend every effort for the relief of the sufferers. Never-

theless, a year later the Aguirre Cerda government announced
a vast Industrialization Program involving the expenditure of
$24 million ($12 million of which came from a loan extended by the
U.S. Export-Import Bank). Great strides were made in electrification and in exploration for oil. The boundaries of Chilean
*Antartica were formally defined, a minimum wage was established,
and the government embarked upon a massive program of social
welfare.

When the Republicans were defeated in the Spanish Civil War
(1936-1939), Aguirre Cerda opened the door to emigrants from
Spain (see: SPAIN, RELATIONS WITH). His wife, Juana Aguirre
Luco de Aguirre, undertook many charitable works for the poor,
especially for children. Of all the Chilean governments to that
date, only that of Aguirre Cerda had a popular base. The President had insisted on identifying himself with the people, gaining
the support of the masses and of the Frente Popular. Before
becoming President, Aguirre Cerda held many important posts
in government. He was Radical deputy from the province of *San
Felipe (1915-18) and from Santiago (1918-21). In 1921 he was
named Minister of Justice and Public *Education, and was responsible for making education compulsory for children through grade
school, thus reducing the number of illiterates in Chile. From
1921 to 1924 he was senator from *Concepción, and in the latter
year he was the leader in the cabinet of the then President (1920-
24) Arturo *Alessandri Palma.

Ownership of extensive vineyards led to his acquiring the nickname "Don Tinto" (Mr. Red Wine).

AIR FORCE. The Fuerza Aérea Chilena (FACh) had its beginnings
in the School of Military Aeronautics set up in February 1913,
but there was no effective aerial fighting force until the end of
World War I when British fliers and engineers began training a
select group of Chilean *army officers for combat, reconnaissance
duties, and aircraft maintenance. The *navy acquired its air arm
in 1919, and the air arms of both services were brought together
in March 1930 to form an independent air force, which was used
the following year to suppress the naval mutiny of *Coquimbo.
The navy was however allowed in 1953 to have its own air arm
again for sea patrol duty, and more recently the army has acquired a few aircraft.

Chilean airmen participated in the coups d'état of 1925 and
1932, both times under the leadership of career officer Marmaduke
*Grove Vallejo. After remaining neutral for the next forty years,
the air force became enmeshed in politics again in 1973, when all
three *armed forces joined in the *coup that toppled President
Salvador *Allende Gossens. Air force commander-in-chief General
Gustavo *Leigh Guzmán helped engineer the coup, in which the
bombardment of the *Moneda Palace by Hawker "Hunters" especially
equipped with rockets was the most spectacular, if not the most
decisive, factor. Leigh was regarded then as the most hard-line
*junta member, but he later became one of President Augusto

*Pinochet Ugarte's most vocal critics. By July 1978 he was per-
ceived as a rival for the leadership and abruptly dismissed from
both the junta and the air force. His departure was accompanied
by the forced resignation of 18 out of the 20 remaining air force
generals, with the implied threat that further trouble would be
resolved by the demotion of the FACh to a mere army air corps.
The two generals who remained, Air General Fernando *Matthey
Aubel and Air Brigadier Javier Lopetegui Torres, became the new
FACh c.-in-c. and chief of staff, respectively. But complete
docility has yet to be attained: in September 1984, Matthey publicly advocated congressional elections for 1986.

The air force has an officer training school, its own staff
college (the *Academia de Guerra de la Fuerza Aérea), and an
all-volunteer strength of 15,000 men, with 85 first-line aircraft
(including 18 F-5 fighter-bombers) and 250 second-line aircraft).
Until recently almost all equipment was American or British, but
France supplied Mirage-50 fighter-bombers in 1979, and Spain has
since sold Chile some other modern airplanes. THe FACh's only
Chilean-built plane is the Pillán T-35 trainer (see: ARMAMENTS).

The FACh is divided into 12 groups, each comprising one
squadron, with 3 combat wings and a support wing. Its main
bases are at Cerro Moreno (near *Antofagasta), Los *Cerrillos
(near *Santiago), *Puerto Montt, and *Punta Arenas. There
are three commands: Combat, Personnel, and Logistics.

AIR TRANSPORT. Chile's difficult topography, with its mountains,
deserts, forests, and glaciers, poses formidable communication
problems which air transport has done much to resolve: a fourth
of all journeys in passenger miles are now made by air. A
Frenchman, Louis Testart, began commercial air service in 1925
in Chile, between *Iquique, *Valparaíso, *Santiago and *Concepción, but ceased a year later when his only airplane crashed.
The need for an airmail service led the government to create
the Línea Aéreo-Postal Santiago-*Arica in 1929, and this became
the national airline of Chile, LAN-CHILE (q.v.) in 1932.

In 1960 the Chilean government set up the Junta de Aeronáutica
Civil (Civil Aviation Board) to decide policy and regulate fares,
and the Dirección General de Aeronáutica Civil (Civil Aviation
General Directorate) to administer *airports and exercise technical
control over the industry. Both bodies are now subordinate to
the Ministerio de *Transportes y Telecomunicaciones.

A privately owned airline, LADECO (q.v.) was established
in 1958 and is now the dominant carrier for mainland Chile's
internal services. There are now four other small domestic air-
lines and about 23 providers of air taxi services.

AIRPORTS. Chile has ten international airports, of which the six
most important are Comodoro Arturo *Merino Benítez (formerly
*Pudahuel) for *Santiago (3,480 meter runway), President Ibáñez
(formerly Chabunco) at *Punta Arenas (2,245 m), Chacalluta for
*Arica (2,175 m), Cerro Moreno for *Antofagasta (2,050 m), El

Tepual for *Puerto Montt (2,050 m) and Mataveri on *Easter Island
(2,007 m). The others are Balmaceda (for *Coyhaique and *Aysén), Carriel Sur (for *Concepción), Pichoy (for *Valdivia) and
Santiago's second airport at Los *Cerrillos. There are 18 major
domestic airports, and another 18 with paved runways. To this
total of 48 airports may be added a further 305 usable airfields.

AISEN. Variant spelling of AYSEN (q.v.).

ALADI (Alianza Latinoamericana de Integración). See: LATIN AMERI-
CAN INTEGRATION ASSOCIATION

ALALC (Asociación Latinoamericana de Libre Comercio). See: LATIN
AMERICAN FREE TRADE ASSOCIATION:

ALAMEDA. Literally a grove or row of plane trees, the name is
given to the principal (and originally, tree-lined) avenue of some
Hispanic cities. The Alameda of *Santiago was laid out by Bernar-
do *O'Higgins and was formally known as the Avenida de las
Delicias. It has since been renamed the Avenida Bernardo
O'Higgins, but is still often referred to as the Alameda.

ALAMEDA VIEJA DE LA CONCEPCION. Site of a battle fought in the
city of *Concepción on November 27, 1820, between the Spanish
forces led by Vicente *Benavides and the Chilean forces led by
Ramón *Freire Serrano. It was an episode of the so-called "War
to the Death" (*Guerra a muerte), during which these two opposing forces committed cruelties and war crimes. The troops
of Benavides, fighting to restore Spanish power in Chile, surrendered.

ALCABALA. A sales tax originating in the Roman gabella, adopted
by the Moors (hence the phonetic form of the word) and brought
to Chile by the Spanish colonial administration. Originally 2
percent, it was increased in the 18th century to 6 percent. The
system of tax farming practiced under the early Republic gave
the businessmen who collected it the unfair advantage of knowing
financial details of their competitors' businesses. For this reason
it was largely abolished by Manuel *Rengifo Cárdenas, who introduced the *Catastro instead.

ALCALDE. Office of town magistrate originated in medieval Spain.
In modern Chile the position corresponds to that of an Anglo-
American mayor (see: LOCAL GOVERNMENT). See also:
ALCALDE MAYOR, ALCALDE ORDINARIO.

ALCALDE BASCUNAN, Juan Agustín (1798-1860). Fourth Count of
the Quinta Alegre who fought in the Wars of Independence (1810)
and held numerous public offices in the newly formed Chilean
state. He was *regidor of the *Cabildo Abierto of 1810. His
parliamentary activities were: deputy from *Santiago at the first

National *Congress of Chile (July 4, 1811); senator in 1818; president of the Conservative Senate from 1820 to 1822; vice-president of the Provincial Assembly of *Santiago (1827); and deputy in *Congress (1827-31). In 1831 he created the Commission on Agriculture and Mining; in 1834, the Commission on War and the *Navy. He was senator again from 1840 to 1860, in which year he died in office.

ALCALDE MAYOR. Royal appointee chosen in the colonies at the recommendation of the viceroy for a three-year period. Alcaldes mayores presided over municipalities (see: CABILDOS) and other administrative units of varying size and importance.

ALCALDE ORDINARIO. Colonial magistrate and municipal clerk, performing functions within the municipality subordinate to the *Alcalde Mayor.

ALDUNATE CARRERA, Luis (1841-1908). Candidate of the Right for the presidential elections of 1866, Aldunate Carrera held many important diplomatic posts. As a lawyer, he was sent to *Peru in 1865 to sign the treaty of *Chincha Alta between Chile and Peru (later Ecuador and Bolivia also signed). In 1866 he was sent to the *United States as secretary of the Chilean delegation in Washington, DC. He then returned to run for President, backed by the Radicals (*Partido Radical), Liberals (*Partido Liberal) and the Nationals (*Partido Nacional), but lost to José Francisco *Vergara Echevers. His other official appointments included that of surrogate judge in Chile's highest court, and positions in the ministries of the interior, of foreign affairs and of the treasury. In 1865 he was designated Minister Plenipotentiary to Chile by the government of Guatemala, an honorary post which he declined. Queen Isabel II (1833-68) of Spain conferred upon him the Cross of the Order of Isabel the Catholic. From 1895 to 1896 he was Minister of the Anglo-Chilean Tribunal. He also wrote numerous treatises on the economic and commercial status of Chile.

ALDUNATE ERRARURIZ, Fernando (b. 1895). A lawyer who exercised his skills in various commercial, *mining and industrial enterprises. After graduating he became Professor of Law at the *Universidad de Chile, and also taught at the *Universidad Católica. From 1930 to 1932 he was a member of the Commission which drew up the Mining Labor Code. As a Conservative, he was elected deputy and later senator to *Congress from 1934 to 1953. Among his civic posts, he was President of the Banco Central de Chile, of the Compañía Acera del Pacífico (*CAP), of the Banco de Crédito e Inversiones, and of various other companies. From 1956 to 1957 he was Chilean ambassador to *Argentina, and from 1959 to 1963, Chilean ambassador to the Vatican. Until the late 1960s he was one of the executive members of the *Partido Conservador.

ALDUNATE PHILLIPS, Arturo (1900-?). Chilean author and critic
who wrote the first book of criticism on the now famous Veinte
poemas de amor y una canción desesperada, a collection of poems
by Pablo *Neruda. From 1940 to 1960 he was president of
*Endesa, the Chilean equivalent of Con-Edison in electricity.
During the 1960s he wrote books on scientific research and space
travel, having become an expert on unidentified flying objects
(UFOs). His A horcajadas en la luz deals with life in the universe.
Aldunate Phillips has taken many trips abroad and has visited
Russian and U.S. space centers, where he has collected materials
for his books. He is a member of the *Academia de la Lengua.

ALDUNATE TORO, José Santiago (1796-1864). A career military officer who participated in the Chilean struggle for *independence
from 1810 to 1818. He was a captain in the *army of Bernardo
*O'Higgins and took part in the battle of *Rancagua. In 1820
he was sent to *Peru by the Argentine liberator José de *San
Martín and fought for that country's independence also. He was
wounded in Peru, and for his military services received the gold
medal. In 1839 he retired from the military. Three years later,
he was named Minister of the Interior in the conservative cabinet
of President (1841-51) Manuel *Bulnes Prieto. In 1847, Aldunate
Toro became director of the *Escuela Militar, a post he resigned
to run unsuccessfully for the presidency of Chile in 1851.

ALESSANDRI PALMA, Arturo (1868-1950). Twice President of Chile
(1920-24; 1932-38). He was born in the central province of
*Linares (south of *Santiago) and died in the capital. In 1893
he received a law degree and became an active member of the
Liberal Party (*Partido Liberal). He entered *Congress as a
representative in 1897. In 1915 he acquired his "Lion of Tarapacá"
nickname for successfully challenging the local political boss for
that province's senate seat. He held many ministerial posts,
including those of Industry and Public Works (1908), Finance
(1913) and the Interior (1918). Backed by the *Alianza Liberal
and the *Partido Democrático, he ran for President of Chile in
1920 and won, being inaugurated on December 23 of that year.
The Alessandri government incurred a period of economic depression (coinciding with the postwar world depression), due to a
drastic decrease in *nitrate exports, and was afflicted by unrest
within the military. In the Senate, conservatives consistently refused to cooperate with the program presented by Alessandri,
which would have drawn funds from a wealthy minority (through
land and income *taxes) to aid the poor and improve working
conditions, health, *education and welfare.
    The general unrest between 1920 and 1924 was increased by
the fact that the pay of public servants and of the military had
fallen in arrears; unemployment was on the rise; the masses were
ragged and hungry. Alessandri reworked his cabinet sixteen
times and finally brought to Congress a majority favorable to his
programs. Although the *army's pay was increased, the military

tried to force the President to devalue the Chilean *peso in order
to alleviate the economic conditions of the population. Unable to
cope with these demands and harrassed by Congress, Alessandri
took the initiative in September 1924 and resigned. Ironically,
Congress would not accept his resignation and granted him a six-
month leave of absence. Alessandri went to Europe, and a military
junta (*junta militar de 1924), headed by General Luis *Altamirano
Talavera, assumed the government of Chile. The junta, in turn,
was forced to resign by junior army officers who accused Altamirano of not bringing about social reforms.

Alessandri was invited by Carlos *Ibáñez del Campo, head of
the new military junta, to return to Chile, and did so in March
1925. A constituent assembly was called immediately to amend
the constitution. *Church and state became separate, and, in
August the new *Constitution of 1925 became law. Because of
a quarrel with Ibáñez, who had been made Minister of War, Alessandri resigned again on October 1, 1925, appointing Luis *Barros
Borgoño to succeed him. New elections were held in the same
year, and Emiliano *Figueroa Larraín became President, resigning
in May 1927 when Ibáñez became President. Ibáñez's government
was seriously affected by the world *depression, and in 1931 he
resigned.

The so-called period of *Anarquía Política ended with the
election of October 1932, which began Alessandri's second term
as President of Chile. The Constitution of 1925 gave him six
years in office with strong powers, which he was determined to
use. One of the first measures he took was to reorganize the
nitrate industry, abolishing *COSACH. As the decade advanced,
Chile made considerable economic progress. Measures were taken
to improve *education, *agriculture and industry. In 1935 the
exports of nitrate were double those of the preceding year. In
April 1937 the *Nacista movement began to spread in Chile. On
September 5, 1938, the Nacistas attempted to carry out a revolution in order to return Ibáñez del Campo to power. Ibáñez was
arrested and Alessandri was given additional extraordinary powers.
Order was kept until Alessandri stepped down from office and
Pedro *Aguirre Cerda was elected as the new President. Temporarily unpopular, Alessandri went to Europe, returning to endorse
Juan Antonio *Ríos Morales in the 1942 presidential campaign. In
1944 he reentered the Senate, becoming president of that body in
1945. He endorsed Gabriel *González Videla for President of
Chile in 1946, and died four years later amidst many "public
honors and middle-class grief."

ALESSANDRI RODRIGUEZ, Fernando (b. 1897). Younger brother of
Jorge *Alessandri Rodríguez. In 1922 he became a law professor
at the *Universidad de Chile. From 1934 to 1953 he was senator
for *Tarapacá and *Antofagasta, becoming president of the Senate
in 1950. In 1942 he was made president of the Liberals (*Partido
Liberal). In the presidential campaign of 1946 the Liberals and

several other parties of the center (*Partido Agrario Laborista, *Partido Liberal Progresista, *Partido Democrático, *Partido Radical Democrático and *Partido Socialista Auténtico) sought to make common cause against Communist-backed Gabriel *González Videla, but could not agree to back Alfredo *Duhalde Vázquez. Fernando Alessandri was then put forward as a compromise candidate. He was adopted, and ran against González and right-wing candidate Eduardo *Cruz-Coke Lassabe, coming third.

ALESSANDRI RODRIGUEZ, Jorge (1896–1986). Son of Arturo *Alessandri Palma, he was President of Chile from 1958 to 1964 and unsuccessful candidate for the same office in the elections of September 4, 1970. He received an engineering degree in 1919 and taught engineering at the *Universidad de Chile. He served in the Chilean *Congress as a deputy (1926–30) and as a senator (1956–58). In 1947, he was minister of the treasury in the cabinet of President (1946–52) Gabriel *González Videla. Urged on by his presidential aspirations, Alessandri ran in the elections of 1958, backed by the Conservatives (*Partido Conservador), the Liberals (*Partido Liberal), a faction of the Radical Party (*Partido Radical), and other minor parties of the center who refused to support their nominee Eduardo *Frei Montalva. The election of 1958 was very close, and was resolved by Congress. Alessandri defeated his major opponent, Socialist Salvador *Allende Gossens, by only 33,000 votes. Although Alessandri had not won a mandate, Congress confirmed him President in October 1958 and he was inaugurated for a six-year term on November 4, 1958.

Backed by the moderates and conservatives, Alessandri was able to bring about some reforms in industry and *agriculture. The first *Agrarian Reform Law was passed in 1962. It permitted the expropriation for cash of some unproductive or inefficient private holdings and provided for the consolidation of *minifundia. A year before, Chile had joined the *Latin American Free Trade Association (LAFTA). In 1963, Chile signed the American Continent Treaty as a de-nuclearized zone; accepted the ruling of Queen Elizabeth II to settle a border dispute at *Palena, between Chile and *Argentina; and signed a Treaty for disarmament in South America. In 1960 Chile was plagued by another major *earthquake. More than 5,000 Chileans died and two million lost their homes. The losses were estimated at more than $800 million. As a result, the country faced one of the severest bouts of *inflation in its history. The *peso was devalued, and a new monetary unit, the *escudo, introduced in its place. The *exchange rate fell from 1,000 pesos (or one escudo) to the dollar, to 1.5 escudos in 1962.

In January 1961 a ten-year development program was announced by the government, with assistance from the World Bank and the U.S. Export-Import Bank. As a result, the *copper, tin, *nitrate and steel industries were able to finance their operations. In 1962 the Chilean government did not sanction the blockade of

Cuba officially, even if it approved it tacitly. But two years
later, in 1964, in accordance with the decision of the *Organization
of American States, Chile broke off relations with Cuba. In the
same year, President Alessandri visited the United States and
toured other Latin American countries. He was succeeded on
November 3, 1964, by Christian Democrat President (1964-70)
Eduardo Frei. In 1970 Alessandri ran again for President, but
was defeated by a narrow margin by Salvador Allende.

In 1973, Alessandri, together with other politicians of the conservative National Party (*Partido Nacional) and the Christian
Democrats (*Partido Demócrata Cristiano), formed the *Confederación Democrática (CODE) to try to have Allende impeached. But
in the congressional elections of March that year CODE failed
to obtain the two-thirds majority it needed for this. Like many
other Chilean politicians, Alessandri was receptive to the *coup
d'état that overthrew Allende later in the year, but was dismayed
at the repression that ensued, and he pretty much retired from
political life. As things were getting difficult in 1984 for the
Augusto *Pinochet Ugarte government and the quest was on to
find a successor, Alessandri had several meetings with former
Christian Democrat vice-president Bernardo *Leighton Guzmán.
The former president, however, now 87, publicly requested that
politicians and the media cease to use his name as that of a
person with a role to play in Chile's future.

ALGARROBO. This largest and newest of the Chilean *iron mines is
located in the province of *Atacama, some 27 miles inland from
Huasco. Purchased by the Compañía de Acero del Pacífico (*CAP)
in 1959, Algarrobo is looked upon as the future supplier for
Chile's integrated iron and steel industry. The deposit has known
reserves of 50 million tons with additional probable reserves of
75 million tons, and is expected to supply ore for two blast furn-
aces for at least 50 years (as opposed to El Romeral's 20-year
supply for only one furnace). Moreover, recent geological surveying and projecting to determine the ore reserves of the Algarrobo mine (and adjacent sector) have led experts to believe the
mineral content of the mine to be substantially greater than
originally estimated. The Penoso hill facing the mine has also
been surveyed and iron ores found there.

Partial operation began in 1960, but full-scale operation only
in 1962. At the time, the mineral extracted from the open-pit
mine amounted to 2.3 metric *tons. A year later production rose
to 2.7 tonnes. Although the world's increased output of iron
ore makes competition more severe, the quality of Algarrobo ore
places CAP in a favorable position. The ore, which has a high
iron and low phosphorous content, is well known and widely accepted in Japan and the United States, and is beginning to find
new European markets.

ALIANZA DE PARTIDOS Y FUERZAS POPULARES. A coalition formed
in 1958 to back the presidential candidacy of Jorge *Alessandri

Rodríguez. The component parties were a faction of the *Partido Radical Doctrinario, the *Partido Social Cristiano, the *Partido Agrario Laborista Recuperacionista, the *Movimiento Nacional del Pueblo and the *Movimiento Republicano. After Alessandri emerged as victor, the Alianza was dissolved to the dismay of many of its members, who were shocked that the President showed so little interest in the organization.

ALIANZA DEMOCRATICA. A coalition of center-left parties created on August 8, 1983, to unite the opposition to Chile's strong man, President August *Pinochet Ugarte, and force him to return the country to democracy by 1985. Its head was Mario *Sharpe Carte, a lawyer. In 1984 he successfully invited the conservatives to join the Alianza. Interior minister Sergio Onofre *Jarpa Reyes opened negotiations, but had to break them off when Pinochet declared that Chile would not be ready for democracy before 1989 at the earliest, and perhaps not even then. Pinochet called the opposition leaders "traitors" who wanted to create chaos by mounting protests against his regime with the aim of returning the nation to Marxism. Pinochet's threats, silencing dissent and dividing the opposition, were an obvious factor in his ability to remain in control.

ALIANZA DEMOCRATICA DE CHILE. A political coalition of Communists, Socialists and Radicals, formed in 1942 to back the presidential candidacy of Juan Antonio *Ríos Morales. Ríos won election, and the Alianza Democrática de Chile remained active until dissolved upon the President's death in 1948.

ALIANZA LATINOAMERICANA DE INTEGRACION. See: LATIN AMERICAN INTEGRATION ASSOCIATION

ALIANZA LIBERAL. A political combination of liberals and radicals formed in 1875 and dissolved in the same year. After the *Civil War of 1891, the Alianza Liberal was organized again, and this time lasted until 1925. During this second period, Chile functioned as a *parliamentary regime, making it necessary for parties to form coalitions in order to attain a majority in both houses of *Congress. The Alianza Liberal achieved its greatest importance during the presidencies of Germán *Riesco Errázuriz (1901-06), Pedro *Montt Montt (1906-10) and--after shedding the more right wing liberals to the *Unión Nacional--that of Arturo *Alessandri Palma (1920-25).

ALIANZA POPULAR. A coalition of five parties formed in 1952 after the triumph of Carlos *Ibáñez del Campo in the presidential elections of that year. The member parties were the *Partido Agrario Laborista, the *Partido Socialista Popular, the *Partido Democrático del Pueblo, the *Partido Radical Doctrinario and the *Partido Femenino de Chile. Their objective was to unite the political groups who had backed Ibáñez. The Alianza was dissolved shortly after its inception.

ALIANZA POPULAR LIBERTADORA. A political alliance which supported the 1938 presidential candidacy of Carlos *Ibáñez del
Campo, formed by the pro-Nazi *Movimiento Nacional Socialista
de Chile, the *Unión Socialista, and a group of military politicos.
The electoral campaign in 1938 was marred by incidents sparked
by the activities of the *Nacistas, and Ibáñez was forced to
withdraw his nomination in order not to be connected with his
extremist sympathizers. These culminated in the September 4
occupation of the *Seguro Obrero building by Nacista students,
and the ensuing clash with the police resulted in many deaths.
Ibáñez was arrested, and the Alianza gave its support to *Frente
Popular candidate Pedro *Aguirre Cerda.

ALLENDE, Hortensia. See: BUSSY DE ALLENDE, Hortensia.

ALLENDE BUSSY, Isabel (1945-). Youngest daughter of assassinated
President Salvador *Allende Gossens, and one of the most outspoken members of her family in regard to the *coup d'état that
overthrew her father in 1973. A sociologist, she was active in
the women's movement (see: WOMEN AND THE WOMEN'S MOVE-
MENT) which flourished in Chile during the *Unidad Popular administration. After the coup she, like her mother and sisters,
went into exile. Isabel accompanied her sister Beatriz *Allende
de Fernández to Cuba, where she lived for a while. Beatriz
decided to remain there, but Isabel began touring Europe, Africa
and Australia, espousing the cause of the restoration of democracy to Chile. She is married with two children and lives in
Mexico.

ALLENDE DE FERNANDEZ, Beatriz (1943-1977). Daughter of President
Salvador *Allende Gossens and wife of Cuban diplomat Luis Fer-
nández de Oña, whom she married when he held a senior position
at the *Santiago embassy. After the *coup she was exiled to
Cuba, where she later committed suicide. See also: WOMEN AND
THE WOMEN'S MOVEMENT.

ALLENDE DE PASCAL, Laura (1914-1976). Socialist deputy elected
for three terms to the Chamber of Deputies, and sister of deposed
President (1970-73) Salvador *Allende Gossens. When she refused to reveal information about her son Andrés *Pascual Allende,
who had succeeded the brothers Miguel and Engardo *Enríquez
as leader of the *Movimiento de Izquierda Revolucionaria (MIR),
she was detained and then arrested. In 1975 Laura was known to
be too sick from cancer to participate in politics or know the
whereabouts of her son. The Washington Post reported that the
*junta was denying her cobalt radiation treatment to encourage
her son to surrender.
    A year later, at the news of her niece Beatriz *Allende de
Fernández's suicide in Cuba, Laura was permitted to leave Chile
for Havana, where she began caring for Beatriz's two children.
    Consumed by cancer and very close to death, she petitioned

the Chilean government to allow her to return to Chile, where she
wanted to die. The government refused. Both Queen Elizabeth
II and the Pope interceded, but to no avail. Very depressed
that she could not return to her homeland, Laura, like Beatriz,
took her own life and was buried in Cuba.

ALLENDE GOSSENS, Salvador (1908-1973). Doctor by profession,
Socialist candidate for the presidency in the last four elections
(1952, 1958, 1964 and 1970), and President of Chile from 1970
to 1973, when he was overthrown and killed in a *coup d'état.
In 1932 he received his degree in medicine and from then alter-
nated his practice with his political career. As a student activist, he helped organize the Socialist Party (*Partido Socialista).
He was arrested twice for political disturbances and regarded by
many potential employers as a troublemaker. In 1937 he was
elected deputy from *Valparaíso, a position he kept until 1941.
In 1939 he became minister of health and welfare in the government (1938-41) of Pedro *Aguirre Cerda, and married Hortensia
*Bussy, a geography student at the *Universidad de Chile. In
1943 he became secretary general of the Socialist Party. In 1952
he was the leftist candidate to the presidency, but was defeated
by Carlos *Ibáñez del Campo, receiving a mere 6 percent of the
popular vote.
    In 1955 he became president of the *Frente Nacional del
Pueblo, a coalition of leftist parties. In 1958 he was the FNP's
presidential candidate, losing to Jorge *Alessandri Rodríguez
by only 33,000 votes: Allende received 28.9 percent of the poll
to Alessandri's 31.6 percent. From 1961 to 1965 Allende was
senator from *Aconcagua and *Valparaíso. In 1964 he ran once
more for president, but lost to Christian Democrat Eduardo *Frei
Montalva, with 38.6 percent of the votes--the highest proportion
he ever received--to Frei's 55.6 percent.
    Even though Allende received only 36.2 percent of the vote
in his last (1970) presidential election, it was enough to edge
former president (1958-64) Jorge *Alessandri Rodríguez (who
received 34.1 percent) and the Christian Democrat candidate
Radomiro *Tomic Romero (who received 28.7 percent). At the
final count, Allende got 1,075,616 votes to conservative Alessandri's 1,036,278 and Tomic's 824,849. Since no candidate had
received an absolute majority, *Congress was required by the
Constitution to choose the new President from the top two vote-
getters. Allende, who was supported by the Communist-Socialist-
dominated *Unidad Popular, could count on 83 votes in Congress
and needed only 13 more to be confirmed. The Christian Democratic Party agreed to support him unanimously, in return for
constitutional guarantees (the ESTATUTOS DE GARANTIAS
CONSTITUCIONALES, q.v.) that he would preserve the democratic process in Chile. Allende signed an agreement to do so,
and on October 24, 1970, Congress confirmed him President by
160 votes to 35 for Alessandri.
    A political assassination that occurred two days before this

confirmation is worth mentioning because such an event had not happened in Chile for 132 years. The *army chief of staff, General René *Schneider Chereau, had announced that the army would support whichever candidate Congress chose. On October 22, General Schneider was mortally wounded by gunmen in an attempted kidnapping. The day before, he had spoken publicly against right-wing plots to keep Allende from taking office. The tale that emerged was one of savage efforts by *ITT and the U.S. *Central Intelligence Agency to thwart Allende's accession to office and his survival in it should he be elected. The general had been included in a worldwide CIA list of its enemies, although it became apparent that the CIA had supported only his kidnapping, not his murder.

On November 3, 1970, Allende was sworn in. Shortly after, he named three Communists to his 15-man cabinet (this being the first time in 25 years that Communists had held cabinet posts in Chile), but he kept four posts, including the key interior and foreign ministries, in the hands of his own Socialists.

Since the *United States could not prevent Allende from taking power, the White House devised two "tracks," both of which were directed to the removal of Allende, but by different means. Track 1 consisted of "cutting off all credits, pressuring firms to curtail investment in Chile, and approaching other nations to cooperate in this venture." To succeed, it required at least the acquiescence of former President Frei. Track 2, entrusted to the CIA, involved direct contact with the Chilean *armed forces; its existence was to be known to only a small group of individuals in the White House and the CIA. When disclosed to the public on July 7, 1975, it was the first confirmation that President Nixon and the CIA had contemplated not merely secret financing of opposition parties and *trade unions, but a military coup and the violent takeover of the government.

Following his election, Allende himself attested to the effectiveness of Track 1 in a celebrated speech he gave at the United Nations in December 1972. There was, he said, "large scale pressure to cut us off from the world, to strangle our economy, and paralyze trade, and to deprive us of access to sources of international financing."

Allende's first year in office saw a government that favored consumption to stimulate an acutely depressed *economy. *Unidad Popular's stated objectives in political economy were to reactivate the levels of productive activities, to effect a substantial redistribution of income in favor of the poorest sector of society, and to initiate changes in the form of property by establishing a dominant state economic sector.

Allende's new policies on salaries, prices and public spending were the key levers for the achievement of the first two objectives. There was substantial readjustment of basic salaries with a notable increase in real wages, outstripping the previous increase in the cost of living; inflation was slowed down considerably. At the end of his first year in office the results were spectacular.

GNP rose by 8.3 percent (the highest rate in 15 years), industrial production rose by 14.6 percent, and unemployment dropped from 8.3 percent to 3.9 percent. The annual rate of *inflation went down from 35 percent in 1970 to 22 percent in 1971.

Allende's success was reflected in the municipal elections of 1971, when Unidad Popular received 51 percent of the vote. Nevertheless, the picture was not necessarily rosy. Consumption, particularly of foodstuffs, increased the demand for imports, and the disastrous fall in the price of *copper on the London exchange created serious difficulties in the *balance of payments. Inflow of foreign capital fell precipitously, *foreign aid from the United States was limited to the military, and massive foreign aid from the socialist block was not forthcoming (see: USSR, Relations with).

These economic woes were clear by the first quarter of 1972 and spelled trouble for a weak *economy. Consumption was expanding at a greater rate than income, and private investment was drying up. Not only did it contract abruptly, but private investors diverted their liquid assets into either foreign exchange or speculative investments, both of which aggravated the already tenuous economy.

In 1973 the economic situation deteriorated and inflation increased reaching an all-time high of 360 percent over the year. Meanwhile, both ITT and the CIA continued to put external pressure on the Allende government. ITT, for example, suggested that "companies should drag their feet in sending money [to Chile], in making deliveries, in shipping spare parts.... Savings and Loan Companies there are in trouble. If pressure were applied, they would have to shut their doors, thereby creating stronger pressures." The CIA was spending an unspecified seven-figure sum in secretly financing strikes of *labor unions and trade groups. These disruptions included the twenty-six-day nationwide truck-owners' strike in October 1972, which presented Allende with his first *labor crisis, as well as the waves of strikes in mid-1973, which at their peak drew 250,000 from work. As a result, production, when it did not actually fall, remained stagnant. Shortages, speculation and the *black market spiraled, and there was a sharpening of class conflict.

In this context, the congressional elections of March 1973 marked a decisive turning point. On the one hand, in spite of the poor economic situation, the results revealed the strength and depth of the popular mass movement. Allende's Unidad Popular received 43.4 percent of the vote, an increase from the 36.2 percent received in the presidential election of 1970 (the Allende government was the only one in Chilean history to increase its popular support midway through its six-year term). On the other hand, the opposition forces, united under the banner of the *Confederación Democrática (CODE), with 53.6 percent of the vote, came close to achieving the two-thirds majority they needed to begin impeachment proceedings against the President, as they had promised to do in their campaign. It was at this point that they decided in favor of a *coup d'état.

In Allende's first two years in power, Chile had seen a consolidation of the forces of the Left. His last year saw an even
greater effort by the Right to unite against his rule. Although
the March 1973 elections had not significantly altered the balance
of power between the UP and CODE, a polarization of the Chilean
electorate and of all Chileans had taken place.

After the elections, Allende set out to accomplish three goals:
to unite his governing coalition into a single party of the left,
as CODE had done with the opposition; to create a stable cabinet;
and to avert the possibilities of strikes organized by the right.
That he was unable to accomplish any of these goals presaged
the end of his tenuous regime.

In office Allende made at least two crucial political mistakes.
The first was to assume that the middle and upper classes would
accept unquestioningly his "Chilean road to socialism" so long as
all his reforms were done through legal means. They never did.
Roberto *Thieme, secretary-general of the Fascist youth organization *Patria y Libertad, had pledged: "If we have to burn half
of Chile to save it from Communism, then we will do it." Indeed,
the violent opposition of these classes contributed in no small way
to Allende's downfall.

His second mistake was made during the much publicized
"*bosses' strike" of October 1972, when, in an effort to reduce
right-wing opposition and frighten the businessmen, Allende persuaded three members of the armed forces to join his cabinet.
This politicized the armed forces, which until that time had attempted to stay above the crisis, into pro- and anti-Allende
factions. As the reform process faltered and the economy deteriorated, extremism and violence in the streets intensified, drawing
the military and the *police away from their proclaimed neutrality.

In 1973 problems rather than progress consumed the attention
of the administration. A series of crises with labor and the
military were responsible for the undoing of Allende.

The most serious crisis occurred when Allende showed himself
incapable of settling a series of strikes--staged not by the leftist
labor unions, but by his implacable middle-class enemies. On
April 18, workers from El Teniente walked out on strike for higher
wages (see: COPPER STRIKES). The strike lasted 76 days and
cost the government some *75 million in lost revenues. It was
finally settled on July 3, when Allende himself went to plead with
union leaders. Three weeks later, however, the powerful truckers,
some 40,000 in strength, also went on strike. This, their second
walkout, was even more political in inspiration. It lasted three
months (or until the *coup itself). In a country largely dependent upon road transport, it cost the government *6 million a
day as fuel shortages increased, food supplies dwindled, and
*agriculture in general suffered because seeds and fertilizers
could not be delivered. Some of the truckers who refused to
go along with the strike met their death on the highways at the
hands of right-wing extremists.

Others to go on strike were taxi drivers, airline pilots, shopkeepers and doctors. Thus the economy became paralyzed. To prevent chaos, the government tried in vain to negotiate with the opposition Christian Democrats, with Raul Cardinal *Silva Henríquez acting as intermediary.

Talk of civil war was already in the air when approximately one hundred members of a *Santiago garrison, led by Lieutenant Colonel Roberto *Souper, attacked the presidential palace on June 29, 1973 (see: TANCAZO). It was a premature attempt to overthrow Allende, with twelve soldiers and civilians killed and twenty-one wounded. The revolt was swiftly put down and Allende declared a state of emergency. Later he asked Congress to declare a state of siege, but it refused.

In the months that followed, Allende tried again to persuade the Christian Democrats to open negotiation, inviting more military into what had become a "revolving door" cabinet. But when General Carlos *Prats González, the army commander-in-chief, was forced to resign, and General Augusto *Pinochet Ugarte replaced him with the promise that the army would remain neutral, Allende was doomed. (See: COUP D'ETAT OF 1973).

ALLENDE LLOREN, Isabel (1949-   ). Daughter of Thomas Allende, cousin of deposed President Salvador *Allende Gossens, and a journalist by profession who lives in exile in Caracas, Venezuela. Today she is one of Latin America's most heralded women writers. Her highly acclaimed Casa de los espíritus, first published in Barcelona by Plaza y Janes, was translated into English by Magda Bogis as The House of the Spirits (Knopf, 1985). Her latest novel, De amor y de sombra (Of Love and Shade), Mexico City, Edivision, 1986 is now being translated into English.

ALLIANCE OF PARTIES AND POPULAR FORCES. See: ALIANZA DE PARTIDOS Y FUERZAS POPULARES.

ALMAGRO, Diego de (1475-1538). A celebrated Spanish *conquistador and the discoverer of the Reino de Chile, who was born in the city of his own name, the illegitimate son of Spanish peasants. In 1524, fleeing a murder charge, he came to Panama, where he became a close friend of Francisco Pizarro. He marched with Pizarro and Fernando de Luque into *Peru, acquiring for Spain territories rich in *gold and *silver. As a result Pizarro was given the governorship of *Peru, whereas Almagro was designated governor of Túmbez at only half Pizarro's salary. This ended their friendship and a long and bitter rivalry began between the two men. Nevertheless, they continued together, and Almagro took part in operations which resulted in the death of the *Inca Atahualpa and the conquest of the Peruvian territories. In 1535, Almagro was granted the title of *adelantado to the regions south of Pizarro's territory (present-day northern Chile and Argentina). He set out to inspect this domain with an expedition of approximately 500 Spaniards and thousands of Indians, but their march was marked by hardships and privations. More than 10,000

Indian carriers died, as did nearly all of the animals and many
Spaniards. Finding no gold, the resentful Almagro returned,
determined that the ancient Inca capital of Cuzco should be his.
In Cuzco he found the Spaniards, led by Pizarro, besieged
by Indians who had rebelled. Almagro's forces, however, soon
forced the rebels to retreat and he claimed the city. Almagro
was victorious in the conflict that ensued with Pizarro and
captured Hernando Pizarro, whom he set free at the entreaties
of his brother Francisco. In 1538, however, there was another
battle between the aging rivals in which Hernando Pizarro took
Almagro prisoner. The latter was executed on July 8, 1538,
leaving Francisco Pizarro the undisputed master of the *Inca
empire.

ALMEYDA MEDINA, Clodomiro (1923–). A lawyer and university
professor, he has been a militant in the Socialist Party (*Partido
Socialista). In 1952 he was named minister of labor, a post he
resigned a year later to become minister of mines. He was the
secretary general of the *Partido Socialista Popular and a member
of the central committee of the Socialist Party. In 1970 he was
named minister of foreign affairs in the cabinet of President
(1970–73) Salvador *Allende Gossens.
During the troubled Allende years, Almeyda was a loyal supporter of the President. After the Chilean *coup, he was imprisoned and sent to one of the first *concentration camps set
up by the military *junta on *Dawson Island in the *Strait of
Magellan. He remained in prison in poor health until an urgent
appeal was made on November 6, 1974, by the *United Nations
General Assembly "to restore basic human rights and fundamental
freedoms in Chile." Secretary General Kurt Waldheim sent the
junta a telegram demanding the immediate release of Almeyda, who
was known to be in a critical condition: he had disappeared
from his place of detention in May, and when his wife located him
several days later in the Air Force Academy, he had suffered a
mental breakdown, the result (it later transpired) of his having
been kept hooded during interrogation and being denied medical
attention. Almeyda was finally allowed to leave for Romania on
January 11, 1975, accompanied by another political prisoner,
former justice minister Jorge *Tapia Valdés.

ALTAMIRANO TALAVERA, Luis. A career military officer who entered
the *Civil War of 1891 as a captain in the *army. Afterward,
he passed through the usual military grades and had commissions
in Europe and South America. He was a lieutenant general of
the army and minister of the interior (September 5, 1924) at
the beginning of the period known as the second *Anarquía Política. He presided over the *junta militar de gobierno which replaced President (1920–24) Arturo *Alessandri Palma on September
11, 1924, and headed that body until the following January, when
a second military coup asked for the return of Alessandri.

ALTO DEL HOSPICIO. Height overlooking the city of *Pisagua, in
the province of *Tarapacá. Its capture on January 23, 1891 by
*congresistas gave them control of the city and allowed them to
proceed with the disembarcation of their army. As this led
eventually to rebel control of the *Norte grande and its mineral
wealth, Alto del Hospicio may be considered the first significant
battle of the *Civil War of 1891.

ALVAREZ SUAREZ, Humberto (b. 1895). Lawyer by profession,
businessman and member of the Radical Party (*Partido Radical).
In 1936 he was minister of justice, and in 1940 minister of the
interior. Between 1941 and 1965 he served in both houses of
*Congress. He was Chilean delegate to the United Nations in
1947 and president of the senate in 1949. He was also very active
in the international business world.

AMERINDIANS. See: ARAUCANIAN INDIANS, ATACEMENOS, INCAS,
MAPUCHES, PATAGONIA, TIERRA DEL FUEGO.

AMPUERO DIAZ, Raul (1917-). A lawyer by profession, he became
very active in the Chilean Socialist Party (*Partido Socialista).
In 1934 he was one of the founders of the Socialist Youth Movement in Chile, and in 1938 he went to New York for the World
Congress of Socialist Youth. In 1946 he was elected secretary
general of the party and has held that post many times. From
1953 to 1973 he was senator for *Tarapacá and *Antofagasta. In
the presidential elections of 1970, he backed Salvador *Allende
Gossens, as he had done in 1951, 1958 and 1964.

AMUNATEGUI ALDUNATE, Miguel Luis (1828-1888). Author of many
books on the history and politics of Chile, and various biographies,
Amunátegui Aldunate was very active in politics and ran for the
presidency of Chile in 1876. In 1867 he was elected vice-president
of the Chamber of Deputies and, in the same year, its president.
In 1868 he was named minister of the interior and of foreign affairs. In 1871 he was once again elected president of the Chamber
of Deputies. In 1874 he presented a proposal for the separation
of *church and state, which was eventually put into law by the
*Constitution of 1925. In 1875 he was nominated by the Liberal
Party (*Partido Liberal) to be candidate for the presidency of the
Republic, but declined. A year later he was persuaded to run,
but lost the election to Anibal *Pinto Garmendia, who was backed
by the *Partido Nacional.
    From 1876 to 1888 Amunategui Aldunate held many important
elective offices and was named president of the Chamber of
Deputies for the third time. His literary contributions have great
historical importance. Among his best known works are:
Títulos de la República de Chile a la soberanía y dominio de la
extremidad austral del continente americano; La Reconquista española: apuntes para la historia de Chile; La Cuestión de límites
entre Chile y Bolivia; and La Crónica de 1810. In 1863 he founded

a newspaper, El Independiente, which reflected the ideology of the *Partido Liberal Doctrinario of which he was a member. He died in 1888 while representing *Valparaíso in the Chamber of Deputies.

AMUNATEGUI JORDAN, Gregorio (b. 1901). Engineer by profession, and member of the Liberal Party (*Partido Liberal). He served in the Chilean *Congress as deputy for *Santiago from 1932 to 1937, becoming president of the Chamber of Deputies in 1937. From 1941 to 1965 he was senator for *Cautín. In the 1940s he was elected president of his party. In the presidential campaign of 1964, however, he refused its nomination, and backed Socialist candidate Salvador *Allende Gossens.

ANACONDA COPPER MINING COMPANY. *Copper is Chile's biggest dollar earner, providing about 68 percent of foreign exchange receipts, and Anaconda has been the giant of the Chilean copper industry, providing twice as much copper as *Kennecott. The largest and best known of Chilean copper mines is *Chuquicamata, located between the *Atacama desert and the western *Cordillera, at an altitude of 10,000 feet. The leading copper producing property in South America, and the largest copper deposit in the world, Chuquicamata was acquired and developed by the Guggenheim brothers, who later sold it to Anaconda. The third of Chile's great copper deposits was located at *Potrerillos in *Atacama province, but in 1959 the Potrerillos mine was exhausted, and Chile was lucky that a new mine was found just 12.5 air miles away. Symbolically, the new mine was called El *Salvador.

Potrerillos was purchased in 1913 by William *Braden, and was later sold to Anaconda. For over 50 years it yielded only low grade ore. From 1927 until production ceased in 1959, it averaged only 50,000 metric *tons of copper a year. El Salvador mine, on the other hand, had by 1970 reached an annual output of 90,000 tonnes. Its rated annual capacity is estimated at 7,700,000 tonnes of ore. El Salvador and Chuquicamata have been producing copper at capacity rate. During the 1960s the tax rate on Anaconda was about 60 percent (10%-20% lower than that levied on Kennecott). This was because Anaconda's policy of expanding production was more in conformity with Chile's national interest. In 1969 the firm drew about 70 percent of its total after-tax profits from its two Chilean subsidiaries, increasing capacity both at the mines and at the refinery.

In 1965, during negotiations with the Chilean government to "chileanize" the copper industry, which would have given the government a greater participation in regulating prices, production and marketing, the Anaconda company insisted on retaining sole ownership of its Chilean subsidiaries. In 1969, fearing that a leftist government would nationalize the copper industry, Anaconda was prepared to make great concessions to the administration of President (1964-70) Eduardo *Frei Montalva. The new agreement, called "nacionalización pactada," or contracted nation-

alization, had the following stipulations: (a) As of 1970 the
Chilean government would have acquired 51 percent of the stock
of the Anaconda mining operations; (b) the Chilean government
would pay Anaconda $197 million, with a 6 percent annual interest;
(c) the sum Chile would pay due to interest would amount to $75
million, meaning that 51 percent of the stock would be worth
approximately $272 million; and, (d) the government and Anaconda
also agreed to the future sale of the remaining 49 percent of
shares. Under stipulated conditions, the government could buy
the entire Anaconda stock after 1973. In spite of these concessions,
the new Chilean administration (1970-73) of Socialist president
Salvador *Allende Gossens had promised to nationalize immediately
not only Anaconda, but also other large U.S. companies (in the
*iron and *nitrate industries) which in the previous sixty years
had taken out of Chile $4,600 million in profits. The significance
of this figure may be seen by a comparison with Chile's G.N.P.,
which totaled only $10,500 million over the country's entire 400-
year existence. According to Chilean government sources, the
conclusion was clear: in a little over half a century, the large
U.S. companies had taken from Chile an amount greater than that
created by Chileans in terms of industries, *highways, schools,
*ports, hospitals, trade, etc. during the country's entire history.
Anaconda was not pleased with the *Unidad Popular copper policies,
and neither were the other two U.S. copper companies, Kennecott
and the *Cerro Corporation. All three began to wage an economic
war on the new Allende regime in order to insure that the companies would be paid in cash for the expropriation of their mines.
When Allende refused to pay any indemnity, on the grounds that
the foreign companies had not paid enough *taxes since purchasing
the mines and had not reinvested sufficiently in the Chilean *economy, all three companies turned to the *United States government
for help.

Anaconda and (even more emphatically) Kennecott called for
Chilean copper to be impounded in European ports, and pressed
French and German courts to sequester shipments of Chilean
copper which they claimed as their property. The case went all
the way to the International Court of Law at the Hague, causing,
along with a lower price for copper on the London Metal Exchange,
an enormous imbalance in foreign trade for the Allende government.

After years of litigation, and after Allende's overthrow, the
government of President Augusto *Pinochet Ugarte decided to
compensate the copper companies nationalized by Allende. The
*junta reached amicable agreements with all three companies: the
Cerro Corporation received $41.9 million; Anaconda received an
initial payment of US $65 million, and an additional payment of
US $188 million; Kennecott was paid a total of US $ 68 million.

ANARQUIA POLITICA. If one excludes the period following the death
of the *conquistador Pedro de *Valdivia, Chile has experienced
two periods of political anarchy: from 1823 to 1830 and from 1924
to 1932. The first period was a result of the struggle for *in-

dependence from Spain. From 1823, when Bernardo *O'Higgins was ousted as Supreme Director of Chile, until 1830 when the Republic was established, Chile lived in a state of constant disturbance. Different Congresses and Supreme Directors succeeded each other amid revolts and military coups. The most important events of this period were: the abolition of *African slavery (1823), the *Constitution of 1823; the *Constitution of 1828; and the *Civil War of 1829-30.

The second period of political anarchy, 1924-32, followed the first administration of Arturo *Alessandri Palma. Alessandri departed before he could end his term of office, and the *armed forces became active in the political arena, the most notable military politician being Carlos *Ibanez del Campo. The most important event during these years of strife was the adoption of the *Constitution of 1925, although this was only fully implemented in 1932. See also: JUNTA DE GOBIERNO DE 1932; JUNTA MILITAR DE GOBIERNO DE 1924; JUNTA MILITAR DE GOBIERNO DE 1925; REPUBLICA SOCIALISTA.

ANCON, Treaty of. A treaty signed by Chile and *Peru on October 20, 1883, to end the War of the *Pacific. Chile was awarded the Peruvian department of *Tarapacá and the Bolivian province of *Antofagasta, which gave Chile its northern frontier on the River Camarones. (The river enters the Pacific at 19° 12' S.).

Under the treaty Chile was to retain part of the Peruvian department of Moquegua, south of the Sama River (which enters the Pacific at 17° 57' S). This territory included the cities of *Tacna and *Arica, but their future status was to be determined by a plebiscite of their inhabitants scheduled to be held in 1893. Since the two countries could not agree on conditions to hold such a referendum, the question remained unresolved until the Treaty of LIMA (q.v.) of 1929.

The Treaty of Ancón made no provision for the *Church administration of the newly acquired territories, which remained part of the Peruvian diocese of Arequipa. Clerical disloyalty remained a problem for the Chilean authorities until 1910, when all Peruvian priests were expelled from the region.

ANCUD. City at the northern end of the island of *Chiloé, at 41° 53' S, 73° 50' W. Founded in 1768 as San Carlos, it began as a center for *whaling, *seal and otter hunting. It received its present name in 1848 on the occasion of its elevation as the see of a new diocese (see: CHURCH ADMINISTRATION). Until the 1974 reorganization of regional government (see: REGIONS AND ADMINISTRATIVE REFORM) it was the capital of the central-southern province of Chiloé (now part of Region X, Los *Lagos). The town's estimated population was 11,000 in 1970 and 26,565 in 1982.

ANDACOLLO. Small *mining town (6,000 population in 1975) in *Coquimbo region, 20 miles SE of Coquimbo, a center for *gold mining since *Inca times and scene of a minor goldrush in 1932.

ANDEAN COMMON MARKET. See: PACTO ANDINO.

ANDEAN PACT. See: PACTO ANDINO.

ANDES. The Andes (*Cordillera de los Andes) usually refer to the
South American ridge of mountains that begin in Venezuela, pass
through Colombia, Ecuador, *Peru, *Bolivia, Chile and *Argentina,
and end in *Tierra del Fuego. Geologically, the Andes are quite
young; they are slowly rising and have many active *volcanoes,
especially in Peru and Chile.
   The entire range is over 4,600 miles long, and a little over a
half of it (2,500 miles) lies in Chile. Its width is scarcely more
than two miles, except in Bolivia, where two parallel border a
broad tableland, the altiplano, of up to four miles across. In
northern and central Chile, the Andes attain an average height
of 11,500 to 13,000 feet, with many individual peaks over 6,000
meters (19,692 feet). Among these, we find Ojos de Salado, at
22,597 feet (Chile's highest peak), and Mount *Aconcagua, just
inside Argentina, at 22,837 feet (the exact height is disputed),
the highest mountain in the Andes. Other peaks averaging
20,000 feet are the Illimani, the Illampu, the Misti, the Chimbo-
razo, and the Cotopaxi. The mean height of the Chilean Andes
decreases in southern Chile to around 10,000 feet, and to 5,000
feet on Tierra del Fuego.
   These mountains, which extend along the northern and western
edge of South America, complicate life in all the countries through
which they pass. Communications are difficult (see: TRANSAN-
DINE RAILWAY), and this has impeded the political integration of
the various republics, whose relations are often exacerbated by
border disputes (see: BOUNDARY TREATY OF 1881).
   Although *agriculture on the Andean slopes is not very rewarding because of poor soil and erosion, the mountains are a
rich source of minerals, even though the mines are often at high
altitudes and difficult to reach. In Chile their principal products
are *copper (see: ANDINA, EXOTICA, CHUQUICAMATA, POT-
RERILLOS, SEWELL) and other nonferrous metals, including
*molybdenum, *silver and *gold. The *Atacama region produces
salt and borax.
   José de *San Martin's great feat in bringing his army of
liberation across the Andes from Argentina in 1817 was a decisive
event in Chile's struggle for Independence from Spain (see:
ANDES, EJERCITO DE LOS).

ANDES, EJERCITO DE LOS. The Army of the Andes was organized
in 1817 by José de *San Martín, governor of *Cuyo in *Argentina,
to fight for the liberation of Chile. San Martín wanted a base
from which the heart of Spanish power in *Peru could be attacked
more effectively than through Tucumán and *Bolivia. Using the
many Chilean refugees in his province, he formed a joint Chilean-
Argentine force, making one of the two rival Chilean leaders,
Bernardo *O'Higgins, his second-in-command, in preference to

the less tractable José Miguel *Carrera Verdugo. The army was
assembled in Mendoza, and consisted of 2,795 foot, 742 horse,
241 gunners (with 21 guns) and 1,400 supply troops (with 9,000
mules and 1,500 horses). After small diversionary units had been
sent on to cross by lesser passes to the north and south, General
Juan Gregorio de las *Heras led his 800 men on January 18, 1817,
through the direct (but difficult) *Uspallata Pass, while San
Martín took the main force through the easier but longer Paso
de los Patos. After 18 days both armies linked up on schedule
on the far slope to defeat the Spaniards at *Chacabuco on February 12, while the diversionary forces occupied their respective
objectives of *Talca, *Copiapó and La *Serena. Just over a year
later, on April 5, 1818, the allied army made Chilean independence
secure at the battle of *Maipú.

ANDINA. A new *copper mine located just northwest of *Santiago,
forming part of what is known as the *gran minería. Its output,
added to that of another new mine, *Exótica, increased total
copper production in the 1970s and early 1980s by about 2 percent. As a result Chile has been producing more copper since
1976 than at any time before: a national annual total of over a
million metric *tons.

ANGELES, Los. City on the *Bío-Bío river in south-central Chile,
founded in 1742 at 37° 28' S, 72° 23' W. It was the capital of
the pre-1974 province of Bío-Bío (now incorporated into Región
VIII, also called Bío-Bío). The city's population was 11,691
in 1907; 18,000 in 1940; 49,179 in 1970; and 76,276 (est.) in
1986.
    Los Angeles was the site of a battle fought on March 1, 1819,
during the *Guerra a muerte ("War to the Death") between
*realistas attempting to take the city and its patriot defenders.
The latter were on the point of defeat when Marshall Andrés de
Alcázar y Zapata came to their assistance and was able to disperse the royalists.

ANGOL, City of. City of southern Chile. Originally founded as a
fort in Indian country at the confluence of the rivers Malleco
and Huequén (37° 49' S, 72° 42' W) by Pedro de *Valdivia in
1553 as Los Confines de Angol, it was abandoned after the disaster of *Tucapel later the same year, refounded in 1559 and destroyed in 1599, temporarily reestablished in 1611, repopulated
in 1637-41 and 1695-1723. The present city dates from the beginning of the final conquest of the *Araucanian Indians in 1862.
The population was 7,391 in 1907; 12,000 in 1940; 49,000 (est.)
in 1985. It was capital of the pre-1975 province of *Malleco.

ANGOL, Territory of. Administrative jurisdiction formed in 1875
from part of the province of *Arauco. In 1887 it became the
provinces of *Cautín and *Malleco.

ANSON, George, [Baron] Anson of Soberton (1697-1762). British admiral. During the War of Jenkin's Ear (the War of the Austrian Succession), while still a commodore, Anson was sent on September 29, 1740, to harry Spanish shipping and possessions in the Pacific. With a squadron of six ships, he arrived at Más Atierra in the *Juan Fernández Islands on June 22, 1741. He used the small island as a base from which to blockade the South American coast. After a westward circumnavigation, he returned to England on June 26, 1744, in the H.M.S. Centurion, his one remaining vessel. With him he carried a booty of £400,000, or about 2 million *pesos.

ANTARCTICA (Territorio Antártico Chileno). Chile's claim to a 1,250,000 km^2 (480,000 square mile) wedge of Antarctica between 53° W and 90° W is based on the presumed inheritance of Spanish rights under the Treaties of *Tordesillas (1494) and Madrid (1670). The Spanish crown entrusted the governance of all its claims south from the *Strait of Magellan to the Pole to Pedro Sancho de la *Hoz in 1539, and subsequently to successive governors of Chile. Independent Chile sought to regulate *seal hunting in Antarctic waters, but attempted no occupation of land until the 1906 establishment of a *whaling station on Deception Island in the South Shetlands. Chile only formally declared her territorial claims on November 6, 1940. They overlap those of the *United Kingdom (defined in 1909) and the Argentine Territory of *Tierra del Fuego (constituted in 1943 and including everything between 25° W and 74° W). Chile currently maintains an observatory, "Capitán Arturo *Prat," on Greenwich Island in the South Shetlands (established 1947); a military base, "General Bernardo *O'Higgins," at Covandonga Bay on Graham Land (Tierra de O'Higgins) on the Antarctic mainland (established 1948); a metereological station, "Presidente *Frei," on King George Island, South Shetlands (established 1969); and three other bases. In 1974 the territory became part of Region XII, MAGALLANES Y ANTARTICA CHILENA (q.v.).

ANTI-COMMUNIST CHILEAN ACTION. See: ACCION CHILENA ANTICOMUNISTA.

ANTISEMITISM. See: JEWS.

ANTOFAGASTA (city). A city and Pacific Ocean seaport in the desert region of northern Chile (23° 40' S, 70° 23' W), 447 miles south of *Arica and 853 miles north of *Santiago. Originally a small fishing harbor called La Chimba in what was then part of *Bolivia, it was upgraded to a minor port and renamed Antofagasta in 1867 to serve the new *silver mine of Caracoles. In 1873 the then British-owned Antofagasta and Bolivia Railway was begun to connect it with La Paz (crossing the present border at Ollague), and in the early 20th century the port was also linked by *railway to Salta in northern *Argentina.

Chile occupied Antofagasta in February 1879 (the immediate cause
of the War of the *Pacific) and after the war the city grew rapidly, soon displacing *Conija as the main port for southern Bolivia.
Antofagasta also exports *nitrate, borax from Ascotán (near
Ollague) and *copper from *Chuquicamata. The population was
5,000 in 1885; 70,000 in 1920; 124,500 in 1971; 193,218 (est.)
in 1982; and 203,067 (est.) in 1986.

ANTOFAGASTA (region). The former province of Antofagasta became
Region II, with the same name, as a result of the 1974 reorganization (see: REGIONS AND ADMINISTRATIVE RESTRUCTURING).
The area is 125,306.3 km^2 (48,381 square miles). Estimated
population was 172,330 in 1920; 271,197 in 1971; and 320,000 in
1982.

API. See: ACCION POPULAR INDEPENDIENTE.

ARAUCANA, La. An epic poem about the Spanish conquest of Chile
and the valiant efforts and sacrifices of the natives, the *Araucanian Indians, who fought the *conquistadores in a war to the
death. Written by Alonso de *Ercilla y Zúñiga (1533-94), La
Araucana portrays a series of events that give a historical account of the wars against the Indians. Ercilla admired the
bravery of the Indians and recorded, in truly Homeric proportions,
the fortitude of men like *Caupolicán, *Lautaro and *Colocolo.
La Araucana is considered today the greatest Spanish epic of
the 16th century.

ARAUCANIA. A new region, made up of the former provinces of
*Malleco and *Cautín, Araucania corresponds to Region IX under
the restructuring carried out by the *junta government in 1974
(see: REGIONS AND ADMINISTRATIVE RESTRUCTURING). Area:
31,760 km^2 (12,263 square miles). Population in 1982: 783,585
(est.). The capital is *Temuco.

ARAUCANIAN INDIANS. The Spaniards termed all the culturally and
linguistically similar nomadic aborigines of central Chile "araucanos"
and their domain "Arauco." Those living north of the River
*Bío-Bío called themselves the Picunche ("north folk") and were
rapidly subjugated after a brief war and soon hispanized through
the *encomienda system. Since those south of the river, the
Mapuche ("people of the land"), unique among South American
Indians, were never conquered by the Spaniards, the term Araucanian came in time to refer to them exclusively. In recent times,
however, it has become more usual to use the aboriginal name
(see: MAPUCHES). See also: GUERRAS DE ARAUCO.

ARAUCANO, El. Newspaper founded in 1830 under government auspices by Andres *Bello López and Manuel José *Gandarillas partly
as a vehicle to publish the texts of new laws and decrees. In
1877 it was replaced by the present official gazette, the *Diario

oficial de la República, founded by José Victorino *Lastarria Santander.

ARAUCO. Province of south-central Chile, formed in 1852, with subsequent boundary modifications in 1869, 1875, 1887. Under the military *junta's reorganization of 1974 it became part of Region VIII, *Bío-Bío. (See: REGIONS AND ADMINISTRATIVE RESTRUCTURING). The population of the province was 60,233 in 1920; 72,289 in 1952; 97,173 in 1970.

ARAUCO DOMADO ("Arauco tamed"). An epic poem of some 16,000 lines, written by Pedro de *Oña to celebrate the deeds of García *Hurtado de Mendoza in the conquest of Chile. It describes the Spanish *conquistador's arrival in southern Chile and his battle with the *Araucanian Indians. Oña's work is inferior to La *Araucana, another epic poem, written by Alonso de *Ercilla y Zúñiga.

ARCHBISHOPS OF SANTIAGO. When *Santiago de Chile was raised to an archdiocese by the Holy See in 1840, the archbishop was regarded as the primate of the *Church in Chile and the spiritual leader of all Catholics in the land. Since then he has been the effective head of the Chilean episcopate. Successive archbishops have been these:

1840-1843	Manuel *Vicuña Larraín (bishop from 1833)
1843-1845	Jose Alejo Eyzaguirre
1845-1878	Rafael Valentín *Valdivieso y Zañartu
1878-1886	Joaquin *Larraín Gandarillas (acting)
1886-1908	Mariano *Casanova Casanova
1908-1919	Juan Ignacio González Eyzaguirre
1919-1931	Crescente Errázuriz
1931-1939	José Horacio *Campillo Infante
1939-1958	José Maria *Caro Rodríguez (Cardinal)
1961-1983	Raúl *Silva Henríquez (Cardinal)
1983-	Juan Francisco *Fresno Larraín (Cardinal)

ARCHIVES. See: NATIONAL ARCHIVES.

AREVALO, Guillermo. *Trade union leader of the now defunct *Central Unica de Trabajadores de Chile and member of the Central Committee of the Communist Party of Chile (*Partido Comunista Chileno). After the *junta came to power with the overthrow of President Salvador *Allende Gossens, Arévalo joined the more militant left, was captured and tortured to death without uttering a single word that could have served his captors.

ARGENTINA, Relations with. Although Chile and Argentina cooperated in the *independence struggle against Spain and in the conflict with Andrés de *Santa Cruz, relations between the two countries have been cool since about 1840 when Chile provided a refuge

for rebels against Argentine dictator Juan Manuel de Rosas (notably Domingo Faustino *Sarmiento and Bartolomé Mitre). Rosas
was also antagonized by the 1843 establishment of a Chilean
settlement at *Punta Arenas, and in 1847 Argentina formally made
claim to all PATAGONIA (q.v.) and the *Strait of *Magellan.
Chile was held responsible for not restraining attacks on Argentine
settlements by *Araucanian Indians, and territorial disputes
increased as both nations pushed effective settlement southward.
War was narrowly averted in 1877 and again at the turn of the
century. The *Pactos de Mayo in 1902 and subsequent arbitration
by British king Edward VII appeared to settle all outstanding
questions, with both countries collaborating in the 1915 A.B.C.
TREATY (q.v.), which endured until the accession of Juan
Domingo Perón to the Argentine presidency.

In 1941 a joint Argentine-Chilean Border Commission was established to help alleviate tension, although it failed to provide a
climate for more harmonious relations. In 1966 Queen Elizabeth
II arbitrated a longstanding dispute along the Río Encuentro on
the *Palena border, but the problem of the BEAGLE CHANNEL
(q.v.) almost led to war in 1982, and explains why Chile, alone
among Hispanic nations, made no endorsement of Argentine claims
to the Falkland Islands that year and was even alleged to have
given covert support to British military operations against Patagonia in the ensuing War of the South Atlantic.

Subsequently there has been some improvement in relations,
and Chile is now Argentina's second largest trading partner in
Latin America.

In recent times a considerable number of Chileans have found
work, or refuge, in Argentina. See: EMIGRATION.

ARICA. Chile's northernmost city, Arica became a Chilean possession
after the War of the *Pacific (1879-83).

Important in early colonial times as the nearest and most convenient port for the Potosí and numerous other *silver mines in
the area, it lost its importance as output in silver declined and
the mines were closed down. At the height of its development
in mid-17th century, Arica's population may have been as high as
100,000. Independence left it in Peruvian territory, separated
from its Bolivian hinterland.

Because of its early wealth, Arica was taken by Sir Francis
*Drake in 1579, who made off with 800 lbs. of silver. The city
also suffered from a number of *earthquakes, the most serious
of which occurred in 1868 and 1877. The epicenter of the first
was under Arica itself, destroying the city; a U.S. warship was
stranded two miles inland by the ensuing tidal wave. The
second earthquake was felt as far away as Hawaii.

In the War of the Pacific, Arica was stormed by the Chileans
on June 7, 1880, twelve days after the fall of *Tacna. The
Treaty of *Ancón in 1883 specified that both cities would be occupied for a period of 10 years, after which time a plebiscite
would determine their nationality. But it was not until 1929,

at the Treaty of *Lima, that Arica became definitively part of Chile and Tacna was returned to *Peru.

Arica's uncertain status was not conducive to development, although a railroad connecting it with La Paz made Arica one of the most important ports for both Chile and *Bolivia (see: RAIL-WAYS).

Nevertheless, the city stagnated even after its future was settled. The 1930 population of 13,200 had risen to only 19,600 by 1952. When Arica became a free port in 1954, a surge in economic development formed the basis of its *automobile industry. Arica's status as a free port remained until rescinded in 1962, but many special *custom privileges remained. The automobile industry and imports remained a monopoly of the city until 1967. (See: AUTO-MOBILE INDUSTRY)

Port installation improvements in the 1960s (see: PORTS) were important to the city's continued economic growth, but by 1979 the number of automobiles assembled in Arica had fallen from a peak of 13,366 in 1970 to 6,945, barely half the national total. Meanwhile *Iquique had been made a free port and the boom it was enjoying in consequence attracted 10,000 emigrants from Arica.

Arica remains important in food production, thanks to the fer-tile valley of the Lluta river, which makes it the only agriculturally efficient area in the entire north. Arica had 87,726 inhabitants (est.) in 1974; about 90,000 in 1980; and 154,422 in 1986.

ARMADA. See: NAVY.

ARMAMENTS. An arsenal, the Fábrica y Maestranza del Ejército (FAMAE) was created in 1811, but most arms were imported. Until World War Two Britain largely supplied those for the *navy, and *Germany those for the *army. Chile's April 1945 declaration of war on Japan, although too late for any participation in the fighting, entitled her to Lend-Lease military supplies from the United States. Between 1950 and 1972 *United States military aid totaled US $65 million. The initial result of the 1973 *coup was to increase this considerably: US $68 million worth was supplied in the first year after the *coup, and a further US $70 million was approved in October 1975, all for the *air force, and including 18 Northrop F-5 fighter-bombers.

Home-produced equipment is still limited to some infantry weapons, light armored vehicles, air defense weapons, light air-craft and small naval craft. The Country's continued dependence on arms imports has been a continual embarassment since the coup. When the Labour Party returned to power in Britain in March 1974 it announced it would accept no new arms contracts for Chile and the AUEW (engineering union) blocked all work al-ready in progress. A U.S. arms embargo was voted by Congress in February 1976, and *France, West Germany and Austria have been among other nations restricting arms supplies to Chile. Such difficulties, however, did not stop the *Pinochet regime from concluding a military aid pact with the Eric Gairy dictatorship in Grenada in January 1977.

There was consequently some attempt in the 1970s to increase the scope of the FAMAE, but its project to modernize the M3-A1 half-track was canceled for lack of funds. Industrial activity by the state was inconsistent with the new regime's economic philosophy and in 1977 FAMAE's budget was slashed by 20 percent to encourage the growth of a private armaments industry. This led to the creation of Carlos Cardoen's Explosivos Industriales Cardoen in 1978, whose Alacrán half-track entered service in April 1983. Since 1981 Industrial Nacional de Aeronaves has been building the Pillán T-35 training airplane (based on the Piper trainer) with 15 percent Chilean components. There is also Astilleros y Maestranzas (ASMER) which provides the navy with vessels up to 1,500 *tons.

Meanwhile foreign supplies had become easier in late 1979 with an Israeli offer of air-to-air missiles and small arms, and a French offer of 16 Mirage-50s (although a new French president, Mitterand, reimposed an arms ban the following year). Soon afterwards West Germany allowed work to begin on two submarines for Chile's navy. Between 1979 and 1981 Brazil's new armament industry made Chile its best Latin American customer, supplying 200 Cascavel EE-9 tanks, 250 Urutú EE-11 amphibious armored troop carriers, 20 twenty-mm gunboats, and a number of aircraft. Britain's new Conservative government lifted its arms embargo in July 1980 (a factor, no doubt, in securing the alleged secret Chilean support in the Falkland War), and in October 1981 Congress agreed to end U.S. restrictions as soon as President Reagan should certify an improvement in the *human rights situation.

Nevertheless, the net result has been a marked decline in Chilean military strength relative to its neighbors. The heavy Argentine build-up begun under the 1976-82 military government has been continued by Alfonsín and has already more than made good that country's 1982 war losses. *Peru has acquired over US $1,000 million worth of arms from COMECON countries since 1970 and is continuing to rearm with Soviet assistance. Nor are Chile's supply difficulties at an end. A barter deal with *Brazil to obtain advanced training aircraft may be frustrated by the return of that country to civilian rule. In February 1985 the *United Kingdom stopped a sale of riot control vehicles for the *Cuerpo de Carabineros, presumably from doubts about the regime's durability.

ARMED FORCES. The *Independence struggle convinced Chile's leaders of the need for effective armed forces. Despite the country's limited resources, Bernardo *O'Higgins had by 1820 established an *army of 5,000 men. The *navy began with two ships in 1813; in 1820 its 8 men-of-war and 16 transports served to transport José de *San Martín's allied army of 2,000 Chileans and 2,400 Argentines to *Peru. The victorious war of 1836-39 against Andrés de *Santa Cruz enhanced the army's prestige,

while the navy saw action in the brief war of 1866-67 with *Spain,
and both services distinguished themselves in the 1879-84 War
of the *Pacific.

After the departure of its Scottish admiral Lord *Cochrane,
the navy continued to model itself on Britain's Royal Navy. The
army developed at first under *French influence, and, then,
following the Franco-Prussian War (1870-71) under that of Prussia.
Very important for the Prussianization of the army was the op-
portunist adherence of Emil *Koerner, German director of the
*Escuela Militar, to the winning side in the *Civil War of 1891.
Among the consequences was the introduction of *conscription
(compulsory military service) in 1900. The *air force, created
by the 1930 merger of the other two services' air arms, was
largely trained by British officers, although there had been a
German air mission in 1924. The gendarmerie, or para-military
*police, dates as a separate force (the *Cuerpo de Carabineros)
from 1927.

Since World War Two the *United States has had a preponderant
influence as the major source of equipment and training for all
four forces. The army was probably most influenced by U.S.
training, but equipment aid benefited primarily the air force
and navy. The navy has a long tradition of being the most
favored service: all through the 1950s and 1960s military expenditure divided roughly in the ratio 8:6:4 between navy,
army and air force. Equipment procurement depends largely on
imports, which since the *coup of 1973 have been plagued by
*human rights disputes with a number of countries. The con-
sequent shortages of *armaments has caused a marked decline
in Chilean military strength relative to her neighbors: in 1980
Argentine military expenditure was almost four times that of
Chile.

In mid-1984 the armed forces numbered almost 120,000 men.
The army's active strength was 50,000 men and 3,000 officers; the
navy had 26,000 sailors and 2,600 marines, the air force strength
was 15,000, and there were 27,000 carabineros. Each of the
services has its own academy for officer training. There is also
an Academia Politécnica Militar for army engineer officers, and
three senior staff colleges: the army's *Academia de Guerra,
the air force's *Academia de Guerra de la Fuerza Aérea, and the
combined services' Academia de Defensa Nacional. Officers of
all four services are also often sent to the USA for specialized
training.

Total defense expenditure during the 1950 and 1960s averaged
about US$ 100 million (2-3 percent of GNP), but it increased
markedly after the coup, reaching 25,600 million *pesos (US$
732.6 million) in 1979 (7.11 percent of GNP); 56,000 million pesos
(US$ 1,436 million) in 1981; and 82,000 million pesos (US$
2,102.6 million) in 1982. But the poor state of the economy
forced a cutback in 1983 and a further one in 1984, to US$
1,600 million--almost the 1980 level. As Chile's economic decline
became even more precipitate, the 1984 figure amounted to almost

10 percent of GNP--or 40 percent of export income.

Well over half the military budget goes toward personnel costs: not that basic salaries are out of line with civilian equivalents, but because of the extremely generous provision of such "perks" as excellent medical facilities, food allowances, subsidized house-purchase loans, indexed pensions (at 100 percent of active pay after 30 years' service), responsibility allowances and hardship-posting compensation (up to 100 percent in parts of mainland Chile, 200 percent on *Easter Island, and 600 percent in the Antarctic). Conscripts, on the other hand, are quite ill paid.

ARMY. In colonial times Chile had a militia, founded in 1760, numbering 1,600 men. The volunteer army raised to fight for Chilean *Independence consisted of a battalion of infantry, 2 squadrons of cavalry and 4 companies of artillery, but this was decimated at *Rancagua and its remnants escaped into *Argentina, eventually returning as part of José de *San Martín's liberating Ejército de los *Andes. San Martín's Chilean second-in-command, Bernardo *O'Higgins, was named *Supreme Director of Chile in 1817 and immediately set about creating a national militia, Hispano-America's first regular army. It consisted of an infantry battalion under Juan de Dios *Vial del Río, and an artillery unit under Joaquín *Prieto Vial. Unfortunately it proved incapable of preserving control of the country during the *anarquía política that followed O'Higgins' fall in 1823, and which culminated in a final defeat of government troops under O'Higgins' successor Ramón Freire Serrano at *Lircay in 1830. Diego *Portales Palazuelos and Prieto Vial, the new rulers of Chile, created a purged and unified army from the forces of both sides, under firm civilian control: 3 infantry battalions, 2 cavalry regiments, a squadron of hussars and a regiment of artillery. Portales also set up a civil militia as a counterpoise, entrusted with such duties as guarding the *Moneda Palace.

Although the purge did not prevent the *Quillota Mutiny, the new army distinguished itself in the 1836-39 war against Andrés de *Santa Cruz. But after that it was mainly occupied in protecting settlers against the *Araucanian Indians. Although increased in 1843 to 5 infantry battalions and 3 regiments of cavalry, it was, at the outbreak of the War of the *Pacific, still a small frontier guard of 400 officers and 2,400 men with 16 artillery pieces from Krupp. During the war, against the even less prepared armies of *Peru and *Bolivia, it expanded rapidly: to 10,000 men by May 1879; 17,000 by the year's end; eventually evolving into an efficient 45,000-strong field army, which, after final victory, was put to offensive use against the Araucanians.

The continuing threat posed by Peruvian revanchisme and by the long-standing border dispute with *Argentina persuaded Chile to retain this enlarged army, and Emil *Koerner Heinze was recruited from *Germany to help in its modernization. The result was the best equipped army and the best educated officer corps in Latin America.

During the *Civil War of 1891 the traditionally conservative
*navy united against President José Manuel *Balmaceda Fernãndez,
but the army split, with a majority of its officers supporting him.
The division of loyalties thus created in the army officer corps
remained politically important for many years, while the war and
its aftermath also exacerbated relations with the navy, seen as
unduly favored by the post-1891 regime. All high-ranking
*Balmacedistas were purged at the end of the war, and 116
(out of 118) loyalist captains were suspended for six years. On
the other hand, Koerner's personal participation in the war on
the rebels' side as their chief-of-staff (itself a key factor in
their victory) strengthened his influence and hastened the
Prussianization of the Chilean army in the period up to World War
One. This was manifested not only in training, organization,
uniforms and equipment (notably the 9mm Mauser rifle introduced
in 1899), but, above all, in the army's attitude to politics and
politicians. This was not improved by the politicians' frequent
use of the army in repressing *labor discontent. One result was
the army's direct political involvement during the so-called second
period of *anarquía política, 1924-32.

Although the army's relative prestige vis-â-vis the navy was
enhanced by the *Coquimbo mutiny, the embarassing events of
1931-32 convinced most officers to return to abstention from
political intervention--even when faced with the *Frente Popular
victory of 1938 and despite suffering a *Depression-induced reduction from 5 divisions and 24,000 men to only 3 divisions and
12,000 men. There were, all the same, a number of attempts
at intervention by isolated army units: in 1935, 1938, 1939,
1945-46 and 1953-55.

The 1964 army take-over in *Brazil gave food for thought.
In 1969 General Roberto *Viaux Marambio attempted a rising
against President Eduardo *Frei Montalva, and the election of
President Salvador *Allende Gossens in 1970 provoked the right-
wing murder of army c.-in-c. Rene *Schneider Chereau, the most
prominent champion of army neutrality. He was succeeded by
another neutralist, Carlos *Prats González, but from then on the
army became increasingly politicized, all the more so when Allende
tried to combat this by recruiting members of the armed forces
into his Cabinet. At the end of August 1973 Allende replaced
Prats with General Augusto *Pinochet Ugarte, both he and Prats
being unaware that Pinochet had been actively plotting rebellion
with the majority of generals, admirals and air marshals since
the previous year.

The successful *coup took place on September 11, 1973, and
officers who had failed to go along with the usurpation of power
were purged.

The new army c.-in-c., General Pinochet, thus became President of the Republic. Command of the army under him devolved
upon Lieutenant General César Raul Manuel *Benavides Escóbar,
who became a member of the new governing *junta in 1980. The

vice-commander-in-chief was Lieutenant General Julio *Canessa, and immediately below him was the chief of the army general staff, Major General Rafael Ortiz Navarro. In 1985 Canessa replaced Benavides as head of the army, and Santiago Sinclair became vice-commander-in-chief.

See also: ARMAMENTS; ARMED FORCES; CONSCRIPTION; ESCUELA MILITAR.

ARQUIVOS NACIONALES. See: NATIONAL ARCHIVES.

ARROBA. An old Spanish measure of weight (25 *libras, or a fourth of a *quintal), equivalent to 11.502 kilograms or 25 lbs 5.72 ozs. See: WEIGHTS AND MEASURES.

ASENTADOS. Peasants who technically did not receive title to the land they cultivated, but who worked cooperatively with other *campesinos on parcels of expropriated land.

ASENTAMIENTOS. *Agrarian reform centers set up during the administration of President Salvador *Allende Gossens (1970-73), in charge of redistributing the land to *campesinos by breaking up the *latifundias, providing bank loans, overseeing farm planning and insuring incentives to the peasants for increased production. See also: COOPERATIVES.

ASICH. See: ACCION SINDICAL CHILENA.

ASMER (Astilleros y Maestranzas). See: ARMAMENTS.

ASOCIACION LATINOAMERICANA DE LIBRE COMERCIO. See: LATIN AMERICAN FREE TRADE ASSOCIATION.

ATACAMA. The great desert of northern Chile. Not only is the direct rainfall minimal, but the *Andes in the latitude of the Atacama desert are too arid to allow effective irrigation from streams and rivers (in contrast to the situation at *Arica, and further north in *Peru). The desert stretches 500 miles north-south (from *Iquique to Chañaral) and is 200 miles across at its widest (between Mejillones and the Argentine frontier).

Administratively, Atacama is the name of the former province to the south of the desert formed in 1843 and which became Region III (with the same name) in the restructuring of 1974 (see: REGIONS AND ADMINISTRATIVE RESTRUCTURING). It has an area of 78,268 km^2 (30,219 square miles), and the population (79,531 in 1920; 118,277 in 1960; 152,045 in 1970) was estimated as 204,488 in 1982.

ATACAMEÑOS. Indians who had settled in the semi-desert provinces of *Atacama and *Coquimbo before the arrival of the Spanish conquerors. They were pastoral and were soon absorbed by the more numerous *Diaguitas hordes, who came from western Argentina. Both tribes have long since been extinct.

AUDIENCIA. A royal *law court established in colonial Spanish America, presided over by a ranking official (viceroy, governor or captain general). It served as the highest court of appeal and exercised practically all the functions of government within its territorial jurisdiction. Its members were judges known as *oidores ("those who hear"). Their number varied according to the importance of each audiencia (that of Mexico, for instance, had ten oidores, while that of Guatemala had only three). The first audiencia was established in Santo Domingo in 1511. Soon the most important trading centers had their own audiencias. Mexico City had one in 1527, and Lima one in 1542. The first audiencia in Chile was that of *Santiago, established in 1609.

AURORA, La. A newspaper published in *Santiago in 1937 to diffuse the ideology of the political party known as the *Acción Republicana.

AURORA DE CHILE, La. Chile's first newspaper. A political weekly, it was founded by Juan *Egaña Risco, and was printed in *Santiago on a press specially imported for the purpose from the United States by Mateo Arnaldo *Hoebel, a Swiss-born U.S. citizen who became *intendant of the city. Edited by Fray Camilo *Henríquez González, the paper lasted from February 13, 1812 till April 1, 1814, when it became the Monitor araucano, under which title it was published from April 6, 1813 until September 30, 1814-- just before the royalists triumphed at the battle of *Rancagua.

AUTOMOBILE INDUSTRY. When the city of *Arica became a free port in 1954, Chile opened its doors to an automobile industry that saw the first assembly plants developed in the country's northernmost city. By 1960, 1,854 passenger cars a year were being produced in Arica. In 1962 twenty different foreign manufacturers assembled 6,615 vehicles, that number reaching 7,797 vehicles in 1964. As a result, automobile imports fell from an estimated 17,500 in 1961 to 9,000 a year later, and reached an all-time low of 2,000 (only 8 of which were passenger cars) in 1964.
But Arica's free port status ended in 1962, and by 1967 the Chilean government, as part of a policy of regional development, permitted other cities to develop car manufacturing plants. Fiat was allowed to build a factory in *Rancagua, Peugeot at Los Andes, and Ford Motors at Casablanca, a small town located conveniently close to both *Santiago and *Valparaiso. In spite of this competition, Arica's output peaked at 13,366 units in 1970, as opposed to a combined total of 11,225 units in the "Zona Central."
The advent of the *Unidad Popular government in 1970, suspicious of multinationals, caused several foreign firms (including Nissan and British Leyland) to end their Chilean operations. The number of foreign car manufacturers in Arica fell to 4. The free-trade policy of the post-1974 *junta government, with its slashing of the high protective *custom duty on imported cars,

was even more disastrous to the automobile industry, especially since the Chilean government decided to withdraw from the *Pacto Andino in 1976.

By 1977 only four firms (two in Arica, two in Central Chile) were left, producing 13,089 units that year, of which 9,896 were passenger cars. During the same year, 34,941 cars were imported. This compares with 30,000 vehicles assembled in Peru, almost 20,000 in Argentina, and just under a million in Brazil.

The 1982 production was 10,255 units, of which 7,926 were passenger cars. Automotriz Arica (formerly Citröen Chile) produced 457 units; General Motors Chile, also in Arica, produced 3,354 units. Automotores Franco-Chilenos (formerly Renault-Peugeot) and Fiat Chile, both located in the Central Valley, produced 3,437 and 3,007 units, respectively. By 1986 only General Motors and Franco-Chilenos remained. A new law of December 1985 introduced a phasing out of all protection of Chilean automobile assembly over two years. Finance minister Hernán *Büchi Buc was reported to believe that it was uneconomic for Chile to have a motor vehicle industry.

AUTORIDAD EJECUTIVA. The executive branch of the newly established (July 4, 1811) Chilean *Congress. It came into existence on August 11, 1811.

AVELLANO. Site of a battle fought on December 10, 1819, between Conservatives, who wanted to retain the Spanish crown to control the affairs of Chile, and the *Independientes, who wanted total separation from Spain.

AVIATION. See: AIR FORCE; AIR TRANSPORT, AIRPORTS; LADECO; LAN-CHILE.

AVION ROJO. The red trimotor Fokker aircraft used by Marmaduke *Grove Vallejo to return from exile in *Argentina on September 30, 1930, in a plot to lead a putsch by soldiers of the *Concepción garrison. Grove and his associates were taken prisoner by loyalist troops and sent to *Easter Island. See: DOVER CONSPIRACY.

AYLWIN AZOCAR, Patricio (1918-). Lawyer by profession, and one of the founders of the Christian Democratic Party (*Partido Demócrata Cristiano). In 1951 he became president of the *Falange Nacional, the precursor of the Christian Democratic Party. From 1958 to 1960, and again in 1965, he was president of the Christian Democratic Party. In 1965 he was elected to an eight-year term in the senate. During the incumbency of President Salvador *Allende Gossens (1970-73), Aylwin, as leader of the Christian Democrats, took on a policy of confrontation with *Unidad Popular. As one of the more conservative members of his party, he applauded the military *coup d'état that overthrew Allende. However, the *junta made it very clear to him that they had set out

on a new course to institute a different kind of "democracy" in
Chile, one that would be devoid of politicians and political parties.
They further instructed the Christian Democrats to keep away
from politicking unless they were willing to face the consequences.

AYSEN. Former province of southern Chile, created as a territory
in 1928 from parts of the province of *Chiloé and of the territory
of *Magallanes, with an area of 108,998 km^2 (42,087 square miles).
The population grew from 1,660 (est.) in 1920 to about 10,000 in
1928; 21,896 in 1960; 48,496 in 1970; and 66,322 (est.) in 1982.
In 1974 the province became the new Region XI, designated variously *Coyhaique (after its capital city) and Aysén del General
Ibáñez del Campo (in honor of Carlos *Ibáñez del Campo during
whose first presidency the territory was first organized). Also
spelled Aisén.

- B -

BACHELET, Angela. See: WOMEN AND THE WOMEN'S MOVEMENT.

BACHELET MARTINEZ, Alberto. General of the *air force who refused to go along with the *coup d'état of September 11, 1973,
and who was killed by the military regime of President Augusto
*Pinochet Ugarte on March 12, 1974. Like so many other officers
who had resisted the military intervention in Chile, he was considered an enemy of the state and had to be eliminated. When
he died, he was in his fifties. His death was widely denounced
by *Church and legal sources in Chile.

BALANCE OF PAYMENTS. Over the years, Chile has suffered chronically from severe balance of payment crises. Frequently foreign
exchange earnings would fall as a consequence of a lower international price of *copper. This would deprive the country of
sufficient foreign exchange to cover the national debt, which
would, in turn, lead to further borrowing. Trade deficits would
grow as imports exceeded exports, and investments would dry
up as confidence in the *economy declined.
Such a sequence occurred in the late 1960s, but when President
Salvador *Allende Gossens came to power in 1970, the balance of
payment position was good and Chile's international reserves were
high. In 1971 these reserves were used to import great quantities
of foodstuffs and other goods, and consumption reached an all-
time high. At the same time, though, there was an exodus of
foreign and domestic capital, as investors were not happy with
Chile's experiment with socialism. This led to a deterioration in
the balance of payments which continued during 1972 and 1973.
Chile suspended repayment of its foreign debts and its foreign
exchange reserves became negative.

When President Augusto *Pinochet Ugarte came to power in September 1973, he immediately set out to curb inflation and to remove *customs and duties on imports and exports, making use of free-market economics under strict monetarist policies. Inflation was reduced from a rate equivalent to 1,000 percent per annum to 10 percent, and the economic recovery some called "a miracle" was on.

From 1973 to 1977 Chile experienced an economic growth of 8 percent to 9 per annum, and foreign capital began to pour back into the country. By 1979 Chile's balance of payments was strong and her reserves were growing. Then something happened and the economic miracle turned into a nightmare.

Chile's economic collapse began in the second half of 1981, as foreign bankers, who had been eager to lend Chile money, suddenly noticed a huge deterioration in the balance of payments. As *foreign investment, which had been surging into the country at an almost exponential rate (rising from US$ 572 million in 1977 to US$ 2,200 million in 1979 and US$ 4,800 million in 1981) began to dry up, some hard facts about the Chilean economy began to surface. The biggest problem was the increasing trade deficit. This had reached US$ 355 million in 1979, but even that was nothing compared to the US$ 2,600 million reached in 1981. This was due almost entirely to a virtual explosion in imports of consumer goods while export earnings had remained constant. Another problem was that the currency had been pegged to the dollar (see: EXCHANGE RATES) so that the *peso had become grossly overvalued, making Chilean products increasingly uncompetitive in world markets.

Worst of all, the Chilean banking system was collapsing. The banks' difficulties in meeting obligations on heavy foreign borrowing were made worse from 1982 when the peso was devalued. The government was forced to liquidate three banks and take over five others, including the three largest (see: BANKS, BANKING AND FINANCIAL INSTITUTIONS).

By 1982, Chile's balance of payments was in total disarray, as the country's foreign debt reached US$ 1,700 million, more than double that of Brazil, and thirty times that of Mexico in relation to population.

Even with a favorable increase in the price of copper in 1983, a balance of payment crisis was developing in 1984, due primarily to a fall in export earnings while the foreign debt burden continued to soar, to US$ 1,800 million. Moreover, just servicing the debt (public and private) had reached US$ 3,200 million, equivalent to more than 80 percent of Chile's 1984 export earnings.

See also: ECONOMY; FOREIGN AID; PUBLIC FINANCE.

BALMACEDA FERNANDEZ, José Manuel (1840-1891). President of the Republic, 1886-91. A member of the *Partido Nacional and one of the most admired orators of his time, Balmaceda was elected President with the backing of the Liberals (*Partido Liberal) and Radicals (*Partido Radical). During the first years of his presidency he was able to increase public revenue and to embark on an ambitious public works program, which included a 600-mile expansion of the *railways, the building of *highways, the improvement of *ports and harbors, the provision of safe water supplies, the lengthening of *telegraph lines, increased *postal services, and better provision of sanitation and *public health services. There were also improvements in *education, in *agriculture, and in *manufacturing. Despite general prosperity, Balmaceda's administration alienated a reluctant *Congress, which was not ready for such radical changes, and relations between them began to deteriorate.

A controversy ensued over congressional criticism of government spending, and the President's programs met violent opposition. He was accused of being extravagant and of attempting to free himself from Congress so that he could rule dictatorially. By 1890 he could count on only a few political supporters. Congress challenged his cabinet choices and refused to approve his budget. He played into the hands of his enemies when, in January 1891, without convening Congress, he appropriated funds for the new fiscal year. A week later, Congress, meeting as a National Assembly, declared the president deposed. Balmaceda, assuming dictatorial powers, refused to yield and the *Civil War of 1891 ensued.

Although the bulk of the *army remained loyal to the President, the revolutionary Congress, with the support of the *navy, which controlled the *ports, defeated the government forces in two encounters: the battle of *Concón, near *Valparaíso, and that of La *Placilla, near *Santiago. Both battles, which left more than 10,000 dead, occurred in August 1891. The defeated Balmaceda found asylum in the Argentine embassy, refusing to resign until the expiration of his term of office on September 18, 1891. A day later he wrote an eloquent statement defending his actions and pleading for mercy for his supporters, and then committed suicide. The death of Balmaceda marked the end of thirty years of liberal rule. See also: COUP D'ETAT OF 1973.

BALMACEDISTA. A partisan or sympathizer of President (1887-91) José Manuel *Balmaceda Fernández. See also: PARTIDO LIBERAL DEMOCRATICO.

BALTIMORE, U.S.S. United States warship whose October 1891 visit to Valparaíso created a serious diplomatic incident. A fight between Chilean workmen and sailors ashore from the ship caused a number of casualties including two American dead. The American ambassador demanded immediate compensation; foreign minister Manuel Antonio *Matta Goyenechea considered this insultingly premature, as the official investigation was yet in progress, and declared the ambassador persona non grata. The U.S. State Department replied with an ultimatum, threatening war if an indemnity of 75,000 pesos were not paid forthwith. The Chilean government decided to give way, whereupon Matta resigned.

BALTRA CORTES, Alberto (1912-). Lawyer by profession and
member of the Radical Party (*Partido Radical). He taught at
the *Universidad de Chile, and was director of the university's
School of Political Economy. From 1942 to 1945 he was General
Director of the economics ministry (Ministerio de *Economía y
Comercio). He was later named minister of economy and trade
by President (1946-52) Gabriel *González Videla. In 1950 he was
president of the Chilean delegation at the third congress of the
*Economic Commission for Latin America (ECLA), held in Montevideo,
Uruguay. In 1958 he became president of the Radical Party.
Since then he has been active in Chilean economic circles and has
written various books on economics.

BANADOS ESPINOSA, Julio (1858-1899). Newspaper correspondent;
writer of various books on Chilean history, professor of law at
the *Universidad de Chile; holder of various ministerial posts
in the government of President (1886-91) José Manuel *Balmaceda
Fernández. In 1885 he was elected deputy in *Congress from
Ovalle, and in 1888 he was appointed justice minister. From 1890
to 1891 he was editor of La *Nación. When the *Civil War of 1891
began he was minister of the interior, but on August 3 he became
minister of war and took part in the battles of *Concón and La
*Placilla (August 27 and 28, respectively). The government
troops having been defeated, he left Chile and went to *Peru,
where he asked for political asylum. He returned to Chile in
1894, was elected deputy to *Congress and was named director of
the *Partido Liberal Democrático. In 1897 he was made minister
of industry and public works. As a newspaperman he won many
awards for his objective reporting. He left many works which
were published posthumously. In 1889 he was honored by the
Brazilian Emperor Pedro II with the cross of the Order of the
Rose.

BANKS, BANKING AND FINANCIAL INSTITUTIONS.
A. History. The Spanish *law inherited by independent Chile,
with its Biblical distrust of usury, was too medieval in outlook
and too protective of the borrower in its practical effects to
permit the growth of a modern financial system. In 1854 a law
introduced the concept of commercial partnerships with limited
liability--the modern corporation ("sociedad autónoma")--but
until Chilean law was generally modernized with the 1856 promulgation of the new Civil Code, Valparaíso merchants were Chile's
de facto bankers, giving credit in the form of goods against
future production (of a farm or a mine). The first and most
important mortgage bank, the Caja de Crédito Hipotecario, was
created by *Congress in August 1855. The first commercial bank
(created in 1854 and incorporated in 1856) was the Banco de
Valparaíso de Depósitos y Descuentos, whose title was simplified
in 1860 to Banco de Valparaíso. In 1867 its chief shareholder,
Agustín *Edwards Ossandón, started his own Banco A. Edwards
y Cia. Other commercial banks, including the Banco de Chile

and the Banco Agrícola, were formed, and by 1890 Chile had 14
banks. In 1884 a Caja de Ahorros (Savings Bank) was opened
for small savings, and this later became part of the Caja de
Crédito Hipotecario. All of these institutions concentrated on
large loans to big landowners, who alone were thought credit-
worthy. The landowners in turn, rather than invest in *agriculture, which they allowed to remain primitive and undercapital-
ized, used such loans to reinvest in more remunerative industrial
and commercial speculation.

A central bank, the Banco Central de Chile, was created in
1929, and its authority and responsibilities progressively increased.
Until 1974 it served as the nation's main credit channel and was
the only institution allowed to issue bank notes. (See: KEMMERER,
Edwin Walter).

When President Salvador *Allende Gossens came to power, one
of the first measures he took was to nationalize the Chilean banks:
this became effective in 1971. After his overthrow in September
1973, the new military *junta had to essentially rebuild the banking
system, which they quickly returned to private ownership.

By 1981 Chile's financial system was relatively well developed
and expanding. The major financial institution in *Santiago,
apart from the Central Bank, was the State Bank of Chile (Banco
del Estado de Chile), founded in 1953. In addition to its four
offices in the capital, it had 146 branches throughout the country.
It acted as a repository of state funds, as a savings institution,
and as a mortgage and loan bank.

There were some sixty other banking institutions, including:
Banco A. Edwards; Banco de Chile; Banco de Concepción; Banco
Continental; Banco de Créditos e Inversiones; Banco Empresarial
de Fomento; Banco Hipotecario de Chile (BHC); Banco Hipotecario
de Fomento Nacional; Banco Industrial y de Comercio Exterior;
Banco Internacional; Banco Morgan Finza; Banco Nacional; Banco
O'Higgins; Banco Osorno y La Unión; Banco del Pacífico; Banco
de Santiago; Banco Sudamericano; Banco del Trabajo; Banco Unido
de Fomento; Colocadora Nacional de Valores; and Banco Comercial
de Curicó.

There were 18 foreign banks operating in Chile, of which
Manufacturers Hanover was traditionally the most active. The
others were: The American Express International Banking Corporation, Banco do Brasil; Banco Real; Bank of America; Bank
of Nova Scotia; Bank of Tokyo; Bankers Trust; Chase Manhattan;
Chemical Bank; Citibank; Crédit Suisse; Deutsche-Südamericani-
shce Bank; First National Bank of Boston; Hong Kong and Shang-
hai Banking Corporation; Midland Bank; and Morgan Guarantee.

The most important financial association was the Asociación de
Bancos e Instituciones Financieras de Chile. The Stock Market
revolved around the Bolsa de Comercio and the Bolsa de Valores
(see: STOCK EXCHANGE).

B. The Collapse of 1981-84. By 1979, restrictions that
forced banks into specialized activities, such as limiting commercial banks to short-term loans, had been removed in order to

broaden bank services in the interest of fostering competition and securing the economies of scale. The sharp fall in *inflation (from the equivalent of 1,000 percent per annum to 19 percent) that had followed the *coup restored the confidence of depositors and investors. Furthermore, interest rates, which had been extremely high for several years, declined in 1979 and 1980, although they were to rise again sharply in the second half of 1981.

Since the coup, Chile's *economy had been managed by a handful of advisers to President Augusto *Pinochet Ugarte known as the *"Chicago Boys" because they had all been educated at the University of Chicago and had adopted the monetarist policies of Milton Friedman. The leader of this group was Sergio de *Castro Spikula, who was economics minister from 1975 to 1976 and finance minister from 1976 to 1982. So committed were they to the free market model that they were impervious to argument and were seen as extremely arrogant. They recommended the pegging of the *exchange rate. They also laid down that the domestic money supply should be increased or reduced in line with the inflow or outflow of foreign currency reserves in the Central Bank.

These measures, however, were not sufficient to avoid a collapse, which began in late 1981. Foreign bankers, who had been falling over themselves to lend Chile money, suddenly noticed a huge deterioration in the country's *balance of payments. As foreign capital began in consequence to dry up, Chilean banks began to have difficulty servicing their debts. In many cases absence of regulation had allowed banks to lend excessively to their own subsidiaries and borrow reserves from them. The hollowness of the economic boom emerged most clearly from the size of Chile's total foreign indebtedness (see: BALANCE OF PAYMENTS). The "Chicago Boys" were sent packing, along with an economic model that had not worked.

In 1981 four banks and four financial institutions were taken over by the government, in reversal of the doctrine that government should play the smallest possible role in the economy. In January 1983, five more banks were taken over (the Banco de Concepción, the Colocadora Nacional de Valores, the Banco Internacional, the Banco de Chile and the Banco Santander) and two banks were liquidated (the BHC and the Banco Unido de Fomento). The consequences this time appeared much more serious than in 1981. The total liabilities of the banks that had been taken over amounted to US$ 3,760 million of which the Banco de Chile accounted for a staggering US$ 2,100 million. The liabilities of the two banks that were liquidated were US$ 2.6 million in the case of BHC, and US$ 138.7 million in that of the Banco Unido de Fomento.

The collapse in the banking system, it was feared, could seriously undermine the entire financial system for several years to come.

BAQUEDANO GONZALEZ, Manuel (1826-1897). A precocious military genius who ran away from home when he was only 12 years old to fight against the *Peru-Bolivia Confederation. At the age of 13 he was promoted to lieutenant, and by the end of the War of the *Pacific (in which he captured the city of Lima) he had reached the rank of general. He was also active in politics as a member of the Liberal Party (*Partido Liberal), and in 1881 he was nominated for the presidency of Chile, an honor he refused. From 1882 to 1888 he was in *Congress as senator from *Santiago. He did not participate in the *Civil War of 1891. As a result, he was named by President (1886-91) José Manuel *Blamaceda Fernández on August 28, 1891, to succeed him as the head of an interim government. This government lasted just the three days it took for Jorge *Montt Alvarez, the rebel leader, to reach Santiago.

BARBOSA BAEZA, Enrique (b. 1882). Lawyer by profession and active member of the *Partido Liberal Democrático. When a faction of the party split off to become the *Partido Liberal Democrático Aliancista, he became its president (1926). In 1925 he supported Emiliano *Figueroz Larraín , who became President (1925-27) of Chile. In 1932 he rejoined the Partido Liberal Democrático and backed the candidacy of Arturo *Alessandri Palma, who became President of Chile for the second time (1932-38). In 1956 Barbosa Baeza joined the newly formed *Movimiento Republicano, becoming its vice-president. From January to May 1956 he served as minister of foreign affairs in the cabinet of President (1952-58) Carlos *Ibáñez del Campo.

BARBOSA PUGA, Orozimbo (1838-1891). A career military officer who fought in *Valparaíso in 1866 during the War of 1865-66 with *Spain. He also fought against the *Araucanian Indians in 1868. He became a colonel in 1876, and in 1880 and 1881 was highly commended for his bravery in the War of the *Pacific. In 1891 he was elected to the Senate and remained loyal to President (1886-91) José Manuel *Balmaceda Fernández during the *Civil War of 1891. He was commander-in-chief of the loyalist troops in the final battle of La *Placilla, where he was defeated in a skirmish, taken prisoner by a superior force of rebel cavalry and barbarously assassinated. His body was then paraded naked through the streets of nearby Valparaíso.

BARRA LASTARRIA, Eduardo de la (1839-1900). Nineteenth-century Chilean author and member of the Radical Party (*Partido Radical). In 1864 he became popular through his book of poems, Poesías líricas. He also wrote various treatises on linguistics and on the rhetoric of the Spanish language. His best work on linguistics concentrates on the Spanish epic Poema de mio Cid. He kept himself immersed in political disputes and in 1891 participated in the *Civil War of 1891, condemning the actions of the revolutionary *Congress. Because of this loyalty to President (1886-91)

José Manuel *Balmaceda Fernández, he was forced into exile in Montevideo, Uruguay. He also spent about three years in Buenos Aires, Argentina. His reputation as an educator and poet led the Argentine government to bestow numerous commissions upon him, but in 1895 he decided to return to Chile. Upon his arrival, he was received and acclaimed by many young Chilean intellectuals.

BARRENECHEA PINTO, Julio César (1910–   ). Member of the Socialist Party (*Partido Socialista). In 1931 as president of the Federation of Students, he led the student movement that overthrew the government of President (1927-31) Carlos *Ibáñez del Campo. In 1932 he was elected president of the student government at the *Universidad de Chile. From 1932 to 1941 he was deputy for *Cautín in *Congress, and from 1941-45 was deputy for *Santiago. In 1944 he was named second vice-president of the Chamber of Deputies. From 1945 to 1952 he was Chilean ambassador to *Bolivia. In 1956 he left the Socialist Party and became president of the *Partido Democrático Nacional (PADENA). Since his youth he has written many books of poetry and in 1960 he received the *Premio Nacional de Literatura. In 1966 President (1964-70) Eduardo *Frei Montalva named him ambassador to India.

BARRIOS HUDTWALCKER, Eduardo (1884-1963). Chilean writer and author of many literary works. He was Director of the *National Library of Chile (1927-31) and held many important ministerial offices. He was minister of public instruction in 1927; minister of the interior in 1928; and minister of public *education (the new name for "public instruction") later the same year. During the 1940s he edited El *Mercurio. In 1946 he won a very coveted literary prize, the *Premio Nacional de Literatura. In 1953 he again became minister of education, and from 1953 to 1960 was General Director of Libraries and Museums. Barrios' best-known novels are: El niño que enloqueció de amor (1915); Un perdido (1917); and El hermano asno (1922).

BARRIOS TIRADO, Guillermo (b. 1893). A career *army officer. He studied at the *Escuela Militar in Santiago (1912-13), an institution which he later directed (1942-43). In 1946 he became general, and from 1947 to 1952 was minister of national defense. From 1958 to 1960 he was governor of *Arica, the northernmost city in Chile. He has written many books and articles on military science.

BARROS ARANA, Diego (1830-1906). Chilean historian and man of letters. He wrote many important biographies, among them the well-known Galería de hombres célebres de Chile and his Historia general de la independencia de Chile. The latter, begun in 1854 and finished in 1858, is one of the best accounts of the wars of *independence. Among his other well-known works are: Historia de Chile (1860), Los cronistas de India (1861), Historiadores chilenos (1862), Vida y viajes de Hernando de Magallanes (1864) and Proceso de Pedro de Valdivia (1873).

In 1858 Barros Arana was imprisoned, accused of conspiring against President (1851-61) Manuel *Montt Torres, and was later exiled. He traveled widely in Europe and other South American countries. In 1862 he returned to Chile, where he continued his literary work, publishing many books on history and diplomacy. He became a member of the *Partido Liberal Doctrinario. In 1881 he represented Chile in the negotiations leading to the *Boundary Treaty of 1881, and was accused of losing seven eighths of *Patagonia to *Argentina. When he died in 1906 Chileans recognized that he was a great historian, but thought of him as a poor diplomat because of this loss of territory.

BARROS BORGOÑO, Luis (1858-1943). Politician and diplomat. Barros received his law degree in 1880 and while still a student taught history at the *Instituto Nacional. In 1883, while holding the office of Chief of Staff in the ministry of foreign affairs, he participated in the final negotiations with *Peru to end the War of the *Pacific. Later he assisted in bringing about peace with *Bolivia too, and he filled various ministerial posts from 1889 to 1918. In 1920, backed by the *Unión Radical, he ran unsuccessfully against Arturo *Alessandri Palma in the presidential election. At the end of Alessandri's term of office Barros was named minister of the interior (1925). As such, Barros succeeded Alessandri when the latter resigned in October 1925, remaining in power for two months. On December 23, 1925, he was replaced by President-elect Emiliano *Figueroa Larraín.

BARROS LUCO, Ramón (1835-1919). President of Chile 1910-15. Barros Luco was born and educated in *Santiago, where he received a law degree from the *Universidad de Chile. After a distinguished political career which saw him elected deputy and then senator and named subrogate minister of war, he participated in the revolutionary *junta de gobierno of 1891 which deposed President (1886-91) José Manuel *Balmaceda Fernández. In 1896 Barros Luco was named president of the Senate, and in 1903, during the illness of Germán *Riesco Errázuriz, he served as acting President of Chile. In the crisis of 1910 all parties turned to him to run for President. As neither of his opponents, Agustín *Edwards MacClure and Juan Luis *Sanfuentes Andonaegui, received the necessary votes to be nominated, Barros Luco was elected President by *Congress and was inaugurated on December 23, 1910.

The government of Barros Luco has been severely criticized by Chilean historians for not being able to put a stop to political quarreling within his administration. His first cabinet, named on December 26, 1910, lasted only 18 days. Subsequent cabinets lasted only a little longer. It became apparent to many that the interests of politicians were being placed above those of the country. In spite of these setbacks, Barros Luco was able to bring some progress to Chile. The School of Engineering was established; the port of San Antonio was opened (see: PORTS); a new building for the *National Library was erected; and the Historical Museum was inaugurated. Many public works were undertaken, including the establishment of sanitary waterways and the construction of bridges and *highways. In 1913 a school for pilots was established, one of the first in South America (see: AIR FORCE). In 1915 Chile signed a commercial and political treaty with Argentina and Brazil, the *ABC Treaty. Also in 1915, Barros Luco was responsible for the electoral law known as "La Ley de las elecciones," a very important measure to stop the scandalous ballot box frauds.

BARROS OREZ, Daniel (1834-1904). A student of engineering and mathematics who is best known as a novelist and writer of fables. Barros Orez was also interested in the theater, especially in dramatic art. He did most of his writing in the city of *Talca in Central Chile, and his *Pipiolos y *pelucones is accepted as a very fine interpretation of Chilean life after Independence was won.

BASQUES. Tall, individualistic and highly enterprising, the Basques (vascos) occupy a region of the central and western Pyrenean foothills contiguous to the Bay of Biscay (Viscaya). Two great influxes of Basque immigrants were registered in Chile, and so important have they been to the ethnic constitution of the nation that Basque Miguel de Unamuno claimed Chile and the Society of Jesus to be "the two great creations of the Basque race." The first wave of Basque immigrants arrived in Chile in the 17th and 18th centuries, when 45 percent of all immigrants were Basques. The second wave occurred as a consequence of the Spanish Civil War (1936-39), when many Basques were forced into exile.

Basques had, however, begun to arrive in Chile from the very beginning of the Spanish conquest. Some Basque merchants accompanied Pedro de *Valdivia. Soon they joined the ranks of *conquistadores, seamen, administrators, miners, farmers and missionaries, leaving a legacy that is evidenced in the frequency of such surnames among the traditional Chilean elite as Echaurren, Echeverría, Errázuriz, Eyzaguirre, Irrarázabal, Izquierdo, Larraín, Lazcano, Undurraga and Urrutia.

In the mid-19th century, Chile hoped to attract Basque immigrants to open up the lands of the south and to engage in farming and animal husbandry (especially *sheep farming). But only a few did so: the unconquered *Araucanian Indians still posed a great threat to settlers. Those that came at that time, and subsequently, generally preferred to settle in *Santiago and the rich Central Valley. With modern industrial development, many Chilean Basques used their skills as entrepreneurs in tanneries, shoe factories, flour mills, canneries, hotels, shop-keeping and *agriculture.

By the 20th century, 10 percent of all Chilean intellectuals

and artists were of Basque descent; 23 percent of the most valuable land was owned by Chilean Basques, and 529 out of the
2,498 wealthiest families in Chile were Basque.

Santiago, together with Buenos Aires and Mexico City, have
the greatest concentration of Basques in Latin America, and are
prime staging areas of support for the Basque separatist movement in Spain.

See also: IMMIGRATION.

BATTLES. See: ADUANA DE IQUIQUE: ALAMEDA VIEJA DE CON-
CEPCION; ALTO DE HOSPICIO; ANGELES, Los; ARICA; AVELLANO;
BELLAVISTA; CALAMA; CALDERA; CANAS, Fundolo; CANCHA
RAYADA; CAPE ANGAMOS; CERRO GRANDE; CHACABUCO;
CHILLAN; CHORRILLOS; CONCEPCION (pueblo.) CONCON;
CURALI; CURAPALIHUE; DOLORES; HUALQUI; HUMACUCHO;
HUARA; HUITO; IQUIQUE; LINDEROS; LIRCAY; LONCOMILLA;
LOROS; MAIPON; MAIPU; MIRAFLORES; MONTE PINTO; OCHA-
GAVIA; PANGAL; PAPUDO; PETORCA; PLACILLA; PUREN;
QUECHEREGUA; QUILMO; QUILO; RANCAGUA; ROBLE; SAN
FRANCISCO; SANTIAGO; TALCAHUANO; TARPELLANCA; TRES
ACEQUIAS; TRILALEO; TUCAPEL; VEGAS DE SALDIAS, Las;
VEGAS DE TALCAHUANO, Las; YERBAS BUENAS; YUNGAY. See
also: COCHRANE, Thomas; HILLYAR, James; PIRATES AND
PRIVATEERS; WARS.

BAUTACANA, La. See: WOMEN AND THE WOMEN'S MOVEMENT

BEAGLE, H.M.S. British naval survey vessel, with Charles *Darwin
aboard, which visited Chilean waters in 1833-34. See: BEAGLE
CHANNEL; FITZROY, Robert.

BEAGLE CHANNEL. Strait between the main island of *Tierra del
Fuego and the islands of Hoste and Navarino to the South, named
after H.M.S. *Beagle, the British naval vessel which surveyed
it in 1833-34. Rights to territory and navigation in the area
were a subject of bitter dispute with *Argentina until 1904,
when (largely owing to the mediation efforts of Archbishop Mariano
*Casanova) both countries accepted the 1902 arbitration of King
Edward VII. This divided Tierra del Fuego between them, with
the Channel as the southern boundary of the Argentine portion,
but protecting Argentine navigational rights throughout its length
and limiting Chilean fortifications in the area. Unfortunately the
British monarch's award did not cover three small islands at
the Channel's eastern entrance, *Picton, *Nueva and *Lennox.
Despite discussion of their sovereignty when the *ABC Treaty
was signed in 1915, and "binding" arbitration by Queen Elizabeth
II in 1978, no settlement appeared in sight until the military fell
from power in Argentina in 1982. The new Argentine president,
Raúl Alfonsín, submitted an arbitration proposal of Pope John
Paul II to a national plebiscite, which accepted it. As a result,
the foreign ministers of the two countries signed a treaty at the

Vatican on November 29, 1984, which has since been formally ratified. The treaty gives Chile possession of all three islands and the waters around them to a distance of three miles from shore. In return Chile has given up some of her claims to the other waters on the Atlantic side of *Cape Horn, except for a limited jurisdiction around other Chilean territory in the area, and the general international boundary is to be the meridian south from Cape Horn.

BELLAVISTA, Battle of. Final battle in the campaign to liberate the island of *Chiloe and incorporate it into the new Republic of Chile. It took place on January 14, 1826; the royalists' capitulation was signed in San Carlos on January 18, and the definitive treaty of TANTAUCO (q.v.) on January 19.

BELLO CODECIDO, Emilio (1869-1941). Grandson of Andrés *Bello López and brother-in-law of President (1886-91) José Manuel *Balmaceda Fernández. Bello Codecido was a lawyer who entered upon an administrative and congressional career at an early age. He was a member of the *Partido Liberal Democrático, served as a deputy and held important ministerial offices from 1894 to 1938. In 1925 he was president of the second *junta militar de gobierno of that year, formed to invite exiled President Arturo *Alessandri Palma to return. This attempt to restore constitutional rule failed and Bello Codecido spent some time in exile. In 1936 he accepted the war portfolio in the second administration (1932-38) of Alessandri.

BELLO LOPEZ, Andrés (1781-1865). Man of letters and founder of the *Universidad de Chile. Bello was born in Caracas, but died in *Santiago, where he spent more than thirty years of his life. In 1802 he was named Secretary in the colonial government of Venezuela. In 1808 he joined the Venezuelan independence movement and was sent to London by Simón Bolívar to woo British aid for the revolutionary cause. In 1810 he returned to England, where he resided for almost two decades. During that time he cultivated the friendship of philosophers, men of letters and scientists. In 1829 he was invited to Chile to fill a high post in the Ministerio del *Interior y Relaciones Exteriores and to lead the intellectual life of the young republic. After founding the *Universidad de Chile (1843), he became its first rector. By then he had obtained Chilean citizenship, and was already active in politics. He was elected to the Senate in 1837, 1846, and from 1855 through 1864. His literary contributions were many. Besides writing poetry, he was the author of one of the best grammars of Spanish, the Gramática de la lengua española (1847).

He was also the intellectual leader of the neo-classical period in Chile, which began around 1830 and lasted for about fifteen years. As a contributor to the literary supplement of the newspaper El *Araucano, Bello was at odds with the Argentine Domingo Faustino *Sarmiento, who had been exiled by Argentine dictator

(1829-52) Juan Manuel Rosas. Sarmiento became a contributor to El *Mercurio of *Valparaíso and attacked Bello for writing unimaginative poetry in the cold, simple and gutless neo-classical style. Sarmiento espoused romanticism in literature, and the polemic which began between the two writers lasted until Sarmiento returned to Argentina.

Bello left behind many outstanding works in addition to his well-known grammar and his poetry. His Tratado de derecho internacional (1834) and his Código civil are among his great contributions to Chilean *law. Among his many disciples are José Victorino *Lastarria Santander and Miguel Luis *Amunátegui Aldunate.

BENAVENTE BUSTAMANTE, Diego José (1790-1867). Chilean patriot who took part in the *independence struggle. In 1811 he formed part of the junta government proclaimed by the patriots in *Concepción. Two years later he was wounded at the Battle of *Roble, but recovered to take part in the Battle of *Rancagua in 1814. He emigrated to *Argentina with José Miguel *Carrera Verdugo after the patriots' defeat at Rancagua, and remained there until 1823. On his return to Chile he married Carrera Verdugo's widow, Mercedes Flotecilla Valdivieso, and held various ministerial posts. He reorganized the Ministerio de *Hacienda (the treasury) and served as counselor and minister of the interior. In 1826 he became a member of the *Partido Federalista, and president of the Chamber of Deputies. He energetically opposed conservative statesman Diego *Portales Palazuelos, but was absolved from participation in his death. In 1857 Benavente became vice-president of the Senate, and later its president. He was one of the founders of the National Party (*Partido Nacional). Before he died he wrote various essays on the struggle for *independence, the most notable of which is the Memorias de las primeras campañas de independencia.

BENAVIDES, Vicente (1777-1822). One of the central figures in the Chilean struggle for *independence. In 1811 he fought against Spain in the *army of Juan José *Carrera Verdugo. Two years later, however, he changed sides and fought at the battle of *Rancagua (1814) as a *realista. He distinguished himself on the side of Spain during the battles for the so-called "Spanish Reconquest." In 1818 he was captured and would have been shot, but some *independientes who had fought with him in 1811 saved his life at the last moment, and he was sent into exile in *Argentina. In 1819 he returned to Chile and became the commander of the Spanish troops fighting to recover territory lost to the patriots. Thus began the so-called "War to the Death" (*Guerra a Muerte). After being defeated by the patriots on numerous occasions, he resolved to leave Chile and fight for Spain in *Peru. He was captured at the border by the Chilean authorities and brought to *Santiago, where he received a summary trial and was executed on the morning of February 23, 1822.

BENAVIDES ESCOBAR, César Raúl Manuel (1912-   ). Career *army officer and former member of the military *junta. He studied at the *Escuela Militar in *Santiago, and rose quickly through the ranks, becoming a major in 1959, colonel in 1968, general in 1972 and commander of the fifth division in the far south in 1974. Like many of his peers, he studied for two years in the *United States. He is considered an expert in *telecommunications and was appointed army telecommunication chief. Under President Augusto *Pinochet Ugarte he has served as interior minister, defense minister and director of the War College (*Academia de Guerra), and became the army's representative on the junta on March 11, 1981. At the time he was regarded as an unconditional ally of Pinochet and one of this three or four most likely successors. On November 7, 1985, however, he was removed from the junta and replaced by Julio *Canessa.

BIBLIOGRAPHY. For an account of the evolution of bibliography in Chile, see: NATIONAL BIBLIOGRAPHY. For bibliographical information about the topics treated in this Dictionary, see the Bibliographic Appendix. This embraces both sources used in compiling the dictionary and additional readings chosen on consideration of both quality and general availability. Needless to say, it has not been practicable to limit these to material in English. A listing of general works is followed by topical listings under broad subjects such as agrarian reform, biography, history, economics, etc.

BIBLIOTECA NACIONAL. See: NATIONAL LIBRARY

BIENESTAR SOCIAL, Ministerio de. The Ministry of Social Welfare was created by Statute No. 7,912 of November 30, 1927. It replaced the Ministerio de *Higiene, Asistencia y Previsión Social y Trabajo (Ministry of Health, Social Security and Assistance, and Labor). It functions were to secure the well-being of all Chileans by providing a minimum working wage, social security and sanitation. In 1932 the ministry was divided into two new ministries, the Ministerio de *Salubridad Pública (Public Health) and the Ministerio del *Trabajo (Labor).

BILBAO BARQUIN, Francisco (1823-1865). Chilean writer who spent many years of his life in exile for his anticlerical views and his opposition to the conservative government (1851-61) of President Manuel *Montt Torres. At the age of eleven he accompanied his father into exile in *Peru. In 1839 he returned to Chile and entered the *Instituto Nacional, where he studied under Andrés *Bello López and José Victorino *Lastarria Santander. In the late 1830s he published La sociabilidad chilena, a book in which he criticized, among other things, the priestly vocation in Chile. Soon a polemic developed when La revista católica, a *Church publication, launched a campaign against Bilbao Barquín. He was brought to trial, and his book was found to be blasphemous, im-

moral and seditious. The author was fined and sent to prison
for non-payment. His admirers paid the fine and threatened to
mob the judges.

Life in *Santiago, however, proved insupportable, and he
went into voluntary exile in *France, where his book was well
received. In 1850 he returned to Chile and founded, with
Eusebio *Lillo Robles, the *"Sociedad de la Igualdad," a society
created to defend the plight of the poor and to organize them into
a political body. Religious polemics continued, and Bilbao Barquín
accused the Church of misusing its vast land holdings. Within
the Church, the young priests sided with the controversial
author on the grounds that Christ himself had accursed the
money-changers and thrown them out of the temple.

The more conservative clergy and the government of Montt
Torres launched a bitter campaign against the Sociedad de la
Igualdad. There was violence, and Bilboa Barquín's life was
threatened. He was exiled and had to leave Chile, disguised as
a priest to cross the Peruvian border. Meeting with further
persecution in *Peru, he went to Europe in 1854 and to *Argentina in 1856. In Buenos Aires, where he died, he devoted himself to the task of unifying Argentina. His second major book
was Los boletines del espíritu (1850). His writings inspired the
formation of the Radical Party (*Partido Radical).

BIO-BIO. A province of Central Chile, created in 1875. The population, which was then 76,498, grew to 97,968 in 1907, and 196,005
(est.) in 1971. The total area was 11,135 km^2 (4,300 square
miles) and the capital was Los *Angeles. In 1974 the old province
was merged with the provinces of *Arauco, *Concepción and
*Nuble to form the new Region of Bío-Bío (Region VIII). This
had a 1982 estimated population of 1,766,627 and its capital is
*Concepción. See: REGIONS AND ADMINISTRATIVE RESTRUCT-
URING.

BIO-BIO RIVER. The major river of central Chile, both in length and
in size of watershed. It crosses the old provinces of *Concepción,
*Bío-Bío and *Malleco, and is navigable for 130 km (80 miles),
with a further 70 km used by logging rafts. From 1640 until the
mid-19th century it formed the northern boundary of the lands
of the *Araucanian Indians (see: QUILLEN, Parlamentos de).

BIO-BIO UNIVERSITY. See: UNIVERSIDAD DE BIO-BIO.

BLACK MARKET. The first year in power of democratically-elected
Socialist President Salvador *Allende Gossens saw a consumption-
led expansion of the Chilean *economy. As the government set
about redistributing income more equitably in favor of the poorest
sectors of society, consumption increased beyond all bounds.
But as early as 1972, a marked imbalance within the economy
manifested itself when a sharp contradiction emerged between
supply and the new level of demand. The state's incapacity

to control the production and distribution of goods resulted in the development of large-scale black marketeering throughout Chile.

The wide gap between supply and demand rapidly led to an explosive situation. This was cleverly used and promoted by the opposition (under the advice of the U.S. *Central Intelligence Agency) for what was euphemistically termed the "destabilization" of the Allende government. The larger and more widespread the black market the better, since the purpose was to aggravate the economic crises, broaden discontent among the population, and prepare conditions for military intervention.

The opposition began skillfully to manipulate the shortages to its advantage in order to generate within the population a collective shortage "psychosis." Anyone with resources and storage facilities began to stockpile commodities just in the hope that they would be scarce in the future. Such concealed goods were sold at very high prices on the black market. A large number of individuals, including some belonging to government circles, engaged in this lucrative activity. Peasants also participated by falsifying production data and refusing to deliver their crops to the agrarian reform centers (see: AGRARIAN REFORM).

As inflation approached 250 percent per annum in 1973, the already-existing dollar black market expanded--it had begun with the election of Allende as the ruling class began to hoard dollars to take abroad. By mid-1973 the shortage of foreign-exchange dollars became even more acute.

As soon as the government of President Augusto *Pinochet Ugarte took power, all black market activities were declared illegal under threat of heavy fines and long terms of imprisonment.

BLACKBERRIES. Among the European plants introduced into southern Chile in the middle of the 19th century by Francois Chabry for the Sociedad de Agricultura, the introduction of the common bramble or blackberry (rubus fruticosus) has been the most unfortunate. In its almost uncontrollable spread it has been compared to the rabbit in Australia.

BLACKS. See: AFRICAN SLAVERY.

BLANCHE ESPEJO, Bartolomé (1879-1970). Cavalry lieutenant colonel who was politically active in the 1924-32 period of *Anarquía política. Along with Carlos *Ibáñez del Campo and Marmaduke *Grove Vallejo, he was one of the three most influential members of the *Junta militar of 1924, and reputedly the real author of its manifesto. As Ibáñez's right-hand man he held the posts of under-secretary of war (1924-25), director general of *police (1925-26) and war minister (1926-31). A stern disciplinarian, he served Ibáñez well by keeping the *army loyal (posting likely dissidents far away from *Santiago). During the disturbances that led to Ibáñez's fall he was given command of all police and army units in the capital. In 1932 it was the politically conser-

vative Blanche who directed the September 13th coup that forced
the resignation of President Carlos Guillermo *Dávila Espinosa,
and when Supreme Court president Abraham *Oyanedel Urrutia
refused to accept the presidency of a military regime, Blanche
himself became interim President of Chile. After further negotiations, however, Oyanedel agreed to become interim President to
restore constitutional government and hold free congressional and
presidential elections, and Blanche handed his office over to
him on October 1, 1932.

BLANCO CUARTIN, Manuel (1822-1890). News reporter, poet and
editor of El *Mercurio from 1866 to 1886. He is credited with
writing various articles and poems that attracted wide attention
in Chile and outside the country, and made El Mercurio one of
the most widely-read papers in South America. Son of the Argentine poet Ventura Blanco Encalada, Blanco Cuartín received
his education in *Santiago at the *Instituto Nacional. He had
planned a career in medicine, but because of deafness turned to
journalism. In 1876, while still on the editorial staff of El
Mercurio, he joined the faculty of philosophy and humanities of
the *Universidad de Chile. He was a member of the Conservative
Party (*Partido Conservador).

BLANCO ENCALADA. Chilean battleship. One of two ironclads
ordered to remedy the deficiencies in Chile's *navy revealed in
the War of 1865-67 with *Spain, it was laid down in Hull, England,
as the Valparaíso, but its name was changed on its 1875 arrival
in Chile. During the War of the *Pacific its sinking of the
*Huáscar at *Cape Angamos gave Chile command of the sea, and
so, ultimately, victory. In the *Civil War of 1891 the Blanco
Encalada became the rebel flagship until it was sunk by government torpedo boats in *Caldera Bay, April 23, 1891. Most of
those aboard, including many rebel congressmen, were drowned.

BLANCO ENCALADA, Manuel (1790-1876). Chilean admiral. Born
in Buenos Aires, he was sent to Spain to complete his education
and returned to South America at the outbreak of the wars of
independence. In 1813 he joined the Chilean patriots in the fight
against Spain. Taken prisoner after the Battle of *Rancagua in
1814, he was condemned to death. His sentence, however, was
commuted to exile on the *Juan Fernández Islands. In 1817,
after the patriots' victory at *Chacabuco, he was freed and was
able to participate as an artillery colonel in the battles of *Cancha
Rayada and *Maipú (both in 1818). After independence from
Spain was won, Blanco Encalada began the organization of the
Chilean *navy, under Lord *Cochrane. When the latter left
Chile in 1823, Blanco Encalada became Admiral of the Navy. For
three months in 1826 he was *President of Chile, the first holder
of that title. In 1837 he participated in the war against the *Peru-
Bolivia Confederation of Andrés de *Santa Cruz. Between 1849
and 1859 he served in the Chilean Senate. He also went to

France in 1852 on a diplomatic mission as Chilean minister pleni-potentiary. At the age of 75 he went to Peru to repatriate the body of Bernardo *O'Higgins. In 1865 he directed naval opera-tions in the War of 1865-66 with *Spain. Blanco Encalada was also grand master of Chile's first masonic lodge.

BLEST CUNNINGHAM, Guillermo (1800-1884). Physician of Sligo, Ireland, who received his medical training in Dublin and Edin-burgh. He went to Chile in 1827 at the invitation of his brother Andrew who had arrived in one of the first British ships legally trading with Chile in 1811 and had gone into business in *San-tiago. Guillermo Blest was elected to the Chilean *Congress several times, but is mainly important as promotor of the Escuela de Medicina, which President Joaquín *Prieto Vial founded in 1833 (see: EDUCATION; PUBLIC HEALTH). Blest's children included the novelist Alberto *Blest Gana, the poet Guillermo Blest Gana and the jurist Joaquín Blest Gana.

BLEST GANA, Alberto (1830-1920). Chilean novelist who considered himself a realist and who described the transformation of Chilean society from "an energetic world of pioneers to a lax, degenerate society." He wanted to become the Balzac of Chile and had a wide knowledge of French literature. Among his best works are Martín Rivas, considered a classic in depicting Chilean mores of the 1850s; Durante la reconquista (1897), which portrays the city of *Santiago during the wars of independence against Spain from 1814 to 1818; and Los transplantados (1904), a critique of Chilean emigrants who leave their country and their traditions to go to Paris to be absorbed in luxury and ostentation.

BLOQUE DE IZQUIERDA ("Leftist block"). A political coalition of leftist parties organized in 1934 and dissolved in 1936. The Com-munist Party (*Partido Comunista) refused to join the coalition, which was formed mainly by Socialists (*Partido Socialista), Socialist Radicals (*Partido Radical Socialista) and Democrats (*Partido Democrático). The Block represented the major oppo-sition to the second administration (1932-38) of President Arturo *Alessandri Palma. When the Alessandri government proposed to use the profits from *copper and *nitrates to liquidate the national debt, the Bloque de Izquierda opposed the idea vehemently. But both houses of *Congress approved it in 1936. As a result, the coalition dissolved and, in the same year, the Popular Front (*Frente Popular) was organized. This was another block of leftist parties, but this time the Communists were included.

BLOQUE DE SANEAMIENTO DEMOCRATICO. A coalition of Christian Democrats (*Partido Democrata Cristiano), Radicals (*Partido Radical), Socialists (*Partido Socialista), Communists (*Partido Comunista) and National Democrats (*Partido Nacional Democrático) formed in 1958 to oppose the presidential candidacy of Jorge *Alessandri Rodríguez. When Alessandri was elected for the term 1958-64, the block was dissolved.

BOLETIN OFICIAL DE LA JUNTA DE GOBIERNO. When the forces backing the revolutionary *Congress of 1891 established a provisional government in the city of *Iquique, their *junta de gobierno published a Boletín oficial. This accused President (1886-91) José Manuel *Balmaceda Fernández of responsibility for the conflict (which claimed some 10,000 lives). The Boletín lasted from May 28th to November 10th, the later numbers being published in *Santiago.

BOLIVIA, Relations with. Chile's first war with Bolivia, In 1837-39, was caused by fear of Andrés *Santa Cruz's *Peru-Bolivia Confederation and had no outcome beyond the break up of the confederation and the exile of its instigator. A little later-- from 1846--development of the *guano industry made it necessary to define more precisely the two countries' common frontier. During the administration of Bolivian president Mariano Melgarejo the Boundary Treaty of 1866 was negotiated. This fixed the boundary at 24°S, with export duties on guano extracted between 23°S and 25°S to be divided equally between them both. Chile claimed that this was never done, but, in any case, *nitrates were becoming much more valuable than guano, and those extracting them were almost all Chileans. A new treaty in 1874 allowed Bolivia to retain all custom revenues from her cisandine lands, on condition that the rate of duty was not increased. When this undertaking was breached, Chile occupied the port of *Antofagasta (February 1879), the causus belli of the War of the *Pacific. The 1884 negotiations to end the war gave the entire region to Chile: it became the province of Antofagasta, but a definitive treaty was not signed until 1904. This provided Bolivia with some compensation for loss of her Pacific coast in the form of a *railway link from La Paz to *Arica, begun in 1906 and completed in 1913. This rail link now carries half of Bolivia's external trade. Its construction cut the time for the uphill journey from the coast to the Bolivian capital from 10 days by mule train to about 20 hours. Bolivia, however, considered that it had signed the treaty under duress and has to this day not accepted its legality.

Relations remained cool, and in 1962, when Chile dammed the river *Lauca to build a hydroelectric project, Bolivia broke off relations. These were resumed in 1975 when Chile agreed to an exchange of territory so as to provide Bolivia with a (demilitarized) corridor to the Pacific. The negotiations were unsuccessful, in part because *Peru objected to Bolivia acquiring former Peruvian territory, and Bolivia again severed relations in 1978. Meanwhile, the *Organization of American States had voted 25 to 0 (Chile and Paraguay being absent) to back "a sovereign and useful access to the Pacific Ocean" for Bolivia.

With the military in power in Chile, it was hoped that the accession to the Bolivian presidency of Luis García Mora in 1980, after a rightist military coup, would lead to a better understanding between the two governments. A lack of diplomatic progress,

however, resulted in relations being broken off yet again in
1982.

BONILLA BRADANOVIC, Oscar (1918-1975). Career *army officer.
Educated at the *Escuela Militar, he rose in the ranks to brigadier
general in 1970, and by the time of the *coup was outranked only
by General Augusto *Pinochet Ugarte himself. In September 1973
he was given the senior ministerial portfolio of the interior. As
interior minister he quarreled with *DINA head Manuel *Sepúlvedo
Contreras over anti-terrorist policy, and in March 1974 was publicly praised by the Vatican for easing repression in Chile. In
July 1974 he was transferred to the ministry of defense. In
November he was reportedly out of favor with Pinochet for having
had dealings with the Christian Democrat leadership. On March
3, 1975, he was killed in a mysterious helicopter accident near
Curicó. Many think his criticism of the *junta's harshness may
have caused his death. Bonilla earned the Grand Star of Military
Merit for thirty years' service, and numerous other decorations.

BORGOÑO NUÑEZ, José Manuel (1789-1848). Chile patriot who fought
in the wars of *independence. In 1821 he went to *Peru to liberate that country from Spanish rule. On his return to Chile, he
was elected deputy in 1823, and in 1827 he was named war minister
in the cabinet of President (1827) Francisco Antonio *Pinto
Díaz. In 1838 he was sent to Madrid to accelerate the conclusion
of a peace treaty between Chile and Spain. There he was decorated by the Spanish monarch but refused to accept the honorary
title conferred upon him. He was justice minister in the government of President (1841-51) Manuel *Bulnes Prieto.

BOSSAY LEYVA, Luis (1912-   ). Active member of the Radical Party
(*Partido Radical) and candidate in the presidential election of
1958; he was defeated by Jorge *Alessandri Rodríguez. In 1939
Bossay Leyva had been president of the Radical convention held
in *Valparaíso. He held various important ministerial offices in
the administration of President (1946-52) Gabriel *González Videla.
In 1946 he was appointed war minister; in 1947 minister of economy
and trade; and, also in 1947, he was subrogate foreign minister.
From 1953 to 1965 he was senator from *Aconcagua and *Valparaíso.
In 1963 he was appointed by Alessandri Rodríguez to be president
of the Chilean delegation to the *United Nations.

BOSSES' STRIKE (Paro de los patrones). There were a number of
strikes by sections of the middle class during the Presidency of
Salvador *Allende Gossens (1970-73). They were ostensibly protests against government economic policies--either against their
effects (principally high inflation, exacerbated by price controls
which squeezed profits and created shortages of all types of goods
and spare parts) or against what was being proposed (mainly
threats of nationalization of small businesses). Most of the
organizers, however, and the political parties who proclaimed

their support, saw the strikes as a political weapon, and they were for this reason liberally subsidized by the U.S. *Central Intelligence Agency.

There were roughly three such strikes, or groups of loosely associated strikes. The first was one of 150,000 *Santiago shopkeepers, August 21-22, 1972. This ended when it was made illegal and a state of emergency proclaimed in the province. The second was a national truck owners' strike, October 10-November 5, 1972, which was joined by many small businessmen, physicians, ships' captains, bank employees, lawyers and *LAN pilots. It cost the country US$ 200 million, and to end it the government had to denationalize the CENADI wholesaling cooperative and undertake not to nationalize the road haulage industry. The final series of strikes began on May 22, 1973, with a strike of privately owned bus companies. Physicians and engineers came out on June 21, the truck owners (again) on July 26, taxi drivers on August 3, and engineers, airline pilots, nurses, lawyers and small businessmen later in the month. Shopkeepers closed down August 24-31. There were some 500 acts of terrorism associated with the strikes, but these decreased markedly after the August 26 arrest of Roberto *Thieme. The strikers returned to work the day after the military *coup d'état of September 11, 1973, and supplies were restored by September 17.

BOUNDARY DISPUTES. Listed under FRONTIER DISPUTES, q.v.

BOUNDARY TREATY OF 1866. See: BOLIVIA, RELATIONS WITH.

BOUNDARY TREATY OF 1881 (Tratado chileno-argentino de límites). Treaty between Chile and *Argentina, signed June 23, 1881 and ratified October 26, 1881. It established the principle that Chilean rights would be paramount on the Pacific side of the continent, and those of Argentina on the Atlantic side. Chile gave up all *Patagonia north of the 52°S parallel, plus all its Atlantic coast. The main island of *Tierra del Fuego was divided along the 68° 34' W meridian. The western frontier of Argentine Patagonia was defined as "las más altas cumbres que dividan las aguas," the signatories being unaware that the line of highest peaks (only 3,500 feet in the south) did not always coincide with the continental watershed divide, which, owing to a freak of nature, was in places well to the east. The treaty was also ambiguous about who owned three small islands at the Atlantic end of the BEAGLE CHANNEL (q.v.). See also: ARGENTINA, RELATIONS WITH.

BOURBON REFORMS. See: CHARLES III.

BRADEN, William. U.S. mining entrepreneur who pioneered the working of Chile's low-grade *copper ore in 1905, later forming the *Braden Copper Company.

BRADEN COPPER COMPANY. An American corporation formed to
exploit El Teniente *copper mine at *Sewell. It is now a subsidiary of the KENNECOTT COPPER CORPORATION (q.v.).

BRADY ROCHE, Hernán Julio (1921-   ). Career *army officer.
Educated at the *Escuela Militar, he rose rapidly through the
ranks: major in 1955, colonel in 1967, general in 1970. Throughout his career he has held various teaching positions at military
schools, and in 1972, during the presidency of Salvador *Allende
Gossens, he directed the Army Staff College (*Academia de
Guerra). After the 1973 *coup that overthrew Allende, in which
he was heavily involved, he was named general of an entire
division. He became the highest ranking officer in the defense
ministry as Chief of National Defense. Upon the 1975 death of
defense minister General Oscar *Bonilla Bradanovic, Brady Roche
was appointed to succeed him. He received the Grand Star of
Military Merit for thirty years' service, as well as many other
decorations, especially for his role in the 1973 coup. In 1981
he became minister in charge of the Nuclear Energy Commission.

BRAZA. Pre-metric measure of length, equal to 1.67 meters. See:
WEIGHTS AND MEASURES.

BRAZIL, Relations with. Perhaps because Chile and Brazil do not
share a common border, relations between them have usually been
cordial, with Brazil often acting as arbiter in various disputes
that Chile has had with contiguous countries. As early as 1838
Brazil and Chile signed a treaty of friendship and trade. After
the War of the *Pacific, when Chile wrested the *nitrate fields
and *copper mines of the *Atacama desert from *Peru and *Bolivia,
Brazil recognized Chile's new expanded frontiers almost immediately.
    At the turn of the century, Chile's strong South American
power position was based in part upon its community of interests
with Brazil, and upon the latter's rivalry with *Argentina, although from 1915 there was a formal agreement for tripartite
cooperation in the *ABC Treaty.
    In the 20th century, relations have remained cordial, with a
few exceptions: after the overthrow of Brazilian President João
Goulart on April 1, 1964, when thousands of Brazilians emigrated
to Chile until 1968 when Eduardo *Frei Montalva agreed to close
the Chilean escape route, and after the election of President
Salvador *Allende Gossens, in 1970, which presented a threat to
authoritarian regimes throughout South America.
    From 1970 to 1973, hundreds of Brazilian political refugees
came to Chile, often telling stories of torture and murder which
discredited the Brazilian military regime. But while official relations between the two countries cooled, relations between their
*armed forces became warmer, especially when the Chilean military
used Brazil as a model in plotting the downfall of Allende.
    Chile's aping of Brazil, and the emergence after September

1973 of a similarly repressive government in Chile, gave credence
to the existence of a Brazilian connection in the overthrow of
Allende (aided and abetted by the U.S. *Central Intelligence
Agency, whose role in Brazil in 1964 was by then all too well
known). In both countries the private sector played a crucial
role in the overthrow of two legitimately-elected governments
of the left. The Brazilian businessmen, who had plotted the
ousting of Goulart, were the very people who advised the Chilean
right on how to deal with Allende.

Soon after Allende's election, thousands of Chilean businessmen
had taken their families and fortunes abroad, mainly to *Argentina,
Ecuador, Venezuela and Brazil. In Brazil these well-to-do
émigrés quickly found work with multinational corporations or
invested their capital in new businesses or on the stock exchange.

The Brazilian "recipe" for Allende's opponents was that they
should create economic chaos, foment discontent and a deep fear
of communism among both employers and employees, block all the
legislative efforts of the government, organize demonstrations and
rallies, and even, if need be, undertake acts of terrorism. All
this required financing, and a great deal of money was raised and
expended to topple Allende. Dr. Glycon de Paiva, a Brazilian
mining engineer with "a lot of other interests," took great pride
in how "we taught the Chileans to use their women against the
Marxists. We ourselves created a large and successful women's
movement, and Chile copied it."

From Brazil came also the model for Chile's *Academia de
Guerra, with its stress on "geopolitics," a science much favored
by General Golbery de Couto e Silva, the eminence grise of the
Brazilian military take-over, and which became President Augusto
*Pinochet Ugarte's own subject. Golbery's geopolitics as adopted
in Chile starts from the political premise of a permanent war
between the forces of international communism and the West.

Relations between the military of both countries continued
affable, as each strove to retain military control over civilian life.
Brazil's President João Batista Figueiredo was warmly welcomed
during an official visit to *Santiago in 1980, when both countries
issued statements condemning terrorism in Latin America. However, by the time Pinochet sought to make a return visit in 1984,
the Brazilian "abertura" (cautious return to civilian government)
was well advanced, and the Brazilian authorities had to politely
decline the now embarassing request as inopportune.

BRISEÑO CALDERON, Ramón (1814-1910). Lawyer and bibliographer,
in charge of the *National Library of Chile 1864-86 (until 1879
as Chief Librarian, thereafter as Director). This was an important period for the building up and organizing of the Library's
collection, which grew under Briseño's management from 37,780
to 65,000 volumes.

BRITAIN. See: UNITED KINGDOM.

BRITISH INFLUENCE. Britons began to settle in Chile from early
in the 19th century. Scots-descended Jorge *Edwards Brown,
founder of the Edwards dynasty, came in 1808; Irishman Guillermo
*Blest Cunningham, father of novelist Alberto *Blest Gana, came
in 1827. British immigration contributed significantly, in influence
if not in absolute numbers, to the growth of the Chilean nation.
It reached its peak during the last quarter of the 19th century,
when businessmen came to set up industries and engineers came
to build the *railways. Thanks to Scottish nobleman Lord *Cochrane and the contemporary prestige of the Royal Navy, British
influence was particularly strong in the *navy. British capital
was important in the *nitrate industry. Many Chilean social customs also derive from the British. Chileans are accustomed to
drinking afternoon tea and are proud of having developed private
schools modelled on the English "public" school system. See
also: IMMIGRATION; UNITED KINGDOM, Relations with.

BROADCASTING. See: TELECOMMUNICATIONS.

BROUWER, Hendrik. Dutch *pirate who occupied *Valdivia in 1643.

BÜCHI BUC, Hernán. Minister of finance since February 1985.
Trained as a civil engineer and holding an MBA from Columbia
University. Büchi became an advisor in the ministry of the
economy in 1975. After being an undersecretary in the ministries
of the economy and of health, he became head of *ODEPLAN.
In 1984 he was made head of the Superintendencia de Bancos,
and the following year succeeded Luis *Escobar Cerda to become
President Augusto *Pinochet Ugarte's sixth successive finance
minister.

BULNES PINTO, Gonzalo (1851-1936). Historian. Son of President
Manuel *Bulnes Prieto, Gonzalo Bulnes served as a deputy 1884-
87 and 1898-1901, and as a senator 1912-24. He was appointed
Chilean minister to Berlin and Rome in 1891 and as ambassador
to Buenos Aires in 1927. See: HISTORIOGRAPHY.

BULNES PRIETO, Manuel (1799-1866). Statesman who served two
consecutive terms as President of Chile: 1841-46 and 1846-51.
As President he continued the conservative rule that had begun
in 1831 and was to last until 1861. His strong regime suppressed
the radical press and exiled the radical leaders, while at the same
time continuing the general prosperity that Chile was experiencing
through economic and educational reforms. As a young career
military officer, Bulnes participated in the struggle for Chilean
*independence. He joined the Chilean patriot *army when he was
only twelve years old, and took part in every major battle, distinguishing himself at *Maipú. In 1838 he commanded the Chilean
army in the war against the *Peru-Bolivia Confederation of
Andrés *Santa Cruz. Elected President in 1841, Bulnes embarked
upon a program of governmental reform. He founded the Office

of Statistics, and organized the country's second complete national *census since independence (the <u>Censo Jeneral</u> of 1843). He also elevated *Valparaíso and *Atacama to the status of *provinces. In 1844 he signed a treaty with *Spain for the recognition of Chile as an independent republic.

The second Bulnes administration was much more tumultuous than the first. Although the first few years were peaceful and many programs of public works were implemented, the President ruled with an iron hand to stifle opposition and to secure the continuation of conservative rule in Chile. As the election of 1851 approached, a military uprising was organized to overthrow the President and prevent Manuel *Montt Torres being elected to succeed him. This revolt, the *Mutiny of Urriola, was headed by Colonel Pedro Alcántara *Urriola Balbontín, but troops loyal to the President were prepared for such an emergency and defeated the rebels. After Montt Torres's election, the *Civil War of 1851 broke out. Bulnes, who was at the head of the army, was able to restore peace.

During Bulnes' second term, the School of Agriculture, the Academy of Painting and the Music Conservatory were erected. *Highways and bridges were built, the first *railway line, between *Copiapú and *Caldera, was constructed, and work was begun on the rail link between the capital and *Valparaíso.

BULNES SANFUENTES, Francisco (1917-   )₀ Lawyer by profession, and member of the Conservative Party (*Partido Conservador). He became involved in politics during his university days (he received his law degree in 1939), and was elected president of the Conservative Youth Movement (*Juventud Conservadora). From 1945 to 1962 he served in *Congreśs, first as a deputy, and then from 1953 as senator for O'Higgins and Colchagón. In 1962 he was elected president of the Conservative Party. In the presidential election of September 4, 1969, he supported the candidacy of Jorge *Alessandri Rodríguez₀

With the defeat of Alessandri and the election of Socialist Salvador *Allende Gossens, Bulnes became a vociferous member of the opposition, urging the *armed forces to intervene when the *Confederación Democrática (CODE) failed to receive enough votes to impeach Allende in March 1973.

Seeing the *coup d'état of September 1973 as a necessary evil to stop Marxism in Chile, he supported the military in their efforts to consolidate power. But after 13 years of military rule in Chile, Bulnes and other members of the Conservative right are demanding a return to democracy. Bulnes, together with interior minister Sergio Onofrio *Jarpa Reyes, made a public call in 1984 for the election of a Congress before 1989. President Augusto *Pinochet Ugarte, however, emphatically denied any intention of calling either congressional or municipal elections urged by right-wing government supporters.

In 1976 Bulnes became ambassador to *Peru.

BUSSY DE ALLENDE, Hortensia Beatriz (1914-). Widow of deposed
President (1970-73) Salvador *Allende Gossens. Born in Valparaíso, Hortensia Bussy (or Bussi) received a degree in geography
from the Instituto Pedagógico of Valparaíso. She met Allende in
1939 when he was minister of health, and shortly afterwards they
were married. They had three daughters, Carmen *Allende de
Paz, Beatriz *Allende de Fernández and Isabel *Allende Bussy.
After Allende's death Hortensia Bussy traveled to Cuba and to
Mexico, where she now resides, and has continued to speak out
against the military *coup d'état that brought about the death of
her husband and the death of democracy in Chile. After touring
the *United States immediately following her husband's overthrow,
she lectured at prestigious universities and colleges until she was
denied an entry visa in 1983. Numerous protests to the U.S.
State Department resulted in the concession of a three-month
visa allowing her to visit the United States again in 1986. The
Mexican government is giving her a pension to live in Mexico
City.

BUSTOS LAGOS, Mariano (b. 1899). Member of the Democratic Party
(*Partido Democrático) who held various important government
posts in the thirty years before military rule was installed in the
1973 *coup. He was labor minister in 1942 and again in 1946.
In 1944 he was vice-president of the International Labor Conference held in Philadelphia. From 1946 to 1950 he was Chilean
consul general in Canada, and in 1953 he was named Chilean
plenipotentiary to Belgium and Luxembourg. On his return to
Chile in 1958, he was named Administrative Director in the
ministry of foreign affairs, a post he held until 1965.

- C -

C.D.T. (Central Democrático de Trabajo). See: TRADE UNIONS.

C.I.A. See: CENTRAL INTELLIGENCE AGENCY.

C.N.M. See: CUBAN NATIONALIST MOVEMENT

C.N.S. See: COORDINADORA NACIONAL SINDICAL.

C.N.T. (Confederación Nacional de Trabajadores; Comando Nacional
de Trabajadores). See: TRADE UNIONS.

C.R.A.C. See: CONFEDERACION REPUBLICANA DE ACCION CIVICA.

C.T.Ch. (Confederación de Trabajadores de Chile). See: TRADE
UNIONS.

C.U.T. (Central Unica de Trabajadores de Chile). See: TRADE UNIONS.

CABILDO. A municipal council, the basic local government authority in the Spanish American colonies. As the Spanish conception of municipality included the surrounding countryside--the cabildo of Port of Spain in the West Indies, for instance, administered the whole island of Trinidad--it would be rather closer in ulti- mate responsibility to an Anglo-Saxon country council than to a town one, were it not for a general tendency to neglect the rural areas. The council comprised several judges, a commissioned officer, a police chief and a board of aldermen: that of late 18th-century *Santiago was made up of 12 *regidores and 2 *alcaldes. In the early days of the colony these officials were elected by the townsmen, but from the 1700s they came to be appointed. The cabildo supervised public works, sanitation and primary *education, regulated prices and wages, enforced the *law and collected *taxes.

CABILDO ABIERTO. An open town meeting, attended by all townsmen. This existed in colonial times beside the ordinary (closed) *cabildo to give every burgess the opportunity to vote and ex- press himself when matters of grave importance were facing the community. This type of open gathering became very important during the struggle for independence from *Spain.

CACABUCO. See: CONCENTRATION CAMPS.

CACERES CONTRERAS, Carlos (1940-). Commercial engineer and industrialist who succeeded Miguel Kast as head of the Central Bank of Chile in September 1972. A trusted advisor of President Augusto *Pinochet Ugarte, he was chosen by the President in February 1983 to replace the controversial Rolf *Luders Schwar- zenberg as minister of finance. In April 1984, however, he was in turn replaced by Luis *Escobar Cerda. Cáceres Contreras received a degree in business administration as well as one in engineering, and worked in the 1960s for the *Kennecott Copper Company. He has written numerous books and articles in the field of banking and finance.

CACEROLAS, Marcha de las. See: POTS AND PANS DEMONSTRA- TIONS.

CAFFARENA DE JILES, Elena. See: WOMEN AND THE WOMEN'S MOVEMENT.

CAJA DE CREDITO HIPOTECARIO. See: BANKS, BANKING AND FINANCIAL INSTITUTIONS

CAJA DE LA COLONIZACION AGRICOLA. Government agency created in 1928 to redistribute state-owned land and badly managed private land holdings. In 1962 it was reorganized as CORA (q.v.).

CALAMA. City of *Antofagasta province on the Antofagasta-La Paz *railway, 238 km (148 miles) from Antofagasta and 4 km (2.5 miles) from the mouth of the Loa river. Estimated population in 1986: 90,056. The city was the scene of one of the earliest actions in the War of the *Pacific, on March 23, 1879, when Chilean troops took it from a stubborn Bolivian resistance. It was then a small *mining and *nitrate center of 1,000 residents.

CALDERA. Small town (3,150 est. 1974 population) in *Atacama region, serving as the port for *Copiapó and for the *iron ore of Cerro Imán. The Bay of Caldera was the scene of a government naval victory in the *Civil War of 1891. The Almirante Condell and Almirante *Lynch, two torpedo boats loyal to President José Manuel *Balmaceda Fernández, engaged and sank the rebels' *Blanco Encalada, which went down in only five minutes with almost all its crew of 140. Among the few who escaped drowning was Ramón *Barros Luco, President of the Chamber of Deputies.

CALICHE. Ground rich in NITRATES, q.v.

CALLAMPAS. The urban shanty-town slums in Chile are referred to as "populaciones callampas" (mushroom communities), because of the rapidity with which they grow. Such squatter settlements became common in the 1950s. By the mid-1960s they housed about 14 percent of Chile's population, and by 1984, 20 percent. Efforts to provide them with basic utilities (electric power and piped water) were increased during the Salvador *Allende Gossens administration (1970-73). See also: HOUSING; INTERNAL MIGRATION.

CALVO DE ENCALADA RECABARREN, Martín (1756-1828). A military officer and conservative politician, and one of the most ardent promoters of the struggle for *independence. In 1811 he was appointed vice-president of the first Naitonal *Congress (July 4th), and he formed part of the ruling *junta de gobierno on August 11 of that year. In 1814 he was exiled by the Spaniards for his participation in the Battle of *Rancagua. When Chile won its independence in 1818 he returned to *Santiago and was elected to the Senate. In 1823 he was a member of the Council of State (Consejo del Estado).

CAMBIASO, Miguel José. See: MUTINY OF CAMBIASO.

CAMELOT. See: PROJECT CAMELOT.

CAMPESINO. A countryman or peasant. Related terms (q.v.) are: AFUERINO; ASENTADO; HUASO; INQUILINO; MEDIERO; OBLIGADO; PEON. See also: AGRICULTURE; AGRARIAN REFORM; INTERNAL MIGRATION; LABOR.

CAMPILLO, Juan José. Royalist Commander at Battle of CURAPALIHUE, q.v.

CAMPILLO INFANTE, José Honorio (b. 1872). *Archbishop of *Santiago, September 1931–August 1939. Previously professor of Canon Law at the *Universidad Católica. Founded the *Acción Católica Chilena. Was forbidden by the Vatican to endorse the *Partido Conservador publicly in 1934. Strongly supported the Nationalist rebels in the Spanish Civil War. In 1939 he was made titular bishop of Larissa and retired into private life.

CAMPINO SALAMANCA, Enrique (1794–1874). Chilean patriot who participated in the wars for *independence. In 1810 he joined the revolutionary *army and distinguished himself in every major battle against the Spaniards. In 1814 he took part in the Battle of *Rancagua, where the patriots were defeated, and he had to flee to *Mendoza, Argentina. He came back to Chile with the legendary army of the Andes (Ejército de los *Andes) under the command of the Argentine liberator José de *San Martín. Campino Salamanca fought in the subsequent battles of *Chacabuco (1817) and *Maipú (1818). In 1820 he accompanied San Martín's army in the campaign to liberate *Peru and was promoted to colonel. Back in Chile, he participated in the "Campaña de *Chiloé" (1825–26). In 1827 he took part, with his brother Joaquín, in the military coup d'etat known as the *Sublevación de Campino. In 1832 he was promoted general. From 1826 to 1861 he served as a deputy in *Congress as a member of the *Partido Federalista, and from 1861 to 1870 he was senator from the province of *Santiago.

CAMPINO SALAMANCA, Joaquín (1788–1860). Brother of Enrique *Campino Salamanca, and by profession a lawyer. An active member of the Federalist Party (*Partido Federalista) and president of the Chilean *Congress, he was minister of the interior and foreign affairs 1825–26. In 1827 he helped his brother organize the military coup d'état known as the SUBLEVACION DE CAMPINO (q.v.). Later the same year he was named Chilean plenipotentiary to the *United States, and in 1830 held the same office in Mexico. After returning to Chile he served as a deputy in Congress, 1840–49.

CAÑAS, Fundo Lo. Site of an action in the *Civil War of 1891. A group of some 60 men were sent by rebels in *Santiago to blow up the *railway bridge over the River Maipu and commit other acts of sabotage against the government of President (1886–91) José Manuel *Balmaceda Fernández. They gathered at Fundo Lo Cañas, a farm to the southeast of the city at dusk on August 18, 1891, but were surrounded during the night by government troops who had discovered the plot. Most were killed; the survivors were brought to Santiago and, after a mass trial, were sentenced to death and executed on August 20.

CANCHA RAYADA. Plains near the city of *Talca, and site of two important battles during the wars of *independence, both won by

the Spanish. The first occurred in 1814, when 450 Spaniards
dispersed more than 1,400 Chileans in a surprise attack. The
second battle, March 19, 1818, was much more important, at
least in a psychological sense. At a time when the Spanish were
losing their grip on their South American colonies and events
in Chile were going very badly for them, loyalist troops pulled
off another surprise attack. The Chileans panicked, thinking
that a massive enemy concentration was surrounding their camp.
They fled north towards *Santiago, but their retreat was cut off.
Of the two patriot commanders, Bernardo *O'Higgins was reported
killed, and José de *San Martín organized the retreat. It was
a humiliating defeat which lowered the morale of the Chilean troops.

Much credit for stemming the rout went to then Lieutenant
Colonel Juan Gregorio de las *Heras.

CANCILLER. Literally "chancellor" but usually means the minister
(or Chile or any other country) responsible for foreign affairs
(ministro de *relaciones exteriores). The chancellor of the exchequer (or finance minister) is the ministro de *hacienda. The
chancellor (or president) of a university is the rector.

CANESSA, Julio. *Army representative on the military *junta since
1985. A lieutenant general who became second-in-command of the
army to General Cesar Raul *Benavides after the *coup, he replaced Benavides both as army c.-in-c. and as its junta representative in November 1985.

In 1982 Canessa attracted public attention when he made a
conciliatory speech calling for national unity, implicitly condemning
President Augusto *Pinochet Ugarte for dividing the Chilean people
into "good" and "bad" Chileans. He was accused of meeting
clandestinely with dissident *trade union leaders, but was later
cleared of such charges. He is seen as a "bridge-builder" who
insists on unity at home and on the need to establish better relations with the rest of the continent. He is reported to be an
austere man who has lived in the same house since he was a
captain. He is viewed as one of three or four military men who
are possible successors of *Pinochet should the *armed forces
remain in power.

CANTO ARTEAGA, Estanislao del (1840-1923). Career *army officer
who commanded the *congresista forces in the *Civil War of 1891.
He fought at *Cerro Grande in 1859, spent 1861-71 fighting the
*Araucanian Indians and took part in the War of the *Pacific.
In 1881 he was promoted to colonel and made sub-director of the
*Escuela Militar. In 1889 he became prefect of *police in *San-
tiago, but differences with President José Manuel *Balmaceda
Fernández led to his being posted to *Tacna in 1890. When the
civil war broke out he immediately went over to the rebels and
largely contributed to their victory. As a result he was promoted general in November 1891.

CAP. An acronym for the Compañía de Acero del Pácifico (Pacific Steel Company). A publicly owned company founded in 1950, CAP has established the basis for national heavy industry development in its integrated steel plant at *Huachipato. CAP is a subsidiary of *CORFO.

CAPE ANGAMOS. Headland near Mejillones (just north of *Antofagasta). Scene of a naval engagement, October 8, 1879, during the War of the *Pacific, when the Chilean ironclad Cochrane, commanded by Juan José Latorre, caught up with the elusive *Huascar. The battle ended with the surrender of the battered Peruvian ship upon the arrival of the *Blanco Encalada to assist the Cochrane.
   The combat is also known as the Battle of Mejillones.

CAPE HORN. A rocky promotory at the southernmost tip of South America, 56°S, 67° 15'W. It marks the end of the mountain chain known as the *Cordillera of the *Andes. Called in Spanish Cabo de Hornos, and located on Horn Island in the Wollaston Islands, it was discovered in 1616 by the Dutch *pirates Jacob Lemaire and Willem Cornelius Schouten, and named for the latter's home town of Hoorn in the Netherlands. Although the earlier circumnavigators got from the Atlantic to the Pacific by threading their way through the *Strait of *Magellan, by the beginning of the 19th century, passage between the two oceans under sail was normally made by "rounding the Horn," despite the enormous seas and gale-force winds that prevail in such southerly latitudes.

CAPELLANIA. A perpetual lien on an estate held by the *Church, usually as the result of a deathbed grant by a previous owner. An 1864 law made capellanías redeemable, with a consequent considerable loss to church revenue.

CAPITULACION DE PURAPEL. Treaty signed December 16, 1851, ending the *Civil War of 1851 in southern Chile following the Battle of *Loncomilla. Rebel commander José María de la *Cruz y Prieto negotiated the surrender of his forces to General Manuel *Bulnes Prieto in return for an amnesty.

CARABINERO. A member of the Chilean national police force, the CUERPO DE CARABINEROS (q.v.).

CARDENAS AVEDANO, Pedro Nolasco. *Partido Democrático politician whose participation in the *República Socialista of 1932 and subsequent membership of the *Junta de gobierno of June 17, 1932, split the party.

CARDOEN, Carlos. Director of Explosivos Industriales Cardoen, a company making explosives and war material. See: ARMAMENTS.

CARLOS. For Spanish kings so named, see the English form, CHARLES.

CARMONA PERALTA, Juan de Dios (1916-). Lawyer by profession, and minister of national defense in the administration (1964-70) of Eduardo *Frei Montalva. He had been a member of the *Falange Nacional and a student leader of the Falange Universitaria. He was a deputy in *Congress 1949-61, and became an active member of the Falange Nacional's successor party, the *Partido Demócrata Cristiano, which is now in recess because of the *coup d'état of September 11, 1973.

CARO RODRIGUEZ, José María (1866-1958). *Archbishop of Santiago and the first Chilean Cardinal. Born in La *Serena he was professor of Philosophy, Theology, Greek and Hebrew in the Santiago Seminary before becoming bishop of *Iquique (1912) and of La Serena (1935). His telegram of congratulation to Pedro *Aguirre Cerda on his electoral victory in 1938 was an important factor in ensuring the peaceful accession of the *Frente Popular government, and the Vatican named him Archbishop of Santiago to replace the archconservative José Horacio *Campillo Infante, who was required to resign (August 1939). In 1945 Caro was named cardinal, an honor due allegedly in part to representations to the Vatican by the Chilean ambassador when prelates in other Latin American countries were so elevated.

Caro's pastoral letter of 1938 supporting "Obedience to lawfully constituted governments" as a Christian duty set a precedent for the *Church's acceptance of Salvador *Allende Gossens' accession in 1970, but Cardinal Caro was nevertheless prepared in 1947 to censure the *Falange Nacional publicly for being too left wing, particularly in regard to its attitudes to the *U.S.S.R. and to the Franco regime in *Spain.

After his death, Pope John XXIII named Raúl *Silva Henríquez to succeed him.

CARRASCO CARRASCO, Arnoldo (b. 1893). A career *army officer. He graduated from the *Escuela Militar, which he later directed (in 1934). He was one of the founders of the present-day Chilean Police (the *Cuerpo de Carabineros). In 1944 he was promoted to general in the army. From 1944 to 1946 he was minister of national defense in the cabinet of President (1942-46) Juan Antonio *Rios Morales. In 1947 he was named Chilean ambassador to Canada, and in 1953 he became Chilean ambassador to *Brazil.

CARRERA CUEVAS; Ignacio de la (1755-1819). Father of José Miguel, Luis, and Juan José *Carrera Verdugo, three Chilean patriots who fought in the struggle for *independence from *Spain. In 1777 Carrera Cuevas was serving the King of Spain as lieutenant colonel in the royal militia (the "Milicias de Príncipe"). Two years later he was promoted to colonel. He retired in 1803, but, because of his sons' activities in the cause of independence, he returned and became a colonel in the patriot army. In 1810 he took part in the first *junta de gobierno, and a year later became a member of the Supreme Court of independent Chile. He closely observed the vicissitudes and adverse fortunes that befell two of his sons, Luis and Juan José, and had to pay the costs of their execution in *Mendoza, Argentina. He died heartbroken shortly afterwards.

CARRERA FONTENCILLA, José Miguel (1820-1860). A political activist in *Santiago against the Conservative government of President (1851-61) Manuel *Montt Torres. In 1851 Carrera Fontencilla participated in the *Mutiny of Urriola, a thwarted military coup d'état. He escaped to La *Serena, where, with Benjamin *Vicuña Mackenna and others he organized an army in the *Civil War of 1851. This was defeated by government forces at *Petorca. As a result he went into exile, but returned to Chile and participated in the *Civil War of 1859. Once again he met defeat, this time at *Cerro Grande. He was condemned to death, but managed to escape to Lima, where he died a year later of a liver ailment.

CARRERA VERDUGO, José Miguel (1785-1821). Chilean patriot who was executed in 1821, in Mendoza, Argentina, where three years earlier the same fate had befallen his brothers Juan José and Luis. Son of Ignacio de la *Carrera Cuevas, José Miguel was sent by his father to study at the military academy in Cádiz, Spain, 1806-11. It was there that, in 1808, he met the Argentine liberator José de San *Martín. In 1809 Carrera Verdugo was promoted to captain in the cavalry. Two years later, learning that Chile had proclaimed the *Junta de Gobierno of 1810, he tried to return to his native land, but was arrested on suspicion of his intention to go back to work for the collapse of Spanish rule in South America. He was soon freed, however, and arrived in *Valparaíso on July 25, 1811.

On September 4, 1811, he participated in the first revolutionary action against *Spain (see: JUNTA DE GOBIERNO DE 1811), and on November 15th that year he replaced the revolutionary junta with a new one, in which both he and Bernardo *O'Higgins, who was later to become his great enemy, took part. O'Higgins soon resigned his position, as did other delegates, leaving Carrera Verdugo in sole charge. From 1812 to 1813 Carrera ruled Chile on a broad basis of political reform. The first provisional *Constitution of 1811 was proclaimed: a step toward complete independence from Spain. A Chilean national *flag was designed, and diplomatic relations were established with the *United States (see: POINSETT, Joel Roberts). Carrera Verdugo refused to recognize edicts from Spain, set up a *printing press, fostered *education by opening primary and secondary schools, established the *National Library, and gave *Santiago its first *newspaper, the *Aurora de Chile.

As a result, his popularity grew and his followers, many of whom were conservatives who still professed allegiance to *Ferdinand VII of Spain, became known as *carreristas. But troubles were in the making for the Chilean statesman, both at home and abroad. In 1813, Fernando de Ascabal y Souza, the viceroy of *Peru, decided to move against the rebellious Chileans, dispatching an expedition 2,000 strong. Because of this imminent danger, Carrera Verdugo had to leave the junta to take command of the Chilean *army. In August that year the royalists routed Carrera in a bloody battle at *Chillán, where the Chileans suffered great losses.

Discouraged by the defeat, the junta appointed Bernardo O'Higgins as Chilean commander. This led to bitter rivalry. Carrera refused to give up his command, and an armed confrontation between the two occurred at *Tres Acequías when O'Higgins approached Santiago from the south. News of another royalist attack reached both camps immediately after this first engagement. Due to the gravity of the situation, Carrera and O'Higgins decided to set their differences aside and to fight together against the common enemy, with Carrera as commander. It is not clear whether the fate of the Chileans would have been different had O'Higgins been in command, but the Battle of *Rancagua (October 1, 1814) was a decisive royalist victory. Both Carrera Verdugo and O'Higgins found refuge in *Mendoza, accompanied by their followers.

The quarrels of Chile were carried over into Argentina. San Martín, who was in Mendoza as governor of *Cuyo, received Carrera Verdugo coldly while accepting O'Higgins' aid in his plans to liberate Chile. As a result, Carrera accused both O'Higgins and San Martín of excluding him from the reconquest of his homeland. Disgusted, he went to Buenos Aires, where he stayed briefly to collect money for the cause, and then sailed to the United States, where he purchased two men-of-war, the Clifton and the Salvaje. When he got back to Buenos Aires his services were once again refused by San Martín and O'Higgins, and he swore to take revenge for their ingratitude. From 1816 to 1821 he perpetrated acts of war in Argentina against the rival forces of San Martín, O'Higgins and Juan Martín de *Purreydón (who had been elected Supreme Director of Argentina at the National Congress of Tucumán in 1816, and who had avowed to help the Chilean and Peruvian struggles for *independence).

Carrera Verdugo published a newspaper, El Hurón, in which he attacked the three of them and demanded justice for the innocent deaths of his two brothers, executed in Mendoza in 1818. On September 1, 1821, Carrera Verdugo was captured near the city of San Juan in northwestern Argentina. He was accused of sowing discord in the revolutionary camp and, two days later, taken to Mendoza and shot as a traitor. Thus was eliminated one of the most controversial patriots of Chilean independence. Even today, the conservatives in Chile praise José Miguel Carrera Verdugo and want him remembered as a misunderstood hero who was, in reality, a real lover of his country.

CARRERA VERDUGO, Juan José (1782-1818). Chilean patriot who was executed in *Mendoza, Argentina. He participated in the Chilean struggle for *independence, and was a career military officer. When his brother José Miguel came back from Spain to aid the cause of independence, Juan José was a major in the patriot army. In 1813 he became president of the *junta de gobierno in *Santiago, and a year later he fought at *Rancagua with his brothers Luis and José Miguel. After the defeat, all three brothers went into exile in Mendoza, Argentina. Juan José was involved in the political contention for power between his brother José Miguel *Carrera Verdugo and Bernardo *O'Higgins, plotting with José Miguel and Luis to bring about the downfall of O'Higgins. In 1818 he was accused of organizing an uprising against the local authorities in Mendoza, was captured and executed, together with his younger brother Luis *Carrera Verdugo. Three years later the same fate was to befall José Miguel.

CARRERA VERDUGO, Luis (1791-1818). Chilean patriot who was executed in Mendoza, Argentina. Youngest of the three Carrera Verdugo brothers, he was involved in the armed conflict to liberate Chile from Spain. He was also involved in the struggle between his brother José Miguel *Carrera Verdugo and Bernardo *O'Higgins, both of whom sought to gain political control of Chile. From 1810 to 1814 Luis participated in the campaign against *Spain fought mainly in southern Chile and around the capital, *Santiago. After the defeat of the Chilean *army at *Rancagua in 1814, he emigrated, with many other patriots, to Argentina. In the same year he killed General Juan *Mackenna O'Reilly, an O'Higgins supporter, in a duel. In 1818 Luis and his brother Juan José *Carrera Verdugo were charged with bringing discord into the Chilean camp in Mendoza, where Chilean and Argentine patriots were organizing a campaign to drive the Spanish out of South America. They were also accused of organizing the overthrow of the local authorities in Mendoza. The two brothers were executed, a fate which later befell their other brother, José Miguel.

CARRERINO. See: PARTIDO CARRERINO.

CARRERISTA. A follower or sympathizer of José Miguel *Carrera Verdugo during the Chilean struggle for independence from Spain.

CARRIL, Delia del (b. 1880). Companion of Pablo *Neruda. Although her real name is Delia del Carril, the woman who lived with the Chilean Nobel Laureate for approximately 18 years (1934-52) is known to the world and to her friends as "Hormiguita," literally "little ant." The explanation is that she always carried on her shoulders a load greater than her weight; as when, for example, she organized and paid for the emigration of thousands of Spanish Republicans to Chile after General Francisco Franco took over in *Spain in 1939.

When she met Pablo Neruda in Spain, Hormiguita was acquainted with the most refined intellectual circles of Madrid. Her closest friends included humanists, poets, artists—Federico García Lorca, Pablo Picasso, Miguel Hernández, Rafael Alberti. During

the Spanish Civil War it was her generosity and her adherence
to the Communist Party that attracted Pablo Neruda to her.
When they began living together, he said that he had found in
Delia all that his other friends put together could not give him.
Delia del Carril's work consists of painting, drawing and
printing, and she has exhibited her work in Moscow, Paris, Madrid,
Mexico, Venezuela, Peru and Argentina.

Although she was born into a wealthy Argentine landowning family, she considered herself a Chilean from the moment
she went to Chile with Neruda. She studied art in the prestigious
Taller 99 and was surrounded by many Chilean artists and intellectuals. She was a staunch supporter of President Salvador
*Allende Gossens. After his overthrow her house in *Santiago
(which Neruda himself had built) became a meeting center for opponents of the repressive military regime of President Augusto
*Pinochet Ugarte。

She was heartbroken when Neruda died in 1973 and held the
*junta government responsible for his death. Many Chilean ar-
tists, including Roser Bru, Florencia de Amesti, Dinora and Mario
Toral, frequently visit her in Santiago.

CARTAGENA AGREEMENT. See: PACTO ANDINO.

CARVAJAL PRADO, Patricio (1929-   ). Career naval officer. Carvajal Prado attended the naval school and then quickly moved up
through the ranks to the position of rear admiral in 1969, and
vice admiral in 1970. As an active participant from the *navy in
the *coup d'état that overthrew Salvador *Allende Gossens in
1973, he was made minister of defense by President Augusto
*Pinochet Ugarte, and in 1974 became minister of foreign relations。
As such he led Chile's *United Nations delegation from 1974 to
1977. He was succeeded in 1978 by Hernán Cubillos Sallato, but
returned to the cabinet as defense minister again in August 1982.

CASA DE CONTRACTACION. An institution developed by the Spanish
crown in 1503 to regulate commerce, navigation and migration.
It was responsible after 1524 to the *Consejo de las Indias (Council of the Indies). Its west coast trading center was in Lima,
*Peru. The casa was abolished in 1790.

CASANOVA CASANOVA, Mariano (1833-1908). Jesuit prelate and
educator and the most distinguished preacher of his day. Elected
to the theology faculty of the *Universidad de Chile in 1859,
he wrote an important work on the *Jesuits in *Santiago, documented the December 8, 1863 burning of the Church of the *Compañía,
and compiled the city's official census. His other works included
La instrucción religiosa, La filosofía de la historia and Manuel
Frutos Rodríguez (all 1860).

Personally tolerant and of a wide classical learning, he was
made *archbishop of Santiago in 1886. The previous incumbent,
Rafael Valentin *Valdivieso y Zañartu, had died in 1878, but

the obvious choice, acting archbishop Joaquín *Larraín Gandarillas, was unacceptable to the government: he even refused a funeral service in the *cathedral for ex-president Aníbal *Pinto Garmendia in 1884 for his having been a free-thinker. The government had proposed Francisco de Paul Taforó, whose friendship with prominent liberals created virulent objection to his candidacy among churchmen. After eight years' stalemate, Casanova was put forward as a compromise candidate on the suggestion of interior minister Carlos Atuñez, his former pupil.

On becoming archbishop, Casanova's concern with the increasing secularization of *education led him to establish the *Universidad Católica de Chile (1888), to which he appointed Larraín Gandarillas as first rector. Rising anti-clericalism (priests were made ineligible for election as deputies in 1892, and the *Partido Radical was campaigning for compulsory--and lay--primary *education, liberalization of the marriage laws and *church disestablishment) made the archbishop inevitably a figure of controversy, especially when he excommunicated the owners, employees and readers of the radical daily La *ley and of the satirical magazine Poncio Pilato for blasphemy. The magazine promptly reentitled itself the Mariano Casanova.

Earlier, as a personal friend of President (1886-91) José Manuel *Balmaceda Fernández, his secret mediation between the President and *Congress had led to the Belisario Prats ministry of August-October 1890, which postponed the crisis but did nothing to resolve it. During the ensuing *Civil War of 1891, Casanova strove (with little success) to keep the Church neutral. Casanova's mediation was also important (and more fruitful) in the turn-of-the-century boundary dispute with *Argentina. His action, however, was widely interpreted as pro-Argentine sympathy and cost him his popularity. The dispute was settled when both countries accepted the arbitration of King Edward VII (1904).

CASSIDY, Sheila. A British surgeon working for the Combined Churches' Committee for Peace (an organization concerned with the welfare of political prisoners and their families), Dr. Cassidy gave medical aid on October 16 and November 1, 1975 to an injured MIR (*Movimiento de Izquierda Revolucionaria) guerrilla, Nelson Gutiérrez. She was caught, arrested and tortured, but this became known in Britain in mid-November and diplomatic protest secured her expulsion from Chile on December 30. Although the only direct consequence was the immediate recall of the British ambassador, memory of the incident probably delayed the lifting of Britain's arms embargo when Prime Minister Margaret Thatcher came to power in 1979. See: ARMAMENTS.

CASTILLO, Carmen. An active member of the *Movimiento de Izquierda Revolucionaria (MIR), now in exile in Paris. In her thirties, she had written a chronicle of the death of her boyfriend Miguel *Enríquez, who was secretary general of MIR and was killed by the Chilean security forces, *DINA, in 1974.

CASTILLO VELASCO, Jaime. President of the *Falange Nacional and later of its successor, the *Partido Demócrata Cristiano. In 1965 he was appointed minister of land and settlement (ministro de tierras y colonización). He is considered the theoretician in the PDC.

CASTRO CABEZAS JIMENEZ, Hugo (1922–   ). A career naval officer. After graduating from the naval academy he rose quickly through the ranks and received the Star of Military Merit for twenty years' service. He is currently a rear admiral, director of the naval academy and chief of the *merchant marine. Rewarded for his role in the overthrow of President Salvador *Allende Gossens, he was named *education minister on September 24, 1973. One of the first decrees he pronounced in that capacity was that all rectors of the country's universities would be replaced by military rectors, who would set out to reorganize the universities and eliminate all elements judged dangerous to the function of the universities. After the "cleansing" process was over, Castro Jiménez was replaced as minister of education in December 1976.

CASTRO PALMA, Baltasar (1919–   ). Sometime leader of the *Frente Nacional del Pueblo, a coalition of leftist parties which later became known as the *Frente de Acción Popular (FRAP). From 1949 to 1953 he served as a deputy in *Congress, backed by the Socialists. In 1953 he became president of the Chamber of Deputies. In 1956 and 1961 he was elected senator. He backed Salvador *Allende Gossens in the presidential elections of 1952, 1958, 1964 and 1970.

CASTRO SPIKULA, Sergio de. One of the young economists in the government of President Augusto *Pinochet Ugarte. He became minister of the economy in 1975. As leader of a handful of economic advisers known as the "*Chicago Boys," De Castro was minister of finance from 1976 until 1982, when Chile's experiment with free-market economics turned sour. Chilean businessmen almost invariably put the blame on Sergio de Castro for the country's economic collapse that began during the second half of 1981. In April 1982 Sergio de Castro and the "Chicago Boys" were asked to leave the government, taking with them an economic model that had appeared at first a "miracle" but had ultimately turned out to be a "nightmare." Castro subsequently became economic adviser to El *Mercurio.

CATASTRO. A 19th century land tax levied as a percentage of agricultural property values and benefits. It was introduced by Manuel *Rengifo Cárdenas to replace the revenue lost when he largely abolished the *alcabala, but was resented for not exempting land left out of production. In 1860 it was replaced by the *Contribución territorial.

CATHEDRAL, The (La Catedral). Santiago's cathedral is located in the Plaza de Armas. Originally a colonial building, constructed 1746-1830, it was transformed during the 19th century. Its treasures are a silver altar standing on the left aisle and a silver custody covered with precious stones, made during the colonial period in Calera de Tango, Chile.

CATHOLIC CHURCH. See: CHURCH, The

CATHOLIC UNIVERSITY. See: UNIVERSIDAD CATOLICA DE CHILE

CATTLE FARMING. Chile's chief agricultural activity in early colonial times was the raising of *creole beef cattle on rough pasture for tallow and hides. Slaughtering was limited to the annual fall round-up--the only time the animals were fat enough--so their meat had to be preserved for year-round consumption by salting and drying into jerked beef (charqui). The development of *wheat growing from the mid-18th century, and particularly its expansion in the 1850s, decreased the area of natural pasture (especially as careless farming led to much soil erosion), and the 1870s saw disastrous outbreaks of hoof-and-mouth disease (aftosa).
    The improvement in middle-class living standards with the *nitrate boom led to a great new demand for red meat: by the 1890s the average per capita beef consumption in *Santiago was 150 kg (330 lbs) a year: twice that of New York City. To some extent Chilean farmers responded by growing alfalfa grass, which made it possible to introduce European breeds of cattle. There was also a considerable importation of livestock (mostly bovine) from *Argentina. Even so, inadequate supply led to riots in 1905.
    Agricultural statistics before the *census of 1935-36 are unreliable: figures for heads of cattle around 1905 range from 1.6 million to 2.7 million, but 2.4 million seems a fair figure for 1930. Despite the intervening increase in population, by 1965 the figure had only climbed to 2.87 million head. Although there was then an increase under President Eduardo *Frei Montalva and in the early part of Salvador *Allende Gossens' presidency, a significant proportion of the increase went for export (200,000 head in 1971). Destabilization of the *economy in the latter part of the Allende administration and the free market policy under President Augusto *Pinochet Ugarte caused a decline: from 4 million head in 1978 to 3.74 million in 1981.
    See also: AGRICULTURE; LIVESTOCK

CAUAS LAMA, Jorge (1934-   ). A brilliant Chilean economist and the architect of the *junta government's experiment with free-market economics, which were implemented in 1974, not without considerable difficulties. He studied at Columbia University and the University of Chicago, where he followed the monetarist policies of Milton Friedman and became known as one of a handful of advisers to President Augusto *Pinochet Ugarte, the "CHICAGO BOYS" (q.v.).

In 1967 he became director of the Central Bank of Chile, and later its vice-president. From 1972 to 1974 he was an international consultant for the World Bank. He then returned to Chile to become finance minister, a position he resigned two years later when he was named Chilean ambassador to the *United States. In 1978 he returned to Chile and was named president of the Bank of Santiago.

Ignoring the staggering social cost imposed on middle-income groups, as well as on lower-income groups, Cauas implemented an austerity program in order to revive the *economy.

CAUDILLO. A leader, political boss or chief, generally one with a military background.

CAUPOLICAN. Famous Indian chief who led the *Araucanians to victory until he was captured and executed by the Spaniards in 1558. He was born in the beginning of the 16th century, and in 1533 was named *"Toqui" (chief) by *Colocolo. During the Spanish occupation and conquest of Chile, Caupolicán surprised the Spaniards in the Valley of *Tucapel, destroying their camp and killing most of them (December 2 and 3, 1553). Pedro de *Valdivia, who fought in the battle, was captured and executed by the Indians on December 25, 1553. In April 1554, with the help of *Lautaro, another Indian chieftain, Caupolicán defeated Francisco de *Villagra, who had succeeded Valdivia. García *Hurtado de Mendoza, who succeeded Villagra, finally defeated Caupolicán at the battle of *Monte Pinto (*Concepción). Aided by an Indian traitor, Hurtado de Mendoza took the Araucanians by surprise, capturing them and sentencing them all to death. It is reported that some 6,000 Indians were executed. Caupolicán promised the Spaniards that in exchange for his life he would give back the sword, helmet and a gold chain which had belonged to Valdivia. An Indian emissary was sent to get these objects, but when he failed to return after some days had gone by, the Spaniards executed Caupolicán. The Indian chief died a horrible death, as he was forced by the Spaniards to sit on a sharp pointed wooden pole.

CAUPOLICANAZO. In 1983 more than 10,000 people met in the Teatro Caupolicán in *Santiago, in what became known as the Caupolicanazo. They protested against the military regime of President Augusto *Pinochet Ugarte and demanded "democracy in the country, and democracy at home." The word rhymes with *Tancazo, which was an aborted coup attempt that took place in 1973 with the aim of removing from power Socialist President (1970-73) Salvador *Allende Gossens. The symbolism of the Caupolicanazo did not escape anyone in Chile. See: WOMEN AND THE WOMEN'S MOVEMENT.

CAUQUENES. Capital city of the former province of *Maule in central Chile. The estimated population in 1982 was 53,262.

In 1974 the province became part of the new Region VII; see: REGIONS AND ADMINISTRATIVE RESTRUCTURING.

CAUTIN. Former province of central Chile, with an area of 18,376.7 km^2 (7,095 square miles), created in 1887 from the Territory of *Angol. The population has grown from 38,141 in 1885 to 139,553 in 1907; 365,072 in 1952; and an estimated 467,217 in 1982. In 1974 Cautín became part of Region IX, *Araucania; see: REGIONS AND ADMINISTRATIVE RESTRUCTURING.

CAVENDISH, Thomas (1560-1592). English sailor. Following the example of Sir Francis *Drake, he circumnavigated the globe, June 20, 1586-September 19, 1588, attacking Spanish shipping en route off the coasts of Chile and of other Spanish possessions. While sailing through the *Strait of *Magellan he found the survivors of Pedro de *Sarmiento de Gamboa's settlement, which he named "Port Famine" (see: PUERTO DE HAMBRE).

CELAM. See: CONSEJO ESPISCOPAL LATINOAMERICANO.

CENSORSHIP. Press freedom was an unknown concept under Spanish colonial rule, and when the liberal *Cortés of Cádiz abolished political (but not religious) censorship throughout the Spanish domains in 1812, the insurgent *junta de gobierno in *Santiago went out of its way formally to confirm the "censura previa." A new junta (*junta de gobierno de 1813) the following year did, however, restrict this to religious matters. Ten years later a general pre-publication censorship was reimposed, but abolished completely by Supreme Director Ramón *Freire Serrano within the year. As most of the press depended on government subsidies to survive, the new freedom was of little practical significance. Any hope of developing an independent press in Chile was squashed by a new press law in 1846. This qualified the freedom to publish by the threat of such draconian punishments for anyone convicted of abusing it that journalists took good care to avoid politically sensitive topics: the maximum sanction was a 1,000 *peso fine and four years in prison, followed by a further six years' exile. A special censorship of imported books was in effect from 1813 to the late 1840s.

The situation changed totally with the law of July 17, 1872. This continued to proscribe any writings that outraged morality or the established Catholic religion, but it reduced the penalties to quite small fines. These were so ineffective that when Archbishop Mariano *Casanova felt the radical press had gone beyond the bounds of decency in the 1890s, he had recourse to excommunication rather than to the courts. The law remained unchanged until *Church disestablishment in 1925.

The new *Constitution of 1925 guaranteed freedom of opinion and speech, but already in the run-up to the plebiscite that adopted it, the authorities closed down rightist La Hora and leftist La Acción for their outspokenness. The Carlos *Ibáñez del Campo dictatorship closed down twenty Communist papers in 1927. President Arturo *Alessandri Palma used a state of siege in February 1936 to muzzle the opposition press, and he placed new restrictions on three opposition papers in January 1938. During the 1950s the LEY DE DEFENSA DE LA DEMOCRACIA (q.v.) restricted Marxist propaganda. Generally speaking, however, Chile rejoiced in almost unlimited press freedom for the 101 years that followed the 1872 law; that is, until the *armed forces' *coup d'état that overthrew President Salvador *Allende Gossens in September 1973. The new regime immediately introduced tight censorship of press, radio and television. All leftist publications were banned, and nine days passed from the time the first shots were fired at La *Moneda Palace (on the morning of September 11) before the first news reporters waiting outside were allowed to enter.

Foreign correspondents' protests against intimidation were ignored. The *junta suppressed whatever it considered "false reporting," freely expelling foreign journalists as personae non gratae and sometimes using violence against them. The arrest and court-martial (on unspecified charges) of Bobi Sourander of the Stockholm Dagens Nyheter caused a diplomatic confrontation with Sweden. And the arrest and torture of Sheila *Cassidy, due in part to her accounts of conditions in Chilean prisons, led to the *United Kingdom's ambassador being recalled.

By the early 1980s, press censorship had relaxed somewhat, the result more of increasing denunciation from abroad than from any softening of government attitudes. There is still an absolute ban on publishing anything that deals with Marxist thought. Although the introduction of the *Constitution of 1980 was accompanied by the ending of overt press censorship, the minister of the interior has the constitutional right to ban any newspaper or magazine if there is a risk of disturbance of public order, and the continuance of a "state of emergency" prevents the reporting of "terrorism" or anything concerning banned organizations (which include all left-wing political parties).

See also: NEWSPAPERS; TELECOMMUNICATIONS.

CENSUSES. Chile has the longest series of published population censuses of any Latin American country. Incomplete colonial censuses were made in 1777, 1784, 1791-93 and 1796; their results were surveyed in the introduction to the XII Censo general de población, published by the Servicio Nacional de Estadística in 1956, and the 1777 census was published by the Academia Chilena de la Historia in 1940. The first post-Independence census, begun in 1813, was published in 1953, but it is incomplete, having been interrupted by the royalist victory at *Rancagua; it is the next census, effected in part of the country in 1831 and in the rest in 1835, that is officially reckoned the first Censo jeneral. Although Chile took the unprecedented step, for a Latin American country, of creating an Oficina Estadística in 1843, the second Censo jeneral (of that same year) is little more than a population count. The next, in 1854, was vitiated by a wholesale evasion by males fearful of its supposed military service implications. Decennial censuses were held regularly from 1865 to 1895, but the gradual increase in their accuracy and geographical extension gives an exaggerated impression of the true rate of population increase; they were also to some extent falsified for electoral reasons. Administrative problems delayed the VIIIth census for two years, till 1907, but the care and efficiency with which it was carried out makes it a landmark in Chilean statistical history. The IXth census was postponed until 1920, to comply with an inter-American agreement for zero-year censuses. The Xth census, in 1930, was the first to be mechanically tabulated, and the XIIth, which was two years late (in 1952) was combined with the first Censo de vivienda (housing census). The XIIIth population (and IInd housing) census, November 29, 1960, was the first to include female fertility.

The last two population and housing censuses (April 22, 1970 and April 21, 1982) have been conducted by the Instituto Nacional de Estadística, which publishes results in both hard-copy and on computer tape. The XVth census, delayed till 1982 by government expenditure cuts, gives the total *population as 11,275,440 (81 percent urban). Population density was 40 inhabitants per square mile, and population growth was 1.71 percent a year.

CENTAUR PLAN. A plan devised by the U.S. *Central Intelligence Agency and designed to make the *Unidad Popular government the object of a financial blockade by foreign capital. The plan also supported right-wing groups that were working for the overthrow of President (1970-73) Salvador *Allende Gossens. Drawn up in Washington, D.C., by a special "Chile group" under the auspices of the National Security Council, the plan, alongside an economic offensive from within and without Chile, relied on the physical removal of undesirable persons, sabotage, subversion and psychological warfare through the radio and the press.

CENTRAL BANK. See: BANKS, BANKING AND FINANCIAL INSTITUTIONS: KEMMERER, Edwin Walter

CENTRAL INTELLIGENCE AGENCY (C.I.A.). The *United States Central Intelligence Agency was directly involved in the *coup d'état that overthrew Socialist President (1970-73) Salvador *Allende Gossens on September 11, 1973. The Nixon administration had been antagonistic to Allende ever since the Socialist leader had come to power, and especially since Allende's nationalization of the *copper industry and the take-over of some forty U.S. companies. The American ambassador, Nathaniel Davis, had left for Washington just three days before the coup, and returned to *Santiago just as the *junta was consolidating power. The U.S. government was in fact forewarned of the coup, as it later admitted, but failed to inform the Chilean government as it was required to do by its obligations under the *Organization of American States (OAS). Evidence has surfaced that the C.I.A., the State Department and certain U.S. corporations (such as

I.T.T., q.v.) were directly or indirectly involved in the coup.

In 1973 the credibility of the C.I.A. was sufficiently intact for it to be able easily to dispose of charges (such as that made by Fidel Castro in New Delhi on September 17) that the United States had aided and abetted the overthrow of Allende. In the *United Nations on the same day, U.S. ambassador John A. Scali repeated earlier denials of any such involvement and branded the Cuban charges as "lie after lie." If suspicions remained, they were based not so much on evidence--the sensational exposés were still to come--as on dissatisfaction with the evasive answers supplied.

The question of C.I.A. collusion in the overthrow of Allende was investigated by the House Subcommittee on Inter-American Affairs in closed hearings on October 11, 1973, and was first exposed by Tad Szulc in the Washington Post on October 21. C.I.A. Director William F. Colby, who had succeeded Richard Helms, confirmed suspicions that his agency had been involved in the overthrow by obstructing credits to the Chilean government and by aggravating Chile's economic situation. Although Washington would have preferred Allende's own mismanagement of the economy to have sufficed to bring his government down, when "destabilization" became necessary the funds were available.

Colby refused to reveal whether C.I.A. operations in Chile were funded by the "Forty Committee," a national security top-secret organization headed by Henry Kissinger. It emerged later that the "Forty Committee," through the C.I.A., had poured over US$ 8 million into Chile between November 3, 1970, the day of Allende's inauguration, and September 11, 1973, the day of the coup. The money was ear-marked to destabilize the Allende government, with final approval coming from Kissinger himself. The US$ 8 million was converted on the *black market at up to 500 percent of the official exchange rate. More than half of the total was used to provide benefit for strikers (see: BOSSES' STRIKE and COPPER STRIKE).

Even before Allende's inauguration, the C.I.A. had allegedly been involved in the assassination of General René *Schneider Chereau. The evidence released by the Senate Select Committee on Intelligence on November 20, 1975, is summarized below.

On October 25, 1970, General Schneider died of gunshot wounds inflicted three days earlier when he resisted a kidnapping attempt. As commander-in-chief of the *army and a constitutionalist opposed to military groups, Schneider was considered an obstacle to efforts to prevent Allende from assuming the office of President of Chile. The United States supported, and sought to instigate, a military coup to block Allende. United States officials supplied financial aid, machine guns and other equipment to various military figures who opposed Allende. Although the C.I.A. continued to support coup plotters up to the time Schneider was shot, the record indicates that the C.I.A. had withdrawn active support of the group that had actually carried out the kidnapping attempt on October 22.

In the three years that Allende was in power, the CIA financed not only the two well known strikes (truckers, miners) but also

*Radio Agricultura, which conducted a smear campaign against Allende, the women who organized the "*pots and pans" demonstrations, opposition political parties who tried to impeach Allende through Congress (see CODE), opposition newspapers such as *El Mercurio, and the subversive right (see Patria y Libertad). It was clear that to the CIA "distabilization" was a euphemism that prepared the way for the military coup they had been plotting all along, and more actively, as President Augusto Pinochet *Ugarte states, ever since the October 1972 strike. The CIA specifically anticipated the fall of Allende and provided money and advice to bring it about swiftly.

CENTRAL NACIONAL DE INFORMACIONES (C.N.I.). Government information agency which replaced DINA (q.v.), the dreaded secret police, on August 6, 1977, after much criticism had been leveled against the former organization. Since then the "National Information Center" has performed the same functions in Chile as those performed in the United States by the *Central Intelligence Agency, the Federal Bureau of Investigation and the Secret Service. The C.N.I. gathers and processes information in all fields necessary for government decision-making, especially where national security is involved.

Instances of persons disappearing (alleged to have been executed and secretly buried or dropped into the ocean, after being detained) ended abruptly after the C.N.I. came into being. But, although *human rights abuses abated significantly, the C.N.I. continued to be the object of criticism during its first six years of existence. In 1982, for instance, it was alleged that many shootouts between police and suspected leftists were, in fact, staged executions. According to the Chilean Human Rights Commission, the C.N.I. has remained the main target of complaints of arbitrary arrests and of torture and other forms of degrading treatment during confinement.

The C.N.I. is solely responsible to President August *Pinochet Ugarte. Critics of his government see only a cosmetic change of name between the C.N.I. and its predecessor, DINA, rather than the significant structural changes that were promised. Its first director was General Odlanier Mena.

CENTRAL UNICA DE TRABAJADORES DE CHILE (C.U.T.) See: TRADE UNIONS.

CEPAL (Comisión Económica para América Latina). See: ECONOMIC COMMISSION FOR LATIN AMERICA.

CERA (Centro de Reforma Agraria). Acronym for the Agrarian Reform Center. This consists of production units which combine several reformed estates, whose workers form a production cooperative with a common investment fund.

CERRO CORPORATION. The third major U.S.-based *copper corporation, after *Anaconda and *Kennecott. Like them, it was nationalized by the government of President Salvador *Allende

Gossens in 1971. After the *armed forces *coup d'état of September 11, 1973, all three U.S. corporations demanded compensation estimated at over US$ 2,000 million. They received, however, a mere US$ 360 million. In 1974, in the first such settlement, the Cerro Corporation received compensation of US$ 41.9 million.

CERRO GRANDE. Site of a battle fought just south of La *Serena on March 29, 1859, during the *Civil War of 1859, between the revolutionary forces of Pedro León *Gallo Goyenechea and troops loyal to President (1851-61) Manuel *Montt Torres. Although Gallo had an army of over 2,000 men, with cavalry and 12 pieces of artillery, the battle was won by the government troops, who were much inferior in numbers and equipment.

CHACABUCO. Site of a decisive battle won by the Chilean patriots during the war of *independence, fought on February 12, 1817. The liberating Army of the Andes (Ejército de los *Andes), led by José de *San Martín and Bernardo *O'Higgins, swept across the Andes and attacked the Spaniards at Chacabuco, inflicting heavy losses on them. The royalist troops of Governor Francisco Casimiro *Marcó del Pont had to retreat, and San Martín and O'Higgins marched victoriously on to the capital city of *Santiago. San Martín was hailed as the country's deliverer, and was unanimously elected governor of Chile, an honor he refused so that it could be conferred on the Chilean O'Higgins.

CHARLES III (1716-1788). King of Spain (as Carlos III), 1759-88, having become previously King of the Two Sicilies (as Carlo VII, from 1734). Son of *Philip V, he succeeded to the Spanish throne on the death of his half brother *Ferdinand VI. Charles' reign witnessed a thoroughgoing attempt to modernize the administration of Spain and her oversea possessions. Known as the Bourbon Reforms, these included the expulsion of the *Jesuits, the creation of the new viceroyalty of the Plate (separating *Cuyo from Chile), the division of the various captaincies general into *intendencias, the ending of Seville's monopoly of American trade, the inauguration of a public *postal service, and the encouragement of *agriculture, *immigration and *education.

CHARLES V, Emperor (1500-1558). First king of a united Spain and its ruler when Chile became part of Spanish America. Born in Ghent to Queen Joan the Mad of Castile (sister to Henry VIII's first wife) and her Burgundian husband Philip the Handsome, Charles became King of Castile and Aragon (as Carlos I) on the death of his maternal grandfather King Ferdinand of Aragon in 1516 and was elected Holy Roman Emperor following the death of his Hapsburg grandfather Maximilian I of Austria in 1520. His wide international connections account for the involvement of many Germans and other non-Spaniards in the early years of the conquest of the Americas. He abdicated in 1556, leaving his Burgundian, Spanish and Italian possessions to his son *Philip II, and his central European inheritance to his brother, the future emperor Ferdinand.

CHARÑACILLO. A veritable *silver mountain, discovered May 16, 1832 by a goatherd working for Juan *Godoy, an Indian who has become *Copiapó's local hero. The site, 60 miles from Copiapó in *Atacama province, developed into a small town with a 4,000 residents by the mid-1850s when it was connected to the Caldera-Copiapó *railway. By 1859 some US$ 60 million worth of silver had been mined, but soon after the ore was exhausted.

CHICAGO BOYS. A handful of President Augusto *Pinochet Ugarte's advisers, known as the "Chicago Boys" because they were all educated at the University of Chicago, the alma mater of strict monetarist Milton Friedman, and who managed the Chilean economy in the years immediately preceding 1983. The free-market economics practiced by the Chicago Boys met with a great degree of success for the eight years that followed the 1973 *coup d'état. Inflation was reduced from the equivalent of 1,000 percent per annum to the equivalent of 10 percent p.a., and the gross national product increased at an annual rate of 8 percent to 9 percent. But what was once considered a miracle turned into a nightmare, as trade deficits soared and the banking system approached a near collapse (see: BANKS, BANKING AND FINANCIAL INSTITUTIONS). Mismanagement of the *economy created conditions of instability and high interest rates, and practically no growth. As a result, the Chicago Boys were out of a job as the search for scapegoats continued, with Pinochet himself likely to bear the blame for his country's recent economic debacle. (See also: ECONOMY, The).

CHICHA. A popular fermented beverage made from grapes or various other products such as maize or pineapple.

CHILE. A. Name. The name Chile comes from the Quechua chilli or tchili ("cold," "snow," or "the deepest point of the earth") and it was used by the Indians to designate the river and valley of *Aconcagua. It was they who called the region Tchilimapu ("land of Chile"). Their language was the Tchili-dugu ("language of Chile"). Upon the arrival of the *conquistadores, the name was changed to Chile. There is another hypothesis about the name Chile: that it comes from the Chilean birds triles, which during their flight emit the sound "chi-lí, chi-lí."

B. Location, Size, Extent and Time. Often referred to as an island, this long and narrow ribbon of land, stretching 2,630 miles (4,233 km) from *Arica to *Cape Horn, is surrounded by formidable natural boundaries that make communication with the outside world difficult by land or sea. Of Chile's total area of 292,258 square miles (756,945 km^2), 7.6 percent is arable, and 2 percent is actually cultivated. At its widest point, Chile spans 221 miles; its average width is 109 miles. It is bordered on the north by *Peru; on the east by *Bolivia and *Argentina (with the latter it shares a 2,000-mile, oft-disputed boundary); on the south by the Drake passage, including a small Atlantic seaboard; and on the west by a deep and cold Pacific Ocean. Chile is compressed between the *Andes and the Pacific, and lies between 17° 25' and 55° 59' south latitude. Chile lies entirely within one time zone; 8:00 a.m. Chile time is 12:00 noon Greenwich Mean Time.

C. Dependencies. Chilean sovereignty extends to the *Juan Fernández Islands, *Easter Island, and to a number of arid, volcanic and uninhabited Pacific islands (the *Diego Ramírez Islands, *Sala y Gómez Island, and the *San Félix and San Ambrosio Islands). A long-standing dispute with Argentina over some small islands in the BEAGLE CHANNEL (q.v.) was only settled in 1985, and Chile, Argentina and the *United Kingdom have conflicting claims to the Palmer Peninsula in *Antarctica. These claims have not seriously disturbed relations among the three nations.

D. Topography. Chile is a long ribbon of land composed of three narrow parallel divisions: to the east is the *cordillera of the *Andes; to the west is a lower coastal plateau; and in the middle is the Central Valley. The Central Valley is poorly defined in the north and in the south, and more precisely defined in the center of the country. The Andes descend more or less abruptly on the Chilean side, while they fall more gradually into Argentina. In altitude there is a gradual decline from north to south; while northern peaks exceed 15,000 feet, those of *Tierra del Fuego attain less than 2,000 feet. The Andes are geologically recent, as is evidenced by their numerous peaks and their frequent *earthquakes. The Central Valley, which is delimited to the west by the older coastal range with its low, rounded hills, is 600 miles long and up to 45 miles wide. In the far south it is drowned by the ocean and interrupted by transverse canyons and fjords. The northern, or *Atacama, desert is one of the world's driest regions. Its three *provinces (*Tarapacá, *Antofagasta and Atacama) include the territory won from *Bolivia and *Peru in the War of the *Pacific. The extensive coastal plateau in this desert region falls some 3,000 feet to the sea, providing an unbroken coastline with no natural harbors. Vegetation and animal life are almost nonexistent. Here are found immense layers of raw *nitrate or caliche, long a source of wealth for Chile. Central Mediterranean Chile extends from 30°S to 37°S. In the *Santiago-*Valparaiso area, climate and vegetation are very mediterranean. The coastal hills are lower than those of desert Chile, but the coastline continues largely unbroken by natural harbors, with the exception of Valparaíso and *Talcahuano. Extensive and fertile transverse alluvial fans have been built by the *Mapocho, *Maipo and *Maule rivers. Natural precipitation and water from the Andes mountains provide an abundant water supply.

For centuries, during both colonial and republican periods, Mediterranean Chile was considered to be Chile. Only during the

CHILE
NATURAL REGIONS

BOUNDARIES:
- - - - PROVINCIAL
——— REGIONAL

DESERT
CHILE

MEDITERRANEAN
CHILE

FOREST
CHILE

PROVINCES

1 TARAPACÁ
2 ANTOFAGASTA
3 ATACAMA
4 COQUIMBO
5 ACONCAGUA
6 VALPARAISO
7 SANTIAGO
8 O'HIGGINS
9 COLCHAGUA
10 CURICÓ
11 TALCA
12 MAULE
13 LINARES
14 ÑUBLE
15 CONCEPCIÓN
16 BÍO-BÍO
17 ARAUCO
18 MALLECO
19 CAUTÍN
20 VALDIVIA
21 OSORNO
22 LLANQUIHUE
23 CHILOÉ
24 AYSÉN
25 MAGALLANES

ATLANTIC
CHILE

last 75 years has natural growth brought increased *population to the north and the south. Southward from the *Bío-Bío River marine climate and vegetation predominate. Still further south, from the island of *Chiloé to Cape Horn, is an almost uninhabited archipelago, a wilderness of rocky terrain, scrub vegetation and tundra, glaciers and ice-sheets. Atlantic Chile includes territory on both sides of the *Strait of Magellan, east of the southern Andes. It also includes the plains of *Tierra del Fuego. The only province in Atlantic Chile that has achieved economic progress to date is *Aysén, in which the wet grasslands support a colony of sheep herders. There is also hope that more *petroleum will be found in this region.

E. Climate. Northern, or desert, Chile is predominantly arid. Most of its uninhabited expanse receives no rainfall at all. Except for the high Andes, its highest annual precipitation is at La *Serena and in the Valley of *Elquí: a mere four and a half inches. The coast, influenced by the *Humboldt (or Peru) Current, is cooler and more even in temperature throughout the year than the inland desert. Coastal skies are sometimes cloudy. Inland, skies are uniformly clear, the daytime temperatures constantly high, and the relative humidity very low, with marked extremes in temperature between day and night. In short, the climate follows a pattern that is typical of inland deserts elsewhere.

In Mediterranean Chile, mean annual rainfall ranges from 19 inches at *Viña del Mar, on the coast, to 38 inches at *Angol, farther inland. Seasonal temperature variation is from 15°F in *Viña del Mar to 22°F in Angol. While total rainfall is adequate for *agriculture, frequent summer droughts have made irrigation projects necessary in the Central Valley.

Forest Chile experiences rainfall throughout the year. Mean annual rainfall varies from 53 inches to 113 inches, and reaches a high as 200 inches in some isolated regions. The mean annual temperature is about 50°F. In the southern archipelago the climate is even colder: rain falls two days out of three. Atlantic Chile is uniformly cold and wet, with an annual temperature variation of less than 6°F. Normal rainfall exceeds 100 inches annually.

F. Flora and Fauna. Botanical and zoological life varies with the topographical and climatic zones described above. Desert Chile is virtually barren of plant and animal life. On the inhospitable slopes of the northern Andes, scattered desert brush and grasses subsist. The Central Valley supports more abundant life in its mediterranean environment, including such native botanical species as the Chilean pine, several varieties of cactus, and the national flower, a red, bell-shaped species known as the *copihue. South of the Bío-Bío, the marine climate has induced dense afforestation, with the beech predominating over other native trees such as laurels, magnolias and diverse conifers (see: FORESTRY).

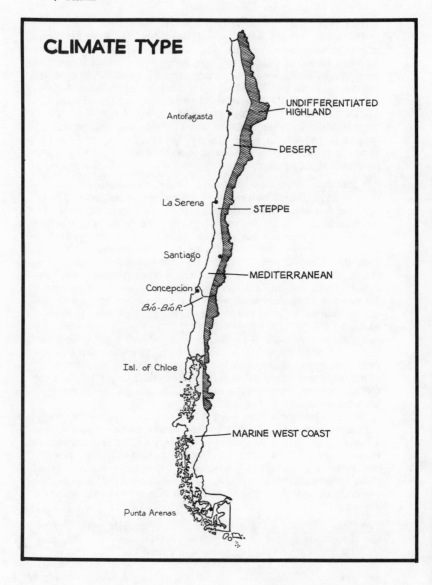

CLIMATE TYPE

UNDIFFERENTIATED HIGHLAND

Antofagasta

DESERT

La Serena

STEPPE

Santiago

MEDITERRANEAN

Concepcion
Bío-Bío R.

Isl. of Chloe

MARINE WEST COAST

Punta Arenas

Further south, cold temperatures and high winds stunt tree growth and inhibit heavy forestation. The grassland of Atlantic Chile has made possible extensive *sheep farming. The dominant Andean barrier has caused a separate botanical and zoological evolution in Chile and Argentina. Chilean faunal life includes the puma, the guanaco and vicuña, the guemal or huemal (a species of deer) and the Andean wolf. The *chinchilla has been harvested almost to extinction. Native to forest Chile are several varieties of marsupials (pouch-equipped mammals related to the Australian kangaroo). The bird population of Chile is without many of the varieties common to the rest of Latin America. The waters of the Humboldt Current abound with fish and support a growing fishmeal industry (see: FISHERIES).

G. History. Pre-colonial Chile had no great cradle of civilization like those of the Middle East and Asia. There were prehistoric inhabitants of a stone-age culture, about whose origin, appearance and climate we remain largely ignorant. Archaeological evidence suggests that their achievements were similar to those of Cro-Magnon man in Central Europe. But historic times in Chile, in the usual sense of a literate civilization, does not antedate the first Spanish explorations under Diego de *Almagro and Pedro de *Valdivia. These *conquistadors had a very hard time trying to subdue the *Araucanian Indians. Like the Seminoles, the Araucanians were never conquered by *Spain. Under *Lautaro, *Caupolicán and other leaders, the Araucanians maintained their hegemony over the territory south of the Bío-Bío River. Legend reports the irony of these Indians rewarding captured greedy Spaniards by pouring molten *gold down their throats. Before the outbreak of the independence movement in 1810, Chile was among the most neglected of Spain's colonies. An agricultural *economy supported about half a million persons, including some 100,000 southern Indians (*Mapuches), 150,000 *Creoles, 20,000 *Peninsulares, 250,000 *Mestizos, 4,000 Negroes, and a handful of European immigrant families of non-Spanish origin. The economic and social pattern was feudal; European culture, land, and *education were the property of the oligarchy. The *Church, after the expulsion of the *Jesuits in 1767, was weak.

Chile's history from the end of the colonial period may be divided into six main periods. (1) The years from 1810 to 1831 saw *independence established, and were characterized by a conflict between the partisans of centralized government and the advocates of *federalism. (2) From 1831 to 1861 there was a highly centralized government based upon the conservative *Constitution of 1833. (3) Liberalism, with greater local autonomy and individual freedom, prevailed during the years 1861 to 1891. (4) A *Parliamentary regime followed the *Civil War of 1891 and lasted until 1924. (5) The period from 1925 to 1973 saw the growth of a relatively stable and democratic nation, characterized by growing *industry, *literacy, *trade unions, *inflation, and the nationalization of natural resources. (6) The *armed forces' *coup d'état of 1973 ushered in a period of counter-revolution. There were three loci of opinion in 1810. The reactionaries or *realistas sought a return of monarchical control; the moderates or *moderados would accept the monarchy, granted certain reforms; and the radicals or *exaltados desired immediate and complete independence. Following the *cabildo abierto of September 1810, a constituent *Congress was assembled. The Congress appointed a ruling *junta, which was promptly deposed by the Carrera Verdugo brothers. Military forces of the new junta, under José Miguel *Carrera Verdugo and Bernardo *O'Higgins, were defeated by the Spanish in 1814. Radical sentiment grew from 1814 to 1817. Independence came to fruition as José de *San Martín's forces, having crossed the Andes, defeated the Spanish first at *Chacabuco and then, irrevocably, at *Maipú. Independence was declared in February 1818. San Martín refused the offer of political leadership; the Carrera brothers were shot; and O'Higgins established a brief dictatorship.

Ruling for five years, O'Higgins created Chile as a nation. Though he promoted education, built a *navy, attempted land and ecclesiastical reforms, and ruled efficiently, O'Higgins alienated the oligarchy. He was overthrown in 1823 as a result, and went into voluntary exile in Peru. The most important development between 1823 and 1830 was the establishment of two major and divergent political parties: the Conservatives (*Pelucones) and the Liberals (*Pipiolos). The Conservatives, constituted by the oligarchy, stood for centralized government, order and the status quo. The Liberals sought constitutional government and land and Church reforms. These two groups, formally organized as the *Partido Conservador and *Partido Liberal in the 1840s and 1850s, dominated Chile during the remainder of the 19th century.

Between 1830 and 1861 three Conservative presidents ruled Chile, each for a ten-year period. The first dominant figure was Diego *Portales Palazuelos, who, though he never occupied the Presidential chair, ruled "over the President's shoulder" until he was assassinated in 1837. He engineered the *Constitution of 1833, which established a highly centralized government, and stood till 1925. He superintended a re-marriage of Church and State, promoted trade, and sought *foreign investment. His was the guiding hand behind President (1831-41) Joaquín *Prieto Vial, under whom the successful war against the Bolivian dictator Andrés de *Santa Cruz was begun in 1837. The President during the 1840s was Manuel *Bulnes Prieto, under whom the first American investment capital entered Chile: *mining developments created prosperity for the wealthy. The first influx of German immigrants resulted from the European disturbances of 1848, and brought new liberal ideas into Chile.

In the 1850s, Manuel *Montt Torres ruled as an "enlightened despot," promoting and improving *agriculture, trade, communications and education. Andrés *Bello López completed his codification of civil *law. Montt's moderate innovations antagonized both landowners and the Church. The Liberals ruled from 1861 to 1891. This period saw a fragmentation of the two major parties and the establishment of the Radical Party (*Partido Radical). The liberal parties were largely dominant and were successful in reducing the old prerogatives of the Church and in curtailing presidential and central government power.

The national educational system provided the basis for today's highly literate (by Latin American standards) population. A technical revolution benefited agriculture, though a depression in the mid-1870s halted economic growth for a time. A notable event was the War of the *Pacific from 1879 to 1883, in which the rich *nitrate deposits of the *Atacama desert were taken by Chile, and *Bolivia was deprived of its border on the Pacific. Growing industry, a mushrooming nitrate plutocracy, and the incipient growth of *trade unions resulted; an optimistic nationalism prevailed. The last Liberal President, José Manuel *Balmaceda Fernández, came to power in 1886. From honest concern for the lower classes, he initiated social, economic and infrastructural programs which offended the landowners and the Church. Congressional opposition and later an armed revolt (the Civil War of 1891) brought down Balmaceda's government. This last strong President finally sought asylum in the Argentine legation and shot himself.

The period from 1891 to 1973 saw the growth of genuine democracy in Chile. President (1891-96) Jorge *Montt Alvarez relieved the bitterness of the civil war by declaring a general amnesty. During the period up to 1920, Chile enjoyed unprecedented prosperity based upon booming sales of its nitrates and *copper. But the prosperity benefited only the wealthy oligarchy and the small plutocracy of the newly rich in business, and it begat political corruption, from the highest officials to the impoverished citizen who sold his vote. The Conservatives were joined by the now-wealthy Liberals. The Radicals included both progressive businessmen and lower-middle-class office workers, united in opposition to the oligarchy. But Radical economics did not satisfy the laborers, who in 1912 established the Socialist Workers' Party (*Partido Socialista de Trabajadores). It became the Communist Party (*Partido Comunista) in 1922.

During this period, the common man had no part in the booming economy. The illiteracy rate (see: LITERACY) was about 50 percent, and nine-tenths of the population were impoverished. Popular unrest led to a demand for reforms and to the election in 1920 of Arturo *Alessandri Palma. President (1920-24) Alessandri promised land, *tax and social reforms, but Conservatives in Congress blocked his legislation. This forced the President to resign in 1924. After two military coups, however, Alessandri was recalled in 1925 and secured the passage of the *Constitution of 1925. The new constitution strengthened the Presidency, separated Church and State, established religious freedom, and gave public welfare theoretical priority over property rights. Damned by the right and left for what he had done, or failed to

do, Alessandri was again deposed, and from 1925 to 1931, Carlos
*Ibáñez del Campo ruled as dictator. The Ibáñez regime lasted
through the boom of the late 1920s, sustained in a free spending
program of U.S. loans totaling US$ 300 million. The Great
*Depression of the 1930s precipitated renewed unrest; Ibáñez was
forced into exile.

There followed two years of disorder under many short-lived
administrations. In 1932, Alessandri, now a convert to economic
conservatism, was returned to the Presidency. His finance
minister, Gustavo *Ross Santa María, brought order to Chile's
financial house, but in the process established an oppressive
regime. He promoted building activity, tightened tax collection
procedures, and increased the government's share of nitrate
profits to 25 percent. An understandably ungrateful electorate
turned in 1938 to the Popular Front (*Frente Popular) and elected
Pedro *Aguirre Cerda. The latter restored civil liberties and
promised national economic planning. The Chilean Development
Corporation (Corporación de Fomento de la Producción, *CORFO)
perhaps the major achievement of the Popular Front government,
was established as a result.

In the elections of 1942, the Conservatives nominated the discredited Ibáñez, while the Radicals, by now the strongest party
in Chile, nominated and easily elected Juan Antonio *Ríos Morales.
The new President signed a treaty with the United States in
1943 to cooperate against the Axis powers. As a result, Chile
benefited from the Lend-Lease program. The Development Corporation received loans from the Export-Import Bank of Washington, D.C., and embarked upon an ambitious program to promote
industrial growth, emphasizing steel, water power, and a search
for *petroleum which met with limited success. The government
enlarged the public school system, extended *public health facilities, and made a small beginning in low-rent *housing and urban
renewal.

Another radical, Gabriel *González Videla, assumed the Presidency in 1946. At first friendly towards Chile's 30,000 to
50,000-member Communist Party, he was later antagonized by the
obstructionism of Communist ministers; eventually, in 1948, González Videla cleared the cabinet and legislature of communists,
banned the party, and broke off diplomatic relations with the
*U.S.S.R., Yugoslavia and other Communist countries. González
Videla, too, pursued the elusive goal of industrialization. Additional Export-Import Bank loans helped build a steel mill at *Huachipato, Near *Concepción. Hydroelectric development continued,
and a sugar-beet industry was established. But copper prices
fell after World War II, and agricultural productivity declined.
*Inflation, a problem in Chile for decades, continued, aggravated
by excessive government issues of paper currency. Working
class discontent rose as the election of 1952 approached.

With the Radicals badly divided, the Conservatives elected
Ibáñez. Faced with economic decline, Ibáñez surprised many by
ruling moderately. He reorganized and economized within govern-

ment while continuing the industrialization program, yet nearly managed to balance the budget. A Conservative coalition in 1958 nominated and elected Jorge *Alessandri Rodríguez, son of Alessandri Palma. Conservative and capitalist in economics, Alessandri Rodríguez nonetheless represented a move to the left in that he believed that government management of the economy was necessary. He urged the landowners to reinvest profits and produce more food. He selected an able, honest cabinet, secured the first balanced budget since 1950, and finished 1959 with a foreign exchange balance of US$ 40 million. Given emergency economic powers, he trimmed the government civil staff by 5 percent, paid delinquent government debts, and took to the courts to prosecute income tax evaders.

This more promising economy was then shaken in May 1960 by a series of devastating *earthquakes and accompanying tidal waves which killed 5,700 people, upset the working of nearly half the nation's farmland, and caused damage estimated at US$ 800 million. In 1961 a grant from the United States of US$ 100 million helped to repair the damage. Also in 1961, the Alessandri administration initiated a ten-year development program (1961-70) which called for the investment of some US$ 10,000 million, and sought a 70 percent increase in mining production, a 76 percent increase in industrial production, a growth of 62 percent in agricultural production, and an increment of 97 percent in hydroelectric power capacity. IBRD (World Bank) experts in 1961 evaluated the plan and pronounced its goals feasible. The Alessandri administration made some progress in tax reform, housing development, and water and sanitation development, but little or no progress in *agrarian reform or in education. Laws enacted in 1962 and 1963 streamlined government administration, broadened the tax base, and provided for conversion to a single progressive income tax.

In September 1964 Eduardo *Frei Montalva, leader of the Christian Democratic Party (*Partido Demócrata Cristiano), was elected President for a six-year term. The congressional elections of March 1965 gave the Christian Democrats a majority in the Chamber of Deputies and increased their strength in the Senate. As a result, Frei was able to fulfill in part his extensive and expensive platform promises: accelerated *housing construction, land reform for some 100,000 peasants, and extended health and educational services. Frei was also able to "chileanize" copper, which meant that his government would have tighter control over all phases of the U.S.-owned copper industry: pricing, production and marketing.

On September 4, 1970, Chilean voters went to the polls to elect a new President. In the month that marked the 160th anniversary of their independence, they elected the first Marxist government in the Western Hemisphere. Socialist Salvador *Allende Gossens received a little over 36 percent of the vote, enough to edge out former President Alessandri, who received 34.1 percent, and the Christian Democrat candidate, Radomiro

*Tomic Romero, who received just over 28 percent. After he was sworn in, Allende pledged to initiate the socialization of Chile.

The new president aimed to achieve four main objectives by the end of his term in 1976: (1) to recuperate basic resources, meaning the nationalization of copper (already underway) and other minerals such as nitrates, *coal and *iron; (2) to radically speed up agrarian reform by expropriating most of rural Chile for conversion into rural farm *cooperatives; (3) to nationalize banking and credit (already underway); and (4) to control exports and imports (Allende's *Unidad Popular program called for the nationalization of domestic and foreign commerce).

In 1964, and again more emphatically in 1970, Chile had begun political processes to change the economic structure of the country and to bring social justice to the nation. The Christian Democratic government of Eduardo Frei and the Socialist government of Salvador Allende had embarked on ambitious programs of reforms that attempted to undo a system in which 5 percent of the nation's families controlled 35 percent of the best agricultural land; 90 percent of Chilean copper was owned mainly by two U.S. firms (*Kennecott and *Anaconda): the banks worked for the established rich; and industry underproduced products that were overpriced.

Allende's transition to socialism angered the oligarchy, the coalition of big business and big landowners that had also opposed Frei. Subsequently, the *army abandoned its neutrality and decided to intervene. The result was a violent *coup d'état which toppled Chile's social, political and economic structures (see: PINOCHET UGARTE, Augusto).

H. Government. The *Constitution of 1833 and that of 1925 represented the pillars upon which democratic Chile rested until the coup of 1973. Up to that time, Chile had been a unitary Republic with a centralized form of government and a division of power into three main branches: the executive, the legislative and the judicial. The *Comptrollership General constituted a fourth branch, although it was an independent and separate body. The division was as follows:

(1) The Executive. The President of Chile was designated as "Supreme Chief of the Nation" and controlled the executive branch of government. Native citizenship, 30 years of age, and eligibility to membership of the Chamber of Deputies were the legal qualifications, prior to the 1973 coup, to holding presidential office. The President was, moreover, to be elected by direct popular vote for a term of six years.

The *Constitution of 1925, to remedy the evils of parliamentary rule (as experienced between 1891 and 1924), specified 17 areas in which the President had sole or primary rule. In general, the constitution allowed him to administer and govern the state, with the authority to implement policies for the preservation of internal order and external security, and for the observance and enforcement of the constitution.

The President had the power to issue decrees, instructions

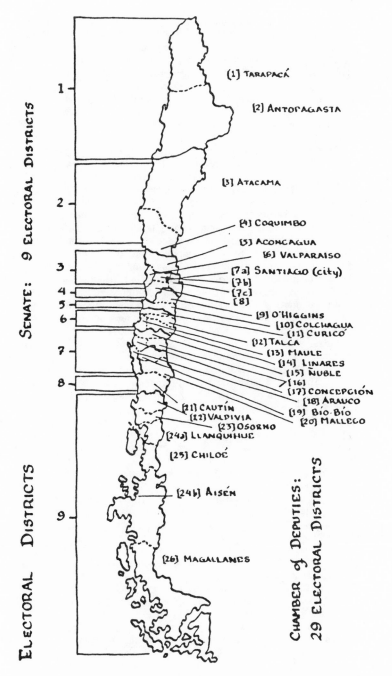

ELECTORAL DISTRICTS

SENATE: 9 ELECTORAL DISTRICTS

CHAMBER of DEPUTIES:
29 ELECTORAL DISTRICTS

[1] TARAPACÁ
[2] ANTOFAGASTA
[3] ATACAMA
[4] COQUIMBO
[5] ACONCAGUA
[6] VALPARAISO
[7a] SANTIAGO (city)
[7b]
[7c]
[8]
[9] O'HIGGINS
[10] COLCHAGUA
[11] CURICÓ
[12] TALCA
[13] MAULE
[14] LINARES
[15] ÑUBLE
[16]
[17] CONCEPCIÓN
[18] ARAUCO
[19] BÍO-BÍO
[20] MALLECO
[21] CAUTÍN
[22] VALDIVIA
[23] OSORNO
[24a] LLANQUIHUE
[25] CHILOÉ
[24b] AISÉN
[26] MAGALLANES

and regulations he deemed necessary for the execution of the law; to supervise the administration of the judiciary; to extend the time of the regular congressional sessions (for no more than 50 days); to call extraordinary sessions of Congress in time of emergency; to appoint a cabinet (see: MINISTRIES), diplomatic agents, provincial governors (*intendants), judges and military and civilian personnel; to raise *taxes, disburse money and raise additional funds (not to exceed 2 percent of the budget); to maintain relations with foreign countries; and to declare a state of siege.

The President had also other legal and extralegal privileges which allowed him to participate in the legislative process through his power to introduce measures and through his suspensive veto. In the event of a President's death, resignation or disability, one of the cabinet ministers became acting President with full executive powers. However, the new chief of state had to call new elections within 60 days. The Minister of the Interior was first in line of succession, followed by the other cabinet ministers, the president of the Senate, the president of the Chamber of Deputies and, finally, the Chief Justice of the Supreme Court.

(2) Legislative. Before the coup of September 11, 1973, legislative powers were vested in the National *Congress (Congreso Nacional). This was made up of a 45-member Senate and a 147-member Chamber of Deputies. Members of both houses were elected by direct popular vote and had to be Chilean citizens. Senators, who had to be at least 35 years of age, were chosen from nine electoral provinces, five from each, for a term of eight years. Half the total Senate membership was renewed every four years; the entire Chamber of Deputies was renewed in 29 electoral districts every four years. Each deputy had to represent at least 30,000 inhabitants.

Legislative powers were exercised by Congress as an independent body, or in concurrence with the executive branch. As an independent body Congress could give the President permission to leave the country; approve treaties; impeach and try government officials, cabinet ministers, high magistrates, military and civilian personnel, and governors. Impeachments were initiated by the Chamber of Deputies but tried by the Senate. Congress needed the cooperation of the executive branch in order to tax and spend, authorize the expropriation of public and private property, authorize the contracting of debts, approve the national budget, establish new currency, provide salaries for all branches of the armed forces, create employment services, restrict civil liberties in time of crisis, and grant pardon and amnesty.

Legislation could be initiated by any member of Congress. In special cases the President could be called upon to take action. Only the President was empowered to initiate changes in the political or administrative division of the country, create new offices, change the salaries of government employees, or draft the budget. Congress was allowed to decrease the amount of money requested by the President, but could not increase it.

After a bill had been approved in both houses, it had to be
forwarded to the President, who could either sign it into law
or veto it entirely or in part. A two-thirds vote in both houses
overrode the Presidential veto.

Congressional sessions were held annually from May 21 (Navy
Day-- Día de la Armada) to September 18 (Independence Day).
Both the President of the Republic and the president of the Senate
had the power to summon extraordinary sessions of Congress
upon written petition from a majority of the members of either
house. The 1925 Constitution granted no reserve powers to the
central government, stating specifically that "no person or group
of persons is empowered to assume any authority or right other
than those that have been expressly conferred upon them by law."
It was this clause that made it necessary for the military junta
to do away with the Constitution of 1925 in order to give any
semblance of legitimacy to the government that came to power
after the overthrow of Allende.

(3) The Judiciary. The judicial branch of government consisted of the Supreme Court and various subordinate courts.
There were 13 judges on the Supreme Court, all appointed by
the President of the Republic from the lower courts (a practice
kept after the 1973 coup). To be eligible for such appointment
to the Supreme Court, a judge had to be 36 years of age and
have a minimum of 15 years' legal experience. The members of
the Supreme Court themselves chose the Chief Justice.

Primarily a court of final appeal, the Supreme Court supervised the lower courts and could declare the application of a law
unconstitutional. It could not, however, declare a law per se
unconstitutional, and hence it exercised only a limited judicial
review. Immediately below the Supreme Court were the courts
of appeal. These courts had jurisdiction over cases involving
members of Congress. On the next lower judicial level there were
two courts: tribunals of major and minor quantities. As their
designations indicated, these courts heard cases involving different
monetary amounts. The courts also heard various criminal cases
involving numerous offenses and fraudulent electoral practices.

(4) The Comptrollership General. This independent branch of
government controlled revenues and expenditures, and generally
dealt with the fiscal aspects of the nation's economy. Only the
accounts of Congress were exempt from this control. The Comptroller General was appointed by the President of the Republic
with the approval of the Senate, and could only be removed by
impeachment. Prior to the coup, the Comptrollership General
had the authority to keep a check on the President of the Republic,
and had grown into a powerful administrative court with powers
to exercise judicial control. It came to be known as the "guardian
of the Constitution." (See: KEMMERER, Edwin Walter.)

I. Provincial and local government. Prior to the coup of 1973,
Chile was divided into PROVINCES (q.v.) and these in turn into
departments, subdelegations and districts, under appointed of-

ficials. The subdelegation corresponded to the local government units known as communes, which were under popularly elected municipalidades (see: LOCAL GOVERNMENT).

Nine months after the coup, the administrative division of Chile was totally restructured. See: REGIONS AND ADMINISTRATIVE RESTRUCTURING.

CHILEAN TRADE UNION ACTION. See: ACCION SINDICAL CHILENA

CHILENO. "Chilean" (both adjective and name of inhabitant). The feminine is chilena.

CHILLAN. Capital city of the former province of *Nuble, which is now part of the new Region VIII, *Bío-Bío (See: REGIONS AND ADMINISTRATIVE RESTRUCTURING).

In August 1813, during the struggle for Chilean independence, Chillán was in royalist hands and besieged by patriot troops led by José Miguel *Carrera Verdugo, then ruler of Chile (see: MAIPON). Due to bad weather conditions, there was a stalemate between besieged and besiegers. The latter had to lift the siege and retreat to *Concepción, but before departing they sacked that part of the city that they had managed to infiltrate. Atrocities were committed on both sides, and many inhabitants were brutally murdered. The death count exceeded 500. During this century, Chillán has been a disaster area in the *earthquakes of 1939, 1960 and 1964.

The city's population was 29,117 in 1907; over 40,000 in 1920; 61,535 in 1952; 98,500 (estimated) in 1971; and 126,531 (estimated) in 1986.

CHILOE. An island off the southern coast of Chile lying across the 42nd and 43rd south parallels and the 74°W meridian, measuring about 100 miles north-south and 40 miles east-west. From the island to *Cape Horn there is an almost uninhabited archipelago, a wilderness of rocky terrain, fjords, scrub vegetation and tundra, glaciers and ice-sheets. Between 1824 and 1826 Chiloé Island was held by Spanish troops under Antonio Quintanilla, who had fled there from defeat on the mainland to make it one of the last strongholds of the Spanish during Chile's struggle for independence. (At that time and since 1787 the island had been administratively severed from Chile and made a direct dependency of the viceregal government in *Peru.) Ramón *Freire Serrano, Supreme Director of Chile at the time, led an expedition to free the island and incorporate it into the national territory. For two years Quintanilla frustrated him; the Spaniard even offered the island to the *United Kingdom (whose foreign secretary, George Canning, turned it down) to avoid having to surrender it to the Chileans. Freire finally defeated Quintanilla on January 13-14, 1826; a treaty signed at *Tantauco made Chiloé definitively part of independent Chile.

Chiloé was also the name of a province, established in 1826, which included several of the adjacent smaller islands and part of the nearby mainland. In 1853 most of the mainland area was separated, to become the new territory of *Llanquihue. The rest of mainland Chiloé was separated in 1928, becoming part of the new territory of *Aysén. That left the province of Chiloé with an area of 27,013.5 km^2 (10,430 square miles). The population in 1853 had been 50,000. By 1920 it had doubled, to 110,331. Since then, however, it has hardly changed: it was estimated as 115,705 in 1982. The province's chief towns were *Ancud and the provincial capital, Castro, both on Chiloé island. In 1974 the province of Chiloé was combined with the provinces of *Valdivia, *Osorno and Llanquihue to form the new Region X, Los *Lagos (see: REGIONS AND ADMINISTRATIVE RESTRUCT- URING).

CHINCHA ALTA, Treaty of. Alliance against Spain, signed by Chile and *Peru, December 5, 1865, soon after the outbreak of the War with *Spain of 1865-66, to which Ecuador and Bolivia adhered shortly afterwards.

CHINCHILLAS. Small rodents with a body length of about 10 inches and fur of exceptional quality. Chinchillas were known to the *Incas, who accepted the pelts as tribute in lieu of gold and made their king's robes of the fur. Large-scale export began in the 18th century and by 1900 reached 500,000 skins a year. The consequent threat of the animal's extinction led the governments of Chile, Argentina, Bolivia and Peru to forbid further exports. In the 1920s eleven of the coastal range species (eryomis langier) were exported to the *United States to form the basis of commercial breeding there, and in 1931 two Chilean commercial fur farms started breeding the almost extinct Andean species (eryomis brevicaudata). This latter variety, found only at elevations of over 12,000 ft., has the finer and denser fur, being in greater need of insulation.

CHONCHOL CHAIT, Jacques. Minister of Agriculture in the administration of Salvador *Allende Gossens. A well-known agronomist who had worked for the *United Nations' Food and Agriculture Organization, he was appointed by President Eduardo *Frei Montalva in 1965 to head the state Institute for Agricultural Development (*INDAP), which he rapidly transformed from a technical agency into a peasant league. He left INDAP in 1967 and in 1969 joined with other radical dissidents from the Christian Democrats to form the *Movimiento de Acción Popular Unitaria (MAPU) from dissatisfaction with the pace of *agrarian reform under Frei. As Allende's agriculture minister he sought to promote large, centralized state-run units rather than extend peasant ownership. Chonchol enjoyed strong support from Christian Democrat trade unionists and in July 1971 he left MAPU to become president of the newly formed *Izquierda Cristiana. Chonchol vigorously opposed the inclusion of the military in the *Unidad Popular cabinet and was consequently replaced as agriculture minister by Socialist Rolando Calderón. Chonchol was able to avoid arrest when the *armed forces took power in September 1973 by taking refuge in a foreign embassy. He was eventually allowed to go safely into exile in Venezuela on June 8, 1974. Since then he has been a professor of Latin American sociology at IHEAL, University of Paris III.

CHORRILLOS, Battle of. Victory of the Chilean forces under General Manuel *Baquedano González on January 13, 1881 (during the War of the *Pacific) over Peruvians guarding the approach to Lima. The defeated Peruvians fell back on *Miraflores. Peace negotiations were begun, but Peru refused the Chilean terms and the war continued.

CHRIST OF THE ANDES. Twenty-five foot statue of "Cristo Redentor" (Christ the Redeemer) made of the bronze of melted-down Chilean and Argentine cannon, erected at the international boundary above *Uspallata Pass (at 13,780 feet) to celebrate the resolution by arbitration of the boundary dispute between Chile and *Argentina, and dedicated March 13, 1904, a jubilee year in the Catholic *Church. The statue can only be seen from the old highway: the *railway and the modern highway are both tunneled at this point. See: PACTOS DE MAYO; ARGENTINA, Relations with.

CHRISTIAN DEMOCRATS. See: PARTIDO DEMOCRATA CRISTIANO

CHRISTIAN LEFT. See: IZQUIERDA CRISTIANA

CHUQUICAMATA. The largest and best-known of Chilean *copper mines, located between the *Atacama desert and the western *cordillera, at an altitude of 10,000 feet. The leading copper-producing property in South America and the largest copper deposit in the world, Chuquicamata was acquired and developed by the Guggenheim brothers, who later sold it to the *Anaconda Copper Mining Company. Chuquicamata is an open-pit mine, and from 1915 to the present, output has been exclusively from upper oxide ores. Practically no underground workings exist. The ore is quarried by blasting and power-shovel work. Over a period of fifty years, the face of the ore-bearing mountain has been blasted off and terraced at various levels which reach a depth of about 1,000 feet. Over 80 miles of railroad tracks run along the terraces to the bottom of the vast crater. To the close of 1969 some 380 million metric *tons of ore had been produced and treated, averaging 1.86 percent in copper content. Copper produced at this mine in a period covering four decades has been more than 6 million tonnes. Estimated reserves exceed 25 million tonnes.

Chuquicamata was expropriated and nationalized in 1971 by the Salvador *Allende Gossens government. Its ownership and management, along with all the other foreign-owned Chilean mines that were nationalized, were assumed by the State Copper Corporation (*CODELCO), which thereby became the largest single producer of copper outside the *U.S.S.R.

Along with El Teniente at *Sewell (the world's largest underground copper mine), Chuquicamata was producing in the 1980s more than 80 percent of the *gran minería output.

CHURCH, The. A. Colonial Period. Under Spanish rule, political and ecclesiastical authority were virtually coextensive, and Church and State worked together as one (see: REAL PATRONATO). Although the State regarded itself as the senior partner in the Church-State combination, there were times when Church authority exceeded secular authority. The State used physical force against the Church's enemies; the Church returned the favor by thundering her excommunications against, and visiting her spiritual punishment upon, those who rose to defy civil authority. When normal devotion appeared insufficient or a challenge to the Church, the threat of the Holy Office of the *Inquisition sufficed to prevent moral lapses from the "Christian way of life."

The splendid work of the Church's missionaries tended to overshadow the work which the Catholic Church did for the urban population: hospitals, orphanages, homes for the aged, and the whole familiar list of charitable enterprises. But it was the Dominicans, the Franciscans, and later the *Jesuits and Augustinians who spread the faith in Chile.

The Church became very rich. The Jesuits alone, prior to their expulsion in 1767, controlled over 50 *haciendas. Church ministrations were largely ineffective among the *Araucanian Indians, but were a strong civilizing influence among the largely illiterate *mestizo population.

Toward the end of colonial rule, popular piety declined somewhat and the early monopoly of the Church in *education was gradually limited by the growth of secular education. When the storm of *independence began to sweep over Chile, the new constitutions recognized Roman Catholicism as the religion of the State.

B. Independence to Disestablishment. Although the Church hierarchy gave vigorous support to the continuance of Spanish rule and the Vatican did not recognize Chile's Independence until 1830, many individual clergy came to the fore in hastening developments. The founders of the new Republic all saw themselves as faithful Catholics.

The *Constitution of 1833, which gave the country a relatively stable regime for sixty years, proclaimed Roman Catholicism as the State religion and further obliged the President, upon taking his oath of office, to swear to observe the Catholic religion and to protect it. Nevertheless, there was disagreement as to what precisely Church establishment should imply.

The political history of Chile from 1833 to 1925 may be regarded very much in terms of a conflict over this, with the *Partido

Conservador endeavoring to safeguard the Church's traditional
prerogatives, the *Partido Liberal seeking to curtail them, and
the *Partido Nacional and the *Partido Radical working to secure
complete separation.

Important stages in this struggle include a quarrel in 1856
between President Manuel *Montt Torres and Archbishop Rafael
Valentín *Valdivieso y Zañartu concerning State power over the
Church's internal affairs. The quarrel was over the dismissal
of a cathedral sexton, which was vetoed by the high court (see:
SACRISTAN, Cuestión del). Other bones of contention were:
the granting of freedom to worship and teach to non-Catholics
(1865); the break-up of the *Fusión Liberal-Conservadora, primarily over Church-State relations (1873); the reforms to secular-
ize cemeteries, subject the clergy to civil and criminal proceedings,
and deprive church marriages of legal validity (1882-85); the establishment of the Catholic University (*Universidad Católica) in
Santiago (1888); and a law making the clergy ineligible to sit
in the National *Congress (1892). But what made the Church
far less effective as a social welfare provider was a law enabling
landowners to redeem censos and *capellanías (ecclesiastical liens
on their estates), thus sharply reducing Church income (1865).

C. Disestablishment. The *Constitution of 1925 ended formal
Church establishment. The State ceased to pay clerical salaries,
but it also ceased to control Church appointments and administrative arrangements. As a result, immediately following disestablishment, the Church increased the number of Chilean bishops
from four to ten, and soon thereafter, to fourteen. The separation
of Church and State was regarded as inevitable and was not
strongly resisted. Its chief author, President Arturo *Alessandri
Palma, consulted the Vatican over its detailed implementation,
which included the granting of tax exemption for Church properties
and a five-year transitional payment of 2.5 million *pesos a year.

D. The Modern-day Church. Chile remains, like the rest of
Latin America, a predominantly Roman Catholic country (nominally
89 percent). But Sunday mass attendance is only 12 to 15 percent, with women and children as the chief participants. The
mestizo population of central Chile seems to be the most traditional
and orthodox in its adherence to the Church; Chileans of other
parts of the country show less attachment to organized religion.
There is today a total of 760 parishes in 24 dioceses. Many
schools, hospitals and large land holdings are in the care of
various religious orders.

The Church has systematically refused to sponsor specific
political parties since 1920 (see: ACCION CATOLICA). Indirectly,
however, it can still exert considerable political influence. The
telegram of congratulation sent by Bishop José María *Caro Rodríguez to President-elect Pedro *Aguirre Cerda, for instance,
did much to secure the peaceful accession of the *Frente Popular
government in 1939.

The immediate post-World War Two period was a difficult time for the Church financially, as inflation eroded much of its wealth. President (1958-64) Jorge *Alessandri Rodríguez, a Conservative, helped the institution by providing subsidies to Catholic schools. The Church also received considerable aid from the exterior: 96.9 percent of current non-State assistance for the Church comes from abroad, as do half of the 2,491 priests in Chile.

Nevertheless the Church enjoys continued success. Both clergy and laity are educated as never before. Theological exclusiveness is no longer basic to the personality of the Chilean Catholic. Changed attitudes among the clergy are nowhere better seen that in the fact that high Church officials are sponsoring, with Church lands, a program of agricultural education and land reform. The Christian Democrat movement (*Partido Demócrata Cristiano) reflects a renewed lay concern with the social and economic application of Christian theological beliefs.

The thorny question of the role of the Church in modern times was taken up when Latin American bishops met in Medellín, Colombia, in 1968. An attempt was made to put into practice the recommendations of Pope John XXIII and the Second Vatican Council. But the Latin American bishops wanted to adapt these to the realities of Latin America. This produced a division within the Church, creating a popular church which gave rise to grass-roots Catholicism. As the economic well-being of the Latin American populace deteriorated with the rise of military dictatorships, this popular church turned to "liberation theology," a different form of religion which sought to "liberate" people from ignorance, poverty and oppression. It also gave rise to "comunidades de base" (Christian base communities) inspired by the Bible's references, in both the Old and New Testaments, to the poor and to oppression.

The aim of such base communities in Chile was to delegitimize the military regime that came to power with the overthrow of President Salvador *Allende Gossens in 1973. As civil society had been undermined by the military regime, the Church in Chile became the surrogate for civil society. Opposed to "institutionalized violence," the Church defended jailed church leaders, lawyers, trade unionists, students, politicians and all those persecuted by the military government. For the Chilean Church, the promised land was getting rid of the military government.

In the bloody days immediately following the *coup, the *archbishop of Santiago, Raúl Cardinal *Silva Henríquez, called on the *armed forces for restraint. Like many other people, he thought that the killing, torture and mass arrests might be a transitional phenomenon. When he realized that the *junta had begun a campaign to suppress the opposition, he became more critical. He made it known that the Church believed in the right to life, liberty and personal security; the right to equality before the law; the right to freedom of worship; the right to freedom of investigation, opinion, expression and dissemination of ideas; the right to a fair trial; and the right to due process of law. The cardinal is a firm advocate of Article 18 of the United Nations Charter and the Geneva Convention, and he wanted the members of the junta to put these into practice. He was assured by the government that harsh measures were necessary to turn the state of "internal war" into one of "internal security." Nevertheless, he began speaking out against alleged violations of *human rights, turning his pulpit into a political forum.

During the rest of his episcopate, the cardinal remained the junta's most outspoken critic. On May Day 1975, for example, he delivered a powerful sermon attacking capitalism, and, indirectly, the junta's economic program. He challenged the traditional laissez-faire tenet that capital should be regarded as the owner of the means of production, and found private property a contradiction in a country where so many people had nothing. Subsequently, he inferred that socialism was more compatible with Christianity than capitalism. He argued further that the economic life of a nation cannot be devoted to profit, and was acclaimed by the faithful, some of whom are members of the Catholic Workers Youth Federation (Juventud Obrera Católica).

See also: CHURCH ADMINISTRATION; RELIGIOUS PRACTICES.

CHURCH ADMINISTRATION. From colonial times to the early 19th century, the Chilean *Church consisted of two dioceses: to the north and south of the river *Maule. The northerly diocese of *Santiago was founded in 1561, the southerly diocese of *Imperial was established two years later in 1563. When Imperial was destroyed by the *Araucanian Indians, the see was moved to Penco, and later to *Concepción. Both dioceses were subject to the Archbishop of Lima.

A law promulgated in 1836, effective in 1840, created two new bishoprics: La *Serena and San Carlos de *Ancud. In the latter year Santiago was elevated to an archdiocese (see: ARCHBISHOPS OF SANTIAGO), separating the Chilean Church from the jurisdiction of the Archbishop of Lima. Acquisition by Chile of the *Norte Grande after the War of the *Pacific, without any provision in the Treaty of *Ancón to make corresponding changes in ecclesiastical jurisdiction, left the church in the former Peruvian territories under the direction of the Peruvian bishop of Arequipa until 1928.

Separation of Church and State by the *Constitution of 1925 gave the Church freedom to arrange its own affairs. As a result, the number of dioceses in Chile was raised from four to ten almost immediately. *San Felipe, *Valparaíso, *Talca and *Rancagua were separated from Santiago; *Linares and *Chillán from Concepción.

In 1926 *Temuco became a bishopric. Two years later the problem of jurisdiction in the territories acquired by Chile from Peru was finally resolved by the creation of two new dioceses in the north, *Antofagasta (1928) and *Iquique (1929). In 1939 La Serena and Concepción were elevated to archbishoprics, while *Puerto Montt was made into a bishopric. Since then, *Valdivia

(1944), *Punta Arenas (1947), *Copiapó (1957) and Los *Angeles (1959) have become bishoprics, while Puerto Montt (1963) and Antofagasta (1967) have been elevated to archbishoprics.

CHURRO. A nice person; good-looking, agreeable.

CIENFUEGOS ARTEAGA, José Ignacio (1762–1847). A priest from *Talca who participated in the struggle for Chilean independence, and who had a distinguished political and diplomatic career. He belonged to the Federalist Party (*Partido Federalista) and took part in the formation of the *junta de gobierno of 1811. After the Battle of *Rancagua and the defeat of the Chilean patriots, he was exiled to the *Juan Fernández Islands. When José de *San Martín and Bernardo *O'Higgins won the Battle of *Chacabuco (1817), he returned to Chile and was elected deputy in 1818, later becoming a senator. In 1826 he was appointed president of *Congress. Among his many diplomatic posts, he held that of Chilean minister to the Vatican. In 1832 Rome named him Bishop of *Concepción, an honor he refused in order to retire to Talca, where he spent the last years of his life rebuilding Talca's mother church.

CIVIC ACTION. See: CONFEDERACION REPUBLICANA DE ACCION CIVICA.

CIVIL AVIATION. See: AIR TRANSPORT

CIVIL WAR OF 1829–1830. The first civil war in Chile was caused by the *Congress electing Joaquín *Vicuña Larraín as Vice-President in spite of the fact that he had come fourth in the presidential election of 1829. President (1827-29) Francisco *Pinto Díaz resigned in order to maintain the peace, but Congress refused to accept his resignation. When he resigned a second time the same year Congress named Francisco Ramón *Vicuña Larraín as President. But the chief of the rebellious troops, José Joaquín *Prieto Vial, commissioned colonel Manuel *Bulnes Prieto to mobilize troops in the south.

On November 9, 1829, Bulnes Prieto occupied the city of *Rancagua and all the territory between the *Bío-Bío and *Maule rivers. The newly appointed President summoned Ramón *Freire Serrano to come to his aid, but Freire refused because he was opposed to the President. The rebel troops, encountering little resistance, forced the President to leave the capital and take refuge in *Valparaíso. But the government refused to come to terms, and the Battle of *Ochagavía ensued between government forces under the command of Francisco *Lastra y de la Sotta and the rebels led by General Prieto Vial.

Lastra y de la Sotta realized he could not defeat Prieto Vial, and a treaty was signed between them which placed both armies under the command of Freire Serrano, who was to supervise new elections for a junta government. The treaty failed as both

armies were disposed to fight. The rebels then occupied the city
of *Coquimbo and captured the President. Freire Serrano broke
with the rebels and pledged to help the government. At the ensuing battle of *Lircay, Freire was defeated, and the number of
dead and wounded totaled well over a thousand. Prieto Vial,
as victor, put an end to the war, and José Tomás *Ovalle Bezanilla became President (1830-31). This marked the beginning of
thirty years of conservative control in Chile.

CIVIL WAR OF 1851. The Civil War of 1851 was the result of liberal
malcontent with the continuation of conservative rule under
Presidents Manuel *Bulnes Prieto (1841-51) and Manuel *Montt
Torres (1851-61). After the February 1851 proclamation of the
presidential candidacy of José María de la *Cruz y Prieto, there
was a rising in *Santiago--the *Mutiny of Urriola--in April.
This was crushed and Montt was chosen President by the electoral
college on July 26. José Miguel *Carrera Fontencilla and Benjamín
*Vicuña Mackenna, who had been captured after the April mutiny,
escaped from prison to La *Serena, where they led a rising on
September 7, 1851. This was crushed at the Battle of *Petorca
in October. Meanwhile, on September 13, Pedro Félix *Vicuña
Aguirre had led another uprising in the city of *Concepción.
Vicuña's troops, under the command of Cruz Prieto, were defeated
at the Battle of *Loncomilla on December 8, and capitulated eight
days later at *Purapel.

La Serena continued to be a center for revolutionaries, but
the strong conservative government of Montt Torres kept a close
watch on developments there, sending troops more than once to
quell uprisings. See also: LINDEROS.

CIVIL WAR OF 1859. The Civil War of 1859 aimed to overthrow the
government of President Manuel *Montt Torres (1851-61). Montt
favored as his successor an ultra-conservative, Antonio *Varas
de la Barra, who was opposed both by the liberals, who desired
to end the long dominance of the conservatives, and by some
dissatisfied members of his own party. Following a narrow government victory in the elections of 1858, the opposition, led by
Benjamín *Vicuña Mackenna, attempted to convene a constitutent
assembly to rewrite the constitution. This was frustrated by the
government, which proclaimed a state of siege (October 1858) and
had a number of its opponents imprisoned and later exiled.

As a result, liberals and radicals rose in rebellion in both the
north and south of Chile. On January 5, 1859, rebels under the
leadership of wealthy mine owner Pedro León *Gallo y Goyenechea
occupied the police headquarters in the city of *Copiapó. Uprisings in *San Felipe, *Talca and *Talcahuano were quickly suppressed, but Copiapó held out. Gallo, at the head of a 2,000-
strong army, marched to its relief and defeated government
forces at Los *Loros, north of La *Serena, which he took. He
was crushed, however, by government forces at *Cerro Grande,
south of the city, in April 1859, when two of his lieutenants

changed sides after accepting government bribes. The civil war, which had cost some 5,000 lives, was then over. The government was victorious and, with order restored, could proceed to prepare for the coming elections of 1861.

CIVIL WAR OF 1891. The Civil War of 1891 was the result of a conflict between the *executive and legislative powers within the Chilean government. On the one side, President (1886-91) José Manuel *Balmaceda Fernández, a Liberal, wanted to unite his badly-split party; on the other hand, a group of liberals opposed to his authoritarian style favored parliamentary control of the executive (see: PARLIAMENTARY REGIME). When the presidential elections of 1891 approached, Balmaceda backed the candidacy of Enrique Salvador *Sanfuentes Andonaegui, but most of his party in *Congress refused to back the President's choice. These Liberals were joined by the Conservatives, antagonized by Balmaceda's anticlerical legislation.

During his years in power, Balmaceda had brought general prosperity to the country, but a controversy had developed over congressional criticism of government spending. The President was accused of extravagance and of attempting to free himself from Congressional control so that he could rule dictatorially. By the time of the elections he could count on few supporters in Congress. Congress challenged his cabinet choices, causing frequent ministerial crises, and refused to approve his budget. Balmaceda played into the hands of his enemies when, on January 1, 1891, he appropriated funds for the new fiscal year without convening Congress.

One week later Congress met as a National Assembly and declared the President deposed. Balmaceda refused to yield and assumed dictatorial powers the very same day (January 7). Although most of the *army remained loyal to the President, the bulk of the *navy supported the rebellion, and the leaders of Congress were able to flee north by sea. There they began organizing armed resistance, greatly aided by Emil *Koerner Henze, who became the rebels' chief of staff. *Iquique fell to the Congressional forces on February 16. Balmaceda's troops in the area were defeated at Pozo Almonte on March 7. By the end of April, Congress controlled all of Chile north of *Coquimbo and La *Serena, with its *nitrate wealth, and on April 12 it formally created a provisional government, the *junta de gobierno de 1891, with rebel navy leader Captain Jorge *Montt Alvarez (son of the late President Manuel *Montt Montt) as provisional President.

Much now depended on whether the rebels could acquire arms. An attempt to secure them from the *United States failed. In July, however, arms arrived from Europe on a British ship, including the first magazine (repeating) rifles ever used in warfare. Even though the rebels' flagship, the Blanco Encalada, had been sunk by government torpedo boats at *Caldera (April 23), the rebel navy still controlled the seas. In August the navy landed 9,000 troops at Quinteros, 20 miles north of *Valparaíso, under the leadership of Estanislao del Canto Artigas, a veteran of the War of the *Pacific. Government forces were defeated in two encounters: the Battle of *Concón, near Valparaíso, and that of La *Placilla, near *Santiago. Valparaíso was occupied at the end of August, and the capital fell three days later. The defeated Balmaceda found asylum in the Argentine embassy, refusing to resign until the expiration of his term, on September 18, 1891. A day later he took his own life.

CLARIN, El. A leftwing newspaper closed down by the *coup of September 1973. See: NEWSPAPERS.

CLARO VELASCO, Benjamín (1902-). Professor of civil law at the *Universidad de Chile who became president of the political party known as the *Unión Republicana. When in 1937 the Unión Republicana fused with the *Acción Nacional to form the *Acción Republicana, Claro Velasco became president of the new party. In the same year he was elected deputy to *Congress. On four occasions he was appointed *education minister (Ministro de Eduacación Pública): in 1942, 1943 and twice in 1946. He has held high office in the defense ministry (1943) and in the justice ministry (1944). In 1950 he was named minister of the economy and commerce by President (1946-52) Gabriel *González Videla.

CLUB DE LA REFORMA. A society founded in 1849 for members of the Liberal Party (*Partido Liberal).

COAL. Coal mining began in Chile in 1840 to supply fuel for the newly-introduced steamships (see: MERCHANT MARINE). Its use in the local smelting of *copper was pioneered by Joaquín *Edwards Ossandón and became important in 1852 when Matías *Cousiño Jorquera built what was then South America's largest copper smelting plant at Lota, just south of *Concepción. There he developed his own coal mines to fuel it, using British machinery and technicians. His annual coal output rose from 5,300 metric *tons in 1852 to 160,600 tonnes in 1858, and in 1875 his company was the first in the world to mine under the seabed. Like most South American coal, Chile's is generally low grade. Facilities for its transport within the country during most of last century were inadequate: railway locomotives in central Chile remained wood-burning until about 1870--a circumstance that accounts for the loss of much of the forests there. The nascent industry also faced strong British opposition. A protective duty, introduced in the 1850s and sharply increased in 1864, had to be given up when British shipping firms raised their freight rates for Chilean exports, claiming that imports of British coal constituted their chief cargo on the inward voyage. When Chilean coal production fell in the 1880s due to flooding in the mines and cholera among the miners, British coal exporters were able to raise prices to Chile fivefold, to the world's highest. World War One, when a shortage of U.K. coal pushed prices from 13 *pesos a tonne in 1914 to 85 pesos in 1919, revived the Chilean industry, even though fewer ships required bunkering in Chile after the 1914 opening of the Panama Canal. Availability of coal was also a factor in the choice of *Talcahuano as the main base for Chile's *navy.

The coal that was not used in copper smelting or by steamships provided power for the *railways: in the mid-20th century steam trains were consuming about 25 percent of Chile's coal production, and the availability of this coal delayed the replacement of steam traction. In 1950, when about 2.2 million tonnes of coal were mined, demand was increased by the opening of the large *Huachipato steel mill, which has since been using 65 percent Chilean and 35 percent U.S. coal.

In the last quarter century Chile has become increasingly dependent on other power sources, mainly oil and hydroelectricity. Coal production fell to 1.5 million tonnes in 1960, 1.38 million in 1973, and 995,561 in 1980. The percentage used by railways and steamships fell from 31 percent in 1957 to 14 percent in 1975, while that used for electric power generation rose from 18 percent to 36 percent. Industrial consumption rose from 39 to 52.8 percent.

Although some coal has been mined in the far south since 1868, a new development has been the shift of emphasis from underground mining (still largely concentrated in the Concepción area) to strip mining of poorer quality coals in *Magallanes province.

COALICION. A rightist coalition of many parties founded in 1891 and dissolved in 1919. It received greatest support from the Conservative Party (*Partido Conservador). This political combination and others like it were typical of the *parliamentary regime in Chile, which resulted from the congressional victory in the *Civil War of 1891. A majority in Congress was needed to make national policies, and the parties saw the advantage of grouping together to achieve such a majority. The Coalición was opposed to the Liberal coalition, the *Alianza Liberal.

In 1901 the Coalición backed as presidential candidate Pedro *Montt Montt, who was defeated by the Liberals' Germán *Riesco Errázuriz. In 1906 the Coalición candidate lost again. Not until 1915 did the Coalición manage to back the winner in the presidential election. Their nominee then was Juan Luis *Sanfuentes Andonaegui, President from 1915 to 1920. During the first three years of his presidency, members of the Coalición formed the cabinet. In 1918, however, the Alianza Liberal won a majority in the parliamentary elections of March 15, and the President was forced to form a new cabinet that included many liberals. A year later the Coalición dissolved, and many of its members joined the *Unión Liberal, formed the same year.

COBIJA. A city founded in 1825 on what was then the Pacific coast of *Bolivia. Located about fifty miles north of where *Antofagasta

now stands, it developed rapidly into the chief port of southern
Bolivia, but was badly damaged in two *earthquakes and then,
with the post-1870 rise of Antofagasta, as rapidly declined. It
is now a ghost town.

COCHRANE, Thomas, [10th Earl of Dundonald] (1775-1860). Scottish
sailor, radical politician and prolific inventor, who fought for
the independence of Chile, Peru, Brazil and Greece, and is re-
vered by all four countries. Chile hails him as one of the heroes
of independence and as father of the Chilean *navy.

Joining Britain's Royal Navy at age 17, in 1792, he had a distinguished fighting record in the Napoleonic Wars, for which he
was knighted, and in 1807 he entered Parliament. In April 1814
he was convicted of fraudulent stock exchange dealing and sentenced to stand in the pillory (a punishment that the government
dared not carry out), to a year's imprisonment and to a £1,000
fine. He was struck off the Navy List, deprived of his knighthood, and expelled from the House of Commons (but promptly reelected by his faithful constituents). He always fiercely maintained
his innocence (which is generally, but not universally, conceded),
and he escaped from prison to secure a new trial--which only
resulted in a further £100 fine (paid, like the other, by public
subscription).

In May 1817, having apparently no future in Britain, he accepted Bernardo *O'Higgins' invitation to take command of the
Chilean navy, arriving in *Valparaíso on November 29, 1818.
Using his characteristic mix of courage, daring, superb seamanship, ingenuity and sheer bluff, his little force soon swept the
Spaniards from the South Pacific--they called him "El Diablo,"
the Devil--and ranged as far north as Mexico. Early in 1820
he attacked the main Spanish strong point of *Valdivia, capturing
15 forts, 128 guns, 50 tonnes of powder and 130,000 *pesos of
Spanish pay. The following October he seized the frigate *Esmeralda (renamed the Valdivia) as she lay at anchor under the
harbor guns of Callao. Cochrane's ships ferried the army of
liberation to Peru, but his intolerance of José de *San Martín's
more cautious style of warfare caused a rift between them. In
1822, unwilling to chose between his friends O'Higgins and Ramón
*Freire Serrano in the threatening civil war, he accepted command
of the Brazilian navy. His fight for Brazilian independence from
Portugal earned him the Marquisate of Maranhao from Emperor
Pedro I. In 1827 he accepted a similar role in the Greek independence war against Turkey, but was largely frustrated by
mutinies provoked by the rebel government's failure ever to pay
its sailors.

In 1831 he inherited his father's Scottish earldom, which
ended his political ambitions by preventing his sitting in either
house of Parliament. In May 1832 his wife successfully petitioned
the new king, William IV, a former naval officer and the last Lord
High Admiral of England, to grant him a free pardon and rein-
statement in the navy without loss of seniority, making him im-

mediately a rear admiral, and ultimately, in 1851, full admiral. In 1846 Queen Victoria restored his knighthood, and in 1848-51 he commanded the navy's West Indies and North America station. Later honors included membership of Trinity House and the titular dignity of Rear Admiral of the United Kingdom. On the 1854 outbreak of the Crimean War he was considered, at 79, for command of the fleet, but was rejected--for fear he might be too reckless! His proposal to take Sebastopol by use of a smoke screen and poison gas (two of his many inventions) was turned down as contrary to the usages of war.

He died in his Kensington, London, home after an operation for kidney stones.

CODE. See: CONFEDERACION DEMOCRATICA.

CODELCO. The State Copper Corporation. See: CORPORACION DEL COBRE.

COIHAIQUE. Variant spelling of COYHAIQUE (q.v.).

COINAGE. Chilean coinage began with the creation of a mint in *Santiago in 1749. Spanish currency under *Charles III consisted of four gold coins (the doubloon--doblón or onza--; media onza; cuarta onza; and *escudo) and five silver coins (the *peso duro; cuatro reales; dos reales; real; and medio real), each coin in the same metal being worth twice the next smallest. The coinage was decimalized in 1851 on a basis of 100 centavos to the peso. Gold coins were minted for 2, 5, and 10 pesos, called respectively escudo, doblón and cóndor: thus the doubloon became worth two and a half escudos instead of eight. Silver coins were minted for 5, 10, 20 and 50 escudos and for one peso. *Inflation led to the withdrawal of gold coins in 1875, paper banknotes being substituted, and to the withdrawal of silver coins in 1932, nickel coins being substituted. See also: EXCHANGE RATE.

Before inflation drove centavos out of use, a 20-centavo coin was known as a chaucha, and a 50-centavo coin continued to be referred to as cuatro reales. At the present time there are coins for 1, 5, 10 and 50 pesos, and bills for 100, 500, 1,000 and 3,000 pesos.

COLCHAGUA. A province of central Chile, located south of Santiago, capital *San Fernando. The province was originally established in 1826, but subsequently had detached from it the provinces of *Talca (1833) and *Curicó (1865), leaving it an area of 8,326.8 km^2 (5,174 square miles). The population has grown from 142,456 in 1865 to 166,342 in 1920 and 219,262 (est.) in 1982.

In 1974 the province became part of Region VI, *Libertador (See: REGIONS AND ADMINISTRATIVE RESTRUCTURING).

COLECTIVO. A route taxi. Colectivos operate in *Santiago and other large cities, carrying from four to six passengers from one determined point in a city to another. They are more expensive than bus or subway transportation, but less expensive than regular taxis.

COLLADOS NUNEZ, Modesto (1916-   ). Christian Democrat politician. Collados Nuñez was born in Argentina and became a Chilean citizen in 1940. He was a member of the Christian Democratic cabinet of President (1964-70) Eduardo *Frei Montalva, first as minister of public works and communications (1964), and later as minister of housing and urban renewal (1965). He held office as economics minister under President Augusto *Pinochet Ugarte, April 1984 to July 27, 1985.

COLOCOLO (1515-1561). An *Araucanian Indian chieftain who fought valiantly against Pedro de *Valdivia and the Spaniards who came to conquer Chile. He distinguished himself during the years 1551 and 1553, and, with the aid of *Caupolicán, defeated the Spaniards at the Battle of *Tucapel. Colocolo continued to fight in 1554 against Valdivia's successor, Francisco *Villagra. When the Spaniards retreated to the city of *Concepción, Colocolo took the city and burned it, wounding Villagra, who managed to escape. In 1555 the Spaniards, led by Villagra, counterattacked, and this time it was Colocolo who escaped. A year later Colocolo was defeated by the Spanish on the shores of the *Bío-Bío river, but returned to fight under Caupolicán two years later. In 1559 Colocolo signed the first peace treaty with the Spaniards, but in 1561 found himself fighting the *conquistadores once again. It was in that year that the aging Indian chief lost his life at the Battle of *Lumanco.

COLOMBIA, Relations with. Chile-Colombia relations were formalized in 1880, after start of the War of the *Pacific, during which Colombia remained neutral. Chile wanted a swift resolution to the conflict with *Peru and *Bolivia, and a convention on arbitration was signed that year in Bogotá. For Colombia, which was having its own border difficulties with Ecuador, Venezuela, *Brazil and Costa Rica, the signing of the convention symbolically pointed to the advantage of diplomatic solutions to disputes.

During the 20th century, relations with Colombia have remained normal for the most part. Colombia, although it has its own history of violence during this century, was surprised by the 1973 *coup in Chile and the degree of violence that followed. During the first years of the regime of President Augusto *Pinochet Ugarte, many Chileans found asylum in Colombia. Colombia's relations with Pinochet were at first cool, and have never reached the classification of "warm."

COLONIAL ADMINISTRATION. Under the supreme authority of the Royal Council for the Indies (*Consejo de las Indias), Spain's

American possessions were administered by viceroys, Chile being included in the Viceroyalty of *Peru. The vice-royalties were divided into reinos ('kingdoms')--Chile being the Reino de Nueva Extremadura--under gobernadores (governors). Early in the 18th century, Chile's status was raised to that of a captaincy general (under a capitán general) who presided over a Real *Audiencia. Local government consisted of towns and their surrounding rural areas, governed by town councils (*cabildos).

In 1776 a new viceroyalty, that of the River Plate, was set up at Buenos Aires, and the province of *Cuyo was detached from Chile and included in the new administration. In 1787, *Chiloé was separated from Chile, to be administered directly from Peru, and the rest of the captaincy was divided into two provinces (*intendencias) under *intendants (intendentes): *Santiago, from La *Serena to the river Maule, and *Concepción, from the Maule to the southern frontier with the *Araucanian Indians. These "intendencias" were divided into departments called partidos: 14 in the case of Santiago, 8 in the intendency of Concepción. The partidos were entrusted to prefects (subdelegados) with similar functions to the *corregidores whom they replaced.

In March 1798 a royal decree set Chile's captain general largely free from viceregal control.

COMANDOS POPULARES. A political party of the right formed originally in 1958, when it backed the presidential candidacy of Jorge *Alessandri Rodríguez. The party was dissolved in 1961 when it failed to win representation in Congress. In 1963 the party was formed again to back the candidacy of Julio *Durán Neumann in the presidential elections of 1964. It participated in the parliamentary elections of 1965, but once again failed to win any representation and so was dissolved for the second time.

COMERCIO Y ABASTECIMIENTO, Ministerio de. The Ministry of Commerce and Supply was created by Statute no. 5149 on October 6, 1941. Its main functions were to supervise the internal and external economy of the country. A year later it ceased to exist and was replaced by the Ministerio de *Economía y Comercio (Ministry of the Economy and Trade).

COMISION ECONOMICA PARA AMERICA LATINA. See: ECONOMIC COMMISSION FOR LATIN AMERICA.

COMMERCIAL AVIATION. See: AIR TRANSPORT

COMMUNE (Comuna). Basic unit of modern Chilean LOCAL GOVERNMENT (q.v.).

COMMUNICATIONS. See: AIR TRANSPORT; HIGHWAYS; MERCHANT MARINE; PORTS; POSTAL SERVICES; RAILWAYS; TELECOMMUNICATIONS.

COMMUNISM. The Communist Party of Chile (PARTIDO COMUNISTA CHILENO, q.v.) is a revisionist, pro-Soviet party which traditionally lacked any revolutionary fervor and maintained close relations with Moscow until 1973, when the military *junta that overthrew Socialist President Salvador *Allende Gossens outlawed it, sending many of its members underground. The Partido Comunista Chileno backed the *Frente de Acción Popular (FRAP) and *Unidad Popular candidate for the presidency in 1952, 1958, 1964 and 1970.

The Revolutionary Communist Party (PARTIDO COMUNISTA REVOLUCIONARIO, q.v.) was the result of a split in the Communist Party in 1966. The Partido Comunista Revolucionario was unhappy with the anti-Marxist line of the Partido Comunista Chileno ever since the latter had adopted the revisionist policies of Khrushchev.

The Communist Rebel Union (UNION REBELDE COMUNISTA) was a Marxist-Leninist party formed in the north of Chile along the same ideological lines as the Partido Comunista Revolucionario. Like the latter, it has maintained a basically underground structure since the fall of Allende.

The MOVIMIENTO DE IZQUIERDA REVOLUCIONARIA (q.v.) was of Castroite inspiration. Founded in 1967, MIR was the most revolutionary party of the pre-*coup period.

See also: ACCION CHILENA ANTI-COMUNISTA; IZQUIERDA COMUNISTA.

COMMUNITY COUNCILS. See: CONSEJOS COMUNALES

COMPAÑIA, Church of The. A church in *Santiago so named for having been built (in 1709) by the *Jesuits ("Compañía de Jesús"), which gave the name to the street, Calle Compañía, on which it was erected. At an evening mass on December 3, 1863, honoring Santa María Purísima, the church was destroyed by one of the worst fires in Chilean history. Over two thirds of the estimated 3,000 worshippers died when the doorways became blocked. The victims were mostly women, hampered by crinolines, then at their most extravagant width. Even many of those rescued by ropes perished because of the highly inflamable petticoats they wore. After the fire the church was not rebuilt, but was converted into what is now the garden of the National *Congress building.

COMPAÑIA DE ACERO DEL PACIFICO. See: CAP.

COMPAÑIA DE JESUS (Society of Jesus). See: JESUITS.

COMPAÑIA DE SALITRE DE CHILE. See: COSACH.

COMPAÑIA SUDAMERICANA DE VAPORES. A steamship company, run at first with British, and then with American, capital. Its main office is in the port city of *Valparaíso.

COMPTROLLERSHIP GENERAL, the. (Controlaría General de la República). Autonomous agency established 1927 to supervise the
fiscal management of national and local government in Chile. See:
CHILE--H. Government. (4) Comptrollership General.

COMUNA. Modern unit of LOCAL GOVERNMENT (q.v.) in Chile.

CONAF. See: CORPORACION NACIONAL FORESTAL

CONCENTRACION NACIONAL. A political fusion of four major parties,
the Radical (*Partido Radical), Conservative (*Partido Conservador), Liberal (*Partido Liberal) and Democratic (*Partido Democrático). It was organized in 1948 during the government (1946-
52) of President Gabriel *González Videla to pass the LEY DE
DEFENSA DE LA DEMOCRACIA (q.v.) to outlaw the Communist
Party (*Partido Comunista Chileno). After this was enacted the
Concentración Nacional continued to work as a coalition until
1950. In that year *Congress passed another law to fix wages
and prices, and this split the coalition: Liberals and Conservatives sided together against the other two parties, which had
backed workers striking for better wages. The Radical and
Democratic parties were accused of conspiring to create a revolutionary alliance with the *trade unions. The Radicals were
also accused of bringing violence onto the streets. When demonstrations ensued, the Concentración Nacional dissolved.

CONCENTRATION CAMPS. Immediately after the *coup d'état that
overthrew Socialist President (1970-73) Salvador *Allende Gossens,
a total of 20 detention camps were established in Chile, ranging
from *Arica, *Pisagua, and *Iquique, in the far north and Cacabuco in the *Atacama desert to *Punta Arenas and *Dawson Island
in the *Strait of Magellan. It was to the remote north and especially to the almost uninhabited south that the majority of the
prominent prisoners were sent (over 30 of Allende's closest advisers were held in the maximum security prison at *Dawson Island). Other detention camps were at *Antofagasta, *Copiapó,
La *Serena, *Valparaíso, *San Antonio, *Tejas Verdes, *Santiago,
*Rancagua, *Chillán, *Quiriquina Island, *Concepción, *Temuco,
*Valdivia, and *Puerto Montt. Conditions in the 20 centers
ranged from unsatisfactory to abominable: prisoners were often
beaten and tortured, and later executed. Many disappeared without a trace, as Chile acquired an increasingly bad name for its
disregard of human rights.

CONCEPCION (city). The third largest city in Chile (after Greater
*Santiago and Greater *Valparaíso). Founded by Pedro de
*Valdivia on March 3, 1550 as Concepción del Nuevo Extremo,
where now stands the tiny port of Penco, Concepción has suffered
badly from *earthquakes, especially that of May 25, 1751, and
its site has been moved several times as a consequence. It is
now on the *Bío-Bío river, not far from its mouth. When the

1751 quake struck, Concepción, with a population of 20,000, was only second to Santiago. Owing to the destruction and to a truce with the *Araucanian Indians (which meant that the city ceased to be a military headquarters), the number of inhabitants fell sharply, to only 6,000 at *Independence. By 1865 it had increased again, to 13,958. It reached 24,180 in 1895; 55,330 in 1907; 77,589 in 1930; 120,099 in 1952; 148,078 in 1960; 178,200 in 1970; and an estimated 213,818 in 1984. The greater metropolitan area, with a 1981 estimated population of 549,659, includes the port and naval base of *Talcahuano, nine miles away, and the Bay of San Vincente, just outside the city, which provide excellent harbors for the commercial needs of the whole province. There are sufficient *iron ore, *coal, water and hydroelectric power at hand for the city to operate its own steel mill: the integrated *Huachipato iron and steel plant is capable of satisfying the basic needs of all Chile. With a new *petroleum refinery just finished, the city promises to become the industrial center of the nation. It lies 350 miles south of Santiago, at 36° 50' S, 73° 03' W.

CONCEPCION (province). The administrative division of Chile in 1787 created the *Intendencia of Concepción, stretching from the river *Maule to the *Bío-Bío (see: COLONIAL ADMINISTRATION), including the later *provinces of *Maule, *Linares, *Nuble and Concepción. The immediate post-Independence province, as established in 1826, lost territory north of the Nuble river, but was extended south of the Bío-Bío, until new provinces were formed there during the course of the 19th century. By 1920 it was left with an area of 5,681.1 km^2 (2,193 square miles) and a population of 247,611. By 1971 the population had increased to 662,679 (est.) and was 797,689 (est.) in 1982. The administrative restructuring of 1974 made the province part of Region VIII, Bío-Bío, but retained *Concepción city as the capital. See: REGIONS AND ADMINISTRATIVE RESTRUCTURING.

CONCEPCION (pueblo). Scene of Chilean heroism in the closing stages of the War of the *Pacific. On July 9, 1882, a large Peruvian force trapped the 70-man garrison of this small outpost in the central highlands of Peru. The Chileans held out for about 18 hours, until they were all killed. The Combate de Concepción is also remembered by both sides for its atrocities: the Peruvians killed the four civilian survivors (women and a child); and a later Chilean punitive expedition razed the village to the ground.

CONCEPCION, ALAMEDA VIEJA DE LA. See: ALAMEDA VIEJA DE LA CONCEPCION.

CONCHA CERDA, Melchor de Santiago (1799-1883). Lawyer and statesman. In 1820, after graduating in law at the University of San Marcos in Lima, Peru, he returned to Chile, where he had a distinguished political career. He held elective office from

1823 to 1876. Together with the Spaniard José Joaquín Mora, he drafted the Chilean *Constitution of 1828.

CONCHA ORTIZ, Malaquias (1859-1921). Member of the Radical Party (*Partido Radical) who in 1887 founded the Democratic Party (*Partido Democratico), a splinter of the *Partido Radical Democra tico. The members of the new party criticized the Radicals for siding with *labor during the *mining strikes of the 1870s, and for being anticlerical. Concha Ortiz became the secretary general of the Democratic Party, and in the *Civil War of 1891 he sided with President (1886-91) José Miguel *Balmaceda Fernández. On Balmaceda's fall he was imprisoned by the victorious *Congress, but was freed shortly afterwards.

Three years later he was framed by the *army authorities on a charge of organizing an uprising in one of the military posts in *Santiago. This, it transpired, was only a pretext to proclaim a state of siege in Santiago province in order to rig the parliamentary elections of 1894. In that year Concha Ortiz wrote a controversial book about the democratic process in Chile, El programa de la democracia. He also wrote a treatise on economic policy, Tratado de economía experimental. In 1896 he became president of the Democratic Party, a post he held until 1909. He remained very active in politics until his death, holding office continuously from 1900, first as deputy and then as senator. In 1915 he became president of his party once again. From 1917 to 1918 and again from 1919 to 1920 he was minister of industry and public works.

CONCHA QUESADA, Miguel (1910-   ). Active member of the Communist Party (*Partido Comunista Chileno) until 1955. He studied economics in Mexico, and in Chile he became the vice-president of a *trade union, Trabajadores en la Industria Privada ("Workers in Private Industry"). In 1946 he was appointed by President (1946-52) Gabriel *González Videla as minister of *agriculture, a post he had to leave when González Videla outlawed the Communist Party in 1948. In the government (1952-58) of President Carlos *Ibáñez del Campo, he was named Superintendant of Prices and Wages (1953-54). In 1955 Concha Quesada was sent as honorary Chilean consul to Milan, Italy. It was then that he renounced membership in the Communist Party.

CONCHA SUBERCASEAUX, Carlos (1863-1917). Lawyer by profession and member of the Conservative Party (*Partido Conservador). Concha Subercaseaux was an enemy of President (1886-91) José Manuel *Balmaceda Fernández during the *Civil War of 1891. From 1894 to 1906 he was a deputy in *Congress and held various diplomatic assignments. In 1903 he became president of the Chamber of Deputies. From 1898 to 1899 he was minister of war in the cabinet of President (1896-1901) Federico *Errázuriz Echaurren. From 1900 to 1903 he was Chilean minister to Argentina.

CONCON. A small town near *Valparaíso, and the site of a bloody
battle fought on August 22, 1891, during the *Civil War of 1891.
The army supporting the rebel *Congress counted 9,248 men and
was commanded by Colonel Estanislao del *Canto Artigas. The
troops supporting President (1886-91) José Manuel *Balmaceda
Fernández numbered some 8,000 and were led by generals Orozimbo *Barbosa Puga and José Miguel Alcérrea. The loyalist army
was routed, losing some 2,000 men killed or wounded. The
congressional troops' losses were estimated at 1,000.

CONFEDERACION DE TRABAJADORES DE CHILE (CTCh). See:
TRADE UNIONS.

CONFEDERACION DEMOCRATICA (CODE). A coalition of four parties
opposed to President (1970-73) Salvador *Allende Gossens.
Founded in mid-1972, the coalition was led by former Christian
Democrat President Eduardo *Frei Montalva and by National Party
senator Sergio Onofre *Jarpa Reyes. The rightist attempt to
paralyze the economy in October 1972 was organized by the *Partido Nacional and fed by the *Partido Demócrata Cristiano's "free
*trade union" base. The most reactionary sector of the CODE
opposition was led by Jarpa. By creating economic social chaos,
the opposition hoped to win the two-thirds majority in the congressional elections of March 1973 that they needed to bring impeachment proceedings against Allende. When that failed, CODE
hoped to provoke the *army into removing the Socialist President,
and this they succeeded in doing on September 11, 1973.
    The four parties that made up CODE were: the Christian
Democrats, the National Party, the Radicals (*Partido Radical)
and the *Partido de la Izquierda Radical--the party which, on
instructions from the *Central Intelligence Agency, pretended to
support the Allende government in order to sabotage it.

CONFEDERACION NACIONAL DE TRABAJADORES (CNT). National
labor organization formed in 1958 under Christian Democrat auspices. See: TRADE UNIONS.

CONFEDERACION REPUBLICANA DE ACCION CIVICA (CRAC). A
political organization backing the rightist government (1927-31)
of President Carlos *Ibáñez del Campo, formed in 1930 and dissolved in 1931. Made up mostly of white-collar workers, its
membership was always relatively small. In the parliamentary
elections of 1930, CRAC elected fourteen deputies but no senators.
When the Ibáñez government fell in 1931, CRAC dissolved.

CONFIN. (Consejo de Fomento e Investigaciones Agrícolas). Agricultural Extension Services.

CONGRESISTA. A term used during the *Civil War of 1891 to designate a partisan of the rebel Congress which was at war with
President José Manuel *Balmaceda Fernández.

CONGRESO DE PLENIPOTENCIARIOS. See: OCHAGAVIA TREATY

CONGRESO NACIONAL. See: CONGRESS

CONGRESO TERMAL. A Congress convened in March 1930 during
the presidency of Carlos *Ibáñez del Campo, and so called because it was held in *Chillán, a summer resort with thermal baths.
The Congress was elected by arbitration ("arbitraje electoral")
to avoid any political repercussions on the parties that composed
it. The basis of its selection was that when the number of candidates equals the number of seats to be filled, a direct popular
vote is unnecessary. The "Thermal Congress" was dissolved
June 6, 1932.

CONGRESS (Congreso Nacional). The Chilean Congress has always
been bicameral, consisting of a Senate and a Chamber of Deputies.
    The first National Congress was established with much solemn-
ity on July 4, 1811. It was convened by the *Junta de Gobierno
of 1810, and was elected by the *cabildos. There were three
loci of opinion in this first congress. The reactionaries (*realistas)
sought the return of monarchical rule; the moderates (*moderados)
would accept the monarchy, granted certain constitutional reforms,
and the radicals (*exaltados) desired immediate and complete independence. The congress of 1811 appointed a ruling junta,
which was promptly deposed by the *Carrera Verdugo brothers,
José Miguel, Juan José and Luis. As a result, it came to an
abrupt end on December 2, 1811.
    The first congress of independent Chile was that established
by the CONSTITUTION OF 1818 (q.v.), subsequently modified
by the CONSTITUTION OF 1823 (q.v.). The CONSTITUTION OF
1833 (q.v.) established an indirectly elected senate and a directly
elected lower house in a form which lasted until 1925.
    For the form of Congress established by the *Constitution of
1925, see: CHILE--H. Government, (2) Legislative.
    At present Chile has no functioning Congress, but the new
CONSTITUTION OF 1980 (q.v.) provides for its coming into existence by 1989.

CONQUISTADOR. Conqueror. Specifically, a Spaniard who took part
in the conquest of the New World.

CONSCRIPTION. Compulsory military service was introduced into
Chile by a law of September 5, 1900, and the principle is now
enshrined in the *Constitution of 1980. Nineteen-year-old males
are normally liable for a year's service in the *army or two years
in the *navy. In practice the actual time served varies according
to the exigencies of the service: army service may last from 9
months to 2 years, and middle-class officer conscripts serve for
a much briefer period. As the 100,000 or so young men becoming
eligible for drafting each year are about three times the number
that can be adequately trained, many are never in fact called

up and avoidance has always been easy for those with wealth or other influence.

The army takes about 30,000 conscripts a year. This includes, as a matter of policy, about 3,000 illiterates: conscription is seen by the authorities in educational as well as military terms. The navy takes only 1,000 or less: its present conscript strength is 1,600. The *air force is usually able to depend wholly on voluntary enlistment.

On completion of their active service, conscripts are reckoned for the following 12 years as being on "active" reserve (although this involves little or no actual duty or training) and after that, for another 13 years, as being on second-line reserve.

CONSEJO DE LAS INDIAS. The supreme governing council for the Spanish American colonies, known as "El Real y Supremo Consejo de las Indias." The Council of the Indies was established in 1524 as a body independent of any other Spanish institution under the crown. It controlled all functions of government in Spanish America and was responsible for preparing the laws, writing the royal decrees, and drawing up royal ordinances by which the colonies were administered. Among its many important functions were those of supervising the treatment of the Indians, granting permission for new expeditions of discovery, creating bishoprics, setting up *universities, and providing for the military defense of the colonies. The council enjoyed wide powers throughout the Hapsburg period (to 1700). In 1714, however, the Bourbon King *Philip V instituted the Secretariat of the Indies, with the Council subordinated to it. By 1790 the Council had been reduced to a merely advisory body. It was abolished by the Cádiz *Cortés in 1812, reestablished by *Ferdinand VII in 1814, but finally abolished in 1834.

CONSEJO DIRECTORIAL. A provisional government established November 13, 1825, when the Supreme Director (1823-26) Ramón *Freire Serrano appointed Miguel *Infante Rojas to subrogate his term of office. General Freire took leave of absence to lead an expedition to conquer *Chiloé. As a result of its annexation, Chile was divided in 1826 into eight provinces: (from north to south) *Coquimbo, *Aconcagua, *Santiago, *Colchagua, *Maule, *Concepción, *Valdivia and Chiloé. On March 6, 1826, Freire returned to Santiago to resume his duties as Supreme Director.

CONSEJO EPISCOPAL LATINOAMERICANO (CELAM). The Latin American Episcopal Council was established in 1955 by Latin America's Catholic bishops. The council's main concern has been the Catholic *Church's role in Latin America. CELAM's functions are: (1) to study matters of interest to the Church in Latin America; (2) to coordinate activities; (3) to promote and assist Catholic initiatives; and, (4) to prepare other conferences of the Latin American episcopate to be convoked by the Holy See. CELAM has a general secretariat and five undersecretariats.

Each undersecretariat has its own special responsibilities to the council, viz.: (1) the preservation and propagation of the faith; (2) the supervision of diocesan clergy and religious institutes; (3) the dissemination of religious education for youth; (4) the increased role of apostolate of the laity; and (5) social action and social assistance.

CONSEJOS COMUNALES. Community councils set up by law as part of the *agrarian reform program of the administration of President Eduardo *Frei Montalva and which became very active during the presidency of Salvador *Allende Gossens. The consejos rationalized health programs, extended educational facilities to the rural areas, planned agricultural production, set up marketing cooperatives, purchased communal farm equipment, and tried to deal with a series of economic crises fomented by striking truck owners and other opposition groups (See: BOSSES' STRIKE). The consejos were made up of farm union members, small property owners and salaried farm workers. Generally they were stauch supporters of Allende's agrarian reform programs.

CONSERVATIVE PARTY. The PARTIDO CONSERVADOR (q.v.) split in 1949 into the PARTIDO CONSERVADOR TRADICIONALISTA (q.v.) and the PARTIDO CONSERVADOR SOCIAL CRISTIANO (q.v.), but united again in 1953 as the PARTIDO CONSERVADOR UNIDO--P.U.C. (q.v.). On May 11, 1966, the P.U.C. merged with the *Partido Liberal to form a united party of the right, which took the name PARTIDO NACIONAL (q.v.).

CONSTITUCIONALISTA. Term used during the *Civil War of 1891 to denote a supporter of President José Manuel *Balmaceda Fernández in his constitutional struggle against the rebel *Congress (whose supporters were CONGRESISTAS, q.v.).

CONSTITUTION. Chile has had nine constitutions since the time of its struggle for *independence from Spain. The following entries detail them in chronological order.

CONSTITUTION OF 1811. Chile's first constitution, the Reglamento para el arreglo de la autoridad ejecutiva provisoria de Chile, was drafted by the *National Congress, which had been selected by the *cabildos. At the time there was still indecision whether to declare a "magna carta" for an independent Chile, or to stay loyal to *Ferdinand VII. The executive power was to be vested in a three-man junta (see: JUNTA DE GOBIERNO DE 1811), although in fact the junta merely executed the orders of Congress. The junta was to appoint a Senate of life-term members. The constitution was invalidated by José Miguel *Carrera Verdugo's coup d'état of November 15, 1811.

CONSTITUTION OF 1812. The Reglamento Constitucional Provisorio was a provisional constitution drafted by José Miguel *Carrera Verdugo (with the help of *United States consul Joel Robert *Poinsett) to give legitimacy to his government. It made purely formal acknowledgement of the authority of *Ferdinand VII while denying the legality of any order emanating from outside Chile. It established a three-man junta as the executive, and a unicameral Congress, the Senado Consultivo.

The constitution for the Spanish empire adopted by the liberal *Cortés of Cádiz was also a "Constitution of 1812."

CONSTITUTION OF 1814. The Reglamento para el gobierno provisorio was another provisional constitution, replacing that of 1812 and drafted to cope with the imminent threat posed by the viceroy's invasion. Promulgated March 17, 1814, it provided for a *Supreme Director with almost dictatorial powers, and a seven-member senate to be appointed by the Director. The rout of the patriots at *Rancagua on October 2 brought back Spanish rule to Chile, and the Reglamento was abolished.

CONSTITUTION OF 1818. The first constitution of an independent and sovereign Chile. It delegated executive powers to a *Supreme Director (Director Supremo) without specifying how many years he would rule, thus establishing a quasi-dictatorship. The legislative power was delegated to a conservative Senate, consisting of ten appointed members, and to a representative chamber, to be elected. The judicial power was greatly modified from the days of Spanish colonial rule and was vested in a Court of Appeal (Corte de apelación), which replaced the Real *Audiencia. A Supreme Court (Tribunal Superior) was also established, replacing the *Consejo de las Indias. The Constitution of 1818 lasted four years.

CONSTITUTION OF 1822. This new constitution was an attempt by Chilean liberals to adopt the Spanish constitution of 1812 of the liberal *Cortés of Cádiz. The Chilean constitution, however, did not vest the executive power in a monarch--as the Spanish did-- but in a *Supreme Director (Director Supremo), thus providing for a semi-republican form of government. The judicial branch conformed to the structure of the constitution of 1818.

CONSTITUTION OF 1823. This constitution was a modification of that of 1818. Chile was to be a unitary republic. The *Supreme Director (Director Supremo) was to rule for four years, with eligibility for one reelection. He had to be a Chilean by birth or a foreign-born Chilean national who had resided in the country for a minimum of twelve years. The executive power was greatly limited through a system of checks and balances. The Supreme Director was responsible to a State Council (Consejo del Estado) of nine members appointed by himself. His power was further checked by a Senate, by an elected House of Representatives, and by an assembly of prominent citizens. The Senate was com-

posed of nine members elected every six years. The House of
Representatives consisted of from 50 to 200 members, elected
every eight years. The assembly of prominent citizens had one
representative for each 200 people. The 1823 constitution had
little success, and only two of its articles were included in later
constitutions: one establishing a national tribunal of justice for
the land, and another securing individual rights.

CONSTITUTION OF 1828. The proposed Constitution of 1828 was made
up of 134 articles and served as a basis for the long lasting
Constitution of 1833. It called for the indirect election of a
President, who would hold office for five years and could only
be reelected after the lapse of a further five years. The Vice-
President, also elected by indirect vote, would succeed the
President in case of death or disability. The executive branch
of government did not dispose of extraordinary powers, but could
veto legislation. The legislative power was vested in a *Congress
made up of a Senate and a Chamber of Deputies. The Senate was
made up of two representatives from each *province, elected indirectly by the provincial assemblies for a period of four years.
The Chamber of Deputies was made up of representatives elected
by direct vote for a period of two years. The judicial power was
vested in a Tribunal of Justice. Supreme Court members were
appointed by Congress.

CONSTITUTION OF 1833. The Constitution of 1833 ushered in a
period of thirty years' conservative rule in Chile, and lasted altogether 92 years. Based on the *Constitution of 1828, it had
168 articles and embodied Diego *Portales Palazuelos's belief that
power should be concentrated in a highly centralized government.
Chile was to be a unitary republic, and Roman Catholicism was
to be the official religion, enjoying full partnership with the state.
The President was to be elected by indirect vote for a period of
five years, with the privilege of one reelection. He had to be
native-born, and not less than thirty years of age. Suffrage
was limited to literate males over twenty-five and literate married
men over twenty-one, with the additional specification that the
voters be property owners.

There was no vice-president; the minister of the interior would
succeed the President in case of death or disability. The Senate
was also to be elected by indirect vote, for a period of six years.
The Chamber of Deputies, on the other hand, was to be elected
by direct vote for a period of three years. Provincial and municipal authorities were subjected to presidential control. Any
foreigner could become a Chilean citizen if he was literate and
owned property, or the equivalent thereof. Ministers had to be
native-born. Although this constitution remained in effect until
1925, it functioned rather differently after 1891 under the so-
called PARLIAMENTARY REGIME (q.v.).

CONSTITUTION OF 1925. On August 30, 1925, a new constitution was adopted to replace that of 1833. The document had been proposed by President (1920–24; 1925) Arturo *Alessandri Palma, and it embodied the liberal ideas of President (1886–91) José Manuel *Balmaceda Fernández, who had presented a similar proposal to *Congress in 1890. Unlike the *Constitution of 1833, the new "magna carta" provided for a presidential term of six years with no immediate reelection. The President was to be elected by direct popular vote. *Congress could no longer unseat a member of the President's cabinet. As a result, presidential powers were increased and the President alone was responsible for his cabinet: the age of the *parliamentary regime was ended. *Church and state were separated, and individual rights were guaranteed. The electorate was extended to include all literate males over twenty-one. See: CHILE--H. Government.

CONSTITUTION OF 1980. The Constitution of 1980 was drafted for the purpose of institutionalizing the MILITARY REGIME, q.v. that had come to power on September 11, 1973, with the overthrow of President (1970–73) Salvador *Allende Gossens. The new constitution provided for a "democratic" structure for Chilean society based on the family, and it rejected the class struggle. It was in marked contrast to the liberal democratic traditions existing in Chile before 1973 and which had been the hallmark of the Chilean political system and the *Constitution of 1925.

With its 120 articles, the constitution of 1980 named General Augusto *Pinochet Ugarte as President of Chile from 1981 to 1989, leaving open the possibility that he could serve for a further eight years. Article 24 gives the President extraordinary powers to quell internal disturbances. He can dissolve the legislature once during his term of office and may declare a state of emergency for up to twenty days. He can censor or prevent the circulation of new publications considered contrary to national security or individual morals; prohibit entry to, or expel from, the country any person deemed harmful to national security; and internally exile a person for up to three months.

The first 23 articles of the constitution define the rights and obligations of citizens, nationality and citizenship. The following rights are guaranteed: the right to life and personal integrity; to a legal defense; to personal liberty and individual security; the right to reside in, cross or leave the country; the right of assembly, petition, association and free expression; the right to religious preference; and the right to work. Men and women are accorded equal rights. No one shall be obliged to join any association or group considered to be contrary to national security, public order or morality, as defined by the state. While collective bargaining is a guaranteed right, a strike that causes grave harm to the public domain, the nation's economy or state security, is prohibited.

Political parties must disclose their membership and finances; they may not coerce citizens into joining, and are not allowed to receive money from foreign countries. All Marxist parties and

and "totalitarian groups" are banned from the political process.

The 1980 constitution is described as a "transition to democracy," and it extends the President's term from six years to eight, while increasing his powers considerably. It provides for no reelection of the President; a bicameral legislature with an upper chamber of 26 elected and 9 appointed senators, who are to serve an eight-year term; and a lower house of 120 deputies elected for a four-year term. All former presidents are to be senators for life. Other appointed senators must include: two former Supreme Court justices; a former comptroller general; a former minister of state; a former director of the *Cuerpo de Carabineros (police), and a former university rector.

There is a National Security Council consisting of the President, the other members of the *junta militar de gobierno (viz. the commanders-in-chief of each of the *armed forces--the *army, *the navy, *the air force and the Cuerpo de Carabineros), and the presidents of the Supreme Court and the Senate.

The bicameral legislature will come into existence by 1989, at which time the junta will nominate the President and the no-reelection clause will be suspended. The nomination will be submitted to a referendum.

All local administrators and members of the cabinet will be appointed by the President of the Republic.

Abortion is prohibited.

CONSTITUTIONAL GUARANTEES. See: ESTATUTOS DE GARANTIAS CONSTITUCIONALES.

CONSTRUCTION INDUSTRY. See: HOUSING AND CONSTRUCTION.

CONTRAGOLPE. A newspaper published in *Tierra del Fuego from 1960 until 1973. It was the official organ of the Socialist Party (*Partido Socialista de Chile) in southernmost Chile.

CONTROLARÍA GENERAL DE LA REPUBLICA. See: COMPTROLLER-SHIP GENERAL.

CONTRERAS LABARCA, Carlos (b. 1899). Lawyer by profession and active member of the Communist Party (*Partido Comunista Chileno). From 1920 to 1922 he was leader of the Federación de Estudiantes de Chile (*FECh). In 1931 he became secretary general of the Chilean Communist Party, a position he held until 1947. From 1926 to 1941 he held elective office as a deputy, and from 1941 to 1949 was a senator. In 1946 he was appointed minister of public works and communications in the 1946-52 administration of Gabriel *González Videla, who had been elected President of Chile with the help of the communists and had to appoint members of that party to his cabinet. In 1961 Contreras Labarca was again elected for an eight-year term as senator. During that time he was head of the Chilean Delegation on *Human Rights.

CONTRERAS SEPULVEDA, Manuel. See: SEPULVEDA CONTRERAS, Manuel

CONTRERAS TAPIA, Victor. Active member of the Communist Party (*Partido Comunista Chileno). He held elective office from 1945 to 1973. In the 1946-52 administration of President Gabriel *González Videla he held the post of minister of lands and colonization from 1946 to 1947. In 1961 he was elected to an eight-year senate term. He backed Salvador *Allende Gossens in the presidential elections of 1952, 1958, 1964 and 1970.

CONTRIBUCION TERRITORIAL. A tax on agricultural income, later called the impuesto agrícola, introduced in 1860 to replace the *Catastro, so as to exempt unproductive land from taxation. In 1875 its annual yield was fixed at one million *pesos, but with no adjustment for the depreciation of the peso its effective burden fell steadily. After the *Civil War of 1891, it was sharply reduced and both assessment and collection were turned over to the municipalities (see: LOCAL GOVERNMENT).

CONVENCION PRESIDENCIAL DE IZQUIERDA. An assembly of leftist delegates convened by the Popular Front (*Frente Popular) in 1938 to organize a strategy for victory in the presidential elections of that year. Some 1,030 delegates participated: 400 from the *Partido Radical, 330 from the *Partido Socialista, 120 from the *Partido Comunista Chileno, 120 from the *Partido Democrático, and 60 delegates from the *trade union federation CTCh (Confederación de Trabajadores de Chile). After many ballots the Convention chose the Radical Party's candidate Pedro *Aguirre Cerda, who went on to win the presidency.

CONVENTILLO. Literally, "little convent." A type of single-story housing for the lower classes. The name derives from its U-shape and central courtyard, which resembles a convent patio.

CONVICTORIO CAROLINO. A colonial secondary school in *Santiago with some 100 pupils. Founded in 1600 by the *Jesuits as the Colegio San Francisco Javier, it was renamed after the Society's 1778 expulsion in honor of King *Charles III. After Independence the school was incorporated into the *Instituto Nacional.

COOPERATIVES. By comparison with the Scandinavian countries, Chile's cooperative organization is still in the formative stage. The greatest expansion of the cooperative system came with Presidents Eduardo *Frei Montalva (1964-70) and Salvador *Allende Gossens (1970-73) as they both tried to break up Chile's *latifundia system of land tenure (see: AGRARIAN REFORM). The most successful cooperatives in Chile are those in the dairy, grape growing and wine making industries. When the *armed forces overthrew Allende, their economic policies deemphasized the cooperative system and emphasized the free-market policies of individual enterprise. See also: ASENTADOS.

COORDINADORA NACIONAL SINDICAL (CNS). A confederation of *trade unions founded in 1978 with the cooperation of the Roman Catholic *Church. It had a membership of 700,000 and was viewed with suspicion by the government of President Augusto *Pinochet Ugarte. The confederation's leadership sought wage increases and the end of political restrictions on trade unions.

COPACHI. (Comité de Cooperación para la Paz en Chile). See: VICARIATE OF SOLIDARITY.

COPERE (Comité de Programación Económica y de Reconstrucción). A government agency for economic programming and reconstruction.

COPIAPO. Capital of the present region and pre-1974 province of *Atacama. Founded in 1772 by Governor José Antonio Manso de Velasco to exploit the area's mineral wealth, by 1830 it had become a booming *mining town with more than 13,000 inhabitants and had displaced La *Serena as Chile's most important metropolis north of *Santiago. Chile's first *railway was built between Copiapó and *Caldera in the early 1850s by William *Wheelwright in order to export *silver from neighboring Tres Puntas and *Charñarcillo. With the decline of silver mining, Copiapó's population fell, decreasing by three thousand between 1865 and 1907. By 1971 the population had reached 48,700 and was estimated as 75,791 in 1986.

The river from which the city is named serves to irrigate a wide area of its valley, rich in fruit and wine.

COPIHUE. The national flower of Chile. The plant, <u>Lapageria rosea</u>, is a native of Chile and was first described scientifically in a Peruvian-Chilean flora of 1802. It was named after Josephine Beauharnais de La Pagerie because she was "a famous and learned woman and Napoleon's wife." It is a climber of the lilac family, with fine bell-shaped flowers and a berry resembling an unripe red pepper. The Chilean variety has red flowers, but in other parts of the Americas there is also a white variant.

COPPER. Chile has been described as a single gigantic copper mine encrusted in a beautiful and varied geography. Perhaps no other region in the world has been more abundantly endowed with the mineral than have the Chilean *Andes. The major mining towns are located in the western *cordillera, extending from the *Atacama desert (in the northern Region of *Antofagasta) into central Chile, south of *Santiago. More than 90 percent of Chile's copper is produced in *Chuquicamata, El *Salvador and *Sewell. The mineral was known to the *Incas, but mining it only became important towards the middle of the 19th century.

Between 1851 and 1880, Chile accounted for approximately 40 percent of world output. At that period numerous small veins of copper oxide containing 8 percent or more of copper were worked in the *Norte Chico (Cerro Blanco, Tamaya, La Higuera).

Most of this activity was on a very small scale, needing little capital as most of the mines were little larger than holes in the ground. Output fell after 1880, partly because of low world prices. In 1909 it was 42,726 metric *tons. By the 1920s most of these rich lodes had been worked out, places like La Higuera had become ghost towns, and Chile's share of world production had greatly diminished.

The industry, as it is known today, depends on the large-scale quarrying of low grade (2-3 percent) copper sulphide ore. This was developed by two United States-owned firms, the *Anaconda Copper Mining Company and the *Kennecott Copper Corporation. Their subsidiaries, the Chile Exploration Company and the Andes Mining Company (Anaconda) and the *Braden Copper Company (Kennecott), constitute what the Chileans call *Gran Minería, composed of large-scale production with a minimum output of 250,000 tonnes annually. The rest of the industry is divided into Mediana Minería and Pequeña Minería, medium- and small-scale production made up of a handful of medium-sized and small enterprises. In 1932, when Chilean *nitrate lost its importance in world markets, copper replaced it as the nation's principal export, reaching 426,670 tonnes in 1947.

Today Chile and the *U.S.S.R. are equal firsts among the world's copper producers. Chile's output in 1960 constituted 14.3 percent of the world's copper supply. Chile's current production has reached over 1.3 million tonnes a year (1984); this accounts for two-thirds of all exports; one quarter of all the copper moving in the free world; and one sixth of the copper used by the *United States.

Plans outlined by the government of Salvador *Allende Gossens aimed to raise copper output from its 1970 level of 1 million tonnes to 1.2 million by 1975 (a feat achieved in 1976). But this was not all his government wanted. Upon being sworn into office on November 3, 1970, Allende pledged that he would nationalize Chilean copper, with compensation to the U.S.-owned firms.

Chilean copper resources, which had been primarily in the hands of foreigners since 1905, have a considerable impact on the national economy in at least four main areas. First is their contribution to the *balance of payments. Since 1932, the copper exports of the Gran Minería have represented around half of Chile's total exports, reaching 64.5 percent in 1955 and dropping to 45.3 percent in 1975 (the reason for the drop was an increase in other exports, rather than any decrease in copper exports). The 1982 production represented 60 percent of the country's export earnings. The returns from the Gran Minería, including the legal cost of production, taxation and importation of the companies themselves, *custom duties, etc., have represented an average of about 52 percent of the receipts collected in U.S. dollars by the country for its exportation.

Second, there is copper's participation in fiscal receipts. The Gran Minería's contribution to the total of ordinary *tax revenue has ranged from a high of 47.4 percent in 1955 to a low of 7 percent in 1955, but has usually been in the area of 15 to 18 percent.

Third is the influence on *employment. Based on the supposition that each worker supports four other persons besides himself, a little more than one per cent of the total population lives directly from the copper industry--not to mention those employed by, and dependent on, business resulting from the copper enterprises.

The fourth impact has been as an influence on the rate of technological advance. The operation of extraction and refining installations in Chile represents a significant contribution to the country's technological progress. In addition, copper-related activities have contributed to an increasing demand for industrial goods, resulting in a stimulation of the production of materials of a more and more advanced technical nature.

When President (1964-70) Eduardo *Frei Montalva was elected, he had pledged to "chileanize" the copper industry. This meant tighter government regulations over pricing, production and marketing. On December 21, 1964, after less than two months in office, Frei announced that negotiations with the Kennecott Copper Corporation, the Anaconda Company and the *Cerro Corporation (a new company which only began operating in 1964) had resulted in an agreement. The pact which was signed aimed at doubling copper production by 1970 (from 617,000 tonnes to 1.2 million tonnes) and almost tripling Chile's refining capacity (from 200,000 to 700,000 tonnes). Most importantly, it made the Chilean government a part owner of the North American companies, which meant that the government would participate decisively in the administration, financing, exploitation and marketing of Chilean copper.

Separate agreements were signed with each firm. The Cerro Corporation agreed to a joint venture of a 75 to 25 ratio in the development of the Río Blanco mine. The cost of this was predicted as US$ 81 million. The Kennecott Corporation agreed to share ownership of the El *Teniente mine at *Sewell, with the Chilean government acquiring a 51 percent holding, for which Kennecott would receive US$ 80 million over a 20-year period. In return Kennecott agreed to use this money to expand production. The government and the corporation would jointly obtain US$ 100 million in loans from international sources to expand El Teniente's output from 180,000 tonnes a year to 280,000 tonnes. The Anaconda Company insisted on retaining sole ownership of its operating mines. A newly-formed company, to be owned 51 percent by Anaconda and 49 percent by the Chilean government, would be developed near Chuquicamata, and any additional mines developed would be jointly owned.

In return for the American companies' cooperation, Frei made two concessions: the management of the companies, despite the government's share in ownership, would remain under American control; and company profits would be taxed at lower rates than previously. By 1970 the Frei administration was insisting that

Chile should own at least 51 percent of the companies' stock, and
new agreements were drawn up. The Chilean left opposed Frei's
program. Economist Vera argued that chileanization (or "nacionalización pactada") would cost the Chilean government US$ 1,195
million. In his calculations he took into account all the possible
variables, using a copper price of 52 cents a pound as his basis.
He came to the conclusion that outright nationalization would
cost the government only US$ 347 million.

Vera's study refuted all the arguments against nationalization.
The possibility of copper being replaced by a substitute was almost nonexistent. The complicated technology in the extraction
and refining of copper was no more than a myth, and Chilean
technicians were just as capable of running these operations as
their North American counterparts. Nor could the financial situation be any worse with nationalization than it was under Frei's
new agreements, and would in all likelihood be better. Vera
predicted that with nationalization a copper exchange could be
created in Santiago, and Chile's output of the red metal could
make up 19 percent of world production by 1972.

Allende agreed with Vera's conclusions. As a result, Chilean
copper was nationalized. The Draft Constitutional Reform he sent
to Congress soon after taking office had as its basic objective
the nationalization of copper and other minerals vital to the interests of the State. First and foremost the Draft reiterated the
principle already embodied in the Mining Code, namely that the
State had absolute, exclusive, inalienable and imprescriptible
ownership of all mines. Most Chileans had been in favor of
nationalization. All three presidential candidates in the election
of 1970 had pledged and proposed various drafts for nationalizing
the copper mines. The following table shows that the North
American companies' profits in Chile had been excessive, whereas
their output increases had been meager:

INVESTMENTS:	A. Worldwide	B. Chile	B as % of A
Anaconda	$1,116,172,000	$199,030,000	16.64
Kennecott	$1,108,155,000	$145,877,000	13.16

PROFITS:	A. Worldwide	B. Chile	B as % of A
Anaconda	$ 99,313,000	$ 78,692,600	79.24
Kennecott	$ 165,395,000	$ 35,338,600	21.37

On Allende's accession the price of copper (which had been
88 cents a pound) fell by one fourth on the London Metal Exchange,
and decreased further, to 48 cents, in 1971. This represented
a serious setback for the economic targets set by Allende in his
socialization campaign. Prices recovered considerably in 1973,
but the *copper strikes at El Teniente and Chuquicamata practically canceled out the gain.

In 1974 the three major U.S.-based copper corporations that
had been expropriated in 1971 demanded compensation and threatened to continue the sequestration of shipments of Chilean copper

that they had begun against Allende. In an abrupt switch from its initially tough stand on the matter, the *junta negotiated amicable settlements with all three companies.

By 1976 Chile, for the first time in its history, exceeded a copper output of 1 million tonnes, a level that has been consistently maintained since. Demand in the 1980s picked up considerably. Chile's 1980 production was 1,067,700 tonnes and exports were valued at US$ 1.8 million. By 1983, ten years after Allende's overthrow, Chile led world production at 1.23 million tonnes, followed by the U.S.S.R. (1.2 million tonnes), the U.S.A. (1.08 million tonnes), Canada (615,000 tonnes) and, in fifth place, Peru (322,000 tonnes). Prospects for a further rise in Chile's production were excellent following the installation of new flash smelters at Chuquicamata.

According to recent CODELCO figures, Chile's proven reserves total more than 7.4 billion tonnes of copper ore, with an average copper content of 1.1 percent. This would yield 81 million tonnes of fine copper, or about 80 years' production at current rates. As new explorations continue, further reserves of 10,800 million tonnes with a 0.5 percent copper content have been estimated, with a potential yield of another 54 million tonnes of copper.

Although public investment in mining is at present considered insufficient, the size, quality and relatively low exploitation costs of its copper reserves indicate that Chile will be an important source of world copper for the rest of this century and beyond.

COPPER STRIKES. On April 18, 1973, in an attempt to bring down the government of Socialist President Salvador *Allende Gossens, copper miners at El *Teniente (near *Sewell), the world's largest underground copper mine, walked out, demanding higher wages. The strike, which was financed by the U.S. *Central Intelligence Agency, lasted 76 days and cost the government some US$ 75 million in lost revenues. It was finally settled on July 3, when Allende himself went to plead with the union leaders.

In the 1980s copper workers' strikes again became politically important (see: TRADE UNIONS).

COQUIMBO (city). Located six miles from La *Serena, it serves as the latter's principal port. Coquimbo was founded in 1850 on a peninsula at the mouth of the River Coquimbo. The Bay of Guayacán, on the peninsula's southern side, is well protected from the wind; during colonial times it was often favored as a lair by *pirates, from Sir Francis *Drake onward. Coquimbo's 1986 population was 70,461 (est.). Before the present city was built, "Coquimbo" was often used to designate La Serena itself.

COQUIMBO (province). A province of north-central Chile. Originally an *intendencia created in 1811, it was reduced to its present size of 39,647 km^2 (15,308 square miles) in 1843 when *Atacama was made a separate province. Its population was 110,589 in 1854; 175,021 in 1907; 262,169 in 1952; and 429,255 (est.) in

1982. The post-1973 *junta has reorganized it as Region IV, but with the same name and boundaries (see: REGIONS AND ADMINISTRATIVE RESTRUCTURING). The three largest towns are La *Serena (the capital), *Coquimbo and Ovalle.

COQUIMBO MUTINY (Sublevación de la escuadra). After President Carlos *Ibáñez del Campo was forced from office on July 31, 1931, by the effects of the Great *Depression, the new government's deflationary policy included reductions of up to 30 percent in the pay of the *armed forces. This provoked a naval mutiny at *Coquimbo, led by petty officers. The mutiny spread to *Talcahuano, from where a flotilla steamed north to join the Coquimbo mutineers. Great apprehension was caused by the fact that this included the battleship Latorre, whose guns had a 15-mile range. On September 6 an air attack was used to break the mutineers' morale and secure the mutiny's collapse. Although the *República Socialista of 1932 freed the mutineers from prison, some 2,000 ratings and 30 officers were dismissed, the fleet was dispersed and several warships were put out of commission, a terrible blow to the prestige of what had always been Chile's senior service. See also: AIR FORCE, NAVY.

CORA (Corporación de la Reforma Agraria). Agrarian Reform Corporation, a decentralized government agency, nominally under the Ministerio de *Agricultura but given considerable operating autonomy, set up under the Agrarian Reform Law of 1962 to replace the *Caja de la Colonización Agrícola. It was given power both to acquire land compulsorily from *latifundistas and to make loans to *campesinos wishing to buy land. It was a key instrument in implementing the agrarian reform programs of both President (1964-70) Eduardo *Frei Montalva and President (1970-73) Salvador *Allende Gossens. Both presidents proposed a fundamental change of the *latifundia system, reapportionment of the land, and the application of more advanced technology to increase agricultural production. But whereas Frei planned to organize ownership and farm operation on a private basis, Allende was in favor of organizing *cooperatives and land cultivation under collective ownership. When Allende was overthrown by the *armed forces in 1973, CORA became subservient to the *junta's program of returning most of the land to its former latifundista owners. In 1978 CORA was dismantled. See: AGRARIAN REFORM; AGRICULTURE.

CORCHAC. The Chilean airport authority. See: AIR TRANSPORT; AIRPORTS.

CORDILLERA. Mountain range. In Chile, the "High Cordillera" (or simply, "Cordillera") refers to the *Andes, but the term is also used for Chile's parallel (but much lower) coastal range. See also: CHILE--D. Topography.

CORDONES INDUSTRIALES. The defense organizations which emerged in the poblaciones *callampas to insure that newly appropriated lands would not be taken away from the poor by the opposition to President (1970-73) Salvador *Allende Gossens, which had set out to sabotage his peaceful road to socialism. During the bloody battle in *Santiago on September 11, 1973, and the days immediately following, the *air force strafed the Cordones Industriales, destroying most of their tin shanties and killing hundreds of people.

CORDOVEZ DEL CASO, Gregorio (1783-1843). A colonel in the army fighting for Chilean independence, he became involved in politics after 1810, taking part in the armed struggle against *Spain. After Chile officially became an independent state in 1818, he became mayor of La *Serena. In 1822, he was elected deputy to Congress representing the province of *Coquimbo. In 1824, he moved that the *Constitution of 1823 be nullified, but *Congress voted down his motion. He continued to be a representative to Congress until shortly before his death.

CORFO. Acronym for Corporación de Fomento de la Producción, the government-controlled Chilean Production Development Corporation. In 1939 the Chilean government created CORFO to promote industrial growth. The principal aim of this agency was to establish a comprehensive economic development plan which was to include hydroelectric power, *petroleum exploration and refining, and steel manufacturing. The ostensible purpose of CORFO was to augment productivity so that Chile could pay off the debts contracted after the earthquake of 1939, but this was merely an excuse. Actually, the unstable Chilean economy needed some form of government intervention to stimulate industrial development, but the *Congress opposed any form of government intervention in economics.

The Popular Front government which won the presidential elections in 1938, on the other hand, espoused a doctrine of collectivism in economic growth. The *United States also favored governmental intervention in Chile in order to guarantee loans it made for purposes of development. CORFO has come to be used as a model for other government development organizations in all parts of the developing world. It created a mixed economy in Chile--i.e., a system which combines private and state ownership and control of the economy. The Corporation was largely responsible for industrial expansion in Chile after World War II, but it has declined in strength and activity since 1950.

With the military take-over of September 11, 1973, one of the major functions of CORFO has been the development of business conditions and research programs for the benefit of the private sector. CORFO has been increasingly performing this function through its affiliate, the Institute for Technological Research. See: INTEC-CHILE.

CORPORACION DE FOMENTO DE LA PRODUCCION. See: CORFO.

CORPORACION DE LA REFORMA AGRARIA. See: CORA.

CORPORACION DE LA VIVIENDA. See: CORVI.

CORPORACION DE REFORMA AGRARIA. See: CORA.

CORPORACION DE VENTAS DEL SALITRE Y YODO. See: COVENSA.

CORPORACION DEL COBRE (CODELCO). The State Copper Corporation established in 1971 when *copper was nationalized in Chile,
to oversee the production, distribution and marketing of copper,
as well as investment in new exploration. Since it came into
being, two new mines have been found and developed: the
*Andina mine just northwest of *Santiago, and the *Exótica mine,
immediately south from *Chuquicamata.

CORPORACION NACIONAL FORESTAL (CONAF). The National
Forestry Corporation, established in 1972 during the administration
of Socialist President (1970-73) Salvador *Allende Gossens, to replace earlier organizations in the development of FORESTRY
(q.v.). It was given primary responsibility for planning and
administering government forestry activities. Until 1978 CONAF
was directly involved in reforestation programs, but since then
tree planting has been taken over completely by the private sector. CONAF has contributed greatly to forestry expansion.

CORREA FUENZALIDA, Guillermo (b. 1900). Lawyer, statesman and
member of the Liberal Party (*Partido Liberal). He became professor of civil law at the *Universidad de Chile in 1922 and director of its law school, 1925-27. From 1930 to 1937 he held elective
office as deputy to *Congress, and subsequently headed various
ministries. He was minister of *education, 1937-38, minister of
justice, 1938, minister of foreign affairs and commerce, 1938,
and once again minister of justice, 1946-47. He was also president
of the Central Bank (Banco Central de Chile) and vice-president
of the Liberal Party.

CORREA LETELIER, Hector (1915-   ). Lawyer by profession and
member of the Conservative Party (*Partido Conservador). From
1941 to 1965 he held elective office. He was also vice-president
and then president, of the Chamber of Deputies. In 1965 he
became Chilean ambassador to *Brazil.

CORREA MORANDE, María. Chilean writer, and member of the Liberal
Party (*Partido Liberal). She was the head of the feminist
section of the Party, and for a brief period, director general
of the Party (1950). From 1957 to 1961 she held elected office
as a deputy in *Congress. She was very active for the Liberals
in the presidential campaigns of 1958, 1964 and 1970.

CORREGIDOR. In colonial times, a royal official administering a
*corregimiento. The corregidor's responsibilities were to collect
local *taxes, maintain the peace by instituting a local *police
force, and supervise the work of the Indians in the economic
development of his district. As the corregimientos were the remote areas outside district capitals, it was easy for a corregidor
to become rich unscrupulously. The corregidores were responsible
for many scandals. They were especially notorious for their maltreatment of Indians. The "Bourbon reforms" under King *Charles
III in the 1780s included the abolition of the office of corregidor
and its replacement by that of *intendant.

CORREGIMIENTO. Administrative unit in colonial times, under a
*corregidor, subordinate to the captaincy-general (see: COLONIAL
ADMINISTRATION), devised to protect the Indians and govern
remote communities by maintaining the peace and collecting *taxes.

CORREOS. See: POSTAL SERVICES.

CORTES. The Spanish parliament. Particularly important for the
history of Spanish America was the constituent cortés of Cádiz,
which met in 1810 to exercise authority during the French captivity of King *Ferdinand VII and prosecute the war against
*France. This cortés, which included deputies from Chile and
the other provinces of Spanish America, had a liberal majority
and enacted many reforms, all repudiated by Ferdinand VII when
he recovered power in 1814. These included the abolition of the
*Inquisition and of political *censorship, and the enactment
of the very liberal Spanish constitution of March 1812, which
provided the basis of Chile's *Constitution of 1822.

CORUÑA, Matanza de La. A clash between the police and striking
workers on June 3, 1925. The workers, employees of La Coruña
*nitrate fields near *Iquique, were protesting the precarious
working and living conditions provided for them and their families.
When the company *pulpería received orders to stop selling any
food, the workers occupied the building and refused to leave
it. Guards were called to the scene and many miners were shot
to death: A group of them were taken prisoner, brought to a
field and executed. The bloodbath had repercussions in other
*mining towns in Chile.

CORVALAN LEPE, Luis (1916-   ). A journalist, university professor
and militant member of the Communist Party (*Partido Comunista
Chilena). He was considered a traditionalist; that is, less a
revolutionary and more in line with the Soviet position. On
foreign policy questions, he supported the *U.S.S.R. as opposed
to the Red Chinese, and cautioned the most fervent admirers of
Fidel Castro. He was the leader of the million-strong Communist-
controlled *trade union federation, the Central Unica de Trabajadores de Chile (CUT), and was named secretary general of the

Party on four occasions. In 1961 he was elected for an eight-year term as senator for *Valparaíso and *Aconcagua. In every presidential election from 1952 onwards he had backed the leftist candidate Salvador *Allende Gossens.

Soon after the 1973 *coup d'état that overthrew Allende, the *junta had Corvalán arrested and sent to the maximum security prison on *Dawson Island in the *Strait of Magellan. In 1975, through the intervention of *human rights groups, he was transferred to a prison in *Santiago, as he was suffering from a bleeding stomach ulcer. Nevertheless he received little, if any, medical attention, and was forced to eat beans in spite of his stomach problem.

Also in 1975 he received the Lenin Peace Prize from the Soviet Union, and in December 1976 he was allowed to leave for exile in Russia, in exchange for the Soviet political dissident Vladimir Bukovsky. Corvalán now lives in East Germany.

CORVI (Corporación de la Vivienda). Housing corporation, a government agency instituted to provide low-rent housing for the Chilean poor and middle-class. It came into existence during the second (1952-58) administration of President Carlos *Ibáñez del Campo. See: HOUSING AND CONSTRUCTION.

COSACh (Compañía de Salitre de Chile). The Chilean Nitrate Company, a government-controlled company created during the first (1927-31) administration of President Carlos *Ibáñez del Campo, with Chilean and American capital, which had a monopoly on *nitrates and their by-product *iodine. The company proved to be a failure because there were not enough sales on the international market to pay dividends to the government and the stockholders. In 1934 COSACh was replaced by a new government company, the Chilean Nitrate and Iodine Sales Corporación, COVENSA (q.v.), which had monopoly control of all sales and exports.

COUNCIL OF THE INDIES. See: CONSEJO DE LAS INDIAS.

COUP D'ETAT OF 1973. Early Tuesday morning, September 11, 1973, *Santiago turned into a bloody battleground (see: SANTIAGO, Battle of). A few hours later, Socialist President Salvador *Allende Gossens, who had been elected to a six-year term with the pledge that he would bring about a socialist revolution through peaceful means, met his death in the presidential palace of La *Moneda, resisting a well-coordinated military coup.

Allende's economic policies had sought to establish national control over the basic means of production, to increase industrial and agricultural activities, and to redistribute Chile's wealth more equitably. These policies had threatened not only a small privileged upper class, but also most of the middle class, and even some sectors of the working class that were relatively comfortable in an economy of scarce resources.

That the country was not functioning well economically was

evident even to the most loyal supporters of the President. He was impotent when faced with striking truck owners and *copper miners (see: BOSSES' STRIKE; COPPER STRIKES). His economic programs, such as land distribution (see: AGRARIAN REFORM) and increased wages for all workers, were often badly planned and badly implemented. But if his attempts to introduce social justice failed, they failed because of the reaction of a growing middle class that cared little or nothing for the poor.

Allende's transition to Socialism angered especially the oligarchy, the coalition of big business and big landowners, that also had opposed President Eduardo *Frei Montalva. Subsequently, the *army abandoned its neutrality and decided to intervene. The result was a violent coup d'état which toppled Chile's social, political, and economic structures, destroying one of the most enduring democracies on the continent.

The intensity of the coup astonished most Chileans, who had believed in the neutrality of the *armed forces. Traditionally, the military had always seemed institutionally loyal; it overthrew the government only twice in its history. In 1891, the military over-threw reformist President José Manuel *Balmaceda Fernández; in 1973, it overthrew Allende. Both times the military sided with the oligarchy. Balmaceda was driven to suicide for refusing to deliver Chile's *nitrate riches to foreign companies. Allende was murdered after he nationalized the copper mines. There is evidence that in both cases the oligarchy incited the army to inter-vene, and that in both cases foreign interests (the British com-panies in Balmaceda's time, U.S. companies in Allende's time), played decisive roles (See CENTRAL INTELLIGENCE AGENCY; ITT).

If Allende's death and the degree of violence that followed were unexpected, the coup was not. Even the staunchest sup-porters of the Allende administration knew that his government coalition could not last. Cabinet crises, runaway *inflation, crippling strikes, food shortages, and general discontent among the upper classes resulted in the political and economic deteriora-tion of Chile. While the governing coalition, the *Unidad Popular (UP), became divided and uncertain of its goals in spite of its successes at the polls, the opposition, led by the Christian Demo-crat and National parties, grew confident and united, forming a new party called *Confederación Democrática (CODE).

When, in the Congressional elections of March 1973, CODE failed to get two thirds of the vote needed to begin impeachment proceedings against Allende, it called on the military to intervene.

Prior to the September 11 coup, there had been at least three instances when a military revolt or a civil war might have erupted. The first, on May 18, involved the Commander of an *air force base in Santiago who threatened to carry out his own coup, but the plot was uncovered by a pro-Allende colonel and the air force commander was arrested. The second episode was the well pub-licized revolt of June 29, known as the *Tancazo, which was also premature as it turned out. And the third incident was the res-

ignation of General César *Ruiz Danyau on August 28. Jets
streaked out of Santiago to the southern city of *Concepción to
prepare for an immediate mobilization. The coup was postponed,
but as soon as General Carlos *Prats Gonzalez resigned--the last
staunch supporter of Allende and commander-in-chief of the army--
all three branches of the armed forces united in the overthrow
of Allende. The *navy immediately occupied the city of *Valparaíso, Chile's principal port, and cut communications to the
capital of September 10. All of Allende's supporters within the
armed forces were rounded up and imprisoned. Early the next
day, the coup was carried out in Santiago, with the military
seizing all radio and television stations. After the take-over, the
military *junta immediately issued a statement that Allende had
committed suicide. Prats was allowed to go into exile, but only
after he had appeared on television a few days after the coup
disclaiming that he was leading an insurgent army from the south
to overthrow the junta.

From the moment Chile fell under the jackboot, the contrast
between Allende and the new President Augusto *Pinochet Ugarte
was striking. Under Allende, political life had almost no surveillance. The radio and the press, as wretched as they were in
their reporting, reflected every political point of view, and the
*universities were open and free from blacklists. No one was
tortured for his or her political beliefs. There were no summary
executions or *concentration camps. All families with small children received at least a liter--just over a U.S. quart--of milk a
day, and unemployment had reached an all-time low of 2.5 percent.

Under Pinochet, things were very different. This was not the
typical Latin American military coup. Thousands were killed in
*Santiago in a matter of days, and there were mass arrests and
mass executions throughout the country. As Pinochet had stated
in a frank interview before the coup, "If we come out of the
barracks, we come out to kill." *Church and legal sources estimated that more than 30,000 Chileans lost their lives in the coup
and its aftermath; more than 40,000 became political refugees (see:
EMIGRATION); and over 5,000 were imprisoned or sent to concentration camps. Many simply disappeared. *Torture was normal.

Nor was the new government a typical Chilean *junta. It
moved ruthlessly to destroy national institutions in a far more
sweeping manner than had ever before been attempted in the
modern history of Latin America.

A succession of decrees dissolved the National *Congress, suspended most civil liberties, including the right to assembly (see:
HUMAN RIGHTS). The one million-member *trade union federation,
the Central Unica de Trabajadores, was banned and strikes and
collective bargaining were suspended for almost a decade. Most
of the hard-won reforms of previous administrations in the land
tenure system were done away with (see: AGRARIAN REFORM).
*Political parties on the left were outlawed; those representing
the center and the right were declared in "indefinite recess."
The junta also managed to emasculate an already weakened court
system (see: CHILE--H. Government. (3) The Judiciary) by

quashing all habeus corpus petitions and by postponing the civil trials of thousands of political prisoners (measures relaxed only recently because of international pressure).

A rigid *censorship was imposed on *newspapers and broad- casting (see: TELECOMMUNICATIONS). The foreign press was kept in check, and many of its members expelled for writing stories unfavorable to the junta. Books of all kinds--not only those of Mao, Marx and Marcuse--were seized by the tens of thousands from homes, bookstores and libraries, and then fed to bonfires in the streets of Santiago. Not even the works of Chile's Nobel prize-winning poet Pablo *Neruda were spared. The *universities were purged of all leftists, both students and faculty, and placed under military *intervención.

At a stroke the military accomplished in a matter of days changes more severe than any ever dared by Allende in three years, wiping out any pretense at pluralism in Chilean society and any vestiges of respect for human life.

The regime's violations of human rights have isolated it and resulted in its ostracism by the international community. Pinochet has become the "solitary dictator," and today most of his right- wing supporters are calling for a return to democracy. See also: JUNTA MILITAR DE GOBIERNO DE 1973; PINOCHET, UGARTE AUGUSTO.

COUSINO JUNQUEIRA, Matías (1801-1862). Chile's leading capitalist of the early 19th century. After making a fortune mining in *Atacama, he returned to *Santiago in 1848 and strove to en- courage *wheat growing for export. In 1852 his Compañía Car- bonífera de Lota became the chief developer of Chilean *coal mining. He was also the largest shareholder in the project to connect *Valparaíso to Santiago by *railway. Elected to the National *Congress in 1843, he was a senator from 1855 until his death. At the end of the century the fortune he had left to his widow was second only to that of Juana *Ross de Edwards. His son Luis Cousiño Squella endowed Santiago with the Parque Cousiño, now known as the Parque O'Higgins, and his daughter- in-law Isidora Goyenchea Gallo de Cousiño presented the Chilean *navy with a warship named after him on the outbreak of the 1879 War of the *Pacific.

COVADONGA. Spanish schooner captured by surprise by Chilean commander Juan *Williams Rebolledo in the *Esmeralda at the Battle of *Papudo, November 26, 1865. As a Chilean warship, the Covadonga took part in the Battle of *Iquique (1879) in which it caused the loss of the Peruvian ironclad Independencia, wrecked when following the smaller Covadonga too close inshore. The Covadonga was later used to enforce the Chilean blockade of the Peruvian coast, and was destroyed on hitting a Peruvian mine in Callao Bay in mid-1880.

COVENSA (Corporación de Ventas de Salitre y Yodo). The *Nitrate and *Iodine Sales Corporation, a government agency created in

1934 to replace COSACh (q.v.). It monopolized selling and exporting, but not production. It functioned until 1968 when the
Chilean government created SOQUIMICA (q.v.).

COYHAIQUE. Capital of the former province of *Aysén and of the
geographically identical new Region XI, Aysén del General Ibáñez
del Campo. The population was 11,782 (est.) in 1982. Also
spelled Coihaique.

CREOLE (Spanish criollo). (1) An American-born Spaniard, whether
descended from the original *conquistadores or from later immigrants. The Creoles made up the bulk of the white population
in South America. It was they who were mainly responsible for
creating colonial Spanish and Portuguese America, but they were
usually excluded from high-ranking official positions. Although
the *law put them on an equal footing with the *Peninsulares,
the Creoles suffered discrimination and disadvantages due mainly
to their American birth. The Creoles were the force behind the
19th century movement for independence from Spain.
    (2) The word was also used, logically but confusingly, for
an American-born Negro, as opposed to one brought from Africa.
    (3) In its more general sense, the word refers to anything
born, grown or developed in the Americas that is not indigenous:
such as creole cattle, cuisine, dialects.

CRISTO REDENTOR STATUE. See: CHRIST OF THE ANDES.

CRUCHAGA TOCORNAL, Miguel (1869-1949). Lawyer, professor of
international law, diplomat and politician. He had a long and
distinguished career as a public servant. From 1900 to 1906
he was a deputy in *Congress. He was finance minister in 1903;
minister of the interior in 1905; minister of industry and public
works, also in 1905; minister of foreign affairs and commerce in
1932. He was also named subrogate minister of the interior in
1935, of health in 1935 and of finance in 1936. As a diplomat,
he held many important offices, first as Chilean minister to
*Argentina, Uruguay and Paraguay, during the years 1907
through 1913, then as minister to Germany from 1913 to 1920.
During the next two years he was Chilean ambassador to *Brazil,
and three years later, in 1925, he became ambassador to the
*United Kingdom. In 1931 he was named ambassador to the
*United States. He also represented Chile in international meet-
ings and was an arbiter in the border dispute of 1915 between
Mexico and the United States. In 1937 he was elected senator,
and, in the same year, president of the Senate. He remained a
senator until his death.

CRUZ-COKE LASSABE, Eduardo (b. 1899). Conservative Party
politician. He joined the Party (*Partido Conservador) while a
student, and graduated in medicine in 1921. In 1925 he became
a professor at the *Universidad de Chile. In 1937 he was named

minister of health and social welfare. From 1941 to 1957 he held
elective office as a senator. During that time he was responsible
for introducing a bill (which became law) sponsoring socialized
medicine. In 1946 he was his party's candidate for the presidency,
but lost to Gabriel *González Videla. In 1948 when González
Videla proscribed the Communist Party (*Partido Comunista
Chileno), Cruz Coke opposed the measure (see: PARTIDO CON-
SERVADOR SOCIAL CRISTIANO).

CRUZ GOYENECHE, Luis de la (1786-1829). Chilean patriot who participated in the campaign for independence, fighting in all the
major battles against Spain: *Rancagua, *Maipú, *Chacabuco.
He was a member of the Federalist Party (*Partido Federalista).
After the Battle of Chacabuco, in 1817, there was news that
another Spanish invasion was going to take place. José de *San
Martín and José Ignacio *Zenteno named Cruz Goyeneche Supreme
Director of Chile, while Bernardo *O'Higgins, who had been
wounded at Chacabuco, tried to reorganize the armies fighting
for independence. Cruz Goyeneche remained in power until the
return of O'Higgins, who in 1818 was proclaimed *Supreme
Director with the founding of the Chilean Republic.

CRUZ TOLEDO, María de la. The first woman to be elected to the
Chilean Senate, in 1953. She had attempted to win a Senate
seat in 1950, but had received very few votes. She organized
and became president of the *Partido Feminista de Chile, a party
responsible for the extension of the suffrage to women in national
elections, in 1952, and for defending women's rights. In the
presidential election of 1952 the Party supported the candidacy
of Carlos *Ibáñez del Campo, who won. During the campaign,
De la Cruz Toledo had traveled throughout Chile to win votes
for Ibáñez. In 1953, when a Senate seat was vacated in *Santiago,
she was urged by the President to run for it. She did and she
won. But her Senate career was short-lived. She soon antagonized her colleagues, who forced her to resign in the same year.

CRUZ Y PRIETO, José María de la (1799-1875). A career *army officer who participated in the campaign for *independence from
Spain. In 1813 he was leader of a battalion during the Battle of
*Chillán, and in 1814 he escaped to Mendoza, *Argentina, after
the disastrous defeat of *Rancagua. He came back to Chile with
the frontier army of the liberator José de *San Martín, the
"Ejército de los *Andes," and in 1817 he fought at the battles
of *Chacabuco, *Maipú and *Pengal. From 1824 to 1830 he held
elective office. In 1830 he was named war minister. In 1838 he
participated in the war against the *Peru-Bolivia Confederation.
Afterwards he was promoted general. In 1851 he took part in
the *Civil War of 1851 against President (1851-61) Manuel *Montt
Torres, who had defeated him at the polls. From 1846 to 1855,
backed by the Liberal Party (*Partido Liberal), Cruz Prieto was
a senator.

CRUZAT INFANTE, Manuel (1940-). Chilean financier involved in
   shady deals with the Banco Hipotecario de Chile (BHC) and with
   the conglomerate known as the *Grupo Cruzat-Larraín (see also:
   LARRAIN PENA, Fernando, and VIAL CASTILLO, Javier).
   Educated at the *Universidad Católica de Chile, the University
   of Chicago and Harvard University, he became known as the
   piranha for his aggressive financial deals, and he was one of the
   *"Chicago Boys" who brought the Chilean government to the brink
   of bankruptcy in 1983.

CUADRA. Traditional Chilean measure. As a linear measure, a
   cuadra was the length of one side of a block: 150 *vergas or
   125.39 m (411 ft., 4.32 ins.). The cuadra cuadrada (or simply
   cuadra), equivalent to 1.572 hectares (3.886 acres) survived
   until recently as the commonest Chilean land measure. See also:
   WEIGHTS AND MEASURES.

CUADRILATERO. A political fusion of four parties, the *Partido
   Nacional, the *Partido Radical and two splinters of the Liberal
   Party: the *Partido Liberal Doctrinario and the *Partido Liberal
   Macetón. It took its name ("quadrilateral" in English) from its
   four-party composition. It was formed to oppose the constitutional
   program of President (1888-91) José Manuel *Balmaceda Fernández.
   After the fall of Balmaceda, the Cuadrilatero instituted the *Par-
   liamentary Regime that lasted until 1925.

CUBAN NATIONALIST MOVEMENT (C.N.M.). A terrorist movement
   founded in 1959 by Guillermo *Novo for the purpose of overthrowing the government of Fidel Castro. The C.N.M., through Novo
   and other Cuban exiles in the *United States, cooperated with the
   Chilean secret police, the *DINA, in assassinating Chilean political
   exiles who might be a danger to the regime of strongman President
   (1973-) Augusto *Pinochet Ugarte. Enlisting the help of C.N.M.
   and of its clandestine-operation arm in New Jersey, *Omega 7,
   the DINA was able to carry out an assassination on "embassy row"
   in Washington, D.C., on September 21, 1976. The target was
   the Chilean ex-diplomat Orlando *Letelier del Solar. Letelier was
   killed with co-worker Ronni Moffit, who was a U.S. citizen. The
   act had grave implications in United States-Chilean relations, since
   a foreign government had conducted an assassination on American
   soil.

CUECA. The national folk dance of Chile. During the first years
   of the Republic, the cueca was part of the celebration in commemoration of the defeat of the Spanish. It has now become the
   traditional dance to celebrate Independence Day (September 18,
   1810) and other festive occasions.

CUERPO DE CARABINEROS. The Chilean national *police force. It
   derives ultimately from the colonial Dragones de la Reina (Queen's
   dragoons), renamed after Independence, the Dragones de Chile.

These were incorporated into the army in 1903 as the Gendarmes del Ejército ("army gendarmes"), so called in opposition to the border police formed in 1896 as the Cuerpo de Gendarmes de las Colonias. In 1906 both gendarme bodies were amalgamated as the army Regimento de Carabineros. In 1927, during the first government of Carlos *Ibáñez del Campo, the Carabineros reverted to a semi-civil status as the Cuerpo de Carabineros, which incorporated all other existing law enforcement agencies. Thus law enforcement was put firmly under central government control: the general director of the paramilitary Carabineros received his orders directly from the Minister of the Interior. But the corps was very professional and acquired a general reputation of impartial efficiency--"South America's finest national police force"-- until the 1960 creation of a special arm, the *Grupo Móvil de Carabineros, used primarily in strike-breaking and in suppressing student and peasant demonstrations. This became the most repressive arm of the Jorge *Alessandri Rodríguez and Eduardo *Frei Montalva governments, and was abolished as soon as the left achieved power under Salvador *Allende Gossens, November 3, 1970. The corps as a whole stayed loyal to the *Unidad Popular government for most of its period in office, but became less so in the months immediately preceeding the 1973 *coup. Then, under the command of General César *Mendoza Durán, the carabineros began to cooperate with the other *armed forces, actively searching for arms believed to be hidden by the left--particularly by the *Movimiento de Izquierda Revolucionaria--but reducing their surveillance of such right-wing groups as *Patria y Libertad. With Allende's overthrow, General Mendoza became one of the governing *junta, while ministerial control of the corps passed from the Interior Ministry to that of Defense.

In August 1985, General Mendoza resigned both his command of the police and his seat on the junta, as the result of the trial of fourteen carabineros for the February 1985 murder of three Communists. He was succeeded by his former assistant Rodolfo Strange.

The corps' strength in mid-1984 was 27,000 men, recruited to higher standards than those of the other services and equipped with heavy modern arms. There are specialized marine and air sections, but the secret police (the *Central Nacional de Informaciones and its *DINA predecessor) are totally separate forces.

See also: ARMED FORCES; GOPE; POLICE.

CUEVAS MACKENNA, Francisco (1910-). Graduated as a civil engineer in 1933. In 1953 he was named minister of mines, a post he resigned in 1954 to become president of the State Bank (Banco del Estado de Chile). In 1955 he left the Bank to become finance minister. In the government of President (1964-70) Eduardo *Frei Montalva, he was appointed president of the National Mining Society (Sociedad Nacional de Minería).

CURALI. Site of a battle during the *Guerra a Muerte, the final

stage of the struggle for *independence from *Spain. It was
fought on April 4, 1817, near the city of *Concepción. The
realistas, under the command of lieutenant colonel Juan José
Campillo, made a surprise attack on Chilean patriots led by Juan
Gregorio de las *Heras. The patriots repelled them just the same.
Casualties were light on both sides.

CURICO (city). A town of Central Chile (35°S, 71° 15'W), capital of
the former province of the same name. Its population was
17,573 in 1907; 60,400 (est.) in 1971; and 70,000 (est.) in 1982.

CURICO (province). A former province of Central Chile, created in
1865 by separation from the province of *Colchagua. Its area
was later reduced from 7,714 km^2 to 5,266.3 km^2 (2,033 square
miles) by the return of one of its three departments to Colchagua.
The population was 89,391 in 1952; 123,600 (est.) in 1971; and
146,294 (est.) in 1982. The administrative restructuring of 1974
made Curicó part of the new Region VII, Maule. See: REGIONS
AND ADMINISTRATIVE RESTRUCTURING.

CUSTOMS AND DUTIES. In colonial times trade with foreign nations
was forbidden, and duties on trade with other parts of the Spanish
empire were levied purely as a source of revenue. Independent
Chile made some experiment with protective tariffs, but from the
end of the 19th century export duties on *nitrates and import
duties on luxury goods came to be levied solely for raising revenue.
  In the early 1930s Chile's trade policies became restrictive
and protectionist. The change was the result of the *Depression
of the 1930s and the policies of finance minister (1932-38) Gustavo
*Ross Santa María.
  A post-World War II development was the introduction of free
ports at *Arica, *Punta Arenas and *Chiloé, as a stimulus to
regional development. These free ports, however, were not
exempted from import duties on luxury goods such as *automobiles
and whiskey.
  Chile is a signer of the Treaty of Montevideo, ratified on May
2, 1961, which established the *Latin American Free Trade Association (LAFTA). By the treaty's provisions the member nations
mutually provided "favored treatment." The other signatories
were *Argentina, *Brazil, *Colombia, Ecuador, Mexico, Paraguay
and Uruguay. Chile was also for a while a member of the *Pacto
Andino (the Andean Common Market), which involved four other
Pacific coast countries: Colombia, Ecuador, Peru and Bolivia.
Chile's generally poor relations with its neighbors was, however,
underscored by her withdrawal from the Andean Pact in October
1976. Chile has bilateral trade agreements with most of the
western European nations and with South Africa. In the Americas
it has bilateral relations with the United States, Canada, Venezuela
and Uruguay, among others, but not with Mexico. During the
presidency (1970-73) of Salvador *Allende Gossens, Chile established bilateral agreements with Cuba, Yugoslavia, the *U.S.S.R.

and most other eastern European countries. These were severed after the *coup d'état of September 11, 1973.

Under Allende no great change occurred in Chile's protectionist and restrictive trade measures. Goods competing with local industry continued to be heavily taxed. Favorable treatment was given to essential imports such as *wheat, beef, aircraft, spare parts for aircraft and buses, and heavy machinery for *agriculture and *copper mining. Luxury goods were taxed at a minimum rate of 62 percent by value, while luxury items such as automobiles were taxed at over 200 percent of their commodity value.

With the advent of the military government in 1973, Chile embarked on a course of free-market economics following the model of University of Chicago professor Milton Friedman. Abiding by the laws of the purest form of laissez-faire, the country lifted most trade restrictions. Chile changed from one of the most protected economies in the world, with average tariffs in 1973 of 105 percent, into one of the most open, with all tariffs slashed to 10 percent by 1979.

Allende had sought to utilize customs and duties to end, or at least minimize, *balance of payments deficits. General Augusto *Pinochet Ugarte and his economic advisers were able to do what Allende was not, with a balance of payments strong and foreign currency reserves growing. But what had seemed at first a "miracle" began in 1979 to turn into a "nightmare." Trade deficits soared, while exports remained constant. In just two years the annual deficit had skyrocketed from US$ 355 million in 1979 to US$ 2,600 million in 1981. And 1983 and 1984 were little better. All of this was the result of a virtual explosion in consumer goods imports and a loss of confidence (read: investments) in the monetarist policies of Pinochet's economic advisors.

In the end the uniform tariff had to be raised: to 20 percent in May 1983 and to 35 percent in September 1984. In July 1985 the principle of a uniform tariff was abandoned, with the custom duty on most products being reduced to 30 percent.

See also: BANKS, BANKING AND FINANCIAL INSTITUTIONS. B. The Collapse of 1981-83; CHICAGO BOYS, The; ECONOMY, The; PUBLIC FINANCE; TAXES.

CUYO. Region of northwestern *Argentina comprising the present-day provinces of Mendoza, San Juan and San Luis. First explored by *conquistador Francisco de *Villagrâ, returning to Chile from Upper Peru. His favorable report led governor García *Hurtado de Mendoza to organize its settlement: the city of *Mendoza, named in his honor, was founded in 1561. The connection of the new province with central Chile by way of the *Uspallata Pass was so tenuous that Cuyo gradually came to look rather towards Tucumân to its north and Buenos Aires to the east, especially after trade with them was legalized in 1690. In 1776 the situation was recognized by the administrative separation of Cuyo from Chile and its inclusion in the new Viceroyalty of the Plate, which was eventually to become the Argentine Republic.

CUZCUZ TREATY. A peace treaty signed on May 17, 1830, between Conservatives (*pelucones) and Liberals (*pipiolos) to put an end to the civil strife that had begun a year earlier (see: CIVIL WAR OF 1829-1830). The victory of the Conservatives at *Lircay delivered the nation to conservative control for the ensuing three decades.

- D -

DAMPIER, William (1652-1715). English privateer who twice circumnavigated the Globe. On the first occasion, 1703-1706, he commanded the expedition from which Alexander Selkirk was marooned on Más Atierra in the *Juan Fernández Islands. On the second occasion, 1708-1711, he was a subordinate of Captain Woodes Rogers who rescued the unfortunate Selkirk.
See also: PIRATES AND PRIVATEERS.

DARIO, Rubén (1867-1916). The great Nicaraguan-born poet spent a brief but important period in Chile, from June 24, 1886 to February 9, 1889, living in *Santiago and *Valparaíso. He had been invited to make the journey south by another Nicaraguan, General Juan J. Cañas, who was a friend of Benjamín *Vicuña Mackenna. In the Chilean capital Darío discovered a group of young poets who were intimately familiar with the French Parnassian and Symbolist writers. He also read Poe and Whitman. After joining the staff of the Santiago newspaper La *Epoca, contributing articles, essays and poems, Darío fell out of favor with the paper's director, Eduardo *MacClure. In 1887 Darío published an anthology of poems, Abrojos, which revealed a writer of intelligence and great linguistic skills. But it was not until a year later that his book Azul made him the undisputed master of a new literature known as "Modernismo." The slim volume of poetry and prose caught the attention not only of young poets in Spanish America but also of the most respected Spanish critics, who acknowledged the emergence of a great poet. In less than two decades, Darío was recognized as the greatest Hispanic poet since Quevedo, and Modernism became a world literary phenomenon.

DARWIN, Charles (1809-1882). English biologist who visited Chile in 1833-35 as the naturalist aboard H.M.S. Beagle, a British naval survey vessel commanded by Captain Robert *Fitzroy which made a westbound circumnavigation December 1831-October 1836, primarily to chart the coasts of *Patagonia, *Tierra del Fuego, Chile and *Peru. He spent some time in Tierra del Fuego, visited *Concepción, *Valparaíso (where he was entertained by Jorge *Edwards Brown) and *Santiago, and went on expeditions to the high *Andes and the *Atacama desert. His Journal of the Voyage of the "Beagle" (1839) describes not only fauna, flora and natural

occurrences such as *earthquakes, but details social, economic
and political aspects of the countries he visited. His observations
gave him the material for his work on evolution, and his ship's
survey work is commemorated in the BEAGLE CHANNEL (q.v.).

DAVILA ESPINOSA, Carlos Guillermo (1887-1955). Lawyer, newspaperman, and provisional President of Chile for almost 100 days;
his government was known as the "gobierno de los cien días."
In 1928 he obtained a law degree from Columbia University. He
also did postgraduate work at the University of Southern California and the University of North Carolina. From 1927 to 1931 he
was Chilean ambassador to the *United States. When the government of Juan Esteban *Montero Rodríguez was dissolved on June 4,
1932, Dávila Espinosa participated in the *junta governments that
followed. On June 17 Dávila Espinosa became junta president
and on July 8 he proclaimed himself provisional President of Chile.
His government lasted until September 13, when a coup d'état by
his minister of the interior, Bartolomé *Blanche Espejo, ended
his incumbency. A member of the Radical Party (*Partido Radical)
and later a Conservative, Dávila had a distinguished career as
a newspaperman and diplomat. He worked on El *Mercurio, became director of La *Nación, and was one of the founders of *Hoy.
In 1946 he was the Chilean representative on the Economic Council
of the *United Nations. In 1954 he became Secretary General
of the *Organization of American States, a post he held until
his death in Washington, D.C.

DAVIS, Edward (fl. 1683-1702). Welsh pirate, "undoubtedly the
greatest and most prudent commander who ever led buccaneers
at sea," who sacked *Arica and La *Serena in 1686. His reported
discovery of land 500 *leagues from *Copiapó and 600 from the
Galápagos Islands renewed the search for a great "Terra Australis
Incognita" and led to Jacob *Roggeveen's discovery of *Easter
Island (which may conceivably have been what Davis had in fact
been referring to).

DAWSON ISLAND. One of Chile's most notorious *concentration camps,
located in the squalid, almost uninhabited island in the *Strait
of Magellan. It was on cold and windswept Dawson Island that
most of President Salvador *Allende Gossen's closest advisers were
sent after the military *coup d'état of September 1973, suffering
lack of food and clothing adequate to the intemperate climate.

DECLARACION DE SANTIAGO, La. A multilateral agreement signed
in 1962 by Chile, Ecuador and *Peru, affirming their rights over
seas within 200 miles of their shores. Other Latin American
countries that claim the same legal extension of their coastal
waters are Uruguay, *Brazil, *Argentina, Costa Rica, Nicaragua
and El Salvador. See: LAW OF THE SEA.

DEFENSA NACIONAL, Ministerio de. The Ministry of National Defense was created in May 1927 to replace the ministries of war and of the *navy. The new ministry lasted until November 1927. In March 1932 the service ministries, which by then also included a Ministerio de Aviación for the *air force, were merged again, by Statue no. 5077. This second National Defense ministry was also short lived, and in July was divided into a Ministry of War and Aviation, and a Ministry of the Navy. On December 25, 1932, however, a Ministry of National Defense was created for the third time. It has lasted to the present. Since the *coup d'état of 1973 the defense minister has ranked third in the cabinet, after the ministers of the interior and of foreign affairs. Holders of the office since then have been: Rear Admiral Patricio *Carvajal Prieto (September 11, 1973); General Oscar *Bonilla Bradanovic (July 1974); Brigadier General Hernán Julio *Brady Roche (March 1975); General César Raúl Manuel *Benavides Escobar (April 1978); General Carlos Forestier (December 1980); General Washington Carrasco García (February 1982); Vice Admiral Carvajal Prieto (again, August 1982).

See also: ARMED FORCES; GUERRA, Ministerio de; MARINA, Ministerio de.

DEFENSE OF DEMOCRACY, Law for the. See: LEY DE DEFENSA DE LA DEMOCRACIA.

DEMOCRACIA AGRARIO-LABORISTA. See: PARTIDO DEMOCRACIA AGRARIO-LABORISTA.

DEMOCRACIA RADICAL. See: PARTIDO DEMOCRACIA RADICAL.

DEMOCRATIC ALLIANCE. See: ALIANZA DEMOCRATIC DE CHILE.

DEMOCRATIC CONFEDERATION. See: CONFEDERACION DEMOCRATI-CA.

DEMOCRATIC FRONT. See: FRENTE DEMOCRATICO DE CHILE.

DEMOCRATIC NATIONAL FRONT. See: FRENTE NACIONAL DEMO-CRATICO.

DEMOCRATIC PARTY. See: PARTIDO DEMOCRATICO.

DEPARTMENT (Departamento). A subdivision of a province, under a governor (gobernador). See: PROVINCES.

DEPENDENCIES. See: CHILE--C. Dependencies.

DEPRESSION OF THE 1930s. The League of Nations dubbed Chile the Latin American country hardest hit by the Great Depression. From 1930 to 1932 Chile experienced an acute economic collapse, due in large part to her dependence on the *mining of *nitrates and *copper and her inability to sell these on the depressed world market. By the end of 1930, mining output was down to 35 percent of the 1927-29 yearly average, and over 60,000 miners were out of work. *Agriculture was also adversely affected, especially by the effects of the depression in other countries (Chile was at this period a net exporter of foodstuffs). Total exports in 1932 were down to 15 percent of their 1927-29 average. The depression in mining and agriculture and the resultant unemployment caused other economic activity to decrease, leading to considerable *internal migration, mostly to the capital, *Santiago, as displaced workers scrambled to find ways of supporting their families.

Soon Chile's international credits faltered as exports declined: during 1930 exports fell by US$ 200 million and gold reserves by US$ 25 million. In 1931 gold reserves fell by a further US$ 30 million (from almost US$ 71 million to a little over US$ 40 million). In 1932 Chile defaulted on her foreign debt for the first time in more than a decade. As a result, a Comisión de control de cambios internacionales was created in April 1932 to impose tight exchange controls.

The constant deterioration of the *economy brought with it extreme political instability, and during 1931-32 there was almost continuous political turmoil. After a series of strikes and riots which left many dead and pitted the *army against the strikers, President (1927-31) Carlos *Ibáñez del Campo was forced to resign (July 27, 1931) and left the country. He was succeeded by his interior minister Juan Esteban *Montero Rodríguez, whose deflationary remedy of savage cuts in all government salaries provoked the *Coquimbo mutiny in the navy (August-September 1931). Montero was overthrown by a military coup of June 4, 1932, which led to a short-lived *República Socialista led by *air force commander Marmaduke *Grove Vallejo. Grove was ousted in a bloodless coup (June 17) by the Santiago garrison which installed Carlos *Dávila Espinosa. Dávila in turn was overthrown by his interior minister Bartolomé *Blanche Espejo (September 13), who organized new elections. These were held in October 1932 and brought back Arturo *Alessandri Palma as President of Chile. He responded rapidly to restore confidence among businessmen and investors, and set out to implement relief policies to stimulate a stagnant economy, put Chile back to work, and increase demand through deficit financing of public works and industrial output.

The negative impact on the economy caused by the Depression of the 1930s was transitory. After a severe crisis in the industrial sector that lasted from 1930 to 1936, industrial expansion began once more. Fishing and *foreign trade, which had languished while ships lay idle in *ports, recovered and expanded as well. Agriculture resumed its full productivity cycle, and forestry became a major industry. Only mining, especially in the nitrate fields, was slowed down for years to come.

DEVELOPMENT, Ministry of. See: FOMENTO, Ministerio de.

DIAGUITAS. Indians who came to Chile from western *Argentina before the arrival of the Spaniards. With the *Atacameños, they
settled in the semi-desert provinces of *Atacama and *Coquimbo.
Both tribes are now extinct.

DIARIO ILUSTRADO, El. A *Santiago daily newspaper founded in
March 1902 by Ricardo Salas Edwards as the official organ of the
*Partido Conservado, of which he was leader. When the Conser-
vatives formed a coalition in 1966 with the *Partido Liberal as a
new *Partido Nacional, the paper became the organ of the new
party. It attained a circulation of 30,000 and ceased publication
in mid-1970. See also: NEWSPAPERS.

DIARIO OFICIAL DE LA REPUBLICA DE CHILE, El. The official
gazette of the Republic, begun March 1, 1877, in succession to
El ARAUCANO (q.v.). During the *Civil War of 1891, the
Diario oficial de la República was the organ of the government of
President José Manuel *Balmaceda Fernández. Since Balmaceda's
overthrow, the paper has discontinued its news and editorial
sections and is now purely a vehicle for formal legal announcements.

DIARIO OFICIAL DEL VERDADERO GOBIERNO, El. A clandestine
newspaper published in *Santiago, May 2-June 4, 1891, in support
of the rebel *Congress during the *Civil War of 1891. See also:
BOLETIN OFICIAL DE LA JUNTA DE GOBIERNO"

DIEGO PORTALES BUILDING. A 22-story high-rise in downtown
*Santiago, taken over as the seat of government after the 1973
military *coup, while the Palacio de La *Moneda was being repaired.

DIEGO RAMIREZ ISLANDS. Dependencies of Chile. A small archipelago located at 56° 36'S, 68° 43'W, about 60 miles southwest of
*Cape Horn. Rocky and uninhabited, the group was discovered
in 1619 by the Portuguese explorer brothers Bartolomeu and
Gonçalo Garcia de Nodal, and named for the cartographer of their
expedition.

DIEZMOS. See: TITHES.

DINA (Dirección de Investigación Nacional). The Chilean secret police
in the early years of the presidency of Augusto *Pinochet Ugarte.
Although formally established by Decree-Law 527 in June 1974,
the National Intelligence Directorate (DINA) had been in operation
since November 1973. Under Pinochet's direct control, it numbered
4,000 men and had approximately four times as many informants.
Secret provisions in its charter gave it the power to arrest anyone, and it routinely used torture as an instrument of state
policy. The DINA was feared because it was fairly ecumenical
in choosing its victims. Although the brunt of its repression was
borne by the left, former parliamentarians and *army officers, as

well as suspect leftist terrorists, were beaten and tortured.

The DINA was blamed for a number of bombings that killed or maimed exiled Chilean leaders who were a possible threat to Pinochet and who were said to be on the government's "hate list." Among them were: General Carlos *Prats González, army chief-of-staff under President Salvador *Allende Gossens, who was assassinated when a bomb exploded in his car in Buenos Aires in September 1974, killing him and his wife; Bernardo *Leighton Guzman, Christian Democrat leader, who, with his wife, was seriously wounded by gunmen in Rome in October 1975; and Orlando *Letelier del Solar, Chilean ambassador to the *United States under Allende, who was killed with a co-worker when a bomb exploded in his car outside the Chilean embassy in Washington, D.C. in September 1976. The Chilean government denied any complicity in these attempts, even though strong evidence pointed to the DINA.

Coincident with the visit to Chile in August 1977 of Terrence Todman, United States assistant secretary of state for inter-American affairs, General Pinochet disclosed that the DINA had been dissolved as of August 6. The agency was replaced by the *Central Nacional de Informaciones (C.N.I.), a specialized military body headed by a general, which gathers and processes information in all fields necessary for government decision-making, especially as this relates to national security. Like the DINA, the new intelligence apparatus is responsible solely to the President and draws from an extraordinarily varied investigative network that covers air, naval, military and *police intelligence. The continuing hegemony of Pinochet's intelligence service seems to indicate that the President overshadows the other members of the *junta and that the change of name from DINA to C.N.I. does not denote a significant structural reform.

DINACOS (Dirección Nacional de Comunicaciones Sociales). The Directorate of Social Communications (DINACOS) was established in 1974, soon after the *junta government came to power. It was in charge of press *censorship, supervision of foreign correspondents and propaganda campaigns inside and outside Chile, and worked closely with the Chilean secret police, *DINA.

DIRECCION DE BIBLIOTECAS, ARQUIVOS Y MUSEOS. See: NATIONAL ARCHIVES; NATIONAL LIBRARY.

DIRECCION DE INVESTIGACION NACIONAL. See: DINA.

DIRECCION GENERAL DE AERONAUTICA CIVIL. See: AIR TRANSPORT.

DIRECCION GENERAL DE CORREOS. See: POSTAL SERVICES.

DIRECCION NACIONAL DE COMUNICACIONES SOCIALES. See: DINACOS.

DIRECTOR SUPREMO. The title of Chile's head of state from 1813 to 1828. See: SUPREME DIRECTOR.

DOCTRINARIO. An epithet meaning "orthodox" (but usually translated by cognates like "doctrinal," "doctrinary" or "doctrinaire"), frequently adopted by splinter groups of Chilean political parties to emphasize their fidelity to what they conceive as the party's true principles.

DOCTRINARY RECUPERATION MOVEMENT. See: MOVIMIENTO DE RECUPERACION DOCTRINARIA.

DOLORES, Pozo de. Locality in the Department of *Pisagua, *Tarapacá province. The surrounding Cerros de SAN FRANCISCO (q.v.) were the site of a battle in the War of the *Pacific and of another in the *Civil War of 1891, to secure possession of this important water source. Both are also known as the first and second battles of Dolores.

DON TINTO. Nickname of President (1938-41) Pedro AGUIRRE CERDA (q.v.).

DONOSO, José (1924-   ). Novelist and short-story writer. He studied at the British Primary School in *Santiago, and was a classmate of Carlos Fuentes, the noted Mexican novelist. Donoso went on to the *Universidad de Chile, and in 1949 was awarded a scholarship to study at Princeton, where he received his B.A. in 1951. From that time he has held high offices in the ministry of education. From 1965 to 1967 he was a writer-in-residence and lecturer at the University of Iowa. Among his better known novels are Este domingo and El lugar. Both works portray the decadence of Santiago society. Two of his short-stories have received wide acclaim in Latin America: "Paseo" and "Santelices." In "Paseo" he satirized the routine of everyday life in a Chilean household, depicting the world of inner feelings as viewed by a child who feels that he is less important than a dog found in the street or than the billiard game that his uncles play. In "Santelices," Donoso criticized the routine life of a boarding house. His hero becomes fascinated by wild animals, rejects the monotony of his office work, and thinks that he can escape society by contemplation. Little by little he becomes alienated from the world surrounding him, until his escapism becomes total when he commits suicide.

DOUBLOON (Doblón). See: COINAGE.

DOVER CONSPIRACY. A conspiracy to overthrow President (1927-31) Carlos *Ibáñez del Campo, hatched on or near the Dover-Calais cross-Channel ferry by exiled politicians and military men who ranged clear across the political spectrum from Agustín *Edwards MacClure to Marmaduke *Grove Vallejo, on February

29, 1928. When Irigoyen was elected president of *Argentina later that year, the plotters moved their activities from England to Buenos Aires, but they took no effective action until the ousting of Irigoyen by the Argentine army in September 1930. A trimotor Fokker, the *Avión Rojo, was then hurriedly purchased and Grove with three other conspirators flew to *Concepción, in the mistaken belief that the garrison there would rise on their arrival. Instead the four were caught and sent to detention on *Easter Island.

DRAGOONS (Dragones). See: POLICE.

DRAKE, [Sir] Francis (1540?-1596). English sailor. In his Pelican (renamed during the voyage, the Golden Hind), he completed the second circumnavigation of the Globe (after that of Ferdinand *Magellan's Captain Elcano), December 13, 1577--September 26, 1580. This made him the first Englishman to visit Chile, but his purpose was privateering against Spain rather than exploration. He attacked *Valparaíso on December 5, 1577, seizing 25,000 *pesos' worth of *gold from a ship in the harbor, made an unsuccessful attempt to raid La *Serena, and captured 800 pounds of *silver at *Arica on February 5, 1578. See also: PIRATES AND PRIVATEERS.

DUHALDE VAZQUEZ, Alfred (b.1888). Radical Party (*Partido Radical) politician. Elected to *Congress as a deputy (1927-37) and as a senator (1937-45). In 1942 he became defense minister, and in 1945 minister of the interior. On September 26, 1945 he was named vice-president of Chile. He became acting President of the Republic on the death of President (1942-46) Juan Antonio *Ríos Morales. Duhalde Vázquez held office until the November 4 inauguration of the new president, Gabriel *González Videla. Duhalde Vázquez had been a candidate himself, but during his brief term the country was plagued by *labor trouble which cost him the electoral support he needed and he withdrew his candidacy.

DUNDONALD, Thomas Cochrane, 10th Earl of. See: COCHRANE, Thomas.

DURAN, César Mendoza. See: MENDOZA DURAN, César.

DURAN NEUMANN, Julio Antonio (1918-). Lawyer and *Partido Radical politician. In *Congress as a deputy (1945-53) and as a senator (1957-64) he was the leader of his party from 1952 to 1964. In the presidential election of 1964 he ran with the backing of the Radicals and of the political party known as the *Comandos Populares. He lost, however, to Eduardo *Frei Montalva, obtaining a mere 4.9 percent of the votes, as opposed to Frei's 55.6 percent. Because of his opposition to the government of President (1970-73) Salvador *Allende Gossens, he was named by the military *junta in 1974 as Chilean ambassador to the *Organization of American States (OAS).

- E -

EARTHQUAKES. Chile, like all lands bordering the eastern Pacific, is liable to seismic violence. Over 100 major earthquakes have occurred in the past 400 years. Most have their epicenters to the north of *Valparaíso, but the most serious have had them to the south. In the colonial period notable quakes happened on February 2, 1570 (*Concepción); March 1575 (*Santiago); December 16, 1575 (*Valdivia, with deaths in three figures); May 13, 1647 (from *Iquique to the River *Maule, with Santiago, which was leveled, suffering its worst colonial quake, and Valparaíso badly affected and a total of two or three thousand dead); March 13, 1657 (Concepción, 12 dead); July 2, 1730 (Santiago, Valparaíso, Concepción badly hit, La *Serena almost destroyed); 1742 (Talca destroyed); May 25, 1751 (Concepción destroyed, Santiago badly damaged, Chillán inundated by the accompanying tidal wave).

Nineteenth-century disasters included Valparaíso (practically destroyed on November 19, 1822); Southern Chile on February 20, 1835 (a particularly severe quake and accompanying tidal wave that killed 120, destroyed *Talcahuano and 70 villages, heavily damaged Concepción and Chillán, and also affected Talca and Santiago); Valdivia and *Chiloé on November 7, 1837; *Copiapó on January 11, 1854, and then again on October 5, 1859; and Coquimbo on September 5, 1859. *Arica, which was then in *Peru, was destroyed on August 6, 1868 (with heavy loss of life from two tidal waves) and *Iquique badly damaged. Both Arica and Iquique were badly hit again on May 9, 1877.

In this century, Valparaíso suffered a very strong quake (which also hit Santiago) just before 8 p.m. on August 16, 1906; a fire followed, the city was almost wholly destroyed and 2,500 died. The provinces of *Atacama and *Coquimbo were shaken by an earthquake during the night of November 10-11, 1922. Talca was destroyed again in 1928. The northern seaport of Taltal was partially destroyed by a quake and tidal wave on July 13, 1936.

The earthquake of January 26, 1939 was the century's worst: 50,000 square miles of southern Chile were affected, Concepción suffered badly and some fifty other towns were wholly destroyed. The total deathtoll approached 30,000, a third of it in Chillán.

On May 22, 1960 a quake and tidal wave along 700 miles of coast caused US$ 800 million worth of damage from Concepción to *Aysén, with Valdivia particularly hard hit. There were 5,700 dead, 3,000 wounded, 60,000 homes destroyed and 300,000 homeless. An April 1965 quake at La Ligua killed 420 and badly shook Valparaíso. Taltal again suffered a quake in 1966. On July 9, 1971 ninety died and perhaps as many as 100,000 were left homeless in the provinces of Coquimbo, Santiago, Valparaíso and *Aconcagua, with the cities of Santiago and Valparaíso seriously affected.

At 7:13 p.m. on March 3, 1985, a quake with its epicenter in the sea off Algarrobo about 25 miles southwest of Valparaíso was felt as far away as Sao Paulo and Buenos Aires. It measured 8-9 Mercali, left 145 dead, 2,000 hurt and 200,000 homeless, and caused about US$ 800 million worth of damage. For Santiago it was the first seriously destructive earthquake since 1906. Chile's struggling *economy was badly affected, particularly since the principal export *ports of *San Antonio and Valparaíso were rendered almost inoperative. Damage to *copper smelting plants was bad enough to raise world copper prices.

Earthquake monitoring and research is the responsibility of the official Servicio Seismológico de Chile, created in the aftermath of the 1906 Valparaíso quake. During its first two years of existence it registered no less than 1,888 perceptible earth tremors.

EASTER ISLAND (Isla de Pascua). A triangular volcanic projection about 10 miles by 15, located 2,300 miles west of mainland Chile at 27° 3' to 12' S and 109° 14' to 25' W, originally colonized by Polynesians, in whose language it is Rapa-Nui. Chile's most famous dependency, famed for the mystery of its huge stone statues, the island was apparently discovered by the Welsh pirate Edward *Davis. It was named—on Easter Day 1722—by Dutch admiral Jacob *Roggenveen, and claimed for Spain by Felipe González y Haedo (who named it San Carlos) on November 15, 1770. The Englishman James Cook visited the island in 1774, as did the French explorer Jean François de Galaup, conte de *La Pérouse in 1786. In the early 19th century U.S. sealers impressed islanders as crew, and in 1855 slavehunters from Peru came to obtain workers for the *guano beds. Later French Catholic missionaries arrived. Chile took control on September 9, 1888, and now administers the island as part of the *Aconcagua region (see: REGIONS AND ADMINISTRATIVE RESTRUCTURING). For some six days in 1914 the German admiral Count von Spee used Cook's Bay as the base for his fleet. In 1985 the *United States held talks with Chile regarding the possible use of Mataveri *airport as an alternative space-shuttle landing-strip, lengthening the runway to 3,335 m (11,000 ft) and so helping the tourist trade by making it adequate for wide-bodied jet airliners. An agreement to this effect was concluded in August 1985.

The population before the sealers and slavehunters arrived was about 4,000. Those left after their depredations were decimated by European diseases, notably smallpox and tuberculosis, so that by 1880 only 150 remained. The numbers have now recovered somewhat, to about 1,600. They still speak a Polynesian dialect and grow bananas, potatoes, sugar cane, taro roots and yams for their own consumption. There is also some *sheep farming.

About 400 mainland Chileans live on the island, and about the same number of Easter Islanders have migrated to mainland Chile.

ECHAVARRI ELORZA, Julian (1911-). Accountant by profession, and member of the Agrarian Labor Party (*Partido Agrario Laborista). From 1937 to 1953 he held elective office as a deputy in *Congress. In 1954 he was the leader of a splinter group within his party which joined what was later to become the National Popular Party (*Partido Nacional Popular). In 1957 he became vice-president of the new party and was elected to the Senate. In the presidential campaign of 1964 he supported the candidacy of Eduardo *Frei Montalva, and in 1966 Frei named him ambassador to *Spain.

ECHEVERRIA LARRAIN, Joaquín (1774-1835). Lawyer by profession, and a deputy in the first National *Congress formed in 1811. He was named governor of *Santiago in 1813, and participated in the *junta de gobierno of 1813. In 1817, because of his activities for the cause of independence, he was exiled to *Peru, where he was held prisoner until 1818. In that year he returned to Chile and was named minister of foreign relations by Bernardo *O'Higgins, a post he held for five years. During the government (1823-26) of Ramón *Freire Serrano he was elected senator, and in the same year he was named rector of the *Universidad de San Felipe. From 1820 to 1822 he assisted O'Higgins, who was supreme director from 1817 to 1823, in governing the province of Santiago.

ECHEVERZ, Santiago (1792-1852). Lawyer by profession and member of the Conservative Party (*Partido Conservador). He was secretary of the *intendencia of *Santiago in 1819, deputy in *Congress in 1823 and 1825, and provincial judge in 1824. In 1826 he was named judge (ministro) of the court of appeal, and two years later he was in charge of reforming the *Constitution of 1828. In 1831 he was named vice-president of the Chamber of Deputies, and in 1833 he signed the new *Constitution of 1833, which remained in effect until 1925. In 1843 he became a judge (ministro) of the supreme court. Active in politics, he was elected senator in 1834, holding that office until 1843. He was again elected in 1849 and remained a senator until his death. As a member of the court martial of Ramón *Freire Serrano in 1836, he was responsible for commuting Freire's death sentence to one of exile. For this Echeverz was arrested, but was later acquitted.

ECLA. See: ECONOMIC COMMISSION FOR LATIN AMERICA.

ECONOMIA, Ministerio de. The Ministry of the Economy was created by Statute no. 88 in 1953, and changed the structure of the Ministerio de *Economía y Comercio (Ministry of the Economy and Commerce) which it replaced. Two secretariats were included in the new ministry: one for commerce and another for industry and transport. In 1960 the Ministerio de Economía became the Ministerio de Economía, Fomento y Reconstrucción (see below), but the shorter title was revived by the government of Augusto *Pinochet Ugarte in 1983. Ministers of the economy since the *coup d'état of 1973 have been: General Rolando González Acevedo (September 1973); Fernando Leniz Cerda (October 1973); Sergio de *Castro Spikula (April 1975); Pablo Baraona (December 1976); Roberto Kelly (December 1978); José Luis Federici (December 1979); General Rolando Ramos (December 1980); Luis Danús Covián (April 1982); Rolf *Luders Schwarzenberg (August 1982); Manuel Martín Sáez (February 1983); Andrés Passicot (August 1983); Modesto *Collados Núñez (April 1984); Juan Carlos Délano (July 1985).

ECONOMIA, FOMENTO Y RECONSTRUCCION, Ministerio de. The Ministry of the Economy, Development and Reconstruction was established in 1960 to replace the Ministry of the Economy (Ministerio de *Economía). The new ministry was created by President (1958-64) Jorge *Alessandri Rodríguez by Statute no. 14171, after the disastrous *earthquake of 1960, which left over 60,000 homes destroyed and 300,000 homeless. The new ministry comprised two secretariats, that of the Economy, Development and Reconstruction, and that of Transport. It incorporated most of the departments of the old (1942-53) Ministerio de *Economía y Comercio, and its main immediate purpose was to alleviate the terrible damage caused by the earthquake. The Chilean *economy was on the verge of collapse; the currency had been devalued from 119 *pesos to the dollar in 1953 to 1,000 pesos to the dollar in 1960; thousands of new housing units were needed to accommodate the poor, as well as all the earthquake victims. In the face of this national disaster, President Alessandri used the new ministry to channel the aid coming mostly from the *United States, but also from many other countries around the world. In 1983 its name was shortened to Ministerio de *Economía.

ECONOMIA Y COMERCIO, Ministerio de. The Ministry of the Economy and Commerce was created in 1942 by Statute no. 6-4817, and replaced the Ministry of Commerce and Supply (Ministerio de *Comercio y Abastecimiento). Within the new ministry were the following departments: transport and navigation; industrialization; mines and petroleum; hunting and fishing; statistics; prices; and control of exports. In 1953 the ministry was replaced by the Ministry of the Economy (Ministerio de *Economía).

ECONOMIC COMMISSION FOR LATIN AMERICA (ECLA). In Spanish, Comisión Económica para América Latina (CEPAL). A regional commission of the *United Nations established in 1948 to help Latin American governments promote the economic development of their countries and improve the standards of living of their people. In recent years ECLA/CEPAL has undertaken research on problems of multilateral trade and economic agreements, and has concerned itself with specific areas such as population, industry, agriculture, energy, science and technology, the environment, and the participation of women in development. ECLA's headquarters are in *Santiago, Chile. It meets biennially, while a Committee of the Whole carries on intersessional work.

ECONOMY, The. In colonial times Chile had a largely pastoral economy but *mining and cereal cultivation were also significant (see: CATTLE, GOLD, WHEAT).

Nineteenth-century Chile was endowed with a risk-taking and forward-looking bourgeoisie, a strong efficient central government keen on development, an export-oriented *agriculture, and its own ample *coal and *iron. There were the beginnings of a capital goods industry; *copper began to be smelted rather than being exported as (less valuable) ore, and it almost seemed for a while that the country would emulate Prussia or Japan and achieve a state-led industrial "take-off." Instead, agriculture declined to the extent that Chile became a net importer of food stuffs, foreigners were able to achieve a substantial share of the ownership of the copper and *nitrate industries, and imported manufactures were increasingly preferred to home-produced goods. There is no consensus as to the reasons for this. Some would see the fall of President José Manuel *Balmaceda Fernández in the *Civil War of 1891 as the decisive defeat of the nationalists by "international capitalism," particularly British. Others would blame the tradition of low wage rates and the consequent limited growth of internal purchasing power.

During the present century, despite renewed attempts by politicians of both ends of the political spectrum, the Chilean economy has never yet managed to "take off." Even the import substitutions fostered by the Great *Depression of the 1930s (and the policies of economic nationalist Gustavo *Ross Santa María) failed to achieve a great deal in the long term, though a very similar situation in contemporary Brazil set that country on the road to its present industrial development.

Chile's has remained a "peripheral" economy, dependent for its survival on the world centers of economic power (such as the U.S.A. and *U.S.S.R.), selling its major export, copper, without being able to control its price, and purchasing its major imports without any real bargaining power in the international markets.

Besides this, there has been the problem of *inflation, endemic since the 1870s, and never really tackled, except for a brief heroic attempt to struggle back to the *gold standard in the 1890s. From the end of World War One until the 1970s, inflation averaged 25 percent or more a year. Since then, with a few brief intervals, it has grown steadily worse (see: EXCHANGE RATES), and has been accompanied by secular stagnation-- "stagflation"--whereby temporary economic upswings have been followed almost immediately by crises and periods of zero or negative growth.

To understand the Chilean economy more clearly, we shall concentrate on its last two experiments, one with socialism under the presidency (1970-73) of Salvador *Allende Gossens, and the other with free-market economics under the military *junta of Augusto *Pinochet Ugarte. The two approaches were diametrically opposed and were both new to Chile. That neither has worked is astonishing, given the fact that Chile has virtually all the pre-requisites for agriculture and for *manufacturing and mining industries. A wide gulf has always existed between the country's huge development potential and the living standards that it has actually offered the majority of its inhabitants.

The economic policies of Salvador Allende attracted attention all over the world, as his constitutional transition to socialism attempted to effect a substantial redistribution of income in favor of the poorest sectors of society and to initiate changes in the forms of property by establishing a dominant state economic sector.

Economic development under Allende had a significance that went far beyond the borders of Chile. During the first year there was a substantial readjustment of basic salaries, outstripping the previous increase in the cost of living; the economy moved closer to recovery; and inflation was slowed down significantly. However, over the next two years, many of Allende's policies proved to be misguided, and a majority of middle- and upper-class Chileans rejected his attempts to bring about fundamental social and economic transformations. His economic programs, such as land redistribution (see: AGRARIAN REFORM) and increased wages for all workers, were often badly planned and badly implemented. But if his attempts to introduce social justice failed, they failed because of hostility on the part of the *United States towards his programs and because of the reaction of a growing middle class that cared little or nothing for the poor.

In a time of rising political and economic difficulties, Allende's second year in power proved to be the year of depletion rather than the hoped-for year of accumulation, as there was an explosion in the level of popular consumption. Consumption began to expand at a rate much greater than income, while private investment contracted abruptly, as both domestic and foreign investors diverted their liquid assets into foreign exchange or into speculative dealings. Loans from the United States began to dry up, clearly limiting the state's capacity for accumulation.

By 1973 the gross domestic product fell 3.6 percent, bringing down real wages, while inflation grew from an equivalent of 250 percent per annum to an incredible 1,000 percent. Production, when it did not fall, remained stagnant. Shortages, speculation and the *black market spiraled. Strikes against the government (see: BOSSES' STRIKE; COPPER STRIKES) increased in every sphere of economic activity, bringing about a sharpening of class conflict. Allende's peaceful road to socialism, as a result, became a blind alley, leading the people not toward economic and social justice, but rather toward corporate statism and militarism by violent means.

The leaders of the *armed forces who overthrew Allende in 1973 moved swiftly to restore order and rehabilitate the economy. Their economic policies boiled down to massive deflation, substantial devaluation, a warm welcome to *foreign investment, and austerity programs for the poor, and were in accordance with the free market theories of Milton Friedman and a group of Chilean economists trained at the University of Chicago and known as the *"Chicago Boys."

With their help, Pinochet tried to modernize the Chilean economy by lowering tariff barriers (see: CUSTOMS AND DUTIES) and reducing state intervention in the economy. New export industries were created; inflation was reduced; government deficits were eliminated; and Chile's *balance of payments showed that reserves were growing.

By 1978 Pinochet had restored Chile's faltering economy to moderate health. Inflation had fallen to 70 percent per annum, and for the second year in a row Chile was able to repay nearly US$ 1,000 million in foreign debt, without having to renegotiate its loan. However, the "Chicago Boys'" economic policies also proved to be catastrophic to the long-run health of the Chilean economy. They had implemented austerity programs to bring the economy around, ignoring the staggering social cost imposed on middle-income groups as well as on the poor. The economy experienced three years of rapid growth; then, in mid-1981, it fell into a severe recession. By 1982 the Chilean economic "miracle" had turned into a "nightmare," and the country was headed toward economic disaster. The gross domestic product fell in 1982 by over 14 percent, while the foreign debt had climbed to a record US$ 17,000 million (more than double that of Brazil's, and 30 percent higher than Mexico's, in relation to population). Of all sectors of the economy, only *mining and *fisheries registered positive growth rates for 1982. Industrial production declined by 21.9 percent, with the largest declines (40-50 percent) occurring in the clothing, electrical machinery and food industries. The high degree of indebtedness in both industry and agriculture had become a major cause for concern. Inflation began rising, from a low of 10 percent per annum, to 30 percent per annum. Unemployment reached 25 percent, while underemployment was estimated at 30 percent.

Extreme poverty had existed in Chile before the coup, but angry union leaders and workers claimed that the government's economic programs were aggravating the situation. They were particularly disturbed by a reduction in 1983 in industrial investment and in public spending on construction (the latter could have absorbed thousands of unskilled workers). They were also convinced that "the cost of privilege for the few was borne by the vast majority of the population, forced to live by the breadline." When *labor called a series of strikes, Pinochet responded with force. Several incidents left over 118 dead in 1983, and labor leaders were put behind bars. Students rioted in many cities, further eroding support for the government's economic strategy. Under pressure even from most of his loyal supporters (bankers, industrialists, large farmers), Pinochet fired the "Chicago Boys" and some government regulations were applied, especially in regard to banking and financial institutions. The extreme laissez-faire policies of the "Chicago Boys" had resulted

in at least three grave errors that had damaged--some say, beyond repair--the Chilean economy: (1) the maintenance of a
fixed *exchange rate from 1979 to 1982; (2) the indexing of wages
during the same period; and (3) the failure to regulate the
financial system. Indexed wages and the fixed exchange rate
produced a rate of exchange which was overvalued when Chilean
inflation failed to fall rapidly enough to international levels. The
unregulated banking system prolonged the economic imbalance
as its dubious accounting practices and questionable loans enmeshed the whole of the industrial and financial sectors. By 1984
there was little doubt in anyone's mind that the state of the
Chilean economy was chaotic.

See also: BANKS, BANKING AND FINANCIAL INSTITUTIONS;
COOPERATIVES; EMPLOYMENT; ENERGY AND POWER; EXCHANGE
RATE; FOREIGN AID; FOREIGN INVESTMENTS; FOREIGN TRADE;
INDUSTRY; INFLATION; INTERNAL TRADE; LABOR; MANUFAC-
TURING; NATIONAL INCOME; PLANNING; PUBLIC HEALTH;
STOCK EXCHANGE; TAXES; TRADE UNIONS; TELECOMMUNICA-
TIONS; TRANSPORTATION; and under individual industries (e.g.
AGRICULTURE; AUTOMOBILE INDUSTRY; FISHERIES; INSURANCE;
TOURISM).

EDITORIAL. Publishing house. See: ERCILLA, Editorial; PUBLISH-
ERS AND PUBLISHING; ZIG-ZAG, Editorial.

EDUCACION PUBLICA, Ministerio de. The Ministry of Public Education was created by Statute no. 7912 on November 30, 1927, replacing that of Public Instruction (Ministerio de *Instrucción
Pública). Its functions were to supervise Chilean education,
and to create and maintain the primary education service and such
special establishments as museums, libraries, archives, astronomi-
cal observatories (see: NATIONAL ARCHIVES; NATIONAL
LIBRARY). The UNIVERSITIES (q.v.), which had previously
been autonomous institutions, were incorporated into the education
ministry's responsibilities after the *coup d'état of September
1973, but are under the authority of the *President of Chile.
The university rectors are appointed by the education minister,
who, in turn, is appointed by the President and is directly responsible to him. The education ministry also oversees the Board
of Scholarships and Fellowships, the Educational Society of Chile,
and cinema *censorship.

In accord with its free market economic model, the government
has since 1980 been pursuing a policy of privatizing education
where possible, and, where it is not (as in the case of most elementary and secondary schools), transfering administration and
financing from the ministry to the municipalities (see: LOCAL
GOVERNMENT). Implementation has however been a very slow
process, and in 1986 many schools were still being operated by
the central government.

Education ministers since the coup have been: René Navarro
Tobar (September 9, 1973); Rear Admiral Hugo *Castro Cabezas

Jiménez (September 24, 1973); Admiral Luis Niemann Núñez (December 1976), Gonzalo Vial (December 1978); Alfredo Prieto (December 1979); Rear Admiral Rigoberto Cruz (April 1982); Monica *Madariaga Gutiérrez (August 1982); Horacio Aranguiz (October 1983); Sergio Caete Rojas (July 1985). Madariaga specifically resigned in protest at the continuance of *"intervención" (direct day-to-day government control) in the universities.

See also: EDUCATION.

EDUCATION. A. Colonial. Although the *cabildos provided some primary education, most colonial education was provided by the religious orders, chiefly the Dominicans and the *Jesuits. Provision was insufficient--parents who could afford to, sent their sons to school in Lima--and at the secondary and tertiary levels limited to white males. Improvement began in the latter half of the 18th century with the creation of the *Universidad de San Felipe (1756) and the Colegio (later Real *Academia) de San Luís (1979). See also: CHURCH, The; CONVICTORIO CAROLINO; JESUITS.

B. Independence to Disestablishment. The patriots of Independence, particularly Juan *Egaña Risco, Bernardo *O'Higgins and José Miguel *Carrera Verdugo, were very concerned to improve education, but lacked the resources. An 1813 enactment to set up primary schools in every locality with fifty familes or more remained a mere statement of intent, although the new regime did oblige convents to open primary schools, and the Lancastrian method (using older pupils to teach the younger) was imported from England, along with English Protestant schoolmasters. In 1839, when Manuel *Montt Torres secured the separation of the Ministry of Justice, Religion and Public Instruction (Ministerio de *Justicia, Culto e Instrucción Pública) from that of the Interior, Chile had 400 primary schools, nearly all *Church-run, attended by only 3,000 of the nation's 200,000 children. In 1842 Montt created the first teacher training college (*Escuela Normal de Preceptores), appointing Domingo Faustino *Sarmiento to run it, and ten years later, in 1852, he set up a similar institution for women, the Escuela Normal de Preceptoras. Montt's presidency (1851-61) saw 500 new primary schools opened, increasing the school attendance to 43,414, and an elementary education act, the Ley Orgánica de Instrucción Pública, passed in 1860 to abolish tuition fees. In 1883 a law provided special funds for school construction, and when, after fifty years' agitation, a compulsory attendance act (Ley de Educación Primaria Obligatoria, 1920) was passed--but not wholly enforced, for want of resources --Chile had 3,500 primary schools, most of them state-provided, with 300,000 pupils.

Secondary education, on the other hand, was long regarded as a privilege to be restricted, in the interests of social stability and a docile *labor supply, to the elite. At Independence Chile had but three high schools, in Santiago, La *Serena and *Con-

cepción. By the 1830s, when liceos were established in *Chillán
and *Valdivia, the number of public secondary schools reached
ten (one in each provincial capital). An 1843 reform introduced
a six-year curriculum including history, science, math and a
modern foreign language, but, as only the *Instituto Nacional
had the staff to implement this, scholarships were introduced to
bring the brightest provincial students to *Santiago. "Private"
(i.e. church-run) high school provision expanded much faster,
numbering 63 schools by 1861, including all the liceos for girls.
Divergent views of the Church's role in education was the prime
cause of the 1873 break-up of the *Fusión Liberal-Conservadora,
and disestablishment-advocate Miguel Luis *Amunátegui Aldunate,
who became Liberal education minister, abolished compulsory Latin
(1873), allowed women into the *Universidad de Chile (to counteract the Church monopoly of female secondary education) and
secured a new basic law of secondary and higher education (Ley
Orgánica de Educación Secundaria y Superior, 1879). The next
decade saw the beginning of German influence on Chilean education: the Franco-Prussian War was popularly supposed to have
been won in the Prussian schoolroom, and when a training college
for high school teachers, the Instituto Pedagógico, was set up
in 1889, almost all the faculty was brought over from *Germany.
New liceos, including the first public high schools for girls, soon
followed, often with German teachers. The 50,000 high school
population achieved by 1938 may be compared with 95,000 at
that time in Brazil, which had eight times Chile's population.

The *Instituto Nacional, which functioned at all three educational levels, was the only institution providing higher education in
independent Chile, until the 1833 creation of the Escuela de Medicina (Medical School) by President Joaquín *Prieto Vial. Manuel
Montt set up schools of art and architecture, of agriculture, and
of technical training ("artes y oficios") in 1842, and the *Universidad de Chile in 1843. The University developed along French
lines as a grouping of professional schools, remaining largely
unaffected by the German model of the university as primarily
a research center. But the church-state conflict of the 1870s onward led to the creation of many church-run professional and vocational schools, and, ultimately, in 1888, to the *Universidad
Católica de Chile. In 1918, Enrique Molina, one of the Instituto
Pedagógico's first graduates, organized the private *Universidad
de Concepción, of which he became rector: Chile's third university, and the first one in the provinces.

C. Since Disestablishment. The modern Chilean educational
system is based on four levels: preprimary, primary, secondary,
and university. The preprimary level consists of a crèche for
infants under 2 years of age, a nursery for children aged 2
to 4 years, and a kindergarten for 4- to 6-year olds. The preprimary, however, represents only a small proportion of the total
enrollment. The primary level consists of an 8-year compulsory
cycle; it accounts for the bulk of enrollment. The optional 4-
year secondary cycle is made up of two curricula: the one, to

further education and prepare students to enter the universities; the other, to prepare students technically to enter a trade.

To expand the educational system, there have been periodic efforts since the 1940s at educational reform. These continued during the presidencies of Salvador *Allende Gossens and of Augusto *Pinochet Ugarte. But while Allende veered the educational system toward the poor by expanding enrollments through government subsidies, Pinochet sought to create an avowedly nationalistic and anti-Marxist educational system. During the Allende years, nearly 95 percent of the population between the ages of 7 and 12 years were attending school, an increase of 15 percent over the 1960s. After the 1973 *coup d'état, educational enrollments fell 3.4 percent at the university level, 3.1 percent at the secondary level, and 0.5 percent at the primary level by 1979. In 1981 two decree-laws instituted, for the first time, tuition fees at all universities.

In 1971 there were eleven universities in Chile: two state institutions and nine private. After 1974 the number was reduced to nine, all controlled by the government (see: EDUCACION PUBLICA, Ministerio de). A decree issued in December 1980 make it likely that new private universities would soon be established: the first two of these were to open in 1982.

In 1974, believing that the universities were foci of Marxist indoctrination, the government instituted several far-reaching measures in an effort to depoliticize them. The government announced that all rectors would be replaced by military rectors charged with complete reorganization. Admiral Hugo *Castro Cabezas Jiménez (education minister, September 14, 1973-December 1976) announced a "cleansing" process designed to eliminate all elements considered dangerous. Known leftists were dismissed from faculty and staff positions, and leftist students had their enrollments canceled. The new rectors could dismiss students, fire and hire professors, and create or disband departments and institutes. Purges of suspected leftists in the years immediately after the coup resulted in the firing, expulsion and often imprisonment of more than 39 percent of all university professors and 15 percent of the student body.

The new laws also cut back on existing university curricula, reducing the number of degrees offered to twelve. Eliminated were degrees in the social sciences and humanities. The arts and some technical skills were to be pursued in institutes which had no status as universities. In 1980 professors continued to be fired for their criticism of the university system or of social and economic conditions. In the summer recess over 200 were fired; in 1981 many critics of new university regulations were dismissed. Student demonstrations have been on the increase, demanding a return to full academic freedom and elected rectors. Despite the regime's efforts, control of the universities is proving to be increasingly difficult. See also: UNIVERSITIES.

In 1980 there were 127,219 pupils in kindergarten, 2.3 million students in primary schools, 628,757 in secondary schools, and

119,008 in the universities. Out of every thousand children entering the primary level, 195 went on to secondary school, 59 took vocational training and 16 were admitted to university. This distribution clearly shows that the system was doing little to promote social mobility. University students, on the average, come from upper or upper-middle class families. With the introduction of tuition fees it has become all the more unlikely that members of the lower classes will attend university, unless they obtain a scholarship or a low-interest student loan. The result is that few students from the lower strata of society proceed beyond the secondary level.

See also: EDUCACION PUBLICA, Ministerio de.

EDWARDS BELLO, Joaquín (1887-1968). Great grandson of both Jorge *Edwards Brown and Andrés *Bello López, and a towering figure in Chilean letters. He gained distinction as a journalist, becoming editor of La *Nación in 1920, and as a writer of historical novels. He also served briefly as a diplomat, being Chilean representative at the League of Nations, 1925-27. His best-known work, El *roto, describes the life of the urban poor. His next best-known work, La cuna de Esmeraldo (Esmeraldo's cradle) likewise contrasts the life of the lower classes with that of the comfortably idle. As a young man he traveled widely, especially in Europe, writing El Chileno en Madrid (the Chilean in Madrid) about his years in Spain, and Criollos en Paris (*creoles in Paris); both works crystalize the vices of the upper middle class. His many novels about Chile include El inútil (the useless ones) and El monstruo (the monster). In 1943 he won the National Prize for Literature, and in 1950 the prestigious Camilo *Henríquez Prize. He spent his last years writing for La Nación.

EDWARDS BROWN, Jorge (1780-1848). Scottish-descended patriarch of the influential Edwards family of wealthy industrialists. Born George Edwards in London to John Edwards and Elizabeth Brown, he trained as a surgeon and arrived at La *Serena in 1804 as ship's doctor on the Scorpion, a privateer operating against French shipping in the Pacific. Taking a liking to the country and to a Basque merchant's daughter, he risked hanging by jumping ship and was hidden by the family of his future wife, Isabel Ossandón Iribarren. After his ship had sailed he was discovered and sent to Callao, but managed to return, and, having accepted Roman Catholicism, was married in May 1807. His medical skill and his wife's $1,500 dowry formed the basis of the sizable fortune he amassed during and just after the Wars of *Independence. His ventures included *silver mining at Arqueros, to which he introduced English technology. His financial contributions to the Peruvian campaign secured him Chilean citizenship, and he became successively intendente interino (acting *intendant) of the province of *Coquimbo, and member, and then vice-president, of the Congreso de Plenipotenciarios (see: OCHAGAVIA TREATY).

He had eight children by Isabel, and after her death he had
more children by Ventura Argandoña viuda de Garriga whom he
married in 1834.

EDWARDS [BUDGE], Agustín R. (b. 1899). Son of Agustín *Edwards
MacClure, educated Eton College and Cambridge University,
England. When socialist President Salvador *Allende Gossens expropriated and nationalized all Chilean banks, Agustín Edwards
became his archenemy, working ceaselessly, and in cooperation
with the U.S. *Central Intelligence Agency, to achieve the
President's overthrow. When an editorial in El *Mercurio openly
called upon the *armed forces to oust him, Allende removed Edwards from control of the newspaper (which he regained after
the 1973 military *coup).

EDWARDS MacCLURE, Agustín (1878-1941). Son of Agustín *Edwards
Ross, immensely wealthy and one of Chile's most distinguished
diplomats and businessmen. After studying journalism under
James Gordon Bennett of the New York Herald, he founded the
*Santiago edition of El *Mercurio (June 1, 1900), the Ultimas
noticias (1902), two other newspapers, and four weekly reviews
in Santiago, *Antofagasta and *Valparaiso, of which the most important was the Revista *Zig-Zag (1905). He also directed the
Banco A. Edwards & Cia. He supported the 1891 rebellion against
*Balmaceda and entered the National *Congress in 1900, becoming
vice-president of the lower house in 1902, and holding several
ministerial posts including that of foreign minister (1903-05 and
1909-10). He was appointed minister to *Spain in 1906 and to
the *United Kingdom in November 1910. He presided at the Third
Assembly of the League of Nations (1922) and at the Fifth Pan-
American Conference (1923). He was among the many politicians
exiled by Ibáñez del Campo in 1927 and was involved in the
*Dover Conspiracy. One of the most powerful conservatives
in Chile, he was also the author of many historical works (e.g.
The Birth and Consolidation of the Republic of Chile), accounts
of his travels, and a book for children.

EDWARDS MATTE, Guillermo (b. 1889). *Unión Liberal politician.
Nephew of Agustín *Edwards Ross. Minister of finance under
Arturo *Alessandri Palma in 1922 and under Luis *Barros Borgoño
in 1925; successively minister of the interior (1928-30) and of
foreign affairs (1931) under Carlos *Ibáñez del Campo. Reputed
to have been more fascist-leaning than Ibáñez himself.

EDWARDS OSSANDON, Agustín (1816-1879). Son of Jorge *Edwards
Brown, he was poorly educated, but had a wonderful talent for
business. Beginning at 17 as a chicken farmer, he made $14,000
and went to *Chañarcillo, financing the *silver miners and buying
their ore. In 1851 he married his niece Juana *Ross Edwards
and moved to *Valparaíso, where he was the chief founding shareholder in the city's first bank, the Banco de Valparaiso de De-

pósitos y Descuentos, 1854. Later he founded his own Banco
A. Edwards & Cia. (1867) and the Cia. Chilena de Seguros,
and contributed a third of the capital of what was then the
largest *nitrate company. He also pioneered *railways (in association with his friend William *Wheelwright) and the export of
smelted *copper to Europe, and became a senator. He died worth
25 million *pesos, the foremost Chilean capitalist of the day, and,
according to his obituary in the London Times, "the world's
premier copper trader."

EDWARDS OSSANDON, Joaquín (1806-1868). Banker and industrialist,
and eldest child of Jorge *Edwards Brown. Sent to Catskill,
New York, for his education, he was then apprenticed to a Boston
firm before returning to La *Serena, where he married his step-
mother's child by her first marriage, Margarita Garriga Argandoña.
His Fundición El Barco at Lirquén pioneered the smelting of *copper with Chilean *coal in 1843, and he became *intendant of *Coquimbo. Joaquín *Edwards Bello was his grandson.

EDWARDS ROSS, Agustín R. (1851-1923). Son of Agustín *Edwards
Ossandón; a diplomat, politician and businessman who purchased
*Valparaíso's leading newspaper El *Mercurio in 1884. This
thereby became the organ of the *Partido Nacional, the party of
rich industrialists representing the interests of the Edwards
family. He was elected deputy in 1876, became José Manuel
*Balmaceda Fernández's finance minister in 1886 and was senator
for his native Valparaiso from 1888-1897. During the *Civil
War of 1891 Balmaceda allowed him to go to Lima, where he made
himself one of the rebels' most effective agents abroad. Afterwards he held several ministerial posts in the Jorge *Montt Alvarez administration and served as vice-president (1892) and
president (1893-94) of the Senate. He retired from public life
in 1896, when his fortune--in land, banking, commerce, *mining
and urban property--was evaluated at $9,124,361: Chile's largest
at that time.

EDWARDS VIVES, Alberto (1873-1932). Politician and writer. Grandson of Jorge *Edwards Brown and his second wife, Ventura
Argandoña. During the *Civil War of 1891 he collaborated with
his cousin Agustín *Edwards MacClure in a clandestine anti-
*Balmaceda newspaper, La causa justa. After the rebels had
won, he entered government service, where he was influential
in reforming government statistics (see: CENSUSES), becoming
Director General of Statistics, 1916-27. He had entered the
*Congreso Nacional as a *Partido Nacional supporter in 1909,
and served as finance minister 1914-15 and 1926-27, and as *education minister October 1930-May 1931. He wrote short stories,
detective fiction and political works, and also articles for El
*Mercurio.

EGAÑA FABRES, Mariano (1793-1846). Lawyer by profession, and active in politics from the establishment of the Chilean Republic. In 1813 he was Secretary of the Interior in the *junta government of José Miguel *Carrera Verdugo, and a year later, after the defeat of the Chilean patriots at *Rancagua, he was exiled, together with his father Juan *Egaña Risco, to the *Juan Fernández islands. After the Chilean victory of *Chacabuco in 1817, he returned to Chile and occupied various high offices in government: chief of *police of *Santiago, member of the Tribunal of Justice, secretary of economy, collector of revenues. In 1823 he was appointed secretary of the junta de gobierno, and in 1824 he was sent to London as Chilean minister plenipotentiary.

In 1830 Egaña Fabres became attorney general of the Supreme Court, and in the same year minister of the interior and foreign affairs. He was on the committee that drafted the *Constitution of 1833 and in 1834 was elected to the Senate. Two years later he was sent as Chilean minister to *Peru, returning to Chile after a few months to assume the post of minister of justice. In 1840 he returned as minister to Peru. Three years later he was named vice-president of the Senate and received the honorary title of official of the Legion of Honor of the Republic for the many services he had rendered his country.

EGAÑA RISCO, Juan (1769-1836). Bachelor of canon law and professor of Latin and rhetoric at the *Universidad de San Felipe. Active in the struggle for Chilean independence, he took part in the first junta government, the *junta de gobierno of 1811, as president of the *education committee. He was a deputy to the first National *Congress, and with Camilo *Henríquez he edited the newspaper La *Aurora de Chile. After the battle of *Ramcagua (1814), the *realistas exiled him and his son Mariano *Egaña Fabres to Más Atierra in the *Juan Fernández Islands. He returned to Chile after the Patriot victory of *Chacabuco (1819) and became a member of the city council of *Santiago. After the fall from power of Bernardo *O'Higgins, he took part in drafting the *Constitution of 1823 and was named plenipotentiary representative from the province of *Santiago to meet with the representatives of *Concepción and *Coquimbo to reconstitute the Republic. Politically he belonged to the Federalists (*Partido Federalista), and was elected senator in 1824, and deputy in 1825. In 1827 he was president of the provincial assembly of Santiago. When he died he left behind many literary works on a multitude of subjects. He bequeathed his large library to his son Mariano; on the latter's death it passed to the *National Library of Chile.

EJERCITO. See: ARMY.

EJERCITO DE LOS ANDES. See: ANDES, Ejército de los.

ELECTIONS. Under the *Constitution of 1833, at the national level only members of the Chamber of Deputies were directly elected

(every three years). Provincial *intendants and other presiden-
tially appointed officials could often influence results. After
1891, under the *parliamentary regime, this influence disappeared,
only to be replaced by that of local municipal political bosses.
Bribery of electors remained a serious problem for many years.
Under the *Constitution of 1925 the President was directly elected
every six years, and members of the Chamber of Deputies and
half the senators were directly elected every four years, by a
system of proportional representation.

The present *Constitution of 1980 does not envisage any "return to democracy" until 1989. There will then be elections for
deputies every four years; 26 of the 35 senators will be elected
for eight-year terms. After President Augusto *Pinochet Ugarte
retires, future Presidents will be elected every eight years.

See also: LOCAL GOVERNMENT; SUFFRAGE.

ELECTRICITY SUPPLY. See: ENDESA; ENERGY AND POWER.

ELQUI. A fertile valley north of *Santiago, and east of La *Serena.
The town of Vicuña, where Gabriela *Mistral was born, is located
in this valley.

EMIGRATION. In the 1850s a number of Chileans joined the gold
rush to California. A little later others moved into *Antofagasta
and *Tarapacá to develop the *guano and *nitrate industries.
These provinces were later incorporated into Chile as a result
of the War of the *Pacific. Chilean laborers were recruited by
Henry *Meiggs to build *railways in *Peru. Low wage rates in
Chile encouraged an emigration in the 1870s that averaged 8,000
a year.

More recently Chileans have gone to work in *Argentina, in
the *coal industry of Río Turbio and the *petroleum industry of
Comodore Rivadavia. There is also some seasonal migration of
agricultural labor into that country, and *Mapuches forced to
seek employment outside their traditional homelands have found
it in Argentine as well as in Chilean cities. The Argentine census of 1970 included 133,150 Chileans, of whom 47,700 had arrived since 1960.

But most Chilean emigration in recent years has been politically
rather than economically motivated. The greatest exodus occurred
in 1970, when Socialist Salvador *Allende Gossens became President
and an estimated one million Chileans fled abroad (see: BRAZIL,
Relations with). Emigration occurred again during the turmoil
following the *coup of September 1973, when the military began
to rule with an iron hand. Although such political exiles have
also gone to Brazil, Mexico, France (some 60,000) and elsewhere,
Argentina, as the nearest refuge, has the largest numbers, perhaps as many as 500,000. The clandestine nature of a large part
of this emigration makes assessment difficult.

EMPLEADO. A white collar employee. White collar and professional

employment (a fifth of the job market) is found chiefly in the
major cities: *Santiago, the capital; *Valparaíso, the largest port;
*Concepción, Chile's most industrial city; and *Valdivia, the site
of new manufacturing industry. There is very little social movement from lower-class to middle-class status, and even though
some skilled workers (*obreros) earn more than some empleados,
they regard their status and lifestyles as inferior. No such
sharp division separates upper-middle-class professionals from
wealthy industrialists and merchants or aristocratic landowners.

EMPLOYMENT. In 1970 Chile's labor force numbered 2.71 million
workers, including half a million women. Of these, 28 percent
were employed in *agriculture, *forestry and *fisheries; 20 percent in *manufacturing; 11 percent in commerce; 8 percent in
construction; 5 percent in *mining and quarrying; and the rest
in government service, domestic service or other occupations.
Approximately one out of every five workers was an *empleado
(white collar worker), and 8 out of 10 did not earn enough to
support a family. Among the lower segments of society, poverty
exerted an overriding influence on family structure.

Actual unemployment remained low in the 1960s and in the
early 1970s, registering a low of 20,000 during the Salvador
*Allende Gossens administration. There was however substantial
hidden underemployment.

Between 1972 and 1979 unemployment increased from 3.9 to
10.5 percent, but was much higher in the capital, where it was
estimated at 13.7 percent. With the economic collapse of the
early 1980s it increased markedly, bringing with it a worsening
poverty, leading to broken homes, illegitimate births and abandoned children. The official rate reached 19.6 percent unemployed in 1982, but attaining 21 to 25 percent in the capital.
The quality of life had deteriorated dramatically in most of the
country due to chronic unemployment and underemployment,
but the collapse of the *economy in the early 1980s made matters
considerably worse. Between 1981 and the end of 1982, 402,000
jobs were lost, and underemployment was affecting 303,000
people, or 4.5 percent of the total work force. And if the
average unemployment rate was high, for the poorest sectors
it was even higher. In 1984 outbursts of rioting and growing
street demonstrations indicated a decreasing tolerance for belt-
tightening among the poor and middle sectors of the population.

The figures for the end of 1984 show some improvement.
There were then 3,798,400 Chileans at work: 615,100 in commerce,
509,600 in agriculture, forestry or fishing, 450,700 in manufacturing 196,400 in transport and communications, 113,600 in construction, 109,600 in government, financial and commercial services, 62,800 in mining and water supply; the
remaining 1,184,500 were in "social and personal services."
Official unemployment rates ranged from 18.1 percent in Greater
*Santiago down to 6.6 percent in *Aysen. The government's
target of reducing the overall national rate of unemployment to

only 15 percent over the next few years, and to 10 percent there-after, seemed however somewhat optimistic.
See also: DEPRESSION OF THE 1930s; INTERNAL MIGRATION; LABOR.

EMPORCHI (Empresa Portuaria de Chile). The state-owned port authority, created in 1960. See: PORTS.

EMPREMAR (Empresa Marítima del Estado). A state-owned shipping line engaged in the coastal trade, where it provides about 75 percent of the passenger and general cargo service. See: MERCHANT MARINE.

EMPRESA. Literally "enterprise" or "undertaking," but the word is in common use to refer specifically to the EMPRESA DE FER-ROCARRILES DEL ESTADO, q.v.

EMPRESA DE FERROCARRILES DEL ESTADO (FF.EE.). Chilean State Railways. Some of Chile's RAILWAYS (q.v.) have been government-owned since 1863, and there has been a national state-operated system since January 4, 1884, although the 590 miles of state system at that time amounted to less than the 779 miles of private lines, and many routes in the north remained in private ownership for many years after that. The present Empresa de Ferrocarriles del Estado has been an autonomous state corporation since 1914, although always dependent on a subsidy until 1979. In 1920 the FF.EE. controlled just over half Chile's total route mileage, and by 1930 some 65 percent. By the 1970s, however, its share was almost 100 percent.
The *Red Sul still enjoys the reputation of being one of the best-run rail networks in South America. But in recent years both track and rolling stock have been poorly maintained, and repairs and upgrading are badly needed. Subsidies have been phased out in conformity with the *military regime's economic philosophy, leaving the FF.EE. to finance its operations solely from revenue. This has been achieved largely by draconian staffing cut-backs.
See also: METRO; RED NORTE; RED SUL.

EMPRESA MARITIMA DEL ESTADO (State Shipping Line). See: EMPREMAR.

EMPRESA NACIONAL DE ELECTRICIDAD, S.A. (National Electricity Undertaking, Inc.). See: ENDESA.

EMPRESA NACIONAL DE MINERIA (National Mining Corporation). See: ENAMI.

EMPRESA NACIONAL DE TELECOMUNICACIONES (National Tele-communication Undertaking). See: ENTEL.

EMPRESA NACIONAL DEL PETROLEO. See: ENAP.

EMPRESA PORTUARIA DE CHILE. See: EMPORCHI.

ENAMI (Empresa Nacional de Minería). The State Mining Enterprise, founded in 1960 to stimulate the pequeña and mediana minería (the smaller-scale enterprises in the *copper industry) by buying and refining their output of ore.

ENAP (Empresa Nacional del Petroleo). The National Petroleum Corporation, a government monopoly created in 1950 to prospect for, produce, and refine *petroleum. It is not engaged in the distribution or sale of petroleum products.

ENCINA, Francisco Antonio (1874-1965). Chile's most cherished historian, and author of the monumental Historia de Chile (Santiago, 1952). Encina, along with Diego *Barros Arana, are considered the country's greatest historians and biographers. He also wrote a comprehensive work on Chile-Bolivian relations (Las relaciones entre Chile y Bolivia, 1841-1963) and a brief history of Chile (Resumen de la historia de Chile). Other well-known works by Encina include a book on the crisis of historiography in Chile (La crisis de la literatura histórica chilena y el nuevo concepto de la historia) and a book on the Chilean economic inferiority complex (Nuestra inferioridad económica). Before dedicating himself primarily to writing, he served as a deputy in *Congress and as Chilean representative at the Pan American Congress in Buenos Aires in 1916.

ENCOMENDERO. A Spanish colonist "entrusted" with an ENCOMIENDA (q.v.).

ENCOMIENDA. A system of forced labor whereby a group of Indians was "commended" to a Spanish overlord for his meritorious services. The overlord (*encomendero) was supposedly to be the material and spiritual guardian of the Indians, and he was to collect tribute from them for providing this protection. Since most of the time the Indians could not afford to pay the royal *tithe, this obligation was transmitted into service. Encountering a stubborn resistance to work on the part of the Indians, the encomendero often turned from guardian to torturer, resorting to violence. Like the *repartimiento, the encomienda system failed in Chile because the *Araucanian Indians for over 300 years refused to be subjugated by the *conquistadores. It was abolished in 1791.

ENDESA (Empresa Nacional de Electricidad S.A.). The National Electricity Co., Inc., created with government money in 1944. The gigantic electrification program it has undertaken has remained entirely under state control, very much like the U.S. Tennessee Valley Authority. ENDESA is a subsidiary of *CORFO, the Chilean Development Corporation.

ENERGY AND POWER. Among the nations of Latin America, Chile ranks second (to Brazil) in hydroelectric power potential, having an estimated reserve of over 8,600 megawatts, with a capacity of producing more than 10,000 million kilowatt-hours (1982 estimate). Over half of the electric power capacity is in hydroelectric generators, which in 1982 supplied 80 percent of the power consumed.

Industry consumes a large percentage (about 66.7 percent) of all electricity produced, with the *copper industry alone accounting for almost 25 percent. *Mining and industrial companies operating their own generators produce almost a third of the nation's electric power. The bulk of Chile's hydroelectric output feeds the grid serving central Chile, which is where the largest cities and most of the population are located. The great length of the country limits the extension of the interconnected system, and the north and the scarcely populated far south have each their own isolated electric power systems.

In 1982 the sources of commercial energy in Chile were *petroleum (60 percent), hydroelectric power (25 percent), *coal (13 percent, and natural gas (2 percent). Chile also has substantial *uranium reserves, the exploitation of which has been left in the hands of foreign companies. The government is contemplating the construction of a nuclear power plant. Geologists agree that there exists a considerable potential for geothermal energy. These alternative energy sources are considered essential to decrease dependence on imported oil, a heavy burden on Chile's *balance of payments.

A 1982 breakdown of Chile's consumption of all types of energy revealed that the mining industry used 30 percent, other industries 20 percent, transportation 25 percent, and all other consumers, including the public services and individual households, accounted for the remaining 25 percent.

ENGLAND. See: UNITED KINGDOM.

ENRIQUEZ, Engardo. Brother of Miguel *Enríquez, he assumed the leadership of the *Movimiento de Izquierda Revolucionario (Left Revolutionary Movement: MIR) on the former's death. After operating clandestinely against the regime of Augusto *Pinochet Ugarte, he went into exile in *France, but later returned to Chile and became one of the many who disappeared in various secret police raids.

ENRIQUEZ, Miguel. University student who took over the leadership of the *Movimiento de Izquierda Revolucionario (Left Revolutionary Movement: MIR) and went underground after the 1973 *coup d'état that overthrew President (1970-73) Salvador *Allende Gossens. For a year he operated clandestinely from a house in *Santiago known as Santa Fé. Then he and his comrade Carmen *Castillo were ambushed by the *DINA in the house of José Domingo Cañas, on October 5, 1974. Enríquez was killed; Castillo, who was wounded, later went into exile in *France and wrote an account of the lives of the revolutionaries. Miguel was succeeded as MIR leader by his brother Engardo *Enríquez.

ENRIQUEZ FIODDEN, Humberto (1907-   ). Lawyer by profession and active member of the Radical Party (*Partido Radical), professor of political economy and public finances at the *Universidad de Concepción, and professor of political economy at the Law School of the *Universidad de Chile. In 1946 he became education minister in the administration (1946-52) of Gabriel *González Videla. He served in *Congress from 1949 to 1961 as a deputy, and from 1961 to 1969 as a senator. In 1965 he became president of the Radical Party.

ENRIQUEZ FIODDEN, Inés. Lawyer by profession and the first woman to be elected to the Chilean Chamber of Deputies. While a student at the *Universidad de Concepción, she had been elected president of the Women's Association. Active in the Radical Party (*Partido Radical), she became president of the party's Feminine Organization. She served in *Congress from 1951 to 1969.

ENTEL (Empresa Nacional de Telecomunicaciones S.A.). The National Telecommunication Company, a subsidiary of *CORFO, set up in 1964 to create a national telecommunication network for all electronic media. See: TELECOMMUNICATIONS.

EPOCA, La. A *Santiago daily newspaper, published November 15, 1881-January 7, 1891 and September 7, 1891-January 28, 1892. Owned by Agustín R. *Edwards Ross, and managed successively by Francisco *Valdés Vergara (1881-82), Benjamín Dávila Larraín (1882-88) and Edwardo *MacClure (1888-91), it was oriented politically to the *Partido Nacional.
    In 1986 the title was revived by Emilio *Filippi M. for a new daily he was seeking permission to publish. See also: NEWS-PAPERS.

ERCILLA. A weekly news magazine published in *Santiago since 1935. Emilio *Filippi M., who became responsible for it in the late 1960s, adapted its style to that of Time or Newsweek. When in March 1976 he was forced to relinquish control to a group of government supporters, he founded the even more outspoken Hoy. See: PERIODICAL PRESS.

ERCILLA, Editorial. Publishing firm founded in 1893, noted in the 1930s for its translations of foreign fiction. It subsequently passed into the ownership of Editorial ZIG-ZAG (q.v.). See also: PUBLISHERS AND PUBLISHING.

ERCILLA Y ZUÑIGA, Alonso de (1533-1594). A career military officer, poet and diplomat, renowned for his epic poem La *Araucana and for his participation in the Spanish wars against the *Araucanian

Indians of Chile. Coming from a noble Spanish family, Ercilla was able to obtain a good university education and to travel widely in Europe. He was in England on the occasion of the marriage of the future King *Philip II of Spain to Queen Mary I, daughter of Henry VIII by his Spanish first wife Catherine, when he heard of the civil wars in *Peru and Chile. In London he met Jerónimo de Alderete, who was embarking for the New World. The young poet decided to go along, and in 1557 he joined García *Hurtado de Mendoza on an expedition to Chile against the Araucanians. It was in the course of the war that Ercilla wrote the first and second parts of the Araucana.

At first he and Hurtado de Mendoza were friends. They were both young and had known each other in Spain. Soon, however, their relationship deteriorated, and when Ercilla drew his sword to duel in the presence of his superior, Hurtado de Mendoza, he was sentenced to death for this act of disrespect and insubordination. The sentence was later commuted. Ercilla was exiled from Chile and on his return trip to Europe he married (1570) doña María de Barzán from Panamá. It was in Spain that Ercilla was able to complete and publish La Araucana, perhaps the greatest epic poem in Spanish (1590). In 1594 the warrior-poet died in Madrid.

ERRAZURIZ ALDUNATE, Fernando (1777-1841). Councilman of the *cabildo of 1810, and deputy to the first National *Congress of 1811. He took an active part in the struggle for Chilean *independence and suffered persecution after the patriot defeat at *Rancagua in 1814. In 1823 he was a member of the *junta de gobierno provisional that succeeded Bernardo *O'Higgins. He was also a member of the convention of 1822 and was a senator for many years. In 1824 he became president of the Senate, and for the next two years he acted as president of the provincial assembly of *Santiago. He served three times as President !ad interim of the Republic: in 1824, when Supreme Director (1823-27) Ramón *Freire Serrano absented himself from the capital; in 1831, when as Vice-President he succeeded President (1830-31) José Tomás Ovalle, who had just died; and, again in 1831, when President (1831-41) Joaquín *Prieto Vial left the capital to undertake an armed campaign to secure his power as ruler of Chile. It was a period of civil strife and Freire Serrano was attempting a return from exile to assume the presidency once again. Those supporting Freire were arrested, and Errázuriz Aldunate demanded that the prisoners be tried by a military court. As acting President of Chile, Errázuriz was responsible for initiating the drafting of the new *Constitution of 1833. During that period, international relations were established with *France, and Chile's independence was recognized by the *United Kingdom.

ERRAZURIZ ECHAURREN, Federico (1850-1901). Lawyer by profession, and President of Chile, 1896-1901. He began his political career as a deputy in 1876, and in 1890 became war minister (ministro de

guerra y marina). This period in Chile was one of political instability, and cabinets were formed and dissolved in a matter of
months, or sometimes weeks. Errázuriz Echaurren became involved in the *Civil War of 1891, in which he opposed the government of President (1886-91) José Manuel *Balmaceda Fernández.
In 1894 Errázuriz Echaurren was elected a senator, and two years
later, backed by a Conservative-Liberal-National coalition, he was
elected President of Chile. A surprising contrast to the ministerial instability of the time was the relatively peaceful and normal
succession of Presidents. Errázuriz Echaurren gave amnesty to
many *Balmacedistas, and allowed the followers of the overthrown
President to form part of his cabinet. During his administration,
Errázuriz Echaurren promoted *education, establishing a school
of nursing and various commercial and technical institutes. He
undertook many public works, and was responsible for increasing
the streetcar service in *Santiago. He resigned as President on
May 1, 1901 and died on July 14 of that year.

ERRAZURIZ ERRAZURIZ, Isidoro (1835-1898). Lawyer, newspaperman
and writer. In 1858 he was imprisoned when he tried to reform
the *Constitution of 1833. He was exiled to *Argentina, but
pardoned and allowed to return, in 1861. Member of the staff of
the newspaper El *Mercurio, he founded his own paper, La Patria
(like El Mercurio, in *Valparaíso) in 1863: it lasted until 1896.
Active in politics, Errázuriz was elected deputy in 1870, 1882 and
1891. He also took part in the War of the *Pacific in 1881. In the
*Civil War of 1891 he sided with the rebel *Congress against
President (1886-91) José Manuel *Balmaceda Fernández. Two
years before, he had founded the political coalition known as the
*Cuadrilatero. With Balmaceda's defeat, Errázuriz became tempor-
ary minister of the interior (1891). In 1893 he became war minister. Three years later he became Chilean minister plenipotentiary to *Brazil.

ERRAZURIZ ZAÑARTU, Federico (1825-1877). Descendant of one of
the most aristocratic families in *Santiago, Errázuriz Zañartu was
a very active member of the Liberal Party (*Partido Liberal) and
became President of Chile for a five-year term in 1871. A lawyer
by profession, he was persecuted politically during the 1851-61
administration of conservative President Manuel *Montt Torres.
He participated in an attempt to prevent Montt from taking office
(see: CIVIL WAR OF 1859) and, as a result, was exiled to *Peru.
By 1861 Errázuriz Zañartu had returned to Chile and was elected
deputy. From 1865 to 1868 he was subrogate war minister and
in 1867 was elected senator, a position he maintained until he became President. His presidency was marked by reforms: he extended Chile's *railways, expanded the *Universidad de Chile,
beautified the streets and boulevards of the capital, and made the
Cerro Santa Lucía a national park. Errázuriz Zañartu was the
first Chilean President to have only one term of office. He amended the *Constitution of 1833 to prevent a President being reelected,

in order to insure that the ruling party would not turn the presidency into a dictatorship.

During his presidency there were fervid religious struggles regarding the abolition of clerical privileges, the separation of *Church and State, the elimination of the ecclesiastical courts, and the burial of non-Catholics in public cemeteries. All these questions were dividing factors between Liberals and Conservatives. The Liberals, although unable to secure church disestablishment, did win on some points: priests were made subject to the jurisdiction of the ordinary civil courts, and the cemeteries sectioned off parcels of land for non-Catholic burials. In the last year of his administration, Errázuriz Zañartu's economic policies experienced an inflationary crisis. The beautifying of *Santiago, under the direction of Benjamín *Vicuña Mackenna, cost the government quite a bit of money. This was the necessary price for transforming the capital from a provincial center into a modern metropolis. At the end of his term, Errázuriz Zañartu threw his support behind Aníbal *Pinto Garmendia, who was elected as the next President of Chile in 1876.

ESCOBAR CERDA, Luis. Commercial engineer and economist. He was dean of the economics faculty at the *Universidad de Chile between 1954 and 1962. On August 30, 1961 he was tapped by President (1958-64) Jorge *Alessandri Rodríguez as minister of the economy, commerce and reconstruction. Then in 1963 he became Alessandri's finance minister. As such he was responsible for raising import tariffs (see: CUSTOMS AND DUTIES). During the following administration of Christian Democrat President Eduardo *Frei Montalva, Escobar Cerda became director of the International Monetary Fund (1963-67). President Augusto *Pinochet Ugarte appointed him finance minister again, in succession to Carlos *Cáceres Contreras, on April 2, 1984. He remained in office for ten months, being replaced by Hernán *Büchi Buc on February 12, 1985.

ESCUDO. The Chilean monetary unit from January 1960 until September 1975. It was introduced to simplify accounting when depreciation of the previous unit, the *peso, had reduced its value to a tenth of one U.S. cent. The escudo was worth 1,000 of the pesos it replaced and was officially at par with the U.S. dollar. Inflation continued, however, and by 1970 the official *exchange rate had fallen to 14.30 to the dollar, and the *black market rate to 55. Immediately after the 1973 *coup d'état it was officially devalued by nearly 70 percent, and two years later the currency unit was changed again, returning to the traditional name. The new peso equalled 1,000 escudos.

Previously "escudo" had been the name of a gold coin, worth one eighth of a doubloon (doblón) in colonial times, and 2 pesos after the 1851 decimalization of the currency.

See also: COINAGE; EXCHANGE RATE; INFLATION.

ESCUELA MILITAR. The Chilean military academy in *Santiago for training cadets to become *army officers was first conceived by Bernardo *O'Higgins in 1817, but its effective foundation was in 1832, as part of *Diego Portales Palazuelos' general reorganization of the army. The Escuela Militar received credit for its contribution to Chile's success in the 1836-39 war against Andrés de *Santa Cruz. Although the school achieved a fine reputation, Portales's main objective was not to professionalize the army so much as to limit recruitment and create a homogenous officer corps representative of the Chilean landowning class. This was achieved chiefly by the severity of the entrance examination, for which only the finest *education would suffice. Chile's rapid economic growth in the 1880s eroded this strong link between the officer corps and the landowning élite, and the need to modernize training revealed by the War of the *Pacific led the Liberal government of Domingo *Santa María in 1886 to appoint the Prussian Captain Emil *Koerner Henze as director. Koerner made the school a model for all Latin America; by 1895 he had recruited 36 other German instructors. Some of these later went to Colombia, Ecuador, El Salvador and Venezuela and introduced German-style military training to those countries. *Bolivia and *Argentina obtained their own military tutors direct from *Germany. By the early 20th century, *Brazil, Mexico and *Peru were virtually alone among Latin American nations in continuing to follow French teaching and practice in their armies.

Since World War II, Germany's influence has yielded to that of the *United States. The school currently has a five-year course (three years of predominantly academic subjects, followed by two years of mainly military ones), and it accepts students from the Dominican Republic, Ecuador, El Salvador, Honduras, Paraguay and Venezuela. Each year a selected group of cadets is sent to the U.S. for more advanced military courses.

Chile has also sent students to the U.S. operated Pan American Escuela de las Américas (United States Army School of the Americas). Noted for its counter-insurgency training, this school was located in the Panama Canal Zone, 1946-85, but has now been moved to Fort Benning, Georgia.

ESCUELA NORMAL DE PRECEPTORES. The first "normal school," or school of education, in Latin America was inaugurated in Chile on June 14, 1842, two years after the first school of education was founded in the *United States. The noted Argentine writer and statesman Domingo Faustino *Sarmiento became its first director. As originally constituted, the school trained only male elementary school teachers. A similar but separate institution to train women to become elementary school teachers was set up in 1852, and a training college for secondary school teachers, the Instituto Pedagógico, came in 1889. See: EDUCATION.

ESCUELA SANTA MARIA, Matanza de la. See: SALITRERAS DE IQUIQUE.

ESMERALDA. Name of three warships. (1) The 40-gun Spanish
flagship captured by Lord *Cochrane in Callao harbor in the
early morning of November 6, 1820 and added to the Chilean
navy as the Valdivia.
(2) The sloop of war that captured the Spanish schooner
*Covadonga at the battle of *Papudo in the War with *Spain of
1865-67, and which was sunk by the Peruvian ironclad *Huascar
at the battle of *Iquique in 1879. The valiant death of the
Esmeralda's commander, Arturo *Prat Chacón made him Chile's
best known naval hero.
(3) Naval sail training ship built in 1952. Its appearance
at the U.S. Independence Day celebrations in New York harbor
in 1976 and again in 1986, provoked protests alleging that the
vessel had been used to detain and interrogate suspected *Unidad
Popular sympathizers in the aftermath of the September 1973
*coup d'état.

ESPEJO, Fundo Lo. See: MAIPU.

ESPINOZA BRAVO, Pedro. A colonel employed by the *DINA, the
Chilean secret police, as Chief of Operations. He allegedly gave
the order to Michael *Townley to plant a bomb in Washington,
D.C. under the car of Orlando *Letelier del Solar. The *United
States extradition request for Espinoza Bravo was denied by the
Chilean Supreme Court. Espinoza was believed to have operated
with the knowledge of the head of the DINA, Manuel *Sepúlveda
Contreras, and perhaps of President Augusto *Pinochet Ugarte
himself. Indicted in 1978 for having ordered Letelier's death,
Espinoza was placed under house arrest for a year and then re-
leased. He later resumed his *army career.

ESTADO, Ministerio del. The Ministry of State was created by the
*Constitution of 1818. It replaced the Secretariat of the Govern-
ment, (Secretaría del *Gobierno) and its main function was to keep
a record of all government business. In 1822 the Ministry of
State was renamed the Ministry of Government and Foreign Affairs (Ministerio de *Gobierno y Relaciones Exteriores) on incor-
porating the Department of Foreign Affairs. See: MINISTRIES.

ESTANCO. A government store where monopolized goods were sold.
Such state monopoly was established in Chile during the government (1823-26) of Ramón *Freire Serrano to alleviate the precarious economic situation of the country following the struggle
for independence (see: PUBLIC FINANCES). Estancos had however already existed in colonial times. Playing cards and dice
had been made state monopolies in the 17th century for the
moral purpose of limiting their use. In 1953 tobacco was added,
primarily to raise revenue, which, in turn, discouraged its cultivation and encouraged smuggling. The custom was extended
later to tea, liquor and other commodities such as salt. Freire
farmed out the estanco: storekeepers could receive a government

concession to sell monopolized goods. The first concessionary was the SOCIEDAD PORTALES, CEA Y CIA., q.v., a company controlled by Diego *Portales Palazuelos, who became a leading political figure in Chile as the strongman in the Conservative Party (*Pelucones), and pretty much controlled the fate of the nation for 17 years, until his assassination in 1837 (see: ESTANQUEROS). The most important estanco, that of tobacco, was finally abolished in 1880.

ESTANQUEROS. Literally, storekeeper given a government concession to sell monopolized goods, such as tobacco, tea and liquors (see: ESTANCO). In 1824 the meaning of the term was extended to embrace political supporters of Diego *Portales Palazuelos, whose objective was to establish a strong centralized government which would prevent anarchy and preserve law and order. Since most of the adherents of this group had associations with the estanco, they became known as the estanqueros. The group was never formally constituted as a political party.

ESTATUTOS DE GARANTIAS CONSTITUCIONALES. (Statutes of Constitutional Guarantees). A political amendment to the *Constitution of 1925 which provided for the following: freedom of all political parties to operate with the Chilean system of government; freedom of the press; the right of public assembly; freedom in *education; no censorship of the mail; and the professionalization of the *armed forces and the *police. A bill to enact these Statutes was sent to both houses of *Congress after the presidential election of September 4, 1970 had resulted in none of the three candidates receiving an absolute majority. Socialist Salvador *Allende Gossens had topped both Conservative Jorge *Alessandri Rodríguez and Christian Democrat Rodomiro *Tomic Romero. Allende had received 36 percent of the vote to Alessandri's 35 percent and Tomic's 28 percent. In exchange for giving Allende the votes needed for his congressional confirmation, the Christian Democrats demanded he sign the Statutes of Constitutional Guarantees after their approval by both houses. He duly signed and was declared President of Chile by a vote of 153 to 36. Allende opposed only one clause, which stated that the Chilean armed forces would take power to see that the amendment was observed to the letter. The clause was dropped.

ESTRELLA, La. Valparaíso daily newspaper, founded in 1921. See: NEWSPAPERS.

EXALTADOS. Members of a political group organized during the struggle for *independence. The exaltados, or radicals, sought to end the Spanish colonial regime and establish a federal republic. Their most notable members included Bernardo *O'Higgins, Juan *Martínez de Rozas and Manuel de *Salas Corvalan. When the first *junta de gobierno was established, the exaltados had only 12 deputies. Fear of being excluded from the junta drove them into extreme federalist and even separatist agitation which led to near anarchy in the provinces. In the first National *Congress the moderates (*moderados) were in the majority and the exaltados were defeated in their attempt to rouse the south to rebellion. José Miguel *Carrera Verdugo, who assumed the directorship of the nation in 1812, did so with the help of the exaltados who rallied around his figure when they saw a possible leader. They were, nevertheless, a minority within his government (1812-13). It seems that what Joaquín Nabuco said about the exaltados in Brazil also applies to the exaltados in Chile: "It is impossible to achieve a revolution without the radicals, and it is impossible to govern with them."

The exaltados should not be confused with the Radicals who were members of the *Partido Radical, organized in 1857.

EXCHANGE RATE. The late 18th century *peso was worth a dollar (it was the same coin!) or roughly a fifth of a pound sterling. This remained the exchange value of Chilean money until the economic difficulties of the late 1870s. Since then *inflation has been almost continuous, with particularly severe bouts from time to time and a generally increasing rate of depreciation since 1945. Until World War Two the peso's value was expressed in pence (240 to one pound sterling): we have inverted this to the more familiar pesos per ₤; for a rough conversion to pesos per $, divide by 4.8. The immediate post-World War Two period, when pesos per dollar became normal, is complicated by a multiplicity of rates. We give the free or "black" rates with the less frequently changing "official" rate in parentheses. Note the cosmetic change of unit to the *escudo in January 1960 and to the new peso in September 1975, each time eliminating three zeros.

Year	Pesos to the Pound	Year	Pesos to the Pound
1851	5.03	1875	5.48
–	–	1876	5.93
1860	5.48	1877	5.71
1861	5.18	1878	6.08
1862	5.28	1879	7.32
1863	5.53	1880	7.79
1864	5.42	1881	7.79
1865	5.22	1882	6.82
1866	5.18	1883	6.82
1867	5.24	1884	7.57
1868	5.21	1885	9.45
1869	5.38	1886	10.04
1870	5.26	1887	9.80
1871	5.22	1888	9.16
1872	5.18	1889	9.06
1873	5.36	1890	10.00
1874	5.39	1891	12.83

Year	Pesos to the Pound	Year	Pesos to the Pound
1892	12.77	1927	39.80
1893	16.00	1928	39.70
1894	19.20	1929	39.60
1895	15.00	1930	40.00
1896	13.80	1931	37.60
1897	13.64	1932	49.10
1898	13.64	1933	54.10
1899	16.55	1934	48.10
1900	14.81	1935	94.70
1901	15.12	1936	96.20
1902	15.80	1937	95.30
1903	14.44	1938	94.30
1904	14.66	1939	84.90
1905	15.61		
1906	16.70	Year	Pesos per $
1907	18.82	1940	31.05 (19.37)
1908	24.94	1941	32.28
1909	22.33	1942	30.98
1910	22.33	1943	33.66
1911	22.59	1944	31.45
1912	23.70	1945	32.05
1913	24.62	1946	34.43
1914	26.97	1947	47.15
1915	29.27	1948	66.00
1916	25.26	1949	99.00
1917	18.90	1950	89.88 (31.00)
1918	14.04	1951	85.43
1919	22.64	1952	123.87
1920	19.83	1953	218.00 (Oct. 110.00)
1921	32.88	1954	315.00
1922	36.36	1955	680.00
1923	36.92	1956	601.00
1924	41.38	1957	785.00
1925	40.68	1958	1,120.00
1926	39.80	1959	1,056.00

Year	Escudos per $	
1960	1.10	(1.00)
1961	1.20	(1.05)
1962	2.40	(Oct. 1.29)
1963	3.10	(from 1.74 in Jan to 2.09 in Dec)
1964	4.50	(from 2.24 in Jan to 2.64 in Dec)
1965	6.10	(from 2.84 in Jan to 3.45 in Dec)
1966	6.60	(from 3.51 in Jan to 4.36 in Dec)
1967	10.00	(from 4.43 in Jan to 5.76 in Dec)
1968	16.30	(from 5.91 in Jan to 7.57 in Dec)
1969	14.90	(from 7.73 in Jan to 9.92 in Dec)

Year	Escudos per $	
1970	28.00	(Aug. 12.21)
1971	74.70	
1972	340.00	(Sep. 25.00)
1973	790.00	(Jun. 65.00; Aug 74.00; Oct 280.00; Dec. 343.00)
1974	2,010.00	(from 371 in Jan to 1,619 in Dec.)
1975	6,400.00	(Jan. 1,870; Apr 3,800; June 4,000)

Year	New pesos per $	
1975	8.90	(Sep. 8.25)
1976	19.00	(from 9.19 in Jan to 17.03 in Dec.)
1977	28.30	(from 17.96 in Jan to 27.59 in Dec)
1978	34.80	(from 28.35 in Jan to 33.84 in Dec)
1979	41.00	(July 39.00)
1980	39.00	
1981	38.90	
1982	73.43	(Jun. 46.00)
1983	80.19	(May 76.00; Dec. 87.00)
1984	115.00	(Jun. 91.00)
1985		
Jan.	133.00	(128.30)
Jun.	184.00	(154.20)
Dec.	207.00	(182.10)

EXCHEQUER. See: HACIENDA, Ministerio de.

EXECUTIVE, The. See: CHILE--H. Government: (1) The Executive; See also: AUTORIDAD EJECUTIVA; COLONIAL ADMINISTRATION; CONSEJO DIRECTORIAL; CONSTITUTION;. GOVERNORS OF CHILE; JUNTA; PRESIDENTS OF CHILE; SUPREME DIRECTOR.

EXOTICA. A new *copper mine, located just south of *Chuquicamata, and part of what is known as the *Gran Minería. With another new mine, *Andina, it increased Chile's total copper production by 2 percent in the late 1970s and early 1980s, ranking Chile with the U.S.S.R. as one of the world's two top copper producers. The ores at Exótica proved, however, to be more complex chemically than anticipated, with consequently higher production costs. As a result, Exótica has been shut down periodically. Despite this, Chilean copper production went above one million metric *tons in 1976, for the first time in history. In the 1980s, with Exótica and Andina both working, that level of production has been maintained.

EXPORTS. See: FOREIGN TRADE.

EYZAGUIRRE ARECHEVALA, Agustín (1768-1837). Statesman active in the revolutionary struggle for Chilean independence. A moderate (*moderado), he was a deputy in the *Congresses of 1811 and 1825. In 1814 he formed part of the *Junta de gobierno

of 1813, which sought complete independence. Elected senator
in 1818, he was president of the Senate from 1823 to 1824. In
1823 he once again formed part of the governing junta (see:
JUNTA DE GOBIERNO PROVISIONAL). When President (1826)
Manuel *Blanco Encalada resigned, Eyzaguirre became provisional
President of Chile, a post he filled until February 1827. His
government had all sorts of difficulties, especially with the rebellious provinces in the south. In finance, there was total
chaos. With no money in the treasury, Eyzaguirre tried to sell
*church-owned property, but this plan failed. Soldiers did not
get paid, nor deputies receive their salaries. This caused trouble
with both the *army and the politicians. In 1827, after a troubled
year in office, Eyzaguirre was deposed and Congress named
Ramón *Freire Serrano as President.

- F -

F.F.E.E. (Ferrocarriles del Estado). The Chilean State Railways.
    See: EMPRESA DE FERROCARRILES DEL ESTADO.

FABRICA Y MAESTRANZA DEL EJERCITO. See: FAMAE.

FACh (Fuerzas Aereas de Chile). The Chilean Air Force. See:
    AIR FORCE.

FALANGE (Phalanx). Name adopted by the young radicals of the
    Conservative Party (*Partido Conservador) in 1935. It was
    originally the FALANGE CONSERVADORA (q.v.), but was changed
    to FALANGE NACIONAL (q.v.) when the new group split com-
    pletely from the Conservative Party to become a party in its own
    right. Chileans insist that there was no connection with Primo
    de Rivera's Falange, formed in Spain in 1933. As Francisco Fran-
    co in 1937, during the Spanish Civil War, made a (compulsorily)
    enlarged Falange into an umbrella group to embrace all parties
    supporting the Nationalist cause, such disclaimer of any association
    is understandable. It does, however, seem a strange coincidence
    that two groups of radical anti-capitalist, Catholic conservatives
    in Hispanic countries should have alighted upon the same term
    within two years of each other.

FALANGE CONSERVADORA. A successor organization to the *Juven-
    tud Conservadora, formed in 1935 by Bernardo *Leighton Guzmán.
    Although it supported President Arturo *Alessandri Palma, it
    became increasingly restive at his reactionary policies and auto-
    cratic style, and in April 1938 Leighton resigned as minister of
    labor in protest at Alessandri's suppression of the satirical
    magazine Topaze. When its efforts to have moderate Liberal
    Jorge Matte adopted as the rightist candidate in the 1938 presi-

dential elections failed, the Falange announced that it would back the candidate chosen instead, Gustavo *Ross Santa María, but "without enthusiasm or ideological support." Following his defeat the Falange decided to support the new *Frente Popular president, broke all ties with the Conservatives and changed its name to *Falange Nacional.

FALANGE NACIONAL. A center party formed in November 1938 from the *Falange Conservadora. Its leaders were young idealists who wished to replace traditional conservatism with the social Christianity of the papal encyclicals Rerum novarum and Quadragesimo anno. In 1938 it had 6 deputies, and with the *Nacistas and the other centrist parties, held the balance between the 67 deputies of the right and the 65 of the *Frente Popular. In 1941 it secured only three deputies, in 1945 four, and in 1949 three deputies and a senator, but in 1957 it achieved 14 deputies and a senator. In July 1957 the Falange Nacional was dissolved to form, in alliance with the *Partido Conservador Social Cristiano, the new *Partido Demócrata Cristiano, the Christian Democrats. See also: FEDERACION SOCIAL CRISTIANA.

FALANGE RADICAL AGRARIA SOCIALISTA. Political combination, organized in 1948, of the *Falange Nacional, the Agrarian Labor Party (*Partido Agrario Laborista) and the Radical Democrats (*Partido Radical Democrático). Its main purpose was to oppose the government of President (1946-52) Gabriel *González Videla, who had been elected with the help of the Communists (*Partido Comunista Chileno). In 1949 the Falange Radical Agraria Socialista was dissolved into the various parties that had originally formed it.

FAMAE (Fabrica y Maestranza del Ejército). The military arsenal and ordinance factory of the Chilean army. See: ARMAMENTS.

FANEGA. A traditional Spanish measure of both land area and capacity. As the former it equals 6,460 m^2 (0.646 hectares) or 1.59 acres. As the latter it equals 55.5 liters: 1.575 US bushels or 1.526 imperial bushels. See: WEIGHTS AND MEASURES.

FARALLONES. A ski resort just outside of *Santiago.

FARMING. See: AGRICULTURE.

FATHERLAND AND COUNTRY. See: PATRIA Y LIBERTAD.

FAUNA. See: CHILE--F. Flora and fauna.

FECh (Federación de Estudiantes de Chile). Federation of Students of Chile. The older of the two leading student organizations in Chile (the other is *UFUCh). FECh was founded in 1906 as a protest movement. Its primary function was to unite local groups within the *Universidad de Chile. Its members today include both undergraduate and graduate students in the various professional schools. Since 1962, FECh has been largely dominated by young members of the Christian Democratic Party (*Partido Demócrata Cristiano). With the election of Socialist President Salvador *Allende Gossens, many members of the FECh struggled to retain student government control of the university, at times confronting students belonging to *Unidad Popular, the leftist coalition of parties that supported Allende. Towards the end of the Allende presidency, students from FECh became militantly anti-Allende, joining the posture of the Christian Democratic Party and other parties of the right that wanted Allende impeached. After the *coup d'état of September 1973, the *military regime's *intervención in the universities emasculated all student organizations as part of the *junta's attempt to depoliticize education. See also: EDUCATION.

FEDERACION CHILENA DE INSTITUCIONES FEMENINAS. See: FIGUEROA GAJARGO, Ana.

FEDERACION DE ESTUDIANTES DE CHILE. See: FECh.

FEDERACION DE IZQUIERDA. A political combination of several leftist groups formed on April 23, 1932, after the fall of President (1927-31) Carlos *Ibáñez del Campo and the defeat of the centrist candidate, Arturo *Alessandri Palma, in the presidential election of September 1931. The Federación drew its support mainly from the left wing of the Democratic Liberals (*Partido Liberal Democrático Aliancista) and the Republican Socialists (*Partido Socialista Republicano). The aim was to oppose the government of President Juan Esteban *Montero Rodríguez, and Alessandri was elected as spokesman. When he renounced this role (May 9, 1932), the Federación dissolved, after barely one month of existence.

FEDERACION NACIONAL POPULAR. A political coalition of various minor parties of the right and center, including the *Partido Nacional Agrario, the Movimiento Nacional Independiente, the *Movimiento Nacional del Pueblo, the *Partido Radical Doctrinario, among others. Founded in January 1956, the Popular National Federation's doctrine was to withdraw from the class struggle advocated by the left and follow a middle-of-the-road course. It dissolved after a few months, whereupon the Partido Nacional Agrario and the Movimiento Nacional Independiente merged with the *Partido Agrario Laborista Recuperacionista to form the *Partido Nacional.

FEDERACION OBRERA DE CHILE (FOCh). The Labor Federation of Chile, a *trade union formed in 1909—originally as the *Gran Federación Obrera de Chile—by Luis Emilio *Recabarren Serrano to represent the interests of *railway workers. In 1916 FOCh

broadened its base to represent the interests of the entire
Chilean working class. In 1921 it adhered to the principles of
the Third (Communist) International, founded by Lenin in 1919
to replace the defunct Second International Workingmen's Association and end the suppression and exploitation of the working
class. FOCH's ideology included belief in a class struggle that
would culminate in the fall of capitalism and the establishment
of an organization of society in which industry, capital and land
would be owned and controlled by the community as a whole. By
1924 FOCh had a membership of 140,000. In 1931 it was outlawed
by rightist President (1927-31) Carlos *Ibáñez del Campo.

FEDERACION SOCIAL CRISTIANA. A political coalition formed in
1955 to unite the National Phalanx (FALANGE NACIONAL, q.v.),
the *Partido Conservador Social Cristiano and a dissident group
of the *Partido Nacional Cristiano--all of them originally offshoots
of the *Partido Conservador (PC) and dissatisfied with the PC's
lukewarm endorsement of the *Church's social teaching. In 1957
the members of the Federación merged to form the Christian Democratic Party (PARTIDO DEMOCRATA CRISTIANO, q.v.), although
some Partido Conservador Social Cristiano members, including
Eduardo *Cruz Coke Lassabe, stayed out of the new party, as-
sociating themselves instead with the rump of the Partido Nacional
Cristiano as the *Partido Social Cristiano.

FEDERALISM (Federalismo). A system of government whereby a union
of *provinces or states is created, with each member state dele-
gating powers to a central authority. In order to oppose the
authoritarian rule of Supreme Director (1817-23) Bernardo
*O'Higgins, Chile was made a federal republic in 1826. As early
as 1822 the provinces had rebelled against O'Higgins. Revolts
broke out in *Concepción (in the south), in La *Serena (in the
north), and he even faced opposition in the province of *Santiago.
In 1823 O'Higgins resigned and went into exile in *Peru. The
South proclaimed its *intendant, General Ramón *Freire Serrano,
as *caudillo, and Freire ruled Chile until 1826, proclaiming it a
federal republic on the model of the *United States of America.
Chile was divided into eight *provinces, with each province to
establish a provincial assembly and elect a governor by popular
vote. The experiment lasted barely a year, being definitively
repudiated in the unitary *Constitution of 1828.

FEDERALISTA. An adherent of *federalism. See: PARTIDO FEDERAL-
ISTA.

FEDERICO SANTA MARIA TECHNICAL UNIVERSITY. See: UNIVERSI-
DAD TECNICA FEDERICO SANTA MARIA.

FELIPE. For Spanish kings so named, see the English form, PHILIP.

FELIU CRUZ, Guillermo (b. 1900). Historian. Became curator of the

Museo Histórico in 1921, and editor of the Revista chilena in 1922. In 1925, at the suggestion of José Toribio *Medina Zavala, he was taken onto the staff of the *National Library of Chile, of which he became director, 1960-66.

FEMALE SUFFRAGE. See: SUFFRAGE; WOMEN AND THE WOMEN'S MOVEMENT.

FERDINAND VI (1713-1759). King of Spain (as Fernando VI), 1746-59. He authorized the construction of a Chilean mint (the Casa de La *Moneda) so that his is the first head to have appeared on Chilean *coinage. He also gave approval to the Real *Universidad de San Felipe, and the city of *San Fernando (founded 1742) was named in his honor.

FERDINAND VII (1784-1833). Last Spanish king to exercise authority in Chile (as Fernando VII). He succeeded his father Charles IV in 1808 but was forced by Napoleon to abdicate in favor of the latter's brother Joseph and remained in enforced exile in *France until 1814. Patriots throughout Spain and its empire who repudiated the authority of Joseph's puppet regime did so in the name of Ferdinand. Only after his restauration and his immediate repudiation of all the liberal reforms of the *Cortés of Cádiz, did it become obvious that continued allegiance to the Spanish crown would be quite incompatible with any degree of autonomy for Hispanic America. Chile formally declared itself a republic on February 12, 1818, almost seven years after de facto independence had been secured with the opening of the first National *Congress, July 4, 1811 (See: INDEPENDENCIA, Declaración de).

FERNANDEZ ALBANO, Elías (1845-1910). A lawyer by profession since 1869, Fernández Albano entered *Congress as a deputy in 1884, beginning a long and distinguished political career. For ten years he directed the Mortgage Bank (Caja de Crédito Hipotecario; see: BANKS, BANKING AND FINANCIAL INSTITUTIONS). He was named Minister of the Interior--equivalent to the office of vice-president in the United States--in the cabinet of President (1896-1901) Federico *Errázuriz Echaurren, and again in that of President (1906-10) Pedro *Montt Montt. On both occasions he became acting President of Chile. The first time, in 1900, was during a three-month absence of Errázuriz; the second time was in 1910 when Montt went on a trip to Europe and died there. Fernández Albano died in office as acting President.

FERNANDEZ LARIOS, Armando (1949-). An *army captain serving in the Chilean secret police, the *DINA. From orders delivered to him by DINA's director, Manuel *Sepúlveda Contreras--some say from President Augusto *Pinochet Ugarte himself--Fernández was sent to Washington, D.C., under an assumed name, to murder Orlando *Letelier del Solar. Letelier had been Chilean ambassador to the *United States under President Salvador *Allende Gossens, and was now feared as the leader of the Chilean opposition in exile, working for the overthrow of the *junta government. Fernández, with the aid of DINA agent Michael *Townley and some Cuban exiles belonging to the *Cuban Nationalist Movement's *Omega 7, set the preliminary stage for the assassination. In 1978 Fernández was placed under house arrest in Chile for a year and then released. He resumed his army career.

FERNANDEZ LARRAIN, Sergio (b. 1901). Lawyer by profession, and active member of the Conservative Party (*Partido Conservador). He sat in *Congress as a deputy 1937-57. He became known for his repressive measures against Chilean *Communism, and he was one of the members of Congress who urged President (1946-52) Gabriel *González Videla to outlaw the Communist Party (*Partido Comunista Chileno). As a result, Fernández Larraín became a member of the executive council (junta) of his party. From 1959 to 1962 he represented the government of President (1958-64) Jorge *Alessandri Rodríguez as its ambassador to *Spain.

FERNANDO. For Spanish kings of this name, see the English form, FERDINAND.

FERROCARRIL, El. *Santiago daily newspaper founded by Juan Pablo Urzúa in December 1855 and owned for a while by Domingo Faustino *Sarmiento's father-in-law Jules Belín (1829-1863). For most of its life the leading Chilean newspaper, it attained in 1894 a circulation of 14,000 (and 17,000 for its Sunday edition) compared with the Valparaiso El *Mercurio's 12,000. It was unable however to meet the challenge of a Santiago edition of El Mercurio (established in 1900), and El Ferrocarril ceased in 1911. See: NEWSPAPERS; PUBLISHERS AND PUBLISHING.

FERROCARRILES DEL ESTADO. See: EMPRESA DE FERROCARRILES DEL ESTADO.

FIGUEROA CARAVACA, Tomás de. Leader of the MUTINY OF FIGUEROA, q.v.

FIGUEROA GAJARGO, Ana (1907-). Promoter of universal suffrage. Born in *Santiago and educated at the *Universidad de Chile and Columbia University, she became a professor of English in 1928, and general inspector of secondary *education in 1946. One of the most active women in Chile in the promotion of universal adult suffrage, in 1948 she became president of the Chilean Federation of Women's Institutions (Federación Chilena de Instituciones Femeninas). Among other things, the Federation promoted and obtained voting rights for *women. These were granted in local *elections in 1934, but only enacted in respect to national elections in December 1948. Between 1950 and 1952 Ana Figueroa was Chilean minister plenipotentiary to the Third General Assembly

of the *United Nations; delegate to the Commission on Human
Rights; president of the Social, Cultural and Humanitarian Commission; and the first woman on the U.N.'s Security Council and
Disarmament Committee. From then until 1959 she held many other
important posts at the U.N.; she was, for example, the representative there for refugees from all over the world.

FIGUEROA LARRAIN, Emiliano (1866-1931). Lawyer by profession
and active member of the Liberal Democratic Party (*Partido
Liberal Democrático). He was named acting President of Chile
in 1910, on the death of acting President (1910) Elías *Fernández
Albano, and was President (1925-27) after Arturo *Alessandri
Palma renounced the office in 1925. As President, Figueroa named
Carlos *Ibáñez del Campo as his minister of war, the first important post held by Ibáñez on his way to the presidency. After
two hectic years in office, Figueroa resigned, and in May 1927
Ibáñez emerged as head of the government. In 1928, as envoy
to Peru, Figueroa negotiated the Treaty of *Lima.

FILIPPI M., Emilio. Publisher of the news magazines ERCILLA
(q.v.) and HOY (q.v.). In 1986 he was seeking permission to
launch a new newspaper, La *EPOCA (q.v.).

FINANCE MINISTRY. See: HACIENDA, Ministerio de.

FISHERIES. Chile's fish production has grown considerably in the
last three decades, making Chile one of the top ten fishing
nations in the world, and second only to *Peru in Latin America.
The total catch in 1950 was 57,000 metric *tons; in 1960 it was
over 300,000 tonnes. Exports of fish products expanded sharply
during the 1970s, with 1976 seeing the record fish catch of over
1.3 million tonnes. Nevertheless, in the early 1980s, fishing and
fish canning contributed only about 3 percent of the gross domestic product and employed less than 1 percent of the labor force.
    Approximately one third of the total catch is whiting, with
anchovies and sardines comprising most of the other two thirds.
Other commercially important fish are haddock, herring, lobster,
oysters, krill, swordfish and tuna. Most of the fish caught are
sold fresh for domestic consumption. There are some 60 fish
canneries with a total of 4,000 employees, and Chile has over
10,000 fishermen. The fast-growing fish-meal industry produced
470,000 tonnes of fish meal and fish oil in 1979; exports of fish
products for the same year were valued at US$ 193 million dollars.
    Fish production was up in 1982, reaching record levels; some
650,000 tonnes of fishmeal were exported (against 455,812 tonnes
in 1981), together with 90,000 tonnes of fish oil (against 77,000
tonnes in 1981).
    Chile (like Peru and Ecuador) claims exclusive fishing rights
in her rich coastal waters up to 200 miles offshore; foreign vessels may only fish these waters with an official permit (see: LAW
OF THE SEA). The Chilean fishing industry has a great potential

for growth, with the bulk of fishing being undertaken off the coast of the northern third of the country and in the waters of *Antarctica.

The fishing fleet in 1975 numbered 275 vessels and 6,300 small fishing boats.

See also: HUMBOLDT CURRENT; WHALING.

FITZROY, Robert (1805-1865). English hydrographer. Entering the British Navy from the Royal Naval College in 1819, he was appointed to the South American station in August 1828, taking command of the 240-ton brig *Beagle on the death of Commander Pringle Stokes, November 13, 1828. He assisted Philip Parker *King in surveying the coasts of Argentina and southern Chile, returning to England in 1830, but setting out again on what was to be a circumnavigation on December 27, 1831, during which he and King ran a chronometric line around the world. He entered Parliament in 1842, served as governor of New Zealand 1843-45, became a vice-admiral in 1863 and committed suicide as a result of overwork as head of the Board of Trade's Meteorological Department in April 1865.

FLAG, National. Chile's national flag consists of two horizontal bands, the upper one white, the lower one red, with a white star on a blue square in the upper corner next to the staff and comprising one sixth of the whole flag. The star represents the unitary republic; the red, the blood shed in the fight for independence; the blue, the purity of the Chilean sky; and the white, the snow of the *Andes. The current flag was designed by Minister José Ignacio Centeno and came into use in 1817. It thus predates the rather similar state flag of Texas, which differs in having the blue area occupy the whole height of the flag next to the staff.

There had been two earlier Chilean flags. The first, hoisted by José Miguel *Carrera Verdugo on July 4, 1812, consisted of three horizontal bands: blue above, white in the middle, and yellow beneath. The second, hoisted by Bernardo *O'Higgins in May 1817, replaced the yellow band with a red one.

FLECHA ROJA, La. A political magazine, organ of the Christian Democrats (*Partido Demócrata Cristiano), published irregularly from August 1971 until the *coup d'état of September 11, 1973.

FLORA. See: CHILE--F. Flora and fauna.

FOCh. See: FEDERACION OBRERA DE CHILE.

FOMENTO, Ministerio de. The Ministry of Development was created by Statute no. 7912 on September 29, 1927 and included the departments of *agriculture, *industry, settlement, public works, commerce and communications. In 1930 the Department of Agriculture became a Secretariat and was separated from the Development Ministry, becoming the Ministerio de *Agricultura in August 1930. Later the same month, public works also became a separate ministry, the Ministerio de *Obras Públicas, but in this case the separation was only temporary: public works again became part of the Development Ministry exactly one year later. In August 1942 the ministry was reformed, dropping the designation "development," to become the Ministerio de *Obras Públicas y Vías de Comunicación.

FOREIGN AFFAIRS, Ministry of. See: RELACIONES EXTERIORES, Ministerio de.

FOREIGN AID. In the present century, Chile has depended on foreign aid for its economic development. Loans and grants to Chile under the Alliance for Progress reached a total of US$ 350 million as of June 1964. While it is difficult to distinguish accurately the uses to which all funds were applied, at least the following amounts were authorized in the areas indicated:

*Education	US$	5,300,000
*Housing		9,000,000
Business and *industry		46,000,000
Sanitation and drinking water		11,000,000
*Agriculture		17,000,000
Infrastructure		87,000,000
Currency stabilization		120,000,000

International agencies that have been active in Chile include the U.S. Agency for International Development (USAID), the Inter-American Development Bank (IDB), the Export-Import Bank of Washington, D.C. (Eximbank), and the Development Loan Fund (DLF). Important USAID projects of the late 1960s included the building of 23 primary schools, financing health clinics, and building *port facilities at San Vicente. IDB projects included loans to farm credit, irrigation projects, low-income housing, college facilities, improvements to city water supplies, and equipment for a *petroleum refinery at *Concepción. Eximbank loans provided for steel mill equipment at *Huachipato, and machinery for industrial development. The DFL loan projects included a savings bank system and the new *Santiago city airport at *Pudahuel (now called Arturo *Merino Benítez). These agencies also supported numerous infrastructure projects.

In 1961 Chile was among the first nations in Latin America to request Peace Corps volunteers. Peace Corps projects, through the Alliance for Progress, have dealt with rural education and urban planning, but they were also marred by scandal (see: PROJECT CAMELOT). For the decade 1960-70, Chile received two thirds of all U.S. development assistance. *United States aid to Chile was, however, reduced drastically during the period 1970-73 when Chile was governed by the first elected socialist president in the Western Hemisphere, Salvador *Allende Gossens. Allende was aware of the vital importance of loans from the

United States and other nations, and he actively sought their
economic support. But the U.S. refused to cooperate, because of
Allende's outright expropriation of the *copper industry. As a
result, Chile was paying over ten times more in servicing past
loans from the World Bank, the Interdevelopment and Reconstruction Bank, Eximbank and USAID than it was receiving in new
loans, which by mid-1973 had fallen to about US$ 30 million.

Prior to Allende's election, the World Bank had loaned Chile
US$ 235 million. On the day of his election, all World Bank loans
were canceled, despite the fact that the Bank was sponsoring the
second stage of a cattle breeding program started under the administration of Eduardo *Frei Montalva, and an ongoing electrification program that it had actively supported for twenty years.
The IDB's boycott of Chile allowed for only two exceptions, as
the Nixon administration put pressure on international lending
institutions to undermine the Chilean *economy: (1) it granted
a US$ 7 million loan to the *Universidad Católica; and (2) it
granted a US$ 4.6 million loan to the *Universidad Austral; both
strongholds of anti-Allende activities. Meanwhile, Boeing refused to sell new planes to *LAN-Chile, despite the company's
impeccable credit record with Boeing.

In November 1971, after the economic squeeze by the United
States, Allende placed a moratorium on the repayment of most
debts (that to the U.S. was US$ 2,300 million, but by the time
of the *coup it had risen to US$ 4,000 million). In February 1973,
Allende turned to the *U.S.S.R. for aid. But the Soviet Union
was not pleased with Allende's economic policies, disapproving in
particular his wage increases to the lowest paid workers, and it
told him plainly that it would not loan Chile another US$ 500
million as it had done in 1972. Although China, Romania, Finland,
Spain, Czechoslovakia, Canada, West Germany, Sweden, *Argentina, and even *Bolivia granted Chile some US$ 200 million in
credits during the period January-September 1973, and in Paris
the ten European nation members of the *Paris Club renegotiated
their Chilean loans, Allende was not able to obtain enough hard
currency to counteract the adverse change in the country's international terms of trade.

In the months following the overthrow of Allende, there was
a turnaround in the availability of loans from the World Bank,
the IMF and private U.S. banks as the virulently anti-Marxist
*junta moved quickly to regain their confidence. Foreign aid
began once more to play an important role in Chile's economic
development, helping create the economic boom that peaked in
1979-80. Foreign projections soon proved wrong, however.
From 1982 imports soared while exports remained constant, creating
a huge *balance of payments deficit, which led in turn to another
severe curtailment of foreign aid. See also: PUBLIC FINANCES;
BANKS, BANKING AND FINANCIAL INSTITUTIONS--B. The collapse of 1981-84.

Another type of foreign aid is that channeled through private
institutions. See for instance: CHURCH--The Modern-day Church.

FOREIGN DEBT. See: BALANCE OF PAYMENTS; PUBLIC FINANCES.

FOREIGN INVESTMENTS. Foreign investment in Chile has been made
mainly by the *United Kingdom and the *United States. In 1970
the total was approximately US$ 1,000 million. British investments,
which had reached a peak of US$ 410 million in 1940, had de-
clined to about a fourth of that amount. U.S. investments, on
the other hand, steadily increased in the 1970s and early 1980s
(except for the 1970-73 period when Salvador *Allende Gossens
was President). There was, however, a sharp decline in U.S.
investment in 1983 and 1984, with the downturn in the Chilean
*economy.

   In 1974 a new Foreign Investment Statute, Decree no. 600,
was introduced to stimulate the inflow of capital and technology
by guaranteeing that foreign investors would receive the same
treatment as Chilean investors, including unrestricted remission
of profits. In contrast to the controlled investment policies of
the Allende government, the *Junta provided many incentives
and guarantees to foreign direct private investment, in recognition
of the medium- and long-term need for substantial capital inflow
to supplement domestic saving and help with the external debt.
When Chile withdrew from the Andean Pact (*Pact Andino) in
October 1976, Decree 600 was rewritten to make investments in
Chile even more attractive. Under the new statute, only investments in excess of US$ 5 million needed the approval of the
Foreign Investment Committee; the only limit on capital repatria-
tion was that it could not begin until three years after its entry.
Foreign investment in Chile soared, to reach a high of US$
2,500 million in 1982. Then, with the beginning of an economic
collapse in Chile, they started to dry up.

   In 1984, as the recession deepened and the financial viability
of both the banks and the large conglomerates was thrown into
question, foreign capital inflows fell sharply. After a nine-year
experiment, the *Chicago Boys' model appeared to have failed,
leading to a loss of confidence on the part of investors both at
home and abroad. In 1982 only US$ 1,200 million entered the
country, less than a third of that received in 1981 (US$ 3,900
million). With the days of easy credit now over, Chile found
she needed US$ 3,500 million just to service her debt. This in
itself increased the apprehensions of foreign investors, who
looked for sounder markets elsewhere in Latin America and in
Asia.

   The government of Augusto *Pinochet Ugarte responded by
firing Finance Minister Sergio de *Castro Spikula, demonstrating
its abandonment of the Chicago model and its desire to restore
Chile's attractiveness to foreign investors by adopting new economic policies. Today, any firm wishing to invest in Chile must
obtain clearance from the office of the President of Chile through
the Committee on Foreign Investment of the Ministry of the
Economy. Arrangements with individual companies specify what
privileges and encouragements to invest will be accorded.

In establishing plants for the processing of Chilean raw materials, foreign investors may bring in capital equipment free of *customs and duties. The government guarantees the applicable *taxes will not be collected discriminately to the exclusive detriment of the foreign firm. Taxes may, of course, be increased for all foreign and domestic producers of given products. Depreciation allowances are provided, and the government may grant the right to re-export capital. Profits and interest on investment may be remitted abroad.

FOREIGN RELATIONS. Prior to September 11, 1973, Chile was one of the few genuinely democratic nations of Latin America. On that day, the *armed forces overthrew the government of socialist Salvador *Allende Gossens, imposing a rigid dictatorial rule that has lasted to date. Like so many other aspects of Chilean life, Chile's relations with the international community were profoundly changed by the *coup. Until Allende's election in 1970, Chile had been staunchly pro-Western, while adhering at the same time to the doctrine of non-intervention. Although Chile was a member of the *Organization of American States (OAS), it initially opposed the OAS move to impose sanctions against Cuba, however it later broke off diplomatic and trade relations. President (1964-70) Eduardo *Frei Montalva restored diplomatic relations with the *U.S.S.R. which had been severed in 1948 owing to disruptive Communist activities in Chile. Allende restored relations with Cuba, and for the first time since 1949 resumed diplomatic relations with China.

Until Allende's overthrow, Chile's relations with other nations had been for the most part friendly and cordial. There had been a tradition of friendship with the *United States, helped in recent decades by the Good Neighbor Policy, World War II cooperation and the Alliance for Progress. This changed in 1970 when Allende nationalized the *copper industry. The U.S. reaction to this, and to Allende himself, was overtly cool (see: UNITED STATES, Relations with).

Chile's friendship with the *United Kingdom was of long standing. The Scottish sailor Thomas *Cochrane had helped found the Chilean *navy. Most vessels in the navy in 1970 were British made. British naval missions had also helped train officers in the Chilean navy prior to the *coup d'état. Trade between the two nations had been substantial before World War II but came to a halt in 1975 when the British broke off diplomatic relations with Augusto *Pinochet Ugarte's regime. While both countries have claimed identical portions of *Antarctica, this never has become a serious problem. When Chile's boundary dispute with *Argentina threatened to lead to war in 1902, the quarrel was arbitrated by King Edward VII. (See: UNITED KINGDOM, Relations with).

Despite the obvious historical ties, Chile's relations with *Spain have been less than fully cordial. Most of the original Spanish settlers of Chile were independent-minded *Basques. After the Spanish Civil War (1936-39) there was a significant emigration of

Republican refugees to Chile, and most Chileans were unhappy with the Franco regime. Pinochet had good relations with Generalísimo Francisco Franco until the latter's death in 1975. Spain has continued to trade with Chile, but relations have been cool since the return to democracy under King Juan Carlos and the advent of a socialist government in Madrid (see: SPAIN, Relations with).

Germans have had somewhat the same influence upon Chile's *army as the British have had upon the navy. Prior to World War II, there was substantial trade between Chile and *Germany, though this commerce has not regained its prewar eminence (see: GERMANY, Relations with). Chile has retained a small but vocal Nazi movement (see: NACISTA). After World War II, some Nazi war criminals settled in Chile, especially in the south and in the city of *Puerto Montt (see, for example: RAUFF, Walter).

Chile's relations with other nations of Western Europe have usually been friendly, although they cooled in 1973 when the military came to power, a fact that has caused particular difficulty in arms procurement (see: ARMAMENTS; FRANCE, Relations with).

Relations with Czechoslovakia, Hungary, Poland, Rumania and Yugoslavia were broken off, along with those with the U.S.S.R., by President (1946-52) Gabriel *González Videla in 1948, but were restored by President Frei. Relaitons with the eastern European countries were cordial under Allende, but since his fall relations have been severed again, except in the case of Rumania. The embassy of the Chinese People's Republic was also allowed to remain. (See: U.S.S.R., Relations with.)

Within South America, Chile has had a tradition of good relations with all its neighbors except three: *Argentina, *Bolivia and *Peru. With regard to Argentina, Chile feels less than fully amicable. Chileans distrust Argentine nationalism and fear economic domination by their larger neighbor. Since the early 1900s, however, border disputes have been settled by arbitration (see: ARGENTINA, Relations with). Chile's relations with Peru and Bolivia, exacerbated by the War of the *Pacific, have moved towards normality, although Chile does not have deep ties with either nation. Both diverge from Chile in geography and political development. After belated negotiations following the war, which dragged on until 1929, Peru recovered *Tacna, Chile was confirmed in possession of *Arica, and Bolivia, the weakest of the three, got the consolation prize: the use of *Antofagasta as a free port, and the construction of a *railway from *Arica to La Paz. It remains, understandably, dissatisfied, and in 1982 once again broke off relations. See: BOLIVIA, Relations with; PERU, Relations with.

The state of Chile's relations with the other Latin American nations, like those with the rest of the world, correlate strongly with political affinity. In the 1960s they were especially cordial with Uruguay, Venezuela, Mexico and, until the March 1964 military takeover, with *Brazil. With the fall of Allende, relations with

Brazil and Uruguay (both by then with military regimes) became warm, but those with democratic Venezuela cooled off considerably, and those with Cuba were broken off. Mexico admitted thousands of Chileans seeking asylum into its *Santiago embassy, and, then, immediately after negotiating their safe conduct to Mexico, broke off relations. See: BRAZIL, Relations with; COLOMBIA, Relations with; PACTO ANDINO.

    see also: RELACIONES EXTERIORES, Ministerio de.

FOREIGN TRADE. Approximately one seventh of Chile's gross national product is exported, and import and export *taxes account for about one third of the state's tax revenue (see: CUSTOMS AND DUTIES; PUBLIC FINANCES). Historically, Chile has been an exporter of minerals, and *copper and its by-products account for almost 70 percent of foreign exchange receipts. The relationship between imports and exports for recent years, in millions of dollars, has been as follows:

	1960	1961	1962	1963	1964	1965	1966	1967
Imports	493	746	710	701	608	604	757	868
Exports	470	465	501	504	625	688	881	913

	1968	1969	1970	1971	1972	1973	1974	1975
Imports	835	934	1,020	1,205	1,330	1,609	2,458	2,094
Export	911	1,129	1,143	999	850	1,309	2,151	1,590

	1976	1977	1978	1979	1980	1981
Imports	1,997	2,815	3,619	5,106	6,561	7,874
Exports	2,116	2,185	2,460	3,835	4,705	3,960

    In 1970 Chile's major exports were: copper and its by-products, 68%; *iron ore and other metals, 13%; cellulose, paper, fishmeal, *cattle and agricultural products, 10%; potassium *nitrate (saltpeter) sodium nitrate and iodine, 6%; and other industrial products, 3%. Chile's major imports were capital goods (machinery and transport equipment, mainly for copper production), 44%; consumer goods, 28%; semi-processed goods (chemicals, raw cotton, crude *petroleum, *railway equipment), 28%. The figures in the above table also include financial and other services (20 percent of the total in 1970). The principal nations receiving Chile's exports in 1970 were: the *United States, 34%; *United Kingdom, 14%; West *Germany, 11%; the Netherlands, 7%; and Japan, 7%. The principal suppliers of Chilean imports for the same year were: the United States, 35%; West Germany, 12%; *Argentina, 8%; United Kingdom, 7%; *France, 5%, and Japan, 4%.

    Marxist President Salvador *Allende Gossens had stated that "the foreign trade policy of the *Unidad Popular government must be considered as a part of the national development plan, and most particularly within the context of the general foreign policy of the nation." And he had pledged to strengthen economic relations with all countries of the world, regardless of their international system, the only limitation being that the national interests of Chile must be served and that the development must be in agreement with Chile's international policy. Allende had in mind particularly Cuba, Red China, and the countries of the Eastern European block.

Between 1930 and 1973, the year Allende was deposed, high tariffs were predominant in an *economy that sought to encourage import substitution in the domestic sector and to control imports of nonessential goods. When the *armed forces came to power with Augusto *Pinochet Ugarte as *junta leader, a phased reduction of import barriers was immediately introduced. By 1979, except for automobiles, where local assembly continued to be protected, the import tariff was down to 10 percent.

Between 1973 and 1980, exports increased at an average rate of 26 percent a year. The bulk of the increase was in non-traditional exports such as manufactured products. In 1981, however, copper prices and those of other minerals were depressed by weak international demand, and export receipts fell by 18 percent over the previous year, beginning a decline that was to continue into 1982 and 1983. In 1980 the United States received 12 percent of Chile's exports; Japan, 10 percent; Western European nations, 41 percent; and Latin American countries (mainly Brazil and Argentina) the remaining 23 percent.

Between 1973 and 1980, imports rose at an average rate of 44 percent a year. Much of the increase was due to greater imports of foodstuffs, and to higher prices for oil. The value of fuel imports increased by 100 percent between 1978 and 1980, constituting 17 percent of all imports in the latter year. In 1978 the United States supplied 27 percent of Chile's imports; Latin American countries (mainly Brazil and Argentina) supplied 29 percent; Western European countries supplied 19 percent; and Japan, 8 percent.

As the *balance of payments began to deteriorate in 1981, measures were taken to raise tariffs on imports of nonessential goods and some foodstuffs, but over the next three years trade deficits soared while exports remained constant, causing an increase in the foreign debt, and a much greater difficulty in servicing it. The overvalued *peso was clearly making Chilean goods less competitive in world markets.

FORESTRY. Of Chile's 741,767 square kilometers (286,396 square miles), about 22 percent (160,000 km^2: 40 million acres) were forested in 1970. "Forest Chile," the primary timber area, lies between *Concepción and *Punta Arenas. Income from lumber exports amounted to US$ 409 million in 1979, an almost tenfold increase since 1969. Of this US$ 181 million was pulp, US$ 165 million was lumber, and US$ 57 million was paper products. However, forestry exports do not seem to have benefited greatly so far from the 1982 devaluation of the *peso, and only a little of Chile's commercially usable timber is as yet accessible by the country's limited *highway network.

Chile's lumber production in the 1960s averaged 6.5 million
cubic meters a year (8.5 million cubic yards), but in the next
decade it increased rapidly: two and one half times between
1973 and 1976 alone. In the early 1980s, lumber accounted for
over half of the wood cut; pulp and paper consumed about 40
percent; the remainder was used for such products as plywood,
veneers, and particle board. Large landowners, after the fall
of President (1970-73) Salvador *Allende Gossens, were mainly
responsible for private sector development of forestry, encouraged
by a government incentive program.

In the early 1980s forestry was given top priority among non-
traditional exports by the Augusto *Pinochet Ugarte government.
In 1982, however, forestry exports were only US$ 322 million,
8.8 percent below 1981 earnings. While earning from pine sawn-
wood fell by 38 percent in 1982 over the previous year, pine logs
increased by 18.3 percent.

In 1980 Chile had approximately 6 million hectares (15 million
acres) of high-value native forests, of which 1 million hectares
were planted with pine (pinus radiata, a long-fibre tree). Pine
is by far the most important softwood in Chile. Others include
the "alerce" (a larch, fitzroya cupressoides), the "araucaria"
(araucaria araucana) and "manio." Hardwoods include the "alamo"
(a poplar), beech, laurel, "lenga" and "olivillo."

While Chilean law provided a 30-year tax exemption on timber
in forest preserves, conservation of forest resources has not been
adequate since planting lagged in the 1960s. However, prospects
were improved by a temporary reduction in tree-cutting imposed
by the government between 1974 and 1979.

In 1983 forestry products showed a modest increase, and projections were good for the late 1980s and thereafter as a result
of the government's reafforestation program.

Leading customers for Chile's wood exports are Argentina,
Brazil, Bolivia, Germany, the United Kingdom and Japan.

See also: CORPORACION NACIONAL FORESTAL.

FRANCE, Relations with. Spain under the Hapsburgs (1516-1700)
was almost continually at war with France: Chile's only contacts
with France during this period were with French *pirates, privateers and smugglers. The War of the Spanish Succession gave
Spain a French dynasty, the Bourbons, and France became an
ally. The Napoleonic invasion of Spain in 1808 ended this period
of alliance, but relations became warmer again with his defeat
in 1815.

France was quick to recognize the new independent republic
of Chile, which was already culturally and intellectually under her
spell (see: FRENCH INFLUENCE). French policies, however,
proved inimical to Latin American interests on several occasions,
from the Plate in the 1830s to Mexico in the 1860s. Chile narrowly averted French annexation of the lands around the Strait of
*Magellan in 1843 (see: PUNTA ARENAS).

Generally, however, relations remained good throughout most

of the 19th and 20th centuries, down to the advent of the *Unidad Popular government in Chile in 1970, with its plans to nationalize the *copper industry. As a result the French government found itself involved in international squabbles over the ownership of the Chilean copper that had been impounded in French ports. Although relations did not improve with the coming to power of the *armed forces in Chile in 1973, the sale of twenty Mirage jet fighters and a number of medium-size tanks in 1979 made France, briefly, one of Chile's most important *armament suppliers. The election of socialist president François Mitterand shortly afterwards, however, led to an interruption of arms sales in 1980. Relations between the two countries have remained cool, and France continues to cite Chile's *human rights record as the reason for this.

Some 60,000 Chileans found refuge in France after the 1973 *coup. See: EMIGRATION.

FRAP. See: FRENTE DE ACCION POPULAR.

FRAS. See: FALANGE RADICAL AGRARIA SOCIALISTA.

FREI MONTALVA, Eduardo (1911-1982). Lawyer and former university professor, one of the founders of the Christian Democratic Party (*Partido Demócrata Cristiano) and President of Chile for the term 1964-70. Active in politics since his university days, Frei took his law degree at the age of 22, graduating with honors. Between 1932 and 1935 he was secretary and then president of Chile's Catholic youth organization, the Asociación Nacional de Estudiantes Católicos y Juventud Católica de Chile. In 1934 he went to Rome to attend the University Youth Congress as a delegate from Chile. A year later he helped organize the youth faction of the Movimiento Nacional Conservador, the progressive wing of the Conservative Party (*Partido Conservador). This took the name *Falange Conservadora, changed to *Falange Nacional in 1938 when it separated completely from the Conservative Party. In 1957, the Falange Nacional United with the *Partido Socialista Conservador to become the Christian Democratic Party (PDC) of Chile.

Frei was minister of public works in the administration of President (1942-46) Juan Antonio *Ríos Morales. Three years later he was elected senator from the region known as the *Norte Chico (the provinces of *Atacama and *Coquimbo). In the congressional elections of 1957 he was elected senator from *Santiago with the largest plurality received by any candidate in that election. In 1958 he was a presidential candidate, finishing third behind President (1958-64) Jorge *Alessandri Rodríguez, who had defeated the runner-up, Salvador *Allende Gossens, by some 35,000 votes. In 1964 Chileans chose Frei as President by an overwhelming majority. With over 2.5 million votes cast, Frei polled over 1.4 million, or 55.6 percent. His nearest opponent, Socialist Senator Allende, polled 975,210 votes, or 38.6 percent.

It was learned later that the U.S. *Central Intelligence Agency had contributed US$ 2.6 million to Frei's successful bid for the presidency: more than half Frei's total campaign budget, and equal to twice as much per voter as Lyndon Johnson and Barry Goldwater together had spent in their presidential campaigns of the same year (1964).

Among his accomplishments as President, Frei passed a series of laws to benefit the people, such as an *Agrarian Reform law, an *education act which made it mandatory for children to go to school until age 16; a law calling for the "chileanization" of the *copper mines--i.e., tighter government control over copper pricing, production and marketing; a law creating a new ministry, the Ministerio de la *Vivienda y Urbanismo (Housing and Town Planning), whose aims were to provide low-income housing for the Chilean middle-class and poor; and a minimum wage law. About this last, a metallurgical worker who had supported Frei in 1964 but had deserted him to support Allende in 1970 complained: "What good are minimum wages when my boss refused to pay them? 'Go find another job,' he'd say." Frei also reestablished diplomatic relations with the *U.S.S.R., Poland, Czechoslovakia, Hungary and Rumania, which had been severed during the administration of President (1946-52) Gabriel *González Videla.

Under Frei's leadership, the Christian Democrats did not remain unified. Even before the presidential *elections of September 4, 1970, the left-wing faction within the party had split off to form a new party, the *Movimiento de Acción Popular Unitaria (MAPU). After the elections, another left-wing faction had split off, forming the Christian Left (*Izquierda Cristiana). Frei, however, remained the number one man in his party and began to organize the center and right wing of the PDC to oppose Allende.

In mid-1972 Frei and Sergio Onofre *Jarpa Reyes, who had emerged as the leader of the right-wing Nationalist Party (*Partido Nacional--a merger of the Liberals and Conservatives), formed a coalition, together with two other small parties of the right, known as the *Confederación Democrática (CODE). Their aim was to stop Allende's socialization of Chile with a clear victory in the congressional elections of March 4, 1973. Both Frei and Onofre Jarpa confidently predicted that CODE would win a two-thirds majority in the Senate and would control the chamber of deputies. Had this come to pass, CODE would have been able to stop most of Allende's programs and could have begun a motion to impeach the President. In spite of heavy C.I.A. financing of CODE's campaign, when the final votes were counted, CODE was found to have failed. The parties supporting Allende had instead picked up six new seats in the chamber of deputies and three new seats in the Senate. Both Frei and Jarpa had been personally successful in winning Senate seats, and they both then began to cooperate with the military for what turned out to be the *coup d'état of September 11, 1973.

Frei had assumed that, once the *armed forces had overthrown

Allende, he would be tapped to be the interim President of Chile.
Like so many other Chileans, Frei was shocked by the degree
of violence that followed the coup, and by the fact that the military had no intention of relinquishing power. They preferred
instead to round up all leftists (sending underground many of
those they failed to apprehend) and put all political parties in
indefinite recess.

When in 1975 Frei dared criticize the economic policies of the
*junta, he was sternly warned to keep out of politics for his
own good. But as the political process became a little less closed,
Frei took on a more active role, urging citizens in 1980, for
example, to vote against the new *Constitution of 1980, which
would extend the presidency of Augusto *Pinochet Ugarte for
another 8 years, with a possible extension for another 8 beyond
that. In the referendum the new constitution was approved 2
to 1, which led Frei to declare the result fraudulent.

A bitter man, Frei died in January 1982. His funeral was accompanied by an anti-government demonstration that numbered
8,000 persons, at least 30 of whom were arrested outside of
*Santiago. Frei had been the favorite of President John F. Ken-
nedy and his Alliance for Progress, and he was seen by the United
States as the man who could have warded off the rise of the left
in Chile, and in the rest of the hemisphere. Frei was blamed
by many Chileans for having incited the coup, which failed to
bring about the results he desired and which had meant a great
deal of suffering for most of the Chilean people. The Pinochet
government viewed him as a nuisance and the politician most
responsible for Allende's having been elected. Christian Democrat
leaders around the world, on the other hand, praised his states-
manship and his courageous opposition to the Pinochet government.

FREIRE SERRANO, Ramón (1787-1851). An active fighter in the
struggle for Chilean *independence, and twice head of the Chilean
state—as Supreme Director (1823-26) and as President (1827).
He fought in all the major battles against *Spain, distinguishing
himself at those of *Rancagua (1814) and *Chacabuco (1817). A
career *army officer, Freire Serrano was acclaimed *caudillo in
the south after a spirit of rebellion had arisen against the authority of Bernardo *O'Higgins, who was forced to resign as Supreme
Director in 1823. The *creole leaders in *Santiago formed a
*junta government to succeed O'Higgins. Because of the distur-
bances in the capital, Freire marched there from the south and
refused to recognize the junta. Instead he named a new one,
which lost no time in proclaiming him Supreme Director.

*Congress produced the new *Constitution of 1823, drawn up
by the eminent Chilean statesman Juan *Egaña Risco, but this was
in force for only six months. Freire staged a coup d'état and
proclaimed himself dictator. As a sympathizer of the liberal
political group known as the *Pipiolos, Freire took strong measures
against the *Church and the Conservatives (known as the *Pelucones). Among his accomplishments were the initiation of the

internal organization of a new Congress, the appointment of a committee to draw up another constitution, and many public works such as the building of roads and schools and the beautification of urban centers. These reforms were costly, and the precarious state of the Chilean *economy was severely affected. In order to alleviate the government's financial straits, Freire developed the *estanco, raising *taxes through the sale of goods such as tobacco which were government monopolies.

In 1824 Freire unsuccessfully attempted to annex the island of *Chiloé, which was still a Spanish possession. In 1826 he returned south and this time his expedition was successful. Chiloé was included within the national boundaries. In the same year Chile was proclaimed a federal republic (see: FEDERALISM) and divided into eight *provinces, each governed by a general assembly. Antagonism between the provincial and central governments soon arose, and Freire, unable to cope with the situation, resigned. Early in 1827 Colonel Enrique *Campino Salamanca led a revolt in Santiago. He dispersed the Congress, but was himself abandoned by his own supporters. Freire was then recalled as President (February 1827). He accepted, but was unable to formulate a workable frame of government and resigned the following May. Congress accepted his resignation and Francisco Antonio *Pinto Díaz attempted to organize a new government.

Freire took part on the Liberal side in the *Civil War of 1829-30 and commanded the losing side at the final battle of *Lircay. He then fled to *Peru, but returned from exile in 1836 and attempted to raise a rebellion on the island of *Chiloé. He failed and narrowly avoided a death sentence, being exiled instead, first to the *Juan Fernández Islands and then to Sidney, New South Wales. He was permitted to return to Chile in 1842 and lived the rest of his life divorced from politics. Freire was superb as a soldier, but lacked any great political ability.

FRENAP. See: FRENTE NACIONAL DEL PUEBLO.

FRENCH INFLUENCE. The beginning of the 18th century saw the accession to the Spanish throne of the French Duke of Anjou, who reigned in Spain as *Philip V. As a result, Spain, for the first time, authorized French vessels to maintain communication with the Spanish empire overseas. In 1701 France was granted the asiento de negros, a limited right to trade in slaves directly with the Spanish colonies. This was used as a cover to smuggle other wares, and soon contraband trade developed between French sailors and Chilean merchants. Although prohibited by Spain, French books began to enter Chile and be read by Chileans.

The 18th century was the period of the great French intellectual awakening that produced first the Enlightenment (with the important Spanish imperial reforms of *Charles III as one manifestation), and then the French Revolution (which influenced all of Latin America). The ideas of the philosophes had enormous impact on the *creole intelligentsia. Prominent among the philosophers and writers was Jean Jacques Rousseau with his Social Contract. The "Declaration of the Rights of Man" especially inspired ideas of independence from Spain.

Napoleon's attempt to place his brother Joseph on the Spanish throne in the place of *Ferdinand VII alienated Chileans (as well as other Latin Americans) who had embraced wholeheartedly the French ideals of liberty and equality. Ashamed of the culture of Spain, seen as an expression of the colonial past, Chileans again turned to France with renewed warmth after the fall of Napoleon. For the élite, a knowledge of French and a trip to Paris were part of the cultural baggage. This attitude explains why movements like Positivism had so great an impact on countries such as Chile.

During the latter half of the 19th century, the prestige of the French language and French culture was felt throughout Latin America, with Chile becoming almost a cultural colony of France. But the Franco-Prussian War of 1870-71 was a severe blow to this prestige, and Chile reacted by turning to the victors for educational and military expertise (see: GERMANY, Relations with). The tradition of France as the center of western civilization remained fixed in the Latin American psyche, nevertheless.

Throughout the world, with the rise of *United States influence, France's importance declined after World War II, notwithstanding the efforts of General Charles de Gaulle, who visited Latin America to revive the idea of a Latin world with Paris as its cultural center. France, however, is still respected in Chile, where movements such as existentialism and writers such as Jean Paul Sartre and Albert Camus were still in vogue before the military takeover of 1973.

See also: FRANCE, Relations with.

FRENTE DE ACCION POPULAR (FRAP). (Popular Action Front.)
A coalition of leftist parties formed in 1956 and dissolved in 1969. The member parties were the Communists (*Partido Comunista Chileno), who operated underground until 1958, the Socialists (*Partido Socialista de Chile), the National Democrats (*Partido Democrático Nacional), the Popular Socialists (*Partido Socialista Popular) and the People's Vanguard (*Partido Vanguardista del Pueblo). Both the Communist and Socialist parties, the strongest members of the coalition, followed a Marxist ideology. Their fundamental postulates were nationalization of the country's natural resources and centralized state control. In the parliamentary elections of 1957, the FRAP elected 17 deputies and 8 senators. In the presidential elections of the following year, the FRAP's candidate was socialist Salvador *Allende Gossens. He was defeated by the conservative candidate, Jorge *Alessandri Rodríguez, by a mere 33,000 votes. Encouraged by such showing, the FRAP intensified its campaign with an eye on the presidential elections of 1964.

Shortly before these 1964 elections, the People's Vanguard Party broke away from FRAP to support Christian Democrat

(*Partido Demócrata Cristiano) candidate Eduardo *Frei Montalva.
Allende lost to Frei, this time by some 430,000 votes. In 1968
FRAP began to lose its power and a year later it was dissolved.
The major member parties formed a new leftist coalition with other
minor parties, known as the UNIDAD POPULAR (q.v.).

FRENTE DEL PUEBLO. (People's Front.) Political combination of
leftist parties organized in 1951 to back the presidential candidacy
of Salvador *Allende Gossens. It was made up of the Communists
(*Partido Comunista Chileno), Socialists (*Partido Socialista de
Chile) and the Popular Socialists (*Partido Socialista Popular).
Allende lost the election to rightist candidate Carlos *Ibáñez del
Campo. The coalition lasted until 1955. One year later the leftist
parties in Chile were grouped into a new coalition known as the
FRENTE DE ACCION POPULAR (q.v.) or FRAP.

FRENTE DEMOCRATICO DE CHILE. (Democratic Front of Chile.) A
political combination of parties from the center and the right,
formed in 1962 to nominate a presidential candidate for the elections
of 1964. The member parties were the Radicals (*Partido Radical),
Conservatives (*Partido Conservador) and the Liberals (*Partido
Liberal). The coalition was formed mainly to stop the Communist
threat in Chile. The Frente Democrático de Chile's choice in
1964 was Julio *Durán Neumann, a Radical. Durán decided, however, to run simply as a candidate of the Radical Party, and the
Frente Democrático was dissolved.

FRENTE NACIONAL DEL PUEBLO. The People's National Front was
a political combination of leftist parties, organized in 1955 to
present a united front in the presidential elections of 1958.
Its candidate was Salvador *Allende Gossens. Socialists (*Partido
Socialista de Chile), Communists (*Partido Comunista Chileno)
and Radicals (*Partido Radical) made up the bulk of the membership. In 1956, however, the Front was dissolved, and a new
coalition was formed, called the FRENTE DE ACCION POPULAR
(q.v.), or FRAP.

FRENTE NACIONAL DEMOCRATICO. The Democratic National Front
was a political party organized in 1949 to oppose the government
of President (1946-52) Gabriel *González Videla. Most of the membership was made up of Communists who in 1948 had gone underground as a result of the measures taken by González Videla under the *Ley de Defensa de la Democracia to outlaw the Communist Party (*Partido Comunista Chileno). In the parliamentary
elections of 1949 the Frente Nacional won only two seats (in the
Chamber of Deputies). In early 1950 there were grave incidents
between striking *trade union members and the *police, which
resulted in several deaths. The party, having instigated the
confrontations, was held responsible. As a result it lost popular
support and was dissolved later that same year.

FRENTE PATRIOTICO MANUEL RODRIGUEZ. The Manuel Rodriguez
Patriotic Front was formed in 1983 "to oblige the army to relinquish power." Named in honor of the guerrilla leader of the
*Reconquista Española period, Manuel *Rodríguez Erdoiza, the
front is said to number 1,000 militants, carrying out systematic
sabotage against power lines, communications, and properties
owned by multinational corporations. A connection with the
*Partido Comunista Chileno has been alleged.

FRENTE POPULAR (Popular Front). A political coalition made up of
several left-of-center parties: the Communists (*Partido Comunista
Chileno), the Socialists (*Partido Socialista), the Radicals (*Partido Radical) and the Socialist Radicals (*Partido Radical Socialista), plus the *trade union federation CTCh (Confederación de
trabajadores de Chile). It was proposed in 1935 as a measure
to keep in check the widespread fascist ideology then prevalent,
especially in Europe, but the Front did not achieve definite form
until May 1937. As the threat of fascism grew, particularly with
the triumph of the Nationalists in the Spanish Civil War (1936-39)
and with World War II imminent, the Popular Front consolidated
its forces and became one of the most powerful political organizations in Chile. In the presidential *elections of 1938 the Front
backed the Radical candidate Pedro *Aguirre Cerda, who won.
In 1941 the Socialists pulled out of the Popular Front, presenting
their own candidates for the parliamentary elections of that year.
Soon the Communists abandoned it too, and when later in the
year President Aguirre died in office, the Popular Front was
dissolved. For the election of 1942, however, the Communists,
Socialists and Radicals came together again in the *Alianza Democrática de Chile (1942-46).

FRESNO DE LEIGHTON, Anita. Wife of Christian Democrat leader
Bernardo *Leighton Guzmán, who was with her husband when
secret police agents machine-gunned them in Rome. Miraculously,
both survived, but Anita Fresno was hit in the spine and has
been paralyzed since the assassination attempt (October 6, 1975).
On the same day as the shooting, the French police arrested
three Chileans as *DINA agents and deported them.

FRESNO LARRAIN, Juan Francisco (1914-). Cardinal Archbishop
of *Santiago. Ordained in 1937, he became Bishop of *Copiapó
in 1958 and Archbishop of La *Serena in 1967. He was also President of the Episcopal Conference of Chile. He succeeded Raúl
Cardinal *Silva Henríquez as Archbishop of Santiago in 1983 and
was made a cardinal in May 1985. In August 1985 he was responsible for drawing up the National Accord (Acuerdo para la transición hacia la plena democracia) signed by eleven parties of
the right, center and moderate left, including the *Partido Demócrata Cristiano, *Partido Nacional, *Movimiento de Unidad Nacional,
*Partido Social Democrático, *Partido Socialista de Chile, *Partido
Radical and *Izquierda Cristiana. Even the radical left alliance

MDP (*Movimiento Democrático Popular), although not invited to sign, indicated its support. The accord's call for dialogue was firmly rejected by President Augusto *Pinochet Ugarte in December 1985, but the group continues to press for an early return to "full democracy."

FRONTIER DISPUTES. See: ABRAZO DEL ESTRECHO; ANCON, Treaty of ANTARCTICA; ARGENTINA, Relations with; ARICA; BEAGLE CHANNEL; BOLIVIA, Relations with; BOUNDARY TREATY OF 1881; FOREIGN RELATIONS; LIMA, Treaty of; PACTOS DE MAYO; PATAGONIA; PERU, Relations with; TACNA; TIERRA DEL FUEGO.

FUENZALIDA CORREA, Osvaldo (b. 1894). Lawyer and Radical Party politician. He joined the *Cuerpo de Carabineros as a lawyer in 1921, became its auditor general in 1927, and professor of penal law in the *Police Academy (Escuela de Carabineros) in 1929. When the Radical Party (*Partido Radical) split in 1938 over participation in the Popular Front (*Frente Popular), Fuenzalida went with the anti-front minority, the Doctrinary Radicals (*Partido Radical Doctrinario), but returned to the Radicals when the PRD dissolved shortly afterwards, becoming vice-president of the Radical Party. In 1943 he was minister of land and settlement in the government (1942-46) of Juan Antonio *Río Morales. From 1945 to 1947 he was Chilean ambassador to Italy. He remained active in the Radical Party.

FUENZALIDA ESPINOZA, Edmundo (b. 1905). Journalist by profession who early in his life entered politics as a member of the Liberal Party (*Partido Liberal) and has since held elective office. He has also had a long and distinguished diplomatic career. He sat in the chamber of deputies from 1932 to 1941 and was appointed vice-president of the chamber in 1935. After World War II he was consul of Chile in Milan and Bilbao. From 1959 to 1961 he was Chilean ambassador to Guatemala. In 1961 he became ambassador to Austria and permanent delegate to the *United Nations' International Atomic Energy Agency. He was ambassador to Uruguay from 1963 to 1964 and in 1965 became ambassador to Switzerland.

FUERZA AEREA CHILENA (FACh). The Chilean Air Force. See: AIR FORCE.

FUNDO. A rural property, large landed estate or hacienda.

FUNDO LO CAÑAS. See: CAÑAS, Fundo Lo.

FUSION LIBERAL-CONSERVADORA. A political union between the Liberals (*Partido Liberal) and Conservatives (*Partido Conservador), both representing conservative interests in Chilean society, organized in 1857 during the conservative administration (1851-61)

of President Manuel *Montt Torres. In 1851 the Liberals had proclaimed the election of Montt Torres to have been fraudulent,
and instigated an armed revolt (the *Civil War of 1851) which
lasted three months and cost some 2,000 lives. While Montt
Torres was unable to mollify the Liberals, he had even more problems with the Conservatives. The Conservative's chief protests
were against the elimination of the *mayorazgos (entailed estates)
and the indignity suffered by the *Church when Montt Torres
became involved in a dispute with the *Archbishop of *Santiago,
Rafael Valentín *Valdivieso y Zañartu, over the dismissal of a
cathedral sexton (see: SACRISTAN, Cuestión del). Montt
Torres' threat to exile the archbishop provoked a very strong
reaction on the part of the conservatives.

The difficulties of both parties with the President produced
the coalition known as the Fusión Liberal-Conservadora. As the
elections of 1861 approached, it was evident that the Conservatives
had to reckon with the power of the Liberals. The latter wanted
to reform the *Constitution of 1833: they demanded a single term
of office for the President, separation of Church and State, and
religious freedom for non-Catholics. Montt Torres wanted Antonio
*Varas de la Barra to succeed him, but, threatened with another
armed revolt, he had to accept the more moderate candidate
backed by the Liberals, José Joaquín *Pérez. The election of
Pérez as President (1861-71) ended thirty years of Conservative
rule in Chile and marked the beginning of a thirty-year Liberal
rule. The Fusión Liberal-Conservadora lasted until 1875, when
disagreements between the Conservatives and Liberals over matters
of Church-State relations brought about its dissolution. Those
Conservatives who remained faithful to the policies of President
Montt founded a new party, the Montt-Varistas, which adopted
the name PARTIDO NACIONAL, q.v.

- G -

GABRIELA MISTRAL, Editorial. See: ZIG-ZAG, Empresa Editorial.

GALLO VERGARA, Manuel (c1790-1842). Silver *mining magnate who
    in 1818 proclaimed Chilean Independence in *Copiapó. From
    1832 he began exploitation of the *Charnarcillo *silver mines in
    association with Juan *Godoy.

GALLO Y GOYENECHEA, Pedro León (1830-1877). Rebel leader in
    the *Civil War of 1859. As an officer in the *Guardia Nacional
    he fought against the 1851 Mutiny of *Urriola. In 1852 he followed
    his father Manuel *Gallo Vergara into *Silver mining in *Copiapó.
    He was elected *regidor on the Copiapó municipal council in 1853
    but was forced out of office when he tried to abolish flogging as
    a disciplinary method in the municipal *police force. Such radi-

calism won him great public sympathy. When the *Civil War of 1859 broke out, he was proclaimed <u>caudillo</u> of the revolution. He organized, largely at his own expense, a 2,000-strong army, a mint, and an armament industry which cast 15 cannon. Although victorious at Los *Loros, the treason of his lieutenants Urrutia and Vallejos caused his defeat at *Cerro Grande and, under sentence of death, he fled to, successively, *Argentina, the U.S. and *Spain. An 1862 presidential amnesty allowed his return and he was enthusiastically elected deputy for Copiapó and *Caldera the following year. This position he kept until his 1876 election as senator for *Atacama.

GALVARINO. Legendary *Araucanian chieftain who was reported to have been born around 1557. The year of his death is unknown. Galvarino became famous for his exceptional bravery. He was captured in Lagunilla, and the Spanish governor requested that both his hands be cut off. Galvarino placed his right hand on the block, and when it had been removed, he, without a word, placed his left hand on the block. At the conclusion of the sentence, he placed his head on the block, but his life was spared so that he might serve as an example to those who would disobey the Spaniards. Galvarino left, swearing to avenge himself. He spent the rest of his life inciting Indian uprisings but was captured again and executed. Some Chilean historians believe that he killed himself in order not to give his enemies the satisfaction of killing him.

GANDARILLAS GUZMAN, Manuel José, (1789-1842). A lawyer by profession who participated in the struggle for Chilean independence with the *Carrera Verdugo brothers. In 1814, he was named secretary of the *<u>cabildo</u> (town council) of *Santiago. After the battle of *Rancagua, he went into exile to Mendoza and from there to Buenos Aires. After the battle of *Chacabuco, he returned to Chile. He went into voluntary exile to Argentina when Bernardo *O'Higgins took power, and returned to Chile once again after the overthrow of O'Higgins. In 1825, he formed part of the governing council which took power in the absence of President (1823-26) Ramón *Freire Serrano. In 1826, he was finance minister, and helped organize the *Estanquero party. In 1828, he was elected a deputy to Congress but resigned. From 1831 he was a senator, dying before the end of his term.

GANDARILLAS LUCO, José Antonio (1839-1913). Lawyer by profession and member of the Doctrinary Liberal Party (*Partido Liberal Doctrinario). From 1870 to 1875 he was a judge (<u>ministro</u>) in the Court of Appeal. In 1876 he was elected a deputy to *Congress. In 1879, he occupied the Ministry of Justice and *Education. He was also subrogate Minister of War and the Navy. From 1869 to 1895, he formed part of the commission for the revision of the Penal Code. In 1888 he was elected a deputy to Congress, and a senator in 1891. In 1892, he was named president of the

Senate. He unsuccessfully ran for President in 1886, backed by the Doctrinary Liberal Party.

GANDARILLA LUCO, Pedro Nolasco (1839-1891). A civil servant without party affiliation who sat in *Congress as deputy (1876-79) and as senator (1882-91). In 1881 he was appointed administrator of the *estanco in *Santiago, and in 1883, fiscal treasurer. In 1885 he was made minister of finance, and a year later became director of the Treasury and president of the Tribunal de Cuentas (the national audit office). At various times during 1889 he was acting minister of the interior, acting minister of justice and education, acting war minister, and acting minister of industry and public works. From January to August 1890 he was again finance minister. His loyalty as a civil servant to the government of President José Manuel *Balmaceda Fernández during the *Civil War of 1891 led to his persecution after the victory of the rebel Congress, and he took his own life, November 1891.

GARCIA CARRASCO DIAZ, Francisco Antonio (1742-1813). Governor of Chile at the beginning of the struggle for *Independence. He had a long career in the *army. He was twice temporary governor of *Valparaíso.
    He was named acting governor of Chile in 1808 and governor in 1809, but his term was shaken by internal and international difficulties. There was a movement in Chile to declare independence and not recognize Napoleon's brother Joseph Bonaparte, who had replaced *Ferdinand VII as King of Spain in 1808. The governor had to sustain a repressive attitude against all those who wished the French to win in Spain. In 1810 the people of *Santiago rejected the role played by the governor to aid the independence movement in Chile. García Carrasco Díaz lost support and left for Callao, *Peru, in 1811.

GARCIA RODRIGUEZ, Ricardo. Appointed interior minister in December 1985, in succession to Sergio Onofre *Jarpa Reyes.

GAY, Claude (1800-1873). French naturalist contracted by Diego *Portales Palazuelos in 1830 to write a physical description of Chile. Justice and education minister Mariano *Egaña Fabres encouraged Gay to extend his task to a Historia física y política de Chile. This took 43 years to write (without ever being finished) and was published in Paris in thirty volumes, 1844-65. The project cost the Chilean government $100,000: one half for the author, the other in printing costs. After his death, his family presented his books and papers to the *National Library.

GENDARMERIE. See: CUERPO DE CARABINEROS.

GENTE DECENTE. (Literally, "decent people.") Middle-class persons.

GENTE HONESTA. (Literally, "honest people.") People of the lower class.

GENTE HUMILDE. (Literally, "humble people.") Poor people.

GEOGRAPHY, Chilean. See: CHILE--D. Topography.

GERMANY, Relations with. The first Germans to arrive in Chile
were among the *conquistadores--thanks to the international connections of Emperor *Charles V of the House of Hapsburg, who
also happened to be King Charles I of Spain. The most renowned
was Barolomäus Blümlein, who founded the resort city of *Viña
del Mar. A number of Germans also came as *Jesuits in the 18th
century.
   Large-scale German immigration began in the 19th century,
at the end of Manuel *Bulnes Prieto's presidency. They settled
mostly in the southern lake district, where they engaged in *agriculture and were able to colonize *Osorno, *Valdivia and *Puerto
Montt (see: LLANQUIHUE). Like the German immigrants in the
southern states of Brazil, those who came to Chile built schools
where the only language spoken was German.
   Latin Americans were particularly impressed with the victory
of Prussia over France in 1870-71, and this ushered in a period
of great German influence in Chile, especially in the *army (see:
KOERNER HENZE, Emil) and in *education. German philosophy
was also important (see: KRAUSISMO), and after the rise of
Hitler in Europe, a Nazi movement, the *Movimiento Nacional
Socialista, prospered in Chile.
   Chile was never really involved in World War I, in spite of the
fact that German warships, particularly the Graf von Spee's
fleet in 1914, made unlawful use of Chilean waters. In April
1945, at the end of World War II, Chile declared war on Japan,
chiefly to qualify for membership of the *United Nations, but not
on Germany.
   In the postwar years, the German Federal Republic has been
a significant source of *foreign aid to Chile, with private German
financial contributions going to the Roman Catholic *Church and
the Christian Democrats (*Partido Demócrata Cristiano). Relations
with the government of Augusto *Pinochet Ugarte were cool in
the period immediately following the overthrow of Salvador *Allende
Gossens. They improved in the mid-1970s (see: ARMAMENTS),
but have remained generally strained in view of Chile's constant
violations of human rights, especially in the mid-1980s.

GOAT FARMING. See: LIVESTOCK.

GOBIERNO, Secretaría de. The provisional government of 1814 created
three secretariats of state: of government, of finance and of war.
The *Constitution of 1818 changed the name of these departments
from "secretariat" to "ministry," and changed the Secretariat
of Government into the Ministry of State (Ministerio de *Estado).

GOBIERNO Y RELACIONES EXTERIORES, Ministerio de. The Ministry
of Government and Foreign Affairs was created by law in 1822

(and approved by the *Constitution of 1822), replacing the
Ministerio del *Estado. It lasted until 1824, when its name was
changed to Ministry of the Interior and Foreign Affairs (Ministerio
del *Interior y de Relaciones Exteriores).

GODOY, Juan. *Silver miner. The son of a white father and Indian
mother, in 1832 he began the exploitation of the *Charnarcillo
silver mines in association with Miguel *Gallo Vergara. For this
he is honored as a local hero in *Copiapó.

GODOY ALCAYAGA, Lucila. Real name of Gabriela MISTRAL (q.v.).

GOLD. Gold in Chile was known to the *Incas who imposed a gold
tribute on the *Araucanian Indians. *Conquistador Pedro de
*Valdivia made an 80,000-*peso profit washing for gold near
*Quillota; others found alluvial gold at Quilacoya, *Imperial,
Villarica, Madre de Dios, *Osorno, Ponzuelas, Illapel and Choapa.
By the end of the 16th century the Spanish had extracted
72.9 *metric tons, averaging 1.5 tonnes a year; production fell,
however, to only 0.35 tonnes a year in the 17th century, as
known sources became depleted. Output revived in the later
half of the 18th century, mainly in *Atacama, and by 1803 Chile
was second only to *Colombia in Latin America, producing 3.1
tonnes a year.
In the 19th century, however, *mining interest turned first
to *silver, then to *copper, so that gold lost its relative significance and production was left to individual prospectors. In 1868
alluvial gold was discovered in the Río de las Minas, near *Punta
Arenas, and also on Navarino, *Picton and *Lennox islands; never,
however, in worthwhile quantities until the 1880s, when *Tierra
del Fuego experienced the gold rush of 1885-1902. A minor gold
rush was also recorded in northern Chile, at *Andacollo, around
1932.
Gold production, which was only 1.27 tonnes in 1909, reached
10.11 tonnes in 1939, but fell to 6.34 tonnes in 1944 and 4.25
in 1947. In recent years it has gone up again. In 1983 Chile's
output reached 20 tonnes out of Latin America's total of 134
tonnes, second only to Brazil, with 51 tonnes. In 1985 17.6
tonnes were produced. Most of Chile's current gold production
(94 percent) is a by-product of copper mining.

GOLD STANDARD (Patrón de oro). Chile's financial difficulties in
the 1870s, due to poorer prices for *copper and a fall in *wheat
exports, and which were an underlying cause of the War of the
*Pacific, led to the replacement of the country's gold *coinage
in 1875 by bank notes, whose notional convertibility was abandoned in 1878. The feeling that paper unbacked by gold was
somehow dishonest and that the ensuing inflation was a sign of
irresponsibility in government led the post-1891 *parliamentary
regime to reintroduce convertibility in 1895 at 18 pence (sterling)
per *peso (see: EXCHANGE RATE). This achievement was made

at considerable cost, and was only possible because of Chile's new found wealth from *nitrates. The arms race with *Argentina soon rendered its continuance impossible and convertibility was suspended "temporarily" in mid-1898. The post-World War I desire, worldwide, for a return to "normalcy" led Chile to restore the gold standard nominally, in 1926, at 6 pence per peso. This was untenable in the great *depression of the 1930s, and the gold standard was definitively abandoned in 1932.

GOMEZ MILLAS, Juan (b. 1900). Professor of history and geography at the *Universidad de Chile, where in 1931 he became secretary general of the university. He was later named dean of the Faculty of Philosophy and Education. In 1953 he was named minister of *education in the cabinet of President (1952-58) Carlos *Ibáñez del Campo. In the same year, he was elected rector of the Universidad de Chile, and was re-elected to that position in 1958. In 1964 he was once again named education minister in the cabinet of President (1964-70) Eduardo *Frei Montalva.

GONDOLA. See: MICRO.

GONZALEZ ROJAS, Eugenio (1903-). A university professor and member of the Socialist Party (*Partido Socialista) who in 1927 was secretary of the Department of Labor. Five years later he was named minister of *education in the government (1932-38) of Arturo *Alessandri Palma. He sat in *Congress as a senator from 1949 to 1957, and from 1948 to 1950 he was secretary general of the Socialist Party. After his Senate term he was invited by the Venezuelan government to organize a Pedagogic Institute in that country. He returned to Chile in 1959, and abandoned politics to dedicate himself to education. In that year he was appointed dean of the Faculty of Philosophy and Education at the *Universidad de Chile. In 1963 he was elected rector of the same university.

GONZALEZ VIDELA, Gabriel (b. 1898). Active member of the Radical Party (*Partido Radical), of which he became president in 1932, and President of Chile, 1946-52. A lawyer in La *Serena, 1923-29, he sat in the Chamber of Deputies from 1930-39, becoming president of the chamber in 1933. During the presidency of Pedro *Aguirre Cerda, González Videla was Chilean ambassador to France and Belgium, 1939-41, and during that of Juan Antonio *Ríos Morales he was ambassador to Brazil, 1942-44. In 1945 he was elected senator for an 8-year term. In 1946 he ran for President as the candidate of his party, and was elected with the backing of the Communists (*Partido Comunista Chileno). The Socialists had their own candidate. As a gesture of gratitude, the new President appointed three Communists to his eleven-man cabinet.

Inaugurated on November 4, 1946, he had to cope with many internal problems, among which the most serious were *inflation

on the one hand, and a serious lag in production on the other.
Not able to woo the Communists who controlled the *trade unions
and who demanded better pay for the workers, González Videla
alienated the Communist members of his cabinet who resigned
after only five months. Anti-inflation laws were passed by *Congress. The workers, however, threatened to strike and disrupt
the *economy even further unless they received better pay.
With his back to the wall, González Videla had to sign into law an
increase in the national minimum wage of at least 25 percent over
that of the previous year. In 1948, feeling that the Communists
were becoming too powerful in their control of the *labor segment
of Chilean society, and urged by the conservative Liberal Party
(*Partido Liberal) and its allies in the *Concentración Nacional,
González Videla outlawed the Communist Party and broke off
diplomatic relations with the *U.S.S.R. and other Communist
countries. The fifteen Communist deputies and five Communist
senators were allowed to finish their terms in office, but some
of them were persecuted (see: LEY DE DEFENSA DE LA DEMO-
CRACIA).

One of those persecuted was the poet Pablo *Neruda, senator
from Tarapacá. Neruda had denounced the steps taken by President González Videla to outlaw the party that had helped him to
achieve power. In a famous discourse read to an open session
of Congress, Neruda said, "Yo acuso" ("I accuse"). He then
went on to criticize the President, calling him a traitor. González
Videla took Neruda to court, and the poet was found guilty by
a kangaroo court. As a result, Neruda lost his Senate seat and
was given a prison sentence, which he avoided by going into
hiding for a year. It was during that time that he wrote the
poem, "Yo acuso," published in the collection Canto general (1950)
and banned in Chile (see: CENSORSHIP).

The government of González Videla had problems not only with
the intellectuals. Strikes and a growing *inflation (which ranged
from 25 to 30 percent yearly) seriously hindered economic progress.
In 1949 there was a sharp decline in the price of *copper, a commodity that accounted for approximately 60 percent of the nation's
foreign exchange. The cost of living had risen in the meantime
to 40 percent over that of the previous year. People became rest-
less. The announcement that bus fares would go up touched off
a series of riots which left seven persons dead and hundreds
wounded. The runaway inflation continued through 1952, when
González Videla's term expired and Carlos *Ibáñez del Campo was
elected for his second presidential term (1952-58).

GONZALEZ VON MAREES, Jorge (1900-1962). Lawyer by profession
and leader of the Chilean Nazi Party, the *Movimiento Nacional
Socialista de Chile, which he helped organize in 1932. In 1937
the *Nacistas elected three deputies, and González Von Marées
was one of them. At the opening session of *Congress, Von
Marées opposed the passage of a bill on social security for workers, which was defeated. He worked to establish a fascist state

in Chile. This caused many disturbances involving Communists and Radicals on the one hand, and the Nacistas on the other. Several of these disturbances resulted in death. He himself always carried a gun, and once fired a shot when President Arturo *Alessandri Palma was addressing an opening session of Congress. For this he was detained and submitted to a medical examination, but later released. In the presidential campaign of 1938 he supported the candidacy of Carlos *Ibáñez del Campo. The violent seizure by party members of the *Seguro Obrero (social security) building in downtown *Santiago led to the arrest of both Von Marées and Ibáñez, whose candidature was withdrawn. Nacista support was then transferred to the *Frente Popular candidate, Pedro *Aguirre Cerda (thus assuring his election). The Movimiento Nacional Socialista was dissolved, and then reborn as the *Vanguardia Popular Socialista. Von Marées continued to sit as a deputy until 1949, then joined the Liberal Party (*Partido Liberal). Not in agreement with the candidacy of Jorge *Alessandri Rodríguez, he left politics in 1951.

GOPE (Grupo de operaciones especiales). An elite unit of the *Cuerpo de Carabineros, modeled on the British Army's Special Air Services (SAS) Regiment.

GOVERNMENT. See: CHILE--H. Government; MINISTRIES.

GOVERNMENT, Secretariat of. See: GOBIERNO, Secretaría de.

GOVERNMENT AND FOREIGN RELATIONS, Ministry of. See: GOBIERNO Y RELACIONES EXTERIORES, Ministerio de.

GOVERNORS OF CHILE during the colonial period:
Pedro de *Valdivia (1541-1553)
García *Hurtado de Mendoza (1557-1561)
Francisco de *Villagra (1561-1563)
Pedro de *Villagra (1563-1565)
Melchor Bravo de Saravia (1567-1575)
Rodrigo de Quiroga (1575-1580)
Alonso de Sotomayor (1583-1592)
Martín García Oñez de Loyola (1592-1598)
Alonso de Rivera (1601-1605)
Alonso García Ramón (1605-1610)
Lope de Ulloa y Lemus (1618-1620)
Luis Fernández de Córdova y Arce (1625-1629)
Francisco Laso de la Vega (1629-1639)
Francisco López de Zúñiga (1639-1646)
Martín de Mujica y Buitrón (1646-1649)
Antonio de Acuña y Cabrere (1650-1655)
Pedro Porter de Casanate (1656-1662)
Francisco de Meneses (1664-1668)
Diego de Avila Coello y Pacheco (1668-1670)
Juan Henríquez (1670-1682)

Marco José de Garro (1682-1692)
Tomás Marín de Poveda (1692-1700)
Francisco Ibáñez de Peralta (1700-1709)
Juan Andrés de Ustáriz (1709-1717)
Gabriel Cano de Aponte (1717-1733)
José Antonio Manso de Velasco (1737-1745)
Domingo Ortiz de Rozas (1746-1755)
Manuel Amat y Junient (1755-1761)
Antonio Guill y Gonzaga (1762-1768)
Agustín de Jáuregui (1773-1780)
Ambrosio de Benavides (1780-1787)
Ambrose *O'Higgins Ballenary (1788-1796)
Gabriel de Avilés (1796-1799)
Joaquín del Pino (1799-1801)
Luis Muñoz de Guzmán (1802-1808)
Francisco Antonio *García Carrasco Díaz (1808-1810)
Mateo de *Toro y Zambrano y Ureta (July 1810-May 1811)
Mariano *Osorio (October 1814-December 1815)
Francisco Casimiro *Marcó del Pont (December 1815-February 1817)

GRAN FEDERACION OBRERA DE CHILE (Great Workers' Federation of
Chile). A *trade union founded in 1909 by *railway employees.
The Marxist leader Luis Emilio *Recabarren changed its name
later the same year to the FEDERACION OBRERA DE CHILE (q.v.).

GRAN MINERIA. Term used in the Chilean *copper *mining industry
to designate that section of the industry made up of large-scale
enterprises, i.e. those with an annual output of 250,000 *metric
tons or more. The Gran Minería, which makes up 90 percent of
Chile's copper earnings, was developed mainly by two *United
States owned firms, the *Anaconda Copper Mining Company and
the *Kennecott Copper Corporation, and later by a third, the
*Cerro Corporation.

GREAT BRITAIN. See: UNITED KINGDOM.

GROUP OF TEN. See: GRUPO DE LOS DIEZ.

GROVE VALLEJO, Marmaduke (1879-1954). A career officer, first in
the artillery, then in the *air force, who led three coups d'état,
of which one succeeded, one failed, and one was temporarily
successful. The first, in 1925, was engineered to bring back
from Italy President (1920-25) Arturo *Alessandri Palma, who
had been forced by the *army to resign in 1924. Alessandri returned but resigned again after seven months. Grove Vallejo,
after heading the army air corps in 1925-26, was sent to London
by President Carlos *Ibáñez del Campo in 1927 as air and military
attaché with the rank of colonel: this was believed by many to
have been a thinly disguised exile. Grove resigned in 1928,
joined the *Dover conspiracy, and two years later returned
secretly to Chile in the *Avión Rojo to stage a coup. His failure

led to exile on *Easter Island, from where he escaped to France
by way of Tahiti. Shortly after the fall of Ibáñez in 1931, the
new government invited Grove to return to Chile, and he was
made chief of the newly formed Chilean air force, with the rank
of air commodore. In 1932, he led a revolt to try to establish
a Socialist Republic (*República Socialista), but his success was
short-lived. Twelve days later he, in turn, was ousted by Carlos
*Dávila Espinosa and exiled once more to Easter Island. From
1933 to 1949 he sat in the National *Congress as a deputy. As
president of the *Frente Popular, he was a candidate in the 1938
presidential elections. His withdrawal in favor of the candidacy
of Pedro *Aguirre Cerda was instrumental in the Frente Popular's
1938 electoral victory. After serving as secretary general of the
Socialist Party (*Partido Socialista), he was expelled in June
1944 when he formed the rival *Partido Socialista Auténtico, but
he left the new party in 1946 when it decided to merge with the
Chilean Communist Party.

GRUPO ANTONIO LUKSIC. Conglomerate owners of the Banco
O'Higgins. In 1985 they acquired the *Antofagasta-La Paz *railway from its British owners.

GRUPO CRUZAT-LARRAIN. Conglomerateurs Javier *Vial Castillo,
Manuel *Cruzat Infante and Fernando *Larraín Peña built two
vast industrial and financial empires known as the *Grupo Vial
and the Grupo Cruzat-Larraín, which later merged to become
Chile's largest controller of banks and company stockholdings.
In 1983 the resounding crash of the three entrepreneurs' empire
brought the Chilean *economy to its knees, leaving some of the
most prestigious banks holding the bag. In fact, Vial, Cruzat
and Larraín had contracted nearly one third of Chile's US$ 18,000
million foreign debt, and the necessary ingredient for their quick
rise (and fall) had been illegal bank credits. In the middle 1980s,
with the Chilean economy turning sour, discontent boiled over
into violent street protests, which rocked the very foundations
of the Augusto *Pinochet Ugarte regime. See also: BANKS,
BANKING AND FINANCIAL INSTITUTIONS; GRUPO VIAL.

GRUPO DE LOS DIEZ (Group of Ten). Christian Democrat *trade
union organization, founded in 1976 to bring together union officials from the *copper, *petroleum, plastic, textile, *railway and
sugar industries, *campesino organizations, the public service
and shipping. In 1981 the Grupo de los diez founded the *Unión
Democrática de Trabajadores (UDT) with nearly 800,000 members.
See: LABOR; TRADE UNIONS.

GRUPO DE OPERACIONES ESPECIALES. See: GOPE.

GRUPO MOVIL DE CARABINEROS. A special *police force organized
in 1960 for the purpose of breaking up workers' strikes and
student and peasant demonstrations. See also: CUERPO DE
CARABINEROS.

GRUPO VIAL. Entrepreneur Javier *Vial Castillo built a vast financial empire in Chile, starting in 1966, when he took over the Banco Hipotecario de Chile. The coming to power of Socialist Salvador *Allende Gossens in 1970 only slowed the pace of Vial's takeovers, and when Allende was overthrown three years later, the pace quickened dramatically. By 1975 the Chilean *economy was in the hands of three young entrepreneurs: Vial, Manuel *Cruzat Infante and Fernando *Larraín Peña, free market economist trained at the University of Chicago. But in 1983 Vial was arrested and the Grupo Vial was dissolved. A similar fate awaited the GRUPO CRUZAT-LARRAIN (q.v.), as the *economy turned sour and popular discontent resulted in violent street demonstrations. See also: BANKS, BANKING AND FINANCIAL INSTITUTIONS.

GUANO. The richness of maritime life along the *Humboldt current and the dryness of the Chilean and Peruvian coasts have created over the centuries enormous beds of accumulated droppings (guano) of fish-eating sea birds. From the times of the *Incas, guano was used as a fertilizer. It was first exported by the Sociedad Chilena de Fertilizantes to Europe in mid-19th century. There are different types of guano, the more recently deposited "white" variety, rich in nitrogen, and the fossilized "red" guano, high in phosphate. Growing interest in exploiting the guano beds led to the first boundary dispute between Chile and *Bolivia, settled by the treaty of 1866. The economic importance of guano was soon eclipsed by that of *nitrates, which led to the War of the *Pacific whereby Chile secured sovereignty over all the territory concerned. There are, however, other guano deposits further north, in Peru.

Chile's production of mainly "red" guano reached 20,000 metric *tons in 1920, and 36,000 in 1975.

GUERRA, Ministerio de. The Ministry of War was created in 1818. It had previously been known as the Secretariat of War (see: GUERRA, Secretaría de). The new *Constitution of 1822 replaced it with a Ministry of War and the Navy (see: GUERRA Y MARINA, Ministerio de). In December 1924, Statute no. 153 set up a separate Navy Ministry, so reviving the title, War Ministry. In May 1927 the Ministry of War and that of the Navy were combined to form the new Ministry of National Defense (see: DEFENSA NACIONAL, Ministerio de). This lasted only six months before being dissolved, and the War Ministry came into existence again. It lasted this time until the second creation of a Defense Ministry in March 1932. The old division was then restored, in July 1932, but a final definitive amalgamation took place on December 25, 1932.

GUERRA, Secretaría de. The Secretariat of War was created in 1814 as one of three divisions of a provisional government independent of Spain, the others being the secretariats of government and finance. The *Constitution of 1818 changed these state secretariats into ministries, so creating the Ministry of War (see: GUERRA, Ministerio de).

GUERRA A MUERTE. A "war to the death" fought during the years 1819 to 1822 between royalists (*realistas) and independents (*independientes). All prisoners taken during this civil war were shot. After the patriot victory of *Maipú, Vicente *Benavides organized the forces loyal to the King of Spain into guerrilla units, waging war on those who had declared the independence of Chile. The fighting in central Chile included battles at *Curalí, *Tarpellanca, *Trilaleo, and *Hualqui. Early in 1822 Benavides was captured as he attempted to reach Peru, and was shot. The war was then momentarily over, but another royalist, Juan Manuel Picó, continued to fight for another two years, his most noteworthy battle being at *Pangal.

GUERRA CIVIL DE 1829-1830. See: CIVIL WAR OF 1829-1830.

GUERRA CIVIL DE 1851. See: CIVIL WAR OF 1851.

GUERRA CIVIL DE 1859. See: CIVIL WAR OF 1859.

GUERRA CIVIL DE 1891. See: CIVIL WAR OF 1891.

GUERRA DEL PACIFICO. See: PACIFIC, War of the

GUERRA Y AVIACION, Ministerio de. The Ministry of War and Aviation was created by Statute no. 173 on July 8, 1932, when the *navy was separated from the Defense Ministry. The separation lasted until December 25, 1932, when the War and Aviation ministry became once more the Ministry of National Defense (Ministerio de *Defensa Nacional), with Departments of War, Aviation and the Navy.

GUERRA Y MARINA, Ministerio de. The Ministry of War and the *Navy was created by the *Constitution of 1822, which united under one ministry the Departments of War and the Navy. This ministry lasted until 1924, when by Statute no. 153 it was separated into two ministries, that of war (see: GUERRA, Ministerio de) and that of the navy (see: MARINA, Ministerio de).

GUERRAS DE ARAUCO. A series of wars against the *Araucanian Indians which lasted for more than three centuries. The sanguinary subjugation of the Araucanians began when Diego de *Almagro led the first expedition into Chile in 1535, and lasted until the close of the 19th century. What has been described as the "bloodiest of all conquests" was ended peacefully in 1883 when the Chilean government signed a treaty with the Indian chieftains assigning in perpetuity certain lands as reservations to the Araucanians (or MAPUCHES, q.v.).
    See also: ARAUCANA, La; ARMY; CAUPOLICAN; COLOCOLO;

GALVARINO; LAUTARO; MONTE PINTO; ORELIE, Antonio; QUILLEN; PUREN; TUCAPEL; VALDIVIA, Pedro de.

GUMUCIO VIVES, Rafael Agustín (1909-). Councilman for the province of *Santiago from 1938 to 1941. He was general director of the Department of Statistics in 1945 and under-secretary of the Treasury, 1946-52. He became president of the *Falange Nacional, and in 1955 president of the *Federación Social Cristiana. In 1957 he entered the Chamber of Deputies at a by-election, and was re-elected from 1961 to 1965 with the backing of the Christian Democrats (*Partido Démocrata Cristiano). In 1965 he was elected senator running as a Christian Democrat. In 1969 he was one of the founders of the *Movimiento de Acción Popular Unitaria (MAPU), a splinter group of the Christian Democratic Party which supported Socialist Salvador *Allende Gossens in the presidential elections of 1970.

GUTIERREZ ALLENDE, José Ramón (b. 1899). A lawyer by profession and a member of the Conservative Party (*Partido Conservador). He was Secretary of the Senate and a member of the Court of Appeal of *Santiago. From 1925 to 1929 he was a deputy in *Congress. From 1929 to 1937 he was principal editor of the Conservative *Diario ilustrado. From 1937 to 1938 he served as foreign minister in the administration (1932-38) of President Arturo *Alessandri Palma. In 1959 he presided over the Chilean delegation to the 14th General Assembly of the *United Nations in New York.

GUZMAN, Jaime. See: UNION DEMOCRATA NACIONAL.

- H -

HACIENDA. A large estate, plantation or ranch. The word is also used for the state treasury and finances. See also: FUNDO.

HACIENDA, Ministerio de. The Ministry of Finance was established in 1817, having previously existed as the Secretariat of the Treasury (Secretaría de *Hacienda). The Ministry's functions are to manage the finances of the state. It is responsible for internal taxation, including income *taxes, for the issuing of money, and for the administration of monetary and fiscal laws, including the regulation of *customs and duties. It oversees banking, credit and the stock market. Such autonomous organs as the Central Bank of Chile (Banco Central de Chile), the State Bank of Chile (Banco del Estado de Chile) and the Savings and Loan Association (Caja Central de Ahorros y Préstamos) are connected to the government through the Finance Ministry (see: BANKS, BANKING AND FINANCIAL INSTITUTIONS). In 1837 the Ministry became responsible for internal and external commerce, *mining, *industry and *agriculture. In 1887 a new Ministry of Industry and Public Works (Ministerio de *Industrias y Obras Públicas) was created to supervise agriculture, industry and public works, thereby relieving the Finance Ministry of these tasks. In 1927 the Department of Mining was transferred from the Ministry of Public Works to the Finance Ministry, but in 1953 a separate Ministerio de *Minas (Ministry of Mines) was set up, so relieving the Finance Ministry of its supervisory duties over mining.

Finance ministers since the 1973 *coup have been: Rear Admiral Lorenzo Gotuzzo (September 1973); Jorge *Cauas Lama (July 1974); Sergio de *Castro Spikula (December 1976); Sergio de la Cuadra Fabres (April 1982); Rolf *Luders Schwarzenberg (August 1982); Carlos *Cáceres Contreras (February 1983); Luis *Escobar Cerda (April 1984); Hernán *Buchi Buc (February 1985).

HACIENDA, Secretaría de. The Secretariat of the Treasury was one of the three secretariats of state created by the provisional government of 1814. In 1817 it became a Ministry; see: HACIENDA, Ministerio de.

HAENKE, Taddäus. Pioneer of the Chilean nitrate industry. See: NITRATES.

HALES JARMARNE, Alejandro. A lawyer by profession, he was a member of the Executive Committee of the Student Federation (*FECh). From 1946 to 1947, after graduating from law school, he served as secretary of the Agrarian Labor Party (*Partido Agrario Laborista), becoming its vice-president in 1949. In 1953 he was appointed minister of *agriculture in the 1952-58 administration of Carlos *Ibáñez del Campo. From 1954 to 1958 he was Chilean ambassador to *Bolivia. In 1960 he was named president of the Chilean delegation to the congress held by the *Economic Commission for Latin America; and in 1966 he became minister of mines in the government (1964-70) of Eduardo *Frei Montalva.

HARBORS. See: PORTS AND HARBORS.

HAWKINS, [Sir] Richard (1562?-1622). English sailor, son of the more famous Sir John Hawkins. On June 22, 1593, he left Plymouth in the hope of imitating Sir Francis *Drake's circumnavigation-cum=privateering expedition, but found the Spaniards prepared for such an attempt. He plundered *Valparaíso in May 1594, obtaining 10,000 *pesos by ransoming ships in the harbor. A superior Spanish fleet, however, caught him in Atacama Bay, June 28, 1594, and battered his ship Dainty into surrender. The Spanish authorities, fearful of allowing his knowledge of the American Pacific coast to reach England, kept him in prison, in Lima, Seville and Madrid, until 1602. See also: PIRATES AND PRIVATEERS.

HEALTH. See: PUBLIC HEALTH.

HENRIQUEZ GONZALEZ, Camilo (1769-1825). Known as the precursor and patriarch of Chilean journalism, Camilo Henríquez founded the first national *newspaper in Chile, La *Aurora de Chile, in 1812. When Henríquez was born, Chile was still a dependency of of the Spanish empire in America. When Chile fought from 1810 to 1818 to obtain complete independence, it was Camilo Henríquez who insisted that Chileans should fight the Spanish yoke. As early as 1783 he had entered the religious order of San Camilo de Lelis in Lima, Peru. On more than one occasion he had been admonished by the *Church not to take part in political squabbles. But in 1810, knowing of his country's struggle for *independence he returned to Chile and wrote fervent articles and speeches to aid the cause of independence, using the pseudonym Quirino Lemánchez.

On January 6, 1811, he wrote a proclamation of Independence, which was published in Buenos Aires and London, and made him famous overnight. He was also a good preacher and used the pulpit to instigate revolutionary fervor in young Chileans. He participated in various *junta governments, was a deputy in 1811, and a senator from 1812 to 1814. In 1813 he had the honor of being named president of the Senate. After the patriot defeat of *Rancagua in 1814 he was exiled to *Argentina. In Buenos Aires he was named by the government editor of the Gazeta de Buenos Aires. He returned to *Santiago in February 1822, thanks to Manuel de *Salas Corvalán, who gave him a position in the *National Library. He was re-elected to the Chamber of Deputies in 1825, dying a few months later.

HERALDO, El. A *newspaper published in *Valparaíso from 1888 to 1953. Founded by Enrique *Valdés Vergara, it was considered the official organ in Valparaíso of the Liberal Party (*Partido Liberal). In 1890 it opposed the government of President (1886-91) José Manuel *Balmaceda Fernández, and as a result was placed under *censorship. Among its most distinguished collaborators was the renowned Nicaraguan poet, Rubén *Darío.

HERAS, Juan Gregorio de las (1780-1866). Argentine-born patriot. Heras joined the army in his native Buenos Aires in 1806 to resist the British invasion of the River Plate. In 1813 he was among a 300-strong force sent by the Buenos Aires government to help Chile's fight for *independence. Heras returned after the Treaty of *Lircay, but was able to help the escape of the patriots to *Mendoza after the defeat of *Rancagua. During the period of the formation of the Ejército de los *Andes, he became José de San Martín's right hand man, and in 1817 he led the advance guard across the *Uspallata Pass. He fought at *Chacabuco, and his action in stemming the panic that followed the second Battle of *Cancha Rayada helped save the patriot army to fight at *Maipo. In 1820 Heras was promoted brigadier general

and made chief of staff in San Martín's campaign in *Peru. Heras
returned to Argentina in 1823, and the following year he succeeded Martín Rodríguez as governor of Buenos Aires. Heras resigned
in February 1826 in favor of Bernardino Rivadavia, Argentina's
first national president, expecting to be given command in the
war with Brazil. When he was passed over, he returned to settle
definitively in Chile. Choosing the losing side in the *Civil War
of 1829-30 cost him his army commission, but he was reinstated
twenty years later and made inspector general of the Chilean army.

HERNANDEZ JAQUE, Juvenal (b. 1889). Lawyer and active member
of the Radical Party (*Partido Radical). Professor of law at the
*Universidad de Chile from 1924, becoming dean of the Law School
in 1931 and rector of the University from 1932 to 1952. A deputy
in *Congress from 1928 to 1932, he served as defense minister
from 1940 to 1942 in the administrations of Pedro *Aguirre Cerda
and acting President Jerónimo Méndez Arancibia. In 1947 he
was again appointed defense minister by President (1946-52)
Gabriel *González Videla. A year later he presided over the
Chilean delegation to the Ninth Panamerican Conference, held in
Bogotá, Colombia. From 1959 to 1964 he was Chilean ambassador
to Venezuela.

HERRERA LANE, Felipe (1922-). Lawyer, banker and politician.
Educated at the *Universidad de Chile and the London School
of Economics, he was president of the student federation *FECh,
1945-46. From 1947 to 1958 he was professor of political and constitutional law. He became well-known in Chile and abroad for
his banking abilities. In 1943 he was an executive in the Central
Bank of Chile (Banco Central de Chile), and from 1953 to 1958
served as its president. In 1953 he became finance minister in
the cabinet of President (1952-58) Carlos *Ibáñez del Campo.
In 1958 he became executive director of the International Monetary
Fund in Washington, D.C., and in 1960 president of the Inter-
American Development Bank (IDB). Originally a member of the
Socialist Party (*Partido Socialista de Chile), he later joined the
Christian Democrats (*Partido Demócrata Cristiano) and considered
entering the 1970 presidential race as a Christian Democrat or
an independent. In the event, however, he stayed at the IDB
until 1971. A close friend of President (1970-73) Salvador *Allende Gossens, he then returned to Chile. UNESCO invited him
to join a Commission for the Development of International Education, and he was appointed president of the Chilean delegation
to UNCTAD III. He has written many works, including his celebrated manual of political economy, Política económica (1950), and
his book on the integration of Latin America, América Latina in-
tegrada (1964). He has received many national and international
prizes for his economic activities, and several honorary doctorates
from United States universities. He has taught in Peru and Chile
and, as a private citizen, has been very critical of the economic
policies of the government of President Augusto *Pinochet Ugarte.

HERRERA PALACIOS, Oscar (1907-   ).   A career *army officer who
attained the rank of lieutenant colonel.   In 1933 he became professor of physical education at the *Universidad de Chile, and
from 1940 taught history, geography and pedagogy at the *Escuela Militar.   In 1952 he graduated in law from the *Universidad
de Chile, and in 1954 became minister of labor in the cabinet of
President (1952-58) Carlos *Ibáñez del Campo.   In 1955 he served
as minister of *education, and, later the same year, minister of
*finance and the *economy, a post he renounced in 1956.

HEVIA, Renato, S. J.   Editor of the renowned Jesuit monthly *Mensaje
who went to jail on December 4, 1985, for protesting *human
rights violations in Chile.   He is liable to five years in prison or
exile.   The charges against him were that, by writing such editorials, he had breached Chile's internal security and had insulted
the President, General Augusto *Pinochet Ugarte.   After an
earlier acquittal on the grounds that the editorials never even
mentioned Pinochet--the charges had been dismissed as "insub-
stantial"--the government had recourse to an unprecedented ex-
trajudicial procedure.   It appointed two government lawyers and
a judge to a three-member board, which then voted 2 to 1 for a
conviction.
      Father Hevia insists that he insulted no one and that his
journal seeks only peace, "but that the peace desired by the
*Church is not the peace of the cemetery."   The government, on
the other hand, which has in the past shut down Mensaje on more
than one occasion, accuses the publication and its editor of aiding
and abetting the opposition, which ranges from the center to the
center-left.   For those who oppose Pinochet, Father Hevia's arrest is a political judgment rather than a juridical one, and is
all the more regrettable because Mensaje has been one of the few
independent journals still operating in Chile.
      See also: CENSORSHIP; CHURCH, The; PERIODICAL PRESS.

HEVIA LABBE, Horacio.   One of the founders of the *Partido Social
Republicano, and its first president.   Hevia Labbe served as
minister of the interior in 1931, and again from 1932 to 1933.
As a member of the first cabinet of Arturo *Alessandri Palma's
second presidency (1932-38), he considered the right-wing political group *Milicia Republicana as too extreme and thus a danger
to public order.   When a parade permit was issued to the Milicia,
Hevia Labbe resigned.   For a short time in 1933 he was also
minister of public health.

HIDALGO.   Nobleman; military officer in the Spanish wars against
the Moors.

HIDALGO PLAZA, Manuel (1882?-1956).   Revolutionary socialist who
joined the Radical Party (*Partido Radical) in 1902 and the Democratic Party (*Partido Democrático) in 1903.   He was president
of the 1910 Workers' Congress (Congreso Social Obrero) and in

1912 was a founder and first secretary general of the Socialist Labor Party (*Partido Socialista de Trabajadores), which in 1922 became the Chilean Communist Party (*Partido Comunista Chileno). In 1913 Hidalgo Plaza was elected as a municipal *regidor in *Santiago. In 1925 he helped draft the new *Constitution of 1925. From 1926-36 he was senator for *Tarapacá and *Antofagasta (except for the period 1928-29 he spent on *Easter Island, exiled by the government of Carlos *Ibáñez del Campo). In 1931 he directed the Trotskyite wing (*Izquierda Comunista) of the Communist Party and ran for the Presidency. Later he joined the *Partido Radical Socialista. From 1939 to 1943 he served as Chilean ambassador to Mexico. When he returned to Chile he was appointed minister of public works. In 1946 he became minister of the economy and commerce. From 1950 to 1953 he was ambassador to Panama.

HIGHWAYS. Roads and highways are under the direct supervision of the Ministry of Public Works (Ministerio de *Obras Públicas). The total length of roads and highways in Chile in 1983 was 78,588 km (48,835 miles), of which 9,541 km (5,929 miles) were paved, 32,258 km (20,045 miles) were stabilized gravel, and the remainder was made up of dirt roads, including seasonal tracks.

The highway system comprises the Pan American Highway, whose Chilean portion extends 3,521 km (2,188 miles) from *Arica in the north, to Quellón, in the south. It is almost wholly paved. The highway system also includes about 55,594 km (35,546 miles) of transversal roads, and the Southern Longitudinal Highway, which is now being resurfaced. The Chilean government, to improve on the inadequate road system of the 1970s, was spending US$ 195.3 million in 1983, mainly for resurfacing and paving.

In 1979 there were more than a quarter million automobiles in Chile, 120,000 trucks, 19,000 buses, and 30,000 motorcycles and scooters. Passenger and freight service fleets accounted for an additional 4,500 new vehicles. See also: AUTOMOBILE INDUSTRY.

HIGIENE, ASISTENCIA Y PREVISION SOCIAL, Ministerio de. The Ministry of Hygiene, Social Security and Assistance was created by Statute no. 44 on October 14, 1924. Two weeks later its name was changed to that of Ministerio de HIGIENE, ASISTENCIA Y PREVISION SOCIAL Y TRABAJO (q.v.).

HIGIENE, ASISTENCIA Y PREVISION SOCIAL Y TRABAJO, Ministerio de. The Ministry of Hygiene, Social Security and Assistance and Labor, was created by Statute no. 66 on October 27, 1924. Its functions were to coordinate all aspects of sanitation and hygiene, and all programs of public welfare and social security. It lasted three years, until 1927, when it became the Ministry of Social Welfare (Ministerio de *Bienestar Social).

HILLYAR, [Sir] James (1749-1843). British admiral. In 1813, during the Anglo-American War of 1812, his ship, HMS Phoebe, a 36-gun

frigate, was sent to the Pacific, where he found Captain David
Porter's *United States frigate Essex was devastating British
*whaling. In February 1814 the then Commodore Hillyar discovered
the Essex anchored at *Valparaíso. As Chile was neutral vis à
vis the U.S. (although allied to the *United Kingdom against
France), Hillyar waited for the Essex to leave port before attacking. This occurred on March 27, when the outgunned Essex
was captured, and Hillyar eventually returned with both ships
to England. During his time in Chile, Hillyar tried to arrange
a truce between the Chilean patriots and the Peruvian viceroy:
this resulted in the ill-fated Treaty of *Lircay.

HIRIAT CORVALAN, Osvaldo (b. 1895). Lawyer and Radical Party
(*Partido Radical) politician. From 1937 to 1945 he served as a
senator. In 1943 he became minister of the interior in the cabinet of President (1942-46) Juan Antonio *Ríos Morales. In 1944
he was acting minister of labor. A year later he became executive
director of *ENDESA, the Chilean National Electric Company. He
has also held important posts in the Chilean Development Corporation, *CORFO.

HISTORICAL MUSEUM. See: HISTORY MUSEUM.

HISTORIOGRAPHY. The publication of historical documents in Chile,
a country that made history its most cultivated field until the
*coup d'état of September 11, 1973, began in earnest more than
a century ago with the Colección de historiadores de Chile (collection of Chilean historians). The two most noted compilers of
documents during that time were Luis *Montt Montt, who wrote
dozens of bibliographical works, and who died in 1909, and José
Toribio *Medina Zavala, who died in 1930, and who compiled the
Colección de documentos inéditos para la historia de Chile (collection of unpublished documents for the history of Chile). Both
authors dealt exclusively with the colonial period. Furthermore,
Medina, in his book La instrucción pública en Chile (public education in Chile), gave a complete sketch of colonial education in
Chile and its documentation. Like Luis Montt, he was a noted
biographer, giving insights into the religious orders that arrived
in Chile to preach and educate as early as Pedro de *Valdivia
and throughout the period of the colony.
  Miguel Luis *Amunátegui Aldunate, Benjamín *Vicuña Mackenna
and Diego *Barros Arana were the three founders of a national
historical literature during the time of the republic. Amunátegui
wrote his first historical work, entitled La reconquista española
(the Spanish reconquest), in cooperation with his brother Gregorio
Víctor. Later he wrote La dictadura de O'Higgins, focusing on
the dictatorship of the Chilean liberator Bernardo *O'Higgins,
considered by many as his finest work. Among his other contributions to the historical literature of Chile, two other books stand
out: El descubrimiento y conquista de Chile (discovery and conquest of Chile) and Los precursores de la independencia de Chile

(the precursors of Chilean independence).

Mackenna wrote many works dealing with the struggle for independence and the internecine wars among the liberators themselves: El ostracismo de los Carreras (ostracism of the Carrera brothers) and El ostracismo del General Bernardo O'Higgins (ostracism of General Bernardo O'Higgins). He also wrote Historia crítica y social de Santiago (critical and social history of *Santiago); Historia de Valparaíso (history of *Valparaíso) and his much celebrated biography of Diego *Portales Palazuelos, Don Diego Portales.

Diego Barros Arana was a great biographer and incessant worker, who at the age of 75, two years before his death, completed his monumental Historia general de Chile (general history of Chile) in 16 volumes, which recounted the Chilean past from primitive times to 1833, the date of the constitutional organization of the country. Among his many other works, two books stand out: Historia general de la independencia de Chile (general history of the independence of Chile) and Historia de la Guerra del Pacífico (history of the War of the Pacific).

Other great historiographers followed. Among them we find Ramón Sotomayor Valdés, with his excellent Historia de la administración del general Prieto, 1831-1841 (history of the administration of General [Joaquín] *Prieto [Vial]); Gonzalo *Bulnes Pinto, with his military histories of Chilean expeditions into Peru (in 1822, 1838 and 1879); José Joaquín Vallejo, who chronicled the history of national customs; and Francisco Antonio *Encina, the greatest of them all.

As a compiler of Chilean modern history, Encina picked up where Barros Arana had left off. Encina's 20-volume Historia de Chile (history of Chile) stands among the most enduring documents on the history of the nation.

Many books and documents have been published on Salvador *Allende Gossens and his experiment with Socialism; others are being written about the military *coup d'état that put an end to constitutional government in Chile, and about Chile's strongman Augusto *Pinochet Ugarte. But it will take years before a sensible documentation of Chilean history since September 11, 1973 will emerge, given the strict *censorship regulations that govern Chile today. See also the "Historiography" section in the bibliography at the end of this book.

HISTORY MUSEUM (Museo Histórico nacional). Recently moved from Miraflores Street to the former Palace of the Real *Audiencia on the Plaza de Armas, the National Museum of History and Prehistory in *Santiago covers the development of Chile to 1925. It contains a good collection of prehistoric ceramics, stones, woods and mummies, as well as a collection of religious objects and collections of colonial and 19th century furniture.

HISTORY OF CHILE. See: CHILE--G. History.

HOEBEL ELCEVON, Mateo Arnaldo (1773-1819). Swedish-born publisher and patriot. Hoebel (or Hoevel) was connected with the revolutionaries who killed King Gustav III and fled to the *United States. Involved in the South American trade, he visited Chile, Peru, Panama and the River Plate. Arriving in Chile for a second time in 1811, he was contracted by José Miguel *Carrera Verdugo to import a printing press and the necessary artisans from New York. This he used to publish the *Aurora de Chile. He accepted Chilean nationality and with the *Reconquista Española of 1814 was exiled to *Juan Fernández. After *Chacabuco he was appointed *intendant of *Santiago and national *police chief. At the end of 1817 he was made treasurer of the *navy in *Valparaíso, where he died.

HOLIDAYS. The 1931 Código del Trabajo (*labor code) specified May Day (May 1) and Sundays as legal holidays. It also provided for paid vacations ranging from 15 to 25 days. Other national and religious holidays are usually treated as legal holidays, even though they are not specifically mentioned in the law. The most important Chilean holiday is Independence Day. To commemorate the event, Chileans celebrate the 18th and 19th of September. See: INDEPENDENCIA, Declaración de. During these two days, public meetings are held, and many eminent speakers are called upon to revive the glory of the past and emulate the days of the *cabildo abierto. José de *San Martín and Bernardo *O'Higgins are honored everywhere, and the *universities in Santiago celebrate the "Semana Universitaria," a week of parading, festivities, and jubilation. On January 1, the New Year is celebrated. May Day is (International) Labor Day: *trade union leaders usually organize parades and public meetings for the laboring classes.

May 21, anniversary of the Battle of *Iquique, is the Día de la Armada (*Navy Day). Chileans pay particular homage to Captain Arturo *Prat Chacón, the hero of the battle. It is on this day that the President of the Republic delivers his State of the Nation address to the National *Congress.

October 12 is Columbus Day, Día de la Raza (day of the [Hispanic] race). It is also the day of the "Big Game." The two rival universities in *Santiago, the *Universidad de Chile and the *Universidad Católica de Chile, play a soccer match in front of huge crowds. Religious holidays in Chile are celebrated according to the dictates of the Roman Catholic *Church. The following are legalized holidays: June 29 (Saints Peter and Paul), August 15 (Assumption Day); November 1 (All Saints'), December 25 (Christmas Day). The following are movable religious holidays: Good Friday, Holy Saturday, the Ascension and Corpus Christi. Many workers in special occupations or in seasonal work are not granted these unofficial holidays.

HOME AFFAIRS, Ministry of. See: INTERIOR, Ministerio del.

HORMAN, Charles (1942-1973). A U.S. Citizen executed in *Santiago shortly after the September 1973 *coup d'état. Besides working on an animated children's film, Horman was investigating *United States involvement in the 1970 assassination of the Chilean *army commander-in-chief, General René *Schneider Chereau. Horman was in *Viña del Mar when the revolt occurred and received the indiscrete revelations of what U.S. military and naval personnel were doing in nearby *Valparaíso. On September 15, 1973, U.S. Captain Ray Davis gave him a ride back to Santiago, where Horman joined his wife. Two days later, he and his wife Joyce decided to turn to the U.S. embassy for help, in view of the continuing fighting in the capital and the declaration of martial law. They asked for safe passage out of the country, but embassy officials said that there was little they could do. Yet, just 15 minutes earlier, the embassy had booked four other Americans on a flight to the U.S., and when the plane took off there were empty seats. That same evening Horman was arrested by the military and taken to the National Stadium. His wife had gone into town and was caught there by the early curfew. The next morning, when she returned home, she found her husband missing and the house ransacked. She immediately notified the U.S. consulate that her husband had disappeared. The consulate allegedly had information that a body identified by the Chilean military as that of Charles Horman was in the morgue, but for an entire month it would not give his wife or family any clues as to his fate. A friend of Horman, Frank R. TERUGGI (q.v.), who had also witnessed the horrors of the coup, was also killed.

Film Director Costa Gravas has documented the disappearance of Charles Horman and U.S. involvement in the coup and subsequent cover-up in the film Missing, which won the Cannes Film Festival Award in 1982. Costa Gravas was sued by the United States government, but later the charges were dropped.

Charles Horman's father, Edmund C. Horman, started a congressional investigation in Washington, D.C., charging the Santiago embassy of not giving protection to American citizens. See also: HUMAN RIGHTS.

HORNOS, Cabo de. See: CAPE HORN.

HOSPICIO, Alto de. See: ALTO DE HOSPICIO.

HOUSING AND CONSTRUCTION. Prior to the administration of Jorge *Alessandri Rodríguez (1958-64), new housing was being built at a rate of only 5,000 dwellings a year. Alessandri was able to build 200,000 new dwellings, mainly for the lower middle class. The deficit when Eduardo *Frei Montalva was elected President in 1964 was estimated at 500,000 units, plus a further 50,000 units a year needed over the next five years to keep pace with Chile's population growth. Frei kept his promise to build 300,000 units by 1970, but that was clearly not enough for the nation's needs.

Rural emigration (see: INTERNAL MIGRATION) exacerbates the housing shortage in urban areas, especially in *Santiago, since more than three out of every four migrants have the capital as their destination. Significant unemployment and limited urban housing were trends characteristic of the 1970s and 1980s. Makeshift shanty town communities have sprung up around Santiago so quickly that they have been dubbed poblaciones *callampas (mushroom towns).

Most housing construction before 1973 was carried out under the guidance of the government housing office, the Corporación de la Vivienda (*CORVI). Salvador *Allende Gossens, who succeeded Frei as President in 1970, promised to resolve the housing shortage for the poor, and earmarked 9 percent of the 1971 budget for housing development. Some 200,000 new units were needed by 1975, but 1972 and 1973 proved to be difficult years economically for Allende.

Then Allende was overthrown, and the programs that ensued under the *junta failed to produce housing within financial reach of the very poor. The policies of the new regime on low-income housing were consistent with President Augusto *Pinochet Ugarte's emphasis on limiting the role of government. By 1978 the ministry of housing and urbanization estimated the deficit at 600,000 units; five years later it had grown to 800,000. The government's goal of building 900,000 units by 1990 seems extremely optimistic. In 1980, a record year, 50,000 new housing units were constructed. But the housing shortage remained acute. And in 1983 the construction industry faced its worst economic crisis in over fifty years. More than 60% of the construction sector workforce were unemployed (see: EMPLOYMENT), and the number of houses started in the first eleven months of that year was a mere 4,752.

HOUSING AND URBAN AFFAIRS, Ministry of. See: VIVIENDA Y URBANISMO, Ministerio de.

HOY. Title of two magazines, the first of which was founded in 1932 by Carlos *Ríos Gallardo and Ismael Edwards Matte. The second, and current, one is a weekly news magazine, subtitled "la verdad sin compromisos" ("the uncompromised truth"), founded on June 1, 1977 by Emilio *Filippi Empresa Editora Araucaria. It was suspended indefinitely following the September 1986 attempt on the life of President *Pinochet.

HOZ, Pedro Sanco de la (1514-1547). *Conquistador rival of Pedro de *Valdivia. Hoz arrived in *Peru with a royal cédula from *Charles V, giving him the right to govern "Terra Australis": any land he should conquer from the *Strait of Magellan to the South Pole. Francisco Pizarro persuaded him and Valdivia to cooperate, but when Valdivia returned briefly from *Valparaíso in 1547, leaving Francisco de *Villagra in charge in his absence, Hoz refused to accept the latter's authority, rebelled and was hanged.

HUACHIPATO. An integrated *iron and steel plant (that is, a plant whose facilities cover the whole gamut of steel-making operations, from the *mining and quarrying of the raw materials to the manufacture of the finished products), located on the Bay of San Vincente, two miles south of *Talcahuano in Greater *Concepción, and 360 miles south of *Santiago. The sheltered Bay of San Vicente has the depth of water needed to receive deep draught ships bringing iron ore from the mines 500 miles to the north. Hydroelectric power is obtainable from the Abanico Plant on the Río Laja in the Andes. The *coal mines at Lota and Schwager are only 25 miles to the south. The 30 million gallons of water per day needed to operate the plant are supplied by the nearby *Bío-Bío River, five miles south of the Bay. There are good *railway and *highway connections with the consumer centers of central Chile. And, lastly, the proximity of cities like Talcahuano and Concepción provides an adequate *labor supply with a minimum of transportation and *housing problems.

Construction of the Huachipato Plant was begun in 1947 by the Compañía de Acero del Pacífico (*CAP) with domestic and foreign capital (most of which came from the United States). Partial operation of the plant began in 1949, and it was fully operational the following year. Since then it has played a significant role in Chile's rapid industrial development. As a result of successive improvement, modernization and expansion programs, steel ingot production increased from 178,000 metric *tons in 1951 to over 600,000 tonnes annually within fifteen years. Output in 1980 was 695,000 tonnes. See also: IRON AND STEEL.

HUALQUI. Site of a battle fought on November 20, 1819 during the *Guerra a muerte. Fifty royalist guerrillas under the leadership of Captain Vicente *Benavides attacked the town of Hualqui, on the right bank of the *Bío-Bío River. The town was defended by 25 patriots commanded by José Tomás Huerta, who beat off the attack. A day later three royalist prisoners, an officer and two soldiers, were publicly executed in the town plaza. This was the custom with prisoners during the so-called "war to the death."

HUAMACUCHO, Battle of. The last important engagement of the War of the *Pacific. On July 10, 1883, Colonel Andrés Cáceres with some 3,000 Peruvian irregulars attacked a Chilean column of 1,600 in an isolated Andean village, but a sudden Chilean sally produced a rout in which the Peruvians abandoned their artillery.

HUARA. *Railway station between *Iquique and *Pisagua, site of a battle during the *Civil War of 1891. On February 17, some 1,000 *congresistas commanded by Estanislao del *Canto Arteaga attacked a well-entrenched government force of 900 led by Eulogio Robles and were defeated in under three hours, losing 240 dead.

HUASCAR. Peruvian ironclad in the War of the *Pacific, commanded by Miguel Grau. At the battle of *Iquique, May 21, 1879, it sank Arturo *Prat Chacón's *Esmeralda, and went on to become the terror of Chilean shipping until it was sunk in its turn by the Cochrane and *Blanco Encalada at the battle of *Cape Angamos, October 8, 1879.

HUASO. The Chilean counterpart of the Argentine gaucho, the horseman of the plains.

HUELGA DE LA CARNE. See: SEMANA ROJA.

HUELGA GENERAL DE ANTOFAGASTA (*Antofagasta general strike). A strike of *railway workers which took place on February 6, 1906 in the northern city of Antofagasta. The workers demanded a one and one-half hour lunch break, as opposed to the one hour allotted to them. The strikers clashed with the *police and several workers and policemen were killed or wounded.

HUERTA DIAZ, Ismael (1917-). Career naval officer who rose fast in the ranks, reaching the grade of admiral. He had started as a naval engineer who had excelled in his field. He traveled widely through Europe and spent some time in France. He had a heavy hand in the overthrow of Socialist President (1970-73) Salvador *Allende Gossens, and, as a reward, he was first named rector of the *Universidad Técnica Federico Santa María, and then Chilean ambassador to the *United Nations. He was also promoted from vice-admiral to admiral. He is now retired.

HUERTA MUNOZ, José Miguel (1919-). Lawyer by profession and active member of the Liberal Party (*Partido Liberal). He was elected deputy to *Congress four times, from 1949 to 1965. In 1962 he served as vice-president of the Chamber of Deputies.

HUIDOBRO, Vicente (1893-1948). A Chilean poet who has achieved notoriety for his poetic manifestoes. He lived for many years in Paris, and was greatly influenced by the French poets Rimbaud, Reverdy, Cocteau, Cendrars, Verlaine and Mallarmé. It was in France that he founded his school of creacionismo, declaring that "the first duty of the poet is to create" and that "the poet is a small god." His most important works are: El espejo del agua (1916-18), Horizón carré (1917), Manifestos (1925) and Vientos contrarios (1926). In his Arte poética (art of poetry), included in the collection El espejo del agua, and in his Manifesto of 1917, Huidobro explained his conception of what a poet should be and what poetry is. His theories attracted wide attention in Latin American and French letters, but his creacionismo did not attract many followers.

HUINCAS. An expression used by the *Mapuche Indians of central Chile to designate the white man.

HUITO. Naval engagement of March 2, 1866 during the War of 1865-
66 with *Spain. Spanish admiral Casto *Méndez Núñez had been
maintaining what was ostensibly a blockade of the Chilean coast,
but, since he had only six ships, was really only a blockade of
*Valparaíso. He risked sending part of this small fleet south to
search for the combined naval forces of the allies, Chile and Peru,
and found them off *Chiloé. He had the advantage of more
modern vessels but as he dared not press his attack in unfamiliar
coastal waters, the result was inconclusive and the Spanish returned to Valparaíso. It was, however, a humiliation for the
Chilean *navy, especially when Núñez later carried out a bombardment of *Valparaíso with impunity.

HUMAN RIGHTS. The human rights situation in Chile as of September
11, 1973, when the *Constitution of 1925 was suspended with the
*coup d'état that overthrew President Salvador *Allende Gossens,
has been described as a "return to the catacombs," an allusion
to the atrocities committed by the military government. Until
that time, Chileans had enjoyed the following human rights guaranteed by the Constitution:
     Article X provided equality before the *law; freedom of re-
ligion, liberty of conscience and freedom of worship; freedom of
speech and of the press; freedom of lawful assembly; freedom of
lawful association; freedom to petition any constituted authority;
academic freedom in state and private schools and *universities;
inviolability of private property; labor laws for the protection of
the workers; and, freedom of movement to settle and travel in
any part of Chilean territory.
     Articles VII, VIII and IX dealt with "universal suffrage" and
specifically stated that all literate adult male Chileans, except
members of the *armed forces (including the *Cuerpo de Carabineros) and the physically or mentally disabled, had a legal duty
to vote. Those who did not were subject to 60 days' jail and a
fine. Women were given the vote in national elections in 1949
(see: SUFFRAGE; WOMEN AND THE WOMEN'S MOVEMENT).
     The law placed restrictions on the employment of women and
children (see: LABOR), and made provision for maternity leave
and child care centers. A female over 12 and a male over 14
could lawfully marry, provided they had the consent of their
parents or guardians and that they notified the officials of the
Civil Register. Divorce did not dissolve the marriage; it merely
separated the parties. A divorced mother, even if she were the
guilty party, received custody of all sons under 14 and of daughters of any age.
     All children under 21 had to be under the care of a parent
or guardian. Compulsory school age was from 6 to 15 years.
     Although the 1925 Constitution provided full rights for all
Chileans, more than 300,000 *Mapuches and other related Indian
groups were living separately from the rest of the community in
1970. Hardly any Indian met, or cared to be bothered with,
voting requirements, and the government interfered little. Chil-

eans of African descent had long been assimilated (see: AFRICAN SLAVERY). Immigrants have always come to Chile in small numbers (see: IMMIGRATION), and the Constitution granted them rights similar to those of the Chilean-born. Naturalization was possible after five years' residence.

These were basically the human rights that protected Chileans until 1973. The contrast with the situation after the coup was striking. The New York Times called the military intervention "the bloodiest political upheaval in Latin America since the Mexican Revolution of 1910," and Newsweek referred to the situation in the Chilean capital as "Slaughterhouse in Santiago."

Under Allende, political life was under almost no surveillance. The radio and the press, as poor as they were in their reporting, reflected every point of view, and universities were open and free from blacklists. No one was tortured for his or her political beliefs, and there were no summary executions or *concentration camps.

In its frenzy to survive, the Pinochet regime let terror run amok. A climate of insecurity and fear pervaded life in the cities and in the countryside. As in every war and state of war, the first casualty was the truth, as press *censorship was imposed immediately after the coup and vestiges of it remain to this day. A state of siege was imposed that lasted until 1978, and the less severe "state of emergency" which followed was only lifted in 1983, when amnesty was granted to some Chilean exiles and political prisoners.

A total of 20 detention camps were established (see: CONCENTRATION CAMPS) and a secret police, the DINA (q.v.), was organized. Repression reached down on every sector of social and professional life, as the Chilean bishops began to speak out against the excesses of the *junta. The climate of violence brought about a general deterioration of cultural life, and some of the best-known figures in artistic life fell victim to the coup, the case of Victor *Jara being among the most notorious.

*Church and legal sources estimated that in the aftermath of the coup some 30,000 Chileans lost their lives, and cited between 6,000 and 10,000 cases of *torture, administered with the use of truncheons, bags of moist material, burning with cigarettes or acid, electric shock in the genital areas, deprivation of sleep, food and drink, truth drugs (notably Pentothal) and psychological pressure on prisoners and their families.

The first concentration camps, to which untold thousands of prisoners were taken, were the small Chile Stadium and then the big National Stadium, with a capacity of 80,000. The nearby Velodrome was used for interrogations. The number of Chilean refugees seeking asylum in foreign embassies exceeded 5,000. Also victimized by the military were thousands of political exiles from countries such as *Brazil, Uruguay, *Argentina, *Bolivia, Ecuador and *Peru, who had been granted asylum by the Allende government. From the moment Chile fell under the jackboot, the rigid censorship that had been set up made it difficult to estimate with accuracy the extent of the repression. More accurate figures, disclaimed by Pinochet, were provided by independent sources and eyewitnesses.

The junta, at first, had little understanding of the international image it was creating by its human rights violations; and it also showed little interest in understanding. In the months and years that followed the coup, brutality was used not so much to interrogate individuals, as to intimidate a nation.

*Santiago, and the country at large, today have an appearance of tranquility. With most of the opposition killed, in exile, or behind bars, the junta's disregard for human rights has diminished. But as the *economy faltered in 1983 and 1984, most Chileans were again taking to the streets in defiance of government ordinances, taking advantage of the new *Constitution of 1980 which had once again guaranteed them basic human rights.

HUMAY, Maria. Organizer of the *Partido Progresista Femenino (Women's Progressive Party), which was formed in 1952 as a splinter of the *Partido Femenino de Chile (Women's Party of Chile). She was named president of the newly formed party.

HUMBOLDT CURRENT. Cold off-shore current some 50-100 miles wide, flowing northward along the western coast of South America, from *Antarctica to Ecuador. Its cooling and stabilizing effect in lower latitudes accounts for the dryness of northern Chile. The abundance of marine organisms explains Chile's wealth in fish, and therefore in seabirds (and hence in *guano and *nitrates), and also why Chilean coastal waters are a migration route for whales (see: WHALING).

HUNEEUS GANA, Jorge (1866-1926). Lawyer by profession, active member of the Radical Party (*Partido Radical), and son of Jorge *Huneeus Zegers. In 1887 he became professor of constitutional law at the *Academia de Guerra, and in 1889 editor of the Boletín de leyes y decretos del supremo gobierno (bulletin of national government laws and decrees). He backed *Congress in the *Civil War of 1891, becoming editor of the rebel *junta's *Boletín oficial. In 1894 he became chief editor of the Radical Party *newspaper La *Ley, and was elected to the Chamber of Deputies in 1897, 1900 and 1907. In 1909 he became minister of justice and *education, and from 1912 until his retirement in 1918 he was Chilean minister in Belgium and the Netherlands.

HUNEEUS ZEGERS, Jorge (1835-1889). University professor, writer, diplomat and conservative politician. He came from a wealthy *Santiago family of German origin and became a professor of mathematics at the *Instituto Nacional in 1855. Graduating in law at the *Universidad de Chile in 1858, he entered the Chamber of Deputies in 1861, becoming its president 1881-84. In 1870 he served as Chilean minister in Austria, and in April-August 1879 as minister of justice and *education. In 1869 he had become professor of law at the Universidad de Chile; in 1883 he was appointed rector. In the year before his death he was elected senator. He was also an eminent writer of jurisprudence, remembered for his Reseña histórica de la constitución chilena (historical summary of the Chilean constitution); La constitución chilena (the Chilean constitution); and Derecho constitucional comparado (comparative constitutional law).

HURTADO DE MENDOZA, García, [4th marquis of Cañete] (1535-1609). Second governor of Chile (1557) and seventh viceroy of Peru (1589). Second son of Andrés Hurtado de Mendoza, 2nd marquis and viceroy 1555-60, García Hurtado de Mendoza, on being named governor set out to recover Chile from the *Araucanian Indians, who had killed his predecessor, Pedro de *Valdivia. In less than a year García was able to push the Indians beyond the river *Bío-Bío. The new native leader, *Caupolicán, was captured, tortured and killed. Early in 1559 Mendoza had to surrender his governorship to his rival, Francisco de *Villagra, but he left Chile with a record of fine achievement. Spanish control of the northern and central parts of Chile had been secured. A start had been made on the conquest of *Cuyo, and exploration had continued of the *Strait of Magellan, which had been claimed in the name of the King of Spain. On his father's death in 1560, Mendoza returned to Spain, but he was back in Lima as viceroy in January 1590. While viceroy he was responsible for sending the English privateer Sir Richard *Hawkins to Spain as a prisoner.

HYDROELECTRIC POWER. See: ENERGY AND POWER.

HYGIENE, Ministry of. See: HIGIENE, ASISTENCIA Y PREVISION SOCIAL, Ministerio de.

- I -

I.T.T. (International Telegraph and Telephone Corporation). I.T.T., a giant transnational made up of 70 companies, and one of the largest conglomerates in the world, played a crucial role in an attempt to block the election of Socialist President (1970-73) Salvador *Allende Gossens.

At the time of the September 4, 1970 elections, I.T.T. controlled 95 percent of the telephone installations in Chile, employing a work force of 6,000, and with company assets estimated at US$ 150 million. Having failed in their efforts to influence the elections through financial subsidies to the nonsocialist candidates (amounting to US$ 400,000), I.T.T. officials were thrown into

disarray with the victory of Allende. Through the offices of
*United States ambassador Edward Korry, I.T.T. officials began
proposing more aggressive direct intervention by the U.S. government. They offered money to the U.S. *Central Intelligence
Agency, pressured the ambassador, and favored efforts directed
toward an immediate overthrow.

Prior to Allende's confirmation, I.T.T. had established contacts with the banking and corporate world, hoping to precipitate
an economic crisis which would have forced the Christian Democrats (*Partido Demócrat Cristiano) to deny Allende the presidency, even though it was customary to elect the presidential
candidate who had received a plurality of the vote (in this case,
Allende).

Former CIA Director (1961-64) and I.T.T. Board member John
A. McCone testified that he had received in 1970 from I.T.T.
Chairman of the Board, Harold S. Geneen, an offer of US$ 1
million to try to prevent the election of Allende. McCone had
passed on the offer to President Richard Nixon's National Security
Adviser, Henry A. Kissinger, who headed the "Committee of
Forty," and CIA Director Richard Helms.

Efforts by I.T.T. in support of anti-Allende activities continued.
William R. Merriam, an I.T.T. vice-president and its former chief
representative in Washington, admitted that he had held several
meetings with William V. Broe, CIA Chief of Clandestine Operations
in the Western Hemisphere. Broe had agreed to an I.T.T. plan
to subsidize anti-Allende forces and prevent Allende from assuming
office. During the interim period between the elections of September 4 and the Congressional run-off on October 24, I.T.T. money
would be used for a propaganda blitz whose aim was to restore
to the presidency the opposition leader Eduardo Frei *Montalva,
who was kindly disposed to I.T.T. interests. The CIA, at the
same time, was to proceed with its plans to create economic chaos
in Chile.

Since under Chilean law Frei could not succeed himself (he had
been president from 1964 to 1970), the I.T.T. plan called for
the Chilean *Congress, with covert U.S. aid, to reelect former
President (1958-64) Jorge *Alessandri Rodríguez, who had barely
lost to Allende in 1970. Alessandri was to resign a short time
later, and Frei was to be reelected in his turn.

But on October 24, after Allende gave Congress guarantees
that he would respect the Constitution (see: ESTATUTOS DE
GARANTIAS CONSTITUCIONALES), a majority of Christian Democratic congressmen voted to confirm him, and Allende was duly
sworn in on November 4.

The initial U.S. government response to Allende's success was
one of shock and hostility. Kissinger warned that Allende was
a Communist and that his election meant the end of democracy
in Chile, with serious consequences for Chile's neighbors, especially *Argentina, *Bolivia and *Peru.

During the next three years, a consensus emerged between

I.T.T., Kissinger, and the CIA, as their goals shifted. Economic pressures were no longer directed to influencing the political process in Chile, but at activating the *armed forces to intervene in political life.

In October 1971, the Chilean government outlined plans to nationalize I.T.T.'s operations in Chile. At this time, I.T.T. officials began to elaborate a strategy of external economic coercion designed to lead to internal economic chaos and the ultimate demise of the Allende government.

In April 1973 the U.S. Senate Foreign Relations Subcommittee on Multinational Corporations, chaired by the late Democratic senator from Idaho, Frank Church, charged that the I.T.T. had "overstepped the line of acceptable corporate behavior." The subcommittee also criticized the Nixon administration, charging that it had apparently approved CIA efforts to engage the I.T.T. in its own plan to create economic chaos in Chile in an attempt to subvert the government. Allende was overthrown five months later. See also: CENTRAL INTELLIGENCE AGENCY.

IBAÑEZ AGUILA, Bernardo (1902-). Schoolteacher by profession and active member of the Socialist Party (*Partido Socialista de Chile). In 1935 he organized a teachers' *trade union, the Unión de Profesores de Chile, and he later joined the CTCh (Confederación de Trabajadores de Chile), becoming general secretary in 1941. When in 1946 the CTCh split into Communist and anti-Communist factions, Ibáñez led the smaller, anti-Communist faction. He sat in the Chamber of Deputies (1941-46) and in 1946 ran as a candidate for the presidency of Chile, losing to Gabriel *González Videla. Ibáñez's subsequent activities in labor organizations have included ten years working at the International Labor Office in Geneva, and after that, two years in Washington, D.C., with the Inter-American Institute for the Development of Free Trade Unions.

IBAÑEZ DEL CAMPO, Carlos (1877-1960). After graduating from the *Escuela Militar in 1896, Ibáñez del Campo became a career *army officer and served twice as President of Chile (1927-31; 1952-58). He participated, as a major, in two uprisings: one on September 5, 1924, the other on January 23, 1925. Both uprisings were conducted by the *armed forces to secure substantial changes in the constitution and the return from exile of President Arturo *Alessandri Palma. Alessandri returned and the *Constitution of 1833 was replaced by the CONSTITUTION OF 1925 (q.v.). In 1925 Ibáñez del Campo, whose political ideology was conservative, was named minister of war by Alessandri. There followed a period of instability in Chile, and new elections returned Emiliano *Figueroa Larraín to the presidency. But after two hectic years in power (1925-27), the well-meaning but weak Figueroa Larraín resigned and Ibáñez del Campo, who had been appointed minister of the interior (February 1927), succeeded him as acting

President in April 1927.

Ibañez immediately called for new presidential elections, presenting himself as a candidate. He was acclaimed the unanimous victor. The army was behind him, and he was able to impose a rigid discipline upon lawmakers and civil servants. Congress went along with his decisions (see: CONGRESO TERMAL). He launched an expensive campaign of public works, increased the pay of the military and provided new *armaments and warships for them. He established a new Chilean Nitrate Company, COSACH (q.v.) at a time when *nitrate, Chile's principal export, was in serious trouble on the world market because of the production of artificial nitrates. Ibañez was able to undertake all these ambitious programs with the help of some US$ 300 million in loans from New York bankers. The coming of the great world *Depression of the 1930s, however, created problems for Chile that Ibañez could not solve, and this foreshadowed his ouster in 1931. Popular discontent increased. Students rioted, and when the *police opened fire, four were killed, as were several faculty members. A nationwide general strike was called, and Ibañez, unable to stop the unrest, was forced to resign and flee to *Argentina.

President Alessandri allowed him to return in April 1937, and in 1938 he ran as the *Alianza Popular Libertadora's third-party candidate with *Nacista support against Pedro *Aguirre Cerda and Gustavo *Ross Santa María, but withdrew in favor of Aguirre after the failure of the *Seguro Obrero coup.

In 1942 he ran for President again, with Conservative, Liberal and Nacista support, but the center and left united behind Juan Antonio *Ríos Morales just to be sure of defeating Ibañez. Ten years later, still a vigorous 75, he ran yet again, promising to "save the nation from the false democracy of Gabriel *González Videla." Despite his dictatorial rule in 1927-31, his repeated plotting, his association with fascism and admiration for Argentine dictator Juan Perón, he won, receiving almost twice as many votes as Liberal Arturo *Matte Larraín: even the left, disenchanted with González Videla's repressive policies, supported him. Congress, well aware of his anti-liberal, even anti-democratic, record, kept him in check, giving him a troubled first year in office. But he did not seek a dictatorial role and was conciliatory with the opposition.

The end of the Korean War in 1953 caused a sharp fall in *copper prices, hindering Chile's economic progress. Ibañez blamed this on the *United States, saying that Chileans were the servants of American imperialism. Ibañez admired Perón for his attacks on the U.S. and his encouragement of Argentine nationalism, and sought to emulate him. But if Chileans went along with his anti-Americanism, they did not appreciate the enthusiastic official reception given to Perón on his 1953 visit to Chile, and Perón's overthrow two years later was joyously received. In 1956 the Chilean left united, as the *Frente de Acción Popular (FRAP), to oppose Ibáñez and his conservative policies. In 1958 FRAP was joined by the *Partido Comunista Chileno, which the President's conciliatory policies allowed to function again.

The second Ibáñez administration had been responsible for the continuation of the democratic process, and for a certain degree of economic progress. A new Ministry of Mining, a state housing corporation (*CORVI), a new state bank (El Banco del Estado--see: BANKS, BANKING AND FINANCIAL INSTITUTIONS) and a *social security institute were created.

IGLESIA CATEDRAL DE SANTIAGO. See: CATHEDRAL, The.

IGLESIA DE LA COMPAÑIA. See: COMPAÑIA, Church of the.

IGLESIA DE SAN FRANCISCO. See: SAN FRANCISCO CHURCH.

ILLITERACY. See: LITERACY.

IMMIGRATION. The basic European component in Chile's population is Iberian in origin. The initial Spanish settlement of Chile was made in 1541 by Pedro de *Valdivia, who was accompanied by 86 men. The *conquistadores were mainly from the Kingdom of Castile, but *Basques came to constitute a significant proportion of later immigrants from the Peninsula. The union of the Spanish and Portuguese crowns from 1580 to 1640 brought also an influx of Portuguese immigrants. There were also some Frenchmen, mostly adventurers engaged in the contraband trade (see: FRANCE, Relations with; FRENCH INFLUENCE).

Mixture with the Indians began almost immediately, and by 1592 there were some 2,000 persons in Chile of either European or mixed descent. By the first decades of the 17th century this number had grown to 10,000 (see: POPULATION).

Later a thin trickle of Irishmen, Frenchmen, Italians and Scots arrived in Chile to escape the consequences of the European wars and revolutions of the 18th and early 19th centuries, leaving their cultural mark on Chilean life. Thus it is that a hero of Chilean independence bears the name of Bernardo *O'Higgins; that a bus line in *Santiago ends on MacIver Street; and that the Alessandri family has been synonymous with Chilean conservative politics in the 20th century.

From the mid-19th century Chile encouraged European settlement to populate and develop the virgin forest lands of the south (see: LLANQUIHUE). After the pacification of the *Mapuches in 1883, the government opened a General Settlement and Immigration Agency (Agencia General de Colonización e Immigración) in Paris to facilitate European immigration. It offered new settlers partial payment of passage, 40 or more hectares--99 acres-- upon arrival (to be determined by the quality of the land), essential farming equipment, and loans to see them through their first year in Chile. By 1887 more than 4,000 immigrants had arrived under this plan. Swiss were followed by Germans, Austrians, Belgians, Scandinavians, Dutch, Frenchmen, Italians and Russians. Some Spaniards from the Canary Islands settled near *Temuco, and, after the Boer War (1899-1902), a few Afrikaners came to Gorbea and *Chiloé. The authorities fostered rapid assimilation by ensuring that adjacent areas were settled by immigrants of different national origins.

Other European groups added to the basic Chilean population mixture. Chile's *nitrate industry and the building of *railways drew a number of British (see: BRITISH INFLUENCE); Yugoslavs arrived during the *Tierra del Fuego *gold rush of 1885-1902; Germans settled *Puerto Montt (see: GERMANY, Relations with). Between 1883 and 1901 more than 36,000 Europeans and a few Americans (see: UNITED STATES, Relations with) had come to Chile.

But migration into Chile never compared numerically with that into *Argentina, Australia or *Brazil. The figures below show the relatively low number of immigrants (the years after 1906, and those in which fewer than 100 migrants arrived, are omitted):

1851	102	1888	805	1898	564
1852	212	1889	10,413	1899	548
1856	460	1890	11,001	1900	936
1857	180	1891	318	1901	1,449
1864	155	1892	286	1902	864
1882	2,466	1893	405	1905	293
1885	1,837	1894	395	1906	1,442
1886	905	1896	1,114		
1887	808	1897	970		

The original requirement that all immigrants be Roman Catholics was dropped long before the peak immigration period of 1883-1901. Soon Chile was harboring an industrious immigrant population to which herding, tanning, meat packing, brewing, commercial and financial institutions, trading houses and other industries gave employment and wealth.

In the 20th century, as European immigration declined, foreign immigration consisted principally of Middle Easterners, especially from Lebanon. These newcomers did not settle exclusively in Chile but went to countries such as Colombia and Ecuador as well, impelled to leave their wartorn lands in search of a better future.

A number of Chileans also left their homeland for other Latin American countries, Europe and the United States (see: EMIGRATION). The greatest exodus occurred in 1970, when Socialist Salvador *Allende Gossens became President and an estimated one million Chileans left their country. At the same time many political exiles from right-wing regimes such as those of Argentina, Brazil and Uruguay, sought refuge in Chile. The overthrow of Allende in 1973 reversed this process, with the return of many who had fled from the prospect of a Socialist government and the flight of many of those, both Chileans and left-wing

exiles, who feared the iron hand of the new military regime.
See also: JEWS; SPAIN, Relations with: TIERRA DEL
FUEGO; WINNIPEG, S.S.

IMPERIAL, La. Colonial city, founded March 1551 by Pedro de *Valdivia at 38° 43' S, 73° 3' W, on the north bank of the river of
the same name. It was Chile's second city and a bishop's see
until it was taken and destroyed by the *Araucanian Indians in
1599. Reoccupied and rebuilt in 1632, it was again destroyed
by the Indians in 1723. In February 1882 the fort (and later
city) of Carahue was built on the site, while, at the same time,
the city of Nueva Imperial was founded nearby, at 38° 45' S,
72° 56' W. In 1887 Nueva Imperial became the capital of the new
department of Imperial in the province of *Cautín.

IMPORT DUTIES. See: CUSTOMS AND DUTIES.

IMPORTS. See: FOREIGN TRADE.

INCAS. The Inca empire was extended south into Chile during the
reign of Tupac Yupanqui, tenth Inca who ruled between 1448 and
1482. The subjugation on the part of the Inca of the fierce
*Araucanian Indians extended south to the River *Maule, undoubtedly facilitating the Spanish conquest of Pedro de *Valdivia in
1541. The splendid Inca highway system helped the *conquistadors' communications and avoided their defeat at the hands of
the Araucanians.

INDAP (Instituto de Desarrollo Agropecuario). A department within
the ministry of *agriculture (Ministerio de *Agricultura) whose
functions are to improve the science of farming, soil cultivation,
crop production and the raising of livestock.

INDEPENDENCE, Wars of. The movement towards self-government
was initially provoked by Napoleon's 1808 attempt to reduce *Spain
to a French satellite (see: FRENCH INFLUENCE), and in 1810
Chilean patriots proclaimed a *junta de gobierno to rule Chile
in the name of the exiled *Ferdinand VII. When the Chilean
junta came to be dominated by advocates of outright independence, notably José Miguel *Carrera Verdugo, the viceroy of
*Peru invaded Chile to reestablish his authority, defeating the
patriots at *Chillán (1813) and *Rancagua (1814). The resultant
Spanish reconquest (*Reconquista española) lasted until the
Ejército de los *Andes, an Argentine-Chilean force led by José
de *San Martín and Bernardo *O'Higgins, invaded Chile from
*Cuyo to defeat the royalists at *Chacabuco (1817). Despite
a patriot disaster at *Cancha Rayada (March 1818), the campaign
was won decisively at *Maipú (April 1818). The Spanish in Chile
were then reduced to an ultimately fruitless guerrilla war known
as the *Guerra a muerte (1819-22).
Meanwhile the Chileans took the war to the enemy, recruiting

Lord *Cochrane to lead the Chilean *navy, occupy *Valdivia
and secure control of the sea. This enabled San Martín to attack
and liberate Peru (1820-22) and Ramón *Freire Serrano to secure
the annexation of *Chiloé (1824-26).

INDEPENDENCIA, Declaración de (Declaration of Independence). On
September 18, 1810, Chilean patriots proclaimed a *junta de
gobierno to rule in the name of King *Ferdinand VII of Spain
(who was then a prisoner of Napoleon). Eight years later, Chile
formally declared itself independent of *Spain. The Supreme
Director, Bernardo *O'Higgins, ordered that in each Chilean
city there was to be a registry with the names of all those favoring independence and those opposing it. The Chilean citizenry
voted almost unanimously for independence. The official proclamation took place in *Santiago on February 12, 1818, a date
that marked the first anniversary of the Battle of *Chacabuco.
Chileans today celebrate their independence on September 18,
in commemoration of the first junta government established in
the country.

INDEPENDENT POPULAR ACTION. See: ACCION POPULAR IN-
DEPENDIENTE.

INDEPENDIENTE. A person who favored independence during the
Chilean struggle for emancipation from *Spain (1810-22). Usually,
the independientes belonged to the political group known as the
*exaltados.

INDIANS. See: ARAUCANIAN INDIANS, ATACAMEÑOS, DIAGUITAS,
GUERRAS DE ARAUCO, INCAS, MAPUCHES, PATAGONIA,
TIERRA DEL FUEGO.

INDIES, Council of the. See: CONSEJO DE LAS INDIAS.

INDIES, Laws of the. See: RECOPILACION DE LEYES DE LOS REY-
NOS DE LAS INDIAS.

INDUSTRIA, OBRAS PUBLICAS Y FERROCARRILES, Ministerio de.
The Ministry of Industry, Public Works and *Railways was created
by Statute no. 2613 on January 17, 1912. Its previous name was
the Ministerio de *Industria y Obras Públicas. In 1924 the ministry was split into the Ministry of Public Works and Highways
(Ministerio de *Obras y Vías Públicas) and the Ministry of Agriculture, Industry and Land Settlement (Ministerio de *Agricultura,
Industria y Colonización).

INDUSTRIA Y OBRAS PUBLICAS, Ministerio de. The Ministry of
Industry and Public Works was established by law on June 21,
1887. It took over from the Interior Ministry (Ministerio del
*Interior) the regulation of public works and the supervision of

the industrial and agricultural growth of the country, including
hunting, fishing, textiles and mining. In 1912 it became responsible for the *railway network and changed its name to Ministerio
de *Industria, Obras Públicas y Ferrocarriles.

INDUSTRY. Chile's industrial development has been extraordinarily
spotty, and for the past 30 years has clearly revealed insuffi-
ciencies in government policies. Chile has done better in the
extractive industries, such as *copper and *iron ore *mining,
which have provided the main source of foreign exchange earnings. In 1982 the mining industries contributed 9.53 percent
of Chile's GNP (compared to 11.7 percent in 1970 and 19.4 percent in 1940). *Manufacturing industry contributed 20.17 percent
(compared to 27.2 percent in 1970 and 11.8 percent in 1940).
The construction industry contributed 5.35 percent (compared
to 4.2 percent in both 1970 and 1940). The public utility industry (electricity, gas, water) made up 2.53 percent (compared
to 1.4 percent in 1970 and 1 percent in 1940). Agriculture and
fisheries accounted for 9.9 percent (compared with 7.9 percent
in 1970 and 13 percent in 1940).

Chile was one of the countries hardest hit by the world *Depression of the 1930s, and its government took a series of measures designed to make the domestic *economy increasingly autar-
chic and hence less vulnerable to the impact of externally genera-
ted shocks. Protection of domestic industry became a government
policy that lasted until General Augusto *Pinochet Ugarte came
to power in 1973, and proceeded almost to eliminate import tariffs
(see: CUSTOMS AND DUTIES) in accordance with a policy of
extreme laissez-faire.

Before this time, however, Chile had already experienced considerable industrial development for a nation of its size and income. In the 1880s, Chilean shops and factories were producing
clothing, footwear, locomotives, heavy mining equipment and
*armaments, and until the 1940s Chile was a net exporter of food-
stuffs.

Industrial output grew rapidly during World War II, when
most of Chile's traditional imports were cut off by the war. As
a result, Chile increased the protectionist measures introduced
by Gustavo *Ross Santa María, and industrial output grew more
steadily, particularly in textiles, chemicals, nonmetallic minerals
and in metal-mechanical industries, such as the *automobile industry. Part of the state intervention to expand manufacturing
and mining was direct. *CORFO was created in 1939 to help a
number of industrial firms get started. By 1970 state-owned
enterprises contributed 12 percent of manufacturing output and
28 percent of industrial assets.

Salvador *Allende Gossens, President from 1970 to 1973, had
done little to change the structure of state interventionism in
industry, but had begun sharply to alter ownership. By the
end of 1971, his *Unidad Popular government had set out to ex-

propriate large-scale mining, banking, telephone and telegraphic services, electricity, and large firms with a capital exceeding 14 million *escudos (one U.S. dollar was officially equivalent to 14.3 escudos). While air and transportation and *postal services were to pass into the public sector, smaller companies were to be given absolute guarantees against expropriation.

It was obvious that the move affected a large number of *United States holdings in Chile. But from the very beginning the Allende government had calculated on strained relations with the United States. By 1973, more than 300 foreign industrial firms had passed into the public sector, and sanctions against U.S. companies became common. The intent of the government was to appropriate profits that had been formerly accrued by private or foreign firms. In retaliation, companies such as *Kennecott, *Anaconda, and *I.T.T. demanded that the U.S. government apply strong pressures against Allende. From early 1973, a number of managers and technicians, mostly trained in the United States and working for U.S. corporations, were leaving the country.

By late in the year, the Chilean economy had reached a chaotic state and industrial output encountered sharp declines which lasted well into 1975. The *coup d'état of September 11, 1973, a drop in copper prices in 1974, and the financial crisis of 1975 had all compounded the problems in the manufacturing sector and in the industrial sector in general. As a consequence, many of the industrial plants became chronically underutilized. Moreover, the inefficiencies of one branch of production were passed on to other branches.

During the rest of the 1970s, industrial production became strong as the Pinochet government decreed nondiscriminatory treatment of foreign investors, hoping to put an end to structural deficiencies in the industrial sector derived from four decades of protectionism and subsidization. Between 1976 and 1979, industrial production reached a rate of expansion of at least 8 percent a year. By the end of 1981, over 700 foreign investment projects had been approved by the government, providing more than US$ 6,500 million of funds for the period 1980-1981.

As Chile tried to diversify its industrial production for export in the early 1980s, the Chilean economy began to deteriorate: trade deficits soared from US$ 355 million in 1979 to US$ 2,600 million in 1981. The only growth in exports during the same period occurred among wood products, processed foods, and chemicals. Foreign capital, which had been invested at an exponential rate (US$ 572 million in 1977; US$ 2,200 million in 1979; and US$ 4,800 million in 1981) began to dry up, and some hard truths about the Chilean economy began to emerge. Chile's currency had been pegged to the dollar since 1979; it was grossly overvalued and made Chile's products increasingly uncompetitive in world markets. As trade deficit soared, exports remained constant or declined. By 1982, only a trickle of foreign investment was reaching the industrial sector.

Industry, construction and transport were the most severely hit sectors during the recession of 1982. Estimates of their overall rates of decline in 1982 were 21.9 percent, 28.8 percent and 10.4 percent, respectively. The main cause for this decline was the collapse of the Chilean economy and, more specifically, the lack of liquidity in the economy which had resulted in reduced demand and consumption; the low level of national and foreign investments in these sectors; and Chile's US$ 17,000 million foreign debt.

Prospects for a recovery in 1984-85 were bleak, as an increasing number of bankruptcies were reported, including some of the country's largest firms.

Besides construction (see: HOUSING AND CONSTRUCTION) and transport, some of the hardest hit industries were the automobile and the textile. The only bright prospect for Chile seemed once again to lie in the extractive metal industries, especially copper, since prices rose in 1983, promising an overall recovery in the export market (see: FOREIGN TRADE).

INDUSTRY, Ministry of. See: INDUSTRIA, OBRAS PUBLICAS Y FERROCARRILES, Ministerio de, and INDUSTRIA Y OBRAS PUBLICAS, Ministerio de.

INFANTE ROJAS, José Miguel (1788-1844). Lawyer by profession, and a distinguished career politician during and after the Chilean struggle for *independence. He was elected secretary of the First National *Congress in 1811. He belonged to the moderates (*moderados) and the federalists (*Partido Federalista) and, in 1814, formed part of the *junta de gobierno of that year. He was in *Argentina on a special mission when the Chilean patriots were defeated at *Rancagua. He returned to Chile after the victory of *Chacabuco, and was named finance minister by Bernardo *O'Higgins. In 1821, to defend his federalist ideas, he founded the *newspaper El Valdiviano Federal. Two years later, he helped organize the Federalist Party. When Bernardo O'Higgins was forced to leave office in 1823, Infante Rojas was one of three men who succeeded him in power (see: JUNTA DE GOBIERNO PROVISIONAL). He also served as vice-president, and later as president, of Congress, having been elected a deputy and then a senator. When in 1825 the *Supreme Director (1823-26) Ramón *Freire Serrano left *Santiago to fight the Spaniards in *Chiloé and include that island within the national territory, Infante Rojas became acting Supreme Director (see: CONSEJO DIRECTORIAL). He thereupon tried to impose the federal system in Chile, but only succeeded in doing so for a short period. In 1843 he was named judge (ministro) of the Chilean Supreme Court and a member of the law faculty of the *Universidad de Chile. He renounced both commissions and died a year later.

INFLATION. Monetary inflation is nothing new in Chile (see:

ECONOMY; EXCHANGE RATE; GOLD STANDARD). In the present
century it has become an endemic part of national life. There
is a wide range of opinion as to the causes of inflation in a
developing country and the reasons for the current debt crisis.
In the case of Chile, we can be sure of three things: (1) the
inefficacy of the industrial program duing the experiment with
socialism (1970-73) and the ensuing experiment with the free
market economic model (1973 to the present); (2) the failure of
*agriculture to supply sufficient food for a growing *population;
and (3) the continuous devaluation of Chilean currency, which
has changed the relationship between the prices of imports and
those of exports. It is assumed that Chile has no control over
the price of the raw materials it exports, nor over the prices
it pays for imported foodstuffs and manufactured goods.

Between 1950 and 1970 the consumer price index rose at an
average rate of 32 percent a year. After 1970 inflation accelerated
and did not begin to slow down until 1975, falling to a low equivalent to 10 percent per annum in part of 1979 (as opposed to a
peak at the end of 1973 equivalent to a rate of 1,000 percent per
annum).

Immediately after the *coup d'état of September 11, 1973,
inflation rose sharply and the economic system became disrupted
in nearly all sectors. For the period 1972-84, the overall annual
consumer price index rise was as follows:

1972	67%	1977	92%	1982	21%
1973	360%	1978	40%	1983	25%
1974	504%	1979	39%	1984	23%
1975	376%	1980	35%		
1976	212%	1981	20%		

Although inflation reached a low equivalent to an annual rate of
9.5 percent in part of 1981 (a remarkable accomplishment in the
wake of triple-digit inflation between 1973 and 1976), it was on
the rise again in 1985, with a projected overall annual rate of
35 percent.

The lack of price stability after 1981 was primarily caused
by large public sector deficits. With the crisis, a debate opened
in Chilean policy-making circles. Supporters of the monetarist
model believed that, since the model was self-regulating, the best
course of action was to allow market forces to return the economy
to equilibrium. Initial government action was to assure the public
that the currency would not be devalued. But the government's
large demands on domestic credit sources eliminated the possibility
of less inflationary deficit financing.

The control of inflation was a priority goal of the government
of Augusto *Pinochet Ugarte. But his advisers were caught in
a dilemma, realizing that contrary to the wishes of the President,
who had aimed at a greater "privatization" of the economy, the
financial crises (see: BANKS, BANKING AND FINANCIAL INSTI-
TUTIONS--B. The Collapse of 1981-84) had caused the private

sector to become more dependent upon the government. If the government rescued certain banks and industrial firms that were saddled with unmanagable debts and loss of capital, then the Central Bank had to purchase the debts of domestic corporations, a solution which ran counter to the government's free market ideas (see: CHICAGO BOYS) and to Pinochet's attempt to control inflation. As a result, many government advisers began to argue in favor of active deflationary measures, in particular for another devaluation, but also for measures such as fiscal stimuli, efforts to reduce interest rates, and a program to rescue overleveraged companies.

Eliminating inflationary financing from the public sector was critical to the government's objective of reducing aggregate demand and stimulating growth and price stability. As trade deficits soared (see: FOREIGN TRADE), exports declined, and the *peso devalued, there seemed little prospect of controlling inflation in the next few years.

INQUILINO. A tenant. In Chile, specifically a tenant farmer. Traditionally, an inquilino occupied his small-holding at his landlord's pleasure, paying his rent in labor on the estate rather than in money. The poorer inquilino would (with his family) perform this labor directly, but still enjoyed a status above that of the landless *peón or day laborer. The better off inquilino would pay a peón to perform the labor obligation for him.

INQUISITION (Tribunal del Santo Oficio). Autonomous institution, functioning more or less in secret, to safeguard morality and religious orthodoxy. It was set up in the New World almost immediately after the Conquest, with *Philip II formally establishing it throughout the Americas in 1569. Many *Church dignitaries were its delegates, and a tribunal was set up in Lima, *Peru, in 1570.

Denunciations were often made out of personal emnity, as in the case of Fernando de *Aguirre or Pedro *Sarmiento de Gamboa. By the late 18th century the Holy Office in the Americas had lost most of its power and influence. In 1811 the Chilean *Congress decreed that funds for the Inquisition were to be used "for other pious purposes." Two years later the *Cortés of Cádiz abolished the Inquisition, but it was restored by *Ferdinand VII in 1814 and brought back to Chile during the royalist restoration (1814-17). The Tribunal del Santo Oficio was ultimately ended by the Spanish liberal cortés of 1820.

INSTITUTE FOR TECHNOLOGICAL RESEARCH. See: INTEC-CHILE.

INSTITUTO DE DESARROLLO AGROPECUARIO. See: INDAP.

INSTITUTO NACIONAL (National Institute of Higher Education). Chile's only institution of higher learning for the first twenty

years of independence, created in August 1813 by Juan *Egaña
Risco, who combined the *Universidad de San Felipe, the *Academia de San Luis technical college and *Santiago's two secondary
schools, the Seminario Conciliar and the *Convictorio Carolino.
As the Instituto also developed a primary school, all three levels
of *education were in effect combined in a single institution.
Chile's *National Library was also originally conceived of as the
library of the Instituto Nacional. The royalist triumph at *Rancagua resulted in the closing of the Instituto, but it was reestablished after the definitive victory of the patriots, opening
again in 1819.

INSTRUCCION PUBLICA, Ministerio de. The Ministry of Public Instruction (i.e., *education) was created by Statute no. 1296
in 1899, which divided the functions of the Ministerio de *Justicia
e Instrucción Pública between newly created ministries of justice
and of public instruction. The latter ministry's functions embraced education at elementary and high school levels. In 1927
its name was changed by Statute 7912 to that of Ministerio de
*Educación Pública (Ministry of Public Education).

INSURANCE. The number of Chilean insurance firms doubled between
1930 and 1960, from 75 to 155 (including 75 foreign-owned firms).
In 1927 the insurance business was reserved by law to Chilean
firms (although foreign firms already operating were not affected).
Private insurance operations were supervised by the government,
and the Chilean Insurance Institute (Caja Reaseguradora de Chile)
had a monopoly of all foreign insurance. The state-owned Insurance Institute (Instituto de Seguros del Estado) carried out
all the fire and casualty insurance of the central government,
and was established in 1953. Seventeen firms wrote life insurance
when Socialist President (1970-73) Salvador *Allende Gossens
came to power. The two leading firms at the time were the
Compañía Chilena de Seguros La Previsión and the Compañía de
Seguros La Chilena Consolidada. Due to endemic *inflation, life
insurance has steadily declined in popularity. Since Allende's
accession, the total value of life policies has declined steadily,
a decline that still continues. The number of policies now in
force is lower than at any time since the 1960s. As with so many
other economic activities, the regime of Augusto *Pinochet Ugarte
has reduced the role of government in the insurance sector.
Today there are 44 general insurance and 18 life insurance companies operating in Chile; most of them are private.

INTEC-CHILE (Instituto de Investigaciones Tecnológicas). The Institute for Technological Research was founded in 1968, and has
become an affiliate of *CORFO. One of its major functions is
to support public and private-sector companies in the creation,
introduction, and adaptation of technology, done through technology transfer programs. Intec-Chile is divided into three

main sectors: food and agroindustry; the chemical and extractive-metal industries; and the development of new industries.

In the food and agroindustry division, Intec-Chile has played a major role in the development of domestic baby food and enriched dairy products; much of the work in the chemical and extractive-metal industries has been concentrated on the *mining sector (successful research was done in the development of Chile's *lithium and potassium reserves, in *coal exploration, and in *uranium mining); among the activities for new industries, the greatest emphasis has been on the energy sector and in the control of pollution in the Greater *Santiago area.

INTELLIGENCE SERVICES. See: SECRET SERVICE.

INTENDANT (Intendente). Under the later colonial regime, a royal appointee in charge of an intendency (*intendencia). Under the *Constitution of 1833, a presidential nominee in charge of a province (*provincia).

INTENDENCIA. An administrative division of a colony, instituted in the late 18th century, designed to relieve the viceroys of such matters as the supervision of financial and military affairs. The competence of the Intendencia extended to the departments of justice, finance, war and *police. The coming of royally-appointed *intendants (intendentes) into the administrative process made possible the elimination of corrupt *alcaldes mayores and *corregidores. Since the intendants were salaried officers of the crown, the temptation for graft and corruption was alleviated. Among their many duties, the intendants were charged with overseeing districts, collecting *taxes, promoting business and trade, and the local militia. Some viceroys regarded the new reforms as inimical to their own power and angrily protested to the crown, but to no avail.

The creation in 1786 of the intendencias of *Santiago and *Concepción (corresponding to the already existing ecclesiastical division of Chile into the dioceses of Santiago and Concepción) was the first administrative division of the captaincy general of Chile (see: COLONIAL ADMINISTRATION). *Coquimbo was made a third intendencia by the first *Junta de gobierno of 1811, but the nomenclature provincia (*province) was substituted for intendencia soon afterwards.

INTERIOR, Ministerio del. The Ministry of the Interior was created on December 9, 1871 on the division of the former Ministerio del *Interior y Relaciones Exteriores. The Minister of the Interior has the most important appointed office in the cabinet of ministers, with responsibility for the country's internal security and for the maintenance of law and order. As Chile has no vice-president, the interior minister is first in line to succeed the President in the event of the latter's disability or death.

The Interior Ministry was also responsible for agriculture,

industry and public works until the Ministerio de Industria y Obras Públicas was created in 1887, and for the *postal service, telegraphs, public health, social security and commerce until new ministries for these were created in 1924. It still administers zoological gardens and the San Cristóbal Park (Cerro San Cristóbal), and had responsibility for the *Cuerpo de Carabineros from 1927 until the *coup d'état of September 1973.

Ministers since the coup have been: General Oscar *Bonilla Bradanovic (September 1973), General César Raúl Manuel *Benavides Escobar (July 1974), Sergio Fernández Fernández (April 1978), Enrique Montero Marx (April 1982), Sergio Onofre *Jarpa Reyes (August 1983), Rodrigo *García Rodríguez (February 1985).

INTERIOR Y RELACIONES EXTERIORES, Ministerio del. The Ministry of the Interior and Foreign Affairs was created on August 14, 1824, replacing the Ministerio de *Gobierno y Relaciones Exteriores. Its functions were many. In addition to being responsible for the internal security of the country, public works and *postal services, it was in charge of all diplomatic and consular activities in and out of the country. Until 1837, when a separate Ministerio de *Justicia, Culto e Instrucción Pública was created, the Interior Ministry was also responsible for the administration of justice, for religious affairs and for *education. In 1871 the Ministry was split into two new entities: the Ministerio del *Interior and the Ministerio de *Relaciones Exteriores.

INTERNAL MIGRATION. Internal migration in the 19th century was largely one of workers moving north to satisfy the labor needs of the *guano and *nitrate industries; the development of south Chile was achieved to a large extent by immigration from abroad (see: IMMIGRATION).

Internal migration in the 20th century has been a rural exodus to the cities that has transformed Chilean society from a predominantly rural one into one that is predominantly urban. The proportion of town dwellers has risen from 27 percent in 1875 and 46 percent in 1920 to 69 percent in 1960 and 80 percent in 1980. This migration has led to urban stratification, particularly in *Santiago, which is the overwhelming choice of the migrants (see: POPULATION).

The rural poor (CAMPESINOS, q.v.), despite an average wage of US$ 1.00 a day, are reluctant to leave, but once jarred loose from the estates on which their ancestors worked, they come to the city looking for work. If the newly arrived *roto (literally "broken," "torn," "tattered") does not find work, which is often the case (see: EMPLOYMENT), he goes to live in a *callampa squatter settlement. Other urban poor live in tenements called *conventillos, whose rooms are strung together under a common roof.

Young women, daughters of impoverished landless laborers, also come to Santiago drawn by the promise of employment. By

1930 Santiago was 54 percent female, and this difference has since increased, while in some rural provinces there are twice as many males as females. By late 1960 the typical migrant to Santiago was a woman: there were 156 female for every 100 male migrants, usually coming from rural areas of central Chile or, increasingly, from other cities. Both male and female migrants were better educated in the 1960s and 1970s than in earlier years, and were relatively younger.

Already by the 1950s, half of Santiago's population growth was the result of migration. So great an influx was hardly accomplished without any dislocations. The elite began to move out to the suburbs, or bought villas away from the larger population centers--often by the seaside.

HOUSING (q.v.) for the mass of the population failed to keep pace with demand, especially when the Augusto *Pinochet Ugarte government began a policy of limiting the role of the public sector. Unemployment, added to the severe housing shortages, led to two protests, in 1980 and 1981, when hundreds of homeless took refuge in churches to bring their plight to the government's attention. The predicament of the migrant has not improved since.

INTERNAL TRADE. In the past two decades, Chile has experienced three profound changes in its model of economic and political development which have affected, among other things, internal trade, an important source of revenues since 1941. Accordingly, the administration of Eduardo *Frei Montalva (1964-70) was widely perceived as a reformist social democracy. During that period, internal trade flourished in Chile. Using 1963 as the base year and 100 as the base figure, we have the following indications of the magnitude of internal trade in Chile: 1964--195; 1965--344; 1966--467; 1967--652; 1968--930; 1969--1,209; 1970--1.453 (*United Nations data). These yearly increases, however, reflected the runaway *inflation which had been endemic in Chile during the previous decades, averaging around 32 percent, and which had reached a high of 35 percent at the end of the Frei administration.

The administration of Salvador *Allende Gossens (1970-73) was perceived as a test of radical Marxist Socialism under a representative government. Between 1970 and 1971, Allende was able to bring down unemployment from 8.3 percent to 3.9 percent, and inflation to 22 percent. As the buying power of all Chileans increased, so did internal trade, doubling from 20 percent of total trade under Frei to 40 percent by the end of 1971. But in 1973, the Chilean economy began to deteriorate and the economic picture changed drastically: internal funds dried up, and inflation rates oscillated between the equivalent of 250 percent per annum and 800 percent per annum in the first eight months of the year. Domestic production, when it did not actually fall, remained stagnant; shortages, speculation and the *black market (which had come into existence when Allende was elected) spiraled; and there was a sharpening of class conflict. Internal trade suffered as a result. Merchants closed their shops and truckers went on strike (see: BOSSES' STRIKE). The *economy had become paralyzed.

Since the *coup d'état of September 11, 1973, a military regime has pursued a policy of a market economy without any of the compromises inherent in the two previous democratic administrations. Internal trade once again doubled between 1976 and 1981. However, the world economic crisis of 1981-83 begun to reveal grave flaws in the Chilean model. As a consequence, there was a decline in internal trade, mainly due to the fact that most imported goods became cheaper than those very same goods manufactured in Chile. For example, it was cheaper to import an automobile part from Ford, General Motors, Europe or Japan, than to have that same part made in Chile and shipped from *Arica to *Santiago (see: AUTOMOBILE INDUSTRY).

During 1983-84, industrial production fell sharply in Chile, but higher *copper prices on the world market and renegotiation of Chile's external debt (which had reached the all-time high of US$ 18,000 million) bode well for internal trade in 1985 and after.

Today the principal production center for commerce, finance and industry is the Santiago-Valparaíso area. Owing to Chile's great length, coastal shipping plays an important role in Chile's internal trade (see: EMPREMAR; MERCHANT MARINE; PORTS). Valparaíso is the port for the Santiago area. The central manufacturing region reaches northern markets through *Antofagasta and southern markets through *Concepción, which is itself a growing center for manufacturing.

Principal cities have both refrigerated and unrefrigerated storage warehouses, as do the leading ports. Typically, the small entrepreneur sells specialized goods in a small retail store. There are only a few chain stores, mostly in the grocery business. While production and consumption of processed and packaged foods is increasing, most staples are still purchased from bulk suppliers. There is little credit buying in Chile. In urban areas, advertising is done through billboards, radio, television (see: TELECOMMUNICATIONS) and in movie houses. Magazines (see: PERIODICAL PRESS) and *newspapers also play an important role in advertising.

INTERNATIONAL ASSISTANCE. See: FOREIGN AID.
INTERNATIONAL RELATIONS. See: FOREIGN RELATIONS.
INTERNATIONAL TELEGRAPH AND TELEPHONE CORPORATION. See: I.T.T.
INTERNATIONAL TRADE. See: FOREIGN TRADE.

INTERVENCION. The assumption by central government of supervision of the day-to-day management of any organization not normally subject to detailed government control, such as private companies during the *Unidad Popular administration, or *universities since the 1973 *coup d'état. The government appointed manager is an interventor.

IODINE. Chile is the world's major source of iodine, which has been produced as a byproduct of *nitrate extraction since the 1840s. Output was 1,263 metric *tons in 1947, and 2,793 in 1983.

IQUIQUE. Capital of the former (ex-Peruvian) province of *Tarapacá, which is now Región I (see: REGIONS AND ADMINISTRATIVE RESTRUCTURING). Originally called Ayquique and founded in 1556, Iquique languished as a small fishing village until the 19th century discovery and development of the rich *silver mines of Huantajaya. Despite being almost destroyed in the *earthquake of August 13, 1868 and again by a quake, fire and tidal wave on May 9, 1877, the city grew further with the *nitrate industry. Iquique became Chilean in November 1879 (see: PACIFIC, War of the). By 1891 it was important enough to be chosen as the provisional rebel capital in the *civil war against President José Manuel *Balmaceda Fernández (see: JUNTA DE GOBIERNO DE IQUIQUE). By 1920, with a population of 50,000, Iquique was exporting as much nitrate as *Antofagasta. Its 1971 population was 61,700 (est.). In 1975 it became a free port and enjoyed a brief but intense boom during the so-called "economic miracle." This attracted several thousand migrants, mainly from *Arica. By 1982 its estimated population was 68,063, and by 1986 it was 127,491. The city is important for its canning industry of tuna and merlin (see: FISHERIES).

Iquique has been the scene of three particularly bloody battles. The most famous, on May 21, 1879, saw the unequal struggle between the *Esmeralda and the *Huáscar which made Arturo *Prat Chacón Chile's national hero. The bloodiest was that known as the *Aduana de Iquique, fought on February 16, 1891 by rebel troops successfully defending the city against forces of President Balmaceda. The most notorious was the brutal repression of a nitrate workers' strike in 1907 (see: SALITRERAS DE IQUIQUE).

IQUIQUE, Junta de. See: JUNTA DE GOBIERNO DE IQUIQUE.

IRIBARREN CABEZA, Juan Antonio (b. 1885). A lawyer by profession and member of the Radical Party (*Partido Radical), Iribarren Cabeza spent many years of his life teaching in the Law School of the *Universidad de Chile. In 1940 he was named *education minister by President (1938-41) Pedro *Aguirre Cerda. In 1946 he became minister of the interior, and served for a short time as interim President of Chile, succeeding Alfredo *Duhalde Vázquez, who resigned. Iribarren Cabeza has been an advisor of *CORFO and is the author of Historia general de derecho.

IRISSARI ALONSO, Antonio José de (1786-1868). Born in Guatemala, Irisarri Alonso came to Chile in 1809 and participated in the struggle for *independence. He was *regidor of the *cabildo in *Santiago (1811) and was secretary of state for government for seven days in 1814, acting as *Director Supremo until the return of Francisco de la *Lastra y de la Sotta, who appointed him *intendant of Santiago. When José Miguel *Carrera Verdugo and his brothers seized power and repudiated the Treaty of *Lircay, Irisarri was among the opponents whom they banished to Argentina. In 1818 he returned to Chile as a supporter of Bernardo *O'Higgins. After the exile of O'Higgins, Irisarri returned to Guatemala, where he remained until 1830. In that year he returned to Chile, once again becoming involved in politics. In 1834 he was named intendant of *Curicó. He then participated in the war against the *Peru-Bolivia Confederation and went to Peru to sign the treaty of *Paucaparta. The Chilean government, however, repudiated the treaty and accused Irisarri of treason for signing it. When he disobeyed orders to return to Santiago, he was tried in absentia and sentenced to death. As a consequence Irisarri returned to Guatemala where, in 1855, he was named minister plenipotentiary to El Salvador and the U.S.

IRON AND STEEL. Iron ore runs a distant second to *copper as Chile's most valuable mineral product. In 1980 proven reserves totaled around 900 million metric *tons at some 100 sites around the country, the most important of which is *Algarrobo, purchased by the Compañía de Acero del Pacífico (*CAP) in 1959. Today Chile is the third largest producer of iron ore in Latin America, behind Brazil and Venezuela, with a production of 8 million tonnes compared with Brazil's 92 million, Venezuela's 16 million and Latin America's overall 120 million.

During the first half of the century, Chile exported iron ore to the *United States. Then, in the early 1950s, a domestic steel industry was established at *HUACHIPATO, q.v. As a result, the Chilean demand for iron ore increased, and for a while all export ceased. In 1951, 3.2 million tonnes of ore were produced, compared with 1.74 million tonnes in 1947, but production fell after 1955 as some of the major ore deposits in central-south Chile were exhausted.

Later, new sites were found, with probable reserves of 2,000 million tonnes. Full-scale operation of the Algarrobo mine began in 1962-63, and one year later annual extraction from the open-pit mine was 2.3 million tonnes. By the late 1960s, Chile's total annual output of iron ore had increased to 5.2 million tonnes.

Algarrobo was essential in the development of a domestic steel industry in Chile. The need for such an industry was based on the premise that steel production measures the material progress of a nation undergoing industrial expansion. The drastic curtailment of steel imports during World War II also gave support to the concept of establishing an integrated iron and steel plant. Chile is one of the few South American countries that has acceptable grade iron ores, limestone and *coal, as well as an abundance of hydroelectric *energy.

Since the construction of the Huachipato plant, completed in 1950, Chile's steel industry has developed into an efficient, modern enterprise capable of supplying the country's basic steel requirements. As a result of successive improvements, steel ingot production reached 695,000 tonnes in 1980, an achievement made possible through financial and technical assistance from the United States. The United States also helped in the construction of a pelletizing plant in 1978. Since Chilean ores contained a high level of impurities, the new plant was producing 3.3 million tonnes of pellets annually, containing 65 percent iron with impurity levels of only 0.03 percent sulphur and 0.5 percent phosphorus.

State activity in iron mining began in 1942 with the creation of the state-owned CAP. With the nationalization of the major privately-owned mines in 1971, CAP took control of about 96 percent of all iron and steel production.

Production in recent years has fluctuated. In 1971 it was 11.2 million tonnes, but fell to 7.8 million tonnes in 1978. This was due to weak demand in both domestic and international markets. There was subsequently a slight improvement, to 8.8 million tonnes in 1980, but in 1984 output was down to only 7.1 million tonnes. In 1984 the iron and steel sectors employed some 5,000 workers.

Most of Chile's iron ore is exported, with about 85 percent of the total going to Japan. Exports in 1977 were worth US$ 82 million, or about 4 percent of total exports. In 1984 iron ore exports totaled US$ 110.6 million, and iron and steel exports, US$ 22.9 million.

IRRARAZAVAL ALCALDE, Jose Miguel (1801-1848). Lawyer by profession and member of the Law School and Political Science Department at the *Universidad de Chile. A delegate to the assembly called by the *junta government in 1823, he also served as a deputy in *Congress and as *regidor to the *cabildo held in Santiago in 1825. In 1827 he was Vice-President of Congress, and, three years later, participated in the Plenipotentiary Congress called in Santiago. From 1834 to 1848 he served in the Senate, having been one of the drafters of the *Constitution of 1833. He was also a member of the Commission on Higher Education, and sat as a judge on the Supreme Court in 1836. Five years later, he was appointed Minister of the Interior and Foreign Affairs by President (1831-41) Joaquín *Prieto Vial. Just before his death in 1848 he was elected President of the *Senate.

IRRARAZAVAL ALCALDE, Ramon Luis (1809-1856). A lawyer by profession and member of the Conservative Party (*Partido Conservador). From 1834 to 1839 he was deputy to Congress, and served as Vice-President of the Chamber of Deputies in 1840. Irrarázaval Alcalde held many high positions in the government (1841-51) of Manuel *Bulnes Prieto. In 1841, he was subrogate Minister of Foreign Affairs, a post he again occupied in 1844. From 1844 to 1845 he served as Minister of the Interior and acting President of Chile, because of the President's illness. From 1845 to 1851 he was Chilean plenipotentiary minister to Rome [the Papal State].

IRRARAZAVAL LARRAIN, Manuel José (1835-1896). A lifelong politician who was a member, and later president, of the Conservative Party (*Partido Conservador). In 1863 he founded the Conservative *newspaper El Bien Público, and a year later another paper, El Independiente. He sat in *Congress as a deputy from 1864 to 1870 and as a senator from 1873 to 1882. In 1874 he became known as the champion of the Catholic cause during the virulent dispute with the Liberals (*Partido Liberal) which broke up the

*Fusión Liberal-Conservadora. Many of the Liberals were Free
Masons and wanted *Church disestablishment and the secularization
of *education. After the outbreak of the *Civil War of 1891,
Irrarázaval became the rebel government's minister of the interior,
and in August 1891 secretary of the *junta de gobierno de Iquique.
For health reasons he abandoned his political activities in May
1892 and emigrated to the United States, dying four years later
in New York.

IRRARAZAVAL LECAROS, Raúl (1906-   ). Lawyer by profession and
member of the Conservative Party (*Partido Conservador). From
1941 to 1949 he was a deputy in *Congress. In 1950 President
(1946-52) Gabriel *González Videla named him finance minister.
As vice-president of his party in the early 1950s, he secured the
union of its two factions as the *Partido Conservador Unido.
President (1952-58) Jorge *Alessandri Rodríguez appointed him
ambassador to the Vatican. From 1957 to 1965 he was a senator.
He has also been a member of various law guilds and was advisor
to the Editorial Jurídica de Chile.

IRRARAZAVAL ZAÑARTU, Alfredo (1867-1934). Member of the Liberal
Party (*Partido Liberal) and a distinguished career diplomat and
politician. During the *Civil War of 1891 he supported the rebel
*Congress, taking part in the battles of *Concón and *Placilla.
Two years later he was named secretary of the Chilean legation
in Berlin. In 1900, with the backing of both Liberal and Democratic parties, he was elected deputy, remaining in Congress until
his appointment as ambassador to Japan in 1911. He subsequently
held ambassadorial posts in *Brazil (1913), *Germany (1920) and
Ecuador (1925).

ISLA DE PASCUA. See: EASTER ISLAND.
ISLAS JUAN FERNANDEZ. See: JUAN FERNANDEZ ISLANDS.
IZQUIERDA, BLOQUE DE. See: BLOQUE DE IZQUIERDA.

IZQUIERDA COMUNISTA ("Communist left"). A political party formed
in 1931 when Carlos *Ibáñez del Campo was ousted from the Presidency of the Republic. A Trotskyite splinter group of the Communist Party (*Partido Comunista Chileno), the Izquierda Comunista was headed by Manuel *Hidalgo Plaza and adhered to the Fourth
International. In the presidential elections of 1931 the party ran
Hidalgo as its candidate, but, with his defeat the party dissolved
and its members joined the Socialist Party (*Partido Socialista).

IZQUIERDA CRISTIANA. In July 1971 a splinter group of the Christian Democrats (*Partido Demócrata Cristiano, PDC), unhappy with
the center-rightist tendencies of the PDC leadership, formed the
"Christian left" (Izquierda Cristiana), a new political movement
led by Jacques *Chonchol Chait which declared its support for
Socialist President (1970-73) Salvador *Allende Gossens. After
the *coup d'état of September 11, 1973, the leadership of Izquierda Cristiana was accused of being Marxist and was persecuted
by the new military regime.

IZQUIERDA NACIONAL. A political party known as the Nationalist Left, formed in 1964 as a splinter of the Radical Party (*Partido Radical). During the presidential elections of that year, the Radical Party supported Julio *Durán Neumann, while the Izquierda Nacional supported Salvador *Allende Gossens. Following the elections, the party dissolved.

- J -

JARA, Victor (?-1973). Composer, singer, actor, theater director, guitarist and poet, who, like Pablo *Neruda, was connected with radical politics. When the news reached Jara that the *armed forces had ousted President Salvador *Allende Gossens in September 1973, Jara left for the Technical University (*Universidad Técnica del Estado) in *Santiago, a leading center of leftist support. He had worked with students during the truck owners' strike (see: BOSSES' STRIKE), handing out food in poor areas, and was taking part in the preparations for resistance against the *coup d'état.

He was arrested and transferred to the National Stadium. An *army officer recognized him and asked him to play the guitar. Jara obliged, but both his hands were broken. The <u>comandante</u> insisted that he continue to play. Jara looked to the stands and asked others to join him in a revolutionary song. The sound roared over the concrete as Jara led the beat. The <u>comandante</u> ordered that Jara be shot. Afterward, the soldiers turned their machine guns toward the grandstands and began to shoot indiscriminately. Later Jara's remains were found outside the stadium, his hands broken and his body mutilated.

Today it is forbidden to mention Jara's name in Chile, the same being true for that of Salvador Allende.

JARPA REYES, Sergio Onofre (1921-). A businessman in the field of *agriculture, he became the first president of the political party *Acción Nacional in 1963. In 1972 he was one of the founders of *CODE, a coalition of political parties of the right which included the Christian Democrats (*Partido Demócrata Cristiano) and the Nationals (*Partido Nacional). The most reactionary sector of the opposition, which also included the former PDC President (1964-70) Eduardo *Frei Montalva, was led by Onofre Jarpa. The intent of the new coalition was to create economic and social chaos in Chile and thus provoke the *armed forces into removing Socialist President (1970-73) Salvador *Allende Gossens. The rightist attempt to paralyze the *economy in October 1972 was organized by the National Party and by Onofre Jarpa himself. A year later the efforts of the CODE came to bear fruit with the fall of Allende.

As a reward for his anti-Allende activities, Onofre Jarpa, who had been elected senator for the first district in *Santiago in 1973, was appointed ambassador to the *United Nations in 1974

and to *Colombia two years later by the *junta government of
General Augusto *Pinochet Ugarte. He held that post until 1978,
when he became ambassador to *Argentina. After the civil disturbances of 1980-81, Pinochet, under pressure, decided to name
some civilian to his cabinet. Onofre Jarpa was tapped for the
post of minister of the interior, which he eventually achieved,
in August 1983.

Since then the former senator has mediated between the military and the political parties of the right, which are held in
"recess," for a return to civilian rule. In 1984 he proposed an
early return to democracy, but his talks with Pinochet on the
subject have been stalemated. He was politely told that Chile
would not be ready to elect a *Congress before 1989 at the earliest. In January 1985 he resigned, being succeeded as interior
minister by Rodrigo *García Rodríguez. Jarpa has been viewed
as a possible successor to Pinochet in the event of a return to
democracy.

JESUITS (Society of Jesus; Compañía de Jesús). The first members
of the Society (founded in 1540) reached Chile in 1593 and became as important--indeed, as dominant--in *education and culture
in Chile as elsewhere in the Spanish empire. Although their mis-
sionary achievements were somewhat hampered by the almost perpetual state of war between the colonists and the *Araucanian
Indians, they established many educational and proselytizing institutions, including the Colegio Máximo San Miguel (the future
*Convictorio Carolino) in *Santiago, and a college in *Concep-
ción which eventually became the Universidad Pencopolitana (1724),
besides others of lesser renown in *Valdivia, La *Serena and
*Chillán. Their scientific contributions included map-making,
historical writings and botanical studies, and the considerable
number of Germans among the Jesuits in the 18th century may be
regarded as the beginnings of German influence in Chile (see:
GERMANY, Relations with). The order's great wealth and power
and its concern to limit economic exploitation of the Indians led
to political pressure on the *Church to abolish it. As a result,
all Jesuits were summarily expelled from Chile in late August 1767
(as they were from the rest of Latin America). The Society was
however reestablished by Pius VII (1814), and its members were
able to return to Chile in the 1840s.

JEWS. Two groups of Jews came to Latin America: the Sephardic,
who were the descendants of Spanish and Portuguese Jews and
who had come to Latin America to escape the tentacles of the
"Holy Office" (the *Inquisition), and the Ashkenazic, who were
Jews from Central and Eastern Europe (primarily Russia, Poland,
and *Germany). The latter had come in the late 1930s and early
1940s, to escape from pogroms, settling mainly in *Argentina,
but also in *Brazil, Mexico, and Chile.

The overwhelming majority of Chilean Jews arrived between

1934 and 1946: 50 percent were Eastern European Jews; 40 percent were German; and 10 percent Sephardic. Consequently, a majority of Chilean Jews had experienced the horrors of the Holocaust, directly or indirectly, and some had also known the rigors of life in the Communist bloc.

After the election of Salvador *Allende Gossens in 1970, many Chilean Jews fled, motivated by common fears. Their experience had made them so wary of totalitarianism that some chose to leave Chile at great personal cost rather than run the risk of being trapped in a non-democratic system. Ironically, Allende had ruled democratically and had met with Jewish leaders in *Santiago hoping to convince them not to leave and to ask those who had left to return. Under Allende there were no discriminatory policies against any single group, and Allende himself had tried to reassure the Jewish leaders that he would never dream of alienating the Jewish community, recognizing the service they had rendered Chilean society.

But fears persisted when Allende nationalized the banks and basic industry, and Jews began to think that his government would come under the influence and control of the *U.S.S.R.

Under the Augusto *Pinochet Ugarte government, there have been many instances of anti-semitism in Chile. More than one percent of Chile's 11,000 Jews had fled abroad during the previous regime, including many of the wealthier members of the Jewish community who were in a position of leadership. When some of these returned after Allende's overthrow, they discovered that the military government had been much more repressive against all groups, including Jews, than had the brief experiment with socialism.

JOBET OJEDA, Ernesto (1922-   ). A 1942 graduate of the Chilean Naval Academy who rose rapidly through the ranks to become rear admiral in 1974. In 1973 he participated in the naval operations that began on September 10, in preparation for the *coup that overthrew President Salvador *Allende Gossens a day later. Since then he has held important positions in the *navy and in government. He is a trusted friend of President Augusto *Pinochet Ugarte.

JOURNALISM. See: CENSORSHIP; NEWSPAPERS; PERIODICAL PRESS.

JUAN FERNANDEZ ISLANDS (Islas Juan Fernández). Pacific dependencies of Chile. Located 360 miles west of *Valparaíso 33° 48' S, 78° 45' to 80° 47' W, the islands are rugged, volcanic, and, on the peaks, wooded. Más Atierra (officially, but not popularly, renamed Isla Piloto Robinson Crusoe in 1966) is 36 square miles in area; Más Afuera (officially renamed Isla Marino Alejandro Selkirk), 33 square miles, is 100 miles to the west. Santa Clara is merely an islet off Más Atierra. Named for their discoverer in 1574, until the mid-18th century they were used only as a lair by *pirates, who stocked them with goats as a permanent meat supply. The goats brought flies and devastated the native vegetation at lower elevations. The islands' chief fame comes from their association with Daniel Defoe's Robinson Crusoe, which was inspired by the experience of Alexander Selkirk, marooned on Más Atierra by his captain Stradling, a member of William *Dampier's privateering expedition of 1704, and only rescued by another privateer, Woodes Rogers, in February 1709.

Soon after the outbreak of the War of the Austrian Succession in 1740, Lord *Anson established the base here of his British naval squadron raiding Spanish shipping. This led Spain to make the first permanent settlement on Más Atierra in 1750, later destroyed by the *earthquake of the following year. During Chile's independence struggle, many patriots were exiled to Más Atierra by Spain. The islands continued to be used as a penal colony and a place of exile for political prisoners for many years after Independence. In 1914 Más Atierra was the scene of a breach of Chilean neutrality by both Germany and Great Britain, when S.M.S. Dresden escaped into Cumberland Bay after the Battle of the Falklands, followed by H.M.S. Glasgow, which engaged and sank her.

At present some 550 fisherfolk live on Más Atierra, exporting lobsters to the mainland from the little town of San Juan Bautista. Más Afuera has only seasonal occupation. Any development of tourism is hampered by the irregularity of sea communication with Valparaíso.

JUDICIARY, The. See: CHILE--H. Government, 3: The Judiciary.

JUNTA. A meeting or committee. Specifically in the political sense, any governing committee appointed for a special purpose, or formed to take over government when normal political institutions have broken down. In particular, during *Fernando VII's captivity in France, 1808-1814, ad hoc juntas were formed throughout Spain and her empire to rule in his name and wage war against the puppet government of Napoleon's brother Joseph Bonaparte. In this dictionary, however, "junta," when used unqualified, is usually to be understood as the JUNTA MILITAR DE GOBIERNO DE 1973 (q.v.).

JUNTA DE GOBIERNO DE 1810. A council of government proclaimed by Chilean patriots in the name of King *Ferdinand VII on September 18, 1810. Its members were Mateo de *Toro y Zambrano y Ureta (president); José Antonio Martínez Aldunate y Garces, bishop of *Santiago (vice-president); Fernando Márquez de la Plata (first secretary), Juan *Martínez de Rozas Correa (second secretary); and Ignacio de la Correa Cuevas (third secretary). The junta immediately voted to form a Chilean *navy and to open trade with all friendly nations. Although formal independence

was not declared for another eight years, September 18 has become the date on which Chileans celebrate Independence Day
(see: INDEPENDENCIA, Declaracíon de).

JUNTA DE GOBIERNO DE 1811. A. September 4. A military coup
led by José Miguel *Carrera Verdugo installed a new junta (Juan
*Martínez de Rozas Correa; Juan Enrique Rosales; Juan *Mackenna
O'Reilly; José Gaspar *Martín Esquivel; and Martín *Calvo de Encalada Recarbarren). The junta temporarily abolished the *cabildo,
created the *intendencia of *Coquimbo, and declared free all offspring of slaves born in Chile (see: AFRICAN SLAVERY).
B. November 15. José Miguel Carrera Verdugo, dissatisfied
with the junta he had installed in September, replaced it with
another headed by himself in which Bernardo *O'Higgins took the
place of Martínez de Rozas.

JUNTA DE GOBIERNO DE 1812. Seeking to consolidate his power,
José Miguel *Carrera Verdugo dissolved the junta of November
15, 1811, replacing it with one made up of himself, Pedro José
Prado Jaraquemada and José Santiago Portales Larraín (father of
Diego *Portales Palazuelos), in January 1812. The new junta,
which was almost a Carrera dictatorship, took significant steps
towards *independence, including the adoption of the *Constitution
of 1812, the first national *flag, the first *newspaper, *Aurora
de Chile, and the opening of diplomatic relations with the *United
States.

JUNTA DE GOBIERNO DE 1813. A new junta government was established in Chile in March 1813 when José Miguel *Carrera Verdugo
left *Santiago at the head of a patriot army to face an invasion
by the Viceroy of *Peru, intent on reestablishing Spanish rule in
Chile. Carrera's brother Juan José *Carrera Verdugo succeeded
him as president of the new junta. Total separation from Spain
was sought, a Supreme Director (*Director Supremo), equivalent
to a head of state, was elected, and a *cabildo abierto summoned.
Francisco de la *Lastra y de la Sotta was unanimously chosen for
the new office.

JUNTA DE GOBIERNO DE 1891. From 1823 to 1891 Chile experienced
an autocratic form of government: conservative until 1861, liberal
thereafter. No junta governments appeared during this period
and the President of the Republic enjoyed wide powers. In
January 1891, however, *Congress rebelled against the rule of
President José Manuel *Balmaceda Fernández in the *Civil War of
1891. The first rebel government was that of the JUNTA DE
GOBIERNO DE IQUIQUE (q.v.). When the victorious *congresistas
entered *Santiago, August 31, 1891, a new junta was set up with
Jorge *Montt Alvarez, head of the Junta de Iquique, as its president. On September 3, a new junta was formed, consisting of
Montt, Waldo *Silva Algüe (vice-president of the Senate) and

Ramón *Barros Luco (president of the Chamber of Deputies). A new law of municipalities was decreed, establishing local autonomy and electoral freedom (see: LOCAL GOVERNMENT). The junta's reforms introduced the PARLIAMENTARY REGIME (q.v.) in Chile, under which the executive was subject to the will of the majority in Congress. New elections were then called, and Montt was elected President for the term 1891-96.

JUNTA DE GOBIERNO DE 1932. A. June 4. A military revolt overthrew the government of Juan Esteban *Montero Rodríguez. It established a junta government of three: General Arturo Puga Osorio (president), Carlos *Dávila Espinosa and Eugenio Matte Hurtado, with Marmaduke *Grove Vallejo as war minister. With this junta begins the so-called *República Socialista.

B. June 13. The first junta was dissolved and another established, with Puga Osorio assuming the executive power once more.

C. June 17. Plots and coups d'état succeeded one another. Carlos Dávila, breaking with his comrades and supported by the *Santiago garrison, seized power and formed a new junta with Alberto Cabero and Pedro Nolasco Cárdenas Avendaño, with Puga Osorio as war minister. Grove and Matte were banished to *Easter Island and accused of being Communists.

D. June 30. The fourth junta of 1932 lasted until July 8. It differed from that of June 17 only in that Eliseo Peña Villalón replaced Alberto Cabero. Dávila then proclaimed himself provisional President of the Republic and remained in power until the *armed forces demanded a return to constitutionality and ousted him in a coup led by Bartolomé *Blanche Espejo, September 13. Blanche handed power over to Supreme Court president Abraham *Oyanedel Urrutia, who called new presidential elections. As a result, Arturo *Alessandri Palma was elected for his second term (1932-38).

JUNTA DE GOBIERNO DE IQUIQUE. At the outbreak of the *Civil War of 1891, the forces opposed to President (1886-91) José Manuel *Balmaceda Fernández fled by sea to the far north. On February 16 the *congresistas occupied *Iquique, and by April controlled also *Antofagasta, *Tacna and *Arica. They then decided to establish a governing junta (April 12) consisting of Jorge *Montt Alvarez (president), Ramón *Barros Luco and Waldo *Silva Algüe, with four ministries: interior; foreign relations, justice and education; finance; and war. The junta organized an army which was victorious at *Placilla, August 27. This permitted the rebels to enter *Santiago and set up a new junta there (see: JUNTA DE GOBIERNO DE 1891) as a temporary government until elections could be held later in the year.

JUNTA DE GOBIERNO PROVISIONAL (1823). A provisional junta government was set up on January 28, 1823, when Bernardo

*O'Higgins resigned as Supreme Director of Chile and went into exile. The junta was composed of Agustín *Eyzaguirre Arechévala, José Miguel *Infante Rojas and Fernando *Errázuriz Aldunate, who assumed the executive power. This junta lasted until March 29, 1823, when it was dissolved and a new junta was established, known as the *Junta de Representantes.

JUNTA DE REPRESENTANTES (1823). This junta government, es-tablished on March 29, 1823, replaced the provisional junta (*Junta de Goberno Provisional) which had been ruling since January 28, 1823. Three representatives from Chile's three *provinces assumed the executive power: Juan *Egaña Risco from *Santiago, Manuel Vásquez de Novoa from *Concepción and Mariano Antonio González from *Coquimbo. The junta immediately called an assembly to elect a constituent *Congress. There would be a nine-member Senate, a governor for each of the six departments into which Chile was now to be divided, and local administrators. The *Supreme Director would be elected by Congress. Two days after the junta came to power, Congress chose Ramón *Freire Serrano as Supreme Director of Chile.

JUNTA MILITAR DE GOBIERNO DE 1924. A junta formed by the *armed forces when President (1920-24) Arturo *Alessandri Palma resigned on September 10, 1924. A conflict had developed between the President and the military over the devaluation of the *peso to alleviate the crisis in the *economy. The military wanted immediate devaluation, and Alessandri's refusal was the cause of his resignation. The junta that then assumed power was composed of General Luis *Altamirano Talavera (president), Vice Admiral Francisco Nef Jaras and General Juan Pablo Bennet Argadoña. A few months later, however, this junta, which had vowed a return to constitutional rule, was overthrown by *army officers in the capital who formed the first JUNTA MILITAR DE GOBIERNO DE 1925 (q.v.).

JUNTA MILITAR DE GOBIERNO DE 1925. A. January 23. The JUNTA MILITAR DE GOBIERNO DE 1924 (q.v.) was ousted in a bloodless coup on the pretext that Luis *Altamirano Talavera had not carried out the reforms he had promised when his junta had been established on September 11, 1924. The new junta (General Pedro Pablo Dartnell Encina, president; and General Juan Emilio Ortiz Vega), which remained in power only six days, wanted President (1920-25) Arturo *Alessandri Palma to return to Chile to govern the land.

B. January 27. After consultation with other military leaders, the Junta of January 23 handed over power to a new junta composed of friends of President Alessandri: Emilio *Bello Codesido (president), General Pedro Pablo Dartnell Encina and Admiral Carlos Ward. It invited Alessandri back from his self-imposed exile in Italy. He arrived in *Santiago on March 20, 1925, to wide acclaim by the nation and by Bello Codesido.

JUNTA MILITAR DE GOBIERNO DE 1973. The military junta that
came to power on September 11, 1973, in one of the bloodiest
coups d'état in the history of Latin America, was made up of
*army representative General Augusto *Pinochet Ugarte, *air
force representative General Gustavo *Leigh Guzmán, *navy representative Vice Admiral José *Toribio Merino, and *police chief
General César *Mendoza Durán, representing the *Cuerpo de
Carabineros.

Many Chileans had condoned the coup as the only way to
avert civil war. But most had underestimated the extent of the
repression that ensued. See: COUP D'ETAT OF 1973.

Pinochet, who emerged as Chile's strongman, promised peace,
progress and unity to a polarized nation that had been traumatized
by hyper-*inflation and violent street fighting during the last
months of the *Unidad Popular government. But the junta aimed
to entrench itself in power by ruthless suppression of all alternative power centers. The coup was followed by a virtual state
of emergency (that lasted until 1983) to "restore national dignity"
and "to uphold legality." Social and economic policies were imposed without regard to their divisiveness.

The social cost of the junta's experiment with free market
economics (see: CHICAGO BOYS; ECONOMY) was borne disproportionately by the poor, whose real wages plummeted while *employment fell to an official low of 75 percent--and a real rate of
70%--compared with 87.5 percent under President Salvador *Allende Gossens. The living standards of many middle-income sectors also declined because of *exchange rate devaluations and consequent sharp falls in purchasing power. Monetary restrictions
in terms of loans and credits also weakened the competitiveness
of many small and medium-sized manufacturers and exporters.
When a decree law signed by Pinochet promised to evict thousands
of shantytown (*callampas) squatters, General Gustavo *Leigh
Guzmán, who had represented the most right-wing elements of
the now defunct *Patria y Libertad, resigned in disgust (July
1978). Leigh was concerned not so much with the effects of the
regime's economic policies, as with its disregard for those affected.
Major General Fernando *Matthey Aubel replaced Leigh as the air
force representative on the junta.

In 1980 Pinochet officially became President of the Republic,
and therefore no longer the army's representative on the junta.
He was replaced in this role by Lieutenant General César Raúl
Manuel *Benavides Escobar.

In August 1985 Mendoza was replaced by the new police chief
Rodolfo Strange, and in November 1985 Benavides was replaced
by his successor as army c-in-c., Julio *Canessa.

The junta's institutionalization of brutality and torture to
guarantee its political control has isolated it internationally. This
in turn caused it to seek a degree of legitimacy by the enactment
of the new *Constitution of 1980. This guarantees more rights
for all Chileans, but was still rejected by most of the political
parties "in recess." It named Pinochet as President until 1989,

with the possibility of reelection for a further 8 years after that. Pinochet's failure to reunite Chile was seen by many as the beginning of his downfall. His support had only come from a small group of élites. But even among them, as the Chilean economy deteriorated, there was much grumbling at the junta's social and economic policies. Since 1981 more and more people have taken to the streets demanding a return to civilian rule. It seems that more than a dozen years of military rule have failed to quench the traditional democratic idealism that has molded Chilean political life since Independence. (See also: PINOCHET, UGARTE AUGUSTO.)

JUSTICE. See: CHILE--H. Government, (3) The Judiciary; HUMAN RIGHTS; JUSTICIA, Ministerio de; LAW, The; POLICE.

JUSTICIA, Ministerio de. The Ministry of Justice was established in 1899 by Statute no. 1296, having previously been part of the Ministerio de *Justicia e Instrucción Pública. Its functions are to maintain a balance between the *executive and the judicial power, and to administer the law of the land. The Undersecretariat of Justice controls the following: the civil registry, the forensic medical service, the Consejo de Defensa del Estado, a pensions service and the budget office. Recent ministers have been: Gonzalo Prieto Gandara (September 1973), Hugo Musante Romero (July 1974), Miguel Schweitzer Speisky (April 1975), Renato Damiliano Bonfante (March 1977), Mónica *Madariaga Gutiérrez (April 1977), Jaime del *Valle (February 1983), Hugo Rosende Subiabré (December 1983).

JUSTICIA, CULTO E INSTRUCCION PUBLICA, Ministerio de. The Ministry of Justice, Worship and Public Education was established by law in 1837, and lasted until 1887. Its functions were to administer the law, watch over *Church-State relations and religious affairs, and oversee public *education, responsibilities that had previously devolved upon the interior ministry (Ministerio del *Interior). In 1887 religious affairs were transferred to the foreign ministry (which became the Ministerio de *Relaciones Exteriores y Culto) as concerning primarily relations with the Vatican. The justice ministry thereon became the Ministerio de *Justicia e Instrucción Pública.

JUSTICIA E INSTRUCCION PUBLICA, Ministerio de. The Ministry of Justice and Public Education was established by law in 1887, when religious affairs were transferred from the Ministerio de *Justicia, Culto e Instrucción Pública to the foreign affairs ministry (Ministerio de *Relaciones Exteriores y Culto). The ministry's functions were to administer the law of the land and to provide public education for all Chileans. It lasted until 1899, when its two functions were divided between separate justice and education ministries (Ministerio de *Justicia and Ministerio de *Instrucción Pública).

JUVENTUD CONSERVADORA. (1) A group of young conservatives, dissatisfied with their elders' lack of a social conscience, organized after the collapse of *Ibáñez del Campos's first government in 1931. In 1935 it became the *Falange Conservadora, and then, following the election of 1938 and its complete dissociation from the *Partido Conservador, its name was changed to *Falange Nacional, which eventually evolved into the *Partido Democrata Cristiano.

(2) Those young conservatives who organized themselves in support of the military *junta that overthrew President Salvador *Allende Gossens in 1973. Avowed anti-Marxists, they worked in the *Diego Portales building itself and their leadership had access all the way up the governmental ladder to President Augusto *Pinochet Ugarte himself. Their main mission was propaganda; they strove to keep the junta's policies active in the *universities and accuse anyone they suspected of being a leftist.

- K -

KEMMERER, Edwin Walter (1875-1945). American economist. Professor of economics at Princeton, 1912, Kemmerer visited many foreign countries as financial advisor, among them the Philippines, Egypt, Colombia, South Africa, Poland, Ecuador, Bolivia and Peru. In 1925 he came to Chile as president of an American financial commission, whose recommendations led to a drastic reform in Chilean banking, finance and government accounting. Banking law was revised, the present Central Bank (Banco Central) was established, and the Comptrollership General (Controlaría General de la República) was created. See: BANKS, BANKING AND FINANCIAL INSTITUTIONS; CHILE--H. Government, (4) Comptrollership General.

KENNECOTT COPPER CORPORATION. The rise of Chile's modern *copper industry dates from 1905, when William *Braden purchased El *Teniente mine at *Sewell, 75 miles southeast of *Santiago. Large capital investments by the Guggenheim brothers, followed by the sale of the mine in 1915 to the Kennecott Copper Corporation, made possible the mechanization of El Teniente and its spectacular production. Block carving extraction of the ore was carried on at various levels within the mountain, connected by aerial tramway to the smelters at Caletones, four miles away in the canyon of El Teniente river. The smelter was operated by the *Braden Copper Company.

After extraction, the ore is crushed and treated; the resulting concentrate is brought to the smelter, and the finished product is transported by rail to the Pacific coast of Chile and, subsequently, shipped abroad. Since it began operation, the annual

copper production of El Teniente--with the relative price of copper
on the U.S. markets, and the percentage of copper in the ore
extracted--is given through 1964.

Year	Copper price (¢ per lb.)	Short *tons produced	Copper percentage
1906-11	----	6,769	2.33
1921	----	13,702	----
1931	----	103,572	----
1941	11.7	141,071	----
1945	11.6	164,000	2.26
1950	21.0	158,000	2.09
1951	24.4	171,129	2.11
1955	36.6	155,000	2.40
1956	41.6	180,000	2.01
1957	28.9	173,000	1.96
1958	25.4	192,000	1.94
1959	30.0	184,000	1.93
1960	31.0	176,000	1.99
1961	29.3	168,000	1.90
1962	31.0	154,000	1.95
1963	32.5	160,000	1.93
1964	35.0	180,000	1.93

In 1966, during the Vietnam War, Chileans were compelled to
sell 90,000 tons of copper at a price of 36¢ per pound (on the
London Metal Exchange Market the price for copper was set at
50¢ per pound), and in 1969, when negotiations were arranged
to "chileanize" the copper industry--i.e., tighter government
regulations over copper pricing, production, and marketing--the
price for copper was set at 42.5¢ per pound (as opposed to
52.5¢ on the London Metal Exchange Market).

As part of the large Chilean copper-mining industry (*Gran
Minería), Kennecott was the largest taxpayer in Chile from 1964
to 1970, when it was nationalized by the Salvador *Allende Gossens government. El Teniente produced approximately 40 percent
of Chilean copper, and four out of every five dollars earned by
the company went back into the Chilean economy. In spite of
this, company profits remained high. Normally Kennecott paid
70 percent of its profits to the Chilean government, but in 1961
the conservative President (1958-64) Jorge *Alessandri Rodríguez
increased the tax to about 75 percent.

In 1962 *taxes were raised again to 82 percent, and the trend
continued in 1963 (86 percent) and in 1964 (87.5 percent). In
1965, and again in 1969, taxes were lowered as the result of an
agreement between the Chilean government and Kennecott, leading
many analysts to believe that the Eduardo *Frei Montalva's
"chileanization" of the copper industry was more favorable to the
U.S. companies than to Chile.

The reason why copper taxation was imposed in a heavier
manner on Kennecott was that during the 1950s and 1960s

Kennecott had not increased its production (unlike *Anaconda, the other giant of the Chilean copper industry). Kennecott had been interested mainly in its total earnings from copper; the corporation had increased the output of its open pit mines in Utah, where the metal was easier to extract, rather than at El Teniente.

The "chileanization" of copper affected Kennecott first. Even prior to 1964 the U.S. owners had been in contact with the Chilean government, negotiating a transfer of 51 percent ownership to Chile. Kennecott offered a proposal to the government by which Chile was to pay Kennecott US$ 81.6 million for the 51 percent share in the Braden Copper operation, estimating the total value of the mine at US$ 160 million. The Frei administration obliged, but the price paid came as a shock to most Chileans; the book value of the 50-year old, poorly maintained, mine, was no more than US$ 72.5 million in 1967, but had been inflated by Kennecott officials with the acquiescence of Frei himself.

When Allende assumed office, Chile accounted for 11 percent of the total copper production in the world, with over 6.2 million metric *tons, and the total value of Chilean exports for the same year amounted to US$ 1,230 million, of which US$ 700 million came from copper. Analyzing the statistics accumulated up to that time, it was estimated that between 1911 and 1970 both Anaconda and Kennecott had taken out of Chile US$ 4,600 million of declared profits, more than one third of Chile's physical assets, ammassed not in 50 years, but in 400 years since the Spanish colonization. More than US$ 1,000 million in "declared" profits were extracted in only four years (1964-68) during the "chileanization" of copper under Frei.

The complete nationalization of the copper industry was on both Allende's and the Christian Democrat's (*Partido Demócrata Cristiano) electoral programs, and was supported by the overwhelming majority of the Chilean people. The *Partido Nacional, the rightist party, could hardly afford to take a position contrary to that of the other two parties. With the election of Allende, not only Kennecott, but also Anaconda were expropriated without compensation. In view of the large profits made by the two companies, Allende felt that the companies had taken from Chile a disproportionate amount of money, exponentially greater than what they had put in. Allende reminded Kennecott officials that the entire company was purchased in Chile for US$ 3.5 million.

As Kennecott and other U.S. firms protested against the assessment of their worth by the Chilean government and demanded compensation, *United States-Chile relations reached a low point. The U.S. government imposed an informal "trade blockade" against Chile, and the *Central Intelligence Agency financed strikes in the El Teniente copper mine (See COPPER STRIKES). Kennecott, in the meantime, joined by Anaconda, succeeded in impounding Chilean assets in New York, and the battleground was also extended beyond the U.S. Claiming that all copper coming from El

Teniente to be sold on the European markets was "stolen property," the company succeeded in stopping the sales of Chilean
copper in France, Holland, and Sweden.

In 1973, Allende was overthrown, and Kennecott (and Anaconda) demanded indemnization from the military government of
Augusto *Pinochet Ugarte. At first, the *junta refused compensation. Then, in an abrupt switch from its initial position, it
reached amicable agreements with Kennecott and Anaconda. Both
received what they considered adequate compensation and promised to assist the new government with copper exploration. See
also: COPPER.

KING, Philip Parker (1793-1856). English hydrographer. He entered the British Royal Navy in 1807, and was employed 1817-22
surveying the coasts of Australia, for which he was elected a
Fellow of the Royal Society. In September 1825 he was given
command of H.M.S. Adventure to survey the south coast of the
Americas from the River Plate to *Chiloé. This survey took over
ten years; for most of the time Commander King was assisted by
Robert *Fitzroy in the *Beagle. Afterwards King settled in New
South Wales. He reached the rank of rear admiral in 1855.

KOERNER HENZE, Emil (1846-1920). German-born reformer of the
Chilean *army. Educated University of Halle, Hanover Military
School and Berlin Military Academy, becoming artillery captain
in 1881 and professor at Charlottenburg School of Artillery and
Military Engineering. In September 1886 Chile's minister in Berlin, Guillermo *Matta Goyenechea, contracted him to direct (from
July 1887) the already prestigious *Escuela Militar at 12,000
marks a year and the rank of lieutenant colonel. His reforms
there greatly enhanced the school's reputation throughout Latin
America. As upper-class Chileans tended to prefer to serve in
the *navy, Koerner looked to high academic standards and a
stress on professionalism in the army officer corps as a counter-
weight to the navy's social prestige. The result was the finest
army in Latin America. At the start of the *Civil War of 1891 he
was dismissed by President José Manuel *Balmaceda Fernández
and went over to the rebels, who made him their chief of staff.
In just four months he organized an army of 12,000 men, and was
largely responsible for the rebel victories of *Concón and *Placilla. In 1895 he made a visit to Germany and recruited a large
contingent of German instructors. With his encouragement many
Chileans also began to go to *Germany for advanced military training. In 1904 he was promoted to general and made chief of the
Chilean general staff. His ambitious 1906 reorganization of the
army on Prussian lines was a partial failure: there were not
enough trained officers and the government made a number of
political appointments which increased army dissatisfaction with
parliamentary democracy. Nevertheless, under his command the
army nearly doubled, from 11,500 in 1904 to 26,000 in 1912.
He retired in 1910 and went back to Germany.

KRAUSISMO. A neo-Kantian pantheistic philosophy which did not
have much success in *Germany where it was originated by Karl
Christian Friedrich Krause (1781-1832), but which gained a wide
following in Spain and Latin America. One of the tenets of this
philosophical system was that humanity would arrive at an organic
completeness which represented the maturity of the human race.
This, in turn, would bring about the unification of all mankind.
In Chile, Krausismo was widely spread among the Free Masons.
But, like Positivism, Krausismo was never very strong in Chile
and soon lost its appeal.

- L -

LA PEROUSE, Jean François de Galaup, [conte de] (1741-1788). A
French sailor who on August 1, 1785 was sent on a voyage of
Pacific exploration, in which he drowned. The voyage included
a visit to *Concepción (February 22, 1786) at a time when even
its precise location was unknown in Europe, and to *Easter Island
in April 1786, to which he introduced a number of European
crops.

LA SERENA. See: SERENA, La.

LABOR. The first demand for labor in Chile outside *agriculture
and *fisheries was in *mining (*gold, *silver, *copper and *coal).
The mid-19th century boom in *railway building absorbed much
Chilean labor, not only in Chile itself, but also in some neighboring countries (see: MEIGGS, Henry). Even more labor-
intensive was another 19th century development, the extraction
of *guano and *nitrates. *Manufacturing industries began in the
later 19th century, but largely developed after the great *Depression of the 1930s had encouraged Chilean governments to
pursue a policy of import substitution.
    Labor militancy becomes significant at the end of the 19th
century with important strikes by nitrate workers and *Valparaíso
dock workers (July 1890), by Valparaíso sailors (May 1903), by
workers in *Santiago protesting about meat prices (October 1905;
see: SEMANA ROJA), by *Antofagasta railway workers (1906;
see: HUELGA GENERAL DE ANTOFAGASTA), by *Iquique nitrate workers (1907; see: SALITRERAS DE IQUIQUE), by workers in Chilean *Patagonia (1919) and at *Punta Arenas (1920), and
by nitrate workers at La Coruña (1925; see: CORUNA, Matanza
de La). These strikes, often brutally suppressed, were accompanied by a growth of labor unions, with the first federation of
unions, the *Federación Obrera de Chile, dating from 1909 (see:
TRADE UNIONS).
    There was also a concomitant development of labor legislation,

beginning with a 1907 act to make Sunday a compulsory rest day. By 1924 government involvement with working conditions had grown sufficiently to justify a special ministry of public health, social security and labor (Ministerio de *Higiene, Asistencia y Previsión Social y Trabajo). By 1932 this had become the ministry of labor (Ministerio de *Trabajo).

Labor law was codified in 1931 as the Código de Trabajo. The effect of this and subsequent legislation was that, by the mid-1970s, working hours were fixed at 8 hours a day, 48 hours a week (with a reduction to 40 hours being contemplated by the *military government) with overtime pay (at time and a half) for anything beyond this. Workers were entitled to a two-week paid vacation annually, provided they had completed 288 days of employment. Women were entitled to six weeks' prenatal and six weeks' postnatal leave on half-pay, with a guaranteed right to return to their employment afterwards. No one under 18 might work in dangerous or unhealthy occupations, nor might they work between 8 p.m. and 7 a.m. without special permission from the labor ministry, and there were restrictions on night work by women. Children between 14 and 18 who had not completed their compulsory elementary education had to attend school for at least two hours a day. Children under 14 who had not completed their compulsory *education could only work in small industrial establishments operated by members of their own families. In 1979 a new Plan Laboral replaced the Código de Trabajo, making changes principally in regard to social security (see: SOCIAL WELFARE) and labor relations (see: TRADE UNIONS).

See also: EMPLOYMENT.

LABOR, Ministry of. See: TRABAJO, Ministerio de.

LABOR AND SOCIAL INSURANCE, Ministry of. See: TRABAJO Y PREVISION SOCIAL, Ministerio de.

LABOR UNIONS. See: TRADE UNIONS.

LADECO. Acronym for Línea Aérea del Cobre. Formed in 1958, LADECO has become Chile's major domestic airline, superseding *LAN CHILE since 1970 as the nation's chief internal carrier. By the 1980s, LADECO was carrying two thirds of all Chilean passengers on domestic flights. It has also some limited international routes to Argentina, Brazil and Paraguay, and provides cargo services throughout South America. LADECO's fleet consists of three Boeing 737s and three 727s.

LAFERTTE GAVIÑO, Elías. See: PARTIDO COMUNISTA CHILENO.

LAFTA. See: LATIN AMERICAN FREE TRADE ASSOCIATION.

LAGOS, Los. A new Región established in 1974 (see: REGIONS AND

ADMINISTRATIVE RESTRUCTURING). Región X Los Lagos comprises the four former provinces of *Valdivia, *Osorno, *Llanquihue and *Chiloé, and is situated in Chile's enchanting lake district (Los Lagos, "the lakes") bordering Argentina. Area 67,090 km^2 (25,903 square miles); 1982 population (est.): 873,248; capital city: *Puerto Montt.

LAIA. See: LATIN AMERICAN INTEGRATION ASSOCIATION.

LAN-CHILE. Acronym for Chile's national airline, the Línea Aérea Nacional de Chile. It was formed as a state corporation in 1929 and originally called Línea Aéreo-Postal Santiago-Arica. Its present name dates from July 21, 1932. The carrier originally had a legal monopoly on commercial air transport within Chile, and, like the Post Office, is subordinate to the Ministerio de *Transportes y Telecomunicaciones.

Until 1941 LAN-Chile provided transport only between *Santiago and *Arica with intermediate stops at *Valparaíso, Ovalle, La *Serena, *Copiapó, *Antofagasta, Calama and *Concepción. Later services were begun to *Puerto Montt (1944), *Punta Arenas (1945), *Temuco (1953), *Valdivia (1953), *Coyhaique (1968) and Puerto Williams, the naval base on Navarino Island (1974).

LAN's international services use the two Santiago airports at Los *Cerrillos and Arturo *Merino Benítez, and extend northeast through Argentina and Brazil to Europe (Madrid, Paris, Frankfurt); north to New York (via Lima, Guayaquil, Cali, Panama City and Miami); and across the southern Pacific to Tahiti and Fiji (via *Easter Island). An experimental transpolar flight to Australia was made in 1974, but no scheduled service was started.

Since the late 1970s, the airline has been losing its share of the domestic market to *LADECO (down to 29.5 percent in 1980). But LAN-Chile retains 94 percent of the total international loads (passenger and freight) carried on Chilean aircrafts. It has a fleet of seven Boeing 707s, two 737s and one DC 10-30.

LAND AND SETTLEMENT, Ministry of. See: TIERRAS Y COLONIZACION, Ministerio de.

LAND OWNERSHIP. See: AGRARIAN REFORM.

LAND TAX. See: CATASTRO; CONTRIBUCION TERRITORIAL; TITHES.

LANGUAGE. The official language of the Republic is SPANISH (q.v.). There still remain 50,000 pure-blooded *Mapuches, and another 200,000 of closely related stock who speak Indian tongues. There are also German and Italian immigrants who are, for the most part, bilingual.

LARRAIN GANDARILLAS, Joaquín (1829?-1897). Acting *archbishop of Santiago from 1878 until replaced in 1886 by Mariano *Casanova Casanova, who appointed him first rector of the *Universidad Católica, a post he held until his death.

LARRAIN GARCIA MORENO, Jaime (b. 1895). A career politician elected to *Congress as a deputy in 1921, and for the Agrarian Labor Party (*Partido Agrario Laborista) as a senator in 1945. After the death in office of President Juan Antonio *Río Morales in 1946, the parties of the right held a joint convention at which the Agrarian Labor Party put forward Jaime Larraín for president. The convention chose instead the Liberal Party's Fernando *Alessandri Rodríguez, who lost the election to Gabriel *González Videla (President 1946-52). In 1951, opposed to his party's decision to support the presidential candidacy of Carlos *Ibáñez del Campo, Jaime Larraín and other dissenters formed a new party, the *Movimiento de Recuperación Doctrinaria (MRD), which supported the Liberal candidate Arturo *Matte Larraín, Jaime Larraín's cousin. When the *Partido Nacional was formed from the MRD and other Agrarian Labor dissidents, Larraín joined the new party.

LARRAIN PEÑA, Fernando. Son of Fernando Larraín Vial (director of the Santiago stock exchange), Fernando Larraín Peña was a successful businessman who, with two other partners, Javier *Vial Castillo and Manuel *Cruzat Infante, got control of the Banco Hipotecario de Chile--(BHC) (see: BANKS, BANKING AND FINANCIAL INSTITUTIONS). In 1976 the three became known as the piranhas for the voracity with which they purchased large blocks of stock in 42 companies. In 1975 the three parted company, with Javier Vial forming the *Grupo Vial and the other two forming the *Grupo Cruzat-Larraín. With the liquidation of the BHC in 1983, all three were charged with fraud and faced prosecution.

LARRAIN VIAL, Bernardo (1914-). Lawyer by profession and active member of the Conservative Party (*Partido Conservador). In the late 1930s he became president of the *Juventud Conservadora. He sat in *Congress as a deputy from 1949 to 1957 and as a senator from 1957 to 1965. In 1965 he was elected president of the Conservative Party.

LASTARRIA SANTANDER, José Victorino (1817-1888). Lawyer by profession and founder of the Liberal Party (*Partido Liberal). He was also one of the most spirited protagonists of POSITIVISM (q.v.). In 1837 he became secretary of the Law Academy (Academia de Leyes), and the following year published three books (a geography textbook and two works on law). On graduating from law school in 1839 he became a law professor at the *Instituto Nacional and the intellectual leader of the Liberal Party. In 1842 he founded the Sociedad Literaria (literary society) of *Santiago, and figured prominently among Chile's intelligentsia.

His major works are in the fields of *law and literature: Teoría del derecho penal (theory of criminal law), Elementos de derecho penal (elements of criminal law), Bosquejo histórico de la constitución del gobierno de Chile (historical outline of the Chilean constitution) and Estudio sobre los primeros poetas españoles (study on the earliest Spanish poets), to mention a few. He founded a newspaper, El seminario de Santiago (July 1842–February 1843) which became the organ of the Liberal Party. In 1843 he became a senior civil servant in the ministry of the interior. In the same year he was elected to the Chamber of Deputies, where he sat until 1846, and again 1849-52 and 1855-61. He founded the literary reviews El crepúsculo (1842-43) and La revista de Santiago (1848-49) (see: PERIODICAL PRESS), and defended the romantic ideas of the Argentine exile Domingo Faustino *Sarmiento. Sarmiento had denounced Andrés *Bello López's devotion to classicism and argued for the creation of an indigenous American literature. Lastarria added his voice in favor of a total break with colonial habits and tradition.

In 1862 Lastarria was named Chilean minister plenipotentiary to *Peru, *Argentina and *Brazil. From 1864 to 1873 he was again a deputy in *Congress, this time for constituencies in the north of Chile which led him to travel in the *Atacama Desert (1872), studying its mineral resources. In 1874 he was appointed to a commission to codify the laws relating to *agriculture and other aspects of rural life. He concluded however that Chile's existing Civil Code already covered the subject adequately and the projected Código rural (rural code) was in consequence never published. In 1875 he became a judge (ministro) in the Santiago Appeal Court, a post he left temporarily in 1876-77 to be minister of the interior in the cabinet of President (1876-81) Aníbal *Pinto Garmendia. He was senator for *Coquimbo, 1876-79, and for *Valparaíso, 1879-85. Because of a disagreement with the president of the Liberal Party, Domingo *Santa María Gonzales (President of Chile 1881-86), Lastarria and a group of dissidents left the party and formed a new political entity called the *Partido Liberal Doctrinario. From 1883 until ill health forced his resignation in 1887, he was a member of the Supreme Court.

LASTARRIA VILLAREAL, Demetrio (1846-1891). Lawyer by profession and member of the Liberal Party (*Partido Liberal). He became a diplomat, being part of the Chilean delegation to *Peru in 1863 and to *Argentina in 1864. He traveled widely in Europe in 1865, and was a deputy in *Congress from 1876 to 1891, assuming other high official posts during this period of liberal rule in Chile. In 1879 he served as vice-president of the Chamber of Deputies; in 1880 he was Chilean minister plenipotentiary to *Brazil; in 1883 attorney general of the municipality of *Santiago; in 1885, president of the Chamber of Deputies; in 1888 minister of foreign affairs; and in 1889 minister of the interior. In the *Civil War of 1891 he sided with President (1886-91) José Manuel *Balmaceda Fernández, and when the latter resigned and later committed suicide, Lastarria Villareal left for exile in Argentina, but died on the way.

LASTRA Y DE LA SOTTA, Francisco de la (1777-1852). Member of one of the most distinguished families in Chile. He was sent to *Spain to pursue his studies and served in the Spanish royal navy until 1807. When he returned to Chile in 1811 he joined the movement for *independence, organizing the military and naval forces fighting against Spain. In 1814 he was appointed Supreme Director of Chile, but lasted only four months in power. During that time he was one of the signatories of the *Lircay Treaty. Soon afterward he was imprisoned by the Spaniards and sent to the *Juan Fernández Islands, where he suffered many privations. Freed after the Battle of *Chacabuco, he was made a colonel and given command of the forces in *Valparaíso. He served in a number of important military and naval positions; was general commander of the *navy at Valparaíso; *intendant of the *province of *Santiago; and three times governor of Valparaíso. He also served as war minister. In 1839 he briefly retired, but reentered public life two years later, becoming a member of the Appellate Court. In 1843 he was elected to the Chamber of Deputies, and continued to serve in government until his death.

LATCHMAN ALFARO, Ricardo A. (1903-1965). Teacher by profession, and a successful diplomat and politician who wrote many books on history and literature. Son of an English-born *mining engineer, he became professor of literature in the *Universidad de Chile in 1931. A founding member of the Socialist Party (*Partido Socialista), in 1937 he helped found the *Unión Socialista. He was in the Chamber of Deputies from 1934 to 1941, and during the following seven years held a number of diplomatic posts in *Argentina, Uruguay and *Colombia. He was Chilean delegate to the Ninth American Conference in Bogotá, and served as Chilean ambassador to Uruguay from 1959 to 1963. In 1963, his last year in public life, he was head of cultural affairs in the foreign ministry.

LATIFUNDIA. A vast landed estate, uncultivated, or poorly cultivated, and of 1,000 acres or more in size, belonging to a single proprietor. See: AGRARIAN REFORM; MINIFUNDIA.

LATIFUNDISTA. Owner of a LATIFUNDIA (q.v.).

LATIN AMERICAN COUNCIL OF BISHOPS. See: CONSEJO EPISCOPAL LATINOAMERICANO.

LATIN AMERICAN FREE TRADE ASSOCIATION (LAFTA). Chile is a founder member of the Latin American Free Trade Association, also known by its Spanish name Asociación Latinoamericana de Libre Comercio (ALALC), constituted by the Treaty of Montevideo of February 18, 1961. LAFTA's aims are to stimulate the economic integration of the Latin American countries. To date this goal has been achieved to only a limited extent; see: CUSTOMS AND DUTIES. See also: LATIN AMERICAN INTEGRATION ASSOCIATION.

LATIN AMERICAN INTEGRATION ASSOCIATION (LAIA). Known in Spanish as ALIANZA LATINOAMERICANA DE INTEGRACION (ALAI), this is an intended successor organization to the *Latin American Free Trade Association, its constitution was drawn up at LAFTA's 19th Extraordinary Conference, Acapulco, Mexico, June 1980.

LATORRE BENAVENTE, Juan José (1846-1912). A career naval officer and member of the Liberal Party (*Partido Liberal). He distinguished himself in the War of the *Pacific, and by the improvements he introduced into the *navy, particularly in gunnery and in the use of electricity in ships. During the presidency (1886-91) of José Manuel *Balmaceda Fernández he was sent to England to supervise the construction of modern naval vessels for Chile. In 1890 he was in *Spain when a rebellious *Congress demanded Balmaceda's resignation. He returned to Chile and remained loyal to the President while most of the navy defected to support the Congress. With the end of the *Civil War of 1891, Latorre was dismissed from the service and exiled. He returned to Chile in 1894, was reinstated by the navy and ran for the Senate, backed by the *Partido Liberal Democrático, which had made him its honorary president. He was elected senator for *Valparaíso for 1894-1900 and reelected for 1900-06. In 1896 the French government made him a commander of the Legion of Honor for his contributions to naval architecture. In 1898 he was appointed foreign minister, and in 1908 was promoted to vice-admiral.

LATORRE [COURT], Mariano (1886-1955). Noted Chilean novelist who headed a literary school known as criollismo, "the novel of the land," i.e. *creole--typically Chilean--manners and customs. Primarily a short-story writer, Latorre has written about the rural regions of his native land. His major works are Cuna de cóndores (condors' nest), 1918; Zurzurlita (little Chilean bird) 1920; Chilenos del mar (Chileans of the sea), 1929; and Hombres y zorros (men and foxes), 1937. For his detailed descriptions, Latorre has often been compared to the Spanish novelist José María de Pereda.

LATORRE GONZALES, Orlando (1916-). Lawyer by profession and member of the *Vanguardia Popular Socialista, a successor to the Chilean Nazi (*Nacista)' Party. He served as a cabinet member during the second presidency (1952-58) of Carlos *Ibáñez del Campo, first as justice minister (1952), and later as minister of public works (1953). He was one of the creators of the government *housing agency *CORVI. In 1954 he joined the Agrarian

Labor Party (*Partido Agrario Laborista), becoming the party's president in 1955.

LAUCA. A river in the northern Region I (*Tarapacá), which rises in Chile but flows into *Bolivia, and has been the cause of a continuing dispute between the two countries since 1953. In 1939, with permission from Bolivia, Chile used the waters of the Lauca to irrigate the Valley of Azapa, near *Arica. Shortly afterward Bolivia also began to use the waters of the river to irrigate land adjacent to the Chilean border. For a little over a decade the irrigation projects of both countries proceeded amicably. Then, in 1953, Bolivia accused Chile of having altered the course of the river, thereby securing more water for irrigation on the Chilean side. The Chileans, in turn, accused the Bolivians of using the Lauca River as a pretext to obtain a port on the Pacific. (Bolivia had lost its Pacific shoreline and, with it, the port of *Antofagasta, in the War of the *Pacific). The quarrel intensified in 1961 when Chile began building a hydroelectric project on the river. The following year Bolivian President Víctor Paz Estensorro broke off diplomatic relations. These were resumed in 1975, but broken off again in 1978. There was a short-lived resumption in 1980-82, but they were then broken off once more over Chile's failure to provide Bolivia with a permanent access to the Pacific. See also: BOLIVIA, Relations with.

LAUTARO (1535-1557). An *Araucanian Indian chief who fought bravely to expel the Spaniards from Chile. In 1550 he was captured by Pedro de *Valdivia and forced to serve as a scout for the Spaniards for the next three years. During his captivity Lautaro maintained contacts with his people, waiting for a propitious moment to annihilate the Spanish camp. Such an opportunity presented itself in the battle of *Tucapel, in which Pedro de Valdivia and his men were killed by the Indians under *Caupolicán and *Colocolo, despite Lautaro's efforts to save the prisoners' lives. Lautaro also participated in the siege of *Concepción in 1554, which saw the defeat of the Spanish under Francisco de *Villagra. In 1557, at the battle of Mataquito, Villagra and his men were able to surprise the Indian camp, annihilating their force and killing Lautaro.

LAW, The. When the Spanish conquered Chile in 1541, they brought with them a legal system based on Roman law, modified by medieval conceptions of Christian morality and equity, which affected particularly the law of matrimony, seen as a holy sacrament, and that of money-lending, castigated as usury. Roman law tried to prescribe for every conceivable human action that might be subject to legal sanction, leaving little room for judicial initiative. The task of the judge was merely to find the correct legal prescription to fit the particular case being heard. Some trials were assigned a jury, especially when the case involved a serious

crime, and the burden of proof was on the prosecution. All
accused were entitled to legal representation, even if the state
had to provide it, but no release on bail was permitted for serious charges.

To cope with the special situation of the Americas, Spain made
piecemeal adaptations which were eventually codified as the Law
of the Indies in 1680 (see: RECOPILACION DE LEYES DE LOS
REYNOS DE LAS INDIAS), but further modifications due to the
great economic and political changes of the 18th century left the
law badly in need of codification again.

The legal system of independent Chile (from 1818) was largely
molded by Diego *Portales Palazuelos' *Constitution of 1833,
which remained in effect for almost a century, and established an
autocratic republic with a strong *executive whose powers bordered on the dictatorial. A new Civil Code of 1855, drafted by
Andrés *Bello López, modernized many aspects of the law, and
was taken as a model by other American nations. A new Commercial Code (1865) took effect in 1867, making possible the
growth of modern financial institutions because of its new approach
to money-lending (see: BANKS, BANKING AND FINANCIAL IN-
STITUTIONS). Codes of Civil and Criminal Procedure appeared
in 1901 and 1906. During the latter half of the 19th century many
steps had been taken towards decreasing the legal influence of
the *Church: the clergy were made fully subject to ordinary law
and the ordinary courts; statistics, records, and the legal celebration of marriage were taken out of ecclesiastical hands.

The process of disestablishing the Church and turning Chile
into a parliamentary democracy was completed by the *Constitution
of 1925, which remained in effect until 1973 when President Salvador *Allende Gossens was overthrown in a *coup d'état. The
1925 document endowed Chile's citizens with individual liberties
and attempted to abolish the privileged classes. *Labor law was
codified in 1931.

The new military regime introduced the present *Constitution
of 1980, which is now the law of the land. In the interim period
between 1973 and 1981, when the 1980 document was ratified by
plebiscite, any vestige of pluralism was eliminated from the Chilean
social system. A lawless reign of arbitrary power was adopted
by a four-man military *junta headed by General Augusto *Pinochet Ugarte.

Operating under a state of siege, the junta government dissolved the National *Congress, prevented unauthorized assembly,
exercised press *censorship, did away with all *political parties,
suspended the right of habeas corpus, and abridged the rights
of *trade unions, no longer guaranteeing the right of the individual to a job, family security or other forms of social welfare.

In contrast to the other branches of government, the judiciary
(see: CHILE--H. Government, 3. The Judiciary) was left practically intact by the new constitution (apart from the purge of
more than 20 judges who had been critical of the military intervention). Before 1970 the 13-member Supreme Court had been

highly respected for its independence and impartiality. With
Allende's election, however, the conservative court became more
politicized, challenging or blocking a number of radical reforms
proposed by Allende to change the land tenure system (see:
AGRARIAN REFORM) and to nationalize the *copper and other
mineral riches of Chile. After the coup, critics of the legal
system under the military cited "a strong political influence in
the appointment and promotion of judges," who traditionally were
appointed for life.

The 1980 constitution gave the Supreme Court limited powers
to rule on the constitutionality of any law. From 1973 to 1981,
political cases were handled by military tribunals. Many lawyers
who defended in such courts usually found themselves in trouble
with the government. As soon as a lawyer defended a suspected
leftist, he or she was accused of being a sympathizer or an outright Communist. District courts heard all criminal cases.

Under the state of siege, the courts were prohibited from
reviewing any decisions made by the military courts; from inter-
fering with the military to free anyone from prison; and from
doing anything about the treatment of prisoners. Furthermore,
the courts could not investigate the cases of people who had
disappeared, and until 1977 they were forbidden to entertain
habeas corpus petitions.

In spite of the new constitutional guarantees, the lack of
judicial independence under the military has lasted to this day.
The 1925 constitution had spoken clearly about the submission of
political leaders to the rule of law, and to a system of checks
and balances within the government to prevent a dangerous concentration of power. The 1980 document was more like the one
drafted by Portales, because it gave the President (Pinochet)
ample powers to entrench his authoritarian rule. See also:
AUDIENCIA; CONSTITUTION; HUMAN RIGHTS; JUSTICIA,
Ministerio de; POLICE.

LAW OF THE SEA. Like most maritime countries, Chile has extended
its claim to territorial jurisdiction over its coastal waters from the
traditional 3 nautical miles from the shore to a present 12 nautical
mile limit. In addition, Chile was the first nation to claim (June
1947) the right to a zone of exclusive economic exploitation out to
200 nautical miles from shore. Several other countries, including
Chile's Pacific coast neighbors, *Peru and Ecuador, have since
made similar claims (see: DECLARACION DE SANTIAGO), but,
despite a series of *United Nations conferences on the subject,
general international acceptance of the new limits is still to be
achieved.

LAZCANO ECHAURREN, Fernando (1848-1919). Lawyer by profession
and active member of the Liberal Party (*Partido Liberal). He
served as a deputy in Congress from 1873 to 1879, and was
elected as a representative to the Constituent Congress held in

*Santiago at the conclusion of the *Civil War of 1891. From 1894 until his death, Lazcano served continuously as senator for *Curicó. He became vice-president of the Senate in 1895, and its president in 1897 and several times subsequently. In 1906 he ran as *Coalición candidate for the presidency of the Republic, losing to conservative Pedro *Montt Montt.

LEAD. Almost all Chilean lead comes from Puerto Cristal in *Aysén. Production is small and fluctuating: 990 metric *tons in 1968; 252 in 1973; 1,816 in 1976; 242 in 1981; and 4,517 in 1984.

LEAGUE (Legua). Three miles. In traditional Spanish measure, where the mile (milla) was 1.852 kilometers, the league was 5.5727 km, or 3.4629 statute (Anglo-American) miles, and 3 leagues equalled 10,000 *brazas. Chile, however, had a shorter league of 36 *cuadras (2,700 brazas) or 4.51386 km (2.805 statute miles). See also: WEIGHTS AND MEASURES.

LEBU. River of south-central Chile which has given its name to a department and a city of the pre-1974 province of *Arauco (now part of Region VIII, *Bío-Bío). The city of Lebu was a township of 2,687 population in 1907. It was later made the provincial capital, even though its population was still very small: 4,500 in 1940; 14,000 (est.) in 1971; and 17,000 (est.) in 1982.

LEFT BLOCK. See: BLOQUE DE IZQUIERDA.

LEFT REVOLUTIONARY MOVEMENT. See: MOVIMIENTO DE IZQUIERDA REVOLUCIONARIA.

LEGISLATURE. See: CHILE--H. Government. 2. Legislative; CONGRESS.

LEIGH GUZMAN, Gustavo (1920-   ). *Air force general. Leigh attended the *Escuela Militar and Escuela de Aviación before joining the FACh in 1944. He was sent for further training to the *United States in 1952-53 and to the *Academia de Guerra de la Fuerza Aérea in 1956, becoming a group captain two years later. From 1966 to 1971 he directed the Escuela de Aviación (the air force academy) and in 1973 was made commander in chief of the FACh. As such he actively participated in plotting and carrying out the *coup d'état of September 1973, and became the air force representative on the *junta militar de gobierno. At that time he was regarded as its most "hard line" member. He opposed, however, the way General Augusto *Pinochet Ugarte was entrenching himself in power and began to criticize some government policies as unnecessarily harsh. In July 1978 he was abruptly dismissed from command of the air force (and ipso facto from his junta membership), along with all but two of the other air force generals. It has been alleged that he was plotting a coup against

Pinochet which was betrayed. Leigh's successor as FACh commander-in-chief was Fernando MATTHEY AUBEL, q.v. In 1986 Leigh predicted civil war if the government should persist in ruling by repression without making any attempt to broaden its base of support.

LEIGHTON, Anita Fresno de. See: FRESNO DE LEIGHTON, Anita.

LEIGHTON GUZMAN, Bernardo (1909-   ). Lawyer by profession and one of the founders of the Christian Democratic Party (*Partido Demócrata Cristiano). While a student he became president of the *Juventud Conservadora, and later was an active participant in the formation of the *Falange Conservadora and its successor the *Falange Nacional. He was labor minister, 1937-38, in the second presidency (1932-38) of Arturo *Alessandri Palma. From 1950 to 1952 he served as *education minister in the cabinet of President (1946-52) Gabriel *González Videla. After the Chileans elected Eduardo *Frei Montalva in 1964 as the first Christian Democrat president in the Western Hemisphere, Leighton was immediately named minister of the interior, thereby becoming acting President for a short time in 1965 when Frei was on a European junket.
    Leighton was less opposed than Frei to the election of Salvador *Allende Gossens in 1970. He voted for Allende's confirmation, and, even though he did not agree with Allende on many of his programs, he was much more critical of the military who overthrew Allende in the *coup d'etat of 1973, doing away with the Constitution at the same time.
    After the new *junta government began jailing thousands of people for political reasons, Leighton decided to go into exile. Before going on to Rome with his wife Anita *Fresno de Leighton, he met with a group of Socialist leaders in Caracas to strengthen the alliance of Chilean exiles opposed to the junta and seeking a swift return to constitutionality. This made him a marked man.
    In October 1975 he was shot in Rome. Miraculously, he was not killed. The attempt on his life was traced all the way back to Chile and the *DINA.
    After an amnesty law of 1983, Leighton returned from Italy, and became one of the few Chileans in public life considered capable of organizing a coalition of opposition forces to fight for a return to constitutional government. Today he still figures among the most influential Christian Democrats in the hierarchy of the party.

LEMACHEZ, Quirino. Pseudonym of Camilo HENRIQUEZ GONZALEZ, q.v.

LENNOX. The largest of three tiny islands in the *Beagle Channel ---the others are *Nueva and *Picton--which have been the

subject of dispute with *Argentina (only settled in 1985). Situated
at 55° 19' S, 67°W, some three miles southeast of *Navarino
Island, Lennox Island was discovered in February 1624 by an
expedition of the Dutch admiral Schapenham, and named Terhalten
after the officer who first sighted it. The present name was
given in 1830 by Phillip Parker *King and Robert *Fitzroy, hydrographers of the British naval survey of *Patagonia and southern
Chile.

LEON DE TARAPACA. Nickname bestowed on President Arturo
ALESSANDRI PALMA (q.v.).

LETELIER, Isabel Morel de. See: MOREL DE LETELIER, Isabel

LETELIER DEL SOLAR, Orlando (1932-1976). Lawyer, economist,
diplomat and cabinet minister in the 1970-73 administration of
Salvador *Allende Gossens, who was assassinated, together with
an associate, Ronni Moffit, in Washington, D.C., on September
21, 1976, by order of the Chilean secret police (DINA, q.v.).
Letelier served at various times as foreign minister, ambassador
to the *United States, and defense minister, and following the
1973 *coup, spent a year in the *concentration camp on *Dawson
Island. Released in 1974 because of international pressure on
the Augusto *Pinochet Ugarte regime, he went first to Venezuela,
where he met with other exiled leaders opposed to the junta government, and then went on to Washington. In the American capital he went back to work for the Inter-American Development
Bank (IDB) and was a senior fellow at the Institute for Policy
Studies.
As a potential leader of a Chile restored to democracy, Letelier
represented a threat to the regime. He was increasingly optimistic about the possibility of evicting the generals, and encouraged
a more forceful and effective resistance in Chile. His murder
had international repercussions, as it became apparent that the
DINA had hired a former *Central Intelligence Agency agent,
Michael *Townley, to carry it out. Townley and a Chilean infantry captain, Armando *Fernández Larrios, had also enlisted
the help of four Cuban exiles living in the United States and belonging to an underground group called the *Cuban Nationalist
Movement (CNM). The Cubans carried out the killings for a
reported US$ 1 million. This was the first time that a foreign
government had planned and carried out an assassination of a
political refugee and an American citizen (Ronni Moffit) on U.S.
soil.
The assassination was executed by a remote-controlled bomb
placed under the car of Ronni Moffit who, because Letelier's car
would not start, had gone to pick him up, accompanied by her
husband (who escaped injury). The device was operated by the
Cubans from within 300 feet of the Chilean embassy, raising the
question of complicity on the part of the Chilean government itself.

The DINA had already carried out assassination plots against two other Chilean leaders in exile: General Carlos *Prats González, who was killed in Buenos Aires, and Christian Democrat leader Bernardo *Leighton Guzmán, who was machined gunned in Rome but had miraculously survived. Just days before Letelier's assassination, the Chilean government had stripped him of his citizenship, to which he had replied, "I was born a Chilean, I am a Chilean and I will die a Chilean. They, the Fascists, were born traitors, live as traitors, and will be remembered forever as Fascist traitors." Letelier was speaking at a rally at Madison Square Garden in New York. The overflow crowd roared its approval, while DINA's agents attended the rally and reported to Santiago.

After years of investigation, DINA's director, Manuel *Sepúlveda Contreras, was placed under house arrest in Chile. But Pinochet refused to extradite either him or two other Chilean secret agents, whom a U.S. grand jury had indicted for the killings. This international incident, which challenged the basis of U.S. sovereignty in its own capital city, illustrated further to what extent the secret police and government of Chile would go to achieve their ends--including the physical elimination of all opposition.

Ley, La. A *Santiago *newspaper, the organ of the *Partido Radical, founded in 1894 and lasting until 1910. Its outspoken anticlericalism led to its directors being excommunicated by Archbishop Mariano *Casanova Casanova.

LEY DE DEFENSA DE LA DEMOCRACIA. The "law for the defense of democracy" was sponsored by President (1946-52) Gabriel González Videla with the purpose of outlawing the Communist Party (*Partido Comunista Chileno). The law (no. 8987), enacted September 3, 1948, banned the Party, removed 40,847 party members from the electoral rolls, and prevented known Communists from running for *trade union office. It also made it illegal to propagate, in writing or by teaching, any doctrine "tending to promote Communism in Chile." Active communists were subject to imprisonment or exile (internal or external) for up to three years. Many, Pablo *Neruda among them, had to go underground. The law, ostensibly "permanent," remained in effect for a decade and was finally rescinded on August 6, 1958.

LEY DE LAS ELECCIONES. See: BARROS LUCO, Ramón.

LEYES DE LAS INDIAS. See: RECOPILACION DE LEYES DE LOS REYNOS DE LAS INDIAS.

LIBERAL ALLIANCE. See: ALIANZA LIBERAL.

LIBERAL-CONSERVATIVE FUSION. See: FUSION LIBERAL-CONSERVADORA.

LIBERAL PARTY.   See: PARTIDO LIBERAL.

LIBERAL UNION.   See: UNION LIBERAL.

LIBERATING POPULAR ALLIANCE.   See: ALIANZA POPULAR LIBER-
TADORA.

LIBERTADOR.   Name of Región VI--in full, "del Libertador General
Bernardo O'Higgins"--, one of the new administrative regions
established by the military government in 1974 (see: REGIONS
AND ADMINISTRATIVE RESTRUCTURING).   Libertador embraces
the former provinces of *O'Higgins and *Cochagua.   It has an
area of 18,193 km^2 (7,024 square miles) and an estimated population of 583,276 (1982).   The capital city is *Rancagua.

LIBRA (pound).   A pre-metrification unit of weight, equivalent to
460 grams.

LIEBRE ("hare").   A minibus which can carry up to 17 passengers.
See also MICRO.

LILLO, Baldomero (1867-1923).   Short-story writer whose themes
of social protest began a new period of "realist literature" in
Chile.   His literature was concerned with man's struggle in an
industrially growing country, the injustice of a stratified society,
the hardship of the *coal miners, and the tragedy of individual
lives drawn into poverty and degradation.   Lillo's most effective
works of social protest were Sub terra (1904) and Sub sole
(1907).   In these stories he sympathizes with the worker's struggle for better working conditions and with the plight of the poor,
especially the *roto, the Indian and the *huaso.

LILLO ROBLES, Eusebio (1826-1910).   A newspaperman who became
famous after 1847 for rewriting the lyrics of the Chilean *National
Anthem.   He was a reporter for El *Mercurio and El Comercio,
both *newspapers printed in *Valparaíso.   In 1850, with Francisco
*Bilbao Barquín, he founded the *Sociedad de la Igualdad.   In
1851 he took part in the *Civil War of 1851 against Conservative
President (1851-61) Manuel *Montt Torres, and was consequently
arrested and exiled to *Peru.   Returning to Chile in 1852, he
became editor of the newspaper La Patria.   In 1858 he returned
to Peru and moved on to *Bolivia, where he spent the next couple
of years in *mining towns, and founded the Banco de La Paz in
the Bolivian capital.   On returning to Chile he joined the faculty
of the *Universidad de Chile (1872-78) and then became *intendant
of *Curicó.   During the War of the *Pacific (1879-83) he held a
diplomatic post with the *army in the field, conducting preliminary
peace negotiations with Bolivia.   He was elected senator for *Talca
in 1882 with the backing of the Liberals (*Partido Liberal), becoming vice-president of the Senate in 1886.   Also in 1886 he was

briefly minister of the interior in the administration of President
(1886-91) José Manuel *Balmaceda Fernández. When Balmaceda
committed suicide, Lillo was entrusted with the President's political testament which he made public. In 1896 Lillo became president of the political coalition known as the *Alianza Liberal.

LIMA, Treaty of. Agreement between Chile and *Peru signed June
3, 1929, to settle differences still outstanding from the War of
the *Pacific, in particular the so-called Tacna-Arica Question.
Peru recovered *Tacna and received an indemnity of Ł 1.25 million
for abandoning all claims to *Arica, which became definitively
part of Chile. The frontier was fixed as a line 10 km (6.2 miles)
north of and parallel to the Arica-La Paz *railway.

LINARES (city). Capital of the former province of the same name.
Its population was 11,122 in 1907; 17,000 in 1940; 60,400 (est.)
in 1971; 67,600 (est.) in 1982. The city was founded by colonial
governor Ambrose *O'Higgins Ballenary.

LINARES (province). A pre-1974 province of central Chile, south of
*Santiago, created in 1873, prior to which it had formed the
eastern part of the province of *Maule. It had an area of
9,413.8 km² (3,635 square miles) and its population was 63,509
in 1854; 118,761 in 1875; 109,363 in 1907; 134,968 in 1940; 197,541
(est.) in 1971. It is now part of Región VII (Maule); see:
REGIONS AND ADMINISTRATIVE RESTRUCTURING.

LINDEROS. Site of a battle fought on January 8, 1852, on the plains
near *Copiapó, the last battle in northern Chile of the *Civil War
of 1851. Government troops led by Victorino Garrido routed a
small force of Liberals commanded by Bernardino Barahona.

LINEA AEREA DEL COBRE. See: LADECO.

LINEA AEREA NACIONAL DE CHILE. See: LAN-CHILE.

LION OF TARAPACA. Nickname of Arturo ALESSANDRI PALMA
(q.v.).

LIRA OVALLE, Samuel. (1934-). Cabinet minister. Made minister
of *mining by President Augusto *Pinochet Ugarte, August 30,
1982.

LIRCAY, Battle of. Fought on April 17, 1830, during the *Civil War
of 1829-30, on the south bank of the River Lircay, near the city
of *Talca, following the breakdown of the Treaty of *Ochagavía.
Troops loyal to interim President (1830) José Tomás *Ovalle
Bezanilla, commanded by General Joaquín *Prieto Vial and Colonel
Manuel *Bulnes Prieto, outmaneuvered the Liberals led by ex-
President General Ramón *Freire Serrano and José Rondizzoni.

Freire tried to retreat, but the bulk of his army was cut off and surrounded. Although Freire was able to escape, his forces were annihilated, with little quarter given to prisoners. Lircay effectively ended the war. Prieto Vial returned to *Santiago, where a year later he was declared President of Chile.

LIRCAY, River. River of central Chile, a tributary of the Río Claro (itself the principal tributary of the *Maule); noteworthy for having given its name to the treaty and the battle (q.v.).

LIRCAY, Treaty of (Compromiso de Lircay). A peace treaty signed on May 3, 1814, between the Chilean patriots and the commander of the Spanish army, General Gabino Gaínza, at the instigation of Commodore James *Hillyar, a British sailor anxious for unity against Napoleon. The treaty stipulated that the royalist army would evacuate the province of *Concepción and that the Chileans would acknowledge the sovereignty of *Ferdinand VII. Although both sides had good reasons for wanting a truce, neither signed in complete good faith. Hostilities soon resumed because, on the Chilean side, José Miguel *Carrera Verdugo ousted the government that had signed it in a coup d'état, and on the Spanish side, Peruvian viceroy José Fernando de Abascal y Sousa repudiated negotiations conducted without his sanction. Soon afterwards, Spanish rule was restored when the patriot armies were crushed at *Rancagua on October 2, 1814.

LITERACY. Although the countries of the "Southern Cone" have long been the most literate in Latin America, Chile for many years lagged behind its neighbors in this group and only began to catch up in the 1930s. Successive percentages of the adult population regarded by the *Census as able to read and write have been: 1875--23%; 1930--56%; 1960--84%; 1970--89%; 1983--(est.) 94.4%.

LITERATURE. Chile's colonial literature is scant but valuable. The earliest literary works were the five letters sent by Pedro de *Valdivia to the king of Spain, recounting his campaign to conquer the fierce *Araucanian Indians and the results of the conquest. But the most notable work of the conquest is La *Araucana, an epic poem by Alonso de *Ercilla y Zúñiga, which praises the valor of the Spaniards but also renders homage to the indomitable "Chilli" Indians. Pedro de *Oña sang of the same wars in his *Arauco domado, but his epic wasted no love on the Indians. The most important characteristic of Oña's work was his detailed description of Chilean nature. Besides these two works in verse, there is one historical account of the conquest and of colonial affairs, written by a participant, Captain Alonso de Góngora Marmolejo. His Historia de Chile was written before 1575 and lacks the depth of later historical accounts. There were other minor works, but none reached the grandeur of Peruvian or

Mexican literature of the same period.

Chile became an intellectual center only after the Wars of *Independence, when the noted Venezuelan writer Andrés *Bello López, with José Victorino *Lastarría Santander and some Argentine exiles, founded a classical literature with strong Romantic overtones. In 1842 they established a literary society (sociedad literaria) in *Santiago with the object of initiating a national literature. In that same year, the *Universidad de Chile was founded, and writers began to devote themselves to belles-lettres. Two other foreigners greatly contributed to the development of Chilean literature: the Argentinian Domingo Faustino *Sarmiento and the Nicaraguan poet Rubén *Darío. Sarmiento had come to Chile to escape persecution by Argentinian dictator Juan Manuel Rosas in 1840; he repudiated the classical tradition of Bello in favor of the ideas of French Romanticism. Darío came to Chile in 1886 and wrote some of his best Modernist poetry in Santiago, beginning a literary movement that was typically Latin American in origin.

Among the most notable Chilean poets of the 19th century we find Pedro Antonio González (1863-1903), author of Ritmos (rhythms) and El monje (the monk); Diego Dublé Urrutia (1877-1964) who wrote Del mar a la montaña (from sea to mountain) and Fontana cándida (candid fountain); Carlos Pezoa Véliz (1879-1908), one of the most important Modernist poets of Chile, and author of Nocturno (nocturne) and Carta a una dama (letter to a lady); and Pedro *Prado Calvo (1886-1952), perhaps the most renowned Chilean stylist and author of many works in poetry and prose. His poetry books are well known to Chilean youth. Among his best are La casa abandonada (the abandoned house), Otoño en las dunas (autumn in the dunes) and Esta bella ciudad envenenada (this fair poisoned city).

In the 20th century, Chilean writers have been greatly respected by the literary public. Chile was the first country in Latin America to win the Nobel Prize for Literature, awarded to poet Gabriela *Mistral in 1945, and in 1971 to Pablo *Neruda. Other towering figures in poetry are Angel Cruchaga Santa María (b. 1893), Vicente *Huidobro, Pablo de Rokha (b. 1894) and Juvencio Valle.

Only a handful of Chilean novelists have reached distinction. Often called the first novelist of Chile is Alberto *Blest Gana, who spent most of his life in Paris, where he died in 1920 at the age of 90. He wrote what became known as the "novel of customs." Among his most appreciated works are Durante la reconquista (during the [Spanish] reconquest), Los transplantados (the transplanted) and El loco estero (the madcap), but Martín Rivas is his best novel, and probably his most popular work in Chile. The hero is a middle-class youth married to a young aristocrat, a convenient theme for showing social stress. Joaquín *Edwards Bello has carried on the tradition of Blest Gana with El *roto and La cuna de Esmeraldo (Esmeraldo's cradle), while

Manuel *Rojas Sepulveda, in his later literary period, wrote
of the alienation of man from society in La ciudad de los Césares
(the city of the Caesars) and Hijo de ladróu (a thief's son).
Eduardo *Barrios Hudtwalcker was a master of the psychological
novel, and José *Donoso has depicted the whole dark world of
passions within the lavishly overfurnished world of the Chilean
upper middle class.

There are many short-story writers in Chile, the best known
of whom are Baldomero *Lillo and José *Donoso. Both depict
*Santiago society with a sense of irony. Theirs is a complex
and suggestive world, but they never lose control over their
infernally driven characters.

With the *coup d'état of September 11, 1973, many Chilean
writers went into exile, as did many other artists and thinkers.
Some, not so fortunate, stayed behind, experiencing *torture
and imprisonment at the least whisper of artistic freedom. Thus
Chilean literature either became subservient to the military regime
or could not be published at all. A group of young writers,
most of them poets or literary critics, continue to write in exile.
Among these are Mahfud Massis, Gonzalo Rojas, Mariester, David
Vallejo, Alfonso González Dagnino, Guillermo Quiñones, Cilia,
José de Rokha, Pablo Sur, Pedro Herrero, Efraín Barquero,
Rocar, Salvatore Coppola, Hernán Lavín Cerda, and Fernando
Quilodrán. Writing under the direction of Chilean critic and
novelist Fernando Alegría, who was the cultural attaché in Washington during the Salvador *Allende Gossens presidency (1970-
73), they have collected their works in a book of poems entitled
Los poetas chilenos luchan contra el fascismo (Chilean poets fight
fascism). As the title suggests, their work is highly political
and critical of the *junta government and of the abuse of *human
rights in Chile. Their mission is to return to a democratic Chile,
abandon what has been a solitary type of creativity, and forget
once and for all the trauma of exile.

LITHIUM. Chile's production of lithium from the Salar (saltflat)
de *Atacama was worth about US$ 18 million in 1985, and repre-
sented 20 percent of world output.

LIVESTOCK FARMING. Chile's extensive grasslands in the central
zone and far south have been a major natural resource for raising
cattle and sheep. Poultry is also important, with large farms
accounting for much of recent expansion. In 1981 livestock accounted for 36 percent by value of the production of Chile's
*agriculture, but remained the weakest segment of the industry.
Production has not kept pace with population growth: meat consumption per capita has fallen and imports of live animals and meat
products have increased.

In 1981 the expanding poultry industry produced 25 million
chickens and 1,100 million eggs, adequate for domestic consumption needs. More poultry (c.79,000 metric *tons a year) was

being consumed than any other type of meat. Sheep (6.2 million head) outnumbered cattle (3.74 million), followed by pigs (1.1 million), goats (600,000), horses (450,000) and asses (30,000). These figures may be compared with the 1909 totals of 4.2 million sheep, 2.3 million head of cattle (including 216,137 dairy cows), 516,764 horses, 343,810 goats, 216,360 pigs and 83,092 asses and mules.

Consumer preference is for beef and chicken over pork, lamb, mutton and horseflesh.

See also: AGRICULTURE; CATTLE; CHINCHILLAS; SHEEP FARMING.

LLANQUIHUE. Former province in the lake district of south-central Chile, created in 1861, with an area of 91,676 km^2 (35,396 square miles), which was reduced to 18,205 km^2 (7,929 square miles) on the 1928 separation of the province of *Osorno. Estimated population: 26,255 (1854); 37,601 (1865); 105,043 (1907); 137,206 (1920); 201,823 (1971); 257,980 (1982). In 1974 Llanquihue became part of Región X, Los *Lagos (see: REGIONS AND ADMINISTRATIVE RESTRUCTURING).

This was the first territory beyond the traditional *Araucanian Indian frontier to be extensively settled by Europeans. Towards the end of the presidency of Manuel *Bulnes Prieto, two simultaneous efforts were afoot to recruit German immigrants for this area. A Chilean government effort through Bernard Philippi (brother to naturalist Rudolf Amandus Philippi) was frustrated by the opposition of the bishop of Paderborn and Münster in whose diocese he was recruiting. A private effort by Franz G. Kindermann, a merchant who sold titles to an enormous tract of virgin forest he claimed to own in Valdivia and Llanquihue, led to the arrival in 1850 of the first two shiploads of settlers: 150 men and women from Suavia (Würtemberg-Baden). As Kindermann's ownership was disputed, the government agent in *Valdivia, Vicente *Pérez Rosales, had a large tract (5 *leagues by 15), of forest between Osorno volcano and the sea, cleared by burning, and a town, *Puerto Montt, was founded at Melipulli on February 12, 1853. By 1858 Puerto Montt was self-supporting, exporting brandy, honey, timber, leather and *wheat flour. By 1864, when the first tide of German *immigration ceased, 1,400 settlers had arrived. In 1861 Puerto Montt was made capital of the new province: it is now capital of the whole Los Lagos region.

LO CAÑAS. See: CAÑAS, Fundo Lo.

LOCAL GOVERNMENT. The towns of colonial Chile and their surrounding rural areas were governed by town councils called *cabildos (see: COLONIAL ADMINISTRATION). Under the *Constitution of 1823 the PROVINCES (q.v.) were subdivided into departamentos under appointed gobernadores. These in turn

came to be divided into subdelegaciones (under subdelegados)
and the latter into distritos (under inspectores). The *Constitution of 1833 established a municipal council of *alcaldes and
directly elected *regidores, presided over by the gobernador
in the capital city of each departamento; the gobernador was
empowered to create similar municipalities in other cities also.
Municipal responsibilities were to include public health, primary
education, highways, bridges and public works. An 1877 Ley
de municipalidades increased the powers and financial autonomy
of the municipalities, but major changes came with the law of
December 22, 1891. This created new units known as comunas
(communes), each governed by a municipalidad of annually elected,
unpaid, councilmen (regidores) under a mayor (alcalde) elected
every three years. Each commune corresponded in area to a
subdelegación. The chief communal revenue source was the
impuesto agrícola (formerly the CONTRIBUCION TERRITORIAL,
q.v.). The council's new powers included command of the
*police, which lasted until the 1924 creation of the national
Cuerpo de Policia, later incorporated into the *Cuerpo de Carabineros. The most important change, however, was that after
1891 the municipalidades supervised *elections, which had hitherto
been done by the centrally-appointed gobernadores. This was
one of the most effective ways in which the 1891-1925 *parliamentary regime curtailed the patronage and power of the President
of the Republic. Municipal ordinances could be vetoed by the
provincial *intendant, but the veto could be overruled by a two-
thirds majority of the councilmen. The communes, with their
limited powers and even more limited resources, were thus the
only democratically controlled units of local government.

The 1973 *coup d'état by the *armed forces led to major
changes. All mayors, except the few who had supported the coup,
were fired and replaced by military officers. All local government
came under the close control of the Ministerio del *Interior, and
all decision-making was centralized. During 1974-75, with the
grouping of the old provinces into new regions (see: REGIONS
AND ADMINISTRATIVE RESTRUCTURING) and the creation of
new provinces (each under a gobernador provincial), there were
some changes of communal numbers and boundaries. In 1981
there were 318 communes.

Following ratification of the new *Constitution of 1980, there
has been some movement toward decentralization, and a law of
1979 increased the communes' financial resources. Mayors are
assisted by communal development councils (consejos comunales
de desarrollo) and appointed by the corresponding regional development council, except in those cases where the President of
the Republic reserves this right to himself (viz. in the most
populous and politically important communes).

LONCOMILLA, Battle of. Last battle in southern Chile in the *Civil
War of 1851, fought between rebel forces led by José María de

*Cruz y Prieto and government troops loyal to President (1851-61) Manuel *Montt Torres, under the command of General Manuel *Bulnes Prieto. The battle took place on the shores of the River Loncomilla, December 8, 1851, and lasted four hours. At the end of that time each side was exhausted, having lost a third of its strength. Cruz Prieto was able to withdraw to the south, but lost so many more men by desertion that he decided to seek an armistice. See: CAPITULACION DE PURAPEL.

LONCOMILLA, River. Tributary of the *Maule, navigable for small craft for 15 km (10 miles).

LOPEZ, Vicente Fidel (1815-1903). Argentine historian, exiled in Chile from 1840 to 1844. During his stay he directed the naval school at *Valparaíso, edited the Revista de Valparaíso, and joined his compatriot Domingo Faustino *Sarmiento in founding a high school and the *Santiago *newspaper El Progreso.

LOROS, Los. Site of a battle, to the north of La *Serena, fought on March 14, 1859, between rebel forces led by Pedro León *Gallo y Goyenechea and government troops led by José María Silva Chávez, during the *Civil War of 1859. After bitter hand-to-hand combat, Silva's army was routed and fled towards *Coquimbo, losing all its artillery, and Gallo was able to occupy La Serena.

LOS ANGELES. See: ANGELES, Los.

LOS LAGOS. See: LAGOS, Los.

LÜDERS SCHWARZENBERG, Rolf (1935-). Economist and banker. Educated at the University of Chicago, he espoused the extreme laissez-faire approach of monetarist Milton Friedman. Dean of the Institute of Economics, *Universidad de Chile, he became one of the *"Chicago Boys," the handful of economic advisers closest to President Augusto *Pinochet Ugarte, who appointed him minister of both finance and the economy, August 1982. As such he had to reverse government policy by intervening actively in Chilean banking and taking over the bank's foreign debts (see: BANKS, BANKING AND FINANCIAL INSTITUTIONS--B. The Collapse of 1981-84).

Closely associated with the business empire of Javier *Vial Castillo since 1965 (see: GRUPO VIAL), he became president of the Morgan Finanza Bank and prior to becoming minister was chief executive (and largest shareholder after Vial) of the Banco Hipotecario de Chile (BHC). In January 1983 Lüders had to order the liquidation of the BHC (which had borrowed excessively from abroad and then loaned heavily to its own subsidiaries) and install a government manager in the Banco de Chile. The following month he was forced to resign, and was under investigation.

In January 1984 Lüders was arrested, together with Vial and

other members of the board of the Banco Andino, a Panamanian subsidiary of the Banco de Chile (which they controlled), allegedly set up in order to circumvent the regulations on bank lending.

LYNCH SOLO DE ZALDIVAR, Patricio (1824-1886). Sailor, administrator and diplomat. Lynch began his career in the Chilean *navy, serving in the war with the *Peru-Bolivia Confederation, after which he was seconded to the British navy, 1840-47, seeing service in the Anglo-Chinese Opium War. During the *Civil War of 1851, he arrested the rebels in *Valparaiso. At the outbreak of the War of the *Pacific he held the rank of vice-admiral and command of the troop transports to *Antofagasta, and he was then given the captured city to administer. In May 1881 he was made an acting army general and given charge of the army of occupation in Peru. When the Chilean occupation ended in August 1884 he was appointed his country's first minister in Madrid following the conclusion of peace with *Spain in 1883. Two years later he resigned because of ill health, dying on the return voyage to Chile, in May 1886.

- M -

M.E.M.Ch. See: MOVIMIENTO DE EMANCIPACION DE LA MUJER CHILENA.

M.I.R. See: MOVIMIENTO DE IZQUIERDA REVOLUCIONARIO.

M.N.S. See: MOVIMIENTO NACIONAL SOCIALISTA DE CHILE.

MacCLURE, Eduardo. Brother-in-law of Agustín R. *Edwards Ross and nephew of Jorge *Edwards Brown's first wife Isabel Ossandón Iribarren. Director of the *Santiago newspaper La *Epoca (1881-1892), which had been founded by Domingo Larraín Dávila and Guillermo Puelma Tupper but was acquired by Edwards Ross and made the principal mouthpiece in the capital of the *Partido Nacional. The paper was never financially successful, Edwards and MacClure had continually to subsidize it, and MacClure soon acquired a reputation of parsimony to his contributors, the most famous of whom was the Nicaraguan poet Rubén *Darío during his brief sojourn in Chile.

MacIVER RODRIGUEZ, Enrique (1845-1922). Lawyer by profession who sat as a Radical (*Partido Radical) in the Chamber of Deputies, 1876-1900, and in the Senate, 1900-1922. In 1878 he became editor of the Radical daily El Heraldo de Santiago and contributed to other *newspapers. In 1880 he was elected vice-president of the Chamber of Deputies. In 1889 he was a founder of the

*Cuadrilatero. When the *Civil War of 1891 broke out he left for Buenos Aires, from where he led a press campaign against the government of President (1886-91) José Manuel *Balmaceda Fernández. The next year President (1891-96) Jorge *Montt Alvarez made him finance minister. In 1894 he became minister of the interior, and was appointed finance minister again in 1895. In 1919 he was elected state counsellor (consejero de Estado) and a member of the Academia Chilena and of the law school of the *Universidad de Chile. A Free Mason, he was from 1883 to 1894 Serene Grand Master of the Masonic Lodge in Santiago.

MACKENNA ASTORGA, Juan Eduardo (1846-1929). Lawyer by profession, and Liberal (*Partido Liberal) politician. He was elected *regidor on the *Santiago city council in 1873 and served in the Chamber of Deputies 1876-79 and 1888-91. He participated in the debate over *Church disestablishment, which he favored. As secretario de la intendencia general, he was responsible for army and navy supplies during the War of the *Pacific. In 1890 he served as foreign minister in the cabinet of President (1886-91) José Manuel *Balmaceda Fernández. In the *Civil War of 1891, Mackenna remained loyal to the President and was elected senator for *Valparaíso in the *Balmacedista Congreso Constituyente, serving as the Senate's vice-president. With the triumph of the rebel Congress, he emigrated to the *United States. All his possessions in Chile were confiscated, and after his return in 1893 he had a lengthy legal battle to recover them. He served from 1905 to 1915 as senator for *Coquimbo, and in 1913 was elected president of the *Partido Liberal Democrático. He also worked as an advisor in the education ministry.

MACKENNA O'REILLY, Juan (1771-1814). Irish-born Chilean patriot. Sent to Spain at the age of 13 under the patronage of his uncle, Count Alejandro O'Reilly, he studied mathematics and engineering and entered the engineer corps of the Spanish army. He took part in the 1787 defense of Ceuta against the Moors and in the 1793-94 Roussillon campaign against revolutionary France. In 1796 he was ordered to *Peru, where Ambrose *O'Higgins y Ballenary was viceroy. In August 1797 he was made governor of the settlement of *Osorno, under the viceroy's direct command, remaining there until his 1808 transfer to *Santiago. Despite his loyalty to Spain, Mackenna supported the Chilean revolution of 1810 and was given responsibility by the *cabildo for planning the city's defenses. In 1811 he was made military governor of *Valparaíso, was promoted to colonel and became a member of the first *junta de gobierno de 1811. Twelve days after José Miguel *Carrera Verdugo had put himself at the head of the junta (November 1811), Mackenna was accused of conspiracy to murder the Carrera brothers and sentenced to a year's internal exile at Cataplico. In the campaign of 1813-14 he fought with Bernardo O'Higgins and was one of the Chilean negotiators of the Treaty of *Lircay. José Miguel Carrera then seized power, repudiated the treaty and exiled Mackenna to *Mendoza as an alleged counterrevolutionary. There, a few months later, he met again with the Carrera brothers, following their escape into Argentina after the Patriots' defeat at *Rancagua. In Buenos Aires, in November 1814, Luis *Carrera Verdugo, the youngest brother, accused Mackenna of insulting his family and killed him in a duel.

MADARIAGA GUTIERREZ, Mónica. Niece to President Augusto *Pinochet Ugarte, and a former cabinet minister. Trained as a lawyer, she was appointed justice minister in April 1977, education minister in February 1983 and ambassador to the *Organization of American States in October 1983. As justice minister she apparently felt she was merely giving legal form to the decisions of other ministers; as education minister she objected to the continuance of *intervención in the universities, and in early 1985 she suddenly resigned and broke completely with the regime, giving wide publicity to her decision.

MAGALLANES. Former province (created 1929) of southern Chile named after Ferdinand *Magellan (Fernando de Magallanes, in Spanish). It was originally organized as a territory in 1848, embracing all Chile south of Tres Montes Peninsula (47°S), an area of 171,438 km^2 (66,192 square miles). In 1928 it was reduced to 132,033 km^2 (50,998 square miles) by losing part of its area to the newly formed Territory of *Aysén. The population was 153 in 1854; 2,085 in 1885; 17,330 in 1907; 29,000 in 1920; 37,913 in 1930; 55,091 in 1952; 85,341 (est.) in 1971; and 112,366 (est.) in 1982. The capital was *Punta Arenas.

MAGALLANES Y ANTARTICA CHILENA. Name of the new Región XII created by the 1974 amalgamation of the former province of *Magallanes with the former territory of *Antártica. The nominal area was about 1,300,000 km^2 (500,000 square miles) and the 1982 estimated population was 112,413. The capital is *Punta Arenas.

MAGELLAN, Ferdinand (c.1480-1521). Portuguese sailor (in Portuguese, Fernão de Magalhães) who sailed to India in 1505 and took part in several other Portuguese expeditions before entering the service of Spain. In 1517, convinced (despite strong evidence to the contrary) that a strait existed in the far south of the American continent giving passage between the Atlantic and Pacific Oceans, he sought the backing of King Manuel I in exploring a westward route to India. Finding the Portuguese court unsympathetic (as had Columbus 25 years earlier), Magellan went to Spain, meeting the young king (the future Emperor *Charles V) at Valladolid and convincing him of the merits of the venture.

On September 19, 1519, Magellan and a crew made up mostly of adventurers set sail from San Lúcar de Barrameda. After a

long voyage they reached Rio de Janeiro and then made their
way southward. On October 21, 1520, they discovered the long-
sought strait, surviving not only severe weather, but a mutiny
that had threatened to put an end to the venture. Their stormy
passage through what is now the *Strait of Magellan took thirty-
six days. The ocean that they then reached had been sighted by
Vasco Núñez de Balboa from a "peak in Darién" and christened
the South Sea. Magellan renamed it Mare Pacificum: the Pacific.
He then sailed westward. Week followed week, food became scarce,
the crew grew mutinous once more, and still no sign of land appeared. Finally they made landfall in March 1521 (probably at
Guam). The natives' acquisitive habits caused Magellan to call
his discovery the Islands of Ladrones (thieves). Ten days later,
Magellan's three small vessels sighted Samar and Cebu in the
Philippine Islands. In Cebu a fight broke out with the natives
in which Magellan lost his life. Juan Sebastián de Elcano was
able to bring one surviving vessel (and 18 men) back to Seville,
where he arrived on May 18, 1522, having completed the first
circumnavigation of the globe.

MAGELLAN STRAIT. See: STRAIT OF MAGELLAN.

MAIPO. River of central Chile, rising in the *Andes a little south
of 34°S, and reaching the Pacific at *San Antonio. *Santiago
stands on one of its tributaries, the *Mapocho.

MAIPON. A stream just outside the city of *Chillán in southern
central Chile, and the site of a battle of the War of *Independence,
fought on August 3, 1813. The Patriot forces, commanded by
José Miguel *Carrera Verdugo, besieging Chillán, had succeeded
in entering the city outskirts, where the troops looted the houses,
getting drunk in the process. Juan Francisco Sánchez, in command of the *realista defenders, allowed the inebriated Chileans
to disperse, and then began hunting them down. Seeing this,
Carrera ordered a withdrawal, whereupon Sánchez counterattacked
in strength and was only repulsed by point-blank cannon fire.
The *independientes' losses were heavy.

MAIPU. The decisive battle of the War of *Independence, fought on
April 5, 1818, on the plain of Maipú, just south of *Santiago.
The Spaniards, under the command of Mariano *Osorio, having
defeated the Patriots at *Cancha Rayada on March 19, were met
by a reorganized Chilean army, commanded by José de *San
Martín, anxious to bar their way to the Chilean capital. Each
army had about 5,000 men. The engagement began at noon and
lasted approximately two hours. Despite losing more than one
third of his men, San Martín was able to force the Spanish to
retreat and take refuge in the houses of Fundo Lo Espejo, a
country estate about a kilometer to the south. There, despite
a heroic resistance, they were overwhelmed, although Osorio

himself and some of his guard managed to escape. San Martín
sent word to Santiago that practically all the south of Chile had
been liberated, and the city burst into a delirium of joy. San
Martín was offered $10,000 for his services, but he declined all
gifts. Although *Peru was yet to be freed and a guerrilla war
would continue in Chile itself, after Maipú Chilean Independence
was secure.

MALLECO. Former province to the immediate south of the *Bío-Bío
River. Formed from part of the province of *Arauco in 1875
as the Territory of *Angol, which was divided into the provinces
of Malleco and *Cautín in 1887. Later extension eastward increased
Malleco's area from 7,701 km^2 (2,973 square miles) to 14,095.1
km^2 (5,442 square miles). The population was 2,158 in 1865;
59,472 in 1885; 109,775 in 1907; 154,174 in 1940; 193,161 (est.)
in 1971. The capital was *Angol. The 1974 restructuring made
Malleco part of Región IX, *Araucania, whose capital is *Temuco.
See: REGIONS AND ADMINISTRATIVE RESTRUCTURING.

MANGANESE. The bulk of Chile's manganese is produced by a *COR-
FO subsidiary, Compañía Manganesa de *Atacama, near Ovalle.
Production is mainly for the home market, but has been increasing
steadily, from 19,600 metric *tons in 1976 to 27,018 tonnes in
1984.

MANPOWER. See: EMPLOYMENT; LABOR; TRADE UNIONS.

MANUFACTURING. Manufacturing has played an important role in
the development of Chile's *economy, providing about one fourth
of the GNP and employing some 20 percent of the *labor force.
Industrial output increased rapidly in the 1960s, growing about
5 percent annually. *CORFO promoted the expansion of manufacturing, power supply and *agriculture, while the Pacific Steel
Company, *CAP, established the basis for new industrial development. Chile is one of the few countries in Latin America that
has both *iron and *coal in quantities sufficient to supply its iron
and steel industry.
    Until 1973 nearly all of Chile's manufacturing was for domestic
consumption. But the military *junta of Augusto *Pinochet Ugarte,
which took power that year, made a clean break with the develop-
mental approach of the preceding four decades. The import-
substitution model of the past was rejected in favor of opening
Chile to the world economy. This meant increased manufacturing
exports. Until then the leading manufactures were: (1) bever-
ages, food and tobacco; (2) textiles; (3) metal and metal products;
(4) chemicals; and (5) leather and rubber goods. Chile was self-
sufficient in cement, cellulose, glass, explosives, newsprint,
paper, shoes, wool textiles and most consumer goods.
    During the first year of Salvador *Allende Gossens' administra-
tion (1970-73), increased real wages for all Chileans caused

aggregate demand to expand rapidly. Employment grew and the real gross domestic product rose 8 percent. Manufacturing increased by 17 percent over the previous year, and there was great progress towards the economic objectives for development. But as the year ended, serious problems began to surface. Nationalization of key industries and the takeover of many textile firms around *Santiago (the center of manufacturing), added to other domestic and international problems, brought about supply shortages, increases in imports, a depletion of government finances, and the growth of the *black market.

The economy bottomed out in 1976, and manufacturing, employment and real wages grew buoyantly from then until late 1981, when once again trade deficits soared and industrial output declined. The Pinochet government sought diversification in manufacturing, giving special emphasis to chemicals, petroleum, fishing and *forestry. Despite the government's export drive, Chile earned only US$ 3,900 million from exports in 1981, compared to the US$ 6,300 million it spent on imports. This was due in part to a reduction in *custom tariffs, which severely undermined domestic industry, unable to compete with imports.

In 1983 trade regulations were tightened, and an import license was required for all goods entering Chile. These measures reflected the gravity of the recession and were an attempt to stimulate domestic industry and increase exports. Manufacturing had suffered an overall decline in 1982 of 21.9 percent, compared to 1981. The major declines were in consumer durables (down by 55.7 percent), transport equipment (down by 38.2 percent), and imputs for construction (down by 31.1 percent). The greatest decline of all was in domestic electrical goods, which tumbled over 62 percent. Union leaders were quick to blame the government. Although the regime's economic policies had reduced Chile's historical dependence on a single primary export commodity, diversification had meant, for the most part during the last ten years, a less sustained growth of output and employment.

MANZANO DE LA SOTTA, Esteban (1793-1830). Chilean patriot. Fought as a guerrilla leader in the War of *Independence, being promoted to colonel. From 1813 to 1822 he was a member of the local *junta in *Concepción, suffering deportation to *Quiriquina Island during the *Reconquista Española. He was elected to the provincial assembly of Concepción in 1822, becoming its president, and the following year was made provincial *intendant. During the *Civil War of 1829-30 he was the leader of the *pipiolos of Concepción. Taken prisoner in Valparaíso, he was incarcerated at *Santiago and died soon afterwards.

MAPOCHO. The river on which *Santiago stands, a tributary of the *Maipo.

MAPU. See: MOVIMIENTO DE ACCION POPULAR UNITARIA.

MAPUCHES. The fierce *Araucanian Indians of central Chile who
called themselves the Mapuches were never conquered in colonial
times. They soon mastered the use of the horses they stole
from the Spaniards, and proved at least as adept mounted guerrillas as were the plains Indians of North America. In 1554
they even captured the leading *conquistador, Pedro de *Valdivia,
whom they tortured and killed. The Spaniards tacitly abandoned
south central Chile (beyond the *Bío-Bío River) to them, limiting
themselves to occasional raiding for slaves. The Mapuches at
that time lived by *cattle raising and fishing, supplemented by
*sheep farming, a limited cultivation of *wheat, and trade with
the Spanish. At the end of the colonial era, Ambrose *O'Higgins
Ballenary negotiated a delimitation of the Indian frontier, to be
patrolled by Mapuches in Spanish service.

When Chilean settlements encroached beyond this after *Independence, the Mapuches resisted fiercely, especially in the
so-called Araucanian Rebellion of 1859-61, which led to the creation of the first reservations in the 1860s. Settler encroachment
on these, and the withdrawal of Chilean troops to fight the War
of the *Pacific, led to a last revolt in 1880 and a consequent postwar punitive expedition. The fall of the Mapuches' stronghold
near Villarica led to a definitive treaty in 1883.

Their traditional way of life depended on a low population density and frequent change of site. Loss of land to continual encroachment since 1883, down to 1.3 million acres in 1929 from an
original 76.6 million, compounded by demographic explosion (a
doubling every 25 years) has forced a gradual change to intensive
settled *agriculture (for which they were wholly inexperienced),
with consequent soil erosion, pauperization and the need to supplement an inadequate subsistence by seeking casual wage labor.
Even so, their communal land ownership and traditional kinship
arrangements allowed them to survive as a distinct, although impoverished, race. The Eduardo *Frei Montalva administration
(1964-70) made a little land restitution (some 3,700 acres), although it sought to break up communal land into private plots.
The Salvador *Allende Gossens government's Ley Indígena (aborigines' act) of 1971 sought to return all illegally occupied Mapuche
lands. In March 1979, however, the Augusto *Pinochet Ugarte
government's Decree 2568 repealed all existing Indian land legislation and called for an end to all collective land ownership: its
continuance was inconsistent with both the regime's economic
philosophy and its nationalist stance that in Chile there were only
"Chileans." By 1984, 70 percent of Mapuche land had been
privatized, leaving a mere 864,500 acres in communal plots. At
the same time, increased mechanization of large farms and a post-
1975 preference by *haciendas for *livestock over *wheat have
drastically reduced opportunities for casual wage labor in the
countryside. The result has been increasing confrontation between
the authorities (supported by *Acción Chilena Anticomunista

terrorism) and the Mapuches' Asociación Gremial de Pequeños
Agricultores y Artesanos de Chile (known by the acronym of its
original name, AD-MAPU), increasingly, albeit ineffectually, supported by concerned outside bodies such as Survival International
and the World Council of Indigenous Peoples. To some extent
the very energy with which government policy is being implemented has been counterproductive, forcing many who had been resigned to assimiliation to redefine themselves as Indians.

Since the Mapuches no longer exist officially, there are no
statistics. Estimates of their numbers in their traditional homeland (the valley of the Toltec river, south of *Temuco, and in
south-central Chile), most of whom remain Mapuche-speaking, go
as high as 405,000. There are also possibly another 200,000
elsewhere: that number doubles if *mestizos are included. The
migrants all over Chile and some in Argentina, who are mostly
in urban jobs (particularly domestic service and as bakers' rounds-
men), still form an essential economic part of their rural families
(who are reckoned to be dependent on their remittances for 25
percent of their income).

MARCO DEL PONT, ANGEL, DIAZ Y MENDEZ, Francisco Casimiro,
General (c.1770-1819). Last royal *governor of Chile. Appointed
to succeed Mariano *Osorio in December 1815, Marcó del Pont was
taken prisoner shortly after the Battle of *Chacabuco (February
1817). Exiled to Argentina, he died shortly thereafter. Command
of the Spanish forces in Chile was then returned to Osorio.

MARIN ESQUIVEL, José Gaspar (1772-1839). Doctor of theology and
law professor at the *Universidad de San Felipe. He was secretary of the *junta de gobierno de 1810, the first patriot government of Chile's struggle for *independence, and of the subsequent
*junta de gobierno de 1811. He became a supporter of Bernardo
*O'Higgins, was elected to the Senate in 1812 and sat on the
Supreme Court in 1823. In 1825 he was elected deputy for *Colchagua and chosen to be vice-president of the provincial assembly
of *Santiago. When O'Higgins was exiled, Marín tried to arouse
the populace to restore him to power. As a result, Supreme
Director (1823-26) Ramón *Freire Serrano had Marín arrested and
exiled (October 1825). He returned and was re-elected to the
Senate (1828-29). In 1831 he was appointed to the convention
charged with drawing up what became the *Constitution of 1833,
and was elected later in 1831 to the Chamber of Deputies, of
which he became vice-president in 1832.

MARINA. Term embracing both the MERCHANT MARINE (q.v.) and
the fighting navy (armada). See: NAVY.

MARINA, Ministerio de. The *navy was administered by the war
department (known successively as the Secretaría de *Guerra,
Ministerio de *Guerra, and Ministerio de *Guerra y Marina) until

December 19, 1924, when Statute no. 163 created a separate Ministry of the Navy. This lasted until May 1927, when a new Defense Ministry (Ministerio de *Defensa Nacional) combined the service ministries into a single department again. The new ministry lasted till November 1927, when the Ministerio de Marina was revived. In March 1932 Statute no. 5077 once again united the service ministries briefly in a single Defense Ministry. This was dissolved again in July, but a final definitive amalgamation took place on December 25, 1932.

MARINA MERCANTIL. See: MERCHANT MARINE.

MARTIN SAEZ, Manuel. Civil engineer and banker. Was minister of the economy from February to August 1983.

MARTINEZ DE ROZAS CORREA, Juan (1759-1813). Native of *Mendoza who migrated to Chile in 1780, graduated in law and became an assistant to Ambrose *O'Higgins Ballenary, who was then *intendant of *Concepción. He organized the troops on the *Araucanian frontier and was promoted to lieutenant colonel in 1790. He took part in the first *junta de gobierno de 1810, and became leader of the *exaltados. On the death in office of Mateo de *Toro y Zambrano y Ureta (May 2, 1811), Martínez de Rosas succeeded him as junta president. When José Miguel *Carrera Verdugo set up the second *junta de gobierno de 1811 in November that year, with himself as president, Martínez de Rozas returned to Concepción, where he organized an army and set up a provisional junta government for the province. To keep the patriots united, Carrera sent Bernardo *O'Higgins to make a pact with the army in Concepción. In spite of this effort, Martínez de Rozas and Carrera came to blows on July 8, 1812. Carrera wanted *Santiago to be the center of revolutionary activities against *Spain, while Martínez de Rozas wanted the *provinces to play the major role in the struggle. The provisional junta of Concepción was dissolved as Carrera marched into the city in triumph. Martínez de Rozas was arrested and exiled to Mendoza, where he died a year later. His body was brought back to Concepción in 1890 by decision of President José Manuel *Balmaceda Fernández.

MARTINEZ SOTOMAYOR, Carlos (1930-). Lawyer by profession and active member of the Radical Party (*Partido Radical). From 1953 to 1957 he was president of the party's Youth Movement. After graduating from the *Universidad de Chile, Martínez Sotomayor began a diplomatic career as Chilean representative to international congresses in Buenos Aires (1955) and Stockholm (1957). He was delegate to the American Conference of Democratic Parties held in Venezuela in 1960, and was Chilean ambassador to the *United Nations from 1960 to 1965. As President Jorge *Alessandri Rodríguez's foreign minister, 1961-63, he accompanied the

President on visits to Mexico, Panama, Ecuador and Peru, held conversations in 1962 with the presidents of the *United States and Mexico, and was president of the Chilean delegation to the meetings of American foreign ministers at Punta del Este (Uruguay) and Washington, D.C. (also in 1962). In May 1963 he was acting interior minister, and in 1964 was president of the Chilean delegation to UNCTAD (United Nations World Conference on Trade and Development) in Geneva. Since 1967 he has worked for UNICEF, becoming in 1974 UNICEF's regional director for the Americas, based in *Santiago.

Martínez Sotomayor also occasionally teaches law and economics at the Universidad de Chile, and has a particular interest in decolonization, witness his book El nuevo Caribe: la independencia de las colonias británicas (the new Caribbean: the independence of the British colonies), 1974.

MAS AFUERA & MAS ATIERRA. See: JUAN FERNANDEZ ISLANDS.

MATAQUITO. Battle in which the *Araucanian Indian chief LAUTARO (q.v.) was killed by the *conquistadores in 1557.

MATTA GOYENECHEA, Guillermo (1829-1899). A Chilean poet and diplomat who was also very active in politics. In 1858 Matta, along with his brother Manuel Antonio *Matta Goyenechea, Benjamín *Vicuña Mackenna and others, was exiled to Liverpool, England, for taking part in anti-government demonstrations. He returned to Chile in 1862 under an amnesty law. In 1870, and again in 1873, he was elected to the Chamber of Deputies, with Liberal (*Partido Liberal) backing. In 1874 he served as the Chamber's second vice-president. From 1875 to 1881 he was *intendant of the province of *Atacama, and in 1881 was sent to Europe as Chilean minister to Germany and Italy. He returned in 1887 and was appointed minister to Argentina and Uruguay. When the *Civil War of 1891 broke out, Matta continued for a while to represent the government of José Manuel *Balmaceda Fernández, but then resigned in order to devote himself to propaganda on behalf of the *congresistas. With the triumph of the revolution, he was made intendant of Concepción, and in 1894 was elected senator for Atacama.

MATTA GOYENECHEA, Manuel Antonio (1826-1892). Radical politician. Like his brother, Guillermo *Matta Goyenechea, he studied in Germany. Upon his return, he led the movement that eventually resulted in the formation of the Radical Party (*Partido Radical). Elected to the Chamber of Deputies in 1855, he held his seat until 1867 and again from 1876-79. Following participation in demonstrations against the government of President (1851-61) Manuel *Montt Torres in 1858, he and his associates (his brother Guillermo and Benjamín *Vicuña Mackenna, among others) were falsely accused of arming revolutionaries and were sentenced to death. To avoid carrying this out, the government secretly placed Matta and the others aboard a ship bound for Liverpool. An amnesty permitted his return in 1862; he founded the *newspaper La voz de Chile, and was elected senator in 1876. During the *Civil War of 1891 he supported the rebel *Congress. Afterward he was reelected to the Senate and appointed foreign minister. As such he was involved in negotiations with the *United States over the U.S.S. *Baltimore affair, resigning on the grounds that the government had failed to support him.

MATTE LARRAIN, Arturo (b. 1893). Lawyer by profession, son-in-law of Arturo *Alessandri Palma, and member of the Liberal Party (*Partido Liberal). In 1943 and 1944 he served as finance minister in the administration of President (1942-46) Juan Antonio *Ríos Morales. In 1950 he was elected to the Senate, and two years later he was the candidate of the right (the Liberals, Conservatives and the *Movimiento de Recuperación Doctrinaria) for the presidency of Chile. He lost, receiving 265,000 votes to the 446,000 of the winning candidate, Carlos *Ibáñez del Campo (who had the support of the *Partido Agrario Laborista, the *Partido Radical Doctrinario and the *Partido Socialista Popular).

MATTHEY AUBEL, Fernando (1925-). A career *air force officer whose name is sometimes spelled "Matthei." He was educated at the German school in *Santiago before entering the air force's School of Aviation. In 1961 he made several trips to the United States as a squadron commander. In 1975 he was promoted to air brigadier, and a year later, in March 1976, was appointed minister of health, a post he retained until July 1978, when he became the air force representative on the military *junta de gobierno. This was occasioned by the dismissal of Gustavo *Leigh Guzmán. Leigh had publicly criticized the entrenchment of power by General Augusto *Pinochet Ugarte, and so was forced to retire both from command of the air force and from the junta. Eight other air force generals also had to retire, and ten others resigned in protest at the firing of Leigh. All were senior to Matthey, who thus became both the fourth member of the junta and commander-in-chief of the air force. Nevertheless, he has proved to be the most open junta member, proclaiming the need for elections in 1986 to prepare for a return to democracy by 1989.

MAULE. A river of central Chile which marked the line of administrative division between the two colonial dioceses (and later also the *intendencias) of *Santiago and *Concepción. In 1826 the northwestern part of the intendencia of Concepción became the province of Maule. In 1848 Maule lost territory to the newly created province of *Nuble, and in 1873 it was again reduced by the creation of the province of *Linares. In this century the province had an area of 5,696.9 km^2 (2,200 square miles). Its population was 110,316 in 1907; 70,497 in 1940; and 94,925 (est.) in

1971.

In 1975 the province was amalgamated with the provinces of *Curicó, *Linares and *Talca to form the new Region VII, Maule. This has an area of 30,518 km^2 (11.783 square miles) and a 1982 estimated population of 726,307. See: REGIONS AND ADMINISTRATIVE RESTRUCTURING.

The capital of the old province was *Cauquenes; that of the new region is *Talca.

MAYORAZGO. An entailed estate. Because it ensured inheritance by primogeniture of undivided landholdings, this form of tenure was regarded as the basis of aristocracy in Chile and was attacked as undemocratic. The *Constitution of 1828 made it possible to disentail an estate; an 1852 law abolished all entails, with some provision for compensation to the former heirs.

MAZA FERNANDEZ, José (b. 1889). Lawyer by profession and one of Chile's most distinguished diplomats. Elected deputy in 1921, he served in the Chamber of Deputies for two terms and then entered the Senate, where he sat continuously from 1925 to 1953, being elected its president in 1936. He was appointed interior minister in 1924, justice minister in 1925 and acting foreign minister, 1925. He was the principal drafter of the *Constitution of 1925. He held ambassadorial posts in Uruguay and *Brazil (1943), *Peru (1945) and *Argentina (1958). In 1945 he was the Chilean delegate to the *United Nations conference in San Francisco, California. In 1954 he was elected president of the General Assembly of the U.N., the only Chilean to receive such an honor.

MEDICINE AND HEALTH PROGRAMS. See: PUBLIC HEALTH; SOCIAL WELFARE.

MEDIERO. Share-cropper.

MEDINA ZAVALA, José Toribio (1852-1900). Hispanic America's greatest bibliographer. Born in *Santiago and educated at the *Universidad de Chile, where he obtained a law degree in 1873, Medina practiced law for two years and then obtained a minor diplomatic post in *Peru. In 1884 Medina was posted to the mission in Madrid, but subsequently his sole occupation became his bibliographic and historical work. He collaborated on a biography of Arturo *Prat Chacón, and in the course of a half a century wrote more than 300 works. Colonial literature received its most adequate treatment in his Historia de la literature colonial de Chile, 2 vols., Santiago, 1878. He was a tireless editor of documents. Among his best works are his Colección de documentos inéditos para la historia de Chile (collection of unpublished documents for the history of Chile) and La instrucción pública en Chile (public education in Chile) which gives us a glimpse of Chilean colonial education. The *Civil War of 1891, by obliging him to leave Chile, resulted in his inventorying the colonial output of the presses of 37 cities throughout Hispanic America--some 70,000 imprints. In 1923 the Universidad de Chile held a special session to honor one of Chile's greatest historiographers. In 1925 he bestowed his private collection of over 20,000 volumes and hundreds of manuscripts to the *National Library.

See also: HISTORIOGRAPHY.

MEDIO PELO. Middle-class person.

MEIGGS, Henry (1821-1877). American *railway entrepreneur. Born in Catskill, New York, he went to San Francisco where success in the lumber business was followed by a sudden crisis that prompted his migration to Chile in 1855. There he built bridges on the Santiago-Valparaíso road and then began the *Santiago-*San Fernando railroad, and in 1861 took charge of the Santiago-*Valparaíso line, which gave him a US$ 1.5 million profit. Soon afterwards he turned his talents to railway construction in Peru, where he built the Lima-Oroya railway and became known as the "Yankee Pizarro." His extensive recruitment of Chilean laborers to work on his Peruvian projects was a source of considerable concern to Chilean farming interests.

MEJIAS CONCHA, Eliecer (b. 1895). Lawyer by profession and active member of the Radical Party (*Partido Radical). In 1919 he became president of the Chilean Students' Association (*FECh). The following year he served as secretary general of the Radical Party. Elected to the Chamber of Deputies in 1930, he served almost continually until 1953. In 1942 he became president of the Radical Party, and three years later was named subrogate minister of the interior in the cabinet of President (1942-46) Juan Antonio *Ríos Morales.

MEJILLONES, Battle of. See: CAPE ANGAMOS, Battle of.

MENDEZ NUÑEZ, Casto (1824-1869). Spanish admiral, and commander of the Spanish fleet in the 1865-66 war between Chile, Peru and *Spain, following the suicide of the original commander, José Manuel Pareja y Septién on November 28, 1865. After the indecisive victories of Abtao (February 2, 1866) and *Huito, Méndez Núñez received orders to bombard the undefended port of *Valparaíso, which he did for four hours on March 31. He then sailed his fleet north and bombarded the Peruvian port of Callao on May 2. This was heavily defended and Méndez Núñez was badly wounded early in the engagement, but his fleet of six frigates managed to put almost all the coastal defense guns out of action. There being nothing further to be done, he then returned safely to Spain. Although the solely punitive objectives of the Spanish government were foolhardy, wasteful and morally inexcusable, their admiral's successful compliance with his orders

so far from base and short of food, fuel and even lubricants
was a triumph of discipline, seamanship, logistics and improvisa-
tion.

MENDOZA. Capital of the formerly Chilean province of CUYO, q.v.

MENDOZA DURAN, César (1918-). General of the *Cuerpo de Carabineros (para-military police). Trained at the Escuela de Carabineros, by 1959 he had reached the rank of major. In 1968
he advanced to colonel, and in 1970 became a general and the
carabineros' commander-in-chief. He is a great horseman and
has taught equitation. He participated in the XVth Olympic
Games in Helsinki (1952) where Chile took a silver medal in the
equestrian events. He also traveled with his team to other countries in Europe, and to Canada and the *United States. He was
decorated for twenty years' service with the *police and received
the Queen Victoria Gold Medal from Elizabeth II.
  He was thought the most moderate of the four-man *junta that
overthrew President Salvador *Allende Gossens in September 1973,
but according to international *human rights organizations, none
of the four could be excluded from complicity in the post-*coup
excesses.
  In August 1985 General Mendoza resigned his command of the
carabineros (and with it his seat on the junta) after fourteen
members of the corps had been charged with murdering three
Communists. He was succeeded by Rodolfo Strange, his former
assistant.

MENSAJE. A Jesuit monthly edited by Renato *Hevia. It has charted
an independent course and has been one of the few journals in
Chile able to operate under the strict press *censorship imposed
by the government of General Augusto *Pinochet Ugarte. Often
reflecting the views of the Christian Democrats (*Partido Demócrata Cristiano), Mensaje has achieved renown for its recording
of *human rights violations in Chile since the 1973 overthrow of
President Salvador *Allende Gossens. Although the post-*coup
government has shut it down from time to time, the journal still
manages to resurface and is a bastion of independent reporting.
  See also: PERIODICAL PRESS.

MERCHANT MARINE. Spanish colonial regulations obliged all commerce
between Chile and Europe to pass across the Isthmus of Panamá,
so that Chilean shipping was limited to the coastal trade. Mail
was exempted from this restriction after 1771 (see: POSTAL SER-
VICES), but was carried exclusively in Spanish vessels.
  After *Independence, Manuel *Rengifo Cárdenas (finance
minister 1831-51) fostered the growth of a Chilean merchant
marine by exempting the fishing fleet from *taxes, encouraging
the cultivation of hemp (for ships' rigging) and restricting the
coastal trade to Chilean flag vessels (a restriction still in force).

In 1840 William *Wheelwright's Pacific Steam Navigation Company introduced the <u>Chile</u> and the <u>Peru</u>, the first steamships to ply between *Valparaíso and El Callao, but his firm was only saved from bankruptcy when the British Post Office awarded him a £25,000 annual subsidy for providing a mail service between Chile and Panamá.

By 1848 Chile had 104 merchant vessels totaling 16,970 tons; of these 45 were engaged in foreign trade (including the growing export of *wheat to California). Forty years later it had 177 merchant ships totaling 77,087 tons, and by 1930 some 119 ships totaling 154,563 tons. In 1983 there were 192 ships totaling 494,939 tons, of which 15 ocean-going ships accounted for 466,000 tons. Of the remaining 177 vessels, all but 60 were of 100 tons or less. Maritime cargos carried in national shipping totaled 14,381,841 metric *tons in 1984. All these recent figures exclude the majority of large Chilean-owned vessels, which nowadays operate under foreign flags of convenience.

The Chilean *navy's Directorate of the National Maritime Territory and Merchant Marine is administratively responsible for Chilean shipping. The country has 1,358 miles of navigable inland waterways, mostly in the lake provinces. The *Bío-Bío is the most important navigable river.

See also: EMPREMAR; FISHERIES; PORTS AND HARBORS.

<u>MERCURIO, El</u>. Chile's leading daily *newspaper. Founded in *Valparaíso by José Ignacio *Zenteno del Pozo y Silva on September 12, 1827, with Pedro Félix Vicuña as editor and Englishman Thomas G. Wells as printer, it is only slightly younger than South America's oldest surviving daily, Recife's <u>Diario de Pernambuco</u> (founded November 7, 1825). Until 1842 (when <u>La Gazeta del Comercio</u> was founded in Valparaíso), <u>El Mercurio</u> was the only daily paper in Chile. The previous year it had been acquired by the Spaniard, Manuel *Rivadeneyra, who appointed its most famous editor, the exiled Argentine statesman Domingo Faustino *Sarmiento; he was succeeded in 1842 by another exiled Argentine, Miguel Piñero. In those early days the paper's news was mainly mercantile. As with other newspapers of the period, it was kept free of political controversy by its dependence on a government subsidy. When this was withdrawn in 1849, the circulation was barely 500. <u>El Mercurio</u> prospered under the editorship (1866-86) of Manuel *Blanco Cuartín. By 1884 when the paper was bought by Agustin R. *Edwards Ross to be the voice of his industrial and financial interests, it had 42 correspondents throughout Chile and 41 abroad, and a rapidly growing circulation that topped 12,000 in 1894. As *Santiago, where it had many of its readers, was now the center of Chilean journalism, Edwards' son Agustín *Edwards MacClure started an edition in the capital, with the most up-to-date equipment, on June 1, 1900. This soon replaced El *Ferrocarril as Chile's most

respected and influential newspaper, and the original Valparaíso Mercurio soon sank to the status of a mere local edition. The paper's coverage of both domestic and foreign news was, and remains, excellent.

During the Eduardo *Frei Montalva administration (1964-70) it supplanted La *Nación as the Christian Democratic government's mouthpiece. Leftist opinion, however, has always regarded it as the tool of the oligarchs, and the Salvador *Allende Gossens government of 1970-73 looked upon it as an enemy. There was, in fact, evidence that owner Agustín *Edwards Budge had received money from the *United States *Central Intelligence Agency to print anti-government editorials. When in 1973 one of these openly invited the *armed forces to overthrow the *Unidad Popular President, Allende closed the paper for six days and ousted Edwards from control for printing sedition. After the *coup d'état of September 11, El Mercurio became the mouthpiece of the new regime. This has not, however, meant financial success: the Edwards family has now lost overall control to the Banco del Estado de Chile (see: BANKS, BANKING AND FINANCIAL INSTITUTIONS) which owns 51 percent of the stock. Circulation in 1984 was 360,000.

MERINO BENITEZ, Arturo (b. 1888). Air commodore, and one of the founders of the Chilean *air force, FACh. From 1952 to 1954 he was vice-president of *LAN Chile, which he had helped found. In 1953 he was undersecretary of transport. In the 1950s he also served as economy minister, and throughout his life received many decorations. General Augusto *Pinochet Ugarte had the name of the national *airport in *Santiago changed from *Pudahuel to "Arturo Merino Benítez" in honor of the man who had contributed so much to Chilean aviation.

MERINO CASTRO, José Toribio (1915-   ). Commander in chief of the Chilean *navy, and member of the *junta militar de gobierno de 1973. He graduated from the Naval School in 1936 as a midshipman and did a stint with the *United States navy from 1944 to 1945. He was a naval academy lecturer and in 1969 became rear admiral and director of armaments. In 1972 he became commander of the first naval zone, and soon afterwards commander-in-chief of the navy with the rank of admiral. The plot to overthrow the government of Salvador *Allende Gossens was developed by Merino himself after gaining the cooperation of the heads of the other services--Augusto *Pinochet Ugarte (*army), Gustavo *Leigh Guzmán (*air force) and César *Mendoza Durán (police). It was thought at first that Merino might emerge as Chile's new leader; then it became clear that Pinochet had began to consolidate power and assume the leadership. It came as a surprise to much of the world, though, when the new leaders unleashed a purge so violent in nature and magnitude as to have been unprecedented in the history of Latin America. Merino, besides being a member of the junta, directs naval headquarters in *Santiago. In 1981 it was thanks to Merino's efforts that Chile was included in the United States' naval exercises in the South Pacific. Chile had been banned from such participation by President Jimmy Carter because of its continued *human rights violations.

MESTIZO. An offspring of a European and an American Indian or the descendant of such a one. In colonial times such a person's share of white blood placed him on a higher social level than the pure Indian or the Black.

METRIC SYSTEM. See: WEIGHTS AND MEASURES.

METRO. The subway (or underground railway) system of *Santiago. Planning and construction began under the administrations of Eduardo *Frei Montalva and Salvador *Allende Gossens, respectively. The first line of the metro was finished after the *coup d'état which overthrew Allende in 1973.

MICRO. The current Chilean word for "bus." It usually refers to a 32-seat vehicle for in-city transportation, built from a Ford or General Motors truck. The word micro was originally used in apposition to the góndola, which in the 1940s designated the larger, pre-World War II vintage bus. As these have long since vanished, micro has become the term in general use. There is now also a smaller minibus, called a LIEBRE (q.v.).

MIGRATION. See: EMIGRATION; IMMIGRATION; INTERNAL MIGRATION.

MILICIA REPUBLICANA. A voluntary militia founded in 1932 by Eulogio *Sánchez Gutiérrez with the purpose of enforcing constitutionality in Chile. Its membership reached 50,000 within its first year of existence. In 1933 the armed and politically conservative Milicia sought permission to parade through the streets of *Santiago. Horacio *Hevia Labbe, the interior minister, opposed this, considering the organization a public danger. When the government conceded permission, Hevia resigned. The Milicia was dissolved in 1935, when the danger of dictatorship had passed, but some of its members then formed a new political party, the *Acción Nacional.

MILITARY FORCES. See: ARMED FORCES.

MILITARY JUNTA. See: JUNTA MILITAR DE GOBIERNO DE 1924; JUNTA MILITAR DE GOBIERNO DE 1925; JUNTA MILITAR DE GOBIERNO DE 1973.

MILITARY REGIME. The JUNTA MILITAR DE GOBIERNO DE 1973 (q.v.) which took power on September 11, 1973, after the demise

of Socialist President Salvador *Allende Gossens and of constitutional government, had considerable problems in establishing its
own legitimacy. A new *Constitution of 1980 was drawn up by a
junta-appointed Consejo de Estado (council of state) which included two of Chile's three living ex-Presidents. This was then
approved by 62.29 percent of the electorate (67.04 percent of
those actually voting) in a plebiscite held on the seventh anniversary of the *coup d'état. By introducing special transitional arrangements until its provisions came fully into operation in 1989,
the constitution sought to legitimize military rule, giving President Augusto *Pinochet Ugarte practically dictatorial power.
Legislative authority is vested in the four-man junta. The President also has a cabinet of 12 ministers (see: MINISTRIES), and
relies on the Supreme Court (see: CHILE--H. Government, 3.
The Judiciary) to uphold the laws of the land.

MILITARY SERVICE. See: CONSCRIPTION.

MINAS, Ministerio de. The Ministry of Mines was created by Statute
no. 16 in 1953, taking over functions previously exercised by
the Ministerio de *Hacienda. Later the same year the title of the
new ministry was changed to Ministerio de *Minería.

MINERIA, Ministerio de. The Ministry of Mining was a renaming of
the Ministry of Mines (Ministerio de *Minas) by Statute no. 231
of 1953. The ministry's functions are to supervise *mining in
Chile and to handle the marketing of minerals both in Chile and
abroad. The most important sectors of the ministry are the
National Mining Enterprise (*ENAMI), the *Nitrate and *Iodine
Sales Corporation (*COVENSA), the National *Petroleum Corpora-
tion (*ENAP), and the *Copper Corporation (*Corporación del
Cobre). Successive ministers of mining since the *coup d'état
of 1973 have been: General Arturo Zúñiga (September 1973);
General Agustín Toro Dávila (July 1974); Captain Roberto Quiñ-
ones (December 1978); José Piñera Echenique (December 1980);
Hernán Felipe Errazúriz (December 1981); Samuel Lira Ovalle
(August 1982).

MINIFUNDIA. A small farm or plantation of less than 1,000 acres.
Division of the large landed estate.

MINIFUNDISTA. A small-holder (owner or occupier of a *minifundio).

MINING. Chile is known as a country of mines. As one of the
principal mining countries of South America, Chile ranks sixth
among mineral producers worldwide and is the world's largest
copper producer. The most important copper mines, the *Gran
Minería, belong to the state. The mining code published in 1982
is supposed to stimulate growth and foreign investments. Chile
also produces iron, coal, nitrate of soda, lead, sulfur, salt and

petroleum. Chile's most important mineral resources in the latter half of the 19th century and the beginning of the 20th was its nitrates; since the 1920s they have yielded primacy to copper (see: ECONOMY, The).

From 1837 to 1887 there was a Department of Mining within the finance ministry (Ministerio de *Hacienda). In 1887 it was transferred to the newly constituted ministry for industry (Ministerio de *Industria y Obras Públicas), but in 1927 it was transferred back to the finance ministry. In 1953 it became a separate ministry, called at first the Ministerio de *Minas, and then shortly afterwards renamed the Ministerio de *Minería.

See also: COAL; COPPER; GOLD; GUANO; IODINE; IRON AND STEEL; LEAD; LITHIUM; MANGANESE; MOLYBDENUM; NATURAL GAS; NITRATES; PETROLEUM; SALT; SILVER; SULFUR; URANIUM; ZINC.

MINISTRIES. Chile's government ministries date back to the time of the wars of *independence, when there was a concerted effort on the part of the leaders of the young republic to systematize government administration. In 1814 three secretariats of state were decreed: finance (secretaría de *hacienda), government (secretaría de *gobierno) and war (secretaría de *guerra). After February 1818 these came to be called ministries (ministerios), a change formalized by the *Constitution of 1818, with the secretariat of government becoming the Ministerio de *Estado (ministry of state). In 1822 this ministry became the Ministerio de *Gobierno y Relaciones Exteriores (government and external relations), while the war ministry's title became Ministerio de *Guerra y Marina (war and navy).

Two years later the Ministry of Government became the Ministerio del *Interior y Relaciones Exteriores (the interior and foreign relations). Its responsibilities also included justice, religious affairs and education until 1837, when a separate Ministerio de *Justicia, Culto e Instrucción Pública was created. In 1871 a separate Ministerio de *Relaciones Exteriores (foreign affairs) was set up. In 1887 industry and public works were also separated from the interior ministry, becoming the province of a Ministerio de *Industria y Obras Públicas; in that same year the foreign ministry took over religious affairs from the justice ministry, as involving Chile's relations with the Holy See. A year later there was another redefinition, due to the foreign ministry's involvement with immigration, and the ministry became de Relaciones Exteriores, Culto y Colonización (foreign affairs, religious affairs and settlement).

In 1899 Education was given its own Ministerio de *Instrucción Pública. The only other change during the *Parliamentary Regime was the addition of ferrocarriles (*railways) to the title of the Industry and Public Works Ministry.

The tumultuous 1920s produced many ministerial changes which would be too confusing to enumerate here. Suffice it to say that

the navy acquired its own Ministerio de *Marina in 1924, and that
the Industry ministry was divided into Public Works and Transport (Ministerio de *Obras Públicas y Vías Públicas), Post Office
(ministerio de Correos y Telégrafos--see: POSTAL SERVICES),
and Agriculture, Industry and Settlement (Ministerio de *Agricultura, Industria y Colonización). There was also a Ministry
of Health and Social Security (Ministerio de *Higiene y Asistencia
y Previsión Social), which later added y trabajo (labor) to its
title.

In 1925 the foreign ministry once again dropped culto (religion)
as a consequence of *Church disestablishment, while Public Works
added domestic and foreign trade to become the Ministerio de
*Obras Públicas, Comercio y Vías de Comunicación. Two years
later the Department of *Mining became part of the Ministerio
de Hacienda (finance), while the rest of the Public Works Ministry
was combined with that of Agriculture and Industry into a Ministry of Development (Ministerio de *Fomento).

Redefinition of ministries continued during the *Depression
years, with some changes lasting only very briefly (e.g. the
amalgamation of the *armed forces ministries as a Ministry of
National Defense) or involving merely a name change--for example,
Instrucción Pública became *Educación Pública, and Higiene y
Asistencia y Previsión Social became *Bienestar Social (Social
Welfare).

Agriculture passed to a separate Ministerio de *Agricultura
in 1930. There was also the creation of a Labor Ministry
(Ministerio de *Trabajo) and one of Health (*Salubridad Pública).
By 1932 the armed forces were finally united permanently in a
Defense Ministry, and older groupings were reintroduced, as in
the case of the Ministerio de Obras Públicas y Vías de Comunicación (1941). In 1953 Mining was once more separated from
Finance, and Trade was dropped from the title of the Ministry
of the Economy Ministerio de *Economía. Social security, too,
was reunited with Labor in a Ministerio de *Trabajo y Previsión
Social, and a new Ministry of Housing (Ministerio de *Vivienda
y Urbanización) was created in 1965. Some changes were more
cosmetic than structural, as, for example, when in 1960 Economía
was changed to Ministerio de *Economía, Fomento y Reconstrucción.
The simpler title was restored in 1983. Such changes continue
to date.

In December 1985 the ministries and their incumbents were as
follows: Foreign Affairs (Jaime del Valle Allende), Finance (Her-
nán *Buchi Buc), Interior (Rodrigo García Rodríguez), National
Defense (Vice Admiral Patricio *Carvajal Prado), Education (Sergio
Rojas), Labor and Social Welfare (Hugo Gálvez Gajardón), Agri-
culture (Jorge Prado), Mining (Samuel Lira Ovalle), Housing and
Urbanization (Miguel Poduje), Land and Settlement (General
René Peri Farstrong), Health (Winstón Chinchón), Public Works
(General Bruno Sievert Held), Justice (Hugo Rosende), Transport
and Communications (General Enrique Escóbar Rodríguez), General

Julio Bravo Valdés (Information, Culture and Tourism).

During recent years Chile has experienced revolving door cabinets. There were major changes in December 1978, December 1979, December 1980, April 1982, February 1983 and August 1983, but changes have been even more frequent at the finance and economy ministries, where there has been little continuity since the "*Chicago Boys" were sent packing. Most cabinet ministers since the *coup have been members of the armed forces, with a handful of civilian ministers usually associated with economic affairs, for which the military have little expertise. Conservative Sergio Onofre *Jarpa Reyes, one of the few civilians, resigned the key Interior portfolio when it became clear to him that the government was dragging its feet in the return to democratic rule. The only woman to reach cabinet rank under Pinochet, Monica *Madariaga Gutiérrez, likewise resigned in disillusionment in early 1985.

See also names of individual ministries.

MIR. See: MOVIMIENTO DE IZQUIERDA REVOLUCIONARIO.

MIRAFLORES. Fashionable suburb to the south of Lima. On January 15, 1881, just two days after *Chorrillos, Miraflores was the site of the last battle before the Peruvian capital. The Chilean victory led to the occupation of Lima on January 17.

MIRISTA. Member or supporter of the *Movimiento de Izquierda Revolucionario.

MISTRAL, Gabriela (1889-1957). Literary name of Lucila Godoy Alcayaga, Chilean poet and the first South American to win the Nobel Prize for Literature (in 1945). Mistral was born at Vicuña, a village in the valley of the *Elqui river in the province of *Coquimbo. She worked for five years as a primary-school teacher in rural Coquimbo, and then from 1911 she taught in secondary schools at, successively, *Antofagasta, La *Serena, *Punta Arenas, *Temuco and *Santiago. In 1922 the Chilean government sent her to study library organization in Mexico. There she accepted the invitation of Mexican education minister José Vasconcelos to help him in his reform of the Mexican school system. In recognition of her poetic gifts, the Chile government appointed her in 1925 to the League of Nations' Institute of International Intellectual Cooperation in Paris. She was then appointed to the Chilean consular service, being posted in turn to Naples (1932), Madrid (1933), Lisbon (1935), Nice (1937), Petrópolis, Brazil (1938), and Santa Barbara, California (1946). She retired from the service in 1948, but served briefly as Chilean representative to the *United Nations in 1953. Gabriela Mistral had first visited the *United States as a professor of Spanish history and civilization at Middlebury and Barnard Colleges in 1930-31, and from 1953 until her death she resided in Long Island, New York.

Early in life she fell in love with a young man, Romelio Ureta, from her native province, but lost him when he committed suicide. To Ureta she dedicated many love poems included in Los sonetos de la muerte (sonnets of death), 1914, and in Desolación (desolation), 1922. In her later writings she turned towards a humanitarianism with religious overtones, pleading with Christ that he save a corrupted humanity as well as the soul of her dead lover. She bemoans the fate of the Jewish race, and of the poor, and shows pity and understanding towards the unmarried mother of forlorn children. But her writings have very little social content of a political or economic nature. Her poetry is very subjective and personal. Her main themes are love and death, desolation and solitude. In her poems there is an idealism which is soft and tender when it deals with love, but becomes a harsh cry when confronted with injustice and cowardice. Her greatest works are considered to be Desolación and Tala (thorny tree), 1938. They both evoke images of burning sands, barren horizons and death.

MODERADOS. Holders of moderate opinions during the Chilean struggle for *independence. The first national *Congress of Chile was established on July 4, 1811. Three loci of opinion were represented: the reactionaries or royalists (*realistas) sought the return of monarchical rule; the moderados were determined to maintain the status quo, accepting the monarchy with certain constitutional reforms; and the radicals (*exaltados) desired complete and immediate independence. The moderados formed the majority in the Congress. Their material interests in many cases had been bound up with the Spanish colonial regime. They wanted the continuation of such a regime, with some modifications. They insisted, for example, that the *creoles be given as much say in the governance of Chile as the *peninsulares. The moderados also wanted a free hand in commerce and the right to choose their own candidates to represent Chile in the *cortés. The moderados, with the help of the realistas, were able to exclude the exaltados from the *junta de gobierno de 1812, choosing José Miguel *Carrera Verdugo as their president.

MOLINA SILVA, Sergio (1928-). Economist. Educated at the *Universidad de Chile, where he later became dean of the School of Economics and taught statistics and micro-economics. In 1952 he worked with the *United Nations as an economic expert on Latin America. A year later he became Chilean delegate to the U.N. Budgetary Committee. In 1954 he became Director of Income Tax in the Finance Ministry and represented Chile at an International Finance Conference held in Rio de Janeiro. In 1955-56 he was Chile's representative on the plenary committee of the *Economic Commission for Latin America, and then went back to teaching at the Universidad de Chile. In the administration of President Eduardo *Frei Montalva (1964-70) he was finance minister (1964-68), president of the Central Bank (1964-68) and president of *CORFO (from February 1968).

MOLYBDENUM. The Chilean *copper industry produced 20,048 metric *tons of molybdenum--just over half the non-Communist world's output--in 1982, as a by-product of copper mining. This represented an increase of more than 30 percent over 1981, but the revenue (US$ 156 million) was less, owing to lower prices. In 1984 output fell to 16,861 tonnes.

MONAP. See: MOVIMIENTO NACIONAL DEL PUEBLO.

MONEDA, Palacio de La. Palace of the Chilean President, in the heart of *Santiago, between the Plaza de la Constitución and the Plaza de la Libertad. Built as the colonial mint (whence its name) in 1805, to the design of Ambrose *O'Higgins y Ballenary's architect Joaquín Toesca, it became the seat of government in 1846. The building contains government offices and the Salón rojo for official receptions, as well as presidential living accommodations. In the first patio there is a beautiful 17th-century copper fountain and two 18th-century cannon. La Moneda suffered considerable damage during the *coup d'état of September 11, 1973, particularly from air attack, and the seat of government was transferred for several years to the *Diego Portales building.

MONEY. See: COINAGE; ESCUDO; EXCHANGE RATE; GOLD STANDARD; INFLATION; PESO.

MONTE PINTO. Site of a battle fought in the hills of *Concepción between the Spaniards and the *Araucanian Indians in 1557. The Spaniards, led by García *Hurtado de Mendoza, easily defeated the Indians, whose losses were reported to be in the thousands. The struggle between the *conquistadores and the aborigines, however, lasted over 300 years. See: GUERRAS DE ARAUCO.

MONTERO RODRIGUEZ, Juan Esteban (1879-1959). Active member of the Radical Party (*Partido Radical) and minister of the interior in the quasi-dictatorial first administration (1927-31) of Carlos *Ibáñez del Campo. On July 26, 1931, Ibáñez was forced to resign and leave for exile in Argentina after a series of student strikes and a revolt of business interests. Chile's *economy was being severely affected by the world *Depression. The national treasury was depleted. With the fall in world trade, its revenue from *nitrate and *copper exports had declined to a trickle.

As interior minister, Montero automatically became vice-president (i.e. acting president) but he resigned on August 22 to campaign for election as president, being replaced by his interior minister, Manuel *Trucco Franzani. In October Montero won by 183,000 votes to Arturo *Alessandri Palma's 100,000, and assumed office on December 4, 1931. Strict foreign exchange controls were introduced to reduce the adverse *balance of trade, but discontent continued, and demonstrations and strikes forced the President to proclaim martial law. On June 4, 1932, the leaders of the three main groups opposed to Montero united to overthrow him in a military coup. This established the *junta de gobierno de 1932, headed by General Arturo Puga Osorio, which set up the so-called *República Socialista.

MONTT ALVAREZ, Jorge (1845-1922). Distinguished naval officer and Commander of the Chilean navy; key figure in the overthrow of José Manuel *Balmaceda Fernández; and President of Chile, 1891-96. As a naval officer Montt Alvarez fought in the War with *Spain of 1865-66 and in the War of the *Pacific, when he participated in the blockade of Callao in 1880. The Congressional rebellion which brough Montt Alvarez to power (the *Civil War of 1891) also brought about the collapse of the political system that had prevailed since 1831. It marked the end of the unitarist presidency with its almost dictatorial powers, and established a *parliamentary regime modeled on that of the U.K.

Montt Alvarez presided over the junta government of April 12 and August 31, 1891, (see JUNTA DE GOBIERNO DE IQUIQUE; JUNTA DE GOBIERNO DE 1891) and on December 26 was duly elected president with the backing of the *Partido Conservador. Presidential powers were limited, and the ruling cabinet became responsible to the party (or coalition) holding a majority in the National *Congress. Montt immediately granted partial amnesty to the *Balmacedistas and stabilized the Chilean electoral system. One of the most important reforms of his administration was to see that Congress would be chosen by popular vote.

Despite these reforms, Chile entered a period of ministerial instability lasting until approximately 1920. During his term in office there were eight complete cabinet changes and eleven ministerial shuffles. His accomplishments as President included a public works program and a strengthening of the *navy. Following his term in office, he traveled widely in Europe, stopping in England where he received high honors from the British government. On return to Chile in 1898 he became Director General of the *navy, and even after leaving the service in 1913 continued to have influence on the navy as mayor of *Valparaíso, until he retired to Santiago in 1918. During this period his power over the navy amounted to a state within the state, aptly dubbed "La *República Chica."

MONTT MONTT, Luis (1848-1909). Bibliographer. Son of President (1851-61) Manuel *Montt Torres. He was professor at the *Instituto Nacional from 1880 to 1886. He then became Director of the *National Library of Chile, a post he held until his death.

MONTT MONTT, Pedro (1846-1910). Lawyer, Son of President (1851-61) Manuel *Montt Torres, elder brother to Luis *Montt Montt, and President of Chile from 1906 to 1910. Elected to the Chamber of Deputies in 1879, he remained a deputy until 1900 when he became senator for *Cautín. A member of the *Partido Nacional (of which he became president in 1891), Montt was named Minister of justice and *education by President (1886-91) José Manuel *Balmaceda Fernández in 1886. In 1887 he became minister of industry and public works, and in 1889, finance minister, but, as such, he opposed Balmaceda's ambitious development plans on fiscal grounds, and resigned in January 1890. During the *Civil War of 1891 Montt sided with the rebel *Congress. Afterwards he became successively Chilean minister to the *United States and minister of the interior. After running unsuccessfully for President in 1901 as *Coalición candidate, he secured election in 1906 with the support of the *Alianza Liberal. Ministerial insta- bility characterized his administration. In 1907 there were *labor problems in the north (see: SALITRERAS DE IQUIQUE) which almost caused him to resign. Montt's government embarked upon an ambitious program of public works, which included programs to beautify the cities and build *highways, bridges and various edifices. He was responsible for finishing the *National Museum of Fine Arts in *Santiago and for inaugurating many new schools. Ill health caused him to hand over his powers to his interior minister, Elías *Fernández Albano, July 8, 1910, and he sailed to recuperate in Germany, but died on arrival in Bremen, August 16.

MONTT TORRES, Manuel (1809-1880). Lawyer, professor, judge, active conservative parliamentarian and minister, and President of Chile from 1851 to 1861. His achievements in communications (the first *railways, first telegraph, first steamships, and the modernization of the *postal service), in education (the *Univer- sidad de Chile, the *Escuela Normal de Preceptores, expansion of primary education), in *law (the new Civil Code), in adminis- tration (three new *provinces, the Oficina Estadística, the *Census of 1843), in banking (the Caja de Ahorro and the Caja de Crédito Hipotecario) and in economic development (*agriculture, *immigration and the metrification of *weights and measures) were so far-reaching as to make him a rival of Diego *Portales Palazuelos for the title of "effective creator of the Chilean state."

He became rector of the *Instituto Nacional in 1835 and presi- dent of the Supreme Court in 1851. He entered *Congress in 1835, becoming president of the Chamber of Deputies in 1840. That same year President (1831-41) Joaquín *Prieto Vial made him interior minister, and he served President (1841-51) Manuel *Bulnes Prieto in a variety of cabinet posts (including the minis- tries of war, of justice and education and of the interior and foreign affairs), and supported Bulnes against recurrent liberal uprisings. In the election of 1851, which returned Montt to the presidency, the Liberals staged another uprising, declaring the ballots fraudulent, and trying to prevent Montt from being in- augurated. The revolt lasted three months and cost an estimated 3,000 lives (see: CIVIL WAR OF 1851).

As President, Montt ruled with a heavy hand, exiling liberal leaders, imprisoning agitators who sought to disrupt the peace, and stifling many of the free voices he had earlier encouraged. During his two terms in office, Montt failed to mollify the Liberals, and also antagonized conservatives by eliminating the *mayorazgo and building railroads through their *latifundias. He became even more unpopular for intervening in *Church matters, particularly in the "Cuestión del SACRISTAN" (q.v.).

Montt's presidency proved an enlightened despotism, as he carried out his many reforms. Toward the end of his second term (1856-61) the Liberal opposition became extremely dissatisfied. When he responded to their agitation by imposing martial law, the Liberals and Radicals took up arms in the *Civil War of 1858. Some 5,000 died in the war, and, although the government was once again victorious, the presidential election that followed brought the conservative's 30-year rule in Chile to a close.

Montt returned to the Chamber of Deputies for the period 1864-67, and served in the Senate from 1876 until his death.

MORALES ECHEVERS DE TOHA, Raquel. Real name of Moy de TOHA (q.v.).

MOREL DE LETELIER, Isabel (1932-   ). *Human rights activist and widow of the exiled Chilean leader Orlando *Letelier del Solar. She is currently a senior fellow at the Institute for Policy Studies in Washington, D.C. Immediately following the *coup d'état of September 1973, Señora Letelier lived under house arrest in *Santiago, simultaneously working with international human rights organizations for the release of her imprisoned husband, former Chilean ambassador to the *United States and Salvador *Allende Gossens' minister for foreign affairs. When he was released from *Dawson Island in 1974, the entire family moved to the United States.

Isabel Letelier is a graduate of the *Universidad Católica in Santiago, and also studied at the Institute of Fine Arts of the *Universidad de Chile. She is an accomplished sculptor and has lectured at many universities and colleges, in the United States and elsewhere, on the current situation in Chile.

She also filed suit against the Chilean government for the assassination of her husband on September 21, 1976, in Washington, D.C. Responsibility for the act was traced all the way back to the *DINA, Chile's dreaded secret police.

MOTOR VEHICLE INDUSTRY. See: AUTOMOBILE INDUSTRY.

MOVIMIENTO DE ACCION POPULAR UNITARIA (MAPU). A splinter of the Christian Democrats (*Partido Demócrata Cristiano) founded in 1969 by Rafael Agustín *Gumucio Vives and Jacques *Chonchol Chait. The principal aim of this left-wing party was to bring about a structural transformation of Chile by fighting capitalism,

imperialism and the exploitation of the Chilean worker. In 1970
MAPU joined five other left-of-center parties to form *Unidad
Popular, a coalition which supported the presidential candidacy
of Socialist Salvador *Allende Gossens. Allende was elected, and
Jacques Chonchol, who had become the secretary general of MAPU,
was named minister of *agriculture. The basic program of MAPU
had seven points: (1) to limit the consumer's aspirations, and
the market, to basic needs; (2) to recover the nation's mineral
wealth from its foreign owners; (3) to accelerate the *agrarian
reform program; (4) to include the workers in the shaping of
Chile's destiny; (5) to nationalize the *banks; (6) to accelerate
the process of industrialization; and (7) to reform the country's
educational system by opening the schools up to all Chileans, and
not just the privileged few.

When the *armed forces overthrew Allende in 1973, the *junta
dissolved all political parties of the left. MAPU went underground,
and by 1975 it had become a much more extremist party, calling
for unity with the *Movimiento de Izquierda Revolucionario (MIR).
The aim of both was to overthrow militarism in Chile.

MOVIMIENTO DE EMANCIPACION DE LA MUJER CHILENA (MEMCh).
The Movement for the Emancipation of Chilean Women was founded
in the late 1930s. The initial demand was for universal adult
suffrage. In this the Chilean movement resembled other feminist
movements of the period in other countries of the world. Women
had been given the vote in municipal elections by a law of 1934.
The vote in parliamentary and presidential elections was conceded
by a law of 1949, which took effect in 1952. Leaders of the movement were Marta *Vergara, Elena *Caffarena de Jiles and Olga
*Poblete de Espinosa, the most politically active of the three.

With the election of Socialist President Salvador *Allende Gossens in 1970, MEMCh became highly organized under the leadership of Moy de *Tohá, wife of cabinet minister José *Tohá
González. Women obtained such benefits as equal pay for equal
work, day care centers for working mothers, the right to divorce
and, in some cases, the right to an abortion. With the coming
to power of the *military regime in September 1973, MEMCh was
eradicated. But ten years later it was resurrected, as more than
10,000 women, using the slogan "Democracy in the nation, democracy in the home," met in *Santiago to form a united front of
opposition to the regime.

See also: WOMEN AND THE WOMEN'S MOVEMENT; CAUPOLI-
CANAZO.

MOVIMIENTO DE IZQUIERDA REVOLUCIONARIO (M.I.R.). The
Revolutionary Left Movement was founded in 1967 and was Castroite in origin. It was strongest in the city of *Concepción;
its members were leftist students, operating mostly underground.
For the MIR, the only way to establish socialism in Chile was
through "the destruction of the reactionary state apparatus."
When Salvador *Allende Gossens became President in 1970, the

MIR tried to force his government to adopt extreme policies to bring about a socialist society. It advocated the expropriation not just of a handful of factories, but of all factories; not just of a handful of estates, but of all estates. It believed, moreover, in arming the people so that they could defend the gains made under what they considered the "reformist policies" of the Allende administration. When the opposition parties combined as the *Confederación Democrática (CODE) in order to impeach the President, the MIR leadership, in a policy turnabout, campaigned for Allende and *Unidad Popular in the March 1973 parliamentary elections.

With the advent of the *military regime, the MIR soon found itself the last armed resistance group still fighting. By 1974, with most of its members underground or dead, the MIR's activities had been seriously curtailed. But the resurrection of what many see as a terrorist organization was in the making by the mid-1980s, with new leaders appearing and increased bombings reported each year in *Santiago and other cities.

MOVIMIENTO DE RECUPERACION DOCTRINARIA (MRD). The Doctrinary Recuperation Movement was formed in 1951 and was made up of dissidents from the *Partido Agrario Laborista (PAL). Its main purpose was to oppose the presidential candidacy of Carlos *Ibáñez del Campo (whom the PAL was supporting). In 1954 the MRD combined with another breakaway group from the PAL to form the National Agrarian Party (*Partido Nacional Agrario) under the leadership of Julián Echavarrí Elorza.

MOVIMIENTO DE UNIDAD NACIONAL (MUN). A political party, sometimes referred to as Unión Nacional, formed after the *coup d'état of September 11, 1973, as a splinter from the *Partido Nacional. The party's creation had the support of *junta president Augusto *Pinochet Ugarte, but it soon became critical of the *military regime for its violations of *human rights, and for its economic policies, which were adversely affecting the middle and lower classes, and in August 1985 MUN became a member of the *Acuerdo Nacional.

MOVIMIENTO DEMOCRATICO POPULAR. An alliance formed in 1983 between the *Partido Comunista Chileno, the *Movimiento de Izquierda Revolucionario and other outlawed parties of the left.

MOVIMIENTO NACIONAL CONSERVADOR. See: PARTIDO CONSERVADOR.

MOVIMIENTO NACIONAL DE IZQUIERDA. The Leftist National Movement was organized in 1964 to back the presidential candidacy of Eduardo *Frei Montalva of the *Partido Demócrata Cristiano. The Movement was dissolved in September of the same year, just before the election, and integrated into the Democratic Socialist Party (*Partido Socialista Democrático).

MOVIMIENTO NACIONAL DEL PUEBLO (MONAP). A conservative political party which tried to attract popular support. It was formed in 1952 to back the presidential candidacy of Carlos *Ibáñez del Campo, and was dissolved after the presidential election of 1958, in which it supported conservative candidate Jorge *Allessandri Rodríguez. The party's full endorsement of Ibáñez was announced in a manifesto published in October 1952.

MOVIMIENTO NACIONAL SOCIALISTA DE CHILE. Modeled on the German National Socialist and Italian Fascist parties, the Chilean Nazi Party was formed in the late 1932 by Jorge *González Von Marées to fight the spread of international Communism. Its basic doctrine was that the individual was a servant of the state and that government had to exercise total control over every facet of national life. Violence would be stopped by violent means. It aroused strong opposition and its short existence was marred by street fighting, violent encounters with the police and a putsch attempt. In May 1938 Von Marées tried to interrupt President Arturo *Alessandri Palma in *Congress and, on being ignored, fired two pistol shots at him. For this he was briefly imprisoned. He then committed his party to supporting Carlos *Ibáñez del Campo's candidacy in the elections of that year, and when electoral failure seemed certain, attempted a putsch (see: SEGURO OBRERO). Fear of being executed for this led him to order his followers to support the candidacy of Pedro *Aguirre Cerda, who pardoned him immediately after the election. The party was dissolved, only to be immediately reincarnated as the *Vanguardia Popular Socialista. See also: NACISTA.

MOVIMIENTO NACIONALISTA CUBANO. See: CUBAN NATIONALIST MOVEMENT.

MOVIMIENTO NACIONALISTA DE CHILE. The Nationalist Movement was a party with fascist tendencies formed in 1941 by Guillermo Izquierdo Araya. Members wore uniforms, and the party's main purpose was to abolish manhood suffrage and bring about the formation of a Chilean corporate state very similar to that of Mussolini in Italy. The defeat of the Axis powers in Europe helped in the downfall of the Chilean Nationalist Movement, and it was dissolved in 1945. Many of its members then joined the *Partido Agrario Laborista.

MOVIMIENTO NACIONALISTA POPULAR. See: THIEME, Roberto.

MOVIMIENTO REPUBLICANO. The Republican Movement was a political party formed in 1956 to regroup the conservative elements within Chilean society who had backed the presidential candidacy of Carlos *Ibáñez del Campo in 1952. In the presidential elections of 1958, the Movimiento Republicano backed Jorge *Alessandri Rodríguez. When the party failed to get representation in Congress in 1961, it was dissolved.

MOVIMIENTO REVOLUCIONARIO NACIONAL SINDICALISTA (MRNS).
The National Revolutionary Syndicalist Movement was formed in
1963 to back the presidential candidacy of Jorge *Prat Echaurren,
considered by many as a man who was trying to revive Nazi
activities in Chile. The main objective of the party was to oppose Communism in Chile and to create a corporate state. In
1964 Prat Echaurren renounced a bid to run for the presidency
and the party was dissolved by the Minister of the Interior for
its fascist tendencies. In spite of this, the party operated underground during the term of President (1964-70) Eduardo *Frei
Montalva.

MÜHLEMBROCK LIRA, JULIO VON, 1913- . One of the founders
and leaders of the Agrarian Labor Party (*Partido Agrario Laborista). He was opposed to the presidential candidacy of Carlos
*Ibáñez del Campo in 1952, causing a split within the party.
Two years later, Rafael *Tarud formed a new party, the *Partido
Agrario Laborista Recuperacionista, which was leftist in orientation. Mühlembrock Lira left the party in 1960 and joined the
*Partido Liberal. In 1961 he was elected to the Senate for an
eight-year term.

MUSEO DE ARTE CONTEMPORANEO. See: MUSEUM OF CONTEMPO-
RARY ART.

MUSEO DE ARTE POPULAR. See: MUSEUM OF POPULAR ART.

MUSEO HISTORICO NACIONAL. See: HISTORY MUSEUM.

MUSEO NACIONAL DE BELLAS ARTES. See: THE NATIONAL MU-
SEUM OF FINE ARTS.

MUSEO NACIONAL DE LA QUINTA NORMAL. See: NATIONAL MU-
SEUM OF QUINTA NORMAL.

MUSEUM OF CONTEMPORARY ART (Museo de Arte Contemporaneo).
Located in the Quinta Normal in *Santiago, this museum exhibits
modern Chilean paintings.

MUSEUM OF POPULAR ART (Museo de Arte Popular). Located in
the Cerro Santa Lucía in *Santiago, this museum contains an exhibit of South American folklore.

MUTINY OF CAMBIASO. A mutiny led by Lieutenant Miguel José
Cambiaso (1823-52), who had been posted to *Punta Arenas for
his violence and lack of discipline. The mutiny at Punta Arenas
was just one of many such anti-government outbreaks in favor of
General José María de la *Cruz y Prieto during the *Civil War
of 1851. Cambiaso's savagery alientated his men, who deserted
him. He was caught, tried and shot.

MUTINY OF COQUIMBO. See: COQUIMBO MUTINY.

MUTINY OF FIGUEROA. A mutiny organized and led by Colonel
Tomás de *Figueroa Caravacá, which took place in *Santiago on
April 1, 1811. Figueroa wished to restore Spanish colonial rule
in Chile, but his mutiny failed, he sought refuge in a convent,
was forcibly taken from it, given a summary trial and executed.

MUTINY OF QUILLOTA. See: QUILLOTA MUTINY.

MUTINY OF SEPTEMBER 5, 1938. See: SEGURO OBRERO.

MUTINY OF URRIOLA. A mutiny organized and led by Colonel Pedro
Alcántara *Urriola Balbontín, which took place in *Santiago on
April 20, 1851, in an attempt to decide the presidential campaign
by force, in favor of José María de la *Cruz y Prieto. It was
doomed by lack of artillery, and Urriola was killed during the
fighting. The mutiny aggravated the division between the supporters of Manuel *Montt Torres, the government candidate and
the Liberals who supported Cruz Prieto. This dichotomy precipitated the events that led to the *Civil War of 1851 later that year.

- N -

NACION, La. (1) A short-lived (1890-91) *Santiago *newspaper,
representing the *Balmacedista faction of the Liberal Party (*Partido Liberal).
    (2) The official government newspaper. Originally founded
as an independent paper on January 14, 1917 by Elidoro *Yáñez
of the *Partido Liberal Doctrinario to provide a platform for a
variety of new social and political viewpoints, it supported the
1920 presidential campaign of Arturo *Alessandri Palma, and
numbered Joaquín *Edwards Bello among its regular contributors.
By 1925 Yáñez (and his paper) had become allies of Carlos *Ibáñez del Campo, who came near to supporting a Yáñez candidature
for the presidency. In June 1927, however, Yáñez's name was
linked with a plot by Carlos Vergara Montero and other infantry
officers to oust Ibáñez. As a result, Ibáñez had Yáñez deported
and his newspaper taken over by the state. Since then it has
remained in government control and been the official mouthpiece
(although the Eduardo *Frei Montalva administration of 1964-70
generally had its views put forward more by El *Mercurio).
Following the *coup d'état of September 11, 1973, La Nacion became a tabloid and changed its name to La Patria. Two years
later it had changed again, to El Cronista. By 1984 it had become
La Nación once more, and had a circulation of 15,000.

NACISTAS. Nazis: used to denote supporters of both the German

National Socialist Party and its Chilean imitations, the MOVIMIEN-
TO NACIONAL SOCIALISTA DE CHILE (1932-38), q.v., and its
successor, the VANGUARDA POPULAR SOCIALISTA (1938-41),
q.v. Other Chilean political parties that have been accused of
being neo-Nazi in their outlook include: *Acción Nacional; *Movimiento Nacionalista de Chile, and *Partido Nacional Socialista
Obrero.

NARBOROUGH, [Sir] John (1640-1688). English admiral. In 1669
he was sent on H.M.S. Sweepstakes to explore the Pacific. Leaving England on October 6, he visited *Patagonia, sailed through
the *Strait of Magellan, discovered Narborough Island, and put
into *Valdivia on December 25, 1670. While they were ashore,
several of his crew were detained and imprisoned on orders from
the governor of Chile, apprehensive that Narborough's real intent
was piracy (see: PIRATES AND PRIVATEERS). Having neither
the means nor the authority to carry out any effective reprisals,
and realizing that all Spanish ports would probably now be closed
to him, Narborough decided to abandon his expedition. He returned the way he had come and reached England in June 1671.

NACIONAL ACTION. See: ACCION NACIONAL.

NATIONAL ANTHEM (Himno Nacional). Chile's first national anthem
was composed in 1819, with words by the Argentine poet Bernardo
de *Vera y Pintado, who had originally come to Chile as representative of the newly independent government of Buenos Aires.
It was sung to the tune of the Argentine anthem until Manuel
Robles (1790-1836) composed music for it the following year. This
was used until 1828, when Mariano *Egaña Fabres, Chile's minister
in London, commissioned the Catalan composer Ramón Carnicer
to write new music for it. Bernardo Vera's words contained
several expressions offensive to Spanish susceptibilities, so after
Spain's 1844 recognition of Chilean independence, the government
sought to change it. In 1847 the Chilean poet Eusebio *Lillo
(the then minister of the interior) composed new lyrics for Carnicer's music. This has been the national anthem ever since,
although the Vera-Robles anthem retained its popularity for some
time. Lillo retained the original chorus ("Dulce patria recibe los
votos/ con que Chile en tus aras juró/ que o la tumba serás de
los libres/ o el asilo contra la opresión"), but the verses are
plainly concilliatory: "Ha cesado la lucha sangriente: /ya es
hermano el que ayer invasor;/ de tres siglos lavamos la afrenta/
combatiendo en el campo de honor" (The bloody fight is over/
the invader is now our brother;/ we have washed away three
centuries of affront/ on the field of honor).

NATIONAL ARCHIVES. The Archivo Nacional de Chile is adminis-
tratively part of the Directorate of Libraries, Archives and
Museums, and until 1982 was housed in the *National Library.
It then began to be transferred to a separate building next

door at 50 Miraflores Street, formerly occupied by the Museo Histórico Nacional, (*History Museum) which had just been moved to the Palacio de la Real Academia.

The first considerable body of manuscript material was acquired by the National Library as part of Mariano *Egaña Fabre's library, and this was notably augmented by the manuscripts acquired with the José Ignacio Víctor Eyzaguirre library and by the papers used by Claude *Gay for his Historia general de Chile which came with the acquisition of his library. Further archival material arrived as spoils of the War of the *Pacific, and in 1886 Luis *Montt Montt, immediately upon his appointment as Director of the National Library, arranged the creation of a separate Sección de manuscritos de la Biblioteca Nacional, adding to it the 5,000 volumes of archives of the Contaduría Mayor (the Chilean treasury) from the 1500s to 1840; the 3,098 volumes of the Real *Audiencia (law courts) from 1568 to 1814; and the 1,045 volumes of archives of the old Capitanía General. The new section held a total of 12,500 volumes by Montt's retirement in 1910. By 1921, when its section head Tomás Thayer Ojeda described it in the Hispanic American Historical Review, it had grown to over 20,000 volumes. A new status and the title of Archivo histórico nacional accompanied the National Library's move to its new building in 1925.

Meanwhile, in 1887 the Archivo General del Gobierno had been formed to preserve official documents of national and local government. In 1927 this was combined with the Historical Archive, becoming the Public Administration section of the new Archivo Nacional de Chile, the relevant law being enacted in 1929 and the historian Ricardo Donoso Novoa being appointed the first director of the enlarged organization.

The collections now occupy eight miles of shelving, range in date from 1502 to the present, and include administrative papers (among them those of the *cabildo), judicial and notary records, real estate deeds, the correspondence of politicians, historians and writers (Pedro de *Valdivia, Bernardo *O'Higgins and Diego *Portales Palenzuelos, for instance), and ecclesiastical records (of the Peruvian *Inquisition, the *Jesuits throughout South America, and other religious orders).

There is an overflow of documents in separate stores scattered throughout *Santiago. Cataloging (incomplete as yet) is mainly according to origin, and only a limited amount of analytical indexing has been done. Material in the Public Administration section is not made available until a specified time (varying up to 60 years) has elapsed since deposit. Since 1978 the Archives have published a twice-yearly Informativo del Archivo Nacional reporting on archival and related materials.

A supporting library on archives and historical research is in process of formation. Other archival collections in Santiago include the Archivo Judicial, Archivo del Registro Civil and the Library of the National *Congress.

NATIONAL BIBLIOGRAPHY. Chile is outstanding among Hispanic
nations for its achievements in bibliography. José Toribio *Medina Zavala is incontestably the greatest name in Hispanic American
bibliography, with an output that embraces the whole of the
Spanish-speaking Americas. The *National Library has a great
tradition of bibliographic work, and many of its directors and
staff have achieved renown in the field. Ramón *Briseño Calderón
(1814-1910), who became director in 1864, compiled an Estadística bibliográfica de la literatura chilena, 1812-1876 (2 vols,
1862-79), cataloguing (at the suggestion of Andrés *Bello López)
everything published in Chile since the introduction of the first
proper *printing press. This would later be complemented by
two works by Medina: Bibliografía de la imprenta en Santiago de
Chile desde sus orígenes hasta febrero de 1817 (Santiago, 1893),
covering the output of the primitive press of the *Universidad
de San Felipe, and Biblioteca hispano-chilena, 1523-1817 (Santiago, 1897-99), for works on Chile from outside the country.
Luís *Montt Montt (1848-1909), son of President Manuel *Montt
Torres, became director in 1886 and immediately began the publication of the Anuario de la prensa chilena, as a regular annual
national bibliography, continued by his Successor Carlos Silva
Cruz only until 1916. It was, however, revived by director
Guillermo *Feliú Cruz in 1962, and by 1965 volumes for all the
intervening years 1917-64 had appeared. Feliú Cruz retired the
following year, and the Anuario lapsed with the publication of
the 1969 volume in 1971, to be revived again in 1977-79 when the
volumes for 1970-75 appeared. The period 1976-79 was covered
in a cumulation entitled Bibliografía chilena, and this title has
now been adopted for a resumed annual series. The production
of the years between Briseño's work and the start of the Anuario
was bridged by David Toro Melo's Catálogo de los impresos que
vieron la luz pública en Chile desde 1877 hasta 1885 inclusive
(Santiago, 1893).

NATIONAL CONFEDERATION OF WORKERS. See: CONFEDERACION
NACIONAL DE TRABAJADORES.

NATIONAL FLAG. See: FLAG, NATIONAL.

NATIONAL FLOWER. The national flower is the COPIHUE (q.v.).

NATIONAL HEALTH. See: PUBLIC HEALTH; SERVICIO NACIONAL
DE SALUD.

NATIONAL HISTORY MUSEUM. See: HISTORY MUSEUM.

NATIONAL INCOME. In 1980 the national per capita income in Chile
was US$ 1,590, a decline from the US$ 1,950 of 1979. In 1984
it was still below US$ 2,000; real wages were less than in 1973,
and per capita purchasing power less than in 1971. Moreover,
there was a much greater concentration of income.

The gross domestic product in 1984 was around US$ 30,000 million. It had grown 7.5 percent in 1980, and 5.3 percent in 1981, but this growth had been effectively canceled out by the *economy's subsequent decline (1982 had seen a negative growth of 14.3 percent). However, at US$ 2,530 per capita in 1984, it was still well above per capita national income.

National income distribution by sector in 1984 was as follows: *agriculture, *forestry and *fisheries 7.2%; *mining 8.9%; *manufacturing 17.7%; construction and *housing 4.6%; commerce 18.2%; transport and communications 4.9%; utilities 1%; government and all other services, 37.5%. Only mining and fisheries had registered positive growth since 1971; commerce had fallen by 14.6%; industrial production by 21.9%; construction by 28.8%; transport and communications by 10.4%, and agriculture and forestry by 3.3%.

Prices of consumer goods in *Santiago and *Valparaíso were noticeably higher than in other principal South American cities, due in part to *inflation of over 30 percent in 1984. The foreign debt had reached US$ 18,000 million, or over 70 percent of the GNP (gross national product). Unemployment was acute (see: EMPLOYMENT). High interest rates, of 30 percent to 40 percent, forced eight major banks to close (see: BANKS, BANKING AND FINANCIAL INSTITUTIONS), put 431 businesses into liquidation and caused more than 1,000 bankruptcies among the self-employed (owners of small businesses and other industries).

NATIONAL INSTITUTE OF HIGHER EDUCATION. See: INSTITUTO NACIONAL.

NATIONAL LABOR UNION. See: UNION NACIONAL LABORISTA.

NATIONAL LIBRARY OF CHILE. The Biblioteca Nacional in *Santiago stands on Avenida Bernardo O'Higgins (the *Alameda) between Miraflores and MacIver streets. The building, erected 1912-24, has oil murals by the Chilean painters Arturo Gordon and Alfredo Helsby. Its 1.8 million volumes make it the largest national library of any Spanish-speaking country outside Spain. The Departamento de Colecciones includes the Sección Chilena (created in 1886 to house all works published in Chile--some 800,000 volumes), the Fondo General (which has now absorbed the old Sección de Américas and has 450,000 non-Chilean works), the Sección Revistas Chilenas y Extranjeras--Chilean and foreign journals and magazines (the former Hemeroteca), the Sección Periódicos (*newspapers), the Mapoteca (maps) and the Archivos Especiales (music, audiovisual material, foreign translations of works by Chilean authors, and authors' manuscripts). There were some 133 staff in 1977, though only 31 of these were professional librarians.

A National Library was proclaimed by the revolutionary *junta in August 1813 on the initiative of Juan *Egaña Risco (who originally envisaged it as the library of the *Instituto Nacional). This amounted to only a few hundred volumes donated by well-wishers, and was closed as "pernicious" by the *realistas when they re-occupied Santiago in October 1814. Bernardo *O'Higgins rees-tablished it, in the building of the colonial *Universidad de San Felipe, by a decree of August 5, 1818, and it took over the books of the university library, itself largely made up of the 6,000 items confiscated from the *Jesuits on their 1767 expulsion. In 1823 the library, which now amounted to 12,000 volumes, moved to the old custom house, where it opened to the public as the "Sociedad de Lectura de Santiago," and the old university library building became the Teatro Municipal.

Successive legal deposit laws (October 25, 1825; July 24, 1834; April 22, 1844; and September 16, 1846), although poorly en-forced, aided the library's growth, and in 1840 its 14,829 volumes were moved into a new two-story adobe building at Catedral and Bandera streets. Holdings were further enhanced by Mariano *Egaña Fabres' 10,000-volume library (added in 1846); the private library of José Miguel de la Barra; 1,606 books of Americana from the library of Benjamín *Vicuña Mackenna (in 1861); 1,560 books from the library of Andrés *Bello López (1868); 4,122 works from the theology collection of Monseigneur José Ignacio Víctor Eyza-guirre (1877); the 1874 gift of the 3,924-volume library of his-torian Claude *Gay; and some 8,790 volumes brought back as spoils of war from *Peru in 1881.

Lawyer-writer-bibliographer Ramón *Briseño Calderón (director 1864-86) organized the collection and modernized its services in imitation of the French Bibliothèque Nationale, and issued the first important printed catalog. When he was succeeded by Luis *Montt Montt, the library's 65,000 volumes exceeded in number those of the national libraries of Colombia and Peru, and the collection was moved again, to the building of the Real Tribunal del Consulado, recently vacated by the National *Congress. Montt built the collection up to 150,000 volumes. His successor from 1910, Carlos Silva Cruz, a great admirer of *United States librari-anship, created the reference department in 1912. Between 1915 and Medina's death in 1930, the library received the books of Spanish America's greatest bibliographer, José Toribio *Medina Zavala.

From 1852 to 1879 the National Library was administered by the Council of the *Universidad de Chile. From then until 1921 it was under the Consejo de Instrucción Pública (public education council) whose chairman was the University's rector. The re-moval of the library to its present building was made in 1925, just before the start of Eduardo *Barrios Hudtwalcker's vigorous first term as director. In 1929, thanks to agitation by the bib-liographer and writer Guillermo *Feliu Cruz, the National Library was made the center of the whole national library system, with the creation of the Directorate of Libraries, Archives and Museums as a department of the education ministry (Ministerio de *Edu-cación Pública). The administration of Gabriel Amunátegui Jordán a few years later (1935-41), is credited with greatly expanding the library's activities.

Like so many Latin American state, provincial and national libraries, the Biblioteca Nacional has failed to dedicate itself clearly to its research function. Director Montt experimented with a home loan service, which led to serious stock losses. Silva Cruz began a service to children, and Alejandro Vicuña Pérez (director 1932-35) even tried the experiment of evening opening to encourage library use by "trabajadores." Guillermo Feliu Cruz (director 1960-67) sought on the other hand to restrict access by the more casual reader, partly in the hope that this would force high schools to comply with their century-old obligation to provide school libraries. His successor, Roque Esteban Scarpa, reversed this policy, granting free access to all those over 19. Scarpa's more positive achievements included the raising of librarians' salaries to a more realistic level, setting up the Archivos Especiales, indexing many important Chilean journals, and expanding the country's public library network.

Two recent periods have been ones of relative stagnation: the second administration of the then ailing Eduardo Barrios in 1953-60, and the immediate post-*coup years. Director Scarpa had been forced to leave in May 1971 under political pressure from President Salvador *Allende Gossens, who appointed the writer "Juvencio Valle" (Gilberto Concha Riffo.) Although the military *junta reinstated Scarpa, it imposed such severe budgetary constraints on the library that even the fabric of the building had to be allowed to deteriorate (with consequent rain damage to the bookstock) and the International Exchange Section ceased to function.

A building restoration and general administrative reform began with the 1977 appointment as director of Enrique Campos Menéndez (since 1973 the Asesor Cultural of the Junta de Gobierno), and the introduction of a controversial tax on books to support the nation's libraries. The *National Archives were transferred to what had been the building of the National Historical Museum, and the library's space problem has been further eased by the acquisition of annexes at the corner of Compañía and De Herrera streets and on Avenida Independencia.

The library's treasures include 87 incunabula, among them the 1474 edition of the Siete partidas of King Alfonso X of Castile ("el Sabio"), the 1491 Vidas delas de Plutarco "traduzidas por Alfonso de Pateçia" and a 1491 edition of Lucan's Pharsalia. The library also possesses a copy of the first (1552) edition of the works of Father Bartolomé de Las Casas (claimed unique in the Western Hemisphere), a 1597 edition of Alonso de *Ercilla y Zúñiga's *Araucana and a 1605 copy of the *Arauco dominado of Pedro *Oña.

NATIONAL MUSEUM OF FINE ARTS (Museo Nacional de Bellas Artes). Located in the Parque Forestal in *Santiago, Chile's national art museum is the oldest museum of painting in South America. It contains a large collection of Chilean paintings by such artists as Juan Francisco González, Alfredo Valenzuela and Alberto Valenzuela Llanos. Foreign artists represented include Monvoisín, Murillo, Guido Reni and Rembrandt. The museum also has a large collection of Baroque art.

NATIONAL MUSEUM OF QUINTA NORMAL (Museo Nacional de la Quinta Normal). A museum of fauna, flora, archeology and minerology, founded in 1830. Its most famous exhibit is that of the mummy of "Cerro Plomo," found in 1954 and probably buried in the snow by an Inca.

NATIONAL PARTY. See: PARTIDO NACIONAL.

NATIONAL PRIZE FOR LITERATURE. See: PREMIO NACIONAL DE LITERATURA.

NATIONAL SECURITY COUNCIL (Consejo Nacional de Seguridad). See: CONSTITUTION OF 1980.

NATIONAL SOCIALIST MOVEMENT. See: MOVIMIENTO NACIONAL SOCIALISTA DE CHILE.

NATIONAL UNION OF CHILEAN WORKERS. See: UNION NACIONAL DE TRABAJADORES DE CHILE.

NATIONAL UNION PARTY. See: UNION NACIONAL.

NATIONALIST LEFT. See: IZQUIERDA NACIONAL.

NATURAL GAS. Chile's reserves of natural gas (mostly methane) are estimated at 80,000 million cubic meters. Output was 7,376,000 m^3 in 1973, but had fallen to 5,064,500 m^3 in 1982. A small proportion is exported. All production since 1978 has been the responsibility of the Sociedad Gas de Chile, which is 51 percent state-owned (*ENAP 31 percent, *COPEC 20 percent).

NAVARINO ISLAND. An island at 55° 7'S, 67° 30'W, of rugged mountains and magnificent woods, measuring 35 miles by 25. It lies south of *Tierra del Fuego, from which it is separated by the *Beagle Channel. On its south side, Nassau Bay separates it from the Wollaston Islands and *Cape Horn. Puerto Williams (population 1,000) with a naval base and a crab-canning factory, is the world's most southerly settlement with a permanent population. The island was named by Philip Parker *King who was surveying its coast when he received the news of the allied naval victory at Navarino in the Greek War of Independence (1827).

NAVY. The Chilean navy (<u>Armada Nacional</u>) traces its origins to

1813, when former Spanish naval officer Francisco de la *Lastra
y de la Sotta, governor of *Valparaíso, seeking to break Spain's
blockade of that port, acquired the ex-U.S. frigate Perla and
the brig Portrillo. Loyalists subsequently secured possession of
both vessels through bribery. But in February 1817 the sloop
Aguila (later renamed Pueyrredón), captured the merchantman
San Miguel and retook the Perla. Aguila was under Iristh mer-
cenary George O'Brien, who had served in the British navy and
was killed in the fight. Naval headquarters were to remain in
Valparaíso until 1927, a factor of considerable importance in
developing an independent-minded service.

After *Maipo, Bernardo *O'Higgins realized that Chilean independence could only be secured by ending Spanish power in
*Peru, and that an attack on Peru was only practicable through
a seaborne invasion, which required an adequate navy. By that
time Chile's strength at sea had grown to 2 large frigates and 3
sloops under artillery colonel Manuel *Blanco Encalada, and was
promptly increased by surprising and capturing the Spanish
Reina Maria Isabel lying at anchor in *Concepción Bay (see:
TALCAHUANO, Battle of); renamed the O'Higgins she became
the flagship. Recruited by O'Higgins, Scottish admiral Lord
*Cochrane arrived to take command in November 1818 and by
daring and tactical skill soon achieved the command of the sea
that made the liberation of Peru possible. He left Chile when
his task was done, in January 1823, and the navy was deactivated.
Ramón *Freire Serrano reconstituted it in 1824, giving command
again to Blanco Encalada. In 1826 the O'Higgins was dispatched
to aid the Argentines against Brazil, but was lost at sea in a
gale off *Cape Horn.

From 1834 the navy undertook important hydrographic work,
and in 1837-38 its command of the sea permitted the transport
of the troops that won the war with the *Peru-Bolivia Confederation. In the war of 1865-66 with *Spain, however, the navy
revealed serious weaknesses which postwar expansion sought to
remedy. But Chile's economic difficulties in the 1870s starved
it of funds, and it entered the War of the *Pacific with insufficient
troop transports, its only seaworthy ironclads handicapped by
badly befouled hulls, and so short of men that it had to recruit
foreign mercenaries (both the Naval Academy--set up in 1818--
and the Seamen's School had been closed in 1876 as economy
measures). After the over-cautious Admiral Juan *Williams
Rebolledo had been replaced, his more dynamic successor, Galvarino Riveros, rapidly won the control of the sea that assured
ultimate victory, and Chile ended the war as the major naval
power in the Americas, superior at sea to even the *United States.

British influence on the Chilean navy, begun with Cochrane,
was perpetuated by U.K. naval missions down to World War II,
which probably explains, in part at least, why the navy developed
a tradition that was more aristocratic and less politically conscious
than that of the *army. That same tradition also made the navy,

when it did become politically involved, much more likely to support the forces of the right. An example was the united support it gave to the conservative rebellion against President José Manuel *Balmaceda Fernández, a rebellion in which naval support was decisive. It consequently emerged from the *Civil War of 1891 as the senior service in both social prestige and national strategic planning: its administrative independence gave rise to the nickname, "La *República Chica."

Britain's 1906 introduction of the revolutionary Dreadnought made all existing battleships obsolete, and led to a naval arms race in Latin America as well as in Europe. Chile at the time possessed one battleship, 6 cruisers, 3 gunboats and 8 torpedo boats; she proceeded to order from Britain two 28,000-ton "dreadnoughts," 3 submarines and 10 destroyers, but the big ships were not ready when World War I broke out. Only one, the Latorre, eventually arrived in 1920. This was South America's largest warship for the next 25 years.

Postwar reorganization split the navy into traditionalists (mainly the admirals) and modernizers (mostly the more junior officers), and this division was exploited by Carlos *Ibáñez del Campo in his struggle to win the presidency. The "new navy," which eventually resulted secured many necessary technical and organizational reforms, but was badly discredited by the *Coquimbo mutiny, and the service lost its primacy to the army from this time.

Since World War II, U.S. influence has replaced that of the U.K. (except for a brief interruption of U.S. advisory missions in 1979, during the Carter administration), but much naval equipment continues to be British-made: 3 of Chile's 7 destroyers, 2 of its 5 frigates, and 2 of its 3 submarines.

By 1980, thanks to arms embargoes by various foreign governments, the bulk of the fleet was obsolete. Of its 3 cruisers, 2 had been built--for the U.S. navy--in 1938 (and transferred to Chile in 1951) and the other was Swedish-built in 1947. Of its 6 ordinary destroyers, only 2 (British-built in 1960) were relatively new. Its 5 frigates, however, included 2 U.K.-built in the 1970s; 2 submarines were being laid down that year in West Germany, and two years later Britain would supply Chile's only guided-missile destroyer, the Prat (ex-Norfolk). Other craft included a corvette (U.S.-built in 1942), 4 Spanish-built torpedo boats, a U.S. submarine chaser, 2 Israeli guided missile boats, 2 ocean-going tugboats, a hydrographic survey vessel, an Antarctic patrol-and-research ship, a training ship under sail, some landing craft, and such auxiliary vessels as a submarine tender, hospital ship, tugs and dry docks. This total may be compared with Argentina's post-Falkland strength of one aircraft carrier, 9 destroyers, 4 frigates, 5 corvettes and 3 submarines (with more building), and Peru's 2 cruisers, 10 destroyers, 12 submarines, 2 frigates and 6 guided-missile destroyers.

Although Chile's original naval air arm was absorbed by the

*air force on its 1930 formation, a small new naval air arm was established in 1953. This now has 40 airplaines (including 6 Brazilian Bandeirantes for sea patrol duty and 3 C-47 transports), plus 30 helicopters.

The navy's overall personnel strength is 28,000: 23,950 sailors, 1,995 officers, 2,000 marines, and 600 marine officers, supported by 6,000 civil servants. A sufficiency of volunteers has meant that only about 1,600 of the men are recruited through *conscription. The commander-in-chief, Admiral José Toribio *Medina Castro, is also a member of the governing *junta. Naval headquarters are now in *Santiago, and for tactical deployment there are three naval zones: the 1st, headquartered at Valparaiso, the 2nd at *Talcahuano (south of Santiago) and the 3rd at *Punta Arenas, facing *Antarctica. The chief naval air base is at El Belloto, near Valparaiso.

Chile has no separate coast guard or lighthouse service. Coast surveillance duties, fishery protection and navigational aids devolve upon the navy's Directorate of the National Maritime Territory and Merchant Marine, equipped with 13 air-sea rescue craft, 10 Brazilian-built patrol boats and a lighthouse servicing ship.

See also: ARMED FORCES, MERCHANT MARINE; PRAT CHACON, Arturo.

NECOCHEA NEMEL, Eduardo (b. 1898). Civil engineer by profession, and one of the founders of the Agrarian Party (*Partido Agrario), becoming its president in 1940. In 1945 he helped organize the merger with the *Alianza Popular Libertadora, resulting in the *Partido Agrario Laborista, of which he also became president. In the 1950s Necochea became vice-president of Chile's national steel company, *CAP.

NEGRO SLAVERY. See: AFRICAN SLAVERY.

NERUDA, Pablo (1904-1973). Chile's second Nobel laureate poet, Neruda was born Ricardo Eliezer Neftalí Reyes y Basoalto, the son of a *railway worker; he made his pseudonym Pablo Neruda his legal name in 1946. By 1927 he had published six books and was already recognized as an influential writer. He was offered a consular post in Rangoon and remained in the diplomatic service until 1944. From 1936, when he was Chilean consul in Madrid at the outbreak of the Spanish Civil War, he was also a political figure of considerable importance. In 1937 he joined the Popular Front (*Frente Popular), a coalition of several left-of-center parties, including the Communists, Socialists and Radicals. In 1939 he was posted to Paris as Chilean consul for Spanish emigration (see: WINNIPEG, S.S.). From 1942 to 1944 he traveled in Cuba, Mexico and the United States and campaigned for a second front in Europe to help the *U.S.S.R. In March 1945 Neruda was elected senator for *Tarapacá and *Antofagasta, and

joined the Chilean Communist Party (*Partido Comunista Chileno)
four months later. In 1948 he publicly accused the President
(1946-52) Gabriel *González Videla of being a traitor; as a result
he had to go underground, spending the next two years as a
fugitive from the law or in exile in Europe and Mexico; in 1950
he won the Stalin Prize for literature. Because of his political
beliefs he was denied admission to the United States on a number
of occasions.

In December 1970 President Salvador *Allende Gossens appointed
him ambassador to France. Neruda had been the Communist
Party's presidential candidate, but had withdrawn just before the
September 1970 elections when the parties of the left united as
*Unidad Popular behind Allende. On October 20, 1971, Neruda
was awarded the Nobel Prize for Literature, the only other
Chilean poet to win such an honor being Gabriela *Mistral. The
Swedish Academy cited him for writing "poetry that with the
action of an elemental force brings alive a continent's destiny
and dreams."

Neruda's poetry begins, as it ends, with the poet's fascination
with nature. But it also reveals the recurrent, even obsessive
imagery, the consistent underlying themes, which weld apparently
disparate volumes of poetry into a kind of spiritual autobiography,
a testament of a man's struggle for existence, and a concern
for the social and political realities of South America and its
people. Considered one of the best poets in Latin America,
Neruda was also a very prolific writer. La canción de la fiesta,
his first book, was written when he was 15 and published in 1921
when he was 17. His second, Crepusculario, followed two years
later. His Veinte poemas de amor y una canción desesperada
of 1925 made him famous immediately. In it he created an original
landscape and a poetry that reflected his personal experience.
Neruda's fame grew even more with Residencia en la tierra, published in two books, first in Chile (1925-31) and then in Spain
(1931-35). They were soon widely acclaimed and Neruda's name
figured prominently with those of Federico García Lorca and the
other poets of Spain's so-called "Generation of 1927." The themes
were anguish, solitude and death, all expressed in an absurd
world. This pessimism was continued in the first two sections of
Tercera residencia (1934-43), but ended with the last poem of
"Las furias y las penas" (Section II of the work). From this
point on, Neruda began a new phase. Section III represented
his political conversion. His social themes, already present in
Crepusculario (in poems such as "Barrio sin luz" or "El ciego de
la pandereta") abandoned the pessimism of the earlier poems and
began to offer a solution for injustice and misery. The poet
abandoned the contemplation of the self in a chaotic world and
began to see order in things. His preoccupation was no longer
with death, but with life. He was willing to put his art at the
service of social realism, being primarily concerned with the
rights of his fellow men.

The earlier period had been one of the lyrical assertion of the natural world and of the individual human being as part of it. After 1936 Neruda's message became more political: the social participation of the poet who identifies himself with his fellow men, as well as an austere vision of the seer who knows that the world is full of tragedy and injustice. The change in the orientation of his work was the product of two major events in his life: his witnessing the Spanish Civil War and his adherence to the Communist Party. The poet became the spokesman of the deprived and sang of their hope. The collection, España en el corazón (Spain in the heart), 1937, defended the legitimacy of the Spanish republican government and accused General Francisco Franco's nationalists of bringing destruction to Spain. Canto general (1950) also expressed a clear political orientation, describing America as it was in 1400 and narrating its history to the present in epic fashion. Las uvas y el viento (1954), inspired mostly by the Chilean landscape and by the workers' struggle to improve their living conditions, likewise attempted to interpret the destiny of America from a historical and political perspective.

Neruda's other major works are these: three volumes of Odes, Odas elementales (1954, 1956, 1957); Estravagario (1958); five autobiographical volumes; Memorial de Isla Negra (1964); Vida, fulgor y muerte de Joaquín Murieta (1966), a social documentary with songs about a Chilean who emigrated to work in California during the gold rush of 1849; and his autobiography in prose, Confieso que he vivido (I Confess to Having Lived), published posthumously at the end of 1973.

Two years before his death, Neruda had asked Allende to relieve him from his duties as ambassador to France. Allende accepted his resignation and the poet returned to Chile with his wife, Matilde *Urrutia. On September 11, 1973, Neruda was listening to the radio in Isla Negra, his house near *Valparaíso. He was already, by then, suffering cancer of the prostate, but had been given several years to live, since the cancer was slow in developing and his health seemed good. Neruda was very shaken by the events that followed the *coup, and by the death of his good friend Allende. The news reports put him in a feverish state. He wanted to go to Santiago for treatment, but no one was allowed to leave home. Three days after the coup, the *junta's emissaries called on Matilde and Pablo Neruda, and on September 19 they were finally allowed to go to the capital by car. They were frequently stopped en route and the car searched, leaving Matilde crying. When they arrived at the hospital, Neruda's condition was very bad. Two days later, the Nerudas learned that their house in Santiago had been ransacked and Neruda's books burned. Neruda died on September 23. He was buried in a humble grave, and for a while no one was allowed, or even knew, where the grave was. Today, in spite of the junta's efforts to keep the grave isolated, many people go to visit it and there is always an abundance of flowers.

The last three pages of Confieso que he vivido give an account of the military takeover and the death of Allende. Although some of Neruda's books are censored, Confieso que he vivido can be purchased in Chile--minus the last three pages. Neruda wanted to be remembered as the poet who made the writing of poetry as a profession respected in Chile and throughout the Hispanic world.

NEW DEMOCRATIC LEFT.   See: NUEVA IZQUIERDA DEMOCRATICA.

NEW PUBLIC ACTION PARTY.   See: NUEVA ACCION PUBLICA.

NEWS AGENCIES.   There is one news bureau in Chile today, the Agencia Informativa Orbe de Chile.   Foreign news agencies include: Agenzia Nazionale Stampa Associata (Italy); Associated Press (United States); Deutsche Presse-Agentur (Federal Republic of Germany); ABC (Spain); Reuters (United Kingdom); and United Press International (United States).   They are all located in *Santiago.

NEWSPAPERS.   Chile's first newspaper, the *Aurora de Chile, and its successor, the Monitor araucano, favored independence and lasted only from 1812 until the defeat of *Rancagua.   The *Reconquista española period saw the royalist Gaceta ministerial del gobierno de Chile edited by Fray José María de la Torre.   With the recovery of patriot control the press blossomed, with over a hundred ephemeral titles appearing during the Bernardo *O'Higgins period.   Until the 1860s, however, the more important (and more informative) newspapers were issued in *Valparaíso, with El *Mercurio as the outstanding name.   *Santiago recovered its importance with the rise of El *Ferrocarril (1855-1911), and by the 1890s the capital's primacy was well established.   In 1894 only El Mercurio among Valparaíso papers had a circulation (12,000) comparable to that of the leading Santiago papers: El Ferrocarril (14,000), La Nueva República (9,000) and the radical La *Ley (8,000).   With the establishment of El Mercurio in Santiago in 1900, the capital's preeminence was incontestable.   Nowadays almost all papers of nationwide circulation originate there, and the Valparaiso Mercurio is little more than a local edition of its Santiago namesake.

Before bringing El Mercurio to Santiago, the Edwards family of wealthy financiers (see: EDWARDS ROSS, Agustín R.; EDWARDS MacCLURE, Agustín; etc.) associated with the right-wing *Partido Nacional had owned Santiago's La *Epoca, directed by Eduardo *MacClure.   Later they founded two other Santiago papers, La Segunda and Las Ultimas Noticias, and they also controlled several provincial papers, including La *Estrella of

Valparaíso. *Partido Conservador leader Ricardo Salas Edwards (a grandson of Joaquín *Edwards Ossandón) founded El *Diario Ilustrado in March 1902. Representing the interests of the large landowners (*latifundistas), this had a circulation of 30,000 when bankruptcy ended its existence in mid-1970 as a virulent opponent of Salvador *Allende Gossens--the *Partido Demócrata Cristiano--acquired it in October 1970 and rechristened it La Prensa. Other conservative papers have included El Independente (founded March 1964) and El Estandarte Católico (1874-91) which became El Porvenir in August 1891 and then La Unión (October 1906-August 1920). El Chileno (1883-1924) championed Social Christianity and reached a circulation of 40,000. *Partido Liberal newspapers have included La Libertad Electoral (1886-1901), owned by Augusto and Eduardo Pérez (brothers-in-law of Guillermo Edwards Ross), La Prensa (March 1908-September 1910) and La Mañana (October 1901-February 1916). La *Nación began in 1917 as a progressive liberal organ, but was acquired by the state ten years later and remains in government ownership. La Tercera de la Hora, which succeeded La Ley (1894-1910) as the *Partido Radical paper, is controlled by the Banco Español-Chile. In 1984 it had the country's largest circulation.

La Unión of Valparaíso (founded January 1885) was pro-Catholic, and the economic elite have pretty much controlled the press in the north and south of the country, with most of the papers leaning toward the traditional parties of the right (fused since 1966 as the new *Partido Nacional).

In the 1891-1925 period there were eleven papers favorable to the *Partido Democràtico, but of these the short-lived La Reforma (1906-08) was the only daily. The socialist press of that period numbered twelve titles in the capital and 17 in the provinces, and there were twelve papers supporting the Chilean Communists (whose party only took that name in 1922). In more recent times the most important leftist papers were El Clarín, a sensationalist morning paper; Las *Noticias de la Ultima Hora, the afternoon tabloid of the *Partido Socialista de Chile; the Communist (*Partido Comunista Chileno) daily El Siglo; the pro-Communist afternoon paper Puro Chile; and the weekly tabloid La Voz.

Generally speaking, the conservative-controlled press did not recognize social problems and devoted very little space to social unrest before Allende came to power. The leftist press was often sensationalist. Objectivity was lost because of the political position most papers reflected. Allende kept press freedom almost intact, but wanted to see the press free of the economic interests of the élite.

In the period immediately following the *coup d'état of September 11, 1973, only El Mercurio and La Nación (renamed La Patria) were permitted in the capital. El Clarín, El Siglo, Puro Chile and Ultima Hora were closed down permanently. Three other papers were later allowed to resume publication: a total of five,

compared to the eleven appearing before the coup. *Censorship,
at times severe, has continued ever since.

The following newspapers were being published in 1984. The
circulation figures were provided by the official Asociación Nacional de la Prensa. Other sources give much lower figures. Dates
are given for the oldest surviving titles.

SANTIAGO: Diario Oficial de la República de Chile (15,000),
   El Mercurio (360,000), La Nación (15,000), La Segunda (48,000),
   La Segunda (48,000), La Tercera (410,000), Las Ultimas Noti-
   cias (85,000).
ANTOFAGASTA: La Estrella del Norte (10,000), El Mercurio,
   founded 1906 (26,000).
CALAMA: La Estrella del Loa (4,000), El Mercurio (5,000).
CHILLAN: La Discusión de Chillán, founded 1870 (8,500).
CONCEPCION: Crónica (20,000), El Sur, founded 1882 (35,000).
COPIAPO: Atacama (6,500).
CURICO: La Prensa, founded 1898 (4,000).
IQUIQUE: La Estrella de Iquique (4,000).
LA SERENA: El Día (10,800).
LOS ANGELES: La Tribuna (10,000).
OSORNO: La Prensa, founded 1917 (26,000).
PUERTO MONTT: El Llanquihue, founded 1885 (6,000).
PUNTA ARENAS: El Magallanes, founded 1894 (6,500), La
   Prensa Austral (9,000).
RANCAGUA: El Rancagüino (10,000).
TEMUCO: El Diario Austral (26,000).
TOCOPILLA: La Prensa (8,000).
VALDIVIA: El Correo de Valdivia, founded 1895 (12,000).
VAPARAISO: La Estrella (34,000), El Mercurio, founded 1827
   (70,000).
VICTORIA: Las Noticias (8,000), El Pehuén de Curacautín (3,000).
   See also: CENSORSHIP; PERIODICAL PRESS.

NITRATE WAR. See: PACIFIC, War of the.

NITRATES. The *Atacama desert between 19° S and 26° S is the
world's sole source of natural sodium nitrate. It is also rich
in other mineral salts, apparently the result of chemical reaction
of the *guano beds deposited on the salts of an elevated former
seabed in an unusually dry climate. These minerals were crucial
for the development of the fertilizer and explosives industries.
The fertilizers were used in Chile first, then they were exported
to Europe. In 1810, Taddäus Haenke, a German, set up the first
nitrate industry. Fifty years later, Alfred Nobel produced nitro-
glycerine and nitrate exports boomed.   1860

By 1830, 800 metric *tons had been produced. Yearly production increased to 30,000 tonnes in 1850; 100,000 in 1870;
670,000 in 1890; and 2,440,800 in 1910. Although the industry
had largely been developed by Chileans, most of the territory
belonged to Bolivia and Peru. Squabbles over the Atacama desert

nitrate rights led to the War of the *Pacific (1879-93). See:
BOLIVIA, Relations with; PERU, Relations with. By the beginning of the 20th century, most of the nitrate industry came to
be controlled by British multinational interests.

Germany's need to be self-sufficient in nitrate production for
military use led to the development of an artificial process just
prior to World War I. This eventually proved cheaper than importing the natural product from Chile. Nitrate output which had
peaked in 1928 with 3.17 million tonnes sharply fell to 433,100
tonnes in 1933 (see: DEPRESSION OF THE 1930s). By 1950,
it had recovered to reach 1.66 million tonnes, but since then it
has steadily fallen to 621,300 tonnes in 1979. World production
of artificial nitrates rose 230 percent between 1950 and 1970.
In 1982, Chile's output was 576,750 tonnes, or some 35 percent
of its 1950 total.

From the late 19th century until the 1920s, nitrates had been
Chile's principal mineral exports. The subsequent decline has led
the Chilean government to create a series of marketing corporations: *COSACh, 1927-31, *COVENSA, 1934-68 and *SOQUIMICA
1968- , but despite such efforts there is little hope for the industry's resurgence.

See also: CORUÑA, Matanza de la; SALITRERAS DE IQUIQUE.

NODAL, Bartolomeu Garcia de. Portuguese sailor. Joint discoverer,
with his brother Gonçalo Garcia de Nodal, of the *Diego Ramírez
Islands in 1619.

NORTE CHICO. The "near north" of Chile, the regions of *Atacama
and *Coquimbo, distinguished from the *Atacama desert area
further north, the *Norte Grande, by having regular rainfall.
This and the mild climate make stock raising (see: LIVESTOCK)
and arable farming (see: AGRICULTURE) possible, particularly
in the valleys of the rivers Huasco, Río de Carmen, Tránsito
and *Elqui, which are noted for fruit, wine, vegetable and flower
growing. *Mining of *copper, *iron, *gold, *silver and *manganese is, or has been, also important.

NORTE GRANDE. Chile's "far north": the desert regions of formerly
Peruvian *Tarapacá and formerly Bolivian *Antofagasta, acquired
in the 1879-83 War of the *Pacific.

NORTHERN UNIVERSITY. See: UNIVERSIDAD DEL NORTE.

NOTICIAS DE LA ULTIMA HORA, Las. (October 1943-September
1973). Daily afternoon *Santiago *newspaper of the *Partido
Socialista de Chile, often referred to as Ultima hora.

NOVO, Guillermo (1939-). Leader of the *Cuban National Movement.
Novo, with three other Cubans and the help of his brother Ignacio, carried out the Washington, D.C., assassination of the

former Chilean diplomat and opposition leader in exile, Orlando *Letelier del Solar, September 21, 1976. After a trial lasting some two years, Guillermo Novo was given life imprisonment. His Cuban accomplices received the same sentence, and Ignacio Novo was sentenced to eight years in prison.

NOVOA LOPEZ DE ARTIGAS, José María Vázquez de (1800-1886). Lawyer by profession and political follower of Ramón *Freire Serrano. In 1824 he was in Peru and Ecuador and fought for the independence of those countries. On return to Chile he was elected a deputy to *Congress, becoming Freire's war minister in 1825. The following year he was elected to the Senate, of which he became president in 1828. He broke with Freire in 1827, participating in the *Sublevación de Campino. But they were reconciled and Novoa was with Freire at the Battle of *Lircay. While Freire was in exile in *Peru, Novoa tried to reinstate him. His plans, however, were frustrated, and Novoa himself was exiled to Peru, where he remained until his death.

NOVOA VIDAL, Jovino (1822-1895). Lawyer by profession and active member of the National Party (*Partido Nacional). A judge of Valparaíso criminal court in 1854 and *intendant of Valparaíso province in 1858, President (1851-61) Manuel *Montt Torres made him finance minister in 1859. He was also acting justice minister in 1860 and 1861. In 1861 he was accused by *Congress of diverting a one-million *peso loan incurred for *railway construction to pay for military expenses in the *Civil War of 1859 and of allowing his political bias to determine his judicial treatment of persons tried for supporting the rebels in that war, many of whom were hanged. Novoa was absolved. He served in Congress as a deputy (1861-67, 1876-82 and 1885-88) and as senator (1882-94). After the fall of Lima in the War of the *Pacific, Novoa shared with Patricio *Lynch Solo de Zaldívar responsibility for the civil administration of Chilean-occupied Peru until the end of the war, when he became Chilean minister to Peru (1884-86). On return to Chile he was appointed to the Tribunales Arbitrales (international courts considering claims from subjects of neutral nations for damages suffered during the war). Novoa's distinguished legal career also included a professorship in the law faculty of the *Universidad de Chile. In 1889 he was one of the founders of the political group called the *Cuadrilátero.

ÑUBLE. Former province of central Chile, created in 1848 by the detachment of the department of San Carlos from *Maule and of that of *Chillán from *Concepción. In the early 20th century Ñuble's area was increased from 8,823 km^2 (3,407 square miles) to 13,951.3 km^2 (5,387 square miles) by the transfer from Maule of the department of Itata. The province's population grew from 100,792 in 1854 to 136,871 in 1875; 166,245 in 1907; 170,425 in 1920; 243,185 in 1940 (after the enlargement); 252,000 in 1952;

328,132 (est.) in 1971; and 351,291 when it was incorporated into Region VIII, *Bío-Bío, in 1975 (see: REGIONS AND ADMINISTRA-TIVE RESTRUCTURING). The provincial capital was Chillán.

NUEVA. A small island, about 9 miles square, located at the mouth of the *Beagle Channel at 55° 15' S, 66° 32' W, some eight miles south of *Tierra del Fuego. Isla Nueva is the most easterly of three small adjacent islands (the others are *Lennox and *Picton) whose sovereignty was long the subject of a dispute with *Argentina.

NUEVA ACCION PUBLICA. The New Public Action Party was founded in 1931 following the overthrow of President (1927-31) Carlos *Ibáñez del Campo. Its founders included Marmaduke *Grove Vallejo and Eugenio Matte Hurtado. Both participated in the *junta de gobierno de 1932 which set up Chile's short-lived *República Socialista. In April 1933 the party merged with other socialist organizations to form the *Partido Socialista.

NUEVA ISLAND. See: NUEVA.

NUEVA IZQUIERDA DEMOCRATICA. The new Democratic left was a political group, formed in 1963, which failed to win representation in *Congress and could not therefore formally constitute a political party. Its organizers were dissidents from the *Partido Democrático Nacional unhappy with their party's membership in the *Frente de Acción Popular, which was backing Socialist Salvador *Allende Gossens in the presidential elections of 1964. The New Democratic Left supported instead Christian Democrat candidate Eduardo *Frei Montalva. The group then dissolved, most of its members joining the Agrarian Labor Democracy Party (*Partido Democracia Agrario Laborista).

NUÑEZ, Casto Méndez. See: MENDEZ NUÑEZ, Casto.

- O -

O.A.S. See: ORGANIZATION OF AMERICAN STATES.

OBLIGADO ("the obligated one"). A peasant or agrarian worker. See also: AFUERINO; ASENTADOS; CAMPESINO; INQUILINO; PEON.

OBRAS PUBLICAS, Ministerio de. The Ministry of Public Works was created by Statute no. 3770 on August 20, 1930, becoming a separate entity from the Development Ministry (Ministerio de *Fomento) under a General Director who would also serve as a minister of state. On August 28, 1931, the ministry once again became a branch of the Development Ministry.

The title was revived following the 1973 *coup d'état, with the separation of communications from public works and the creation of a separate Ministerio de Transportes y Comunicaciones.

Public works ministers since the *coup have been: Brigadier General Sergio Figueroa Gutiérrez (September 1973), Hugo León Puelma (April 1975), General Patricio Torres (December 1980), General Bruno Sievert (April 1982).

OBRAS PUBLICAS, COMERCIO Y VIAS DE COMUNICACIONES, Ministerio de. The Ministry of Public Works, Trade and Communications was created by Statute no. 408 on March 24. It was an extension of the Ministerio de *Obras y Vías Públicas to include responsibility for internal and foreign trade. In September 1927 it was replaced by the Ministry of Development (Ministerio de *Fomento).

OBRAS PUBLICAS Y VIAS DE COMUNICACIONES, Ministerio de. The Ministry of Public Works and Communications was a renaming on August 26, 1942, by Statute no. 6-4817 of the Ministry of Development (Ministerio de *Fomento). Its functions are to plan urban and rural development and to facilitate internal communications. Its under-secretariats deal with: architecture, urban development, *highway construction, irrigation programs, sanitation, and maintenance of *ports and *airports. Public works were the responsibility of the interior ministry until 1887, when the ministry of industry and public works (Ministerio de *Industria y obras públicas) was formed. In 1912 the department of *railways was added, making its title the Ministerio de *Industria, obras públicas y ferrocarriles, and in 1925 it acquired a department of trade and became the Ministerio de *Obras públicas, comercio y vías de comunicaciones. From 1927 to 1942, with a brief twelve-month interruption, the ministry had the title Ministry of Development (Ministerio de Fomento).

Following the 1973 *coup d'état, communications became the responsibility of a separate *Ministerio de Transportes y Comunicaciones, and the works ministry became once more just the Ministerio de *Obras Públicas.

OBRERO. A blue-collar worker, in contrast to a white-collar worker or EMPLEADO (q.v.).

OCHAGAVIA. Site of the first battle of the *Civil War of 1829-30, fought on December 14, 1829, between government forces led by Francisco de la *Lastra y de la Sotta and rebel troops commanded by Joaquín *Prieto Vial. After an inconclusive engagement, an armistice, the OCHAGAVIA TREATY (q.v.) was signed.

OCHAGAVIA ERRAZURIZ, Silvestre (1820-1883). Lawyer by profession and active member of the National Party (*Partido Nacional).

He became a foreign ministry official in 1846 and was sent on a mission to Europe to study agricultural methods, 1847-50. He served in the Chamber of Deputies (1852-58), becoming its vice-president in 1855, in the Senate (1858-67), and in the Chamber again, (1870-73). From 1852 to 1855 he served in the Manuel *Montt Torres administration as justice and education minister, having succeeded Fernando Lazcano Mujica. In 1861 Ochagavía was offered the conservative candidacy in the presidential election, but declined.

OCHAGAVIA TREATY (Acuerdo de Ochagavía). A peace treaty signed on December 16, 1829, after the indecisive Battle of *Ochagavía, in an attempt to end the *Civil War of 1829-30. Command of both armies was to be entrusted to Ramón *Freire Serrano, who would proceed to the election of a provisional *junta. A Congreso de Plenipotenciarios to enforce the constitution was then to be elected. José Tomás *Ovalle Bezanilla, Isidoro *Errázuriz Aldunate and Pedro Trujillo were chosen as the *junta, and the Congreso was elected (it lasted from February 1830 to May 1831). But the treaty was otherwise a failure, as both sides resumed fighting almost immediately, and the civil war went on until May 1830.

ODEPLAN (Oficina de Planificación Nacional). Department of the President's office established during the administration (1964-70) of Eduardo *Frei Montalva to coordinate government policies with economic implications and to prepare an overall national plan. Recent directors, who have held cabinet rank, have been: Naval Captain Roberto Kelly Vásquez (September 1973); Miguel Kast (December 1978); Alvaro Donoso (December 1980); General Gastón Frez (April 1982); Sergio Pérez Hormazábal (August 1982); Hernán *Büchi Buc (August 1983);
    See also: PLANNING.

O'HIGGINISTA. A supporter of Bernardo *O'Higgins.

O'HIGGINS. (1) A former province of central Chile, formed in 1883 and consisting mainly of the former *Rancagua department of the province of *Santiago, giving it an area of 6,066 km^2 (2,342 square miles), between the rivers *Maipo and Cachapoal and a 1885 population of 87,641. In the first half of this century it lost its department of Maipo to Santiago, but gained that of Caupolicán from the province of *Colchagua, with a resultant area of 7,105.5 km^2 (2,742 square miles). The population was 200,297 in 1940; 224,593 in 1952; 303,565 (est.) in 1971; and over 315,000 when the province was incorporated into Región VI. The capital was *Rancagua.
    (2) Name of the new Region VI, in full, "del Libertador General Bernardo O'Higgins," created in 1975 (see: LIBERTADOR).

O'HIGGINS, Bernardo (1778-1842). The national liberator of Chile.

Son of Irish-born governor Ambrose *O'Higgins Ballenary and his
mistress Isabel de Riquelme of Chillán, the young Bernardo
O'Higgins studied in Lima, where his father later served as viceroy, and in Richmond on Thames near London, where he learned
of his background. In London he met the Venezuelan Francisco
de Miranda, who was the first advocate of South American independence. After Ambrose O'Higgins' death, Bernardo came under the tutelage of Juan *Martínez de Rozas Correa, a Liberal
and a Free Mason. Both men conspired to overthrow the Spanish
yoke in Chile. On September 18, 1810, Chilean patriots proclaimed the *junta de gobierno de 1810 to rule in the name of
King *Ferdinand VII. It would be another eight years before
Chile finally declared herself independent of Spain, and O'Higgins
played an important role during that stormy period. In November
1811 José Miguel *Carrera Verdugo ousted Martínez de Rozas
from the governing junta and appointed O'Higgins in his place,
but when he sought to consolidate his power by reforming the
junta in January 1812, O'Higgins was dismissed. He retired to
his *hacienda but rejoined the patriot army when a new threat
from Spain developed in March 1813. Carrera's despotism alienated
the first families of *Santiago who deposed him in January 1814
and made O'Higgins commander-in-chief. Carrera seized power
again following the Treaty of *Lircay, and only Mariano *Osorio's
advance from *Talcahuano toward the capital interrupted an incipient civil war in which Carrera and O'Higgins had already
come to blows. At the Battle of *Rancagua (October 1-2, 1814),
Osorio routed the combined forces of both men. They fled to Mendoza in Argentina, where the quarrel between them and their
supporters continued. In Mendoza, the Argentine liberator,
José de *San Martín, who was preparing an army for the invasion
of Chile, welcomed the Chilean refugees as allies, but found
Carrera's behavior intolerable, ejected him from *Cuyo province
and chose O'Higgins as his second-in-command.

On February 12, 1817, after a legendary crossing of the
*cordillera, the allied Ejército de los *Andes defeated the Spanish
at *Chacabuco. Three days later a *cabildo abierto in Santiago
proclaimed O'Higgins *Supreme Director (director supremo) of
Chile--a post San Martín had refused. During a stormy five-year
rule, O'Higgins was able to expel the Spanish from all Chile,
except the southern island of *Chiloé. With the aid of Lord
*Cochrane (whom he recruited in London in 1817), O'Higgins cre-
ated a modern *navy, which raided Spanish shipping from southern Chile to Mexico and transported San Martín's liberating army
to *Peru. But the cost of the war caused him to lose the support of wealthy taxpayers.

O'Higgins also introduced reforms that further alienated the
Conservatives. He abolished titles of nobility, substituting a
"legion of merit" which honored accomplishment without regard
to social position, and he proposed abolishing the *mayorazgo
(estate inheritance by primogeniture). He also insisted upon the

state's right of patronage over ecclesiastical appointments. The *Church felt even more threatened by his intention to tolerate religious dissent and to open public cemeteries to non-Catholics. He sought to develop Chile by encouraging the importation of books, increasing the number of public schools, improving *highways and beautifying the city of Santiago--thereby increasing *taxes. The aristocracy became increasingly disenchanted with O'Higgins, and the *Carreristas blamed him for the death of their hero and his brothers. Promulgation of the *Constitution of 1822, which extended the supreme director's term of office for a further ten years, caused an uprising in *Concepción led by the provincial *intendant, Ramón *Freire Serrano. The northern province of *Coquimbo quickly joined the revolt, and on February 28, 1823, a *cabildo abierto in the capital demanded o'Higgins's resignation. He surrendered power to a four-man junta (promptly ousted by Freire) and submitted himself to a juicio de residencia (inquiry into the probity of his conduct in office). This exonerated him, but, discouraged by the turn of events, he went into voluntary exile in Peru. For the next five years his followers sought unsuccessfully to return him to power.

Following the Chilean occupation of Lima in the war with the *Peru-Bolivia Confederation, he was at last invited to return to Chile, but he fell ill when about to embark at Callao and died in exile on October 24, 1842, without ever having gone back to his homeland. In 1869 the Chilean *navy transported his remains back to Santiago, where he lies buried.

O'HIGGINS BALLENARY, Ambrose, [marquis of Osorno] (1720-1801). Irishman in Spanish colonial service, and natural father of Bernardo *O'Higgins; known in Spanish as Ambrosio O'Higgins y Vallenar. Son of an Irish tenant farmer, he was sent as an adolescent to Spain where his uncle was a prominent churchman. Ambrose later became a successful trader in South America, and settled in *Santiago. In 1760 he entered government service, campaigned successfully against the *Araucanian Indians, and became, *intendant of *Concepción (1786) and captain general of Chile (1788). In May 1796 he was transferred to Lima, where he ruled as viceroy for four months, and finished his active life in charge of the country's defenses.

O'HIGGINS Y RIQUELME, Bernardo. See: O'HIGGINS, Bernardo.

OIDOR. Judge of an AUDIENCIA (q.v.).

OIL INDUSTRY. See: PETROLEUM.

OLAS. See: ORGANIZACION LATINOAMERICANA DE SOLIDARIDAD.

OLLAS VACIAS, Marcha de las. See: POTS AND PANS DEMONSTRATIONS.

354 / OMEGA 7

OMEGA 7. An organization of anti-Castro Cubans in the *United States who worked closely with the Chilean secret police, *DINA, to carry out a successful assassination plot in Washington, D.C., against former Chilean ambassador Orland *Letelier del Solar, the leader of Chilean exiles who wanted to overthrow the *military regime in Chile. See: CUBAN NATIONALIST MOVEMENT.

OÑA, Pedro de (1570-1643?). The first Chilean-born poet. Son of a Spanish captain, Ona was born in *Angol. His epic *Arauco domado (Lima, 1596) celebrates the deeds of Diego *Hurtado de Mendoza and the conquest of Chile.

ORDEN SOCIALISTA. The Socialist Order was founded in 1931 by two architects, Arturo Bianchi Guandián (b. 1897, a former vice-president of *FECh) and Luciano Kulczewski García (b. 1896). Two years later the party participated in the Socialist Convention of April 19, 1933. This resulted in the merger of the Orden Socialista with five other similar organizations to form the *Partido Socialista.

ORDOÑEZ, José. Brigadier general in the royalist army. At the time of the Spanish defeat at *Chacabuco, Ordóñez was in command in the south. Rallying the royalist remnants there, he retired into the port of *Talcahuano, which he strongly fortified. Aided by a very wet winter and an alliance with the *Araucanian Indians, he was able to hold it against patriot attacks throughout 1817, thus keeping a base for a counter-offensive. Reinforced by sea, his garrison had grown from 1,000 men to an army of 4,500 when Mariano *Osorio arrived to take command in January 1818.
One of the most brilliant officers and tacticians on the *realista side, he played an important part in their victory at *Cancha Rayada, near *Talca, after they had gone over to the offensive, in March 1818. The Patriot Army of the South had to fall back on *Santiago. Cries of "viva el rey" were heard in Talca and vicinity.
A few weeks later, however, the Patriots were able to recover and defeat the royalists at the decisive battle of *Maipo (April 2, 1818), the date of effective Chilean independence. Ordóñez, who had been one of the last obstacles to that goal, was taken prisoner in the battle.

ORELIE, Antoine (1820-1878). French adventurer and self-styled Antoine Orélie I, roi d'Araucanie et de Patagonie. Born Orelie Antoine Tounens at Chourgnac (Dordogne), he practiced law in Périgueux before settling among the *Araucanian Indians in 1861 and persuading them to unite under his authority. An attempt to finance his venture by floating a loan in France failed miserably, but he managed to raise an army of 40,000 *Mapuches. Betrayed by some of the less enthusiastic among these, he was captured by the Chilean government at Los Perales, January 4, 1862, and, after French official intercession, was declared mad and returned to France. There he strove to publicize his cause and made a second journey to his "kingdom" in 1869. He was so coldly received by the Indians that he soon went back to journalism in France. In April 1874, with four companions, he set out again, but the Argentine navy, in response to a request from the Chileans, intercepted his ship at sea. He was sent back to France, where he died in penury, still full of his delusions of grandeur.

ORGANIZACION DE ESTADOS AMERICANOS (OEA). See: ORGANIZATION OF AMERICAN STATES.

ORGANIZACION LATINOAMERICANA DE SOLIDARIDAD (OLAS). The Organization of Latin American Solidarity was established in Havana, Cuba, in 1966 to coordinate and support wars of national liberation on the American continent. Chile is one of 27 countries that took part in the first OLAS Convention, held in July 1967, sending delegates from the Communist and Socialist parties. When Socialist President (1970-73) Salvador *Allende Gossens came to power, he pledged continued support for OLAS. Chile, however, like the other Latin American countries that pledged support, did not play any active role in wars of national liberation, although it did give verbal support to such movements in Latin America.

After Allende's overthrow, Chile withdrew from OLAS and broke off relations with Cuba.

ORGANIZATION OF AMERICAN STATES (OAS). The Organization of American States, of which Chile is a member, was established on April 30, 1948, at the Ninth Conference of American States held in Bogotá, Colombia. The OAS charter was signed by the (then) 21 American republics, including Cuba. In 1954 a Chilean, Carlos Guillermo *Dávila Espinosa, became the OAS's second secretary general. The government of Fidel Castro (but not Cuba as a state) was excluded from the OAS in 1962. In the past Chile has traditionally voted with the *United States, the most influential member within the organization. It abstained, however, on the vote to exclude Castro, although it later adhered to the majority decision by breaking diplomatic and trade relations. Since 1965 Chile has followed a more independent course. In April that year it opposed the U.S. intervention in the Dominican Republic, and in November 1970, Socialist President (1970-73) Salvador *Allende Gossens resumed diplomatic and trade relations with Castro's Cuba. In his presidential campaign Allende had pledged that Chile would withdraw from the OAS if the Latin American republics continued to vote according to the dictates of the United States, as most of them had done in the past. The Chilean President was in favor of establishing a Union of Latin American Republics, without the presence or the influence of the "Colossus of the North."

After the military *coup d'état that overthrew Allende, the OAS issued numerous statements, both in the immediate aftermath of the coup and during subsequent years, deploring the *junta's systematic violence toward the Chilean people.

ORTIZ NAVARRO, Rafael. *Army major general, and a close associate of President Augusto *Pinochet Ugarte, thought to be one of his possible successors. Ortiz is a telecommunications expert who has served in Germany as an attaché and is fluent in German. He has also been the sub-chief of the President's general staff, director of recruitment and director of army operations. He is professor of military geography, strategy and geopolitics (Pinochet's subject) at the *Academia de Guerra.

OSORIO, Mariano (1777-1819). A Spanish-born career officer in the royalist army during Chile's wars of *independence. In 1814, after his victory over the patriots at *Rancagua, viceroy José Fernando de Abascal y Sousa appointed him governor of Chile, an office he held from October 9, 1814, to December 26, 1815. He exiled many patriots to the *Juan Fernández Islands and, under pressure from the viceroy, ruled with an iron hand. Arbitrary arrest and the suppression of free speech characterized his government, and the mild reforms introduced by Juan *Martínez de Rozas Correa and José Miguel *Carrera Verdugo were repealed. He was not harsh enough, however, to satisfy Abascal, who recalled him to Peru and appointed Francisco Casimiro *Marcó del Pont Angel Díaz y Méndez governor in his stead.

The brutal despotism of the restored royal government convinced Chilean patriots that the time had come for independence. After the defeat and capture of Marcó del Pont at *Chacabuco, Osorio was again given command of the royalist armies in Chile, and he landed with a new expeditionary force at *Talcahuano, January 4, 1818. Four months later his army met defeat at *Maipu (April 5, 1818). Osorio managed to escape back to Peru, but he contracted a contagious fever on his way back to Spain and died in Havana, Cuba.

OSORNO. A province of southern central Chile, formerly a department of the province of *Llanquihue, from which it was separated in 1928. It had an area of 9,236.3 km^2 (3,566 square miles) and a population of 107,341 in 1940; 123,059 in 1952; and 170,409 (est.) in 1970. A large proportion of this population was concentrated in the capital, also called Osorno--101,948 (est.) in 1986.

In 1975 Osorno province became part of Región X, Los *Lagos (see: REGIONS AND ADMINISTRATIVE RESTRUCTURING).

OVALLE BEZANILLA, José Tomás (1788-1831). President of Chile 1830-31. He entered public life on completing his legal studies, becoming a deputy (1823-25) and vice-president of the *Santiago provincial assembly (1826). Chosen as president of the three-man junta that was set up as a consequence of the *Ochagavía Treaty of December 1829, he was also a member of the Congreso de Plenipotenciarios of February 1830, which elected him vice-president of Chile. On March 31, 1830, Ovalle became President when Francisco *Ruiz Tagle was forced to resign by Diego *Portales Palazuelos (who became minister of foreign affairs, the interior and war). Portales sent General Joaquín *Prieto Vial south against the forces of ex-President Ramón *Freire Serrano, which were defeated at the Battle of *Lircay, so ending the *Civil War of 1829-30. Ovalle died suddenly on March 21, 1831, and was succeeded by vice-president Fernando *Errázuriz Aldunate.

OYANDEL URRUTIA, Abraham (b. 1874). Vice-president of Chile, October-December 1932, an office he succeeded to by virtue of being President of the Supreme Court when interim President Bartolomé *Blanche Espejo resigned. After holding new presidential elections, Oyandel handed over power to Arturo *Alessandri Palma.

- P -

P.C. See: PARTIDO CONSERVADOR.

P.C.Ch. See: PARTIDO COMUNISTA CHILENO.

P.C.R. See: PARTIDO COMUNISTA REVOLUCIONARIO.

P.C.U. See: PARTIDO CONSERVADOR UNIDO.

P.D. See: PARTIDO DEMOCRATICO.

P.D.C. See: PARTIDO DEMOCRATA CRISTIANO.

P.D.Ch. See: PARTIDO DEMOCRATICO DE CHILE.

P.L. See: PARTIDO LIBERAL; PATRIA Y LIBERTAD.

P.N. See: PARTIDO NACIONAL.

P.R. See: PARTIDO RADICAL.

P.S. See: PARTIDO SOCIALISTA.

P.S.A. See: PARTIDO SOCIALISTA AUTENTICO.

P.S.Ch. See: PARTIDO SOCIALISTA DE CHILE.

P.S.D. See: PARTIDO SOCIAL DEMOCRATICO.

P.S.P. See: PARTIDO SOCIALISTA POPULAR.

PACIFIC, War of the. War waged by Chile against *Peru and Bolivia, 1879-83, to take possession of the *nitrate-rich *Atacama Desert: it was consequently also known as the Nitrate War. Chile possessed originally only the province of *Copiapó, but Bolivia did little to develop its *guano and nitrate resources, allowing them to be exploited by Chilean firms. In 1866 the Chile-Bolivian boundary had been fixed by treaty at 24°S, just south of the port of *Antofagasta (see: BOLIVIA, Relations with). In 1873, however, Peru and Bolivia, apprehensive of Chilean expansionism, signed a secret treaty of alliance. Despite this, Bolivia bound herself, by treaty with Chile the following year, not to increase the rate of duty on the exports of the Chilean mining firms. In 1875 Peru nationalized all nitrate exports from her province of *Tarapacá, which effectively ruined Chilean-owned mining companies in Peru. Three years later the new Bolivian President Hilárion Daza broke the 1874 treaty and raised the taxes levied on nitrate exports. Then on January 6, 1879, Daza embargoed exports by the Chilean-owned Compañía de Salitre and imprisoned its manager. Fearful, it was claimed, that Bolivia's 40 policemen in Antofagasta would be overwhelmed by the town's 6,554 Chileans (out of a total population of 8,507), Chilean President Anibal PINTO GARMENDIA (q.v.) sent his fleet north on February 4, 1879, breaking off diplomatic relations on the 12th. On February 14, Chile occupied Antofagasta and proclaimed 23°S as the new boundary. Daza declared war on March 1.
   The government of Peruvian President Mariano Ignacio Prado, desperate to gain time to prepare for the war, offered to mediate. Chile refused the offer and, learning of the secret treaty of 1873, demanded that Peru renounce it. When this was refused, Chile declared war on Peru. Thus Chile was at war with two countries whose combined population was double its own. The Chilean *army and *navy were in a poor state, but a far better one than those of its adversaries, and its comparative degree of preparedness accounts for its aggressive attitude.
   Command of the sea, which Chile needed for an advance into Peru, was denied by Miguel Grau's ironclad *Huáscar until it was captured at the Battle of *Cape Angamos (October 8, 1879). A month later an expeditionary force was landed at *Pisagua, defeated the Peruvian army of Juan Buendía at the battle of *San Francisco on the plain of *Dolores, and took *Iquique. Chile now controlled the entire province of Atacama, and with it Bolivia's coastline, plus the Peruvian department of *Tarapacá. The disaster overturned the governments of both Peru and Bolivia.
   Early in 1880 General Manuel *Baquedano González landed at

Ilo and Pacocha with 13,000 men, and marched south on *Tacna, which was occupied after a very hard-fought battle on May 26, 1880. The Morro de *Arica (and, with it, the city of Arica itself) was taken by assault on June 6. The fate of Tacna and Arica remained a bone of contention between Chile and Peru until the Treaty of *Lima of 1929.

After abortive peace negotiations with the new Peruvian President, Nicolás de Piérola, Chile began a campaign against the Peruvian capital. A 25,000-strong force disembarked at Pisco and Curayaco, near the mouth of the Lurín, in late 1880. After bloody victories at *Chorrillos and *Miraflores, Lima was occupied on January 17, 1881. Following further unsuccessful negotiations, Piérola fought on, waging a largely guerrilla campaign against Chile's army of occupation under Patricio *Lynch Solo de Zaldívar, with *Huamachuco (July 10, 1883) almost the only set battle. A rump Congress appointed Miguel Iglesias provisional president of Peru; he signed the Treaty of ANCON (q.v.) on October 20, 1883, but was vilified for doing so and had to resign soon after the Chilean army of occupation was withdrawn. Bolivia only accepted a truce on April 4, 1884, after the fall of Arequipa cut off her foreign trade and Chile threatened an invasion of the altiplano.

The war extended Chilean territory to beyond 18°S and Chile entered upon a period of economic prosperity from exploitation of the new lands' wealth in nitrates, *copper ore and their by-products--at the cost of chronically embittered relations with her two northern neighbors.

PACIFIC STEAM NAVIGATION COMPANY. See: MERCHANT MARINE; WHEELWRIGHT, William.

PACTO ANDINO. The Andean Pact or Andean Common Market (AN-COM). This commercial treaty was initially signed in 1969 by five members of the *Latin American Free Trade Association (LAFTA): Ecuador, *Colombia, *Peru, *Bolivia and Chile. Chile was the main promoter: its industrial development was restricted by the small size of its internal market. The treaty was formally ratified in December 1970 in Cartagena, Colombia.

One provision was that profits (e.g. of multinational corporations) should remain within the member countries and not be channeled abroad. There was to be a program of joint or parallel production to foster import substitution and eliminate inefficiencies. Preferential treatment was to be given to Ecuador and Bolivia, in recognition of their relatively lesser economic development.

During the presidency (1970-73) of Socialist Salvador *Allende Gossens, Chile was an active participant in the Andean Pact, which had increased its membership to include Venezuela. But as Chilean industrial production fell by 28 percent in the years immediately following the *coup d'état that overthrew Allende, there were increasing reasons for the country to abandon ANCOM.

Chief among these was the free-trade economic policies of the
*"Chicago Boys" and the new government's subsequent removal
of trade protectionism. The generally poor state of relations
between Chile and her South American neighbors was underscored
when Chile withdrew from the Pacto Andino in October 1976.

PACTOS DE MAYO. A series of four agreements with *Argentina
signed on May 28, 1902, of which the most important were the
acceptance of arbitration by King Edward VII to resolve the disputed interpretation of the *Boundary Treaty of 1881, and an
arms limitation treaty. The latter, possibly the first of its kind
in modern history, resulted from the terrible financial consequences for both Argentina and Chile of the arms race that had been
promoted by the fear of war over their boundary dispute. Unfortunately, the revolution in battleship design caused by Britain's
1906 introduction of the Dreadnought caused a new arms race
in Latin America, and the repudiation of the treaty. See also:
NAVY; ARGENTINA, RELATIONS WITH.

PADENA. See: PARTIDO DEMOCRATICO NACIONAL.

PALENA. A disputed territory situated on the Chile-Argentine border
between 43° 30'S and 44°S, in the region of the Palena, Encuentro
and Falso Engaño rivers and Lake Palena. The dispute dates
back to 1902, and was legally settled in December 1966 through
arbitration by the United Kingdom. Although this gave a greater
acreage to Argentina--with the demarcation line passing through
the Encuentro River---Chile was happy with it because its share
was land that could be cultivated. Most of Argentina's share,
on the other hand, is inaccessible and unproductive, located
high on the *Andes mountains. Chilean Palena is part of Los
*Lagos Region.
    Occasional disturbances over possession of the area have been
reported since the arbitration award.

PALTA. The avocado pear.

PANAPO. See: PARTIDO NACIONAL POPULAR.

PANGAL, El. Battle during the *Guerra a muerte fought on September
25, 1820, in which the *realistas led by Juan Manuel Picó defeated
*independientes commanded by Carlos María O'Carrol and Benjamín
Viel Gomets. O'Carrol was taken prisoner and shot.

PAPUDO, Battle of. Chilean naval success in the War with *Spain of
1865-67. The Spanish commander José Manuel Pareja y Septién
had dispersed his fleet in an attempt to maintain a blockade of
the entire Chilean coastline. This afforded the Chilean Captain
Juan *Williams Rebolledo in the *Esmeralda an opportunity on
November 26, 1865, to take the *Covadonga by surprise, while

it was blockading *Coquimbo, and capture it. This defeat occasioned the suicide of Pareja, who was succeeded by Casto
*Méndez Núñez.

PAREJA Y SEPTIEN, José Manuel. See: PAPUDO, Battle of.

PARIS CLUB. A group of twelve nations which met in Paris in August 1973, when Chile sought a rescheduling of its US$ 700 million
debt. Chile asked that it not have to pay 10 percent for servicing the debt during 1973 and 1974. An arrangement was reached
with the most important creditor countries: the *United States,
West Germany, the *United Kingdom and *France. A generous
rescheduling was agreed a month before President (1970-73)
Salvador *Allende Gossens was overthrown by the *armed forces.

PARLIAMENTARY REGIME. Name often given to the way the *Constitution of 1833 functioned after the 1891 overthrow of President
José Manuel *Balmaceda Fernández, with the National *Congress
empowered to determine the choice of ministers. Although this
was superficially similar to the British system of parliamentary
government (whence the name), the President (unlike the British
monarch) was still regarded as head of government as well as
head of state. Congress was concerned to limit his power rather
than to replace him, and so felt no responsibility for the resultant
administrative chaos. Political parties, concerned with narrow,
partisan interests, splintered and formed unstable coalitions that
forced repeated changes of government ("rotativa ministerial").
After the economic crisis of the immediate post-World War I era,
the parliamentary regime disintegrated into the *Anarquía política
of 1924-32.

PARO DE LOS PATRONES. See: BOSSES' STRIKE.

PARRA, Nicanor (1914-). Contemporary Chilean poet; author of
Cancionero sin nombre 1937), Poemas y antipoemas (1954), La
cueca larga (1957), Versos de salón (1962), Canciones rusas
(1967), Poemas de emergencia (1972), Sermones y prédicas del
Cristo de Elqui (1977), Chistes para desorientar a la policía
(1983) and others. A native of Chillán and brother of the singer
and songwriter Violeta Parra, he trained as a physicist at the
*Universidad de Chile, and Brown and Oxford universities. In
his early poems Parra experimented with surrealist images. He
was attracted by the Chilean landscape and expressed a feeling
of nostalgia for the values of his land. In his later poems he
creates an atmosphere of intense reality and writes verses of
social protest such as "Autorretrato" and "Los vicios del mundo
moderno" (both from Poemas y antipoemas). Parra has declared
that in his early poems one finds only irony and humor, and that
a feeling of tenderness and a humanitarian approach to life can
only be found in his later poems, especially the ones dealing with
social protest.

PARTIDO AGRARIO. The Agrarian Party was formed in 1931 in
*Temuco by a group of concerned agriculturalists belonging to
the Sociedad Agrícola de Concepción, many of whom, such as
Braulio Sandoval, were ex-Radicals. They believed that agriculture should be considered the nation's principal economic activity,
with the state simply a coordinator of national economic forces.
They passed from simply representing the farming interest to
the advocacy of a corporate state. The party elected four deputies in 1932 and supported the presidential candidature of Juan
Antonio *Ríos Morales in 1942. In 1945 it merged with the *Alianza Popular Libertadora to form the *Partido Agrario Laborista.

PARTIDO AGRARIO LABORISTA (PAL). The Agrarian Labor Party
was formed in 1945 by a merger of the *Partido Agrario with the
*Alianza Popular Libertadora and elements of the *Movimiento
Nacionalista de Chile, all advocates of a corporate state. In 1946
it supported the unsuccessful presidential candidacy of the Liberal
Party's Fernando Alessandri (younger brother of Jorge *Alessandri
Rodríguez). The party then grew rapidly and was the first to
support the presidential candidacy of Carlos *Ibáñez del Campo
of 1952. This split the party: the minority formed the *Movimiento de Recuperación Doctrinaria (MRD). In 1954 a further
group of dissidents broke away to join with the MRD as the
*Partido Agrario Laborista Recuperacionista. The 1958 presiden-
tial elections split the party again, and the PAL began a rapid
decline. In October 1958 it merged with the *Partido Nacional
as the *Partido Nacional Popular, which lasted until 1960. A few
PAL members, headed by Benjamín Videla, who had not gone along
with the merger, tried to resuscitate the party in 1963 as the
*Partido Democracia Agrario Laborista, but the party finally went
out of existence when this failed to have any success in the
elections of 1965.

PARTIDO AGRARIO LABORISTA RECUPERACIONISTA (PALR). An
offshoot of the *Partido Agrario Laborista (PAL), founded in
1954. Although both parties wanted to unionize agricultural labor,
the PAL was rightist-oriented, whereas the PALR sought a more
middle-of-the-road course. In 1956 PALR joined with the *Partido
Nacional Agrario to form the *Partido Nacional.

PARTIDO CARRERINO. The political faction supporting José Miguel
Carrera Verdugo subsequent to his break with Bernardo *O'Higgins in January 1812. Carrera summoned a new *Congress, ber-
eft of objectionalbe members, which he was able to dominate.
The reforms that he was then able to introduce (see: CARRERA
VERDUGO, José Miguel) contributed to his popularity and the
growth of his party, whose rivalry with the *Partido O'Higginista
increased during 1813 and later. The march on *Santiago of the
royalist army of Mariano *Osorio in October 1814 obliged Carrera
and O'Higgins to unite for the common defense. But even at the

vital Battle of *Rancagua, the patriot forces were split between
Carrerinos and *O'Higginistas. The Chilean defeat only in-
creased the rivalry between them, and this was carried over into
exile in Mendoza, where it hampered the efforts of José de *San
Martín to form a united Argentine-Chilean army of liberation.
San Martín's choice of O'Higgins as his second-in-command led
to the latter becoming Supreme Director of Chile after the 1817
victory of *Chacabuco. Carrera's brothers Luis and Juan José
*Carrera Verdugo tried to enter Chile to foment rebellion against
O'Higgins, but their plot was discovered and they were executed
in Mendoza. Three years later José Miguel tried to avenge his
brothers' deaths and was also executed. With his death the Partido Carrerino dissolved.

PARTIDO COMUNISTA CHILENO (PCCh). The Chilean Communist
Party--South America's strongest--was founded as the Partido
Comunista de Chile at the January 1922 convention of the *Partido
Obrero Socialista, when it was decided to seek membership of
the Third International (the Comintern). The party's trade
union wing, the *Federación Obrera de Chile (FOCh), had already
joined the Red International of Labor Unions two years earlier.
The PCCh's early strategy, following Lenin's formula, concentrated
on the destruction of social democratic parties--even to the extent of opposing Marmaduke *Grove Vallejo's short-lived *República
Socialista.
    The party's first leader, Luis Emilio *Recabarren Serrano,
was succeeded in 1924 by Elías Lafertte Gaviño. Lafertte ran
for President in 1927 (while the party was outlawed and he himself banished to *Easter Island), and again in 1931 and 1932.
The bitter Stalin-Trotsky fight split the PCCh: the Trotskyite
faction, led by Manuel *Hidalgo Plaza, eventually became the *Izquierda Comunista.
    In 1935 the *U.S.S.R. abandoned the Leninist formula in favor
of a "popular front" policy, seeking a broad alliance of leftist
parties to obtain power through the ballot box. In February
1937 the PCCh was again outlawed, but continued to exist by
changing its name to *Partido Nacional Democrático. As such it
was a founder member of Chile's *Frente Popular (FP) of May
1937. This led to the 1938 election of President Pedro *Aguirre
Cerda, a Radical, as the FP's candidate.
    The Frente Popular dissolved in 1942, but Communist support
of the Radicals secured the election of President Gabriel *González Videla in 1946, and three PCCh members were given ministerial office. They were, however, dismissed in April 1947: they
were militantly anti-American, and González did not want to strain
relations with the *United States at a time of increasing friction
between the U.S. and the U.S.S.R. In reply, the PCCh opened
hostilities against the González administration by instigating a
series of strikes. This coincided with Moscow's announcing an
international policy of class warfare. In 1948, after thousands

of party members had been arrested, *Congress passed the LEY DE DEFENSA DE LA DEMOCRACIA (q.v.), outlawing the party once again. The law was supposed to be "permanent," but Carlos Ibáñez del Campo repealed it in 1958. Meanwhile PCCh members had continued to be active in politics under the disguise of other parties.

In 1947, the year before the ban, the PCCh garnered 16.5 percent of the vote and was the third largest block (after the *Partido Conservador and the *Partido Radical). In 1960, however, in the municipal council elections, it received only 9 percent. Since then its share of the vote has continually increased: to 11.3 percent in 1961; 12.7 percent in 1963; 15.9 percent in 1970; and 17.3 percent in 1971.

In 1964 the Communists joined the *Frente de Acción Popular coalition backing the presidential candidature of Socialist Salvador *Allende Gossens. In 1969 the party joined another Popular Front coalition, the *Unidad Popular, to back Allende once more. This time the Popular Front strategy was fully successful for the first time in any Western Hemisphere country: on September 4, 1970, Chilean voters gave a plurality to Allende and so put into office the first democratically-elected Socialist government in the hemisphere.

But the victory of the left was short-lived. The opposition united in a frantic effort to impeach Allende and, when that failed, to convince the *armed forces to intervene. The transition to socialism had angered the parties of the right and center, as well as the oligarchy--the coalition of big business and big landowners that had also opposed Eduardo *Frei Montalva. The armed forces obliged, with a violent *coup d'état in September 1973 that toppled Chile's social, economic and political structures. The Communist Party was once again outlawed, and many of its members were killed, imprisoned or exiled.

In 1981, the Party, under the leadership of Luis *Corvalán Lepe, who is in exile in East Germany, joined the leftist opposition in asking for the violent overthrow of the *military regime. This is a reversal of its previous position of not using violence and only seeking power through the ballot box.

See also: CONTRERAS LABARCA, Carlos.

PARTIDO COMUNISTA REVOLUCIONARIO (PCR). The Revolutionary Communist Party split from the *Partido Comunista Chileno over the latter's lack of revolutionary fervor and failure to endorse armed struggle. It diverged also over the PCCh's adoption of what it considered the anti-Marxist theses of Khrushchev. Originally Maoist, the PCR is now among those who regard the Albanian Party of Labor as the only truly Marxist-Leninist party in power. After the 1973 *coup d'état, most PCR members went underground or into exile.

PARTIDO CONSERVADOR (PC). The term "conservative" (conservador) to denote those favoring the status quo (the elite, the

*Church and the landed aristocracy), as opposed to the "liberals" (liberales) seeking political change, derives from the 1810 Spanish *cortés of Cádiz. In Chile, however, the corresponding factions were better known until the 1850s as the *pelucones and *pipiolos. The former achieved effective power with the overthrow of Ramón *Freire Serrano, and the period 1830–61 is sometimes known in consequence as that of the Conservative Republic. During the second term of Manuel *Montt Torres, however, many pelucones became estranged by the President's antagonism to the *Church (see: SACRISTAN, Cuestión del) and formally constituted themselves as the Partido Conservador in 1857. Allying themselves with the Liberals, they backed José Joaquín *Pérez Mascayano in the presidential election of 1861, but the *Fusión Liberal-Conservadora broke up in 1876. Out of office from then on, the PC supported dissident Liberals to overthrow President José Manuel *Balmaceda Fernández in the *Civil War of 1891. During the resultant *parliamentary regime, the PC was the main constituent of La *Coalición, which backed the winning presidential candidates in 1891, 1896, 1910 and 1915.

The *Constitution of 1925, by disestablishing the Church, and thus ending the chief controversy between Conservatives and Liberals, served to bring the two traditional parties together, and from 1932 onward they gradually came to work together. The party's youth movement, the *Falange Conservadora, was however unenthusiastic about the PC's backing of the 1938 Liberal candidate for the Presidency, Gustavo *Ross Santa María, and disassociated itself from the main party immediately after the election.

President Gabriela *González Videla's 1948 decision to ban the Communist Party (see: LEY DE DEFENSA DE LA DEMOCRACIA) divided the Conservatives, and in 1949 the PC split into two parties, the PARTIDO CONSERVADOR SOCIAL CRISTIANO (q.v.) opposing the new law, and the PARTIDO CONSERVADOR TRADICIONALISTA (q.v.) in favor of it.

PARTIDO CONSERVADOR SOCIAL CRISTIANO (PCSC). The Social Christian Conservative Party was formed when the original PARTIDO CONSERVADOR (q.v.) split in 1949 over President Gabriel *González Videla's outlawing of the *Partido Comunista Chileno. Led by the PC's executive committee, including party president Horacio *Walker Larraín and its 1946 presidential candidate Eduardo *Cruz-Coke Labasse, the new party sought to orient its activities around a framework of Christian ethics. It opposed all restrictive action against the Communists. In the 1953 parliamentary elections the PCSC won only two lower house seats against the PARTIDO CONSERVADOR TRADICIONALISTA's (q.v.) 17. As a result many PCSC members, including Senator Cruz-Coke and both its deputies, came together with the PCT to form the PARTIDO CONSERVADOR UNIDO (q.v.). The rump of the party was left without parliamentary representation until the 1957

parliamentary elections, which it fought as part of the FEDERA-
CION SOCIAL CRISTIANA (q.v.). In June 1957 the Federación
became the *Partido Demócrata Cristiano.

PARTIDO CONSERVADOR TRADICIONALISTA (PCT). The Traditionalist Conservative Party was created by the 1949 division of the
original PARTIDO CONSERVADOR (q.v.). The split came when
the two factions of the PC put forward rival senatorial candidates
in the parliamentary elections of that year. Following the 1953
elections many members of the rival PARTIDO CONSERVADOR
SOCIAL CRISTIANO (q.v.), including the party leadership, joined
up with the PCT to form a new united party, the PARTIDO CON-
SERVADOR UNIDO (q.v.), even though the *Ley de defensa de
la democracia which had caused the split remained in force until
1958.

PARTIDO CONSERVADOR UNIDO (PCU). The United Conservative
Party was formed in 1953 by the fusion of the PARTIDO CONSER-
VADOR TRADICIONALISTA (q.v.) with a large section of the
PARTIDO CONSERVADOR SOCIAL CRISTIANO (q.v.). This
merger virtually reinstated the old PARTIDO CONSERVADOR
(q.v.). It represented the same interests, and was often referred to as the Partido Conservador. Although markedly traditionalist and right-oriented, the PCU found its strength in
rural Chile, where the most orthodox adherents of Roman Catholicism are concentrated. Its 1961 platform declared that its
"fundamental doctrine was in keeping with the teachings of the
*Church." The platform also called for no government interven-
tion in business or agriculture, and encouraged *foreign investments in Chile.
    Although the PCU and its predecessors received strong sup-
port until the 1950s (17 percent of the vote in 1941; 23 percent
in 1945; and 25 percent in 1950), its strength declined steadily
after 1960. In the 1963 *local government elections it polled
a mere 11 percent of the vote, and the parliamentary elections
of 1965 cut its representation from 17 deputies and 4 senators to
3 deputies and 2 senators; its share of the vote falling to 5.4 percent. The last conservative presidential candidate to secure
election was Jorge *Alessandri Rodríguez in 1958.
    On May 11, 1966, the PCU merged with the *Partido Liberal
to form a new united party of the right, the PARTIDO NACIONAL,
q.v.

PARTIDO CORPORATIVO POPULAR. The Popular Corporative Party
was a small party of the right, founded during the *República
Socialista of 1932. It advocated a corporate state, modeled after
that of fascist Italy. It never won any congressional seat and
was dissolved in 1938, when many of its members joined the newly
established *Falange Nacional.

PARTIDO DE LA IZQUIERDA RADICAL (PIR). The Left Radical
Party was a right-wing faction which split from the *Partido Radical in 1971. On instructions from the United States *Central
Intelligence Agency, the PIR stayed with *Unidad Popular after
the split, pretending to support the government of Socialist President Salvador *Allende Gossens in order to sabotage it from within.
It left when Allende refused to ratify an agreement with the
*Partido Demócrata Cristiano that a PIR member of the cabinet
had negotiated in his name, and in the March 1973 parliamentary
elections PIR formed part of the common opposition slate.

PARTIDO DEMOCRACIA AGRARIO-LABORISTA. Agrarian Labor
Democracy was a political party of the center constituted on December 20, 1963, by the fusion of the *Nueva Izquierda Democrática with the remnant of the *Partido Agrario Laborista.
It went out of existence in March 1965 when it failed to achieve
any electoral success, and most of its members then joined the
*Partido Demócrata Cristiano.

PARTIDO DEMOCRACIA RADICAL. The Radical Democracy Party
was formed in 1969 as a splinter group of the Radical Party
(*Partido Radical). It represented the right wing of the Radicals
which had refused to go along with the party's endorsement of
the *Unidad Popular candidate, Salvador *Allende Gossens, in
the presidential elections of 1970. It put forward instead its leading theoritician, Julio *Durán Neumann, although the party eventually backed the *Partido Nacional's Jorge *Alessandri Rodríguez.

PARTIDO DEMOCRATA. The Democrat Party came into existence
in September 1932, when the PARTIDO DEMOCRATICO (q.v.)
split over the party's participation in the short-lived *República
Socialista. The dissidents, who rejected the class struggle, took
the Democratic Party's alternative name of Partido Demócrata. A
unity convention in July 1933 secured a reunion that lasted less
than six months. In the parliamentary elections of 1937 the Democrat Party supported the right-wing administration of Arturo
*Alessandri Palma and won five seats. The leftist Democratic
Party opposed him and won seven. The Democrats continued to
support the right in the presidential election of 1938. Nevertheless, the two factions came together again in a united party in 1941.

PARTIDO DEMOCRATA CRISTIANO (PDC). The Christian Democratic
Party was founded in 1957 through the merger of two conservative
parties, the FALANGE NACIONAL (q.v.) and the PARTIDO SOCIAL
CRISTIANO (q.v.). Members from other small parties also joined,
namely the FEDERACION SOCIAL CRISTIANA (q.v.) and the *Partido Nacional Cristiano. The historical antecedent of the PDC date
back to 1931, when the youth organization (*Juventud Conservadora) of the *Partido Conservador (PC) was established. All the
parties involved in the formation of the PDC were originally offshoots
of the Partido Conservador. Unlike the PC, however, the PDC was

more centrist and less a party of the oligarchy. Its political philosophy is based on the papal encyclicals Rerum Novarum, Quadragesimo anno and Pacem in terris. Like its most important constitutent, the *Falange Nacional, the PDC proposes to bring about radical
reform in Chile's semifeudal economic and social structure, and
achieve a readjustment of society within a framework of Christian
ethics. Unlike the Falange, however, which never acquired a
large popular base, the PDC rapidly became a mass party. In
1949 the Falange had four seats in *Congress. In 1957 the
Federación Social Cristiana won 17. In the 1958 presidential
election, the PDC's Eduardo *Frei Montalva ran a poor third, with
20.7 percent of the vote, against Conservative Jorge *Alessandri
Rodríguez's 31.6 percent and Socialist Salvador *Allende Gossens'
28.9 percent. In the 1961 parliamentary election, however, the
PDC won 27 seats to become the largest party in Congress, and
in the *local government elections of 1963 it won the largest share
of votes, 22.7 percent. In 1964 Frei became the first Christian
Democratic President in the Western Hemisphere; he received an
impressive 55.6 percent of the vote, as opposed to his nearest
rival's (Allende) 38.6 percent. A year later the PDC elected
82 deputies in the 147-member lower house, while raising its total
number of senators from 1 to 12. In the 1971 municipal elections,
Allende's *Unidad Popular coalition claimed 50.8 percent of the
vote, but the most popular single party in the country remained
Frei's Christian Democrats, who polled 25.8 percent, 3 percent
more than Allende's Socialists.

During the Allende administration, the PDC became allied with
the *Partido Nacional and other parties of the right in seeking
to oust the Socialist President. In the March 1973 parliamentary
elections this alliance was formalized as the *Coalición Democrática
(CODE). When CODE failed to win the two-third majority needed
to begin impeachment proceedings, it organized a series of strikes,
aiming to paralyze the economy, create economic and social chaos,
and so provoke the *armed forces into removing Allende. In this
it succeeded (see: COUP D'ETAT OF 1973).

At first Frei and the PDC publicly supported the military
*junta, expecting it to stay in power only briefly until order was
restored and then return the country to civilian rule. Furthermore, it was supposed that Frei would eventually become President
once again. But both the PDC leader and the *United States
government were misled. The U.S. had preferred such a scena-
rio. But the high commands of the three services and the *police
preferred an idea expressed in the Rockefeller Report on the
Americas, which suggested the replacement of party government
by military rule. Like the other parties of the center and right,
the PDC was declared in "indefinite recess." Soon Frei came
out in opposition to the *military regime, but in 1975 he was
warned to keep out of politics. As things relaxed in the late
1970s and the military gave the appearance of an apertura in
Chilean politics, the PDC leaders called for a return to constitutionality. Like the PCU, they were unhappy with the new

*Constitution of 1980 and became more vociferous against the government. As a result, party leader Gabriel *Valdés Subercaseaux was imprisoned, amid international protest. Even the Reagan administration showed its displeasure and demanded Valdés's release. On the eleventh anniversary of the coup, the PDC was openly calling for a quick return to democracy and the retirement of President Augusto *Pinochet Ugarte.

PARTIDO DEMOCRATICO (PD). The Democratic Party was established in 1887 by dissidents from the *Partido Radical—practically those who had participated in the *Partido Radical Democrático—and labor leaders, concerned about the failure of the Radicals to interest themselves in the plight of the working class. The party program stressed: (1) civil equality for men and women; (2) land reform to convert tenants into property owners; (3) social security for the workers, the sick and the aged; and (4) the abolition of capital punishment. The party was in a sense Latin America's first socialist party and was for a while in tenuous connection with the Second International, but it lacked any firm ideological base and suffered repeated schisms. It supported President Juan Manuel *Balmaceda Fernández in the *Civil War of 1891 and suffered persecution afterwards. In 1892 it won its first seat in *Congress. In 1912 Luis Emilio *Recabarren Serrano left the PD to form the more revolutionary *Partido Obrero Socialista, but the Democrats continued to grow, achieving six congressional seats in 1915, and 16 in 1924. The party's decline began with the Carlos *Ibáñez del Campo dictatorship of 1927-31. In 1932 Pedro Nolasco Cárdenas Avendaño, a former party president, served as agriculture minister (and briefly as a *junta member) during the *República Socialista. This caused a schism, with the dissidents taking the party's alternate name of *Partido Demócrata. In 1952 the party split into the PARTIDO DEMOCRATICO DEL PUEBLO (q.v.) and the PARTIDO DEMOCRATICO DE CHILE (q.v.) over the choice of which of two presidential candidates to endorse. Both splinters joined the Social-Communist backed *Frente de Acción Popular (FRAP) in 1956, and in 1960 they came together (within FRAP) as the PARTIDO DEMOCRATICO NACIONAL, q.v.

PARTIDO DEMOCRATICO DE CHILE (PDCh). The Democratic Party of Chile was a splinter of the *Partido Democrático (PD), founded in 1952 to support the presidential candidature of the Radical Party's Pedro Enrique Alfonso Barrios rather than that of Carlos *Ibáñez del Campo favored by the rest of the PD. The PDCh was leftist in orientation, and in 1956 joined the *Frente de Acción Popular coalition. In 1960 it became part of the PARTIDO DEMOCRATICO NACIONAL, q.v.

PARTIDO DEMOCRATICO DEL PUEBLO. The People's Democratic Party was the splinter of the *Partido Democrático that backed the

1952 presidential candidacy of Carlos *Ibáñez del Campo as part of the *Alianza Popular. In 1956 it joined the *Frente de Acción Popular, and in 1960 it merged with the PARTIDO DEMOCRATICO NACIONAL, q.v.

PARTIDO DEMOCRATICO NACIONAL (PADENA). The National Democratic Party was formed in 1960 by the merger of: the two factions of the *Partido Democrático (united again in 1957), the *Partido Nacional Popular (PANAPO), the bulk of the *Partido Socialista Democrático, and that faction of the *Partido Radical Doctrinario that had participated in the *Alianza de Partidos y Fuerzas Populares. Some of these constitutent parties already belonged to the Socialist-Communist backed *Frente de Acción Popular (FRAP), and the new party decided to stay in membership. The PADENA platform has been characterized as a moderate leftism with socialist tendencies, but absolutely democratic.

In the parliamentary elections of 1961, PADENA received 6.9 percent of the poll and elected 12 deputies. In the *local government elections of 1963, its share of the vote was down to 5.2 percent. The 1965 parliamentary elections reduced its representation to 3 deputies and one senator.

Membership of FRAP was a source of dissension. It caused a split in 1963, when dissidents left to form the *Nueva Izquierda Democrática, and not all members supported the 1964 FRAP candidate for the presidency, Salvador *Allende Gossens. When Allende lost, PADENA decided to leave FRAP and support the government of Eduardo *Frei Montalva. This produced a schism with those who wished to stay within FRAP, and they formed the *Partido Social Democrático.

PADENA continued its cooperation with Frei's *Partido Demócrata Cristiano during the *Unidad Popular period (1970-73), but that did not prevent its being banned by the *military regime that came to power in September 1973.

PARTIDO DEMOCRATICO SOCIALISTA. The Socialist Democratic Party was formed in 1964 by a merger between the *Movimiento Nacional de Izquierda, the *Partido Socialista del Pueblo and factions of the *Partido Democrático that had not joined the *Partido Democrático Nacional, to support the presidential candidacy of Eduardo *Frei Montalva. The party failed to win any seats in the parliamentary elections of 1965 and was consequently dissolved.

PARTIDO FEDERALISTA. When Bernardo *O'Higgins resigned as Supreme Director in 1823, those in favor of FEDERALISM (q.v.) organized themselves into Chile's first formal political party, in support of Supreme Director (1823-26) Ramón *Freire Serrano. They proved to be very strong as a party, electing 56 deputies in the parliamentary elections of 1826. The federal republic that they established proved unworkable, and was effectively ended with Freire's resignation of May 1827. With it, the Federalist Party disappeared too.

PARTIDO FEMENINO DE CHILE. The Feminine Party of Chile was organized in 1946 to campaign for women's rights and, in particular, to secure them the vote in national elections (enacted in 1949). Its president, María de la CRUZ TOLEDO (q.v.), ran unsuccessfully for the Senate in 1950. After the party had backed Carlos *Ibáñez del Campo in his successful presidential bid of 1952, De la Cruz stood for Ibáñez's vacated Senate seat and won. But she caused a number of scandals in the Senate and was disqualified. Her demagoguery provoked a schism, resulting in the formation of the *Partido Progresista Femenino, and the Partido Femenino de Chile rapidly declined in importance, being dissolved in 1953.

PARTIDO LIBERAL (PL). The Liberal Party was one of the oldest political parties in Chile. It was founded during the 1841-51 presidency of conservative Manuel *Bulnes Prieto by Victorino *Lastarría Santander to oppose the "authoritarian and ecclesiastical bias of the Conservative Party." The exact date is unknown, but the party was in existence by 1846.

Basing their philosophy on the principle of laissez-faire and the ideas of contemporary European liberalism, the Liberals advocated separation of *Church and State, limitation of executive authority, no presidential reelection for a second term, civil rights and manhood suffrage. Traditionally the party represented the wealthy industrialists and the upper middle-class. In contrast to the Conservatives (*Partido Conservador), the Liberals were more progressive, emphasizing the need for *education and social reform, and had strength in urban as well as in rural areas.

Lastarría, dissatisfied with President Domingo *Santa María González's alleged autocracy and religious intolerance, left to form the *Partido Liberal Doctrinario in 1885. The quarrel between *Congress and the next President, Juan Manuel *Balmaceda Fernández, which culminated in the *Civil War of 1891, caused another rift in the party, resulting in the schism of the *Partido Liberal Democrático. In October 1933, however, all the various Liberal splinter groups were reunited and the parliamentary elections of 1934 made the PL Chile's premier party with 34 seats in the lower house and 11 in the Senate.

In 1941 the PL got 15 percent of the national vote. In 1949 this climbed to 18 percent, its post-World War II high. The party remained strong during the 1950s, thanks in part to growing voter dissatisfaction with the 1952-58 government of Carlos *Ibáñez del Campo. But, like the Conservative Party, the PL suffered a rapid erosion of popularity in the 1960s. In 1961 its 222,485 voters represented 16.5 percent of the poll, but the 262,919 votes it received in 1963 were only 13.2 percent of a much increased total vote. In the parliamentary elections of 1965, PL representation fell from 28 deputies to 6, and from 7 senators to 5, none of their senatorial candidates being successful.

In 1966 the PL merged with the *Partido Conservador Unido to form a new united party of the right, the National Party (see: PARTIDO NACIONAL). In the 1970s the abbreviation PL was used to designate the neofascist PATRIA Y LIBERTAD, q.v.

PARTIDO LIBERAL DEMOCRATICO. The Liberal Democratic Party was founded in 1875 to support the presidential candidacy and aspirations of his founder, Benjamín VICUNA MACKENNA (q.v.), and dissolved at his death in 1886. The party's ideology was that of other Liberal parties of the epoch, based on a principle of laissez-faire and anti-clericalism. But the novelty of Vicuña Mackenna's American-style campaign, his popularity among working-class Chileans, and his disdain for Chile's semi-feudal land system, frightened the oligarchy, who persuaded him to withdraw from the elections in order to avoid a civil war.

The Liberal Democratic Party was revived in 1891 by Manuel Zañartu Zañartu, shortly after the *Civil War that saw the overthrow of President José Manuel *Balmaceda Fernández. A former Balmacedista, Zañartu now saw Vicuña Mackenna's ideas as closely resembling those of the deceased president. The objectives of the party were 1) to establish the independence of the executive and legislative branches of government; 2) decentralize government power; 3) maintain public order to protect the country's infant industry; and 4) re-establish administrative integrity in government.

In 1924 there was a split in the party and two new parties emerged, the *Partido Liberal Democrático Aliancista and the *Partido Liberal Democrático Unionista. In 1932, the Liberal democratic Party was incorporated with the other two factions into the PARTIDO LIBERAL (q.v.).

PARTIDO LIBERAL DEMOCRATICO ALIANCISTA. A splinter of the Liberal Democratic Party (*Partido Liberal Democrático) formed in 1924 to support the *Alianza Liberal coalition government of President Arturo *Alessandri Palma. In 1926 it supported the presidential candidacy of Emiliano *Figueroa Larraín. In October 1932 it was absorbed in the reunited Liberal Party (see: PARTIDO LIBERAL).

PARTIDO LIBERAL DEMOCRATICO UNIONISTA. A splinter of the Liberal Democratic Party (*Partido Liberal Democrático) formed in 1924 to support the *Unión Nacional opposition to the government of President Arturo *Alessandri Palma. In 1926 it joined with the Aliancista faction in supporting the presidential candidacy of Emiliano *Figueroa Larraín, but in 1931 supported the Radical Party's Juan Esteban *Montero Rodríguez. In October 1932 all factions of the Liberals were merged in a reunited Liberal Party (see: PARTIDO LIBERAL).

PARTIDO LIBERAL DOCTRINARIO. The Doctrinary Liberal Party

split from the *Partido Liberal during the 1881-86 administration of Domingo *Santa María González. It had advanced liberal views, especially in regard to *suffrage and civil liberties, attacking Santa María for his intolerant anticlericalism. In April 1932 it joined the short-lived *Federación de Izquierda, and in October 1932 was absorbed in the reunited Liberal Party (see: PARTIDO LIBERAL).

PARTIDO LIBERAL INDEPENDIENTE. Alternative name for the PARTIDO LIBERAL DOCTRINARIO (q.v.), used in a manifesto of 1885, highly critical of the government of Liberal President Domingo *Santa María González.

PARTIDO LIBERAL PROGRESISTA. The Liberal Progressive Party was founded in 1944 by Augusto Smitmans Rothanel and others, mostly ex-Liberals. It was committed to laissez-faire, the establishment of "authentic liberalism," and the modernization of Chile. In the 1953 elections it won no congressional seats and so was dissolved, most of its members joining the Liberals (*Partido Liberal).

PARTIDO LIBERAL UNIDO. The United Liberal Party was an attempt made in 1930, during the Carlos *Ibáñez del Campo dictatorship, to reunite the various Liberal splinter groups. Although it at first embraced only the *Partido Liberal itself, the *Partido Nacional and some of the Liberal Democrats (*Partido Liberal Democrático), its aim was eventually achieved in October 1932, under the name Partido Liberal.

PARTIDO MONTT-VARISTA. See: PARTIDO NACIONAL, A.

PARTIDO NACIONAL (PN). There have been three successive Chilean parties calling themselves "national."

A. 1857-1933. The *pelucones (who often referred to themselves as conservadores), the party of the elite and the landed aristocracy, were split by the quarrel of their President Manuel *Montt Torres with the *Church (see: SACRISTAN, Cuestión del). Those who sided with the Church and its vested interests in Chile formally constituted themselves as the *Partido Conservador. Those opposed to ecclesiastical supremacy and Church control over the civil power and supported the President formed the Partido Nacional. Known at first as the Partido Montt-Varista, it was opposed by an alliance of the other parties known as the *Fusión Liberal-Conservadora. It lost its congressional majority in 1861 and allied itself with the *Partido Radical in 1867-76, and with the *Partido Liberal in 1876-91. During the *Civil War of 1891 the Nationals sided with the rebel *Congress against President José Manuel *Balmaceda Fernández. During the *parliamentary regime the now much less powerful National Party vacilated between the *Alianza Liberal and the *Coalición. After splitting over which candidate to support in the presidential election of 1920, the party declined rapidly, winning no seats in the elections of 1924. In 1930 it joined the Liberals and other smaller parties of the right to form the United Liberal Party (*Partido Liberal Unido), which became part of the reunited Liberal Party (*Partido Liberal) in October 1933.

B. 1956-58. A second National Party was formed in August 1956 by various splinters of the Agrarian Labor Party: the *Partido Nacional Agrario, *Partido Agrario Laborista Recuperacionista and some independents. In the 1957 elections it won 9 seats. In 1958 it supported the presidential candidacy of Jorge *Alessandri Rodríguez and was dissolved in October 1958.

C. 1966- . Much more important was the founding of the present National Party by the June 1966 merger of the *Partido Liberal and the *Partido Conservador Unido, plus *Accion Nacional and some independents. This new coalition of the right proposed to incorporate all rightist elements in society for the purpose of opposing the Marxist threat in Chile. In the presidential elections of 1970 the PN chose the 74-year-old former President Jorge *Alessandri Rodríguez. He was considered to have a very good chance of beating Socialist Salvador *Allende Gossens, but Allende won, albeit by a narrow margin. In the 1971 *local government elections, the PN received 18.5 percent of the vote, as opposed to the 50.8 percent won by Allende's leftist coalition, *Unidad Popular.

From 1971 the PN began to conspire with the *Partido Demócrata Cristiano to secure Allende's overthrow. In 1972 the two parties joined with the Radicals (*Partido Radical) to form the *Confederación Democrática (CODE), an electoral alliance that hoped to have Allende impeached. The most reactionary sector of CODE was led by PN senator Sergio Onofre *Jarpa Reyes, and the attempt to paralyze the Chilean *economy was led by the Partido Nacional. By creating economic and social chaos, the opposition hoped to provoke the *armed forces into intervening (see: BOSSES' STRIKE). It became clear that the PN had a weak commitment to participatory democracy and constitutionalism. After the *coup d'état of September 1973, many PN members cooperated with the *military regime and were assigned high posts in government. Those who disagreed with the violence and repression that ensued kept a low profile and were allowed to go their way so long as they were not openly critical of the government.

The *junta declared the PN, like other parties of the right and center, in "indefinite recess." Even the new *Constitution of 1980 is extremely restrictive of the political process. As a result, the Partido Nacional is now calling for a return to democracy.

PARTIDO NACIONAL AGRARIO. The National Agrarian Party was formed in 1954 by a merger of the *Movimiento de Recuperación Doctrinaria with another splinter group from the *Partido Agrario Laborista led by Julian *Echavarri Elorza, who became president of the new party. The National Agrarian Party was nationalist, and opposed to the class struggle. In 1956 it became part of the *Federación Nacional Popular. Later the same year it merged with the *Partido Agrario Laborista Recuperacionista to form a new National Party (see: PARTIDO NACIONAL--B.).

PARTIDO NACIONAL CRISTIANO (PNC). The National Christian Party was created in 1952 by some disenchanted members of the Conservative Party (*Partido Conservador) who wanted to bring about social reform, working within a framework of Christian ethics. They won four congressional seats in 1953, but two of these representatives, together with other dissidents, left the PNC in 1955 to join the *Federación Social Cristiana. The rump of the party became the PARTIDO SOCIAL CRISTIANO (q.v.) in February 1958.

PARTIDO NACIONAL DEMOCRATICO. Name adopted by the Communist Party (*Partido Comunista Chilena) in order to maintain its existence after Law no. 6026 of February 1937 had declared it illegal. The law was rescinded shortly afterwards and the party reassumed its old name.

PARTIDO NACIONAL POPULAR (PANAPO). The Popular National Party was formed in October 1958 by a fusion of the *Partido Nacional with the bulk of the *Partido Agrario Laborista. Its doctrine was right-of-center and its platform called for the economic and social "modernization" of the Republic. In September 1960 PANAPO merged with the *Partido Democrático and others to form the PARTIDO DEMOCRATICO NACIONAL, q.v.

PARTIDO NACIONAL SOCIALISTA OBRERO. The National Socialist Workers party was founded in 1964. Its ideology was *nacista, but without any of its predecessors' militarism. Unable to win any seats in *Congress, the party was dissolved shortly after its inception.

PARTIDO NACIONALISTA. The Nationalist Party was founded in 1914 and was based on the positivist principle that science was the only valid knowledge and that religion should be divorced from civil matters. But the party went much further than that. It called for a strengthening of the executive power, nationalization of the country's basic mineral resources, reforms in *education and in the monetary system, and state intervention to protect the working class. Its only congressman was its founder, Guillermo Subercaseaux. In 1920 when he failed to get reelected, the party was dissolved.

PARTIDO OBRERO REVOLUCIONARIO. The Workers' Revolutionary Party was founded in 1941. Affiliated to the Fourth (Trotskyite) International, it preaches a relentless class struggle against capitalism to create a socialist state. Never having won any congressional seat, it has no legal existence as a political party.

PARTIDO OBRERO SOCIALISTA. The first avowedly socialist party in Chile, the Socialist Workers Party (also called in Spanish, Partido Socialista de Trabajadores) was founded in 1912. One of its founders was Luis Emilio *Recabarren Serrano, who also founded the *Federación Obrera de Chile (the Chilean Workers Union). The party aimed to fight capitalism and establish a classless society. In January 1922 it decided to join the Third (Communist) International, changing its name to PARTIDO COMUNISTA CHILENO, q.v. In the same year it elected two deputies to *Congress.

PARTIDO O'HIGGINISTA. A political party formed in 1812 by the followers of Bernardo *O'Higgins in opposition to the PARTIDO CARRERINO (q.v.) supporting the virtual dictatorship of José Miguel *Carrera Verdugo. The *Reconquista Española ended Carrera's power, and when O'Higgins and José de *San Martín liberated Chile in 1817, O'Higgins became *Director Supremo, and the Partido O'Higginista had practically no opposition for some five years. Public opinion, however, turned slowly against O'Higgins. He was too liberal for the landed aristocracy and his style of government was regarded as too autocratic. He was also blamed for the deaths of the Carrera brothers. In 1823 he was overthrown by the aristocrats and went into exile in *Peru. For the next five years the O'Higginistas tried to bring him back and reinstate him as Supreme Director. They failed, and the Partido O'Higginista was dissolved in 1830.

PARTIDO PROGRESISTA FEMENINO (PPF). The Progressive Feminist Party of Chile was founded in 1952 as a splinter from the PARTIDO FEMENINO DE CHILE, (q.v.) by Dr. María Humuy, who became its president. The party supported the presidential candidacy of Carlos *Ibáñez del Campo. When the PPF failed to win any representation in the *local government elections of 1953, it was dissolved.

PARTIDO PROGRESISTA NACIONAL (PPN). The Progressive National Party was the name used by the Communists (*Partido Comunista Chileno) during a period of illegalization in the 1940s, caused by President Pedro *Aguirre Cerda's strong pro-British views and the Communists' pro-German neutrality in the period between the Soviet-German Non-agression Pact of 1939 and the German invasion of the U.S.S.R. in 1941. In the parliamentary elections of 1945 the Communists, still using the PPN label, won 15 house and 3 senate seats (compared with 7 and 1 in 1937).

PARTIDO RADICAL (PR). The Radical Party, although not formally organized as a party until 1888, originated with the Liberals who refused to join the *Fusión Liberal Conservadora of 1857. The first radical deputies were elected in 1864, and the first senator (Pedro León *Gallo y Goyenechea) in 1876. The party's doctrine was oriented toward 19th-century liberalism and laissez-faire, but evolved slowly toward a "collectivist orientation," being the party of the middle class. By the 1930s the Radical Party had greatly expanded its basis of support. It had become the party of white-collar workers, farmers and other segments of what might be called the upper middle-class. More important, it had become the strongest political party in Chile. However, before the advent of the Popular Front (*Frente Popular), no Radical had ever been elected President of Chile.

The election of President Pedro *Aguirre Cerda in 1938 enabled the Radicals to replace many of the Liberal and Conservative holders of official posts; thus the Radicals' goal of controlling government patronage was reached. For the next fourteen years the Radicals controlled Chile. In 1958, however, the PR presidential candidate Luis *Bossay Leyva ran a poor fourth. Immediately afterwards the right-wing of the party became dominant, joining in 1962 the *Frente Democrático de Chile alliance with the Liberals and Conservatives.

This change of alliance, coupled with internal dissention, cost the party its leading role in Chilean politics. During the 1940s the PR polled 20-25 percent of the vote. In 1953 the party suffered heavy losses, falling to a mere 13.5 percent of the vote, although in 1956 its share climbed right back to 22 percent. During 1961-63 it averaged 20 percent of the vote. In the parliamentary elections of 1965, however, its representation in the Chamber of Deputies fell from 38 to 20. In 1969 the left wing became the dominant faction in the PR, and the right wing formed a splinter group known as the *Partido Democracia Radical. In the 1970 presidential elections the PR joined the Communist-Socialist backed *Unidad Popular coalition supporting the candidacy of Socialist Salvador *Allende Gossens. In the *local government elections of 1971, however, the PR vote dropped to 8.1 percent, from 13 percent the previous year.

As a part of Unidad Popular, the Radical Party was outlawed immediately after the *coup d'état of September 1973. Only its right-wing splinters were tolerated by the *military regime. Thirteen years later, what was left of the PR leadership wanted a swift end to militarism and a return to constitutionality.

PARTIDO RADICAL DEMOCRATICO (PRD). The name Democratic Radical Party has been borne by three schisms from the *Partido Radical.

A. 1885. A left-of-center group left the Radicals in 1885, aiming to woo the working class. When it failed in this it was dissolved. Two years later some of its members helped found the *PARTIDO DEMOCRATICO.

B. 1946-49. A splinter group differing in doctrine from the PR solely in its absolute anti-Communist position. This caused it to support the Liberal presidential candidate, Fernando Alessandri Rodríguez against the Communist-Supported Radical candidate Gabriel *González Videla. In 1948 the PRD entered the *Falange Radical Agraria Socialista. Following González's break with the Communists, the PRD was able to negotiate its reincorporation into the Radical Party in 1949.

C. 1969- . When the Partido Radical joined the *Unidad Popular coalition supporting Salvador *Allende Gossens for President, the Radical Democrats split from it and joined other extreme right-wing groups working for Allende's overthrow.

PARTIDO RADICAL DOCTRINARIO (PRD). The name Doctrinary Radical Party has been given to two schisms from the Radical Party (*Partido Radical).

A. 1938. When the Radicals joined the *Frente Popular, those on the right who did not wish to participate in a coalition with Communists and Socialists formed their own party to support the Liberal Party's candidate, Gustavo *Ross Santamaría. Ross lost and the PRD was dissolved shortly afterwards.

B. 1948-64. When the 1946-52 government of Gabriel *González Videla outlawed the Communist Party (see: LEY DE DEFENSA DE LA DEMOCRACIA), part of the left wing of the Radicals broke away, accusing the Radical President of opposing the working class. In 1952 the PRD supported the candidacy of Carlos *Ibáñez del Campo, and in 1957 entered the *Frente de Acción Popular to support the presidential candidacy of Salvador *Allende Gossens. This led to a schism, with one faction joining the *Alianza de Partidos y Fuerzas Populares. By 1964 the PRD had no seats in *Congress and disappeared.

PARTIDO RADICAL SOCIALISTA (PRS). The Radical Socialist Party was a splinter of the Radical Party (*Partido Radical) founded in 1931. Its leftist platform called for: (1) the total reform of the educational system; (2) the domestic exploitation of the country's natural resources, to be undertaken by collective ownership; (3) the redistribution of wealth, with better pay for the working class; (4) the institution of a state-controlled banking system to issue notes and extend credit; (5) the recognition of the class struggle; (6) opposition to imperialism; (7) civil rights; (8) separation of *Church and State; (9) the economic integration of the Latin American countries; and (10) the elimination of the existing unitary form of government and the establishment of a federal republic in Chile. In the 1938 election some PRS members joined the *Unión Socialista, favoring the candidacy of Carlos *Ibáñez del Campo rather than the *Frente Popular nominee. In 1943 most of the party's members joined the *Partido Socialista, and the PRS dissolved.

PARTIDO SOCIAL CRISTIANO. The Social Christian Party was formed in February 1958 as a reorganization of the *Partido Nacional Cristiano. It was then joined by those members of the *Partido Conservador Social Cristiano who objected to their party's merger with the *Falange Nacional to form the *Partido Demócrata Cristiano. Its orientation was rightist and its political philosophy was based on the papal encyclicals Rerum novarum and Quadragesimo anno. It supported Jorge *Alessandri Rodríguez in the presidential election of 1958, joined the *Alianza de Partidos y Fuerzas Populares, and shortly afterwards became part of the United Conservative Party (*Partido Conservador Unido).

PARTIDO SOCIAL DEMOCRATICO. The Social Democratic Party was formed in 1965 by PADENA (*Partido Democrático Nacional) members who opposed PADENA's withdrawal from the *Frente de Acción Popular. It sought to offer an alternative, similar to the German and Italian Social Democratic Parties, to Chilean socialists who did not profess Marxism. In 1968 it had one senator and three deputies. It put forward its own candidate, Rafael *Tarud Siwady, for the 1970 presidential election, with the support of *Acción Popular Independiente (API). In December 1969, however, both the Social Democratic Party and API joined *Unidad Popular (UP), and a few months later Tarud withdrew to give his support to the UP candidate Salvador *Allende Gossens. Early in 1972 the Social Democrats merged with the Radical Party (*Partido Radical).

PARTIDO SOCIAL REPUBLICANO (PSR). The Social Republican Party was founded in 1931 after the fall of President (1927-31) Carlos *Ibáñez del Campo. Its principal objective was to defend public liberties and the democratic institutions of the Republic. Arturo *Alessandri Palma, who was elected President of Chile for the second time in 1932, was one of the founders. In mid-1935, with the stability of Chilean political institutions assured, the PSR was dissolved.

PARTIDO SOCIALISTA (PS). Chile's original socialist party, the *Partido Obrero Socialista, founded in 1912, joined the Third International (the Comintern) and changed its name to the *Partido Comunista Chileno in 1922. For the next ten years the Communists more or less monopolized the Marxist left. It was after the end of the Carlos *Ibáñez del Campo dictatorship in 1931 that independent socialist groups emerged. These groups evolved as a consequence of dissatisfaction on the part of the left with the badly-organized and ultra-leftist Communist leadership. The military rising of June 4, 1932 (see: JUNTA DE GOBIERNO DE 1932), marked the birth of the present Socialist Party, even though it was not formally organized until a year later. Marmaduke *Grove Vallejo, head of the Chilean *air force and a proclaimed nationalist, led the revolt, which established a 12-day *República Socialista. The Partido Socialista was constituted on

April 19, 1933, by the merger of the *Acción Revolucionaria Socialista, the *Orden Socialista, the *Partido Socialista Marxista
and the *Partido Socialista Unificado with Grove's *Nueva Acción
Pública.

By 1935 the Socialist Party had obtained control of the majority of Chile's *trade unions, and had become the principal party
of the Chilean working class. In the presidential elections of
1938 the Socialists backed Grove Vallejo, while the Communists
backed the Radical Party's Pedro *Aguirre Cerda. This provoked
additional resentment among the Socialists. Just before the
election, however, Grove withdrew when it became evident that
he had little chance of winning, and the Socialists joined the
Communists in supporting Aguirre (see: FRENTE POPULAR).

In 1948 the party split over President Gabriel *González
Videla's outlawing of the Communist Party (see: LEY DE DEFENSA
DE LA DEMOCRACIA), those against it becoming the *Partido
Socialista Popular, while the bulk of the party which went along
with the new law became the PARTIDO SOCIALISTA DE CHILE,
q.v.

PARTIDO SOCIALISTA AUTENTICO (PSA). The *Partido Socialista
was divided at its 1943 congress on whether to continue supporting
the government of Juan Antonio *Rios Morales. The minority who
favored continuing to support it, led by Marmaduke *Grove Vallejo, formed their own "Authentic Socialist Party" in June 1944.
In 1946 the PSA backed the Liberal presidential candidate, Fernando Alessandri Rodríguez. Later that year the PSA, without
Grove, fused with the *Partido Comunista Chileno.

PARTIDO SOCIALISTA DE CHILE (PSCh). The Socialist Party of
Chile was formed in 1948 when the *Partido Socialista was split
by the *Ley de defensa de la democracia, although it has continued
to use also the old, shorter name, particularly after the split was
healed in 1958.

Although the history of relations between Socialists and Communists in Chile has been one of hostility, they have often been
allies. There has been no mass infiltration of the PSCh by the
Communists. Many Communists joined the Socialist Party when
their own party was outlawed by the Gabriel *González Videla
government's 1948 Ley de defensa de la democracia. Most of them
withdrew, however, when the Communist Party regained its
legality in 1958.

Socialist Party ideology has not been consistent. It began with
a strong anti-Communist bias, but was quick to join the Communists in the Popular Front (*Frente Popular) once it was given
the opportunity. Then it broke with the Popular Front in 1946
and adopted the Peronist line. Afterwards the party favored
Titoism, and during the 1960s they were partial to Peking in the
Sino-Soviet conflict. This ideological flexibility does not however
connote any lack of basic principles. All the various doctrines
to which they have adhered have contained the same fundamental
concepts: nationalism, anti-parliamentarianism, socialism and pro-

letarianism.

The Chilean Socialist Party may thus be defined as a nationalist party of the left, Marxist in ideology, profoundly anti-oligarchic and anti-parliamentarian, committed to social and economic reform through the organization of the industrial and agricultural workers. The party obtained its greatest voting strength in 1941 (when it polled 18 percent) and in 1971 (when it received 22.8 percent). In 1947 its share fell to only 8.9 percent, but since then the party climbed steadily. In the 1971 *local government elections the PSCh emerged as the strongest party with the Unidad Popular coalition, replacing the Communists. A year before, their candidate, Salvador *Allende Gossens, had shocked the opposition, and the *United States, by winning the presidential election.

As part of the UP coalition, the Socialists were harshly repressed by the military *junta that overthrew Allende in 1973. Many party members were imprisoned, tortured or killed, and the lucky ones were exiled. In the 1980s the Socialist leadership in exile is afflicted by ideological confusion and factional struggle. It has put some distance between itself and the Communists, and two groups have merged: one led by Luis Altamirano, who resides in West Germany and has embraced the anti-Marxist line of the European social democrats; the other, led by Clodomiro *Almeyda Medina, who remains an avowed Marxist in exile in East Germany, is less interested in fighting with the Communists and more in forming a united opposition to overthrow President Augusto *Pinochet Ugarte, by whatever means.

PARTIDO SOCIALISTA DE TRABAJADORES. See: PARTIDO OBRERO SOCIALISTA.

PARTIDO SOCIALISTA DEL PUEBLO. The People's Socialist Party was founded in 1964 as a non-Marxist organization supporting the candidacy of Christian Democrat Eduardo *Frei Montalva in the presidential election of that year, rather than that of the Socialist candidate Salvador *Allende Gossens. The party was not entered in the Electoral Register (Registro Electoral) and so ceased to exist. Many of its members joined with the *Movimiento Nacional de Izquierda to form the *Partido Democrático Socialista.

PARTIDO SOCIALISTA DEMOCRATICO. The Democratic Socialist Party was founded in 1959 as a splinter from the *Partido Socialista de Chile. Its principle aim was the establishing of a socialist society without a class struggle. A year later it was incorporated into the National Democratic Party (*Partido Democrático Nacional). It was not connected with the *Partido Democrático Socialista.

PARTIDO SOCIALISTA INTERNACIONAL. The International Socialist Party was founded in 1931 by Santiago Wilson, merging later that year with the *Partido Socialista Revolucionario to form the Unified Socialist Party (*Partido Socialista Unificado), a precursor of the Socialist Party (*Partido Socialista) of April 1933.

PARTIDO SOCIALISTA MARXISTA (PSM). The Marxist Socialist
Party was formed following the end of the Carlos *Ibáñez del
Campo dictatorship (1927-31) by Eliodoro Domínguez Domínguez,
a director of commercial education. In April 1933 the PSM became a founder member of the *Partido Socialista.

PARTIDO SOCIALISTA POPULAR (PSP). The Popular Socialist Party
was formed by the extreme left-wing faction of the PARTIDO
SOCIALISTA, q.v., when they split over their attitude to Gabriel
*González Videla's 1948 *Ley de defensa de la democracia, which
outlawed the Communist Party (*Partido Comunista Chileno). In
1952 the Popular Socialists backed Carlos *Ibáñez del Campo as
the presidential candidate most clearly opposed to the "false democracy" of González Videla, while the rival *Partido Socialista de
Chile (which had participated in the González Videla government)
put forward its own candidate, Salvador *Allende Gossens. In
1956, however, the PSP joined the new leftist coalition, the
*Frente de Acción Popular, and two years later it was reunited
with the Partido Socialista de Chile.

PARTIDO SOCIALISTA REVOLUCIONARIO. The Revolutionary Socialist
Party was founded in 1931 by Albino Pezoa Estrada, but shortly
merged with the *Partido Socialista Internacional to form the
Unified Socialist Party (*Partido Socialista Unificado), a precursor
of the Socialist Party (*Partido Socialista) of 1933.

PARTIDO SOCIALISTA UNIFICADO. The Unified Socialist Party was
formed by a 1931 merger of the *Partido Socialista Internacional
and the *Partido Socialista Revolucionario, in an attempt to bring
all Marxist-socialist groups together into one party. After the
collapse of the *República Socialista in September 1932 it was
joined by the *Acción Revolucionaria Socialista, and changed its
name to the Socialist Revolutionary Union (*Unión Revolucionaria
Socialista). As such it became a founding member of the PARTIDO
SOCIALISTA (q.v.) in April 1933.

PASCAL ALLENDE, Andrés (1945-). Sociologist. Nephew of the
late President (1970-73) Salvador *Allende Gossens and son of
Laura *Allende de Pascal. He became head of the Left Revolutionary Movement (*Movimiento de Izquierda Revolucionario, MIR)
after its secretary general, Miguel *Enríquez, had been killed
in 1974 and his successor, Edgardo *Enríquez, had disappeared
in Chile a few years later. Pascal Allende is now operating
clandestinely against the *military regime.

PATAGONIA. The now extinct aborigines found by early explorers
on the Atlantic side of the southern tip of South America were
of remarkably large physique, which apparently accounts for
Ferdinand *Magellan having dubbed them Patagones ("big feet"),
hence the name Patagonia for all the mainland east of the Andes,
south of about 40°S.
    The Reino de Chile, as defined by *Charles V's royal cédula

of 1551, extended inland for 100 *leagues, and thus included
most of present-day *Argentina, and all of it south of about 45°S.
Early exploration and settlement attempts in southern Argentina
were all effected from Chile: Francisco de *Villagra in 1553 and
Pedro *Sarmiento de Gamboa in the 1580s, but Puerto Deseado
(now just Deseado) on the Atlantic coast was the only effective
colonial Chilean settlement beyond the *Andes. Patagonia remained, nevertheless, legally part of Chile, even after the 1776
creation of the Viceroyalty of the River Plate separated the then
province of *Cuyo. The southern boundary of the new viceroyalty was fixed along the Rio Negro between 39° and 40°S.

Soon after Chile became independent, Supreme Director Bernardo *O'Higgins advocated the construction of a line of forts along
the Patagonian coast, for fear that Great Britain harbored designs against the South American mainland. It was almost mid-
century, however, before Chileans began settling along the
*Strait of Magellan (founding the town of *Punta Arenas in 1849)
and in the Santa Cruz area. Further north the *Cordillera imposed so formidable a natural boundary that it was almost inevitable for exploration and settlement to proceed south from the
River Plate rather than inland from the Pacific. Already in the
late 18th century expeditions had been sent into the region from
Buenos Aires. By 1847 the Argentine government had laid formal
claim to all Patagonia. In 1856 Chile and Argentina signed a
treaty agreeing to abide by their colonial boundaries, but this
failed through dispute as to what those boundaries were. In
1872 Argentina asserted her claim to lands south of the Deseado
River (roughly 47°S) by expelling Chilean settlers. The Pierro-
Sarrates Treaty of December 1877 patched up a peace by confirming the status quo. The *Boundary Treaty of 1881 gave
Argentina possession of all the mainland down to the 52°S parallel
(and a trifle more along the Atlantic coast), fixing Chile's western
boundary above this as "the highest peaks dividing the waters,"
an unfortunately ambiguous demarcation which led the signatories
to the brink of war again in little more than a decade. Negotiations begun in 1899 led eventually to a 1904 compromise award by
King Edward VII fixing the frontier midway between the summit
line and the continental divide.

See also: ARGENTINA, Relations with; BOUNDARY TREATY
OF 1881; ORELIE, Antoine; PUERTO DE HAMBRE; PUNTA AREN-
AS; TIERRA DEL FUEGO.

PATRIA NUEVA ("New homeland"). The period in Chilean history
of recovered independence, 1817-23, so called in contrast to the
PATRIA VIEJA, q.v. (1810-14).

PATRIA VIEJA ("Old homeland"). Geographically, the traditional
heartland of Chile, between the province of *Coquimbo and the
*Bío-Bío River. It thus corresponds to what is nowadays usually
referred to as the "Zona Central" (Central Zone), viz. Regions
V, VI, VII and VIII. The country to the immediate north of the

Patria Vieja is known as the *Norte Chico. The lands to its south were left to the *Araucanian Indians, and only began to be settled in the second half of last century.

In its (more usual) chronological sense, <u>Patria Vieja</u> designates that period in Chile's struggle for *independence before the *Reconquista Española, i.e. 1810-1814.

PATRIA Y LIBERTAD (PL). An ultra-rightist organization whose title (literally, "Fatherland and freedom") is usually given in English as "Fatherland and Country." It was founded by Paulo *Rodríguez Grez and Roberto *Thieme when it became clear that Socialist Salvador *Allende Gossens would assume the presidency after the September 4, 1970, election. Known mostly as a terrorist group which formed the guerrilla arm of the extreme right before and after Allende's inauguration, its aims were to disrupt normal life, organize and finance strikes, sabotage bridges, *airports, *ports, and *railways, blow up embassies of countries friendly to the Allende government, and, ultimately, to bring the Allende regime down through chaos and economic sabotage.

Patria y Libertad received funds from the *United States *Central Intelligence Agency (C.I.A.) for a variety of purposes, ranging from propaganda broadcasts by *Radio Agricultura to violent demonstrations at political rallies, which the organization's militants attended in full riot gear. These funds came from the then U.S. embassy secretary Keith Wheelock, as well as from sources close to National Security Advisor Henry Kissinger. The tactics of Patria y Libertad were parallel to those of the *Movimiento de Izquierda Revolucionario, but whereas the Chilean *armed forces and the C.I.A. characterized the *Miristas as "goon squads," Patria y Libertad was allowed to act with impunity.

During Allende's three years in power, the organization took credit for over seventy attacks on government offices, public works and the pro-Allende media; assassinated Allende's naval aide, Commodore Arturo; abetted a C.I.A.-funded truck owners' strike that lasted several months and paralyzed the country-- murdering those truckers who failed to participate--(see: BOSSES' STRIKE); and organized the *Tancazo of June 29, 1973, a C.I.A.-sponsored coup attempt, for which it took public responsibility in the Chilean press and which was a prelude to the successful *coup d'état of September 11, 1973. After the coup, several of the organization's members were employed by General Augusto *Pinochet Ugarte as *police interrogators; others joined the *DINA, the secret police responsible for the torture and murder of thousands of Chileans.

PATRONATO NACIONAL. See: REAL PATRONATO.

PAUCARPATA, Treaty of. Peace treaty with the *Peru-Bolivia Confederation negotiated by Manuel *Blanco Encalada (as commander of Chilean forces in Peru) and Antonio José de Irisarri Alonso (as Chilean minister in Peru) and signed on November 17, 1837, under which the Chileans evacuated Arequipa and returned to *Valparaíso. On the *army's return the Senate unanimously repudiated the treaty and the war continued.

PELUCONES ("those who wear large bushy wigs"). A scornful epithet bestowed on their opponents by the *Pipiolos, or liberals, circa 1823, and which came to be the general designation for the small but powerful class of large property owners allied to the *Church. The pelucones, who came to power in 1830 and governed Chile for nearly thirty years, called themselves conservadores (conservatives), but the Conservative Party (*Partido Conservador) as such only came into formal existence in 1857 when President Manuel *Montt Torres' quarrel with the Church (see: SACRISTAN, Cuestión del) split the Pelucones into Conservatives and Montt-Varristas or Nationals (see: PARTIDO NACIONAL).

PENINSULAR. A European-born Spaniard in the Americas, as opposed to the American-born *creole. The Peninsulares were numerous, but they occupied all the positions at the top of the social ladder in the colonies: viceroys, captains-general, governors, archbishops, bishops and most other high officials and high clergy.

PEON. Originally a foot soldier, "peón" has come to mean an unskilled workman, and specifically a rural day laborer. Although, in contrast to the *inquilino (small-holder), the peón is landless, the term usually denotes someone resident on the estate where he works, as opposed to the migrant *afuerino. In the 19th century the peón was in theory paid a money wage, but actually had to purchase all his needs from his employer's *pulpería against his account.

PEOPLE'S FRONT. See: FRENTE DEL PUEBLO.

PEOPLE'S NATIONAL FRONT. See: FRENTE NACIONAL DEL PUEBLO.

PEREZ MASCAYANO, José Joaquín (1801-1889). Member of the National Party (*Partido Nacional) and President of Chile, 1861-71. He served in the diplomatic corps as secretary of the Chilean legation in the *United States, chargé d'affairs in Paris (1829), and minister in Buenos Aires (1830). He entered *Congress in 1834, and held cabinet office under President Manuel *Bulnes Prieto. Elected unopposed to the presidency when Antonio *Varas de la Barra withdrew his candidacy, Pérez, a political moderate, governed with support of both Conservatives and Liberals (see: FUSION LIBERAL-CONSERVADORA). His two terms were a period of material progress, although marred by political and religious conflict. Constitutional developments included the concession of the

right of public worship to non-Catholics (1865) and the enactment
of a ban on the immediate reelection of a President (1871).
Pérez worked for greater political and religious tolerance, but the
presidency continued to enjoy wide powers. The government, in
essence, was still an oligarchy, as it had been under the three
previous Conservative Presidents (1831-61). Pérez's presidency
is regarded as marking the beginning of thirty years (1861-91)
of Liberal ascendency.

Pérez's administration waged the War of 1865-67 with *Spain
(in which Chile was allied with *Peru) and a campaign against
the *Araucanian Indians in 1868.

PEREZ ROSALES, Vicente (1807-1886). A Chilean writer of some importance, and a pioneer of European settlement in *Llanquihue.
His adventurous early years included accompanying his father into
exile in Mendoza in 1814, visits to England and France, a spell
in northern Chile as a miner and smuggler, and travel in Mexico
and California, from where he returned in 1848. In 1850 he was
appointed agent for settlement in Llanquihue; as such he founded
*Puerto Montt. In 1858 he became Chilean consul in Hamburg,
where he wrote Ensayos sobre Chile (essays on Chile) to encourage
*immigration. The following year he was made *intendant of *Con-
cepción, and in 1861 entered *Congress as a Conservative deputy.
From 1876 to 1882 he represented Llanquihue in the Senate. One
of his best known works is his Recuerdos del pasado (memories
of the past).

PEREZ SALAS, Francisco Antonio (1764-1828). A Chilean patriot who
participated in the struggle for *independence from Spain, and
uncle of José Joaquín *Pérez Mascayano and of Vicente *Pérez
Rosales. In 1810 he was one of those who proclaimed the *junta
de gobierno de 1810 to rule in the name of King *Ferdinand VII,
and two years later he collaborated in drafting the Chilean *Constitution of 1812. On April 13, 1813, he succeeded Juan José
*Carrera Verdugo as president of the *junta de gobierno de 1813,
a position he held until August 5. A year later he was exiled by
José Miguel *Carrera Verdugo because of his conservative views,
and following the *Reconquista Española was exiled to the *Juan
Fernández Islands by Mariano *Osorio, November 9, 1814. In 1817
Pérez was freed and appointed president of the Tribunal of Justice. The following year he entered the Senate, becoming its
president. Later in 1818 he was appointed a judge (ministro) of
the Supreme Court.

PEREZ ZUJOVIC, Edmundo (1912-1971). Leader of the Christian Democrats (*Partido Demócrata Cristiano, PDC) who was assassinated
by the Left Revolutionary Movement (*Movimiento de Izquierda
Revolucionario, MIR) in retaliation for assassinations of left-wing
leaders by the "Fatherland and Country" (*Patria y Libertad)
group. The slaying of Zujóvic convinced Socialist President (1970-

73) Salvador *Allende Gossens of the need to eliminate all illegally armed groups in Chile, but this was something he was
unable to accomplish. Christian Democrat leaders, including
former President (1964-70) Eduardo *Frei Montalva, angered by
Zujóvic's death, accused Allende of not being in control. As
the country became more and more polarized, the PDC's opposition
to Allende became more organized and vociferous, contributing
to his overthrow on September 11, 1973.

PERIODICAL PRESS. The earliest periodical publications in Chile
were *newspapers. Periodical publications of a more general
nature only began in the 1840s with the appearance of the first
literary reviews, such as the Revista de Valparaíso (165 numbers
beginning in 1842), El crepúsculo of *Santiago (June 1843-August
1844), the Revista de Santiago (1848-49), the Revista del Pácifico
(1858-61), La Semana (published 1859-60 by the Arteaga Alemparte brothers), and, a little later, the Revista chilena. Of
these early reviews, the Revista católica (founded by Archbishop
Rafael Valentín *Valdivieso y Zañartu in 1843) and the Anales de
la *Universidad de Chile (from 1846) are still published. In the
1860s came the first satirical magazines, such as La linterna
del diablo (from 1867), El charivari (1867-69), and a little later,
El chicote (June 1875-June 1876) and La comedia humana (from
1904). The Revista de ciencias y letras, Chile's first scientific
periodical, began in April 1857, and the Country's first specialist
title, the Revista médica de Chile, in 1869. Important intellectual
periodicals of the later 19th century include La Estrella de Chile
(1867-79) and the Conservative Revista de artes y letras (1884-
1890). The first general illustrated magazines followed the introduction of the halftone method of reproducing photographs in
print: Sucesos of *Valparaíso, which lasted from 1902 to 1934,
and the Revista *Zig-Zag (from 1905).

In this century most magazines are controlled by the economic
elite. Exceptions have included the satirical *Topaze (briefly
banned by President Arturo *Alessandri Palma in 1938), *Hoy
(representing the interests of the *Partido Demócrata Cristiano)
and *Mensaje (a Jesuit journal of high quality, dealing primarily
with the role of the *Church in bringing about socioeconomic reform).

With the imposition of a rigid CENSORSHIP (q.v.) following the
military *coup d'état of September 1973, almost all criticism of
the government ceased. Weekly and monthly periodicals, which
had proliferated during the *Unidad Popular period, disappeared
in large numbers. Almost the only journal of opinion that continued and dared publish commentary critical of official policies
was the monthly Mensaje. In March 1976 an edition of the news-
weekly Ercilla was seized, and the magazine was later sold to a
group of government supporters. Hoy replaced Ercilla as the
most informative news magazine for the foreigner studying day-to-
day events in Chile, but was suspended for its outspokenness,
and only allowed to resume in 1980 (see: FILIPPI, Emilio M.).

The *Constitution of 1980 restricted media coverage of acts of terrorism and gave the government formal powers to censor new periodicals. Existing ones practiced self-censorship to avoid intervention. There was however some increase in the government's tolerance of press criticism from the early 1980s.

Periodicals being published in Chile in 1984 were: Análisis; Arquitectura y construcción; El campesino; Chile aéreo; Chile-agrícola; Chile filatélico; Chile textil; Cosas; Economía y finanzas; Economic and financial survey; Ercilla; Estrategia; Gestión; Hoy; Mensaje; Negocios and Paula.

See also: NEWSPAPERS; MENSAJE.

PEROUSE, Conte de la. See: LA PEROUSE, Jean François de Galaup, [Conte de]

PERU, Relations with. Chile in colonial times was part of the viceroyalty of Peru, administered from Lima. Not only did Chile's struggle for *independence entail repudiation of Peruvian control, but Peruvian independence itself was, in a sense, imposed on that country by the joint Chilean-Argentine army of José de *San Martín. In 1837-39, however, the Chilean war with the *Peru-Bolivia Confederation was supported by many Peruvian nationalists and in the war of 1865-66 with Spain, Chile came to the help of Peru. By this time Chileans had begun working the *nitrate and *guano beds in both the (then) Peruvian province of *Tarapacá and Bolivian *Antofagasta. Feeling they had a common interest in resisting Chilean penetration, Peru and Bolivia entered into a secret alliance, so that when war broke out between Chile and Bolivia in 1879, Peru was necessarily involved. At the conclusion of this War of the *Pacific, Chile annexed Tarapacá but also retained *Arica and *Tacna against payment of a war indemnity (see: ANCON, Treaty of). The so-called Tacna Question embittered relations and was not settled until 1929, when Peru recovered Tacna and received compensation for the definitive loss of Arica (see: LIMA, Treaty of). Peru remained resentful and, in anticipation of further conflict, the two countries began an arms race that continues to this day (see: ARMAMENTS).

In the early 1970s Peru and Chile experimented with leftist governments and attempts at reconciliation were made. But even if governments were willing to establish normal relations, a deep distrust persisted among their people. When more conservative regimes were imposed in both countries, Chile became worried that Peru might launch an attack to recover its lost territory.

In December 1978, Peru expelled various Chilean diplomats and military personnel accused of "spying," while the Chilean ambassador in Lima was declared persona non grata and Peru's ambassador in Santiago was recalled. One hundred years after the War of the Pacific, diplomatic relations were severed. The centennial was a reminder to Peru of her humiliating defeat, while being a cause for celebration in Chile. It was only in 1981 that ambassadors were exchanged and full diplomatic relations resumed. As is true with most Latin American countries having a common border, a great deal of antipathy remains between Chile and Peru.

PERU-BOLIVIA CONFEDERATION, War with. When in 1836 the Bolivian dictator Andrés de *Santa Cruz y Calahumada moved to federate his nation with Peru as the Confederación Peruboliviana, Diego *Portales Palazuelos saw this as a political and economic threat, and Chile declared war. A small force of only 3,500 men was despatched in October 1837 under Admiral Manuel *Blanco Encalada in expectation that its arrival would trigger a rising of Peruvian nationalists. Arequipa was occupied, but the rising failed to occur, the expeditionary force was surrounded, and Blanco Encalada could only save his army by signing the ignominious Treaty of PAUCAPARTA (q.v.), which the Chilean Senate repudiated as soon as the army was safely returned. In August 1838 a larger and better organized expedition, 6,000 strong, was despatched under Manuel *Bulnes Prieto, President Joaquín *Prieto Vial's nephew, accompanied by a number of Peruvian émigrés led by Agustín Gamara, whom Santa Cruz had displaced as president of Peru. This new force disembarked at Ancón, north of Callao, where its presence stimulated an anti-Bolivian rising in southern Peru. Fighting, however, was largely confined to skirmishes until the decisive battle of YUNGAY (q.v.) on January 20, 1839. The victorious Chilean army returned in triumph to *Santiago in November, and Bulnes's enhanced prestige largely contributed to his election to the presidency of the Republic in 1841.

PESO. The traditional Hispanic American, and present-day Chilean, unit of account. Literally "weight," the word was first used in a colonial South America lacking minted coins for a standard weight of precious metal. Eventually coins of the same value (28.5 grams of gold) were minted. Under Charles III, the peso duro became the largest silver coin, known in English as the silver dollar or "piece of eight," since it could be legally cut into eight wedgeshaped "bits" worth one real each.

In 1851 Chile decimalized its currency, making the silver peso ($) the unit, worth five French francs, and divisible into a hundred centavos. After the 1932 withdrawal of silver *coinage, the peso existed only as a bank note. To compensate for Chile's chronic post-World War II inflation, the peso was replaced in 1960 by the *escudo at the rate of 1,000 pesos to the escudo. Further loss of value led the *Pinochet regime to introduce in 1975 a new peso, at the rate of 1,000 escudos to the new peso. See also: EXCHANGE RATE.

PETORCA. Name of a river of central Chile and of a small town on its north bank at 32° 16'S, 70° 59'W, which has given its name to the province (formerly department) in the region (formerly province) of *Atamaca. Founded in 1754, the town (*comuna) had a population of 1,671 in 1907 and 8,472 in 1986.

During the *Civil War of 1851, Petorca was the site of a battle on October 14, when 600 rebels (under Justo Artega Cuevas and José Miguel *Carrera Fontecilla) making for *San Felipe were intercepted by 942 government troops (under Juan Vidaurra Leal) and defeated, losing half their strength as prisoners.

PETROLEUM. All of Chile's domestically produced petroleum comes from the *Magallanes region in the far south. Oil was discovered on the north shore of *Tierra del Fuego in 1945, and first produced commercially in 1949, when 8,800 cubic meters of crude were obtained. The following year, when the government monopoly *ENAP was established, 100,000 m^3 were produced. This amount was quadrupled by 1955. In 1974 some 1,598,562 m^3 were produced from 325 wells on either shore of the *Strait of Magellan. Ten years later output had grown to 2,236,800 m^3. Output growth has not however kept pace with the increase in consumption. Whereas Chilean production met 54 percent of national consumption in 1965, this share had fallen to 36 percent in 1980. Reserves, which include uptapped deposits in other parts of the country, are estimated at 300 to 800 thousand million m^3.
See also: NATURAL GAS.

PHILIP II (1527-1598). King of Spain from 1556 (as Felipe II) and of Portugal from 1580 (as Filipe I); also King of Naples and ruler of the Netherlands (from 1554). The first Spanish Hapsburg, he began the restriction of American *immigration to *peninsulares (ending the more open policy of his cosmopolitan father, *Charles V) and was largely responsible for developing the excessively centralized bureaucracy that characterized Spanish colonial administration. His policies towards England, the Netherlands and France led to the incursions of *pirates and privateers from these countries into American waters that began with Sir Francis *Drake in 1577. The pirate threat led in turn to the first attempt at settling Chile's far south, to guard the *Strait of Magellan (see: PUERTO DE HAMBRE).

PHILIP V (1683-1746). Duke of Anjou, grandson of Louis XIV of France, who secured for him the position of King of Spain (as Felipe V) on the death of the last Spanish Hapsburg, Charles II, in 1700. This was achieved through the War of the Spanish succession (1700-15). His reign, as the first of the Spanish Bourbons, marks the beginning of *French influence on Spanish policies and administration, and of the so-called Bourbon reforms-- although most of these were introduced during the reigns of his sons *Ferdinand VI and (especially) *Charles III. The city of *San Felipe and the colonial *Universidad de San Felipe were so named in his honor.

PICTON. An island, 18 km by 4 km (11 x 2 miles) at 55° 4'S, 67°W, in the BEAGLE CHANNEL, q.v., northeast of Navarino Island, named by British hydrographers Robert *Fitzroy and Phillip Parker *King in honor of Sir Thomas Picton, first British governor of Trinidad who was killed at Waterloo. Picton Island, along with *Lennox and *Nueva, was the subject of a dispute with *Argentina that was only settled in 1984.

PICUNCHES. Aborigines related to the *Mapuches. See: ARAU-CANIAN INDIANS.

PIÑERO, Miguel. Argentine writer who came to Chile in 1840 and succeeded Domingo *Faustino Sarmiento as editor of El MERCURIO, q.v.

PINOCHET UGARTE, Augusto (1915-). President of Chile, 1974- ; Commander-in-chief of the *armed forces; and head of the *junta militar de gobierno de 1973, which overthrew the Socialist government of Salvador *Allende Gossens in the *coup d'état of September 11, 1973. Just two weeks earlier he had been appointed *army c.-in-c. by Allende on his promise that the military would stay out of politics.

As a career army officer, Pinochet had won rapid promotion and received many decorations. He had been sent on several military missions, including one to Washington, D.C. In 1968 he became chief of the Second Army Division, and in 1971 he took command of the garrison in *Santiago. A year later he was promoted chief general of the army.

As army representative on the post-coup junta, he quickly succeeded in making himself the dominant member of what had been intended to be a council in which all four services shared power. Ruling by decree, he set aside once and for all the notion that Chile would shortly return to democracy, or that he would share power with civilians. In 1974 he declared himself President. Later, the *Constitution of 1980 would assure him of retaining that position until at least 1989.

The extent of his rule by decree was unprecedented in Chile. Those civilian politicians not killed, imprisoned or exiled were legally proscribed from any political activities. By 1986 he had ruled for thirteen years, the longest continuous period for any Chilean chief executive since the early 18th century.

Few Latin American countries have seen such a sharp, rapid and intense process of political transformation as that suffered by Chile since Pinochet came to power. Until then, Chile had been one of the most durable democracies in Latin America. Although under Allende the political situation had been difficult, frustrating and sectarian, the integrity of the political system was preserved; there were few cases of imprisonment on political grounds; the press, radio and television, wretched as they were, were free to give their (often hysterical) version of events (see:

CENSORSHIP); the *universities were completely autonomous; and political life was almost entirely devoid of secret police surveillance. Pinochet has reversed all that and has imposed changes more severe than any conjectured by Allende. Every vestige of pluralism has been eliminated from the social system. The initial state of siege and its continuation as one of emergency, lasted ten years, only finally lifted in 1983. He dissolved *Congress, effectively eliminated all *political parties, introduced a rigid press censorship, forbade unauthorized assembly, suspended rights of habeus corpus, and abridged the rights of *trade unions. In a frenzy to ensure their survival, Pinochet and the junta let terror run amok. Despite close international scrutiny and massive exposure, a relentless war was waged on opposition in any form. Security was vested in a secret police organization, the *DINA, created by Pinochet himself; this controlled the operations of the individual intelligence services of all four armed forces (see: SECRET SERVICE). After DINA's establishment, maltreatment of political prisoners, which had at first been random, became systematic. Brutality was used not so much to interrogate an individual, as to intimidate a nation. Pinochet became Chile's undisputed leader, and a reign of arbitrary power was imposed on a cowed populace.

Arrest and unexplained detention by the military became rarer after the adoption of the 1980 Constitution, and a new decree prohibited summary shootings and required *police to notify a prisoner's family within 48 hours of the arrest. The report that *concentration camps were operating in Chile, however, angered many governments around the world, giving credence to the charge that terrorism had become institutionalized in Chile.

The harsh political reality introduced by the Pinochet regime extended also to the economic sphere. The priority of the CHICAGO BOYS (q.v.), the economic managers with whom Pinochet surrounded himself, was to bring *inflation down and increase growth. In order to achieve this, four decades of protectionism and of increasing state intervention in the *economy were abandoned. State ownership was ended in all but a handful of industries, and the Chilean domestic market was opened to foreign competition. The policy was initially successful. Chile's annual growth of 8 percent far outpaced that of the sluggish economies of most countries in the region, and Chile was held up as an example to other developing countries. When it was pointed out that the improved economic picture had come at a great cost to middle- and lower-income groups, Pinochet replied that sacrifices had to be made somewhere.

But in 1981 inflation picked up again, unemployment soared (see: EMPLOYMENT), and the per capita foreign debt became the largest in Latin America. As the price of bread, sugar, flour and oil rose to unprecedented levels, resentment and discontent began to build up dangerously. Outbursts of rioting and street demonstrations on the eve of the *military regime's eleventh anniversary in 1984 indicated a decreasing tolerance for belt-tightening among the poor, and demands for a return to civilian rule increased. All this narrowed President Pinochet's already minimal political base.

The strongest indictment against Pinochet was his failure to reunite Chile, despite ruling longer and more absolutely than any other President. If most Chileans had condoned the bloody coup in 1973 as the only way to avoid a civil war, they had not expected the military's unwillingness to give up power, nor their gross and systematic violation of human rights. Pinochet had promised peace, progress, and unity to a polarized nation that had been traumatized by hyperinflation and violent street fighting. Eleven years after, however, Chileans were suffering from the same malaise.

Reconciliation was hampered by unfair rules of the free market economic model adopted by Pinochet, which had widened income disparities to a degree common throughout Latin America but seldom seen in Chile. The social cost of these policies, as indicated, had been borne disproportionately by the poor and middle-income families, whose real wages had plummeted while unemployment rates had reached 30 percent.

Pinochet's attitude toward his opposition, particularly his harsh repression of peaceful dissent, had also sown division among Chileans. To make matter worse, Pinochet's relations with the Roman Catholic *Church had become very fragile. The police repeatedly raided parishes, accused priests and bishops of being Communists, and showed little respect for religious beliefs.

Critics of the regime complained that reconciliation was impossible as long as critics of Pinochet were labeled "traitors, conspirators, or foreign agents." There was plenty of grumbling among Chileans who had lost patience with the continued repression and bloodshed perpetrated by the regime.

Pinochet's share of troubles by late 1984 was mounting, as he continued to show defiance for an early return to civilian rule and was being blamed for an economy on the brink of disaster. Even his most staunch supporters were abandoning him (bankers, large landowners, industrialists), as the economic recession had begun to affect every sector of Chilean society. The consumerism of a few oligarchic families, accused of ransacking the nation by greedy speculations and fraudulent practices, was offset by proliferating soup kitchens, street peddlers, and beggars.

Thousands of Chileans defied a dusk-to-dawn curfew to storm the streets of Santiago and other cities on the eve of the 11th anniversary of the coup (as they had done the year before). It was the fourth mass protest in as many months, as Chileans demanded an end to military rule and to an economic program that favored only the rich. The oratorical tongue-lashing of the Chilean President was answered by his warning that "I am not giving an inch."

Pinochet was quick to put 18,000 armed troops on alert. To quash the disturbances, police and soldiers attacked with clubs, tear gas, water cannons, and machine guns, firing at people randomly. Hundreds of demonstrators were arrested, at least 7 people were killed, and more than three dozen wounded. Once again, Pinochet had made it clear that he would stop the opposition using any means necessary, and that he cared little about the international image he was creating abroad. Only Air Force Chief, General Fernando *Matthey, said his troops would not participate in further repression.

The most recent disturbances left Pinochet a besieged President, or as Le Monde described him, a "solitary dictator," foreshadowing the possibility of more bloodshed ahead. Opposition political and labor leaders, together with the Roman Catholic Church, issued statements condemning Pinochet's intolerant attitude toward a return to democratic rule. The Chilean leader was at variance with the impression he had left in July 1984 that he was preparing the foundations for a return to civilian rule with a new political-parties law, a new Congress, and new elections by 1989. On the contrary, Pinochet refused to discuss any reduction in the length of his term (although he may soon have little choice), and told Chileans they were not ready yet, in light of recent events, with the election of a Congress by 1989. Pinochet's acrimonious response contrasted with the quiet negotiation that had been going on between his Interior Minister, Sergio Onofre *Jarpa Reyes, the Christian Democrats, and the conservative parties that had traditionally supported him but now wanted a timetable for a return to constitutionality.

Defiantly, Pinochet vowed to stay on, belittling his foes, especially the Christian Democrats, and disregarding the loud bangs of *pots and pans in the streets of *Santiago calling for his resignation (an ominous sign during the last days of Allende's presidency). In a tough speech on September 11, 1984, commemorating the eleventh anniversary of the coup, Pinochet accused ten opposition leaders, including ex-foreign minister Gabriel *Valdés Subercaseaux, of trying to overthrow the regime during the violent protests of the week before. He then reintroduced the state of emergency (only lifted the year before) for at least another six months. In November he upgraded this to a state of siege (previously lifted in 1974). Hundreds of people were arrested, opposition magazines were shut down (see: PERIODICAL PRESS), habeas corpus was suspended, and hundreds were sentenced to internal exile--summary removal from their homes to some remote village in the far north or far south of the country, where they would have to try to find housing, work and food among a population that had been specifically warned against having anything to do with them.

Throughout 1985 Chile was ruled under conditions in which due legal process was suspended: a state of siege; a state of emergency; a state of risk of disturbance of internal order; and, as a consequence of the *earthquake, a state of catastrophe. The government's heavy hand is largely the result of mounting protests by a nation discontented with Pinochet's economic and social policies.

When, in March 1985, two Communist Party (*Partido Comunista Chilean) leaders were assassinated by the secret police, even the Supreme Court had difficulties in rubber stamping what Pinochet wanted. José Manuel Parada, a lawyer working with the *Vicariate of Solidarity, and Manuel Guerrero, president of Santiago Teachers' Association, were abducted by armed civilians and founded beheaded on an abandoned road. The outcry was immediate. Twenty thousand people attended the funerals, defying the state of siege. But Pinochet's message was clear. If the military government had to resort to the same practices as those used in the period immediately following the coup, it was willing to do so.

In 1984, relations with the Church also reached their lowest point since the coup. Monsignor Ignacio Gutiérrez, a *Jesuit who had been in charge of the Vicariate of Solidarity, was informed that he would not be allowed to return to Chile from a trip to the Vatican. The move was seen as a direct challenge to the Chilean Catholic Church, which has been bearing whatever meager witness it could during the years since Pinochet's seizure of power.

Even Pinochet's opponents acknowledged that he was a "true believer," a stern man who questioned the strength of democracy in the face of what he saw as the evil of Communism. After thirteen years of authoritarian rule, it was difficult to assess how long he would remain in power without having gained a minimal degree of popular support. Indeed, by mid-1986 even the leaders of the other armed forces seemed to be wavering in their allegiance and the regime was coming to depend almost wholly on the loyalty of the army.

This situation was changed abruptly by the unsuccessful attempt on Pinochet's life of September 7, 1986. His motorcade, returning to Santiago from his country residence at El Melocotón was ambushed at 6:40 p.m. on a narrow part of the highway, 18 miles from the capital by members of the *Frente Patriótico Manuel Rodríguez led by "Juan Carlos" (identified by the government as César Bunster Ariztía, son of Allende's ambassador to the *United Kingdom). Five of Pinochet's escorts were killed, ten wounded and several vehicles destroyed. A state of siege was reintroduced; opposition papers were banned (although *Hoy was allowed to resume publication a week later), many arrests were made and several alleged Communists were murdered by right-wing terrorists. The following day the government even risked a diplomatic breach with the Netherlands by arresting four *Universidad de Chile students traveling under embassy protection in the second secretary's car. The ruthlessness of the FPMR attack, and the nearly simultaneous discovery of several hidden arms caches caused the armed forces to close ranks, markedly strengthening Pinochet's position, at least in the short term.

PINTO DIAZ, Francisco Antonio (1775-1858). Lawyer by profession
and Chilean patriot. In 1813 the *junta de gobierno sent him
on a diplomatic mission to Buenos Aires and London. He returned
in 1817, fought the Spanish in Upper Peru (modern Bolivia), and
in 1822-24, under José de *San Martín in Peru, reaching the rank
of brigadier general. A liberal (*pipiolo) and supporter of Bernardo *O'Higgins, he became minister of the interior and foreign
relations in July 1824. In May 1827 he became acting President
of Chile in succession to Ramón *Freire Serrano, having already
replaced Agustín *Eyzaguirre Arechevala as vice-president on
February 13.
  Pinto Díaz governed for two years, solidifying the Republican
form of government with the implementation of the *Constitution
of 1828. In October 1829 Pinto was formally elected President,
but a dispute over the election of his vice-president led to a
pelucón (conservative) uprising in *Concepción organized by one
of the disappointed candidates, General Joaquín *Prieto Vial.
Pinto resigned in favor of the successful vice-presidential candidate, Francisco Ramón *Vicuña Larraín, and the *Civil War of
1829-30 ensued. Pinto retired into private life until 1841, when
he became leader of the *Partido Liberal.

PINTO GARMENDIA, Aníbal (1825-1884). President of Chile, 1876-81,
son of President Francisco Antonio *Pinto Diaz, and son-in-law
of General José María de la *Cruz y Prieto. He had a brief university career as a professor of philosophy and the humanities,
but devoted his life mainly to politics. A member of the *Partido
Liberal, he was in Rome (1845-51) as secretary to the Chilean
legation. He sat in *Congress as a deputy, 1852-58 and 1865-70,
and as senator, 1870-76. From 1862-71 he was *intendant of
Concepción, becoming in 1871 President Federico *Errázuriz
Zañartu's war minister.
  At the beginning of Pinto's presidency Chile was suffering
a severe economic depression, due in part to over-extension at
home, aggravated by natural disasters (an *earthquake and subsequent floods), and the effect on world markets of the American
Civil War and the Franco-Prussian War. Pinto's government, confronted with this crisis, fought *Peru and *Bolivia for the possession of the *Atacama desert with its rich *nitrate, *guano and
other deposits. By the end of the resulting War of the *Pacific,
Chile had occupied Peruvian *Tacna and *Arica and Bolivian
*Antofagasta. The economic situation improved, and the election
of 1881 put another liberal President (Domingo *Santa María González) in to succeed him.

PIPIOLOS ("novice, rawhand, beginner"). A name given contemptu-
ously to a political group formed in Chile in 1823, after the fall
of Bernardo *O'Higgins. The pipiolos were inspired by the
liberal, democratic and anti-clerical ideals of the French Revolution. Many of their members were of lower social rank than

their opponents, the PELUCONES ("big wigs"), q.v., hence the nickname. In a sense they were the successors of the *exaltados and the antecedents of the *Partido Liberal, although separated historically and chronologically. Ramón *Freire Serrano, *Supreme Director of Chile 1823-26 and President in 1827, became the champion of their cause. His government began the so-called Pipiolo Era, characterized by such liberal reforms as the abolition of *African slavery, and by economic instability and political anarchy. The era of pipiolo power ended in the *Civil War of 1829-30, which brought the pelucones into power for thirty years.

PIR. See: PARTIDO DE LA IZQUIERDA RADICAL.

PIRATES AND PRIVATEERS. Spain's determination to keep the wealth of the Indies to herself naturally encouraged foreign interlopers, as smugglers, as privateers in time of war, and as outright pirates. The first to penetrate Chilean waters was the Englishman Sir Francis *Drake, who entered the *Strait of Magellan on August 21, 1578. He attacked *Valparaíso, La *Serena and *Arica before sailing farther up the Pacific coast and eventually completing the second circumnavigation of the globe. His example was followed by Thomas Cavendish, who raided Arica in 1586, and then by an increasing number of other English, Dutch and French captains. A few (Walter and Edward Tillert in 1592, Richard *Hawkins in 1594) were captured, but most used their advantage of surprise to plunder ships and coastal towns with impunity. The pirate Bartholomew *Sharp plundered La Serena in 1680, a feat repeated by Edward *Davis in 1686. The 1703 expedition of the privateer William *Dampier is memorable for the stranding by one of his ships' captains, of sailing-master Alexander Selkirk on Más Atierra in the *Juan Fernández Islands. Others are remembered for directly naming some of the places they sailed by. Dutchmen Willem Cornelius Schouten of Hoorn and Jacob Le Maire of Amsterdam, sailing together in 1615, named Staten (Estados), Maurice and Barnvelt islands, Cape Horn and Le Maire's Strait. Sir John *Narborough in 1669 named Desolation and Narborough islands.

PISAGUA. Small (and now decayed) nitrate port in *Iquique province, Tarapacá region, at 19° 36' S, 70° 13' W. Its capture on November 2, 1879, during the War of the *Pacific gave the Chilean army a base from which it could march on *Iquique. Similarly, in the *Civil War of 1891, its capture by the *congresistas under Estanislao del Canto Artigas on February 6, after a naval bombardment and the capture of the dominating *Alto del Hospicio, was the first step in the rebel conquest of the *Norte Grande. Pisagua's population was 2,500 in 1960, but only 327 in 1981.

PLACILLA, La. Height overlooking *Viña del Mar, the site of the last battle of the *Civil War of 1891. Some 9,500 loyalists under Orozimbo *Barbosa Puga sought to defend the approaches to

*Valparaíso against 10,000 rebel troops under Estanislao del Canto Artigas. On the morning of August 27 the government army lost a third of its strength in three hours, and the victorious rebels lost one fifth. Valparaíso was captured and looted and the Congressional forces were free to march unopposed on *Santiago.

PLAN CENTAURO. See: CENTAUR PLAN.

PLAN ZETA. See: ZETA PLAN.

PLANNING. Chile was one of the first nations in Latin America to establish a National Economic Development Plan. The government agency responsible was the Production Development Corporation, CORFO, q.v. The ten-year plan proposed by CORFO in 1960 was reviewed by experts of the International Bank for Reconstruction and Development (IBRD) and the United States Agency for International Development (USAID). It was found to be a feasible plan, calling for the attainment of an average annual increase of 5.5 percent in the GNP, and for total investment of nearly US$ 10,000 million from 1961 to 1970. The plan was successful in its first three years, and GNP growth exceeded the goal by 2 percent. Consumption of goods and services rose 5 percent above the goal, but total investment fell short by 4 percent.

For the rest of the decade, achievement under the plan was uneven. While *mining, construction and services each exceeded their goals by 18 percent or more, *agriculture fell short by 11 percent, and industry by 32 percent. Local and regional planning were assisted by the activities of the Central Planning Bureau (*ODEPLAN), the Economic Planning Center of the *Universidad de Chile, and the Chilean Society for Planning and Development. In 1970 President Salvador *Allende Gossens did not merely propose a new Economic Plan, but stated that "the economic policy of the *Unidad Popular government, in its fundamental approach, aims substantially at replacing the present economic structure with another, one which allowed the realization of a socialist and pluralistic society to begin."

Allende's experiment with socialism was short-lived. His effort to develop three areas of ownership--state, mixed, and private--were repudiated by the *military regime that replaced him in 1973. Although the state retained ownership of the *copper mines which Allende had nationalized, all other sectors of the economy were returned to private hands. Augusto *Pinochet Ugarte's government believed that the state should play the smallest possible role in the *economy. However, the director of ODEPLAN was promoted to cabinet rank in the early 1980s. As Chile's economic collapse became acute in 1982, the government decided to play a more decisive role in regulating *banks and banking, imports and exports, imposing more controls and economic planning.

POBLACIONES CALLAMPAS. See: CALLAMPAS.

POBLETE DE ESPINOSA, Olga. Leader of the *Movimiento de Emancipación de la Mujer Chilena, of which she was president, 1946-50,
immediately following her return from graduate education at
Columbia University. She later became a professor of history
and geography at the *Universidad de Chile, and was awarded
the Lenin Peace Prize in 1962.

PODER POPULAR ("Popular Power"). Mass organizations of workers
and *campesinos during the 1970-73 *Unidad Popular government.
These organizations, which were especially active during the
last few month's of the Salvador *Allende Gossens presidency,
answered such needs as how to get food and supplies to the population at a time of economic crisis and sabotage, how to get
a greater yield from a plot of land, how to organize a people's
supply store (almacén popular), or how to set up a production
committee in a factory. There were also times during the struggle
when these organizations would temporarily distance themselves
from the action in order to discuss the nature of the socialist
state that was then in the first stages of being constructed.
Their leaders would develop the theoretical aspects of socialism,
based on their practical experience. Working women organized
such services as day-care centers and milk distribution to families
with children, and discussed the rights of working women.
    See also: WOMEN AND WOMEN'S MOVEMENT.

POINSETT, Joel Roberts (1779-1851). *United States politician and
diplomat. Sent to South America by President Madison at the
beginning of the independence struggle in 1809, he arrived in
Chile during the *Patria Vieja and had considerable influence
on José Miguel *Carrera Verdugo, particularly in such matters
as the adoption of a national flag, publication of the *Aurora
de Chile and the drafting of the *Constitution of 1812. On the
completion of his mission, Poinsett was obliged to return overland
through Argentina because of James *Hillyar's presence in Valparaíso.

POLICE. The evolution of a national police force took several centuries in Chile, and was only achieved in the 1920s. Some
colonial *cabildos appointed night watchmen known as serenos;
those in the capital were put on a regular footing by Supreme
Director Bernardo *O'Higgins. In 1830 Diego *Portales Palazuelos
organized a complementary daytime force of vigilantes. For more
general enforcement of internal order, the colonial government
had created in 1758 a force of 50 mounted police, with the high-
sounding name of Dragones de la Reina (the Queen's Dragoons).
After independence, they became known as the Dragones de
Chile (Dragoons of Chile). Municipal police forces on the Anglo-
American pattern were introduced with the reform of *local government in 1891, but there was no effective policing of the countryside

until the formation of the Cuerpo de Policia in 1924. This was incorporated into a new national police force, the CUERPO DE CARABINEROS (q.v.) in 1927. The Carabineros have since then constituted Chile's only police body (if we exclude Chile's dreaded secret police, the *DINA, established by the *junta militar de gobierno de 1973, and the DINA's successor, the *Central Nacional de Informaciones).

POLITICAL ANARCHY. See: ANARQUIA POLITICA.

POLITICAL PARTIES. Until September 11, 1973, Chile was unique in Latin America for its almost uninterrupted tradition of democratic legality, which had evolved from a one-party rule at the time of independence to the multi-party system prevalent at the time of the overthrow of Socialist President Salvador *Allende Gossens. Soon afterwards, the *junta militar de gobierno de 1973 which replaced Allende outlawed all political parties that had been members of *Unidad Popular (i.e. all parties of the left), and declared the others (i.e. those of the right and center) to be in "indefinite recess." Through Decree Law no. 28 of November 16, 1973, the junta took over "the constituent, legislative and executive powers."

Although in 1936 Chile had had the incredible number of 36 political parties, as the 1970 presidential election approached, the political arena was largely dominated by just six parties. Imitating the French and Italian political spectrum, these six fell into a right-center-and-left framework. The right was represented by the *Partido Nacional, supported by the landed aristocracy, the wealthy industrialists and the upper middle class, and was a 1966 merger of the two historically dominant parties, the Conservatives and the Liberals. The *Partido Radical, the party of the middle class, and the *Partido Demócrata Cristiano, the strongest party in Chile and supported by the Roman Catholic *Church, constituted the center. The left was represented by the Socialist-Communist dominated six-party coalition known as Popular Unity (*Unidad Popular): the three major parties among these six were the *Partido Comunista Chileno, the *Partido Socialista, and the *Movimiento de Acción Popular Unitaria.

The triumph of Allende's leftist coalition brought to power a political elite pledged to the working class and to revolution. But the revolution was not to take place through a violent destruction of the country's political structure. Socialism was to be implemented peacefully and gradually through electoral and parliamentary procedures; it was to be multiclass and multiparty. The uniqueness of this Chilean experiment raised many questions both in Chile and abroad, and placed constraints on Allende's ability to effect such a revolution within the framework of a capitalist constitution.

Entries for individual Chilean parties and alliances will be found under the Spanish forms of their names. Most begin with the word "partido." Those that do not are as follows:

Acción Católica Chilena
Acción Chilena Anticomunista
Acción Nacional
Acción Popular Independiente
Acción Republicana
Acción Revolucionaria Socialista
Acuerdo Nacional
Alianza de Partidos y Fuerzas Populares
Alianza Democrática
Alianza Democrática de Chile
Alianza Liberal
Alianza Popular
Alianza Popular Libertadora
Bloque de Izquierda
Bloque de Saneaminento Democrático
Coalición
Comandos Populares
Concentración Nacional
Confederación Democrática
Confederación Republicana de Acción Cívica
Cuadrilátero
Dover Conspiracy
Estanqueros
Exaltados
Falange
Falange Conservadora
Falange Nacional
Falange Radical Agraria Socialista
Federación de Izquierda
Federación Nacional Popular
Federación Social Cristiana
Frente de Acción Popular
Frente del Pueblo
Frente Democrático de Chile
Frente Nacional del Pueblo
Frente Nacional Democrático
Frente Popular
Fusión Liberal-Conservadora
Izquierda Comunista
Izquierda Cristiana
Izquierda Nacional
Juventud Conservadora
Moderados
Movimiento de Acción Popular Unitaria
Movimiento de Emancipación de la Mujer Chilena
Movimiento de Izquierda Revolucionario
Movimiento de Recuperación Doctrinaria
Movimiento de Unidad Nacional
Movimiento Democrático Popular

Movimiento Nacional de Izquierda
Movimiento Nacional del Pueblo
Movimiento Nacional Socialista de Chile
Movimiento Nacionalista de Chile
Movimiento Republicano
Movimiento Revolucionario Nacional Sindicalista
Nacista
Nueva Acción Pública
Nueva Izquierda Democrática
Orden Socialista
Patria y Libertad
Pelucones
Pipiolos
Poder Popular
Realista
Regionalistas de Magallanes
Unidad Popular
Unión Demócrata Independiente
Unión Liberal
Unión Nacional
Unión Nacional Laborista
Unión Rebelde Comunista
Unión Republicana
Unión Revolucionaria Socialista
Unión Social Republicana de Asalariados de Chile
Unión Socialista
Unión Socialista Popular
Vanguardia Nacional del Pueblo
Vanguardia Popular Socialista

See also: CONSTITUTION OF 1980; REGISTRO ELECTORAL.

POPPER, Julius. Romanian adventurer who arrived in *Tierra del Fuego during the 1880s gold rush. Having great ambitions, he brought with him a uniformed private army and sought to exercise sovereignty, issuing his own stamps and coinage. Returning to Buenos Aires to defend himself in a civil law suit, he was found dead in his hotel room, allegedly of a heart attack.

POPULAR ALLIANCE. See: ALIANZA POPULAR.

POPULAR COMMANDOES. See: COMANDOS POPULARES.

POPULAR FRONT. See: FRENTE POPULAR.

POPULAR POWER. See: PODER POPULAR.

POPULAR SOCIALIST UNION. See: UNION SOCIALISTA POPULAR.

POPULAR UNITY. See: UNIDAD POPULAR.

POPULATION. Colonial. When the first Spaniards arrived in 1535,
Chile's inhabitants may have numbered as many as one million.
As elsewhere in the Americas, the introduction of European diseases (see: PUBLIC HEALTH), allied to the *conquistadors' excessive labor demands on those they brought under their control,
decimated the population. By 1570 there were perhaps 600,000
Indians (450,000 of them in *encomiendas), 7,000 whites, 17,000
of mixed race and a small number of Black slaves (see: AFRICAN
SLAVERY). The numbers of free *Araucanian Indians recovered
somewhat, but although estimates for the early 17th century have
gone as high as 270,000, there seems to have been little more
than 150,000 at the end of the colonial period. The population
under Spanish rule fell to about 275,000 (including 10,000 whites)
by the end of the 16th century. It did not grow significantly
until the 18th century, during the course of which it roughly
doubled to reach about 500,000 in the late 1790s.

Post-Independence. *Censuses begin in the 1830s: these naturally
exclude the *Mapuches prior to their effective incorporation into
the Republic in the 1880s. Successive totals are as follows:

Census of 1831-34	1,103,036
Census of October 1, 1843	1,083,701
Census of April 19, 1854	1,439,120
Census of April 19, 1865	1,819,223
Census of April 19, 1875	2,075,971
Census of November 28, 1885	2,507,005
Census of November 28, 1895	2,695,625
Census of November 28, 1907	3,231,022
Census of December 15, 1920	3,730,235
Census of November 27, 1930	4,287,445
Census of November 28, 1940	5,023,539
Census of April 25, 1952	5,932,995
Census of November 29, 1960	7,341,115
Census of April 22, 1970	8,884,768
Census of April 21, 1982	11,275,440

The 1980s. In the first quarter of 1984 the population was estimated as close to 12 million, increasing at an annual rate of 1.7
percent, one of the lowest rates of increase in South America.
This total did not include the more than one million Chileans who
live abroad (over 500,000 in Argentina alone), most of whom left
in the 1970s for political or economic reasons (see: EMIGRATION).
   Eight-tenths of these 12 million live in the Zona Central, which
stretches from the basin of the Aconcagua river (north and east
of *Valparaíso), to the *Bío-Bío river, some 300 miles to the south.
This is the country's historic heartland; it is also where most of
its economic development has been concentrated, and it has the
highest population density. Its center is the national capital,
*Santiago, the major magnet for internal migration, where some
four million Chileans now live (4,294,938 in Greater Santiago, 1982
census total).

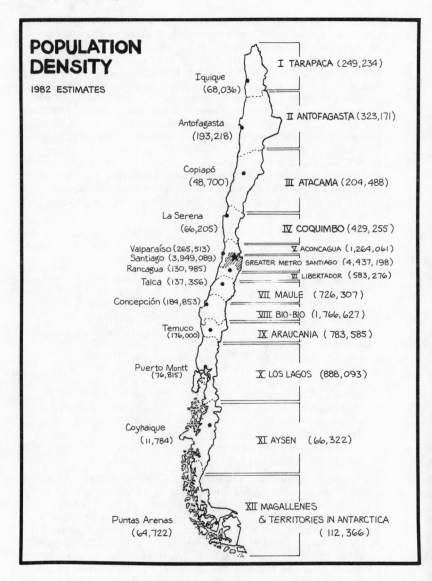

POPULATION DENSITY

1982 ESTIMATES

Iquique (68,036)

Antofagasta (193,218)

Copiapó (48,700)

La Serena (66,205)

Valparaíso (265,513)
Santiago (3,949,089)
Rancagua (130,985)
Talca (137,356)

Concepción (184,853)

Temuco (176,000)

Puerto Montt (76,815)

Coyhaique (11,784)

Puntas Arenas (64,722)

I TARAPACA (249,234)

II ANTOFAGASTA (323,171)

III ATACAMA (204,488)

IV COQUIMBO (429,255)

V ACONCAGUA (1,264,061)
GREATER METRO SANTIAGO (4,437,198)
VI LIBERTADOR (583,276)

VII MAULE (726,307)

VIII BIO-BIO (1,766,627)

IX ARAUCANIA (783,585)

X LOS LAGOS (888,093)

XI AYSEN (66,322)

XII MAGALLENES
& TERRITORIES IN ANTARCTICA
(112,366)

Chile's population is young: one third of it is under 15 years old, and only 15 percent are (in the early 1980s) older than 50 years. The crude birth rate was 37 per 1,000 in 1960, but dropped to 28 per 1,000 in the 1970s and was estimated as 22.3 per 1,000 in 1983. The family planning programs of the Eduardo *Frei Montalva and Salvador *Allende Gossens administrations are claimed to have affected over 70 percent of women of childbearing age. The post-1974 regime, however, has launched a "back to maternity" campaign, eliminating the availability of contraceptives and birth control information. The aboriginal birth rate is high; see: MAPUCHES.

Since 1920, the transformation of Chilean life has been reflected in the growth of urban centers. The proportion of town dwellers in the total population, which was 27 percent in 1875 and 46 percent in 1920, grew to 29 percent in 1960 and 80 percent in 1980. Because of this rapid urbanization, Chile suffers an acute *housing shortage. In Greater *Santiago alone, one of every five inhabitants lives in a shanty town (población *callampa). With rural migration rising continuously, all Chilean cities share this problem, but Santiago is unique, quantitatively and in its response.

Half the nation suffers malnutrition. According to the International Labor Office, 12 percent suffer simple malnutrition, 27.3 percent serious malnutrition and 11 percent desperate malnutrition. More than 600,000 children under 9 years of age are suffering acute malnutrition.

Chileans are remarkably homogenous. An estimated two-thirds are *mestizo (of mixed European and Indian—predominantly Araucanian) descent. The slow, consistent amalgamation of diverse European groups (see: IMMIGRATION) with Amerindians has produced a highly uniform culture. Since last century only a trickle of new people have moved across the mountains, desert and sea into the central zone. Today less than 2 percent of the population are foreign born. Population density varies from 82 per square mile in central Chile, to 16 per square mile in Forest Chile, down to a mere 2 per square mile in the Archipelago (from *Puerto Montt to *Punta Arenas). Overall infant mortality is 56 per 1,000 live births (see: PUBLIC HEALTH).

Nearly 90 percent of the population consider themselves Roman Catholics (see: CHURCH, The—The Modern-day Church; RELIGIOUS PRACTICES). The highly patriarchal family life of Chileans is similar to that of other Latin countries. Among the lower segments of society, poverty exerts an overriding influence on family structure (see: EMPLOYMENT).

See also: HOUSING AND CONSTRUCTION; INTERNAL MIGRATION; LABOR; LITERACY; SANTIAGO; WOMEN AND THE WOMEN'S MOVEMENT.

PORT FAMINE. See: PUERTO DE HAMBRE.

PORTALES CEA Y CIA. See: SOCIEDAD PORTALES CEA Y CIA.

PORTALES PALAZUELOS, Diego (1793-1837). Born to a prosperous
and important family--his father was a member of the *junta de
gobierno de 1812--Portales became a very astute businessman and
a powerful politician. He spoke for the landed aristocracy and
the wealthy traders, showing contempt for the poor and the
toilers in the fields. In 1824 Supreme Director Ramón *Freire
Serrano granted his company, the *Sociedad Portales Cea y Cia.,
a monopoly of tobacco, tea and liquor retailing (see: ESTANCO).
The concession stirred up a storm of abuse, but Portales insisted
that it was time for business to play a greater role in politics.
He then organized a conservative political group known as the
*estanqueros, who later became members of the *pelucones' party.
On April 3, 1830, Portales became President José Tomás *Ovalle
Bezanilla's minister of the interior and foreign affairs and of
war. The rout of the *pipiolos at the Battle of *Lircay two
weeks later delivered the country into the hands of the pelucones,
and for all practical purposes Portales became dictator of Chile,
retaining effective power until his death. His mission was to
impose law and order in government, and he even spoke of the
"religion of government."
     The *Constitution of 1833 embodied Portales' belief in the con-
centration of power and in a highly centralized government. The
1836-39 War with the *Peru-Bolivia Confederation of Andrés de
*Santa Cruz y Calahumada is generally attributed to Portales
determination to destroy the newly united state which he saw as
a political and economic threat to Chile. Early in the conflict,
however, Portales was killed in the Mutiny of *Quillota, an uprising attributed to the machinations of the Confederation's minister in *Santiago.
     By then, however, Portales had practically created the modern
Chilean republic in a form that was not substantially changed until the overthrow of President José Manuel *Balmaceda Fernández
in the *Civil War of 1891.

PORTILLO. A ski resort in central Chile, three hours (139 km) by
train from *Santiago, on the *Transandine Railway near the
Argentine border. The finest ski resort in Chile, it was the site
of the 1966 Winter Olympics.

PORTS AND HARBORS. While Chile's difficult topography has always
made sea transport extremely important, especially in the south,
the country has few natural harbors affording adequate protection
against the prevailing southwesterly winds, hardly any rivers are
navigable for oceangoing vessels, and the steeply sloping seabed
along most of the coast makes artificial harbor construction difficult
and costly. There are in all about 70 ports. Twelve of these
are considered major and are for general cargo: all are administered by the state-owned *EMPORCHI. *Valparaíso is the chief

and best known, with a 1,747,000 metric *ton annual capacity,
but *San Antonio, almost as capacious (1,600,000 tonnes), is
actually nearer *Santiago. The *Bío-Bío complex (*Talcahuano,
Lirquén and San Vicente) is being expanded to a capacity of 4
million tonnes. *Antofagasta is very important, being an outlet
for southern *Bolivia as well as for the mineral wealth of northern
Chile. *Arica was an open roadstead until 1966, moving only
120,000 tonnes a year, but its new harbor (whose hinterland includes western Bolivia and the extreme south of *Peru) can move
one million tonnes. *Iquique, *Puerto Montt and *Coquimbo have
annual capacities of 700,000, 400,000 and 220,000 tonnes respectively. The remaining major ports are *Punta Arenas, *Chañaral and
*Valdivia. Twenty other ports are considered minor, and the
rest are used mainly for fishing boats.

During the 19th century Punta Arenas and Valparaíso had
importance as ports of call on the route through the *Strait of
Magellan or around *Cape Horn to the west coast of the Americas,
but such trade ended with the 1914 opening of the Panama Canal.
Even Punta Arenas is nearer New York via the canal (6,863
miles) than via the Strait (8,000 miles). More recently the extension of *highways and the growth of road and *air transport
has taken some traffic away from Chilean coastal shipping.

Chile's ports have also been affected by *earthquakes and their
accompanying tidal waves, and not always entirely for the worse.
The 1960 'quake removed sandbanks and improved navigation at
the mouths of several southern rivers.

See also: MERCHANT MARINE.

POSTAL SERVICES. Colonial. Before the reforms of *Charles III,
government mail between Spain and the Indies was conveyed in
special navíos de aviso, small, swift naval vessels used exclusively
for this purpose. Commercial and private mail was left to hap-
hazard private arrangements with individual ship owners. A
regular, government-provided service for all types of mail, the
Correo Marítimo de las Indias, was decreed in August 1764. The
first ship on the South American run sailed from Coruña March
11, 1767, arriving in Montevideo on May 31. Frequency was increased from four to six sailings a year in 1771, and a connecting
overland service was added via Mendoza and the *Upsallata Pass
to *Santiago. At the same time Chile acquired an internal service
between 50 post offices from *Copiapó in the north to *Valdivia
in the south. An overland service to Lima was introduced by
way of Mendoza, Tucumán and Potosí.

Although Chile's normal trading route continued to be via
Panamá, mail was sent via the River Plate for speed: a sailing
vessel could take as long as eight months to battle contrary winds
from Panamá to *Valparaíso. There were also dangers from
*pirates in the Pacific.

This colonial mail service to Europe declined in regularity in
face of war conditions after 1779, and finally ceased with the

Buenos Aires May Revolution of 1810.

Since Independence. William *Wheelwright's Pacific Steam
Navigation Company provided a private mail service to El Callao
Peru, from 1841. This was soon extended to Panamá City, whence
the U.S.-owned Pacific Steamship Company provided a link to
San Francisco, and, after 1846, mule trains to Chagres connected
precariously with the Royal Mail Line's service to Southampton.
This link with Europe improved greatly with the 1855 construction
of an American-built railroad from Panamá City to the new Port
Colón (which replaced Chagres).

Modern inland postal facilities (and issue of the first postage
stamps) began in Chile in 1853, but the government did not take
over responsibility for international mail until 1888. Chile did
not join the Universal Postal Union until July 24, 1908. Chile
was a founder member of the Convenio Postal Hispanoamericano
(November 15, 1920) and of its successor, the Pan-American
Postal Union of September 15, 1921.

The Dirección General de Correos (General Post Office) was
a branch successively of the ministerios del *Interior (to 1887),
de *Industria y Obras Públicas (1887-1912) and de Industria,
Obras Públicas y Ferrocarriles (from 1912). In 1924 it briefly attained ministerial status as the Ministerio de Correos y Telégrafos
but was demoted the next year to a mere Departamento de Correos
(Post Office Department) under the Ministerio de *Obras Públicas,
Comercio y Vías de Comunicaciones (and its successors), until
the creation in 1973 of a Ministerio de Transportes y Telecomunicaciones.

In 1985 Chile had 1,486 post offices, handling annually some
68 million pieces of domestic mail and 35 million of foreign mail.

POSITIVISM. A philosophical system based on science as the only
valid knowledge, and facts as the only possible objects of knowledge. Positivism was originated by the French thinker Auguste
Comte in the 1820s, and by the end of the 19th century it had
become widespread in Western Europe and in three Latin American
countries: Mexico, Brazil and, to a lesser degree, Chile. Comte
believed that knowledge had to go through three different theoretical states: the fictitious state (theology), the abstract state
(metaphysics) and the positive state (science). His system was
based solely on positive, observable, scientific facts and their
relation to each other. All speculation or search for ultimate
origin was rejected. Progress through law and order for Comte
was a necessary norm of human history, and capitalism was the
ultimate stage that man would reach after industrialization.

Comte believed that society would regain its unity and its
organization based on a new spiritual power, that of the scientists,
and a new temporal power, that of the industrialists. The system
would also create a "religion of humanity" and a sociocracy made
up of a corporation of positivist philosophers. Education would
be in the hands of the élite, as would government. It is easy

to see how the cult of "law and order" and "government by the élite" turned into dictatorship in Mexico and Brazil. If the same did not happen in Chile, it can be explained by the fact that Chilean Presidents, from the time of independence through the end of the 19th century, had quasi-dictatorial powers. Positivism, never very strong in Chile, found adherents from two groups: the Liberals and the Free Masons. These groups were opposed to the excesses of theology, to ecclesiastical supremacy, and to religious training in the public schools. With the advent of the *parliamentary regime (1891-1925), Positivism lost its appeal in Chile.

POTRERILLOS. The third of Chile's great *copper deposits acquired by *United States capital in the early 20th century, Potrerillos lies in a ravine in *Atacama province at about 12,000 ft. Its discoverers, Felipe Tapia and Patricio Vinuelas, sold it in 1906 to the Compañía Minera de Potrerillos, which was purchased in 1913 by William *Braden and later sold to *Anaconda. Building the 90-km (56-mile) access *railway from the main line at Pueblo Hundido was a masterpiece of engineering by Swiss George Montandon, who was killed during the construction. This and other difficulties of installation delayed any effective exploitation of the deposits until 1923, and even then the mine proved a disappointment. The ore was low grade (1.4) and between 1927 and 1959, when it was exhausted, only 50,000 short (U.S.) tons of copper were produced. In the latter year the Chileans were lucky to find a new mine located 12.5 air miles from Potrerillos. See: SALVADOR, El.

POTS AND PANS DEMONSTRATIONS. During the administration of Salvador *Allende Gossens (1970-73) middle- and upper-class women began to organize to protest shortages in food and the government's imposition of rationing of milk and other basic foodstuffs, by marching in the streets banging empty cooking vessels: the Marchas de las ollas vacías. Such demonstrations had a precedent in Brazil during the João Goulart administration (1961-64) which was overthrown on the night of March 31/April 1, 1964, by the Brazilian army, assisted by the *United States government through its *Central Intelligence Agency. In Chile, too, the C.I.A. was involved in providing financial assistance to the protesting women. After the economy took a downturn in the early 1980s, women once again took to the streets to protest the monetarist policies of strongman Augusto *Pinochet Ugarte. This time, however, women from every social class participated--and clearly now without the encouragement or help of the C.I.A. Pots and pans have become an effective tool for the expression of discontent in Chile. Nor is it necessary to march. The cacophony of pans beaten in unison throughout the city (el caceroleo) by women in their kitchens is an audible outburst of protest as effective as the more visible (and more easily repressed) street march.

POULTRY FARMING. See: LIVESTOCK.

PRADO ARANGUIZ, Jorge José. Minister of *agriculture since April 1982. A lawyer who studied agriculture in France and Norway, he was vice-president of the Confederación de Productores Agrícolas, 1973-75.

PRADO CALVO, Pedro (1886-1952). Chilean novelist and poet of distinction, considered Chile's leading stylist of modernist prose. From 1915 to 1916 Pedro Prado presided over "Los Diez" (the Ten), an association of writers, painters, poets, architects, sculptors and musicians. His major works are Alsino 1920, an allegory based on the myth of Icarus, in which the author dramatized the condition of the Chilean peasant, and Un juez rural (a country judge), 1924. He has also written La casa abandonada (the deserted house), 1912, in poetic prose, and La reina de Rapa Nui (the queen of Easter Island), 1914, a novel of adventure. Prado is also known for his essays, parables and prose poems. In the 1940s he was Chilean minister in Bogotá.

PRAT CHACON, Arturo (1848-1879). Chilean naval hero of the War of the *Pacific. After a few years of schooling in *Santiago, he entered the Naval Academy in *Valparaíso. He took part in the War of 1865-67 with *Spain, and became a captain in 1873. Throughout his career he pursued studies in mathematics, astronomy and other sciences associated with naval operations, and also managed to obtain a law degree. During the War of the Pacific he was commander of the *Esmeralda. His martyrdom at *Iquique made him the naval hero of the war. The anniversary, May 21, is now Chilean *Navy Day, when the country remembers its national hero who, although his ship was hopelessly outgunned by the Peruvian ironclad Huáscar, preferred to die rather than surrender.

PRAT ECHAURREN, Jorge (1918-   ). Lawyer and right-wing politician. In 1941, the year he graduated, he became president of the Youth section of the Conservative Party (Juventud del *Partido Conservador). He entered banking in 1952, becoming president of the State Bank (Banco del Estado de Chile) a year later. In 1954 President Carlos *Ibáñez del Campo made him finance minister. In the 1964 presidential election he revived the neo-Nazi *Acción Nacional party as a personal vehicle to back his candidacy. He withdrew just before the election, but ran unsuccessfully for the Senate in 1965. The following year Acción Nacional was a founder member of the new *Partido Nacional.

PRATS GONZALEZ, Carlos (1915-1974). Commander-in-Chief of the Chilean *army from October 1969, when he was appointed to succeed the murdered René *Schneider Cereau until August 1973, when he was forced to resign in favor of General Augusto

*Pinochet Ugarte. A loyal supporter of Socialist President (1970-73) Salvador *Allende Gossens, his ousting was a necessary preliminary to the *coup d'état then being plotted by other military leaders. He was obliged to go into exile after the coup, and left for Buenos Aires with a safe-conduct pass on September 15. He was, allegedly, followed by agents of the *DINA (secret police) and a year later, on September 30, 1974, he and his wife Sofía Cuthbert de Prats were blown to pieces by a bomb planted in their car.

While in exile, Prats had been careful to avoid any involvement in Argentine politics, as well as any comments regarding the Chilean *junta. But Chile's strongman, Pinochet, feared him all the same, seeing him as a threat to the *military regime. It was in fact obvious from letters Prats sent to Allende's widow, Hortensia *Bussy de Allende, and other exiles, that he had little respect for his former subordinates who had usurped power. He had also maintained contacts with members of the former *Unidad Popular coalition, and had been visited by members of the *Partido Demócrata Cristiano. In a letter to Allende's widow he wrote that he was being watched by a "curious and mixed network of informants." After his death, his apartment was raided and many documents, including his memoirs, disappeared. His diary, however, was found, and was later published in Mexico with the title Una vida por la legalidad (a life within the law), 1976; in Buenos Aires, as Diario, 1984; and finally in Santiago, as Memorias, 1985.

In it Prats complained that neither Allende nor the government parties knew "how profound the North American influence is in our armed forces, and especially on the mentality of the Chilean military man." He was especially critical of military personnel being subservient to the Pentagon and being trained at *United States military schools of counter-insurgency in Panama, Peru and the U.S. He accused them of not liberating a nation from "the enemy within," but rather making it dependent upon "the enemy without," an oblique reference to the role of the United States in Allende's demise.

Prats had a distinguished military career, including a year spent at Fort Leavenworth, Kansas. He also taught at the *Escuela Militar. During the last months of the Allende government, he became convinced that the politization of the Chilean *armed forces was unavoidable. Nevertheless, as commander-in-chief, he urged soldiers and officers to remain loyal to the President, respect Chile's social realities, and participate in the task of developing the country. He was angered that some of the top brass were zealous in curbing terrorism perpetrated by the left, but lax when it came to stopping the right from dangerously stockpiling more arms. He had called such practice the regionalization of terror, from Washington, D.C., to the tip of South America.

Prats was not the only Chilean leader in exile to be reached by the tentacles of the DINA (q.v.). Other victims included Orlando LETELIER DEL SOLAR and Bernardo LEIGHTON GUZMAN (qq.vv.).

PREMIO NACIONAL DE LITERATURA (National Literature Prize). The Chilean equivalent of the *United States Pulitzer Prize for Literature. Given each year to the country's most outstanding literary figure.

PRESA CASANUEVA, Rafael de la (1907-   ). Businessman who was elected to the Chamber of Deputies in 1954 as an Agrarian Labor Party (*Partido Agrario Laborista) member. That same year he was one of a splinter group that left to form the *Partido Agrario Laborista Recuperacionista. In 1960 he joined the *Partido Democrático Nacional (PADENA), a left-of-center party belonging to the *Frente de Acción Popular, which backed the presidential candidacy of Salvador *Allende Gossens. This caused dissention during the 1964 presidential campaign and Presa Casanueva led a schism in 1963 which formed a new party, *Nueva Izquierda Democrática, to support the presidential campaign of Eduardo *Frei Montalva. Frei won and in 1965 appointed Presa Casanueva as ambassador to Portugal.

PRESIDENTS OF CHILE. The decision to name the head of the Chilean Republic the President, rather than SUPREME DIRECTOR (q.v.), was taken by *Congress July 4, 1826. Holders of that office have been the following (vp = vice-president or interim president):

Manuel *Blanco Encalada (July-September 1826)
Agustín *Eyzaguirre Arechavala (September 1826-January 1827), vp
Ramón *Freire Serrano (February -May 1827)
Francisco Antonio *Pinto Díaz (May 1827-July 1829)
Francisco Ramón *Vicuña Larraín (July 1829-February 1830)
Francisco *Ruiz Tagle Portales (February-March 1830)
José Tomás *Ovalle Bezanilla (March 1830-March 1831)
Fernando *Errázuriz Aldunate (March-September 1831), vp
Joaquín *Prieto Vial (September 1831-September 1841)
Manuel *Bulnes Prieto (September 1841-September 1851)
Jorge *Montt Torres (September 1851-September 1861)
José Joaquín *Pérez Mascayano (September 1861-September 1871)
Federico *Errázuriz Zañartu (September 1871-September 1876)
Aníbal *Pinto Garmendia (September 1876-September 1881)
Domingo *Santa María González (September 1881-September 1886)
José Manuel *Balmaceda Fernández (September 1886-August 1891)
Manuel *Baquedano González (August 1891), vp
[*Junta de Gobierno de 1891 (August-December 1891)]
Jorge *Montt Alvarez (December 1891-September 1896)
Federico *Errázuriz Echaurren (September 1896-May 1901)
Aníbal *Zañartu Zañartu (May-September 1901), vp

Germán *Riesco Errázuriz (September 1901–September 1906)
Pedro *Montt Montt (September 1906–August 1910)
Elias *Fernández Albano (August–September 1910), vp
Emiliano Figueroa Larraín (September–December 1910), vp
Ramón *Barros Luco (December 1910–December 1915)
Juan Luis *Sanfuentes Andonaegui (December 1915–December 1920)
Arturo *Alessandri Palma (December 1920–October 1925; interrupt-
ed by the *Junta militar de gobierno de 1924 and *Junta
militar de gobierno de 1925, September 1924–March 1925)
Luis *Barros Borgoño (October–December 1925)
Emiliano Figueroa Larraín––again (December 1925–April 1927)
Carlos *Ibáñez del Campo (April 1927–July 1931)
Pedro Opazo Letelier (July 1931), vp
Juan Esteban *Montero Rodríguez (July–August 1931), vp
Manuel Trucco Franzani (August–December 1931), vp
Juan Esteban Montero Rodríguez––again (December 1931–June
1932)
[*Junta de gobierno de 1932 (June–July 1932)]
Carlos *Dávila Espinosa (July–September 1932)
Bartolomé *Blanche Espejo (September 1932), vp
Abraham *Oyandel Urrutia (October–December 1932), vp
Arturo Alessandri Palma––again (December 1932–December 1938)
Pedro *Aguirre Cerda (December 1938–November 1941)
Jerónimo Méndez Arancibia (November 1941–April 1942), vp
Juan Antonio *Rios Morales (April 1942–June 1946)
Alfredo *Duhalde Vázquez (June–October 1946), vp
Juan Antonio Iribarren Cabezas (October–November 1946), vp
Gabriel *González Videla (November 1946–November 1952)
Carlos Ibáñez del Campo––again (November 1952–November 1958)
Jorge *Alessandri Rodríguez (November 1958–November 1964)
Eduardo *Frei Montalva (November 1964–November 1970)
Salvador *Allende Gossens (November 1970–September 1973)
[*Junta militar de gobierno de 1973 (September 1973–)]
Augusto *Pinochet Ugarte (Head of Junta from September 1973;
Supreme Head of State from June 26, 1974; President of Chile
from December 17, 1974)

PRESS, The. See: NEWSPAPERS; PERIODICAL PRESS.

PRESS FREEDOM. See: CENSORSHIP.

PRIETO [LETELIER], Jenaro (1889–1946). Journalist on the staff of
El *Diario ilustrado and deputy for *Santiago. His works include
the novels Un muerto de mal criterio (a defunct of poor judgment),
1926 and El socio, 1928 (translated as The partner, 1931); Humo
de pipa (pipe smoke), 1955; his reminiscences La casa vieja (the
old house), 1957 and the posthumous Antología humorística (humor-
ous anthology), 1973.

PRIETO VIAL, Joaquín (1786–1854). A career *army officer who was

President of Chile for two terms, 1831-36; 1836-41. Runner-up for the presidency in 1829, he was passed over by a partisan *Congress for the position of vice-president in favor of Joaquín *Vicuña Larraín. This was regarded by the *pelucones (conservatives) as a breach of the constitution and led to the *Civil War of 1829-30 in which Prieto Vial led the insurgent army. The rout of the *pipiolos (liberals) at the Battle of *Lircay delivered Chile into the power of the pelucones. In February 1830 the Congreso de Plenipotenciarios had elected Francisco *Ruiz Tagles Portales provisional President, but six weeks later he was persuaded by Diego *Portales Palazuelos to resign in favor of his vice-president José Tomás *Ovalle Bezanilla. When Ovalle resigned for health reasons a few days before his death, the Congreso de Plenipotenciarios elected Prieto Vial president, March 15, 1831, and a thirty-year Conservative rule began.

Prieto Vial sought to impose order on Chile's unruly factions, retaining Portales as war minister. Prieto Vial embodied Portales' belief in the concentration of power in a highly centralized government, and promulgated the *Constitution of 1833--a document that stood until 1925. Prieto paid considerable attention to the Republic's economic problems. Government expenditure was curtailed and fiscal administration tightened. New port facilities were built at *Valparaíso and steps taken to encourage the growth of a *merchant marine. In 1832 Portales had left political life, satisfied that his work was done, and had gone back into business. He returned however as interior and foreign minister in November 1835, becoming also acting justice minister in February 1837. Rivalry between the ports of Valparaíso and El Callao in Peru, and Portales' fear of the potential power of the new *Peru-Bolivia Confederation, led to war (1836-39). Chile won, the confederation was broken up, and its instigator, General Andrés de *Santa Cruz y Calahumada, was sent into exile.

During Prieto Vial's second term, the government became more stable. Material and cultural progress was made, and Chileans began the task of building a nation. Venezuelan-born Andrés *Bello López was commissioned to stimulate intellectual activities and improve education. Chile had shown its military superiority over *Peru and *Bolivia (in a surprise attack on El Callao, her *navy had captured the entire enemy fleet). So, by the time of the presidential election of 1841, Chileans were satisfied with their Conservative government and chose to continue it with Manuel *Bulnes Prieto, victor in the war with Santa Cruz, and President Prieto's nephew. Prieto himself became military governor of Valparaíso, and sat in the Senate from 1843 to 1845.

PRINTING. For a long time the history of printing in Chile was shrouded in mystery. It now seems that the country's first printing press was that of José de los Reyes, which was functioning by 1697. This was only used however to produce playing cards and engraved pictures of saints. The first typographic press was brought to the *Universidad de San Felipe in *Santiago by a German Jesuit, Father Carlos Haimhausen, on May 6, 1748. It was used in a desultory fashion by the university beadle, José Camillo, to print invitations, official announcements and other trifles. If any books were printed before 1776, none has survived. We only know that Father Haimhausen died in May 1767, four months before the *Jesuits were expelled from Chile, leaving the press behind.

The first known Chilean imprint was a nine-page pamphlet entitled <u>Modo de ganar el jubileo santo</u> (method of gaining holy indulgences), which appeared, poorly printed, in 1776. José Toribio *Medina Zavala records 21 other Chilean publications between 1780 and 1811, and 36 others have since come to light. There is strong evidence that all were printed on Haimhausen's press. Almost all were concerned with religious matters. It is, however, essentially correct to say that Chile had no press before independence. Apart from these 47 works, all writings intended for publication were sent abroad: either to Spain, or occasionally to Lima (which had had a press since 1583) or to Buenos Aires (from about 1800).

Chilean printing really begins with the American press imported by Mateo Arnaldo *Hoebel in 1812 to produce the country's first newspaper, the *<u>Aurora de Chile</u>.

For subsequent developments, see: NEWSPAPERS; PERIODICAL PRESS; PUBLISHERS AND PUBLISHING.

PROJECT CAMELOT. A social science project that came into being in 1964 with funds provided by the *United States Department of the Army. Its purpose was to study the likelihood of insurgent movements developing in Chile, and the ways that might be used to arrest them. According to the U.S. army, the project was to be a three-to four-year effort funded at about US$ 1.5 million annually. A large amount of primary data collection in the field was planned, as well as the extensive utilization of already available data on social, economic and political functions. The project, with its implicit connotations of counterrevolution and possible U.S. intervention, was strongly criticized by the Chilean government, causing an uproar in political as well as academic circles. After a year of adverse publicity, a Congressional hearing, State Department censure, a Presidential veto, and growing leftist agitation in Chile, the project was cancelled.

PROPRIEDAD AUSTRAL, Ministerio de. The Ministry of Southern Property was created by Statute no. 4660 on October 31, 1929. Its primary function was to supervise Chilean possessions in the south, including *Antarctica. Its name was changed on April 3, 1931, to the Ministerio de *Tierras, Bienes Nacionales y Colonización.

PROTESTANTISM. Although Roman Catholicism was the established *church in Chile until 1925, Protestant worship in private was tolerated from the early days of the Republic, and a gradually widening freedom of worship was tacitly conceded as the 19th century advanced. English immigrants brought Anglicanism with them, and the later waves of German *immigration included many Lutherans. These creeds, however, have hardly expanded beyond the original immigrant communities and their descendants. Active proselytizing has been virtually confined to the more populist American Pentecostal sects. Their success, particularly among the poor in the big cities, has been considerable, and current estimates of the total number of Protestants in Chile range from 500,000 to 800,000.

    See also: RELIGIOUS PRACTICES.

PROVINCES. The two intendencies (*intendencias) of *Santiago and *Concepción into which Chile was divided in 1786 were subdivided into 14 and 8 partidos, respectively (see: COLONIAL ADMINIS-TRATION). The northern part of Santiago was made the separate intendency of *Coquimbo in 1811, and shortly afterwards the intendencies were redesignated provinces (provincias). During the brief flirtation with *federalism, the provinces were so increased in number as almost to equal in size the old partidos: there was in fact some correspondence in boundaries. Following the conquest of *Chiloé, a law of August 1826 fixed them at eight: Coquimbo, *Aconcagua, Santiago, *Colchagua, *Maule, Concepción, *Valdivia and Chiloé. Given Chile's small population at the time, most of these were too small to be viable as federal units, which largely accounts for the failure of federalism.

    In 1833 a new province of *Talca was carved out of Colchagua. Manuel *Bulnes Prieto's presidency saw the elevation of *Valparaíso to provincial status, at the expense of Santiago and Aconcagua (1842); the creation of *Atacama province from the northern part of Coquimbo (1843); and the formation of Nuble in 1848 from parts of Maule and Concepción. Maule also lost territory in 1873 when *Linares was made a province.

    The settlement of the territory of the *Araucanian Indians caused further loss of area by Concepción in 1852 and 1869 to form, and then enlarge, the province of *Arauco. In 1861 *Llanquihue, newly settled by German immigrants, was carved out of Valdivia and mainland Chiloé. In 1875 the vast province of Arauco was reduced by the formation of *Bío-Bío (which also took territory from Concepción) and the Territory of *Angol. Following the suppression of the last Araucanian rising (see: MAPUCHES) in 1883, the new southern provinces of *Malleco and *Cautín were formed from the Territory of *Angol (with accretions from *Arauco), 1887.

    Meanwhile, in densely populated central Chile, the department of *Rancagua, minus its coastal section, had been taken from Santiago to form the new province of *O'Higgins (1883). Further north, Chile's acquisitions in the War of the *Pacific were

REGION	CAPITAL OF REGION	PROVINCES	CAPITALS OF PROVINCES
I TARAPACÁ	IQUIQUE	ARICA IQUIQUE	ARICA IQUIQUE
II ANTOFAGASTA	ANTOFAGASTA	TOCOPILLA ANTOFAGASTA EL LOA	TOCOPILLA ANTOFAGASTA CALAMA
III ATACAMA	COPIAPÓ	CHAÑARAL COPIAPÓ HUASCO	CHAÑARAL COPIAPÓ HUASCO
IV COQUIMBO	LA SERENA	ELQUI LIMARÍ CHOAPA	LA SERENA OVALLE ILLAPEL
V ACONCAGUA	VALPARAÍSO	VALPARAÍSO SAN ANTONIO QUILLOTA PETORCA SAN FELIPE LOS ANDES ISLA DE PASCUA	VALPARAÍSO SAN ANTONIO QUILLOTA LA LIGUA SAN FELIPE LOS ANDES HANGA ROA
VI DEL LIBERTADOR GENERAL BERNARDO O'HIGGINS	RANCAGUA	CHACAPOAL COLCHAGUA	RANCAGUA SAN FERNANDO
VII DEL MAULE	TALCA	CURICÓ TALCA LINARES	CURICÓ TALCA LINARES
VIII BÍO-BÍO	CONCEPCIÓN	ÑUBLE CONCEPCIÓN ARAUCO BÍO - BÍO	CHILLÁN CONCEPCIÓN LEBU LOS ÁNGELES
IX DE LA ARAUCANÍA	TEMUCO	MALLECO CAUTÍN	ANGOL TEMUCO
X DE LOS LAGOS	PUERTO MONTT	VALDIVIA OSORNO LLANQUIHUE CHILOÉ	VALDIVIA OSORNO PUERTO MONTT CASTRO
XI AYSÉN DEL GENERAL CARLOS IBÁÑEZ DEL CAMPO	COYHAIQUE	AYSÉN GENERAL CARRERA CAPITÁN PRAT	PUERTO AYSÉN CHILE CHICO COCHRANE
XII MAGALLANES Y ANT- ARTICA CHILENA	PUNTA ARENAS	ÚLTIMA ESPERANZA MAGALLANES TIERRA DEL FUEGO ANTÁRTICA CHILENA	PUERTO NATALES PUNTA ARENAS PORVENIR PUERTO WILLIAMS

SANTIAGO, THE SEAT OF GOVERNMENT, AND THE GREATER METROPOLITAN AREA, ARE LOCATED WEST OF ACONCAGUA (REGION V), BUT ARE NOT INCORPORATED IN ANY OF THE TWELVE REGIONS. (LIKE THE DISTRICT OF COLUMBIA IN THE UNITED STATES, WHICH IS NOT PART OF ANY OF THE FIFTY STATES.)

constituted the provinces of *Tacna and *Tarapacá in 1884, plus *Antofagasta in 1888: a grand total of 23 provinces.

The early 20th century saw a number of changes, most of them during the presidency of Carlos *Ibáñez del Campo (1927-31). With the settlement of the *Tacna question (1929), Tacna itself was returned to Peru, and the remaining portion of Tacna province (which included *Arica) was made part of Tarapacá. A number of small exchanges of territory were effected between central provinces. O'Higgins lost to Santiago and Colchagua; Colchagua was also enlarged at the expense of Curicó. Maule's department of Itatá was accreted to Ñuble; Valdivia lost Villarica to Cautín, and so on. In the south, *Osorno was carved out of *Valdivia and *Aysén out of Magallanes at the same time as the Territory of Magallanes was raised to the status of a province (1929). Thus the final number of traditional provinces was 25.

Each province was headed by an *intendant, appointed by the President for a three-year term, and assisted by assemblymen. After 1833, provinces were divided into departamentos (under appointed gobernadores): they totaled 82 in 1920 and 87 in 1973. The departments, in turn, were subdivided into subdelegations (under appointed subdelegados), and these into districts under inspectors. Provinces generally had three to four departments each, although *Santiago had six, Tarapacá before 1929 only two, and Aysén, one. For LOCAL GOVERNMENT (q.v.), the basic unit after 1891 was the commune, corresponding in area to the subdelegation.

The traditional provinces were abolished by the 1974 reorganization (see: REGIONS AND ADMINISTRATIVE RESTRUCTURING), although some of the 12 new regions correspond exactly to former provinces. The regions, each under an intendant (aided, on paper, by a regional council), were subdivided into 40 redesigned provinces (some of which corresponded to former departments), with a special regime for Gran Santiago. The table on page 417 lists the present regions and the new provinces, with their respective capitals.

PROYECTO DE REGLAMIENTO PROVISORIO PARA LAS PROVINCIAS.
The "Project for the Provisional Ordinance to Demarcate the Chilean Provinces" was put forward in 1825 by members of the *Partido Federalista. It recommended a division of the Republic into eight provinces, as federal units, with each province to elect its own governor. In respect of the division into provinces, the project was enacted by a provisional decree of January 31, 1826, and a definitive law of August 30, 1826. See: PROVINCES.

PUBLIC FINANCES. At the time of independence, Chile was one of the poorest South American states. Revenue from TAXES (q.v.) was only 2.1 million *pesos a year in the 1830s and 8.2 million in the 1860s. The government depended heavily on foreign loans, which before World War One were mainly British, beginning with the £1 million raised on the London money market in 1822. Although exports (*copper, *wheat, *silver, *guano, *nitrates) increased tenfold in value over the half-century from 1825, an economic downturn in the mid-1870s produced a fiscal crisis that was an important cause of the War of the *Pacific. The resultant acquisition of new territories in the north produced a nitrate boom which revolutionized Chile's finances: state revenue rose from 28.9 million pesos in 1882 to 138.5 million pesos in 1902.

The slump following World War I and, in particular, falling nitrate sales (taxes on which were the government's chief revenue) imposed severe financial constraints on the first presidency of Arturo ALESSANDRI PALMA (q.v.). Government revenue suffered even more in the DEPRESSION OF THE 1930s (q.v.), and Chile's fiscal recovery owed much to the policies of Gustavo ROSS SANTA MARIA (q.v.) who was finance minister from 1932 until 1938. Taxes were not, however, increased sufficiently. Despite quite considerable inflows of FOREIGN AID (q.v.) since World War II, growing public sector deficits fueled an INFLATION (q.v.) that eventually peaked in 1974 at 504 percent per annum.

Drastic deflationary fiscal reform under President Augusto *Pinochet Ugarte, including the introduction of a 20 percent value-added tax (which was soon providing a third of all government revenue), slashed the public sector deficit and, consequently, the inflation rate. When the ECONOMY (q.v.) collapsed, however, in the early 1980s, foreign pressure was able to force the Chilean government into assuming responsibility for the country's enormous private foreign indebtedness, thereby increasing the public sector deficit once again--and inflation with it.

PUBLIC HEALTH. During the colonial period, Chile's aboriginal population was decimated by smallpox, typhus, tuberculosis, and even--in the north--bubonic plague, diseases brought to the New World by the *conquistadores (see: POPULATION). Vaccination was introduced in the 18th century by Don Chaparro, a priest, but was not used in earnest until a century later, when Manuel Julián Grajales educated most of the population against the killer disease, smallpox. In the early 1900s annual smallpox deaths were still between five and ten thousand.

A scarlet fever epidemic in 1831-32, with high mortality in overcrowded *Santiago and *Valparaíso, resulted in the creation of the Junta de Beneficiencia de Santiago, the first body in the country devoted to public health concerns. Urbanization also led to cholera outbreaks, which were particularly severe in the 1880s.

Until the 1833 creation of the Escuela de Medicina (promoted by Guillermo *Blest Cunningham), physicians were in short supply. Even the country's increasing prosperity with the nitrate boom in the 1890s, and consequent increase in working class incomes, did little to improve the nation's health. Instead, Chile saw a dramatic rise in alcoholism.

A particular success in the early 20th century was the eradication of malaria, which had affected 70 percent of the population in the far north and required a government campaign by the Instituto de Parasitología that lasted from 1913 to 1946. Real progress in public health began with the 1918 creation of the Dirección General de Sanidad, which in 1924 became the Ministerio de *Higiene, Asistencia y Previsión Social y Trabajo. For example, the death rate, which urban overcrowding had increased from 20 per 1,000 in 1850 to 30.7 per 1,000 in 1920, was reduced to 17 per 1,000 in 1947, 11.5 per 1,000 in 1970, and 6.4 per 1,000 in 1983. The infant mortality rate, which in 1920 had been 370 per 1,000 even in Santiago, also fell. The national average of 163.6 per 1,000 in 1945 decreased to 100 per 1,000 in 1970, 56 per 1,000 in 1980, and 21.9 per 1,000 in 1983. Life expectancy at birth was a little over 50 years during the early 1970s, but had reached 63 years by 1980. The leading causes of death were heart disease and cancer, the same as in the United States.

These figures, however, mask significant regional differences. During the 1960s, for example, infant mortality in rural *Arauco was twice that in Santiago, and Chagas disease remained a problem in the rural areas of the north. In Santiago there is one doctor for every 900 persons, and the figures for *Valparaíso and *Concepción are also favorable. But in other provinces the ratio is approximately one doctor per 5,000, with some rural areas having only one doctor per 10,000. In 1970 there were some 250 hospitals in Chile, with over 40,000 beds: five beds per 1,000 population. In the same year, the Socialist government of Salvador *Allende Gossens spent 9 percent of its budget on public health.

Public health was strengthened and extended in structure during the three-year (1970-73) experiment with socialism. The SERVICIO NACIONAL DE SALUD (q.v.) provided a compulsory and comprehensive health insurance program for the working class as an integral part of the Social Security program (see: SOCIAL WELFARE). When Augusto *Pinochet Ugarte came to power, extensive changes were introduced. Public health services, like so many socially provided services, were reduced as Pinochet sought to eliminate subsidies, minimize assistance to the poor and reduce government involvement in the economy. Whereas before the overthrow of Allende, about 80 percent of Chileans received free health care, under Pinochet they have to seek private health care, with the government reimbursing 50 percent of the charges (70 percent in the case of the very poor).

PUBLIC HEALTH, Ministry of. See: SALUBRIDAD PUBLICA, Ministerio de; SALUD PUBLICA, Ministerio de.

PUBLISHERS AND PUBLISHING. No sustained piece of *printing occurred in Chile until the independence struggle created a demand for *newspapers. By mid-century almost a hundred items a year

were being printed, but 80 percent of these were newspapers
and periodicals. Before 1840 the country did not have a single
bookshop: what few books were available were sold in dry goods
stores or by peddlers. A little publishing was done by newspaper
firms (newspaper and book printing was still being done on the
same simple hand-presses), notably El *Ferrocarril, the leading
Santiago paper, which was owned for a while by Jules Belin
(1829-1863), a French printer who came to Chile in 1848 and published the works of his father-in-law Domingo Faustino *Sarmiento
during the Argentine statesman's Chilean exile. One of the owners of the rival Valparaiso El *Mercurio was the Spanish publisher
Manuel *Rivadeneyra, in Chile from 1829 to 1842. Other presses
included the Cervantes (from the 1880s), the Barcelona (from the
1890s) and that of the Librería Central, owned successively by
A. Raymond and M. Servat.

Any author who used such firms had to provide his own finance and undertake his own distribution, and editions were
limited by the small size of the market to about 200 copies--with
an upper limit of perhaps 500 for a successful novel--even in the
1920s. It was in any case cheaper to have one's works printed
abroad--preferably in Paris, where there were firms, notably
Garnier Frères, ready to publish in Spanish for distribution
throughout the Hispanic world--and share some of the financial
risk. One of the most notable 19th-century Chilean works published in Paris was commissioned and funded, at the instigation
of Diego *Portales Palazuelos, by the Chilean government. This
was Claude *Gay's thirty-volume Historia física y política de Chile,
1844-1865.

The first work of comparable proportions published in Chile
was Diego *Barros's 16-volume Historia general de Chile, 1884-
1902, published by the Casa Editorial de Libros Ilustrados in
Santiago, owned by the Spaniard Rafael Jover (1845-1896) and his
widow Josefina Mariscal de Jover. But the first important Chilean
publisher was Miranda, also in Santiago, whose "Biblioteca de
autores chilenos" series began in the 1890s and was even exported
to Argentina, Colombia and Uruguay. *Ercilla followed in 1893,
and by the early years of the 20th century a number of firms
were in existence. Manuel Guzmán Maturana specialized in school
textbooks, Carlos George Nascimento in literature, and there
was Universo, the forerunner of *Zig-Zag. But all had a hard
struggle competing with the increasing flood of low cost imports
from Spain, and only survived by restricting their output to
works of purely local interest.

This situation was dramatically changed by the Depression of
the early 1930s which brought the *peso down from twelve U.S.
cents to four, making imported books prohibitively expensive
while giving Chilean publishers a considerable price advantage
even abroad. Spurred on by the limits of their small domestic
market, Chilean houses became the first large-scale book exporters
in Latin America, and Nascimento, Zig-Zag, Ercilla, together with

newcomers like Letras, Cultura, Splendor, Lux, Paz, Nueva Epoca, Mundo Nuevo and Osiris, became familiar names throughout Spanish America for everything from philosophy to children's books. By 1936 Ercilla had a backlist of 800 titles. Translated fiction sold particularly well, helped by the fact that authors from countries of the Berne Copyright Convention could be freely "pirated" in the area of the Pan-American Convention. Some 57 European authors were published in this way by Chilean publishers in 1931; 257 in 1932; 346 in 1933.

But inexperience, the need to create a distribution network from scratch, plus the incompetence and sometimes downright dishonesty of foreign middlemen, caused the industry heavy losses. When the market was suddenly enlarged by the collapse of the Spanish publishing trade in the Civil War, Chilean publishers lost out to Argentina, whose industry could learn from the Chileans' mistakes and had a much larger home market to build upon. Also, although both countries benefited from the large influx of refugee publishers and writers fleeing the war, most of these preferred large, more cosmopolitan and more accessible Buenos Aires to distant Santiago. Those who did come to Chile included Joaquín Almendros, who set up Oribe in 1940, Arturo Soria, who created Cruz del Sur, and Mauricio Amster, who became important as a book designer.

World War II, by cutting off almost all oversea supplies of books, enlarged the Latin American market even more, and Chile held on to a sizable export trade, helped by the high standard of Chilean translations. It was about this time that Ercilla passed into the ownership of Zig-Zag, which published Pearl Buck, William Somerset Maugham, F. Scott Fitzgerald, John Dos Passos, John Steinbeck, Charles Webb and Virgil Gheorghiu. Pacífico was formed in 1941, followed by the Editora Universitaria a year or so later and the Chilean branch of Paulinas in 1946. In 1945 the *Universidad de Chile's law and social science faculty set up Editorial Jurídica de Chile, which also used the imprint Andrés Bello for its non-legal titles (history, literature, economics, sociology and technology).

But Argentine books were cheaper, and by 1944 they had far overtaken their Chilean rivals: in that year Argentina published 46 million copies of which two-thirds went abroad, 2.5 million of them to Chile. Chile published only one million, exporting one third of these. Chilean editions seldom exceeded 3,000 copies, and were often smaller. The postwar weakness of the peso led to complicated regulations to prevent book exporting being used as a cover for illicit currency dealing, which made things even more difficult for the legitimate book trade. The industry continued selling a modest amount to Peru and Bolivia, but generally turned back to works of purely local interest, as may be seen by the steady fall in the number of foreign works published in Chile in translation: from 45 in 1959, to 15 in 1964, and just 5 in 1969, compared with a sustained 300 a year at that time in Mexico or

Argentina--and 600 in Brazil. Writers aiming at an international readership increasingly chose to publish abroad. Pablo *Neruda, published by Nascimento before the war, turned to Losada of Buenos Aires. José *Donoso in 1966 started using Mortiz of Mexico City.

By the early 1960s, 90 percent of trade books sold in Chile were imported: two thirds of them from Spain and one fourth from Argentina. Chilean costs were so high that even Chilean imprints were often printed in Spain (at a third of the cost). Paper was particularly expensive, production being a virtual monopoly behind high tariff protection. Chile's two biggest publishers, Nascimento and Universitaria, retreated to the safety of the school textbook market. And anyone who found a publisher for a work outside his field was usually charged for the privilege of getting into print.

The heady years of the *Unidad Popular government led to a spate of political pamphleteering and all the problems of runaway *inflation. Editorial *Zig-Zag, after a dispute with its employees, was nationalized as Editorial Nacional Quimantú. Production measured in number of titles remained at the level of the 1950s-- between 1,000 and 1,500 a year--but the number of copies rose to 9 million, implying an average print run of 15,000. The market had increased through both population growth and the spread of *literacy, but the amount of material of popular appeal in this period was also an important factor.

The September 1973 *coup reversed this tendency. Left-wing houses were forced to close. Wholesale confiscation and destruction of anything Chile's new masters disapproved of meant an additional monetary loss on top of the industry's other economic difficulties, and many other publishers were unable to continue in business. Only 796 titles appeared in 1974; in 1976 the total was 529.

High production costs, high inflation and a home market necessarily small in international terms, now further limited by government social policies, continue to bedevil the industry. To these difficulties have been added a rigid *censorship that has continued ever since the coup (albeit with modifications in the law), the depressed state of the *economy since the collapse of the Chilean "miracle," and the 1977 introduction of a controversial tax on books to support public libraries. There is also the obligation, under Press Law 16643 of 1967, to make copyright deposit of no less than fifteen copies of each book. Houses currently battling these odds include Ediciones Paulinas, Ediciones Universitarias de Valparaiso, Editorial Jurídica y Social de Chile (now owned by a consortium of the Universidade de Chile and the library of the National *Congress), Editorial El Sembrador, Editorial Nascimento SA, Editorial Universitaria SA, Empresa Editorial Zig-Zag SA (now back in business) and Piñeda Libros--not all of them private firms, but all members of the Cámara Chilena del Libro (Chilean Book Association).

See also: CENSORSHIP; PERIODICAL PRESS; PRINTING.

PUDAHUEL. *Santiago's newer airport, built in the 1960s with a loan from the Development Loan Fund, to accommodate larger aircraft and handle the city's international flights. The post-1973 *military regime renamed it the Comodoro Arturo *Merino Benítez. See: AIRPORTS.

PUENTE ALTO. City of Greater Santiago, founded in 1898, with a 1986 estimated population of 126,297.

PUERTO AYSEN. Also spelled "Aisén." Capital of the pre-1974 province of *Aysén, and now in Región XI (see: REGIONS AND ADMINISTRATIVE RESTRUCTURING). A *port classed as minor, but of importance in the coastal trade of southern Chile, Puerto Aysén was founded in 1928 at 45° 27' S, 72° 58' W. Its population was 6,000 in 1940; 14,700 in 1971; and 16,000 in 1982.

PUERTO DE HAMBRE (Port Famine). A site on the mainland shore of the *Strait of Magellan, where there were unsuccessful attempts to establish a fortified town in early colonial times. Alarmed by the incursion into the Pacific of Sir Francis *Drake in 1579, viceroy Francisco de Toledo sent an expedition under Pedro de *Sarmiento de Gamboa to survey the southern regions with a view to shutting the Strait. After doing so, Sarmiento sailed to Spain, and was sent back on September 25, 1581, with a large fleet and 600 potential settlers. Although plagued by foul weather and losses to desertion and piracy, he eventually founded two settlements: Ciudad del Nombre de Jesús (February 5, 1584) and Ciudad del Rey Don Felipe (March 25, 1584). He planned to return with supplies, but was captured by Sir Richard Grenville in August 1586, and the settlers were left to fend for themselves. On January 19, 1586, Thomas Cavendish visited "King Philip's Citie" and found only 15 men and 3 women still alive in both settlements. Hence the name "Port Famine." Another English ship in 1590 found a single survivor, who died after being taken aboard.
   In 1843, Fuerte Bulnes, the predecessor of PUNTA ARENAS (q.v.), was founded close to the site of Puerto de Hambre.

PUERTO MONTT. Capital of the pre-1974 province of *Llanquihue and of the present Región X, Los *Lagos. Founded in 1853 at 41° 28' S, 73° W, the city's population was 3,480 in 1895; 5,408 in 1907; 22,000 in 1940; 82,000 in 1971; and 85,058 (est.) in 1986.

PUEYRREDON, Juan Martín (1777-1850). Supreme Director of the *Argentine, 1814-19, who gave wholehearted backing to José de *San Martín's plan to attack Peru, the seat of Spanish power in South America, by way of Chile (see: ANDES, Ejército de los). For this he was held in exceptionally high esteem by contemporary Chileans. One of the Chilean *navy's first warships was renamed the Pueyrredón, and Pueyrredón was the first person to be awarded Bernardo *O'Higgins' Legion of Honor.

PUGA OSORIO, Arturo. See: JUNTA DE GOBIERNO DE 1932.

PULPERIA. The store on an *hacienda (or other place of employment
such as a nitrate quarry), where employees had to purchase
their food, clothing, tools and other needs. Since in isolated
rural areas there would be no alternative source, the employer
could grant credit at his store instead of paying money wages.
This created a system of indebtedness from which the worker
could hardly ever escape, with the result that the *latifundista
came practically to own his labor force.

PUNTA ARENAS. Also known as *Magallanes. A city and port in
southernmost Chile, located on the neck of the Peninsular de
Brunswick and beside the western shore of the *Strait of Magellan
at 53° 10' S, 70° 56' W. It was the capital of the pre-1974 province of Magallanes, and is now capital of Región XII, Magallanes
y *Antarctica.
    Steamships, being independent of the wind, preferred the
shorter route through the Strait to rounding *Cape Horn, so their
introduction made control of the Strait essential for Chile. In
1843 President Manuel *Bulnes Prieto dispatched a schooner to
establish Chile's claim to the area. It arrived just days before
a French warship, which had been sent to make a similar claim
for France. Bulnes ordered the establishment of a small permanent
settlement to justify Chile's pretensions. Fuerte Bulnes was
built wholly of wood, close to the site of *Puerto de Hambre, but
burned down in 1849. A new site was then chosen, and the
settlement rebuilt as Punta Arenas. This was the most southerly
town in the world until Argentina established Ushuaia further
south in *Tierra del Fuego.
    For many years Punta Arenas's communications were exclusively
maritime. By the end of World War II it had been connected by
road to Puerto Natales, 150 miles away. A *highway to Río
Gallegos, the southernmost town of Argentine *Patagonia, has also
been built. In the 1960s there was a once-weekly air connection
with *Santiago; this has since increased in frequency.
    The population of Punta Arenas was under 200 in 1865; it in-
creased to 3,227 by 1895; to 8,300 by 1907; 25,000 by 1920;
37,000 by 1950; 60,000 by 1970; and 76,800 by 1982. It was
estimated in 1986 to be 107,064.

PURAPEL. Site at 35° 4' S, 72° W where rebel forces in the south
of Chile during the *Civil War of 1851 negotiated the CAPITULA-
CION DE PURAPEL, q.v.

PUREN. Town of Región IX in south central Chile, at 38° 3'S, 73°
5' W, on the river of the same name, founded in 1553. In January
1571 some 2,000 *Araucanian Indians made a surprise attack on
an encampment of 130 Spaniards. The Spanish fled towards
*Angol; their defeat represented a great loss of prestige for the
*conquistadores.

- Q -

QUECHEREGUAS, Hacienda de. Estate at 35° 4' S, 71° 15' W, adjoining the River Claro in the pre-1974 province of *Talca, on the direct route north from Talca toward *Rancagua and *Santiago. During the war for Chilean *independence, Quechereguas was the site of two patriot victories over royalists seeking to advance on Santiago. In the first battle, on April 8, 1814, forces under Bernardo *O'Higgins defeated *realistas led by Gabino Gaínza, who fell back on Talca. In the second, on March 15, 1818, some 170 men commanded by Ramón *Freire Serrano faced 800 troops, led by Mariano *Osorno, whom they succeeded in driving out of the hacienda and back to Camarico.

QUILLEN, Parlamentos de. Negotiations between the Spanish colonial authorities and the *Araucanian Indians which took place on the banks of the River Quillén at 38° 30' S, 72° 30' W, in 1641 and 1647. The result was a treaty, unique in the history of Spanish conquest, whereby the Spaniards officially recognized Indian territorial sovereignty south of the *Bío-Bío river, and undertook to remain to the north of it. In return the *Mapuches were to return their Spanish captives and allow missionaries to convert them. These provisions were unacceptable, however, and the war (see: GUERRAS DE ARAUCO) was soon resumed.

QUILLOTA. Town at 35° 54' S, 71° 16' W, about 20 miles northeast of *Valparaíso on the old road (and present *railway) to *Santiago.

QUILLOTA MUTINY. On June 3, 1837, Diego *Portales Palazuelos stopped at Quillota, on his way to Valparaíso, to review the Maipo Regiment. Mutineers led by Colonel José Antonio Vidaurre Garretón seized the opportunity to arrest him and take him prisoner to Valparaíso. Before arriving the mutineers came under fire from loyalist troops sent by the military governor of the city, Manuel *Blanco Encalada. Thereupon, Portales' guard, Captain Santiago Florín, had his prisoner shot out of hand, June 6, 1837. The mutiny was overcome the next day and its leaders tried and executed.

The mutiny had international overtones. According to Chilean historians, it was organized by the Bolivian minister to Chile, Manuel de la Cruz Méndez, because of Portales' determination to overthrow the *Peru-Bolivia Confederation.

QUILMO. River near *Chillán, the site of a victory of patriots led by the governor of Chillán, Pedro Nolasco Victoriano, over royalists led by Vicente *Benavides' second-in-command, Vicente Elizondo, on September 19, 1819, during the so-called "War to the Death" (*Guerra a muerte).

QUILO, Alto del. Site of a battle fought just outside *Concepción on March 19, 1814, between a patriot army under Bernardo *O'Higgins and a detachment of royalists led by Baraño, well dug-in on the hillside. The ferocity of the patriot attack secured them the hill.

QUIMANTU, Editorial Nacional. See: ZIG-ZAG, Empresa Editorial.

QUINTAL. A unit of weight, quintal métrico, more than double its traditional value. The old colonial and Spanish quintal or hundredweight (100 libras or 4 *arrobas) equalled 46.192 kilograms (101 lbs, 13.4 oz). The metric quintal is a tenth of a metric *ton, i.e. 100 kg (220 lbs, 7.4 oz).

QUINTANA, Hilarion de la (1774-1843). Argentine patriot who fought with the Ejército de los *Andes at *Chacabuco, *Cancha Rayada and *Maipú. From April 16 to September 7, 1817, when Bernardo *O'Higgins was away fighting in the south of Chile, he appointed Quintana interim governor of Chile in his stead. During that time Chile adopted its first blue, white and red national *flag, and coined its first money as an independent state. Quintana stayed on in Chile to fight in the patriot cause until 1819, when poor health forced him to return to Buenos Aires. In 1823 he was sent to Peru on a commission by the Argentine government to fight for that country's liberation. He died in poverty.

QUIRIQUINA ISLAND. A tiny island in *Concepción Bay at 36° 40' S, 73° 5' W, used, like *Dawson Island, as a detention center for political undesirables, established by the *military regime of Augusto *Pinochet Ugarte, to put all suspected leftists behind bars. Of the *Junta's twenty *concentration camps, Quiriquina Island, Dawson Island and *Tejas Verdes were considered the three most brutal.

- R -

RADICAL DEMOCRACY. See: DEMOCRACIA RADICAL.

RADICAL LEFT PARTY. See: PARTIDO DE LA IZQUIERDA RADICAL.

RADICAL PARTY. See: PARTIDO RADICAL.

RADIO AGRICULTURA. A popular Chilean radio station which received millions of dollars from the *United States *Central Intelligence Agency for the purpose of disseminating propaganda aimed at bringing about the downfall of the Salvador *Allende Gossens government.

RADIO BALMACEDA. A *Santiago radio station owned by the *Partido
Demócrata Cristiano which became the voice of the opposition to
the government of Augusto *Pinochet Ugarte. As a consequence
it was confiscated by the government in early 1977.

RADIO COOPERATIVA. A *Santiago radio station started by the
*Partido Demócrata Cristiano in the early 1980s to replace *Radio
Balmaceda, expressing the views of opposition politicians and of
activists within the Roman Catholic *Church.

RADIO NACIONAL. Located in *Santiago, Radio Nacional is the
government station of the *military regime, with a domestic service
and international broadcasting in Arabic, English, French, German
and Italian.

RADIO TRANSMITTING. See: TELECOMMUNICATIONS.

RAILWAYS. Chile has a rich history of railroad expansion that dates
from 1850, when North American engineer William *Wheelwright
built a 52-mile line between *Caldera and *Copiapó. This was
only the second railroad built in South America (the first being
the Demerara line in British Guiana), and served the *silver
mines of *Chañarcillo and Tres Puntas. After that, a policy
was pursued of centering the rail network on *Santiago, the administrative capital, even though this meant bringing rails and
equipment overland by oxcart in the early stages. In 1856 a
line was built south from Santiago to San Bernardo, and extended
to *San Fernando in 1862. Another American, Henry *Meiggs,
began connecting the capital with *Valparaíso, Chile's second city
and main port. He started in 1852, and although the first section,
from Valparaíso to *Viña del Mar, opened in 1855 and *Quillota
was reached in 1857, the difficult terrain imposed a circuitous
route and delayed completion to Santiago until September 1863.
The Santiago-Valparaíso line was of extreme importance because
it reduced traveling time between Chile's two major cities from
two days by stagecoach to four hours (although the modern
*highway, taking a more direct route, reduces the time to about
2 hours 30 minutes by car).
     Most of Chile's subsequent railway construction until World
War I was done by the British, and most late 19th-century immigrants from the *United Kingdom came to Chile to work for the
British companies doing this construction. Swiss railroad engineers also made notable contributions, especially in bridge, tunnel
and mountain-railroad building. Chile came to have some of the
most remarkable examples of mountain railway building in the
world. One such feat was the 278-mile climb at a 4 percent
grade from the sea at *Arica to 13,000 foot high La Paz, built
in 1906-13 as a part of the 1904 treaty with Bolivia (see: BOLIV-
IA, Relations with).
     The nature of the country made constructing Chile's rail

system an outstanding engineering achievement, particularly in
bridge building, and Chile's railway construction expertise has
benefited several other Latin American countries.

After World War I, *United States technology largely replaced
that of Britain, modernizing track and rolling stock. More
recently, the demand for better service has forced Chile
since 1981 to turn to Japan for all aspects of railway technology,
and Chileans are being sent there for training in railway engineering.

Unlike most of her neighbors, Chile now has a railroad network
of almost national extension. The present EMPRESA DE FERRO-
CARRILES DEL ESTADO, q.v., controls practically all the current
5,076 route miles (roughly equal to Chile's 5,995 miles of paved
highways). There are three distinct networks. From Arica
there is a 40-mile line to *Tacna in Peru, as well as the line to
La Paz already mentioned. Between *Iquique and La Calera are
950 miles of meter guage line, the *Red Norte. This includes
two more transandine lines. The older, British owned until 1985,
has connected *Antofagasta to La Paz since 1873, crossing the
frontier at Ollagüe. The other, from Antofagasta to Salta in
northern Argentina, opened in 1948. From Calera southward are
the 3,750 miles of broad guage *Red Sur.

Although the rail network has shrunk from the 1920 total of
8,980 miles, Chile's railways are still vital to the *economy, with
the most heavily used lines, for both freight and passengers,
in the Santiago-Puerto Montt corridor. Passenger travel by train
is still very popular, especially on the Red Sur. The national
total in passenger-kilometers was 1.45 million in 1940 and peaked
at 2.38 million in 1977. In 1983 it was 1.56 million.

In the early 1980s, rail still carried over half the total cargo
shipped in Chile. This had grown from 2.03 million tonne/kilo-
meters in 1940 to a peak of 2.5 million in 1970, but fell to 1.3
million in 1982.

In 1984 Chilean railways possessed 670 locomotives, 650 passenger cars and 10,350 freight cars--almost the same amount as in
1913. Track and rolling stock were inadequately maintained, and
the rail system was in a state of disarray. The exception was
the recently opened underground rapid transit railway in Santiago,
the METRO, q.v.

Besides the Metro, Chile has 564 miles of electrified line--that
between Santiago and Valparaíso was electrified in 1924, the
earliest anywhere in South America. There are plans for a further
electrification of 375 miles of tracks. But availability of Chilean
*coal has meant that steam traction has yet to be wholly displaced.

RANCAGUA. City of central Chile 75 miles from *Santiago on the
direct route south from the capital to *Talca and *Puerto Montt.
Founded in 1743 as Santa Cruz de Triana at 34° 12' S, 70° 46'
W, it became in 1883 the capital of the new province of *O'Higgins,
and in 1975 capital of Region VI *Libertador O'Higgins. The

population was 10,380 in 1907 and 25,000 in 1940, but then grew rapidly because of its proximity to the *Teniente *copper mine at *Sewell, reaching 75,800 (est.) in 1971 and 157,209 (est.) in 1986.

RANCAGUA, Battle of. Decisive defeat of the patriots which ended the phase of the *independence struggle known as the *Patria vieja, and led to the *Reconquista española. On October 1, 1814, some 5,000 realistas commanded by Mariano *Osorio unsuccessfully attacked the entrenched 1,180 patriot defenders of the city, led by Bernardo *O'Higgins. During the night Osorio managed to cut off the defenders' water supply. An attempt at relief by a force under José Miguel *Carrera Verdugo on October 2 was beaten off, and at the end of the day O'Higgins' men were forced to try to break out and retreat. Only a third of them managed to do so. Osorio then made for Santiago, and the patriot remnants sought sanctuary across the *Andes in *Mendoza.

RAPA NUI. Polynesian name of EASTER ISLAND, q.v.

RAUFF, Walter (1907-1984). A former colonel in the Gestapo (German secret police) who had been convicted in absentia by the Nuremberg War Crimes Tribunal for the extermination of some 250,000 Jews at Auschwitz and other concentration camps. He had fled to Chile in 1945, becoming a prominent businessman in *Puerto Montt (a city with many German immigrants), and later in *Santiago. After the *coup d'état that overthrew Socialist President (1970-73) Salvador *Allende Gossens, Rauff became chief adviser to Manuel *Sepúlveda Contreras, director of the Chilean secret police (DINA). In that capacity Rauff had a hand in setting up one of *Chile's 20 *concentration camps at *Tejas Verde, where the enemies of the *military regime were held without charge, interrogated, and kept in maximum security cells or in forced-labor camps. Many were killed, and the lucky ones were eventually released (often into exile), to bear witness against the repressive regime. In 1984 Chilean Jews protested in front of Rauff's elegant house in a wealthy suburb of Santiago, wearing yellow stars, a grim reminder of the Nazi death camps. They demanded Rauff's extradition to Israel to face charges as a war criminal, but this President Augusto *Pinochet Ugarte refused. Rauff eventually died in the same year, aged 77.

REAL ACADEMIA. See: ACADEMIA DE SAN LUIS.

REAL AUDIENCIA. See: AUDIENCIA.

REAL PATRONATO (Royal patronage). The agreement whereby the Papacy surrendered to the Spanish crown almost complete control over all nondoctrinal *church matters (appointment of officials, delimitation of dioceses, collection of *tithes, etc.). After independence, the Republic's assumption that it had automatically inherited such rights (as a patronato nacional) was a constant source of friction until church disestablishment in 1925. See: SACRISTAN, Cuestión del.

REALISTAS (Royalists). Those who, during the Chilean struggle for *independence, 1810-22, favored the continuance of colonial rule and supported the authority of the Spanish crown.

RECABARREN CIENFUEGOS, Manuel (1827-1901). Lawyer and Radical (*Partido Radical) politician. A founder of the *Sociedad de la Igualdad, Recabarren took part in the *Mutiny of Urriola, which led to his being exiled abroad until the amnesty of 1862. He was elected a deputy, 1864-67, and served in the Senate, 1876-1900. President Aníbal *Pinto Garmendia made him interior minister in 1880, and he held cabinet posts under the next three Presidents. He also became president of the Radical Party. During the *Civil War of 1891 he supported the rebels.

RECABARREN SERRANO, Luis Emilio (1876-1924). Revolutionary leader of humble origin who worked as a printer. Born in Valparaíso, he moved north and in 1906 was elected Democratic (*Partido Democrático) deputy for *Antofagasta, but the Chamber refused to seat him when he would not take the oath in the name of God and the Scriptures. He settled in *Iquique and in 1908 founded the socialist newspaper El despertar de los trabajadores (awakening of the workers). A year later he formed the *trade union federation *FOCh. In 1912 he left the Democrats and founded the Socialist Workers Party (*Partido Obrero Socialista), forerunner of the Chilean Communist Party (*Partido Comunista Chileno). He was elected a deputy in 1921, visited the *U.S.S.R. in 1922, returning in 1923. He committed suicide on December 19, 1924.

RECONQUISTA ESPAÑOLA (Spanish reconquest). The period between the battles of *Rancagua and *Chacabuco (October 1814-February 1817) when the Spanish colonial regime in Chile was temporarily restored. Mariano *Osorio, the victor of Rancagua, entered *Santiago on October 5, 1814. As most of those who were irreconcilable to Spanish rule had fled to *Mendoza, he was easily able to consolidate his rule. But the need to maintain an effective army meant heavy *taxes on an *economy ravaged by civil war. Many patriots were exiled to the *Juan Fernández Islands, and when Osorio was replaced by Francisco Casimiro *Marcó del Pont in December, arbitrary arrest became frequent and freedom of speech and assembly were suppressed. Commerce was hampered by the government's failure to end the predations of *pirates. From January 1816 fear of an invasion from *Cuyo increased the government's insecurity and the violence of its repression. Marcó del Pont also weakened his position by scattering his forces to cover all possible directions of attack and cope with the guerrilla activities of Manuel *Rodríguez. The Ejército de los *Andes

eventually arrived early in 1817 and decisively defeated the
royalists at Chacabuco on February 12. Three days later Bernardo
*O'Higgins was named Supreme Director of Chile in Santiago, and
a year later Chile formally declared its independence from Spain.

RECOPILACION DE LEYES DE LOS REYNOS DE LAS INDIAS (Laws
of the Indies). A first collection of laws and regulations relating
to the Spanish American colonies was published in 1563 by the
viceroy of New Spain (i.e. Mexico), Luis Velasco. A more complete collection appeared in Spain in 1596, another in 1628, and
in 1681 the Spanish government of Charles II promulgated a
definitive code in nine volumes. Changes during the 18th century, particularly in financial administration and commercial matters, resulted in a three-volume supplement in 1791. Finally,
a new compilation (or part of it) appeared in twelve volumes in
1805 under the title Novísima Recopilación de las Leyes de Indias.
The code covered all phases of colonial life. It contained
numerous humanitarian regulations protecting the Indians. But
many of its provisions were not effectively enforced.

RED NORTE. The northern network of the Chilean State *Railways
consists of 950 miles of meter (3 feet, 3 inches) gauge line between *Iquique and La Calera. Much of it was originally built
as separate private lines connecting *mining areas to their respective *ports. Extension of the state-owned lateral network
northwards to link up these transverse lines (often of different
gauges) proceeded very slowly, and was barely completed by 1914.
Lack of such a south-north trunk was decisive during the *Civil
War of 1891: President José Manuel *Balmaceda Fernández,
having lost command of the sea, had no way to reinforce his
troops in the *Norte grande, which became the rebels' base of
operations.

RED SUR. The southern network of Chile's *railway system extends
from La Calera southward and totals 3,750 route miles. Except
for the stretch linking central Chile via the *Uspallata Pass to
Mendoza and Buenos Aires (see: TRANSANDINE RAILWAY), the
Red Sur is broad gauge (5ft., 6 ins.; 1.676 m). The most
southerly section, to *Puerto Montt, and its *Ancud to Castro
extension on *Chiloé Island, were completed in 1913. Glaciers
preclude any overland route further south; goods are sent by
sea or through *Argentina. The Red Sur is electrified as far
south as San Rosendo, and there are plans for further electrification.

RED WEEK. See: SEMANA ROJA.

REDUCCION. An Indian village established in the Spanish American
colonies, under a *corregidor, from which all Europeans except
priests were banished. It was hoped that such a system, under

direct royal or ecclesiastical control, would be a more effective
and more humane method of christianizing and hispanizing the
Indians than the private *encomienda. More often than not, however, the reducciones served primarily to provide a much needed
labor force. The most famous reducciones under religious control
were those established by the *Jesuits in Paraguay in the 17th
century.

REGIDOR. In colonial times, an alderman or councilman in the *cabildo, elected by the townsmen to represent them. But as early
as the 17th century, the whole municipal system was honeycombed
with patronage and graft. As a result, local officials came to be
appointed rather than elected, and the office of regidor usually
went to the highest bidder.
   The word continues in use in modern Chile for an elected town
councilor, see: LOCAL GOVERNMENT.

REGIONALISTAS DE MAGALLANES. A group of politicians in the
southernmost province of *Magallanes, whose main objective was
to obtain a decentralized form of government in the province and
defend the free port status of *Punta Arenas. In 1951-52 the
group supported Arturo *Matte Larraín, the presidential candidate
of the right, who lost to Carlos *Ibáñez del Campo. The Regionalistas de Magallanes never achieved election to *Congress (which
would have given them the status of a legal political party) and
were only influential at the local level.

REGIONS AND ADMINISTRATIVE RESTRUCTURING. The pattern of
pre-1974 administrative division of Chile is described under
PROVINCES (q.v.). Nine months after the *coup d'état of
September 1973, this division was totally restructured into twelve
new regiones, plus Greater Santiago, as follows:

REGION I. *Tarapacá. Capital: *Iquique. (the former province
   of Tarapacá)
REGION II. *Antofagasta. Capital: Antofagasta. (the former
   province of Antofagasta)
REGION III. *Atacama. Capital: *Copiapó. (the former prov-
   ince of Atacama)
REGION IV. *Coquimbo. Capital: La *Serena. (the former
   province of Coquimbo)
REGION V. *Aconcagua. Capital: *Valparaíso. (the former
   provinces of Aconcagua and Valparaíso, the former department
   of San Antonio from the former province of *Santiago, plus the
   *Juan Fernández Islands and *Easter Island)
AREA METROPOLITANA DE SANTIAGO. Capital: Santiago.
   (the former province of Santiago, less the department of San
   Antonio)
REGION VI. *Libertador Bernardo O'Higgins. Capital: *Ran-
   cagua. (the former provinces of *O'Higgins and *Colchagua)
REGION VII. *Maule. Capital: *Talca. (the former provinces

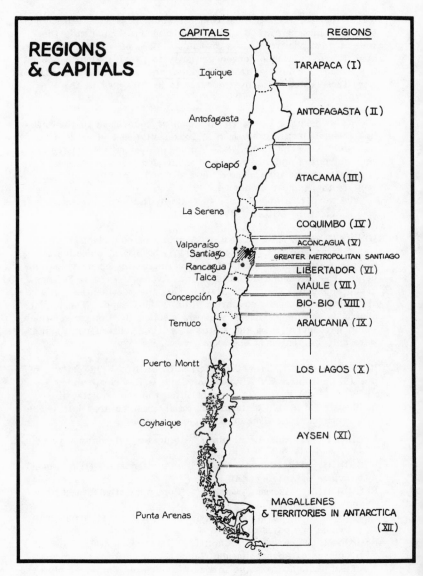

REGIONS & CAPITALS

CAPITALS

REGIONS

Iquique

TARAPACA (I)

Antofagasta

ANTOFAGASTA (II)

Copiapó

ATACAMA (III)

La Serena

COQUIMBO (IV)

Valparaíso
Santiago

ACONCAGUA (V)

GREATER METROPOLITAN SANTIAGO

Rancagua
Talca

LIBERTADOR (VI)

MAULE (VII)

Concepción

BIO-BIO (VIII)

Temuco

ARAUCANIA (IX)

Puerto Montt

LOS LAGOS (X)

Coyhaique

AYSEN (XI)

Punta Arenas

MAGALLENES
& TERRITORIES IN ANTARCTICA
(XII)

of *Curicó, Talca, Maule and *Linares)
REGION VIII. *Bío-Bío. Capital: *Concepción. (the former
provinces of *Nuble, Concepción, *Arauco and Bío-Bío)
REGION IX. *Araucanía. Capital: *Temuco. (the former
provinces of *Malleco and *Cautín)
REGION X. Los *Lagos. Capital: *Puerto Montt. (the former
provinces of *Valdivia, *Osorno, *Llanquihue and *Chiloé)
REGION XI. *Aysén, del General Carlos Ibáñez del Campo.
Capital: *Coyhaique. (the former province of Aysén)
REGION XII. *Magallanes y la Antártica Chilena. Capital:
*Punta Arenas. (the former province of Magallanes and the
former territory of Chilean Antartica)

This restructuring was carried out with two objectives in mind:
to speed up the socioeconomic development of the country, and
to reinforce national security by having well-delineated borders
between the regions, facilitating the location of check points.
See also: CONSTITUTION OF 1980; LOCAL GOVERNMENT;
POPULATION.
The new regions are divided into provinces. see: PROVINCES.

REGISTRO ELECTORAL. The electoral register in Chile lists political
parties as well as voters. To register, a party needs the sig-
natures of 10,000 registered voters, and must apply not less
than 240 days before an election. If it fails to maintain a seat
in either house of *Congress, the Dirección del Registro Electoral
may order it struck from the Register. Parliamentary candidates
must also register 120 days before the election and have been
a member of their sponsoring party for 180 days. See also:
ELECTIONS; SUFFRAGE.

REGLAMENTO CONSTITUCIONAL PROVISORIO (Provisional Constitutional Ordinance). See: CONSTITUTION OF 1812.

REGLAMENTO PARA EL ARREGLO DE LA AUTORIDAD EJECUTIVA
DE CHILE (Ordinance to determine executive authority in Chile).
See: CONSTITUTION OF 1811.

REGLAMENTO PARA EL GOBIERNO PROVISORIO (Ordinance for the
provisional government). See: CONSTITUTION OF 1814.

RELACIONES EXTERIORES, Ministerio de. The Ministry of Foreign
Affairs was created in 1925 when *Church disestablishment removed religious affairs from the purview of the Ministerio de
*Relaciones Exteriores y Culto. It lasted until 1930 when it be-
came for eleven years the Ministerio de *Relaciones Exteriores
y Comercio. On October 6, 1941, the shorter title was restored.
Ministerial departments include Immigration; Foreign Policy; Pro-
tocol; Frontiers; and the Foreign Service. Foreign ministers
since the 1973 *coup have been: Rear Admiral Ismael Huerta
Díaz (September 1973); Vice admiral Patricio Carbajal Prado (July

1974); Hernán Cubillos Sallato (April 1978); René Rojas Galdanes (December 1979); Miguel Alex *Schweitzer Walter (February 1983); Jaime del Valle (December 1983).

RELACIONES EXTERIORES, CULTO Y COLONIZACION, Ministerio de. Title of the Chilean foreign office from 1888 until October 1924, when it became also responsible for religious affairs and agricultural settlement.

RELACIONES EXTERIORES, JUSTICIA, CULTO E INSTRUCCION PUBLICA, Ministerio de. The department of the rebel *congresista government during the *Civil War of 1891, responsible for foreign and religious affairs, justice and *education. See: JUNTA DE GOBIERNO DE IQUIQUE.

RELACIONES EXTERIORES Y COLONIZACION, Ministerio de. Foreign affairs were originally a responsibility of the interior ministry, known successively as the Secretaría de *Gobierno (1814-18), Ministerio de *Gobierno (1818-22), Ministerio de *Gobierno y Relaciones Exteriores (1822-24) and Ministerio del *Interior y Relaciones Exteriores (1824-December 9, 1871). On its separation from the interior ministry, the Chilean foreign office added colonización (agricultural settlement) to its title, because it was at this time actively involved in the recruitment in Europe of immigrants to settle southern Chile (see: IMMIGRATION; LLANQUIHUE). On June 21, 1887, the ministry temporarily lost its responsibility for settlement, but gained that for culto (*Church affairs) from the Justice and Education Ministry (*Justicia, Culto y Instrucción Pública), becoming the Ministerio de Relaciones Exteriores y Culto.

RELACIONES EXTERIORES Y COMERCIO, Ministerio de. From January 8, 1930, until October 6, 1941, the Chilean foreign office had responsibility for trade, previously the domain of the Ministerio de Fomento, and subsequently transferred to the newly created Ministerio de *Comercio y Abastecimiento (trade and supplies). Afterwards the foreign office reverted to its previous short title of Ministerio de *Relaciones Exteriores.

RELACIONES EXTERIORES Y CULTO, Ministerio de. The title Ministry of Foreign and religious affairs first appeared in June 1887 when religious affairs were transferred from the justice and education ministry as concerning relations with the Vatican. A year later, the title was changed to Ministerio de *Relaciones Exteriores, Culto y Colonización, when the foreign office recovered its responsibility for agricultural settlement. The earlier title was resumed in October 1924, when settlement was transferred to the new Ministerio de *Agricultura, Industria y Colonización. With the disestablishment of the *Church, on the adoption of the *Constitution of 1925, religious affairs ceased to be an administrative concern and the foreign office became simply the Ministerio de *Relaciones Exteriores.

RELIGIOUS PRACTICES. Most Chileans are, at least nominally, Roman Catholics: 98.05 percent at the census of 1907; about 89 percent today. Protestants, who totaled only 31,621 (two thirds of them foreigners) in 1907 now number perhaps as many as 800,000 (see: PROTESTANTISM). The number of *Jews has increased in the same eighty years from 90 (almost all foreigners) to about 11,000. There are also a small number of Indians who still practice indigenous religions (less than one percent of the population). Roman Catholicism was the state religion in colonial times, and this did not change with independence. Article 5 of the *Constitution of 1833 affirmed the Republic's religion to be Catholic, Apostolic and Roman, prohibiting the public practice of any other. No action was taken when a Protestant church opened in *Valparaíso in 1837, but proposals to modify the law accordingly encountered stiff opposition. Only in 1865 was the constitution amended to allow dissenters to worship legally on private property, and to provide private schools for the religious education of their own children. In 1871 a lot was provided by law in each public cemetery for the burial of non-Catholics and the obligation was imposed on parish priests to perform marriages of dissenters. In 1884 cemeteries were made nondenominational, and civil registration of marriage was peremptorily substituted for the church ceremony. Since then a church wedding has had no legal standing. Further gradual liberalization followed (see: CHURCH, The). The *Constitution of 1925 formally disestablished the Church and guaranteed liberty of conscience and worship to people of other faiths. Nevertheless, the association between the Chilean state and the Roman Catholic Church remained very strong, at least until the end of the presidency of Christian Democrat Eduardo *Frei Montalva in 1970.

RENGIFO CARDENAS, Manuel (1793-1846). Merchant and Chilean patriot who was exiled to Argentina after the Battle of *Rancagua. When the Spanish were routed at the Battle of *Chacabuco, he returned to Chile, taking an active part in politics. A conservative (*pelucón), he held various ministerial posts during the first two decades of conservative rule in Chile (1831-51). In 1831 newly elected President Joaquín *Prieto Vial chose Rengifo as his finance minister. As such he paid great attention to the financial and commercial problems of the young republic. He introduced measures to curtail government expenditure, to develop new *ports and to encourage the development of a national *merchant marine. He reorganized the taxation system (see: TAXES; CUSTOMS AND DUTIES); negotiated the rescheduling of Chile's foreign debt, reestablishing the country's credit; reduced the size of the civil service; and took action to suppress smuggling. His reforms provided the means to pay for important public works and even for

the War against the *Peru-Bolivia Confederation. He left office
in November 1835 but served as finance minister again under
President Manuel *Bulnes Prieto from October 1841 to February
1844. He was deputy for *Chiloé, 1828-29, and for *San Felipe,
1840-43; from 1834 to 1837 and again from 1843 until his death
he served in the Senate. He also served as acting interior
and foreign minister (1833 and 1841) and as Chilean minister to
*Peru.

REPARTIMIENTO. Apportionment of Indians to the colonists to carry
out public works. Theoretically the Indians were free men, subject to the Crown of Castille. They were therefore liable to tribute, but entitled to be paid for their labor. This system of
forced labor had previously been used by Spain in its earlier
oversea acquisitions--Majorca, the Canaries, Morocco. It was
legally distinct from the *encomienda system, but in practice both
resulted in a state little different from slavery. The Indians
usually turned a deaf ear to any inducement to work, and, since
manual labor was unacceptable to a Spaniard, the natives were
forced to work in the mines or on public construction under pain
of very severe punishment. In Chile, however, the repartimiento
was never a success: the *Araucanian Indians were never effectively subjugated. The system was abolished after the Tupac
Amaru revolt in Upper Peru of 1780. See also: ENCOMIENDA;
REDUCCION.

REPUBLICA CHICA, La. Nickname meaning "the little republic,"
given to the personal rule exercised over the Chilean *navy
by ex-President Jorge *Montt Alvarez as its director general,
1898-1913, and subsequently, in an informal capacity, as mayor
of *Valparaiso, 1913-18.

REPUBLICA DE CHILE. Official title of the Chilean state. Colonial
rule effectively ended in Chile with the creation of the *Junta
de gobierno de 1810. The real *audiencia was then dissolved,
trade freed from the mercantilist restrictions, and relations entered into with the newly independent government of *Argentina.
For the next eight years a war of *independence was fought to
prevent a restoration of Spanish power. However, although the
word "Republic" in its broadest sense may be used to refer to
the whole period from September 18, 1810, it is more accurately
reserved for the period subsequent to the formal declaration of
independence on February 12, 1818. Until then Chile still
owed allegiance in constitutional theory to *Ferdinand VII. In
an even narrower sense, the term is often reserved by historians
to the post-1830 period; the two previous decades are divided
into the *Patria Vieja (1810-14), the *Reconquista Española (1814-
17), the Patria Nova, which saw independence assured with the
liberation of *Peru (1817-23), and the *Anarquía política, characterized by the conflict between the partisans of centralized

government and those who wanted *federalism (1823-30).

The history of the Republic in this last, narrow, sense can be divided into five main periods. From 1831 to 1861 there was a highly centralized government based on the ideas of Diego *Portales Palazuelos, which were embodied in the conservative *Constitution of 1833. Liberalism, with greater local autonomy and individual freedom, prevailed during the years 1861 to 1891. The period 1891 to 1924 is known as that of the *Parliamentary Regime. The fourth period, 1925-1973, that of the *Constitution of 1925, saw the establishment of a relatively stable and democratic nation characterized by growth in *industry, *literacy, *trade unions, and *inflation, and by nationalization of the country's natural resources. The entrenched oligarchy seemed to be losing its traditional prerogatives and was beginning to give in to the growing demands for radical social and economic reform. Since September 1973 the Republic has been governed by a *military regime concerned with ridding Chile of Marxism, whatever the cost.

See also: CHILE--G. History. and--H. Government.

REPUBLICA SOCIALISTA (Socialist Republic). On June 4, 1932, a military coup d'état overthrew the government (1931-32) of Juan Esteban *Montero Rodríguez, and the *junta de gobierno de 1932 assumed the executive power. The leader of the coup, Air Commodore Marmaduke *Grove Vallejo, was not one of the junta, although he was made war minister and was the main mover of the idea to declare Chile a Socialist Republic. After dissolving the *Congreso termal, the junta ordered the Caja de Crédito Popular to return to its borrowers all clothing and household and working tools being held in pawn, a very popular move in the depths of the *Depression. This moment also marked the beginnings of the present *Partido Socialista (Socialist Party), but the Socialist Republic lasted only 12 days. The middle and upper classes were near panic, the members of the new regime were disunited, and one of the junta, Carlos *Dávila Espinosa, had personal presidential ambitions, which he pursued through a second coup d'état, June 17, 1932.

In September 1970, Chileans elected Socialist Salvador *Allende Gossens. He was sworn into office on November 3, pledging to initiate the socialization of Chile and to establish a Socialist Republic. His experiment with socialism ended abruptly, however, three years later in the military *coup d'état of 1973.

REPUBLICAN ACTION. See: ACCION REPUBLICANA.

REPUBLICAN SOCIAL UNION. See: UNION SOCIAL REPUBLICANA DE ASALARIADOS DE CHILE.

REPUBLICAN UNION. See: UNION REPUBLICANA.

RETTIG GUISSEN, Raul (1909-   ). *Partido Radical politician.
Originally a schoolteacher, he qualified as a lawyer in 1935 and
first ran for Congress in 1937. He has since served both as a
deputy and as a senator, distinguishing himself by his oratorical
brilliance. He was president of the Radical Party in 1950 and
again from 1960 to 1964. He has also been dean of the law school
of the *Universidad de Chile.

REVOLUCION DE LA INDEPENDENCIA. The Revolution for Independence refers to the period from the end of colonial rule to the
declaration of independence (Declaración de *Independencia),
1810-18. See: INDEPENDENCE, Wars of; REPUBLICA DE CHILE.

REVOLUTIONARY COMMUNIST PARTY. See: PARTIDO COMUNISTA
REVOLUCIONARIO.

REVOLUTIONARY LEFT. See: MOVIMIENTO DE IZQUIERDA REVO-
LUCIONARIO.

REYES BASOALTO, Neftali Ricardo. Original name of Pablo NERUDA,
q.v.

REYES PALAZUELOS, Vicente (1835-1918). Lawyer, journalist and
politician. On qualifying as a lawyer in 1857, he associated himself with El *Ferrocarril, eventually becoming for a while its
editor. At first he supported President Jorge *Montt Torres and
the *Partido Nacional, but then became a Liberal, succeeding
Jeronimo Urmeneta in 1869 as president of the *Club de la Reforma. When the more progressive liberals split from the party
in the 1880s, he went with them to become president of the *Partido Liberal Doctrinario (1885). He served in the Chamber of
Deputies, 1861-63, 1870-73 and 1876-82; and in the Senate,
1885-1903, and from 1909 until his death. He served as finance
minister in 1866, interior minister in 1877 and as president of the
Senate in 1889, 1895 and 1909. He ran for President of the Republic on the *Alianza Liberal ticket in 1896, but was narrowly
defeated by Federico *Errázuriz Echaurren. Reyes had a reputation for honesty and personal integrity, and distinguished himself as a forceful debater and able political orator.

REYES VICUNA, Tomás (1914-1986). Architect by profession and a
member of the Christian Democratic Party (*Partido Demócrata
Cristiano, PDC). A founder member of the *Falange Nacional, and
its president in 1951, he joined the PDC when this was formed by
the amalgamation of the Falange with the *Partido Conservador
Social Cristiano. In 1965 he was elected senator for *Santiago,
later becoming president of the Senate and one of the PDC's executive directors.

RIESCO ERRAZURIZ, Germán (1854-1916). President of Chile, 1901-

06. Riesco qualified as a lawyer in 1875, served ten years as an official in the justice ministry, became a public prosecutor, and in 1900 was elected senator for *Talca on the *Partido Liberal ticket. He then ran successfully for President, backed by the *Alianza Liberal, succeeding Vice-president Aníbal Zañartu Zañartu in September 1901. During his administration, the boundary conflict with *Argentina was settled by the PACTOS DE MAYO (q.v.) in 1902. The agreement was celebrated by the erection of the *Christ of the Andes statue on the international border in 1904.

Chile also signed a peace treaty with *Bolivia (1904), confirming Chilean possession of *Antofagasta. In 1906 diplomatic relations were reestablished with *Peru.

Serious strikes in the provinces of *Valparaíso, Antofagasta, and *Santiago forced Riesco's government to promote the construction of low-income workers' *housing. His presidency also witnessed the devastating Valparaíso *earthquake of August 16, 1906.

New legal codes of civil and criminal procedure were adopted in 1902 and 1906, respectively, and Riesco's administration also embarked on a large-scale public works program (the erection of public buildings, paving of streets, construction of *highways and bridges), but much of this was not completed until the presidency of his successor, Pedro *Montt Montt (1906-10).

After stepping down from the presidency, Riesco dedicated himself to his law practice, while at the same time remaining active in politics. He died in 1916 from a cardiac seizure.

RIOS GALLARDO, Conrado (b. 1896). Diplomat and journalist. A prominent member of the *Partido Liberal, he joined the staff of La *Nación in 1918, becoming editor in 1926. As foreign minister, 1927-29, he was largely responsible for negotiating the Treaty of *Lima with *Peru. He served as ambassador to Spain in 1929, to Peru in 1930 and to Argentina in 1939-44 and 1953-56. In 1932 he and Ismael Edwards Matte turned the Editorial *Ercilla into a sociedad autónoma (business corporation), and, in association with Edwards, Carlos Guillermo *Dávila Espinosa and Aníbal Jara Letelier, he founded the magazine *Hoy.

RIOS MORALES, Juan Antonio (1888-1946). President of Chile, 1942-46. Lawyer, businessman and member of the Radical Party (*Partido Radical), he was Chilean chargé d'affaires in Panamá before entering Congress as deputy for *Arauco in 1924. He was appointed interior minister in June 1932, and justice minister in September 1932. In 1942 he ran for the presidency, backed by the *Alianza Democrática de Chile, the Falange Nacional and the personal endorsement of ex-President Arturo *Alessandri Palma, against Carlos *Ibáñez del Campo. Ríos won by 260,000 votes to 204,000.

After his inauguration, Chile declared a policy of neutrality in World War II. Economic difficulties and popular pressure, however, induced Ríos to sever relations with the Axis powers in 1943. As a result, Washington included Chile in its Lease-Lend Program, and the Export-Import Bank made new loans to Chile's developing industry. Industrialization was among the priorities of the Ríos administration. A mill for making copper wire was built, a hydroelectric plant erected, and plans were drawn up to begin work on a new steel mill (at *Huachipato). Improvements were made in the *railways, and the educational system was expanded. Nevertheless, although Chile signed the *United Nations pact on February 14, 1945, it delayed declaring war until April 12, and then only against Japan. Ríos's last year in office was troubled by economic difficulties due to a fall in the price of *copper, by rising *inflation and by *labor strikes. He was strongly criticized for traveling abroad in October 1945 (he visited the United States, Mexico, Costa Rica, Cuba and Ecuador) and his entire cabinet resigned. Labor trouble continued through the early months of 1946. Ill health caused Ríos to resign in January 1946, and he was succeeded by Radical leader Alfredo *Duhalde Vásquez. Like his predecessor, Ríos Morales failed to live to the end of his elected term, dying on June 27, 1946.

RIVADENEYRA, Manuel. Spanish publisher, in business in Chile 1839-42. In 1840 he took charge of La Opinión of *Santiago, whose presses printed the official El *Araucano. In 1841 he acquired El *Mercurio of *Valparaíso, and appointed Domingo Faustino *Sarmiento to be its editor. After his return to Spain, Rivadeneyra became famous for embarking on the monumental *Biblioteca de Autores Españoles."

RIVAS-VICUÑA, Manuel (b. 1880). Statesman, diplomat, law professor and journalist. Member of a wealthy and respected family, he was one of the idealogues of the Liberal Party (*Partido Liberal) at the turn of the century. Elected to the Chamber of Deputies in 1909, he was reelected in 1915, 1924, 1926 and 1930. In 1912 he became finance minister, and in 1913 was named interior minister. Later he was undersecretary of war. In the 1920s he became interested in the plight of the Chilean worker, but the legislation he proposed was never passed. In November 1926 he headed Emiliano *Figueroa Larraín's last ministry before that President resigned. Exiled by Carlos *Ibáñez del Campo, Rivas Vicuña later became Chile's ambassador to Italy and delegate to the League of Nations.

Within the structure of the Liberal Party, Rivas Vicuña placed in the center, trying to assume the role of moderator between the reformers who wanted the party to be more socially conscious and those who opposed any changes.

ROBLE, El. Ford on the Itatá, 9 miles above its confluence with the River Nuble, site of a battle on October 17, 1813, during Chile's struggle for *independence. José Miguel *Carrera Verdugo and Bernardo *O'Higgins were leading a small force of 800 patriots in the direction of *Chillán when they were surprised by a dawn attack by a superior *realista force commanded by Juan Antonio Olate. A body of patriot troops under Joaquín *Prieto Vial managed to seize the high ground and hold out long enough for reinforcements to arrive and attack the Spanish flank and rear. The enemy then retired, but had inflicted heavy losses on the patriots, who were forced to hold up their advance on Chillán.

RODRIGUEZ ERDOIZA, Manuel (1785-1818). Hero of the struggle for *independence. Qualifying as a lawyer in 1809, he championed the patriot cause as a *moderado and supporter of José Miguel *Carrera Verdugo, whose secretary he became. The *junta de gobierno de 1811 made him Secretary of War, and a year later he joined the *army with the rank of captain. Becoming involved in the internecine quarrels among the patriots, he was accused of conspiring against Carrera Verdugo in 1813 and arrested. After being released he took part in the Battle of *Rancagua and then sought refuge in Argentina. In 1815 José de *San Martín sent him back to Chile with a small force to wage a guerrilla war against the royalist authorities in *Colchagua. By encouraging the Spaniards to disperse their forces, Rodríguez contributed significantly to the patriot victory at *Chacabuco. Soon afterwards, Bernardo *O'Higgins, suspecting him of continued loyalty to Carrera Verdugo, sought to send him on a mission abroad. He refused to go, was arrested, escaped from prison, and sought out San Martín, who appointed him to his staff. In San Martín's absence he was again arrested and was not released until December 1817. After the defeat of *Cancha Rayada (March 20, 1818) he was asked by the *cabildo to take charge of the defense of *Santiago, being given the status of acting Supreme Director. In two days he organized an army known as the Húsares de la muerte (hussars of death) and restored calm to the capital. On O'Higgins' return, two days later, he handed over his powers. He fought at *Maipu, but by then even San Martín was alarmed by his popularity. His hussars were disbanded and he himself arrested again. On the way to *Quillota he was assassinated, but Chilean historians are not in agreement as to who was responsible. Miguel Luis *Almunátegui Aldunate has hypothesized that O'Higgins was, whereas Justo Abel Rosales was convinced that Bernardo de Monteagudo gave the order.
    See also: FRENTE PATRIOTICO MANUEL RODRIGUEZ.

RODRIGUEZ GONZALES, Pedro Jesús (1907-   ). Lawyer by profession and member of the Christian Democratic Party (*Partido Demócrata Cristiano, PDC). In 1949 he became president of the *Falange Nacional and a trustee of the Catholic University (*Universidad Católica). After the election of Christian Democrat President Eduardo *Frei Montalva in November 1964, Rodríguez Gonzales was made foreign minister.

RODRIGUEZ GREZ, Pablo (1937-   ). Lawyer, university professor
and writer by profession, Rodríguez Grez is best known as
founder of the right-wing terrorist organization *Patria y Libertad
(known in English as "Fatherland and Country"). With industrialist Roberto *Thieme as his second-in-command, he directed an
armed offensive against the democratically elected government of
Socialist Salvador *Allende Gossens. He plotted the *Tancazo of
June 29, 1973, and on its failure fled to Ecuador.
    As a student, Rodríguez Grez had traveled to Brazil and
Argentina and graduated from the *Universidad de Chile with
honors. After Allende's overthrow he became a member of the University of Chile law faculty. He has written books on Chilean nationalism and a critical account of the Allende government, Entre la democracia y la tiranía (between democracy and tyranny). Although
Patria y Libertad has been formally in self-declared dissolution
since 1973, it has insisted on generating a "national civic movement" for the perpetuation of an authoritarian coalition of the
right once democracy is restored in Chile. Rodríguez's aim since
the coup has been to do away with the traditional party system.
Unlike Thieme, however, he has stayed loyal to the *military
regime.

ROGGEVEEN, Jacob (1659-1729). Dutch sailor. In July 1721 he was
sent from Amsterdam by the Dutch West India Company to re-
discover the "Terra Australis Incognita" which the Welsh *pirate
Edward *Davis was supposed to have found in the South Pacific.
On Easter Day 1722 he came to Rapa-Nui, which he named Oster
Eiland, i.e. *Easter Island.

ROJAS DENEGRI, Rodrigo (1967-1986). United States citizen burned
to death in Santiago in July 1986. The son of a Chilean exile
living in Washington, D.C., Rojas was on a visit to Chile when
on July 2, 1986, first day of a two-day politically motivated general strike organized by the ANC (Asemblea Nacional Civil), he
attempted (according to anti-government sources) to photograph
soldiers beating up a young woman protester, Carmen Quintana.
The soldiers thereupon set both Rojas and Quintana alight, but
then doused the flames and abandoned both on a lonely road.
Rojas died of burns and trauma, but Quintana recovered in the hospital. A crowd of 2,000 at the funeral, including U.S. ambassador Harry Barnes, were tear-gassed when an attempt was made
to stage a demonstration. The Chilean government insisted that
Rojas and Quintana were burned while carrying petrol bombs, but
(perhaps as a result of U.S. government pressure) army lieutenant Pedro Fernández Dittus was charged with manslaughter
and negligence.

ROJAS SEPULVEDA, Manuel (1896-   ). Chilean novelist whose am-
bition was to create the modern Chilean novel. His work may be
divided into two main periods: the first from 1926 to 1936, and

the second from 1936 to 1951. The first period is characterized
by regionalism. The novelist describes primarily the seamy side
of Chilean life--city slums, tenements, centers of vice, prisons,
waterfront districts--in such works as Hombres del sur (men of
the south), 1926; El delincuente (the delinquent), 1929; Lanchas
en la bahía (boats in the bay), 1932; and Travesía (crossing),
1934. The second period emphasized the alienation and despair
of modern man, in such works as La ciudad de los Césares (the
city of the Caesars), 1936, and Hijo de ladrón, 1951, which appeared in English as Born guilty, 1956. In these works the influence of existentialist writers, especially Fyodor Dostoyevsky,
can be detected. Rojas portrays life in a realistic manner, and
his greatest achievement is his remarkable study of lower-class
Chilean society.

ROSS DE EDWARDS, Juana (1833-1914). Wife of Agustín *Edwards
Ossandón (her uncle) and sister to Agustín *Ross Edwards. Renowned in her widowhood for her charitable work and her opposition to José Manuel *Balmaceda Fernández (motivated by her
ultramontane views, especially in regard to civil marriage), for
which she was exiled in March 1891. The enormous wealth that
she inherited from her husband--and increased through shrewd
investment--largely bankrolled the congresista forces in the
*Civil War of 1891.

ROSS EDWARDS, Agustín (1844-1926). Important financier with
*nitrate interests; son of David Ross, a successful *Valparaíso
merchant of Scottish descent, and of Jorge *Edward Brown's
daughter Carmen Edwards Ossandón.

ROSS SANTA MARIA, Gustavo (b. 1879). Financier, businessman
and *Partido Liberal politician; son of Jorge Ross Edwards. He
had many investments in the *mining industry, especially *nitrates,
and was founder and president of the Nitrate Company of Chile.
In 1921 he became a *Valparaíso *regidor (city councilor), and in
1927 was one of the many political figures exiled by President
Carlos *Ibáñez del Campo. During his exile he made a fortune
speculating on the Paris bourse, and was the chief fundraiser
for the *Dover conspiracy. Called back to Chile by President
Arturo *Alessandri Palma in 1932 to be finance minister, he was
largely responsible for Chile's recovery from the Great *Depression
of the 1930s. A fiscal conservative, yet at the same time a strong
economic nationalist, he increased tariff protection of Chilean industry, squeezed the foreign-owned *copper industry for higher
taxes, nationalized the British-owned *Transandine Railway,
secured effective state control of central Chile's United States-
owned electric power company, and replaced *COSACH with the
Chilean Nitrate and Iodine Sales Corporation (*COVENSA), a
monopoly in which the Chilean government exercised effective
control and had a right to 25 percent of the profits. His unprecedented six years in office saw government revenue double,

unemployment fall markedly, and import-substitution foster a
modest growth of Chilean industry, but little of this prosperity
trickled down to the masses.

A cold, uncharismatic personality known as "Monsieur Gustave"
for his un-Chilean ways, Ross made no secret of his racist contempt for the Chilean lower classes (who would, he claimed, dis-
sipate in drink any income over subsistence level), nor of his
intense dislike of the *Partido Radical, whose members he forced
out of the government in 1937. His adoption as presidential
candidate over Alessandri's opposition split the right. The *Falange Conservadora was so lukewarm in its support as to be immediately blamed when Ross lost by 218,609 votes to Pedro *Aguirre Cerda's 222,700. Ross had campaigned on a slogan of
"Orden y trabajo" (order and work) and on wholesale bribery
of voters, made possible by a 40-million-*peso slush fund acquired
through illegal foreign exchange manipulation. Unfortunately
for Ross, Alessandri's brutal suppression of the *Seguro Obrero
occupation had led the third party candidate, Carlos Ibáñez del
Campo, to withdraw and urge his partisans to work for a *Frente
Popular victory. Ross cried fraud and appealed to the Electoral
Tribunal, but the archbishop-elect of *Santiago formally congratu-
lated the victor, and Ross's ultimate hope was frustrated when
the army c.-in-c. and the director of the *Cuerpo de Carabineros,
on persuasion by Alessandri, announced they would accept the
verdict of the electorate. Ross withdrew his charges with ill
grace, returned to France, and then settled in *Argentina, where
Aguirre forced him to remain, by revoking his passport.

ROTO. Literally "torn"; hence "ragged"--a term used for the inhabitant of an urban shanty town, or indeed for any lower-class city
dweller and, by extension, to any poor person. Outside Chile
it is sometimes used as a slang term for any Chilean. It furnished
the title, El roto, of Joaquín *Edwards Bello's 1920 novel of the
life of the city poor, published in implicit support of presidential
candidate Arturo *Alessandri Palma's social reform platform. See
also: YUNGAY.

RUIZ DANYAU, César (1918-). A career *air force officer who
joined the cabinet of Socialist President Salvador *Allende Gossens
on August 9, 1973, as minister of public works and transport.
The purpose of Ruiz's appointment was to end the month-old
truck owners' strike that was paralyzing the nation (see: BOSSES'
STRIKE). Unable or unwilling to do so--he claimed he had not
been delegated enough authority--Ruiz was forced to resign ten
days later. He also resigned his position as air force commander-
in-chief. Allende appointed Air Marshall Gustavo *Leigh Guzmán
to replace Ruiz as c.-in-c. Ruiz's resignation was suspected of
having been encouraged by the *armed forces' top brass, who
were plotting the *coup d'état that was to remove Allende in mid-
September.

After the coup Ruiz was briefly Rector of the *Universidad de Chile (1974-75). In 1979 he was appointed ambassador to Japan.

RUIZ TAGLE PORTALES, Francisco (17??-1860). Proprietor of an entailed estate (*Mayorazgo) at Los Andes, cousin to Diego *Portales Palazuelos, and a *pelucón (conservative). He was a deputy in the *Congress of 1811 and participated in the struggle for Chilean *independence. Nevertheless, he was not proscribed during the *Reconquista Española (Spanish reoccupation of Chile, 1814-17), but held office in the *Santiago *cabildo under the occupation. As governor ad interim he delivered the city of Santiago to the Patriots after their victory at *Chacabuco. After the Battle of *Maipú he again became an avowed Patriot, holding various offices in Congress during the *anarquía política period following Bernardo *O'Higgins's abdication. In 1829 he ran for President, and as he came second, the pelucones considered he should have been chosen vice-president. When a partisan Congress preferred Francisco Ramón *Vicuña Larraín, who had come fourth, but was a *pipiolo, the *Civil War of 1829-30 ensued. As a result of the Treaty of *Ochagavía, a Congreso de Plenipotenciarios was charged with electing a new President. They chose Ruiz Tagle (February 17, 1830). The country was still in turmoil, with many areas refusing to recognize the new President, and Ramón *Freire Serrano threatening to depose him by force. In light of this, Diego Portales persuaded his cousin to resign in favor of vice-president José Tomás *Ovalle Bezanilla, which he did on March 31, 1830. Ruiz Tagle then retired from active politics.

RUSSIA. See: U.S.S.R.

- S -

S.N.A. See: SOCIEDAD NACIONAL DE AGRICULTURA.

SAAVEDRA RODRIGUEZ, Cornelio (1821-1891). A career *army officer who fought the *Araucanian Indians in the 1860s and in the last punitive expedition against them in 1882, driving them as far south as Villarica. He also fought on the government side in the *Civil War of 1851 and the *Civil War of 1859. For his role in the extermination of the Indians and his participation in the War against *Spain of 1865-66, he was promoted brigadier general. He also fought in the War of the *Pacific, served in Congress as a deputy, 1861-73, and as a senator, 1885, until his death. In 1878-79 he was war minister.

SACRISTAN, Cuestión del. Bitter Church-State dispute of 1856.
Some canons of *Santiago cathedral objected to the dismissal of
a cathedral sexton. When they in turn were suspended for insubordination, they appealed to the Supreme Court and won.
The *archbishop protested on the ingenious grounds that the
canons' suspension, since it involved only their spiritual duties,
was not a matter within the purview of the state, the patronato
nacional. The government eventually resolved the quarrel by
persuading the canons to submit. Even so, the matter split the
*pelucones into a minority who supported President Manuel
*Montt Torres (and eventually formed the *Partido Nacional) and
the majority who in 1857 formed the ultramontane *Partido Con-
servador--and promptly allied themselves with the Liberals in the
*Fusión Liberal-Conservadora, the better thereby to weaken the
government.
See also: CHURCH, The; REAL PATRONATO.

SALA Y GOMEZ ISLAND. A small island dependency of Chile, situated
at 26° 28'S, 105° 28'W, some 2,100 miles west of Chile and 250
miles east-northeast of *Easter Island. A volcanic outcrop measuring only 4,000 feet by 500 feet and reaching 100 feet above sea
level, it is uninhabited and was discovered in 1793 by the Spanish
sailor whose name it bears. It is administered as part of the
province of *Valparaíso.

SALARIES. See: WAGES AND SALARIES.

SALAS CORVALAN, Manuel de (1754-1841). Politician and lawyer
who participated in the struggle for Chilean *independence.
Elected *alcalde of *Santiago in 1775, he subsequently spent some
years in Europe, where he became acquainted with the latest
ideas in political and economic thought. In the 1790s he was
Governor Ambrose *O'Higgins Ballenary's superintendant of public
works, and founded the *Academia de San Luis, forerunner of
the *Instituto Nacional. In 1811 he was one of the promoters
of the *junta de gobierno de 1811, set up to achieve separation
of Chile from Spain. He was one of the drafters of the *Constitution of 1812 and was associated with Juan *Egaña Risco in
starting La *Aurora de Chile, the country's first newspaper.
One of the *exaltados, he was made secretario de *gobierno--
interior and foreign minister--that same year of 1812, but came
into conflict with José Miguel *Carrera Verdugo and had to go
into exile in *Mendoza. When he returned in 1814, Supreme
Director Francisco de la *Lastra y de la Sotta appointed him to the
Senate. Following the patriot defeat at *Rancagua, he was exiled
by the Spanish into the *Juan Fernández Islands. Returning after
*Chacabuco, he devoted himself to civic matters, working un-
ceasingly to encourage *agriculture, *mining, *industry and *education. He introduced new crops and industries, such as flax
and silkworms. He was given charge of the refounded *National

Library in 1818, recruiting Camilo *Henríquez González as librarian. He was also instrumental in the founding of the Hospicio (orphanage). When Bernardo *O'Higgins abdicated, Manuel de Salas formed part of the *Junta de gobierno provisional de 1823. In that year he was elected president of *Congress.

SALDIAS, Vegas de. See: VEGAS DE SALDIAS, Las.

SALITRERAS DE IQUIQUE. The *nitrate (saltpeter) refinery of Iquique was the scene of many *labor disturbances during the first quarter of the 20th century, as the workers organized to improve their economic and social condition. The depression of 1906 led to demands for pay increases and an end to the abuses of the *pulpería. The authorities offered to mediate and invited the workers to come into the city and lodge at the Santa María elementary school. When, however, they were told to leave the school for another destination, they became suspicious, refused to move and were machine-gunned, some 3,000 workers and their wives and children (out of some 7,000 total) being killed or wounded in the few minutes of the "Matanza de la Escuela Santa María" (December 21, 1907). In the years that followed, armed conflicts between workers and police were frequent. Many labor leaders were imprisoned for years, and the need for stronger TRADE UNIONS (q.v.) was recognized. It was not until 1927 that labor-management relations improved and labor demands were finally met in part.

SALT. The salt flats (salares) of the *Norte Grande produce some 2 million metric *tons of sodium chloride a year.

SALUBRIDAD, PREVISION Y ASISTENCIA SOCIAL, Ministerio de. The Ministry of Health, Insurance and Social Assistance was the result of the Ministerio de *Salubridad Pública changing its name (February 20, 1936) to one making explicit its social security responsibilities. In 1953 the name was changed again, to Ministerio de *Salud Pública y Previsión Social.

SALUBRIDAD PUBLICA, Ministerio de. The Ministry of Public Health was created by the June 5, 1932, division of the Ministerio de *Bienestar Social into a Labor Ministry (Ministerio del *Trabajo) and one for its public health and social security functions.

SALUD PUBLICA, Ministerio de. The Ministry of Public Health created October 14, 1959 by the transfer of the Social Security functions of the Ministerio de *Salud Pública y Previsión Social to the Ministry of Labor (*Ministerio de Trabajo y Previsión Social). The ministry's main functions are: to provide health care for all Chileans (including those unable to pay the full cost); to fight venereal diseases and birth defects; to lower the infant mortality rate; and to conduct research for the prevention of disease. Ministers since the 1973 *coup have been: Col. Alberto Spoerer Covarrubias (September 1973); General Francisco Herrera Latoja (July 1974); General Fernando *Matthey Aubel (March 1976); Col. Carlos Mario Jiménez (July 1978); General Alejandro Medina Lois (December 1979); Rear Admiral Hernán Rivera Calderón (December 1980); Winston Chinchón Bunting (August 1983).

SALUD PUBLICA Y PREVISION SOCIAL, Ministerio de. The Ministry of Public Health and Social Insurance was formed in 1953 by a change of name of the former Ministerio de *Salubridad, Previsión y Asistencia Social. It lasted until 1959, when its social security responsibilities passed to the Labor Ministry and its name was consequently shortened to Ministerio de *Salud Pública.

SALVADOR, El. El Salvador is a relatively new *copper mine, discovered in 1959 and located only 12.5 air miles from *Potrerillos in the province of *Atacama. Providentially discovered just when Potrerillos had been exhausted, it was appropriately named "The Savior." Production at the new mine grew from 42,298 short tons (38,372 metric *tons) in 1959 to about 90,000 tonnes of *copper in 1970. Since then, however, it has declined slightly, producing 76,500 tonnes in 1981. See also: ANACONDA.

SAN AMBROSIO ISLAND. See: SAN FELIX AND SAN AMBROSIO ISLANDS.

SAN ANTONIO, City of. City of central Chile, a major resort and the nearest port to *Santiago, founded 1848. Capital of the province of the same name. Its population has grown from 1,327 in 1907 to 28,000 in 1952 and 73,800 (est.) in 1980. It was the site of one of the post-*coup *concentration camps. See also: PORTS AND HARBORS.

SAN ANTONIO, Province of. Area on the Pacific coast immediately to the west of *Santiago, which in the earlier part of this century was a subdelegación of the department of Melipilla. With the growth of the importance of San Antonio city as a port, it was first made a department (within Santiago province), and then, in the administrative restructuring of 1974, it was transferred to the new Region V, *Aconcagua, as the Province of San Antonio. Capital: San Antonio.

SAN BERNARDO. City of Greater *Santiago, founded 1834, with a population that has grown from 8,269 in 1907 to 136,224 (est.) in 1986.

SAN FELIPE. City of central Chile, on the north bank of the *Aconcagua river, at 32° 44'S, 70° 42'W, founded in 1740 and named for King *Philip V. Before 1974 it was the capital of Aconcagua province. It is now the capital of San Felipe province within the new Region V, Aconcagua. Its population was 10,426 in 1907 and was estimated at 34,562 in 1982.

SAN FELIX AND SAN AMBROSIO ISLANDS. Uninhabited dependencies of Chile at 26° 17'S, 80° 7'W. San Felix and San Ambrosio, its small satellite, are volcanic, and were discovered in 1574 by Juan Fernández.

SAN FERNANDO. City of Chile's central valley, founded in 1742 at 34° 36'S, 70° 59'W and named for the king's eldest son, the future *Ferdinand VI. It was the capital of the pre-1974 province of *Colchagua and is now capital of the new province of Colchagua within Región VI, *Libertador.

SAN FRANCISCO, Cerros de. Site of two battles fought for control of the near-by oasis (pozo) of *Dolores in Tarapacá province, which are also known as the battles of Dolores.
  A. In the War of the *Pacific, a Chilean army of 6,000, after landing at *Pisagua, advanced and took Dolores, but were threatened by Daza's Bolivians advancing south from *Tacna and Buendía's Peruvians coming north from *Iquique. The latter arrived first, on November 19, 1879, and were completely routed. Daza then returned to Tacna, and the Chileans were able to occupy all of *Antofagasta and most of Tarapacá.
  B. The second battle occurred during the *Civil War of 1891, on February 15. Some 350 government soldiers led by Eulogio Robles Pinochet were advancing on the rebel base of Pisagua from Iquique when they were attacked by 1,000 *congresistas under Estanislao del *Canto Arteaga and defeated after a three-hour combat.

SAN FRANCISCO CHURCH. Located at Alameda Avenue and Londres Street, the 16th century *Santiago church, which survived the *earthquake of 1647, is the oldest church in Chile. The simplicity of the interior is typical of American colonial art. The walls are broad and plain, and the confessionals were wood-carved by Indians. The church's most valuable relic is a wooden statue of the Virgin brought by Pedro de Valdivia.

SAN MARTIN, José de (1777-1850). Argentine patriot who, with Simón Bolivar, is considered one of the liberators of the South American continent. He studied in Spain and then returned to his native land, where in the brief span of eight years he led a highly successful military career. He was a lieutenant colonel at the age of 31. In Chile he is remembered for his invaluable help in overthrowing the Spanish yoke. As governor of *Cuyo he provided a refuge for the Chilean patriots fleeing after the *Reconquista Española, and, with the support of Argentine Supreme Director Juan Martín *Pueyrredón, he incorporated them into his legendary Chilean-Argentine Army of the Andes (Ejército de los *Andes), which was victorious in the two key battles of *Chacabuco (1817) and *Maipú (1818). He then led his army north to break the seat of Spanish power in *Peru. However, at the historic meeting in Guayaquil (Ecuador) on July 26, 1822, between San Martín and Simón Bolívar, the two leaders could not reach an agreement to insure the independence of Peru. San Martín decided to withdraw and let Bolívar finish the arduous task of liberation alone. He returned to *Mendoza for a few months, and then traveled to France where he spent the rest of his life, dying in modest circumstances.

SANFUENTES ANDONAEGUI, Juan Luis (1858-1930). President of Chile, 1915-20. From a distinguished *Santiago family, he graduated in law at the *Universidad de Chile in 1879. After a brief service in the *navy during the War of the *Pacific, he entered politics, being elected as a Liberal deputy in 1888. During the *Civil War of 1891 he supported President José Manuel *Balmaceda Fernández; on Balmaceda's fall he temporarily abandoned politics for business. In 1900 he entered the Senate as a member of the *Partido Liberal Democrático (which he had joined in 1891) and in 1903 President (1901-06) Germán *Riesco Errázuriz appointed him finance minister.

An expert in financial affairs, as well as an astute politician, Sanfuentes was a counselor of the Caja de Crédito Hipotécario (Mortgage Loan Bank) since 1888, and the Banco de Ahorros (Savings Bank). In 1915 he won his party's nomination to run for President and was elected by a narrow margin. Immediately he embarked upon the task of rebuilding the nation, especially in the economic field. He succeeded in reducing the public debt, in pushing through a program of extended public works and in making elementary education compulsory. Never very popular with the electorate, he remained neutral in the presidential election of 1920.

SANTA CRUZ Y CALAHUMADA, Andrés de (1792-1845). Bolivian president at the time of the 1836-39 war with Chile. He was born in La Paz to a Peruvian officer in Spanish service and his wife of royal Incan descent. Santa Cruz had a distinguished career in the Wars of Independence, first in the Spanish army and then on the insurgents' side, where he served successively under José de *San Martín and Simón Bolívar. Finally, he served as second-in-command to Marshall Sucre, liberator of *Bolivia, then known as Upper Peru. From 1826-27, while Sucre was serving as Bolivia's first president, Santa Cruz administered *Peru but succeeded Sucre when the latter resigned and returned to Colombia. Although Santa Cruz proved a capable administrator of Bolivia, his heart was set on creating a united republic of Bolivia and Peru. In 1835 civil conflict in Peru gave him the excuse to intervene, and in 1836 he attempted to force a *Peru-Bolivia

Confederation (Confederación Peruboliviana) with himself as Supreme Protector. Brazil made a formal protest and *Argentina
made an unsuccessful attack on the new state. But the Argentine
president Rosas was distracted by his own problems with the
French, and, of all Bolivia's alarmed neighbors, it was Chile
that finally took effective action. War was declared December
1836, and after a frustrated first invasion, Chile's second expeditionary force triumphed at the battle of *Yungay. Santa Cruz
was forced into exile in Ecuador, and when his subsequent attempt to return to power in Bolivia was frustrated by a Peruvian
occupation of La Paz, he left for France, where he died four
years later.

Chilean intervention against Santa Cruz has been variously
seen as a response to fear of an aggressive Bolivia whose further
designs for expansion would in all likelihood be directed southward; as an insurance policy against a statesman whose reformist
energies were turning a weak neighbor into a relatively strong
one; or as the first stage in Chile's own expansionist policy,
which would culminate in the War of the *Pacific.

SANTA MARIA GONZALEZ, Domingo (1825-1889). President of Chile,
1881-86. A professor at the *Instituto Nacional, he qualified as
a lawyer in 1847. Having supported the reelection of Manuel
*Bulnes Prieto, twice President of Chile (1841-46; 1846-51), he
was appointed *intendant of *Colchagua as a reward (1848-50).
A member of the *Partido Liberal, he took part in the *Civil War
of 1851 and was exiled to Lima until 1853. Elected to the Chamber
of Deputies in 1858, he took part in the *Civil War of 1859 and
was exiled again: first to *Magallanes and then to Europe. He
returned in 1862 and President (1861-71) José Joaquín *Pérez
Mascayano appointed him finance minister (1863) and then made
him an Appeal Court judge (ministro). In 1865 he was sent on
an unsuccessful diplomatic mission to forestall the war with *Spain
of 1865-66. Subsequently he helped organize the plan of defense
agreed upon with Peru. During the War of the *Pacific he was
in turn foreign minister, interior minister and war minister, before being elected President in 1881. As President he insisted
on a Chilean occupation of Peru (administered by Patricio *Lynch
Solo de Zaldívar) until a settlement (the Treaty of *Ancón) was
reached in 1884. This was however only a provisional agreement
in certain respects, and the definitive Treaty of *Lima was not
signed until 1929. As chief magistrate Santa María undertook
the last war against the *Araucanian Indians in 1883. The resultant treaties with the *Mapuche chieftains the following year
pushed the tribes further south, but assigned them certain lands
in perpetuity. During the last two years of his presidency,
Santa María faced numerous political and religious controversies,
making his administration the stormiest since that of Manuel
*Montt Torres (1851-61). His secularization of cemeteries, the
introduction of civil marriage and civil registration of births,

plus the long quarrel with the *Church over the appointment of a successor to Archbishop Rafael Valentín *Valdivieso y Zañartu (only resolved by the next administration) led to particularly bad relations with the *Partido Conservador. After leaving office he was elected president of the Senate. He was also appointed to draw up the Código de enjuiciamiento civil (Code of civil procedure), a task his declining health obliged him to abandon after a few months.

SANTIAGO (city). Capital of Chile. It was founded February 12, 1541, by Pedro de *Valdivia as Santiago de Nueva Estremadura, but was almost entirely destroyed in September of the same year by the fierce *Araucanian Indians. It was leveled by an *earthquake in May 1647 and badly damaged by others in July 1730, May 1751, February 1835, August 1906, July 1971 and March 1985. The city also suffered periodically from the torrential *Mapocho river until this was controlled in the 19th century. Liberated by José de *San Martín in 1817, the historic capital of colonial Chile became the capital of the new *Republic of Chile when *independence was declared on September 18, 1818.

Situated at 33° 30'S, 70° 40'W, at an altitude of 550 meters (1,800 feet) on a wide plain between the *Andes and the coastal range, Santiago de Chile is watered by the *Maipo and Mapocho rivers and overshadowed by Mount *Aconcagua (28,835 feet), the highest peak in the Americas. The metropolitan area approximates 8 square miles and lies 60 miles southeast of its main port, *Valparaíso.

Although it retains neoclassical government buildings and baroque churches from colonial times, Santiago is essentially a modern capital with skyscrapers, big department stores, modern hotels, a subway system (the *Metro), and traffic problems. The population, which was about 12,000 in 1700 and 40,000 at independence, reached 115,377 in 1865; 129,807 in 1875; 189,332 in 1885; 256,403 in 1895; 332,724 in 1907; 507,296 in 1920; 712,533 in 1930; 952,075 in 1940; 1,350,409 in 1952; 1,907,378 in 1960; 2,861,900 in 1970 (census figures); 3,730,600 (est.) in 1980; and 4,364,500 (est.) in 1986. Greater Santiago is now the fifth largest conurbation in South America (after São Paulo, Buenos Aires, Rio de Janeiro and Bogotá). The climate is temperate, with generally warm days and cool nights, and little seasonal change other than a two-month rainy period in winter. The city's growth, however, has created pollution problems, particularly in respect to atmospheric smoke.

Santiago dominates Chile's commercial, industrial and cultural life. Its development has been steady, especially since the end of the 19th century, when many European immigrants contributed to its culture, embellishment and charm. More than half the country's manufacturing is done in the capital, and 54 percent of all Chile's industrial activities are carried on in the greater metropolitan area. There have been a number of regional develop-

ment efforts (such as the establishment of a duty-free industrial
zone in *Arica) to reduce Santiago's industrial primacy, but these
have had no significant impact on it.

Gran Santiago is the trading and distributing center for the
fertile central valley (cereals, fruit, wine, vegetables, *livestock);
for textiles (cotton, silk, wool, rayon, hosiery, clothing); for
chemicals (plastics, explosives, paints, varnishes, pharmaceuticals,
cosmetics); for metal products (*iron and steel parts, machinery,
appliances); for banking (national and international); and for a
myriad of other activities, including *printing and paper products,
leather goods, rubber, tobacco, food processing, brewing, meat
packing, flour milling, distilling and tanning.

Two of Chile's leading institutions of higher education, the
*Universidad Católica and the *Universidad de Chile, are both in
the capital, as are the academies of the *armed forces, the
*National Library, the *History Museum and the municipal theater.
Santiago's principal artery is the wide Avenida Bernardo *O'Higgins,
also known as the *Alameda, which crosses the whole city. The
most famous of its fine downtown plazas and parks is the Plaza
de Armas, across from the *Cathedral. The centrally located
Palacio de la *Moneda is the seat of government.

Santiago is linked by *highway, *railway and air to all Chilean
cities. Its north-south rail system (see: RED SUR) is well
traveled, as is the Panamerican Highway from Santiago to Arica.
Its longitudinal rail line links it with the *Transandine railway
to *Argentina. The international airport, named in honor of Arturo *Merino Benítez is 16 miles away to the northeast, at *Pudahuel, and there is another airport for domestic services at Los
*Cerrillos to the southwest.

See also: TOURISM.

SANTIAGO (province). One of Chile's three original provinces, Santiago lost all its territory south of the River Cachapoal in the 1826
restructuring of Chile's *provinces by the *Partido Federalista.
Its subsequently lost its departments of Valparaíso and Casablanca
to the new province of *Valparaíso in 1842, and its department
of Rancagua to the new province of *O'Higgins in 1883, leaving
it with some 14,672 km^2 (5,665 square miles). During the first
presidency of Carlos *Ibáñez del Campo (1927-31), however, it
received the department of Maipo from O'Higgins, increasing its
area to 17,686 km^2 (6,828 square miles). The population grew
from 207,930 in 1854 to 516,870 in 1907; 1,754,954 in 1952; and
3,038,397 (est.) in 1971. The administrative restructuring of
1974 lost it the department of *San Antonio and gave it the new
designation of "Area Metropolitana de Santiago" with an area of
16,895.6 km^2 (6,523 square miles). The 1984 estimated population
was 4.8 million.

SANTIAGO, BATTLE OF. On September 11, 1973, the Chilean capital
turned into a bloody battleground as Salvador *Allende Gossens,

the *Unidad Popular President of Chile, met his death, along with
thousands of other Chileans, trying to resist a well-coordinated
*coup d'état by the *armed forces. Although La *Moneda Palace
was taken in a few hours, fighting continued for some days.
Many downtown government offices, including La Moneda, were
bombed, obliging the new military regime to function from the
Diego Portales building instead. Rebuilding is now at long last
complete.

SANTIAGUINO. An inhabitant of Santiago de Chile, who is thus distinguished from a Santiagueño (from Santiago del Campo or Santiago del Estero), a Santiaguero (from Santiago de Cuba), a
Santiaguês (from Santiago de Campostela), etc. The name owes
its popularity (there are more than fifty cities called Santiago
in the Spanish-speaking world) because it honors Spain's patron
saint, James (Sant'Yago).

SARMIENTO, Domingo Faustino (1811-1888). Argentine educator,
writer and statesman who spent two periods of political exile in
Chile. In 1831 he fled from the local *caudillo of La Rioja, Domingo Faustino Quiroga. On that occasion he was a poor unknown
schoolteacher who took a variety of jobs to make ends meet,
including one as a mine foreman at *Copiapó. He returned to
Argentina in 1836, but soon had to flee again, this time from
dictator Juan Manuel de Rosas. He arrived back in Chile in 1841
and became editor of El *Mercurio. In 1842 he was sent by the
Chilean government to study education abroad, spending time
in both the *United States and *France. He returned with a
great deal of enthusiasm for the ideas of United States educator
Horace Mann, and for those of the French Romantics, such as
Victor Hugo. He was then given charge of the newly created
*Escuela Normal de Preceptores (see: EDUCATION). This second
period of exile was one of the most creative stages of Sarmiento's
life and saw the publication of his classic biography of Quiroga,
Civilización y barbarie (Civilization and barbarism) and his less
well known Educación popular (Popular education).
    Sarmiento took up the defense of a progressive concept of
culture, espousing "romantic" freedom of expression and the vital-
izing effects of French writers on Spanish-American literature.
He was the first to introduce Romanticism in Chile, but was
challenged by the Neo-classicists headed by the Venezuelan-born
scholar Andrés *Bello López. Soon a controversy arose between
these two outstanding foreigners who had made Chile their home.
Bello defended the aristocratic concept of literary standards,
preferring the purity of the Castilian tongue and the values of
Spanish culture over the French. Sarmiento defended French
linguistic influence, saying that Spanish Americans had to turn
to the French language for new expressions. The polemic between
the two writers lasted until Sarmiento returned to Argentina, soon
after the overthrow of Rosas. Eventually he became President
of Argentina himself (1868-74).

SARMIENTO DE GAMBOA, Pedro (1550-1592). Spanish sailor and discoverer of the Galápagos Islands. On October 11, 1579, he was
sent by viceroy Francisco de Toledo to survey the area of the
*Strait of Magellan and to establish permanent settlements to
guard the passage. He sailed through the Strait in February
1580 and returned to Spain on August 15. Appointed Governor
of the Strait, he was again dispatched with a large fleet on
September 25, 1581, but lost five ships in a storm. Further
losses occurred during a long stay in Rio de Janeiro. Bad weather induced Diego Flores de Valdes, nominal commander of the
expedition, to desert, and another ship was lost to pirates. With
a much reduced number of ships and men, Sarmiento reached the
Strait, planted two settlements (see: PUERTO DE HAMBRE), and
returned to Brazil for more supplies. Two attempts to deliver
these were frustrated by gales and Sarmiento sailed for Spain
to get further help. On the way he was captured and taken to
England, where Sir Walter Raleigh secured his release and paid
for his return. While crossing France in December 1586, he was
imprisoned and held for ransom in a dark, rat-infested dungeon
until October 1589. He died three years later.

SCHNEIDER CHREAU, René (?-1969). Commander-in-chief of the
Chilean *army who was abducted on October 22, 1969, and then
murdered in an attempt to prevent Socialist Salvador *Allende
Gossens from being sworn in as President of Chile. Only two
days before, General Schneider had announced that the army
would respect the *constitution and would support whichever
candidate *Congress chose. Fearing that the candidate chosen
might be Allende, several retired army officers, led by General
Roberto *Viaux Marambio and helped by the *United States *Central Intelligence Agency, prepared to stage a coup. Schneider
had been included in the C.I.A.'s worldwide "list of enemies."
As part of the C.I.A.'s attempt to block Allende's accession,
U.S. officials supplied financial aid and equipment (including
machine guns) to various military figures and right-wing groups.
On October 15 (a week before Schneider was killed) it became
apparent to the C.I.A. that Viaux's plot had little chance of
success. Efforts were made to dissuade Viaux, but to no avail.
On the fatal day, just 48 hours before Congress was to vote on
their choice for President, a gang of assailants intercepted
Schneider's car as it was being driven to his office in the Defense
Ministry. Schneider drew a gun, whereupon the gang panicked
and shot him dead. The C.I.A. had supported the original idea
of a kidnapping, but not the murder, which effectively ruined
its hopes of provoking a military takeover to prevent Allende
from taking office (see also: CENTRAL INTELLIGENCE AGENCY).

SCHWEITZER WALTER, Miguel Alex. Foreign minister of Chile,
February 14 to December 15, 1983. Previously justice minister
(April 1975-March 1977) and then ambassador in London, Schweitzer

succeeded René Rojas Galdanes as foreign minister. He resigned after making claims that the Chilean government enjoyed enormous popularity according to a Gallup poll. The claims were made on a U.S. television program but were denied by Gallup. His successor was Jaime del *Valle Alliende.

SEA, Law of the: See: LAW OF THE SEA.

SEAL HUNTING. The southern fur sea (arctocephalus) was formerly found in the South Atlantic and Pacific from South Africa westward to Australia, and along the American Pacific coast from *Magallanes to Mexico. Intensive hunting began on the Falklands in 1784: the seals there were wiped out in 15 years and hunting spread to the islands off Antarctica and to southern Chile. By 1801 there were an estimated 60 vessels (U.S., British, Portuguese, Russian among them) hunting seals in the region and then trading the furs in Canton for tea and silk. Unused to predators on land and unable to move rapidly ashore, the seal populations were soon drastically depleted. Although international treaties sought to conserve stocks in the northern Pacific, no such efforts were made in the south and hunting only ceased there after World War II, when most of the seal populations were extinct or believed to be so. Some recovery, even of varieties that were thought to have been completely exterminated, was noted in the 1970s. *Valparaíso and *Ancud were among the *ports on which Chilean sea hunting was based in the early 19th century.
See also: EASTER ISLAND.

SECRET SERVICES. See: CENTRAL INTELLIGENCE AGENCY; CENTRAL NACIONAL DE INFORMACIONES; DINA; SERVICIO DE INTELIGENCIA....

SECRETARIA DE ESTADO. Original name of the three administrative departments of the Chilean state, 1814-18. The name was then changed to ministerio and the designation of the department head from secretario de estado to ministro. See: MINISTRIES.

SECURITIES. See: BANKS, BANKING AND FINANCIAL INSTITUTIONS; STOCK EXCHANGE.

SEGUEL MOLINA, Rodolfo (1954-). Leader of Chile's largest *copper miners' union, the 23,000-member Confederation of Copper Workers (Confederación de Trabajadores del Cobre, CTC). Politically close to the *Partido Demócrata Cristiano, although not a member, Seguel was jailed in 1983 by the Augusto *Pinochet Ugarte regime for calling for a "national day of protest" against the government. He was released after 34 days, but shortly afterwards his employer, the state *Corporación del Cobre (CODELCO, or Copper Corporation), fired him.
Although relations with Pinochet had deteriorated as a result, Seguel was considered a hero by the trade union movement, which

had shown support for him throughout the country. Seguel was most disturbed by the *junta's economic policies, which had caused unemployment to reach 30 percent (see: EMPLOYMENT). In a Newsweek interview with Mary Helen Spooner, Seguel disclosed that union members had to work almost clandestinely, since they were closely watched and their phones were tapped. He drew a comparison with Poland, saying that Polish and Chilean workers suffered similarly. The regimes were different: one was politically on the left, the other on the right, but both were repressive dictatorships. He also recalled another Chilean union leader, Tucapel Jiménez, who had been killed by the military for seeking to establish a broad-based labor union movement, as Seguel himself was attempting. Like so many leaders of the opposition, Seguel was demanding a return to democracy. In the disturbances of September 4, 1984, he was one of those singled out for a warning to keep out of politics. He was demanding a change because, as he saw it, "the situation in Chile was chaotic, critical and desperate." In October–December 1985 he spent a further two months in jail.

See: LABOR; TRADE UNIONS.

SEGUNDA, La (July 1931-). *Santiago daily newspaper, originally entitled La Segunda de las Ultimas Noticias. Although closed down in the wake of the September 1973 *coup d'état, it was subsequently allowed to resume publication. See: NEWSPAPERS.

SEGURO OBRERO, Matanza del. The Social Security building in Santiago, scene of a putsch attempt by the *Movimiento Nacional Socialista de Chile during the 1938 presidential election campaign. On the previous day, September 4, apparently realizing that they stood no chance at the ballot box, the *Alianza Popular Libertadora (the *Nacistas and other supporters of the *Ibáñez del Campo candidacy) staged a 12,000 strong "march of triumph" in downtown Santiago, and followed this on September 5 with a violent seizure of the main building of the *Universidad de Chile and the Seguro Obrero (opposite La *Moneda), killing a carabinero in the process. An *army regiment whose support they had counted on stood idly, while loyal carabineros stormed the university and then used the Nacistas captured there as a human shield in their attack on the Seguro Obrero. As soon as resistance was overcome, all 61 rebels were shot out of hand, allegedly on the orders of President Arturo *Alessandri Palma (who had personally intervened to drag away the dying carabinero).

Nacista leader Jorge *González von Marées, who had been directing the protest with a radio transmitter, was arrested together with Ibáñez del Campo. With fears of judicial execution, Ibáñez del Campo withdrew his candidacy and both men urged their supporters to work for a *Frente Popular victory. The Chilean press deplored the violence used in the demonstration and accused the Right of extremism.

On October 5 Chileans peacefully voted Frente Popular candidate *Aguirre Cerda into office.

SEMANA ROJA. "Red Week," also known as the Huelga de la carne (meat strike), began with a public protest meeting in *Santiago's *Alameda on Sunday October 22, 1905, demanding the abolition of the import tax on Argentine cattle (see: CATTLE FARMING). Although President Germán *Riesco Errázuriz undertook to study the question, the protest degenerated into rioting, which lasted until the city garrison (then away on maneuvers at *Quechereguas) could be brought back to restore order. This they did on the Monday, October 23, killing some 200 demonstrators. The violence of the repression provoked a national general strike in which *railway workers used the red flag for the first time in Chile as a symbol of revolution. Four years later these railway workers would form Chile's first national *trade union, the *Gran Federación Obrera de Chile. The tax on meat imports was abolished, but without having any impact on the high price of meat in the shops.

SENATE. See: CONGRESS.

SENDET (Servicio Nacional de Detenidos). The National Prisoners' Service, an institution created to handle the administration of the dozens of prison camps set up in Chile after the *coup d'état of September 1973 which overthrew the government of socialist President Salvador *Allende Gossens. SENDET's offices were established in the basement of the deserted National *Congress building, and families were advised that anyone seeking news of an arrested person should go there. SENDET worked closely with the Chilean secret police, *DINA, to determine the degree of dangerousness of each prisoner, and, ironically, to keep families from finding out where their missing relatives were being held. See also: CONCENTRATION CAMPS.

SEPTEMBER 5th MUTINY. See: SEGURO OBRERO.

SEPTEMBER 11th COUP. See: COUP D'ETAT OF 1973.

SEPULVEDA CONTRERAS, Manuel. Colonel (later, General) who founded and headed Chile's dreaded secret police, the *DINA. He enlisted the aid of former S.S. colonel Walter *Rauff, first in converting the Chilean resort of *Tejas Verdes into a *concentration camp, and then employing him as his chief advisor. Sepúlveda was implicated in the murder of Orlando *Letelier del Solar, Chile's pre-*coup ambassador to the *United States, and Letelier's co-worker, Ronni Moffit—a murder that took place in Washington, D.C., and so raised issues of United States sovereignty, especially since Moffit was an American citizen. The U.S. government demanded the extradition of those involved: Sepúlveda,

his agent Michael Vernon *Townley (a U.S. citizen) and two
other Chileans, Pedro *Espinoza Bravo and Armando *Fernández
Larios. The Chilean government returned Townley but refused
to extradite the others, who were placed instead under house
arrest while it conducted its own investigation. A year later
they were freed. It was widely reported internationally that
Sepúlveda was obeying the orders of his superiors, and that
President Augusto *Pinochet Ugarte (who was believed to have
stonewalled the investigation) was possibly involved himself.

SERENA, La. Capital of the northern Region IV, *Coquimbo, and one
of Chile's oldest cities, located a mile from the sea, near the
mouth of the River *Elqui, at 29° 54'S, 71° 18'W. Its port, the
town of Coquimbo, was founded in 1850; before then La Serena
itself was often referred to as "Coquimbo." In colonial times La
Serena was the major city of northern Chile, even though its
18th-century population was a mere 5,000. It was founded in
1543 by Juan Bohón, who named it Extremadura, after Pedro de
*Valdivia's native province. Destroyed by Indians in 1549, La
Serena was rebuilt six months later by Francisco de *Aguirre
as San Bartolomé de la Serena, after his homeland of La Serena,
a district of southeastern Extremadura. Late in the next century
the city was plundered and burned by the *pirates Bartholomew
*Sharp (1680) and Edward *Davis (1686). In July 1730 an
*earthquake leveled half its buildings. It saw the outbreak of
the *Civil War of 1851 and was held by the rebels in the *Civil
War of 1859. The city's population was 15,712 in 1895; about
20,000 in 1940; 71,200 (est.) in 1971; and 89,998 (est.) in 1986.

SERVICIO DE INTELIGENCIA DE CARABINEROS (SICAR). The Intelligence Service of the *Cuerpo de Carabineros, with a strength
of 2,500 to 3,500 men. After June 1974 it came under the supervision of the Chilean Secret Police, the DINA, q.v.

SERVICIO DE INTELIGENCIA DE LA FUERZA AEREA (SIFA). The
intelligence service of the air force. After June 1974 its activities
were supervised by the Chilean Secret Police, the DINA (q.v.)
which was the apparatus for coordinating all intelligence work in
Chile.

SERVICIO DE INTELIGENCIA MILITAR (SIM). The *army's intelligence
service. After June 1974 its activities, like those of the other
intelligence services, were coordinated by the DINA, q.v.

SERVICIO DE INTELIGENCIA NAVAL (SIN). The Naval Intelligence
Service played a key role in the 1973 overthrow of Socialist
President Salvador *Allende Gossens by identifying all naval commissioned officers sympathetic to Allende and disposing of them
before the *coup. Like the other intelligence services, the SIN
came under the supervision of DINA (q.v.) after the founding of
the agency in 1974.

SERVICIO DE SEGURO SOCIAL. See: SOCIAL WELFARE.

SERVICIO NACIONAL DE SALUD (SNS). Government involvement in health care began with the labor legislation of the 1920s and the creation of the Ministerio de *Higiene, Asistencia y Previsión Social in 1924. Provision was however very fragmented until the 1952 creation of the Servicio Nacional de Salud (National Health Service). Even this was primarily directed toward the working class (*obreros) and (nominally, but not very effectively) the indigent. White-collar workers (*empleados) and members of the *armed forces usually had their own programs outside the SNS. By the early 1960s about 60 percent of Chileans were covered by SNS. The service was strengthened and extended during the three-year experiment with socialism under the *Unidad Popular administration, 1970-73. SNS was then providing a comprehensive and compulsory health insurance program for obreros and their families. It was paid for through social security contributions (see: SOCIAL WELFARE). The program covered medical needs from birth to funeral expenses. Those who could not pay received free medical care. Emergency hospital treatment, even if requiring a complicated operation, was free even for the wealthy. The SNS also provided one of the most effective birth control programs in Latin America, which significantly reduced the previously very high rate of death and sickness resulting from illegal abortion--the cause of 40 percent of all maternal deaths in the 1960s.

After 1973 the *military regime implemented extensive reforms as part of its general policy of trying to eliminate subsidies and minimize assistance to the poor. General provision of free health care (which had reached about 80 percent of the population before the *coup) was ended in 1980. Henceforth SNS members had the option of seeking private treatment, for which 50 percent of the charges (70 percent in the case of the very poor) would be reimbursed by government.

SEWELL. Mining town, formerly called Machalí, at 2,140 m (6,955 ft) above sea level in the foothills of the *Andes, which has grown up to exploit the nearby *copper mine of El *Teniente. Some 75 miles southeast of *Santiago, Sewell has been connected since 1911 by an electric *railway from *Rancagua, which climbs 1,627 m (5,288 ft.) in its 72 km (45 miles).

SHARPE, Bartholomew (fl.1679-1682). English *pirate who occupied La *Serena on December 13, 1680, eventually evacuating it in return for a ransom of 9,000 *pesos. Shortly afterwards, on February 8, 1681, he attacked *Arica, but was repulsed.

SHARPE CARTE, Mario (1918-). Lawyer by profession who was elected to Congress on several occasions up until the *coup of September 1973. As deputy from *Bío-Bío province, he was best remembered for advancing the agricultural interests of the region he represented. Not wanting Chile to become Marxist, he reluctantly supported the overthrow of Socialist President Salvador *Allende Gossens as a necessary evil. But like so many other politicians, he was shocked at the violence perpetrated by the *armed forces in the aftermath of their takeover. In 1983 he became the head of the *Alianza Democrática (Democratic Alliance), a coalition of center-left parties seeking a return to civilian rule. As protests against the *military regime grew in 1983 and 1984, Sharpe invited the *Partido Nacional to join the Alliance's demand for a return to democracy by 1985. But Chile's strongman, Augusto *Pinochet Ugarte, stalled the talks between his government and the opposition parties (all nominally "in recess" according to government edict). Pinochet proclaimed that the nation was not yet ready for democracy, and might not be even in 1989, the date set in his own *Constitution of 1980 for a promised return to civilian rule.

During the week of September 4-11, 1984, two anti-government protests resulted in nine deaths at the hands of the police, one of them being that of a French priest, André Jarlan, who was shot in his rectory while reading his Bible. Pinochet contended that the regime was trying to preserve order in society, with the support of the majority of Chileans. He accused Mario Sharpe and the other opposition leaders of seeking to create chaos and wanting to return the country to Marxism. He even threatened another "September 11th," referring to the bloody coup that had brought him to power. Despite such threats, Sharpe pledged that the Alliance would continue its work, stating: "We will continue protesting, because it is the people's only form of expression, and the only language the government will listen to."

SHEEP FARMING. Chile is second only to Australia in total area dedicated to sheep farming. The earliest colonists brought sheep with them, some of which were acquired by the *Araucanian Indians. Soon these became adept shepherds, reputed to have possessed 50,000 head by the end of the 16th century. The present development of the industry, however, began in 1877, with the settlement of some Falkland Islanders on *Tierra del Fuego, backed by British capital. The immigrants' animals were crossed with the Spanish merino and later with other English and New Zealand breeds. Within twenty years their flocks totaled 800,000 head. Only the wool was of economic importance then. It was not until 1905 that the first meat-packing plant was built at *Punta Arenas. Sheep are also raised on the southern mainland of Chile, around Puerto Natales and *Aysén, and until 1953 most of *Easter Island was given over to sheep. By 1920 Chile had 5 million sheep, of which the 2 million in the province of *Magallanes produced four fifths of the wool crop. More recent figures show that in 1948, 5.5 million sheep provided 10,000 metric *tons of wool and 12,000 tonnes of meat. In 1978 there were 7 million sheep in Chile, but by 1981 the total had fallen to 6.2 million. Wool production was then 20,000 tonnes. Since Chilean dietary habit strongly prefers beef to mutton, most of the meat produced by shepherding is exported: 120,000 head from Magallanes in 1971. Chilean sheep produce a fine, heavy fleece which sells at premium prices on the world market.

SHIPPING. See: MERCHANT MARINE.

SICAR. See: SERVICIO DE INTELIGENCIA DE CARABINEROS.

SIFA. See: SERVICIO DE INTELIGENCIA DE LA FUERZA AEREA.

SIGLO, El (October 1952-September 1973). Communist daily *newspaper.

SILVA ALGUE, Waldo (1820-1892). Lawyer by profession and member of the National Party (*Partido Nacional). Embarked on a legal career, he was regente of the court of appeal in *Concepción when in September 1856 President Manuel *Montt Torres appointed him minister of justice and *education. As such he created the library of the *Instituto Nacional and founded a number of provincial high schools and public libraries. In 1860 he joined the law faculty of the *Universidad de Chile and entered Congress as a deputy. In 1891, as president of the Senate, he helped organize the revolt against President José Manuel *Balmaceda Fernández (see: CIVIL WAR OF 1891) and was a member of the *Junta de gobierno de Iquique.

SILVA HENRIQUEZ, Raul [Cardinal] (1907-). *Archbishop of Santiago, May 1961-April 1983. Ordained a priest of the Salesian order in 1938, he became bishop of *Valparaíso in November 1959 and was made a cardinal in March 1962, receiving a doctorate honoris causa from Iona College in New Rochelle, New York the same year. He was compulsorily retired as archbishop on reaching the age of 75, being succeeded by Juan Francisco *Fresno Larraín.
   Within the *Church, Silva Henríquez is considered a moderate. He taught for a number of years at the *Universidad Católica, but is best known for his charitable work on behalf of Chile's poor. During the three year-presidency of Socialist Salvador *Allende Gossens, 1970-73, Church-State relations remained correct but cool, with Silva Henríquez steadfastly refusing to condone the teachings of the Cristianos por el Socialismo (Christians for Socialism). His unwillingness to compromise with either the left or the right enhanced his prestige in Rome and in Chile, where he became the chief intermediary between the Christian Democrats (*Partido Demócrata Cristiano) and the ruling *Unidad Popular. During the last year of the Allende regime, the Socialists sought a dialog with the recalcitrant Christian Democrats, who were by then allying themselves with the right and inviting the *armed

forces to intervene. The Cardinal, however, failed to avert the ensuing coup.

For several months after the military takeover, Silva Henríquez remained silent. His only intervention was to offer prayers for those who had fallen in the struggle, and especially for President Allende. This led to criticism of his passivity, until he began to speak out, no longer accepting the institutionalized violence that the new regime was perpetrating. As a result, the Chilean Church has emerged as perhaps the strongest institutional bridge to future social progress. Silva Henríquez called on the armed forces for restraint, especially when the government began to persecute prominent laymen, including leaders of the Christian Democratic Party. He made it known that the Church believed in the sanctity of human life, in the right to liberty, and in personal security. At the local level, he founded the *Vicariate of Solidarity, which he placed under the Church's protection. He also took an active role in providing an "umbrella" for organized opposition groups. At the national level, the Church provided legal aid to political prisoners whose *human rights had been violated, and it protected lawyers who defended such cases. It also set up institutions where scholars who had been dismissed from the universities could continue to work.

The Pinochet government began a campaign against the aging prelate and continues to discredit his work with the poor, the imprisoned and the homeless. The Cardinal, for his part, did not ignore the poverty and political violence that had resulted from the imposition of military rule on the country. In the anti-government demonstrations marking the 11th anniversary of the coup, he joined opposition party leaders in calling for an end to violence and a return to constitutionality.

SILVER. Silver *mining in colonial Chile, although dwarfed in importance by Potosí in upper Peru, began around 1600. There were rich mines near the *Uspallata Pass, but these were worked out before the end of the colonial era. Other early mines were at Huanatajaya, Tres Puntas and Arqueros. The high point of Chilean silver mining was the discovery of a virtual silver mountain at *Chañarcillo in 1830, which occasioned the construction of Chile's first *railway. This, however, ran out in little more than thirty years. Also important was the discovery of Caracoles in 1870, and production in the period 1875-1900 averaged 1.8 million *pesos a year. The exhaustion of the richest veins, and the general decline of the industry, brought this down to one million pesos in 1915.

There has been some recovery since. In 1982 Chile produced some 379 metric *tonnes, and in 1984 some 489 tonnes, compared with 44.3 tonnes in 1909 and only 23.2 tonnes in 1947. But only 0.8 percent of current production comes from silver mining: 98 percent is a by-product of *copper mining, and 1.3 percent is a by-product of *gold, *lead or *zinc mining.

SIM. See: SERVICIO DE INTELIGENCIA MILITAR.

SIMIAN GALLET, Eduardo (1915-   ). Mining engineer. He studied
in *Santiago, graduating in mining engineering in 1938. He has
worked for *CORFO, and was sent to *Magallenes, in the far
south, to probe the terrain for oil. In 1945 he was responsible
for the first commercial production of *petroleum in its by-
products in Chile. In 1950 he became manager of the national
petroleum corporation, *ENAP. In November 1964, newly elected
Partido Demócrata Cristiano (PDC) President Eduardo *Frei
Montalva appointed him minister of mines.

SIN. See: SERVICIO DE INTELIGENCIA NAVAL.

SLAVERY. See: AFRICAN SLAVERY.

SOCIAL SECURITY. See: SERVICIO NACIONAL DE SALUD; SOCIAL
WELFARE.

SOCIAL WELFARE. Between 1920 and 1973 Chile had built one of the
most advanced welfare states in the world. Almost every Chilean
had become dependent on it. With personal savings wiped out
by the country's chronic *inflation, even the middle and upper
middle classes made use of state provided health, accident and unemployment insurance and pensions. The expansion of Chile's
social services over more than five decades can be explained by
the continually unstable condition of the *economy, which led
wage and salary earners to press government for unemployment
benefits, old age pensions, health care, accident insurance, family
allowances for parents with several children, and other such
provisions. Population growth and increasing urbanization added
to this pressure. So great did the benefits become, and so easy
was it to retire on an attractive stipend that the system became
a significant factor in the continuance of inflation.
    State welfare provision in Chile dates from the first adminis-
tration of Arturo *Alessandri Palma (1920-25), which laid down the
basic pattern. Subsequent governments, particularly the Popular
Front (*Frente Popular) administration of 1938-41 and the *Unidad
Popular government of 1970-73, strengthened and extended the
structure of this provision, creating a system far ahead of most
western European countries and equalled in Latin America only
by pre-1968 Uruguay. Social benefits were administered by 42
cajas de previsiones (guilds) and covered some 80 percent of the
population.
    After the *coup d'état of September 11, 1973, and its imposition
of a *military regime, it was only a matter of time before the total
reorganization of a system so antagonistic to the free market
philosophy of the new government. This philosophy, plus the
desire to eliminate subsidies and minimize assistance to the poor,
has resulted in a drastic reduction of Chilean social welfare.

SOCIAL WELFARE, Ministry of. See: BIENESTAR SOCIAL, Ministerio de.

SOCIALISM. Chile has made two experiments with socialism in the present century. The first was the short-lived REPUBLICA SOCIALISTA (q.v.) of 1932. The other was the 1970-73 UNIDAD POPULAR (q.v.) administration of Salvador *Allende Gossens.

From the time of the República Socialista (with which the Chilean *Communists refused to collaborate), Chilean socialists have always stayed clear of the Communists, even though the *Partido Socialista has formed various alliances with the *Partido Comunista Chileno in order to win elections.

See also: ACCION REVOLUCIONARIA SOCIALISTA; ALIANZA DEMOCRATICA DE CHILE; FRENTE DE ACCION POPULAR; FRENTE POPULAR; PARTIDO OBRERO SOCIALISTA; PARTIDO SOCIALISTA; PARTIDO SOCIALISTA AUTENTICO; PARTIDO SOCIALISTA DE CHILE: PARTIDO SOCIALISTA DEL PUEBLO: PARTIDO SOCIALISTA INTERNACIONAL; PARTIDO SOCIALISTA MARXISTA; PARTIDO SOCIALISTA REVOLUCIONARIO; PARTIDO SOCIALISTA UNIFICADO.

SOCIALIST REPUBLIC. See: REPUBLICA SOCIALISTA.

SOCIALIST REVOLUTIONARY ACTION. See: ACCION REVOLUCIONARIA SOCIALISTA.

SOCIALIST UNION. See: UNION SOCIALISTA.

SOCIEDAD DE FOMENTO FABRIL (SOFOFA). National Manufacturers' Association.

SOCIEDAD DE LA IGUALDAD. The Society for Equality was founded on April 14, 1850, by Francisco *Bilbao Barquín and Eusebio *Lillo Robles. Its aims were to give power to the people and to recognize the equality of all Chileans. It was based on the French Revolution's slogan, "Liberty, Equality, Fraternity," and it proposed to create free schools for all who wished to attend. The society was anticlerical and had hostile encounters with the authorities. An attempt was made on Bilbao's life, with the purpose of destroying the Society and its leaders.

SOCIEDAD PORTALES, CEA Y CIA. Commercial association between Diego *Portales Palazuelos and José Manuel Cea, formed just after Portales lost his wife in 1821. The two partners left Chile for Peru the following year, where their trading enterprise prospered. Returning in 1824, they purchased the government's tobacco, tea and liquor monopoly, the *Estanco, undertaking in return to service the one million-pound loan the Republic had contracted in London (see: PUBLIC FINANCES), an annual obligation of 355,250 *pesos. The government however was unable to take effective measures against illicit tobacco cultivation, and the resultant black market eroded the estanco's profitability. When, in consequence, Portales, Cea y Cía refused to make the agreed payments in London, Supreme Director Ramón *Freire Serrano abrogated the concession (1826). It was largely the difficulty he had in getting the matter equitably settled that drew Portales away from commerce and into politics.

SOCIEDAD QUIMICA Y MINERA DE CHILE. See: SOQUIMICh.

SOCIETY OF JESUS. See: JESUITS.

SOFOFA. See: SOCIEDAD DE FOMENTO FABRIL.

SOLIDARITY, Vicariate of. See: VICARIATE OF SOLIDARITY.

SOQUIMICh (Sociedad Química y Minera de Chile). Government-sponsored *nitrate marketing corporation which replaced *COVENSA in 1968. Originally the majority of its shares were privately owned; the Chilean government (through *CORFO) owned only 37.5 percent. This proportion was increased to 51 percent in July 1970, and in May 1971 SOQUIMICh was wholly nationalized.

SOTOMAYOR VALDES, Ramón (b. 1830). See: HISTORIOGRAPHY.

SOUPER, Roberto. Perpetrator of the TANCAZO (q.v.) of June 29, 1973, a premature attempt to overthrow President Salvador *Allende Gossens. The son of a Chilean diplomat, Souper was a career *army officer who at the time was a lieutenant colonel and in charge of the *Santiago garrison. The attempt failed and he was arrested, only to be released later in 1973 when Augusto *Pinochet Ugarte staged his successful *coup against Allende.

SOUTHERN UNIVERSITY. See: UNIVERSIDAD AUSTRAL.

SOVIET UNION. See: U.S.S.R.

SPAIN, Relations with. After the wars of *independence, it took Chile several decades to normalize relations with Spain. These began to improve with the conservative government of Diego *Portales Palazuelos, architect of the *Constitution of 1833. Formal recognition by Spain of Chile's independence was achieved in 1844. But twenty years later Chile supported *Peru in what seemed a threat by Spain to revive her imperial pretensions (see: SPAIN, War of 1865-66 with). Partly because of the unsettled state of Spanish internal affairs after 1868, that conflict was not formally ended by Spain until 1879, and the peace treaty was only signed in 1883. When Spain fought the Spanish-American War of 1898, however, Chilean sympathies were with Spain rather than with the "Colossus of the North," the United States.

During the 20th century, Chileans regarded Spain as the mother country, preserved their Spanish culture and language, and looked to Spain for intellectual guidance in literature and the arts. The governments of Carlos *Ibáñez del Campo and Miguel Primo de Rivera were particularly friendly and Chile and Spain raised the status of their respective diplomatic missions to embassies in 1928.

When the Spanish Civil War of 1936-39 broke out, Chileans were divided. The government of Arturo *Alessandri Palma, the right-of-center politicians, and the hierarchy of the Catholic *Church, generally supported the rebellion of General Francisco Franco. Those to the left-of-center, including the *Frente Popular government of Pedro *Aguirre Cerda, backed the democratically elected government of the Republic. When Franco prevailed, in one of the bloodiest civil conflicts of the century, Aguirre opened Chile's doors to republican refugees. Pablo *Neruda, as consul in Paris, arranged the voyage of the S.S. *Winnipeg that brought over two thousand Spaniards to Chile. Aguirre delayed recognition of the Franco regime until April 5, 1939, making Chile the last Latin American country to do so (Mexico never did).

Relations with Franco's Spain were cool when Socialist Salvador *Allende Gossens assumed the presidency in 1970. Three years later, when Allende was overthrown by a military junta, relations improved. President Augusto *Pinochet Ugarte attended the funeral of Generalissimo Franco, whom he admired for having saved Spain from Marxism. Ironically, King Juan Carlos pledged to return Spain to democracy, and Spain, in the first free election since 1934, voted a Socialist prime minister into office. Although the two governments continue to have trade relations, Spain has been cool towards Pinochet because of the persistency of *human rights violations by his regime.

SPAIN, War of 1865-66 with. *Peru had failed at independence to make a satisfactory arrangement with Spain regarding her debts to that country, while Spain for her part had persisted in regarding the ending of the independence struggle as nothing more than a temporary truce. In 1865 Spain tried to force a settlement of the debt squabble by seizing the Chinchas *guano islands. This fresh assertion of Spanish sovereignty in South America was seen by her other former possessions as a threat to their independence, and Chile declared war in support of Peru on September 17, 1865. Spain replied with a blockade of the Chilean coast which Chile's navy proved unable to break, even though Admiral Juan *Williams Rebolledo in the *Esmeralda managed to capture the Spanish gunboat *Covadonga, thereby provoking the suicide of Spanish admiral José Manuel Pareja y Septién. At the subsequent battle of *Huito, the Chilean navy was saved from total destruction only by Spanish commander Casto *Méndez Núñez's unfamiliarity with Chilean waters. But the blockade could not force a Chilean capitulation, and after the gesture of bombarding the undefended

port of *Valparaíso (March 31, 1866) the Spanish fleet withdrew.
Núñez was badly wounded while bombarding El Callao (May 2,
1866) and a peace was negotiated.

The war revealed South American weakness, especially since
the Spanish had been able to knock out all Callao's coastal defense guns. But the only long-term results (apart from the
final abandonment by Spain of her pretensions to a South American empire) were the fortifying of Valparaíso and a moderate
expansion of the Chilean *navy.

SPANISH. The official language of Chile, often referred to as Castilian (castellano) to avoid the political overtones of "Spanish"
(español). Like other Hispanic American countries, Chile pro-
nounces some phonemes differently from the pronunciation of
northern Spain, possibly due to a predominance of early settlers
from Andalucía. Typical of Chilean Spanish is the replacement of
the lisplike "th" sound (ceceo) of z (or c before i or e) with the
sound of s (seseo). Chileans also replace the Spanish palatalized
11 with a y sound, or even with the "zh" sound of English azure
(the j of modern French). In conversation, s is dropped when
final, or before another consonant.

The influence of Andrés *Bello López in Chile led to wide
adoption of his ideas on spelling (notably i for y, and j for g
before a front vowel). These idiosyncracies have largely been
abandoned today, but are frequent in mid-19th century writing.

Idiomatic expressions that pertain to Chile are called chilenismos,
as are borrowings from the *Mapuche, Guaraní and Quechua languages. Most of the latter designate animals, plants, flowers
and terms to do with family life. For example, the Chilean national flower is the *copihue, and a boyfriend is a pololo, both deriv-
ing from the Mapuche.

In Atlantic Chile, many words are anglicisms, whereas in the
northern territories formerly held by Peru and Bolivia, linguistic
characteristics inherited from those two countries are still used
in everyday language. Spanish immigrants from Andalusía and the
Basque region have also contributed their own speech peculiarities
to Chilean Spanish. Some of the descendants of 19th century immigrants from other parts of Europe and the world are bilingual,
and Mapuches are usually bilingual in Spanish and Araucanian.

STATE TECHNICAL UNIVERSITY. See: UNIVERSIDAD TECNICA DEL
ESTADO.

STEEL. See: IRON AND STEEL.

STOCK EXCHANGE. Chile's securities market was one of the most
active in Latin America until the advent of the *Unidad Popular
government in 1970. The first stock exchanges were the one in
*Valparaíso (opened in 1892) and the Bolsa de *Santiago of 1893.
Since that time the stock market had grown as corporate business

increased. The securities market dealt in about 350 stocks, plus government mortgages, industrial bonds in gold, and in foreign exchange. Mining and industrial shares accounted for more than 30 percent of the total value in stock transactions, with another 10 percent accounted for by marine, banking and agricultural stock. Stock transactions together made up 90 percent of the total value of trading, bonds accounting for the rest.

Following the 1970 election of Salvador *Allende Gossens, there was a panic among stockholders. Chilean investment abroad has always been largely flight capital, and in 1965, when the dollar stood at 4.5 *escudos, it was estimated at 900 million escudos. Allende's election intensified this flight of capital. This increased even more as many shares failed to keep their original value in face of inflation. As Allende proceeded to nationalize the *copper mines and other large businesses, the volume of share trading fell so much that the Stock Exchange closed.

It took six years, and a sharp decline in the inflation rate, for the Chilean investor to regain confidence. The "economic miracle" from 1976 produced a robust pick up. But the depression that began in late 1981, with the collapse of the Chilean *economy, eroded confidence in the government's free market model, and there occurred a new flight of capital abroad.

See also: BANKS, BANKING AND FINANCIAL INSTITUTIONS; ECONOMY, The.

STRAIT OF MAGELLAN. Named after Ferdinand *Magellan, who discovered the long-sought passage that separates the Atlantic Ocean from the Pacific, on October 21, 1520. This winding, mountain-bordered channel connects the two bodies of water at the southern extremity of South America, separating *Tierra del Fuego from the continental mainland. The length of the Strait is 370 miles, with a width ranging from one to 30 miles.

The enclosed nature of the strait makes its winds uncertain and navigation for a sailing vessel difficult. But even after the open sea route around *Cape Horn was discovered in 1616, the Strait remained the preferred route until almost the end of the 18th century. This was because the small and relatively slow-sailing vessels of the period were usually short of victuals by the time they reached these latitudes from Europe, and mariners welcomed the opportunity to hunt penguins and seals along the Strait to replenish their stock of food on board. When steamships arrived in the early 1840s, being independent of the wind, they preferred the Strait route because it was shorter, and *Punta Arenas became an important port of call until the opening of the Panama canal rerouted almost all shipping.

The Strait is also memorable as the location of the 1899 meeting of the Presidents of Chile and Argentina known as the ABRAZO DEL ESTRECHO, q.v.

STRIKES. See: LABOR; TRADE UNIONS. See also: BOSSES' STRIKE.

SUBLEVACION DE CAMPINO. A military revolt, led by Colonel Enrique *Campino Salamanca with the support of the *Santiago garrison and a number of liberal politicians, including his brother
Joaquín *Campino Salamanca and José María Vázquez de *Novoa
López de Artigas. The revolt took place on the night of January
24/25, 1827. Chile's experiment with *federalism was a period of
weak, short-lived governments which left Chile in a state of near
anarchy. Frequent revolts and coups, such as the one led by
the Campino brothers, made achieving political stability even more
difficult. The coup forced President Agustín *Eyzaguirre Arechavala out of office, but Congress refused to appoint Campino's
nominee, Francisco Antonio *Pinto Díaz, and named instead the
plotters' enemy, Ramón *Freire Serrano, who immediately left the
capital to raise a loyalist army. Diego *Portales Palazuelos, whom
they had imprisoned, persuaded one of the rebels, Nicolás Maruri
(1788-1866), to change sides and lead a counter-coup. This took
place successfully in the early morning of January 29th. Freire
returned the next day and took over the government. Campino
was arrested, but later released. All he had achieved was a
transfer of power to his enemy, although Pinto Díaz was made
vicepresident, and eventually succeeded Freire, four months
later.

SUBLEVACION DE LA ESCUADRA. See: COQUIMBO MUTINY.

SUELDO VITAL. Officially established subsistence wage.

SUFFRAGE. The *Junta de Gobierno de 1810 granted the vote to
anyone with standing in the community ("que gozan de alguna
consideración") "by virtue of his wealth, employment, talent or
quality", and was a Spanish-speaking male of 25 or over. A
law of 1813 reduced the qualifying age to 23, added the prere-
quisite of literacy, and defined "wealth" as having a $300 ($500
in *Santiago) annual income. A so-called "universal suffrage"
law of 1874 simplified the qualifications, but the vote remained
limited to adult male property owners, although the number did
increase appreciably--from 26,000 (1.3 percent of the total population) in 1873 to 104,000 (4.7 percent) in 1879. The *Constitution
of 1925 extended voting rights to all literate males over 21 years,
except N.C.O.s and enlisted men in the *armed forces and the
*police, and made voting (in theory) compulsory. In fact only
7.7 percent of Chileans were on the voting register for national
elections in 1925, and only 12 percent twenty years later.
    A law of 1934 gave women the right to vote in *local govern-
ment elections. Female suffrage at the national level was enacted
in 1949. As a result the percentage of the population on the
electoral register reached 18.41 percent in 1952, with 15.95 percent actually voting. Eleven years later these figures had increased to 33.22 percent and 26.76 percent. In April 1971 the
voting age was lowered to 18, and in 1973 the number of actual
voters was 37.3 percent of the population.

SULFUR. Sulfur deposits of volcanic origin occur at Tacora, Concola, Oyagüe, *Copiapó and other places along the Bolivian and Argentine frontier in northern Chile. Production varies widely according to world demand (18,000 metric *tons in 1976; 114,624 tonnes-- all from *Antofagasta Region--in 1981), and although Chile has the largest output in South America, it is insignificant compared to that of Mexico or the U.S., whose annual production is on the order of several million tonnes.

SUPREME DIRECTOR (Director Supremo). Title of the Chilean chief executive from 1814 to 1826. The *Constitution of 1814 stated that the critical situation of the country necessitated the concentration of the executive power in one individual, the Supreme Director, with unlimited powers for an 18-month term of office. The *Constitution of 1818, the first constitution of an independent Chile, provided that the executive power should be vested in a Supreme Director, without specifying for how many years he should rule. Thus a quasi-dictatorship was established. Successive holders of the title were the following:

Francisco *Lastra y de la Sotta (March 7-July 23, 1814) [*junta headed by José Miguel *Carrera Verdugo (July 23-October 4, 1814)]
[*Reconquista española (October 5, 1814-February 12, 1817)]
Bernardo *O'Higgins (February 15, 1817-January 28, 1823)
Ramón *Freire Serrano (March 29, 1823-July 4, 1826)

When O'Higgins was away campaigning against Mariano *Osorio in southern Chile, he appointed Luis de la *Cruz Goyenache to act as Supreme Director (December 10, 1817-March 24, 1818). When Freire was in *Chiloé commanding the campaign to liberate that island, his authority was delegated on the first occasion to Lastra de la Sotta (December 30, 1823-January 3, 1824) and Fernando *Errazuriz Aldunate (January 3-June 14, 1824); on the second occasion to Francisco Ramón *Vicuña Larraín (May 6-17, 1825); and on the third to a CONSEJO DIRECTORIAL (q.v.) headed by José Miguel *Infante Rojas (November 13, 1825-March 6, 1826). The title of acting Supreme Director was also held for two days in October 1825 by José Santiago Sánchez Alfaro. When Freire resigned in July 1826, *Congress changed the title of the chief executive to that of Presidente de la República (see: PRESIDENTS OF CHILE).

- T -

TACNA. Town and district of southern Peru. Occupied by Chile in May 1880, during the War of the *Pacific, and held until 1929. The 1883 peace treaty of *Ancón indicated that *Arica, Tacna and

Moquequa were to be held as surety for payment by Peru of a war indemnity. The fate of Tacna and Arica was then to be determined by a plebiscite in 1894. Attempts to hold this were frustrated, however, by disagreement over how to proceed. By 1907 only 4,000 Peruvians remained in Tacna, a mere fifth of the population, thus discouraging Peru's interest in a plebiscite. The so-called Tacna Question embittered relations between Chile and Peru, and led to a mutual severance of diplomatic relations in 1920. The *United States, which had been involved as a would-be mediator since 1880, eventually persuaded the two countries to resume relations and negotiate, in 1928. The following year, the Treaty of *Lima (June 3, 1929) gave Arica to Chile, and Tacna, plus compensation of 1,250,000 pounds, to Peru.

TALCA (city). City founded by colonial governor José Antonio Manso de Velasco in 1742 at 35° 25'S, 71° 39'W on the eastern slopes of the coastal cordillera. Its population was 38,040 in 1907; 56,735 in 1940; and 137,621 (est.) in 1986. Capital of the pre-1974 province of Talca, it is now capital of the new Region VII, *Maule. As the center of a wide agricultural zone, its principal industries are food processing.

TALCA (province). A province of central Chile established in 1833, when it was separated from *Colchagua, lying between the rivers Mataquito on the north and *Maule to the south. It had an area of 10,141.1 km² (3,915 square miles) and a population of 79,439 in 1854; 133,472 in 1885; 131,957 in 1907; 133,957 in 1920; 157,141 in 1940; 173,793 in 1952; 282,146 (est.) in 1982. Under the administrative restructuring of 1974, Talca became a province within the new Region VII, *Maule. Its estimated 1985 population was 267,311.

TALCAHUANO. The port city of *Concepción. Founded in 1764, it lies at 34° 42'S, 73° 6'W, within the deeply indented Bay of Concepción. It is the best naturally protected haven on the Chilean west coast, and is one of Chile's major ports (see: PORTS AND HARBORS). During the Chilean wars of *independence, the Spanish commander José *Ordóñ made Talcahuano into the main royalist base after the defeat of *Chacabuco and consequent loss of *Santiago. His fortifications held off attacks by the Patriots led by José Gregorio de las *Heras and Bernardo *O'Higgins in April and May 1817, and a renewed assault by Miguel Bayer in December 1817. In the 19th century Talcahuano was chosen as the premier base of the Chilean *navy due to its closeness to the country's chief *coal mining area, as well as for the advantages of its harbor.

The population was 16,261 in 1907; about 34,000 in 1940; and estimated at 217,660 in 1985.

TALCAHUANO, Battle of. A naval battle which took place on October

28, 1818, between a Spanish frigate, the 50-gun María Isabel, and the Chilean fleet under Manuel *Blanco Encalada, composed of the 56-gun San Martín, the 44-gun Lautaro, the Chacabuco, and the Arauco. The María Isabel was captured and subsequently renamed the O'Higgins.

TALCAHUANO, Vegas de. See: VEGAS DE TALCAHUANO, Las.

TANCAZO. A tank attack on La *Moneda Palace, which occurred on June 29, 1973. Lieutenant Colonel Roberto *Souper and his 100 men fired on the building in the hope of provoking the *army and the other *armed forces into removing Socialist President Salvador *Allende Gossens. It was premature, but prefigured the *coup d'état of September 11. Some 12 soldiers and civilians died, and 21 were wounded. Souper was arrested, but released after Allende's overthrow.

TANTAUCO TREATY. A treaty signed at Tantauco (42° 5'S, 73° 44'W) on January 19, 1826, to surrender Castro, the last Spanish-held city on *Chiloé. This marked the end of the four-year struggle to incorporate the island of Chiloé into the national territory of an independent Chile.

TAPIA VALDES, Jorge Antonio (1925-). Lawyer, writer and university professor. An expert in constitutional law, he was appointed justice minister by President Salvador *Allende Gossens. After the *coup d'état of September 1973 he was imprisoned and spent the next fifteen months in *concentration camps. He was finally released, at the same time as Clodomiro *Almeyda Medina, on January 11, 1975: both men went into exile in Romania.

TARAPACA. Area of northern Chile acquired from *Peru as a result of the War of the *Pacific, and constituted a province in 1884. In 1929 it was enlarged from 46,957 km^2 (18,130 square miles) to 58,073 km^2 (22,422 square miles) with the addition of the department of *Arica. In the restructuring of 1975 it became Región I, keeping the same name and the same capital city, *Iquique. The population (including Arica) was 54,294 in 1885; 120,527 in 1907; 102,789 in 1952; 155,908 (est.) in 1971; 236,345 in 1980.

TARAPACA, Lion of. Nickname given Arturo ALESSANDRI PALMA, q.v.

TARPELLANCA. Ford on the River Laja (a northern tributary of the *Bío-Bío) at 37° 13'S, 72° 34'W; the site of a battle fought on September 26, 1820, during the so-called "War to the Death" (*Guerra a Muerte). A Patriot force of 600 under Andrés Alcázar y Zapata, retreating from Los *Angeles towards *Chillán, encountered 2,400 *realistas under Vicente *Benavides. After a

13-hour combat, the Patriots ran out of ammunition, surrendered and were massacred.

TARIFFS. See: CUSTOMS AND DUTIES.

TARUD SIWADY, Rafael (1918-   ). Independent leftist candidate in the presidential campaigns of 1964 and 1970. A farmer and industrialist, and director of the Chamber of Commerce, he was president of the students' federation while at the *Universidad de Chile, and began his political career at an early age. In 1953 he became president of the *Partido Agrario Laborista and two years later was made minister of the economy. Elected to the Senate in 1957, he was reelected in 1965. He has been president of the Senate's Business and Economic Commission, and a member of its Foreign Affairs Committee. In 1969 he was put forward as presidential candidate by the *Partido Social Democrático and his own tiny *Acción Popular Independiente. Both these parties, however, became members of the *Unidad Popular coalition, and Tarud withdrew his candidature in favor of that of Salvador *Allende Gossens.

TAXES. The chief colonial taxes were *tithes (diezmos) on agricultural income, the *alcabala (a sales tax), profits from state monopolies (*estancos) and *custom tariffs. Manuel *Rengifo Cárdenas, finance minister 1831-51, revised this system, replacing the alcabala by the *catastro (based on agricultural property values) and introducing a new custom tariff. Later the catastro was replaced by the *contribución territorial, and the tithes and estancos were abolished. From 1879 Chile turned for revenue to an export tax on *nitrates; the state came to rely so much on this source that in 1915 taxes on nitrates was contributing three quarters of all custom revenue. The steep fall in nitrate exports that followed the end of World War I was a disaster for Chilean public finance. Panic measures, such as a heavy duty on luxury imports, were taken to plug the resultant deficit. Between the two world wars, a 2.5 percent sales tax was introduced, with an additional 5 percent tax on industrial production, and an income tax.

Laws of 1962 and 1963 broadened the tax base and provided for conversion to a single progressive income tax. Chile's tax administration, already among the most efficient in Latin America, rapidly became stricter. Income tax evasion became punishable as a crime, although some 40 percent of those who should have paid taxes did not do so and got away with it. During the Salvador *Allende Gossens administration (1970-73), income taxes brought in about 30 percent of all government revenue; sales taxes about another 30 percent; and export taxes the remaining 40 percent. In the 1960s the base income tax for unincorporated *copper firms was 22.5 percent, and for incorporated copper firms, 19.5 percent. Foreign-owned copper companies paid a

50-percent tax on basic production, plus a surtax on 25 percent, which was progressively reduced as the firm increased its production. The non-mining corporate income tax was 23.4 percent.

There was a progressive tax on personal income that ranged from a minimum of 8 percent to a maximum of 50 percent. Minimum property taxes were about 1.5 percent of assessed valuation. Inheritance and gift taxes were scaled progressively up to 50 percent. The basic sales tax was 6 percent, and there was a 10 percent tax on luxury goods such as cigars, cigarettes, grain alcohol, beer, matches and wine. There was also a tax on electric power consumption, as well as on rail fares, telegrams, pharmaceuticals and gasoline. Most legal documents paid a government stamp duty. A special tax of 200 percent by value was levied on all motor vehicles, whether imported or nationally manufactured.

In 1975 President Augusto *Pinochet Ugarte proposed new tax laws in order "to minimize the distortion in resource allocation" and "to improve the horizontal equity of the tax system," i.e., equal treatment for equal incomes. Pinochet modified the progressive tax system, taking less from the top. But his measures to reduce corporate income taxes were regressive, i.e., taxes not paid by big business were largely shifted onto the consumer. The government accorded preferential treatment to capital accumulation and capital investment, dramatically reduced import taxes (which favored the consumer but not local industry), and imposed a value-added tax (IVA) of 20 percent on all consumer goods (the highest in the hemisphere). The maximum tax on luxury goods was reduced from 200 percent (under Allende) to the flat IVA level of 20 percent, so making automobiles and jewelry (for example) more affordable by the rich. But these measures, rather than advancing the proposed horizontal equity of the system, in fact made taxation even more of a burden on middle and lower income groups (since indirect taxes are inherently regressive).

The complexity of the new laws encouraged both evasion and corruption, and resulted in high administrative costs (all of which must have had significantly regressive distribution implications). Small businesses faced bankruptcy because of their inability to compete with imports, while large businesses formed conglomerates, becoming more and more monopolisitic.

From 1976 to 1981 the new taxes worked well as incentives promoting economic growth (which averaged 8 to 9 percent a year), but in 1982 a reversal occurred, the *economy deteriorated and went into a deep recession. The GNP plummeted, falling by 14.1 percent, *inflation began to increase again, and capital inflow decreased sharply, as did industrial output. Wages and salaries were squeezed, leaving the performance of the conglomerates in a dismal state, and *banks and other financial institutions teetering on the verge of bankruptcy.

The economic collapse forced the government to intervene in banks and financial institutions, and to try to save small and medium-sized businesses in the extractive industries. Some old taxation schemes were reintroduced: trade regulations were tightened, taxes on luxury goods and tariffs on imports were raised. While such indirect taxes as IVA, sales and production taxes continued, direct taxes (on property, incomes, and copper and other metals) were increased. Although bread, wheat, flour, milk and other basic food items continued to be zero-rated for value-added tax, their price rose sharply (bread by 80 percent, other basic foods such as rice and beans by 78 percent), adding to the already severe economic problems of the poor and the unemployed.

By the mid-1980s it was obvious that the government had shifted its tax policy toward an increasing reliance on indirect taxation (which favored the rich), and had lowered the tax rate on corporate and personal income. Whatever might be the long-term effect of such measures on promoting economic growth, they certainly represented an increased burden on the poor and middle-income sectors.

See also: ECONOMY, The; NATIONAL INCOME; PUBLIC FINANCES.

TEATRO CAUPOLICAN. Scene of the CAUPOLICANAZO (q.v.) protest against the *military regime.

TEJAS VERDES. A former resort adjoining Llolleo at 38° 40'S, 71° 40'W, on the north bank of the *Maipó river, near its mouth. Soon after the *coup d'état of September 11, 1973, Tejas Verdes, conveniently situated on the *Santiago-*San Antonio railroad, was made the site of a *concentration camp for political undesirables who had supported the ousted regime of Socialist President Salvador *Allende Gossens. Believed to be one of the most cruel squalid camps in Chile, it was set up by *DINA director Manuel Sepúlveda Contreras, allegedly with the advice of former Gestapo colonel Walter *Rauff.

TELECOMMUNICATIONS. For the 1980s, telecommunications in Chile were considered adequate. They relied on extensive radio relays and two satellite stations (Longovilo and *Coyhaique), both linked to the INTELSAT system.

A. Radio. Daily public broadcasting began with Radio Chilena in 1923. By 1968 there were over 150 commercial stations (long-, medium- and short-wave, and FM). By 1984 the number had grown to 301 (of which 149 were FM): these included non-commercial stations operated by the *Church and by the Christian Democrat (*Partido Demócrata Cristiano) opposition. Some two million receivers were in use, equivalent to 183 per 1,000 population. Ninety percent of Chileans had at least one radio in their home.

See also: RADIO AGRICULTURA; RADIO BALMACEDA; RADIO COOPERATIVA; RADIO NACIONAL.

B. Telegraph. Chile's first telegraph line, between *Santiago and *Valparaíso, opened in 1852. The first line to Europe, via Buenos Aires, was connected in 1875. The government-run telegraph service has some 600 offices, but the volume of domestic traffic is falling: down from 8 million telegrams in 1979 to 2.5 million in 1983.

C. Telephone. There were 635,157 telephones in service in 1983, of which 391,830 were in Greater *Santiago. The national total is equivalent to 54.4 per 1,000 population, and it has increased over 75 percent in the last decade: in 1970 there were 312,042 sets in use. Two-thirds of subscriber lines are residential, and one third is business. In 1970 nine tenths of the service was provided by one company, CHITELCO. This was 70 percent owned by *I.T.T., and the prospect of nationalization by a socialist government (which did in fact happen on September 29, 1971) helps explain the American company's virulent hostility to the *Unidad Popular government of Salvador *Allende Gossens.

D. Television. Television came to Chile in 1959. The technology is American (e.g. the color system is NTSC) and there is as yet no UHF. Besides the government's Television Nacional de Chile, there are four other channels, all combined commercial-educational and operated by universities. Two of these are in Greater Santiago: Channel 11 (*Universidad de Chile) established 1959, and Channel 13 (*Universidad Católica), established 1962. Channel 3 (*Universidad del Norte) operates out of *Antofagasta, and Channel 5 (*Universidad Católica de Valparaíso) operates from *Valparaíso. All are regulated by the National Telecommunication Corporation, *ENTEL. Thanks to her two satellite stations, Chile can receive programs from all over the world. Currently only 40 percent of Chilean TV programs are nationally produced, compared with 60 percent of Peruvian TV, 70 percent of Argentine and 75 percent of Brazilian. Some 2.6 million TV receiving sets were in use in 1984.

TELEVISION. See: TELECOMMUNICATIONS--D. Television.

TEMUCO. City founded in 1881 at 38° 48'S, 72° 46'W, in Chile's central valley, on the banks of the Cautín river, a tributary of the Imperial. Temuco became the capital of Cautín province when this was established in 1887, and since the administrative restructuring of 1974, it has been the capital of the new Region IX, Araucania. The city's population has grown from 16,037 in 1907; 45,000 (est.) in 1940; 130,000 (est.) in 1971; to 168,120 (est.) in 1985.

TENIENTE, El. The world's largest underground *copper mine, located 3 km (2 miles) southeast of *Sewell at an elevation of 8,000 feet, on the crater wall of an extinct volcano. The mine tunnels stretch for 1,000 km (620 miles) and are being extended at a rate of 20 km (12 miles) a year. Output in 1981 was 291,900 metric *tons; reserves are estimated at 20 million tonnes.

TERCERA DE LA HORA, La. See: NEWSPAPERS.

TERHALTEN ISLAND. See: LENNOX.

TERUGGI, Frank R. A *United States citizen executed by the military in the aftermath of the *coup d'état of September 11, 1973, some say with the assistance of the United States government. Like Charles *Horman, Teruggi was sympathetic to the *Unidad Popular government of Salvador *Allende Gossens, and was witness to alleged U.S. participation in the coup. See also: HUMAN RIGHTS.

THAYER ARTEAGA, William (1918-   ). Lawyer and member of the Christian Democrats (*Partido Demócrata Cristiano, PDC). In 1941 he was national president of the Catholic youth organization Juventud Católica. After graduating in 1945 he became a legal adviser of the *copper workers' union, the Confederación de Trabajadores del Cobre, and of the union of employees of the Banco del Estado de Chile. He worked for the election of PDC candidate Eduardo *Frei Montalva in the 1964 presidential campaign. Upon being elected, Frei made Thayer his minister of labor.

THERMAL CONGRESS. See: CONGRESO TERMAL.

THIEME, Roberto. A rich industrialist from *Temuco who, as second in command to Pablo *Rodríguez Grez, helped found the neo-fascist youth organization *Patria y Libertad, known in English as "Fatherland and Country." Thieme (who became the organization's secretary-general) engaged in numerous acts of terrorism against the government of Salvador *Allende Gossens, pledging "if we have to burn down half of Chile to save it from Communism, we will do it." He was involved in (and was believed to have been the mastermind behind) the abortive coup of June 1973 known as the *Tancazo. He and Rodríguez had both publicized their intention to "unleash a total armed offensive to destroy the government." Indeed, Patria y Libertad's violent opposition to Allende contributed in no small way to the Socialist President's downfall. It has been alleged that the organization was subsidized with funds from the United States *Central Intelligence Agency, although Thieme has claimed that his was in fact the only anti-Allende organization that was not so subsidized. After the failure of the Tancazo, Thieme fled into hiding. In 1980 he founded the Movimiento Nacionalista Popular: wanting an autarchical fascist revolution, he was disillusioned by the liberal trade and mone-tarist policies of the *military regime, and he was behind another failed coup in October 1982. He then fled to Argentina.

TIERRA DEL FUEGO. A triangular-shaped archipelago located at the
southern extremity of South America, and separated from the
mainland by the *Strait of Magellan. It lies between 52° 27' and
55° 59' south, and 63° 43' and 74° 44' west. The total area is
28,434 square miles, two thirds of which is Chilean and one third
Argentine. The Chilean portion comprises the southern tip of
the former province of *Magallanes (now part of Region XII,
Magallanes y Antártica Chilena). The terrain is varied but rugged, comprised chiefly of mountains, volcanic rock and glacial
lakes; the climate is cool in summer and cold in winter, with up
to 200 inches of rainfall in some areas.

Tierra del Fuego ("land of fire") was discovered by Ferdinand
*Magellan in 1520 and named from the many fires seen on it, lit
by the inhabitants for warmth. Bartolomeu Garcia de *Nodal and
his brother Gonçalo were the first to circumnavigate the archipelago in 1619, but no systematic exploration occurred until 1826-
36, when Phillip Parker *King and Robert *Fitzroy surveyed the
whole area. For 350 years after Magellan's voyage the region was
left to its indigenous Alacaluf, Ona and Yahgan Indians, for whom
an Anglican mission was established by W. H. Stirling in 1869.
With the introduction of *sheep farming and the discovery of
*gold, an influx of European *immigration began in 1880. The
Argentine-Chilean *Boundary Treaty of 1881 divided the main
island at the 68° 34' west meridian, but this failed to determine
navigational rights and sovereignty over the smaller of the islands
and the surrounding seabed (see: BEAGLE CHANNEL), which
were only finally determined in 1985.

Epidemics of European diseases and assimilation have left few
identifiable Indians. By 1946 there were only 136 persons claiming to be Alacalufs, 37 to be Onas, and 24 Yahgans. The current
population of the Chilean territories (9,100 in 1980) includes
Yugoslavs, Spaniards, Britons (many of them of Falkland Islander
stock) and Italians, as well as Chileans and Argentines. The
economy is based chiefly on sheep raising and *petroleum exploration (begun in 1945).

TIERRAS, BIENES NACIONALES Y COLONIZACION, Ministerio de.
Ministry created by law on April 9, 1931, to replace the Ministerio
de *Propiedad Austral, but its title was changed almost immediately
to that of *Tierras y Colonización.

TIERRAS Y COLONIZACION, Ministerio de. The Ministry of Lands
and Settlement was created by Statute no. 243 of May 15, 1931,
to replace that of Lands, National Property and Settlement
(*Tierras, Bienes Nacionales y Colonización). Its main functions
were those of safeguarding all public land within Chile's national
territory, and of giving protection to the Indians and their right
to own all lands assigned to them by the peace treaty of 1883
(see: MAPUCHES).

Ministers of Land since the *coup have been: General Diego

Labra Valdés (September 1973); General Mario Mackay Jaraquemada (July 1974); General Lautaro Recabarren (July? 1976); General René Peri Farstrong (December 1979).

TITHES (Diezmos). A 10 percent tax on agricultural income, dating from biblical times, which was universal throughout medieval Europe, to provide for the support of the *Church. Because of the intimate relation between Church and State in Spain (see: REAL PATRONATO), the tithe became an integral part of royal revenue in colonial times. As the Chilean state considered it had inherited the king's ecclesiastical prerogatives (the "patronato nacional"), tithes continued to be collected by the state after Chilean independence, although Manuel *Rengifo Cárdenas exempted from them land dedicated to flax and hemp cultivation. This attempt to encourage these crops, and thereby stimulate Chilean manufacture of rope for ships rigging, failed. Tithes were finally abolished in 1854.

TOCORNAL GREZ, Manuel Antonio (1817-1867). Lawyer son of Joaquín *Tocornal Jiménez, and a member of the *Partido Conservador. He entered Congress as deputy for *Rancagua in 1846, and three years later was made justice minister. Encouraged by Andrés *Bello López, he wrote El primer gobierno nacional, 1847, which did much to clarify the order of events after 1810. He acquired a reputation both in law and in oratory, and in 1862-63 was interior minister in the cabinet of President José Joaquín *Pérez Mascayano. In 1865 he succeeded Bello as rector of the *Universidad de Chile, and just before his death he was elected to the Senate.

TOCORNAL JIMENEZ, Joaquín (1788-1865). Chilean patriot who fought in the struggle for *independence and served his native city of *Santiago in numerous municipal offices, both before and after his 1814-17 exile in Argentina. He was one of the youngest present in the National Assembly that set up a Chilean government, the *junta de gobierno de 1810, of which he became a member. He was president of the Chamber of Deputies in 1832, when he was appointed interior and foreign minister. He also presided over the convention that drafted the *Constitution of 1833. From then until 1837 he held nearly every cabinet post in the administration of Joaquín *Prieto Vial. In 1841 he was a presidential candidate, but lost to Manuel *Bulnes Prieto, and shortly afterwards became superintendant of the Casa de la *Moneda. He held a seat in the Chamber of Deputies from 1831 to 1843 and was a founder-member of the *Partido Conservador in 1857.

TOCORNAL TOCORNAL, Ismael (1850-1929). Prominent *Partido Liberal politician. He graduated as a lawyer in 1873, entered *Congress as a deputy in 1879, and became a senator in 1915. President Germán *Riesco Errázuriz made him minister of industry and public

works in 1901, and Pedro *Montt Montt made him interior minister
in 1909. As such he acted as President during Montt's official
visit to *Argentina of May 21-31, 1910. In the preliminaries to
the presidential election of 1920 he was selected to be the candidate of the *Unión Liberal. Just before the election, however, he
made way for Luis *Barros Borgoño, who became the candidate of
all the forces opposed to Arturo *Alessandri Palma. In 1925
Tocornal became president of the Banco Central de Chile.

TOHA, Moy de (1934-). Widow of *Unidad Popular minister José
*Tohá González, and an active member of the women's movement
(see: WOMEN AND THE WOMEN'S MOVEMENT). "Moy" is a nickname: she was born Raquel Morales Echévers. During the presidency of Salvador *Allende Gossens (1970-73), Moy de Tohá organized the women of Chile, setting up women's centers to provide
day-care and other facilities, such as the sale of food to factory
workers, whereby they could buy a balanced meal for their entire
family for a minimal amount of money each day. The centers
were particularly important when the distribution of food was
jeopardized by the truck owners' strikes (see: BOSSES' STRIKE).
These were years when women made unprecedented advances, obtaining equal pay and improved pregnancy benefits. After the
*coup d'état of September 1973, Moy de Tohá remained in Chile,
working hard for her husband's release. After his death, however, she decided to leave to tour other countries, particularly
in North and South America, speaking out about the achievements
of the women's movement under Allende and of its subsequent
repression and the human rights abuses perpetrated by the *military regime. In 1983 she returned to resume residence in *Santiago. There she took part in the *Caupolicanazo and the revival
of the *Movimiento de Emancipación de la Mujer Chilena. She also
joined the "Comité de Retorno," made up of women whose immediate relatives had "disappeared" after being arrested by the military. Moy de Tohá has become a rallying point for the concerns
of Chilean women.

TOHA GONZALEZ, Jaime. Minister of *agriculture in the last cabinet
of President Salvador *Allende Gossens (August-September 1973).
Brother to José *Tohá González.
    Tohá was with Allende in the attack on La *Moneda during the
*coup d'état of September 11, 1973. He was arrested there and
sent to the *Dawson Island concentration camp, where his health
suffered from the severity of the interrogating, the poor food
and the harsh climate. Like many other detainees, he fell criti-
cally ill. He was consequently sent to a military hospital in
*Santiago, from where he was removed for further interrogation
at the Air Force Academy, February 15-28, 1974. After his return
he was reported to have hanged himself on March 15, by a strap
from the ceiling of his room. This alleged suicide, coming two
days after the death of Air Marshal Alberto *Bachelet Martínez,

was widely denounced by ecclesiastical authorities and independent observers, on the grounds that Tohá had been too weak to stand up, let alone hang himself. The *Church expressed its feelings by celebrating a requiem mass, which it could not have done for a suicide. Some three thousand mourners, led by family members and friends, defied the police by reviving a chant seldom heard in Chile: "el pueblo unido / jamás será vencido" (a united people shall never be vanquished), a rallying cry for Allende's supporters.

TOMIC ROMERO, Rodomiro (1914-). Lawyer, member of the Christian Democrats (*Partido Demócrata Cristiano, PDC) and the Party's presidential candidate in the election of September 4, 1970. Born in *Antofagasta, he was educated at the *Universidad Católica, becoming president of its student federation, and later president of its law center, and editor of its law journal. In 1935 he was one of the founders of the *Falange Conservador and its *Falange Nacional successor, becoming president of the latter, 1946-52. Director of the *Iquique newspaper El Tarapacá, he became deputy for *Tarapacá in 1941. He was a delegate to the international Christian Democrat conferences of 1957 (São Paulo) and 1958 (Brussels). After Eduardo *Frei Montalva's election to the presidency in 1964, Tomic was made ambassador to the *United States. He returned to Chile in 1969 and won his party's nomination for the presidential election of the following year. He won 28 percent of the vote, coming third to Socialist Salvador *Allende Gossens with 36 percent.

Tomic had represented the left wing of the PDC, with a program more or less similar to that of Allende's *Unidad Popular coalition. After the violent *coup d'état that overthrew Allende in September 1973, Tomic and his family went into exile in Switzerland. As an opposition leader abroad, he narrowly escaped the tentacles of the *DINA, and after the 1975 assassination attempt on fellow PDC exile Bernardo *Leighton Guzmán, he toned down his criticism of the *military regime. In recent years, however, Tomic, along with other opposition leaders, has become more vociferous in demanding the end of militarism in Chile.

TON. Three different tons are used in Chilean statistics, particularly in relation to *copper mining. The U.S. short ton equals 907.18 kg (2,000 lbs); the Imperial (long) ton equals 1,016 kg (2,240 lbs); and the official Chilean metric ton (tonelada métrica), also known by its French name, "tonne," weighs 1,000 kg (2,204.6 lbs) and is roughly the equivalent of a cubic meter of fresh water at 4° centigrade. It equals 0.9842 long tons or 1.11022 short tons. Measurements in this dictionary have in most cases been converted to tonnes.

TOPAZE (August 1931-1970?). Weekly magazine. See: PERIODICAL PRESS.

TOPOGRAPHY. See: CHILE--D. Topography.

TOQUI. *Mapuche word for an Indian chief, originally meaning a
stone ax (a traditional symbol of authority).

TORDESILLAS, TREATY OF. The circumstance that Castillian exploration was seeking a western route to India at the same time
as Portugal was exploring an eastern one led Pope Alexander VI
on May 4, 1493, to divide the whole unchristianized globe between
these two countries, an award that was confirmed (and slightly
revised) by the June 7, 1494, Treaty of Tordesillas between them.
The treaty, which is the ultimate legal basis of Chilean claims
to *Antarctica, gave Castille (and so, Spain) title to all lands
more than 370 leagues west of the Cape Verde islands, i.e.
(approximately) everything west of the 43°W Greenwich meridian.

TORIBIO MEDINA, José. See: MEDINA ZAVALA, José Toribio.

TORIBIO MERINO, José. See: MERINO CASTRO, José Toribio.

TORO RODRIGUEZ, Jaime (1915-). A former Radical (*Partido
Radical) expelled from the party in 1969, whereupon he founded
*Democracia Radical, a right-wing splinter group.

TORO ZAMBRANO Y URETA, Mateo de (1727-1811). Original president of the *junta de gobierno de 1810. A man of considerable
fortune who held positions of high rank, including those of
governor of La *Serena (1750), corregidor of *Santiago (1763),
subintendant of the Casa de La *Moneda (1772). He received
the title of Conde de la Conquista on March 6, 1771, and was
made a brigadier general in 1799. When the French invaded
Spain, Toro Zambrano swore that Chile would not serve Joseph
I, Napoleon's brother, as King of Spain, declaring his loyalty
to the exiled *Ferdinand VII (1809). A year later the Santiago
*cabildo forced the unpopular governor Francisco Antonio *García
Carrasco Díaz to resign, chosing the *creole Toro Zambrano to
replace him. As governor he presided over the first junta government. Some Chileans wanted an immediate declaration of independence; some wanted the Real *Audiencia to exercise authority.
Toro Zambrano chose the middle course of ruling Chile independ-
ently of Spain but in the name of Ferdinand VII. He continued
as president of the junta until his death early in 1811, but largely
as a figurehead: the really influential junta member was his
eventual successor, Juan *Martínez de Rozas Correa.

TORTURE. Since the *coup d'état of September 11, 1973, the *junta
has institutionalized brutality and torture to guarantee its political
control. Numerous examples have been cited by an impressive
list of international agencies, but the best substantiated reports
have come from Amnesty International, the International Commission

of Jurists and the Human Rights Commission of the *United
Nations.
See also: DINA; HUMAN RIGHTS.

TOUNENS, Orelie Antoine. See: ORELIE, Antoine.

TOURISM. Buildings of interest to the tourist in *Santiago include
La *Moneda palace, the *Cathedral, the venerable Church of *San
Francisco, the *National Museum of Fine Arts, the *History
Museum, the *Museum of Contemporary Art, the Cerro (hill) de
Santa Lucía (a centrally located park, with a colonial fortress--
now a museum--on the summit) and the San Cristóbal Hill, on the
top of which stands a statue of Our Lady. There is also the
108-yards wide *Alameda, the city's main artery, with its statues
of José de *San Martín and Bernardo *O'Higgins.
    A day-trip to *Valparaíso, 90 miles away, affords the tourist
a chance to see small towns and farms typical of rural Chile,
while the climb to cross the coastal range provides wide vistas
of Chilean beaches, with the snow-capped *Andes in the opposite
direction. *Viña del Mar, a five-minute drive from Valparaíso,
is South America's Riviera, with lovely homes, quaint fishing
boats, and luxurious hotels and casinos. *Portillo, *Farellones
and other spots in the Chilean Andes are becoming popular ski
resorts. The northern cities of *Iquique and *Antofagasta have
fine beaches and are also noted for their fine deep-sea fishing.
The very popular lake district in the south (see: LAGOS, Los)
is often compared with the lake regions of Switzerland and northern Italy. A five-day trip from Santiago to Buenos Aires by
way of the lake district is a most rewarding experience. Most
hotels in Santiago make tour arrangements and offer excursions
to Valparaíso, Viña del Mar, the ski resorts and the lake district. Good *highway and *railway facilities extend almost the
whole length of the country. Interesting to visit are *Arica
(Chile's northernmost city), *Puerto Montt (south of the lake
district, with a mainly German population) and *Punta Arenas
(once the world's southernmost city).
    The number of tourists visiting Chile has grown from 65,000
a year in the late 1950s to 76,000 in 1970 and over 400,000 a
year in the early 1980s. They are drawn chiefly by the fine
skiing and fishing, the beaches and mountains, or by archaeological expeditions. Chilean tourism is regulated and promoted
by two organizations: the Servicio Nacional de Turismo (National
Tourist Service) and the Asociación Chilena de Empresas de
Turismo (Chilean Association of Tourist Agencies), both located
in Santiago.

TOWNLEY, Michael Vernon (1942-). A *United States citizen con-
victed of complicity in the murder of Orlando LETELIER DEL
SOLAR (q.v.) and Ronni Moffitt. Son of an Iowa businessman,
Townley accompanied his parents to Chile in 1957, remaining

there except for the period 1967-70, until he reentered the United States in September 1976 in the company of *DINA associate Captain Armando *Fernández Larios (under assumed names) to carry out the assassination. Townley, who had married a Chilean, had allegedly been a *Central Intelligence Agency armament trainer before being recruited by the DINA (although the C.I.A. has denied this). Townley and Fernández, with the help of members of the Cuban exile terrorist organization *Omega 7, detonated a bomb under Letelier's car near the Chilean embassy in Washington D.C.'s "embassy row." Townley escaped back to Chile, but his role was discovered by the F.B.I., and the United States government secured his extradition in 1978. For testifying on behalf of the prosecution at the trial of the Cubans involved, Townley was given a ten-year sentence, of which he served three years and four months, before being paroled and given safe passage back to Chile under an assumed identity.

TRABAJO, Ministerio de. The Ministry of Labor was created by statute no. 2 as one of the first acts of the short-lived *República Socialista, on June 5, 1932. Previously, all that was pertinent to Chilean labor laws had been handled by the Ministerio de *Higiene, Asistencia y Previsión Social y Trabajo (from 1924) and its predecessors, the Ministerio de Industria, Obras Públicas y Ferrocarriles (1912-24), and the Ministerio de *Industria y Obras Públicas (1907-12).

TRABAJO Y PREVISION SOCIAL, Ministerio de. The Ministry of Labor became the Ministry of Labor and Social Insurance in 1959. It had always had responsibility for workers' insurance and old age pensions, but the title change accompanied a broadening of social security provision and coverage.
    Labor ministers since the *coup have been: General Mario Mackay Jarquemada (September 1973), General Nicanor Díaz (July 1974), Sergio Fernández (March 1976); José Piñera Echenique (December 1978); Miguel Kast (December 1980); Máximo Silva Bafalluy (April 1982); Patricio Mardones (August 1982), Hugo Gálvez Gajardón (August 1983); Alfonso Marquez de la Plata Irrazaval.

TRADE UNIONS. Chile's trade unions grew out of the mutual aid societies organized during the 19th century. But in 1903 union membership totaled only 63,000 and was largely limited to stevedores and workers in manufacturing and *mining. The first labor federation, the *Federación Obrera de Chile (FOCh), was formed in 1909; almost from the beginning it was under the control of the *Partido Socialista de Trabajadores, forerunner of the *Partido Comunista de Chile. In 1921 FOCh affiliated to the Communist Trade Union International. By 1928 it claimed 136,000 members. After growing slowly in the years before the Great *Depression, organized labor became very influential politically during the 1930s. Labor union growth was stimulated by the founding in 1933 of the *Partido Socialista de Chile.

The mid-1930s witnessed the formation of the Confederación de Trabajadores de Chile (CTCh), a merger of the Communist FOCh, the Socialist Confederación Nacional de Sindicatos Legales and the anarchist Confederación General del Trabajo (CGT), although the last soon withdrew. The CTCh was an important element in forging the Popular Front (*Frente Popular) of 1937, but the World War II period was marked by a bifurcation of the labor movement into Socialist and Communist-oriented unions. Socialist-Communist rivalry led to such extensive labor unrest that Gabriel *González Videla's administration in 1948 passed the *Ley de defensa de la democracia, which outlawed the Communist Party. Ironically, this law, which also gave the government the right to intervene in union affairs, provoked a remarriage of convenience between the Communist and Socialist forces; the result was a new national labor organization, the Central Unica de Trabajadores de Chile (CUT). This new union was sponsored by the government in order to frustrate Communist influence, yet it remained strongly Marxist in its orientation. The growing power of the Christian Democrats (*Partido Demócrata Cristiano) led to the formation in 1958 of a rival national labor organization, the Confederación Nacional de Trabajadores (CNT), which has since succeeded in attracting dissident CUT unions into its fold.

By 1960, labor was thus polarized into two camps: the Marxist, larger but disunited, affiliated with international communism, and the Christian Democratic, smaller but more united, democratic and anti-communist, and growing rapidly. The country's total union membership was 230,000, out of a labor force of 2.75 million (35 percent of the population).

In 1964, with the advent of Eduardo *Frei Montalva, and again more emphatically in 1970 with that of Salvador *Allende Gossens, Chile began political processes to change the economic structure of the country and to bring social justice to the nation. The trade union movement boomed, bringing CUT membership up to over a million, and CNT membership to about half that number. Other unionized industries, such as *copper mining, transport, and *agriculture, brought two out of every three Chilean workers into their fold during the years of the *Unidad Popular government (1970-73).

With the overthrow of Allende in September 1973, the trade union movement suffered severe repression. The CUT, the nation's preeminent labor federation, was outlawed because it was believed to be a political organization of the Communist Party. Seven other trade union federations, representing 529 unions and 400,000 workers, were banned, along with the one-million member CUT, and all their property confiscated. Some unions were allowed to continue but were unable to function normally, as strikes were forbidden, as were collective bargaining, union meetings and elections. A series of decrees in 1978 further restricted the

rights of Chilean workers--to the extent that many labor unions
in other countries, including America's AFL-CIO, threatened to
boycott all Chilean shipping.

Responding to this international pressure, the government of
General Augusto *Pinochet Ugarte, in its Plan Laboral of 1979,
enacted legislation that allowed some strikes (but not those dama-
ging to the nation at large) and permitted collective bargaining
and the election of union officials. Some of this was incorporated
in the CONSTITUTION OF 1980, q.v. The right to strike was
however limited to 59 days, after which employers could hire
other workers to replace those on strike. Chile's labor and social
insurance ministry declared that the new labor code would deal
"a death blow to Marxism."

In 1983 and 1984 a series of strikes took place to protest the
government's economic policies. A loose grouping of labor union
leaders, the Comando Nacional de Trabajadores--National Workers'
Command (CNT)--organized the first mass demonstration against
the government on May Day, 1983, headed by Rodolfo *Seguel,
leader of the Confederación de Trabajadores del Cobre (CTC), the
*copper workers' union. Chileans from all walks of life joined in
the protest, banging *pots and pans and honking automobile
horns. The government moved swiftly to meet the challenge,
anxious to discredit the protesters. Seguel was arrested. This
led to violence, and with the subsequent arrest of the Christian
Democrat (*Partido Demócrata Cristiano) leader Gabriel *Valdés
Subercaseaux, repression was intensified. Some 27 demonstrators
died when troops opened fire. The government later released
both Seguel and Valdés and made immediate concessions to the
striking copper workers. The success of the protest led to other
demonstrations and another May Day mass gathering which involved the majority of Santiago's nearly four-million population.
This clearly indicated the strength of the trade unions and the
widespread dissatisfaction with the Pinochet government. In
October 1984 a national strike was called for jointly by the
Christian Democrat Central Democrática de Trabajadores and the
largely leftist CNT.

TRANSANDINE RAILWAY. The most spectacular *railway route across
the Andes is that of the Ferrocarril Transandino Chileno (FCTC).
Its route leaves *Santiago via Llay Llay, climbs through Los Andes
and into the *Uspallata Pass, to connect with the Argentine railroad to Mendoza and Buenos Aires, in one of the most remarkable
examples of mountain railroad building in the world.

William *Wheelwright suggested such a line to the Argentine
government in 1852, envisioning it as a way for Buenos Aires to
secure the bulk of Chile's export trade. The project that eventually got under way, however, was the one proposed by the
brothers Juan and Mateo Clark in 1872. They wanted a line
connecting *Mendoza with *Valparaíso, Chile's principal port, as
a way to secure *Cuyo's export trade for Chile. Swiss expertise

in mountain railroad building was drawn upon (as elsewhere in Chile) and Swiss engineer Schatzmann designed the most difficult section in 1889. But construction was so costly that in 1892 the Clarks' capital ran out. Meanwhile, in 1888, Mendoza had been linked to Buenos Aires, 1,048 km away, defeating the primary object of the line. A London-based firm took over the line in 1904, completing it in April 1910.

The old mule track that the railway followed crossed the *cordillera at 14,500 ft. A two-mile summit tunnel permits the rail link to cross at only 10,500 ft., but even so, because of its latitude, the FCTC suffers much more from snow than the higher transandine lines further north (*Arica-La Paz, *Antofagasta-La Paz and Antofagasta-Salta), and is sometimes blocked for up to four months a year. With more money, an eight-mile tunnel could have reduced the maximum altitude to only 3,000 ft. Lack of money also accounts for the line's having been built to meter (3 ft., 3 ins.) gauge, unlike other lines of the *Red Sur, which are broad gauge.

The FCTC is electrified to the Argentine border, but with the fall in demand due to the growth of air and road travel it no longer provides a through passenger service.

TRANSPORTATION. See: AIR TRANSPORT; HIGHWAYS; LADECO; LAN-CHILE; MERCHANT MARINE; METRO; PORTS AND HARBORS; POSTAL SERVICES; RAILWAYS; RED NORTE; RED SUR; TRANS-ANDINE RAILWAY; TRANSPORTES Y TELECOMUNICACIONES, Ministerio de.

TRANSPORTES Y TELECOMUNICACIONES, Ministerio de. The Ministry of Transport and Telecommunications resulted from the division of the Public Works and Communications Ministry (Ministerio de *Obras Públicas y Vías de Comunicaciones) into separate Transport and Works ministries not long after the *coup d'état of September 11, 1973. Ministers since then have been: General Enrique Garín (July 1974); General Raúl Vargas (March 1976); José Luis Federici (April 1978); General Caupolicán Boisset Mújica (December 1979); General Enrique Escobar Rodríguez (August 1983).

TRATADO DE.... See: TREATIES.

TREASURY. See: HACIENDA, Ministerio de; HACIENDA, Secretaría de.

TREATIES. See: ABRAZO DEL ESTRECHO; ANCON, Treaty of; BOLIVIA, Relations with; BOUNDARY TREATY OF 1881; CAPITU-LACION DE PURAPEL; CHINCHA ALTA, Treaty of; CUZCUZ TREATY; DECLARACION DE SANTIAGO: LIMA, Treaty of; LIR-CAY, Treaty of; OCHAGAVIA TREATY; PACTO ANDINO; PACTOS DE MAYO; PAUCARPATA, Treaty of; QUILLEN, Parlamentos de; SPAIN, Relations with; TANTAUCO TREATY; TORDESILLAS, Treaty of; UNITED KINGDOM, Relations with; WORLD WAR II.

TRES ACEQUIAS. A village by the *Maipo river at 33° 38'S, 70° 45'W, which was the scene of a battle on August 26, 1814, in the brief civil war between *carreristas and *o'higginistas. Bernardo *O'Higgins, advancing on *Santiago from *Talca, crossed the river with only his advance guard, and made a precipitate attack on a well dug-in and numerically superior enemy army. He was routed, but José Miguel *Carrera Verdugo then found himself threatened by the army of Mariano *Osorio and entered into negotiations with O'Higgins to form an alliance against the common foe. The result was the Battle of RANCAGUA, q.v.

TRIBUNAL DEL SANTO OFICIO. See: INQUISITION.

TRILALEO, Fundo. Farm near *Chillán, at 36° 54'S, 71° 57'W, the site of a battle in the so-called War to the Death (*Guerra a Muerte), on November 1, 1819. Pedro Nolasco Victoriano flung his 100 *independientes in a futile attack on 500 *realistas defending the farm. Losing all but 20 of his men, he had to retire, leaving Chillán undefended. The Spanish commander, Vicente *Benavides, was then able to occupy the city, where his troops committed all sorts of atrocities.

TRIVELLI FRANZOLINI, Hugo (1913-). Agrarian engineer and economist, and member of the Christian Democrats (*Partido Demócrata Cristiano). In 1944 he was the drafter of an *agrarian reform program in the government of Juan Antonio *Ríos Morales. From 1949 to 1950 he was an agrarian economist on the National Economic Council (Consejo Nacional de Economía), serving also as Chilean representative on the *United Nations' *Economic Commission for Latin America (ELLA). From 1953 to 1954 he was general director of agriculture and director of the Agrarian Development ment Program for ECLA. From then until 1964 he served on the U.N.'s Food and Agriculture Organization (FAO). When Eduardo *Frei Montalva became President in November 1964, he made Trivelli his minister of *agriculture.

TRUCCO FRANZANI, Manuel (b. 1875). Civil engineer, Radical Party (*Partido Radical) politician and vice-president of the Republic, August 20-November 15, 1931. A teacher at the *Instituto Nacional, he was appointed director general of the State *Railways (*Empresa de Ferrocarriles del Estado) in 1918, and entered the Senate in 1926. Appointed interior minister, August 7, 1931, he became acting President when Juan Esteban *Montero Rodríguez resigned as vice-president in order to run in the coming presidential election. During his short administration, Trucco imposed a 12 percent salary cut on government employees to help reduce the budget deficit caused by the Great *Depression. This was the direct cause of the *Coquimbo Mutiny in the *navy. After Montero Rodríguez's election victory, Trucco became Chilean ambassador in the *United States (until 1938).

TUCAPEL. Fort on the river Fortuna, a tributary of the Curanilahue, at 37° 40'S, 73° 20'W, built by Pedro de *Valdivia in 1552, destroyed by the *Araucanian Indians in 1553, rebuilt several times subsequently, but finally abandoned in 1723. The first destruction was the consequence of the Indian victory at the Battle of Tucapel on December 26, 1553, which marked the beginning of the three-hundred year *Guerras de Arauco. Pedro de Valdivia, seeking to put down an Indian revolt, found his force surrounded by a much larger Araucanian army, which attacked ceaselessly until only Valdivia and the priest Bartolomé del Pozo were left. These two tried to escape, but were captured. The chieftains *Caupolicán and *Lautaro tried to spare them. Valdivia pleaded for his life, promising to leave Chile for good, but another *toqui, Leucotón, killed him with a blow on his neck. Tucapel was one of the most disastrous defeats suffered by the Spanish in their campaign to conquer Chile.

- U -

U.D.T. See: UNION DEMOCRATICA DE TRABAJADORES.

U.F.U.Ch. See: UNION DE FEDERACIONES UNIVERSITARIAS DE CHILE.

U.N. See: UNION NACIONAL; UNITED NATIONS.

U.P. See: UNIDAD POPULAR.

U.S.A. See: UNITED STATES.

U.S.S.R., Relations with. Chile broke off diplomatic relations with Russia in 1917 and did not establish any with the Soviet Union until December 11, 1944. These were broken off on October 21, 1947: the government of Gabriel González Videla accused the *Partido Comunista Chileno of fomenting a *coal miners' strike on instructions from the U.S.S.R. President Eduardo *Frei Montalva reestablished relations on November 24, 1964, soon after assuming office. In 1967 an agreement was reached between the Soviet Union and Chile for the construction of industrial enterprises and the granting of credits. On February 6, 1970, an agreement was signed on cultural exchanges and scientific cooperation. After the election of Socialist President Salvador *Allende Gossens in November 1970, relations became warmer, with both governments expressing their willingness to develop trade under more beneficial terms. Agreements were signed on cooperation in the development of Chile's fishing industry (see: FISHERIES) with economic and technical help from the U.S.S.R.

In 1972, when Chile's *economy showed signs of deterioration, the Soviet Union loaned Chile $500 million on very favorable terms. A year later, as the economic situation became desperate, Allende turned again to the Soviets for help. But the U.S.S.R. was not pleased with the way Allende was handling the economy, disapproving in particular of his wage increases for the lowest paid workers: the Soviets told Allende plainly that they would not lend Chile another $500 million.

Ten days after the September 11, 1973, *coup d'état that brought down the Allende government, the U.S.S.R. broke off relations with Chile. The military *junta that came to power viewed itself as a leader in the international struggle against Soviet Marxism.

See also: FOREIGN RELATIONS.

ULTIMA HORA. See: NOTICIAS DE LA ULTIMA HORA, Las.

ULTIMAS NOTICIAS, Las. (November 1902-). *Santiago daily newspaper founded by the Edwards family. See: NEWSPAPERS.

UNEMPLOYMENT. See: EMPLOYMENT.

UNIDAD POPULAR (Popular Unity). A coalition of six left-of-center *political parties formed in 1969 to support the presidential candidacy of Socialist Salvador *Allende Gossens, viz.: the Communist Party (*Partido Comunista Chileno), the Socialists (*Partido Socialista de Chile), the Radicals (*Partido Radical), the Social Democrats (*Partido Social Democrático), the United Popular Action Movement (*Movimiento de Acción Popular Unida, MAPU), and Independent Popular Action (*Acción Popular Independiente, API). Unidad Popular's (U.P.) basic program was: (1) to establish a revolutionary government which would put an end to imperialism and to the capitalist structure prevalent in Chile; (2) to establish a new social order; (3) to give power to "the people", i.e. the working class; (4) to begin the structural change of society with the elimination of the class system; (5) to undertake a comprehensive *agrarian reform which would eliminate the *latifundio and set up a collective system of farming with the establishment of farm cooperatives; and, (6) to make Chile a power within Latin America.

One of U.P.'s goals was the abolition of the *Organization of American States (OAS), considered by the Latin American left to be an instrument of imperialism and of *United States domination in the Hemisphere. A new organization, truly representative of the Latin American countries, would then be instituted.

Unidad Popular won a plurality in the 1970 presidential election with only 36.8 percent of the votes. In the March 1971 municipal elections it obtained 50.8 percent, an impressive increase. Within the coalition, the Communists increased their vote from 15.9 percent of the total (1970) to 17.3 percent. The biggest increase

went to the Socialists, Allende's own party, who replaced the
Communists as the strongest faction within the coalition; their
vote almost doubled, to 22.8 percent. The relatively small Radical
Party obtained 8.1 percent in 1971, and the rest of the U.P.
vote (2.6 percent) went mainly to MAPU.

During Allende's first two years in power, Chile saw the consolidation of the forces of the left under the hegemony of the
Unidad Popular government. During his last year, Chile saw
an even greater effort by the forces of the right to unite against
him. In early 1973 both the Unidad Popular and the opposition
focused on the upcoming March parliamentary elections. The
U.P. had proposed a new unicameral legislature in order to deal
more effectively with the country's economic crisis, particularly
with regard to the production and distribution of foodstuffs. The
opposition, united in a new coalition, the *Confederación Democrática (CODE), had hoped to win two thirds of the seats in
*Congress, the majority it needed to begin impeachment proceed-
ings against the President, whom it blamed for the country's
economic woes. All 150 seats in the Chamber of Deputies and half
of the 50 Senate seats were up for reelection. Unidad Popular
obtained a solid vote of confidence from the working class, winning 43.39 percent of the vote, against 56.61 percent for CODE.
As the UP share was 7 percent more than Allende had achieved
running for President, the left regarded the result as a victory.
No other government in Chile, after all, had increased its voting
strength midway through a six-year administration. But CODE
also claimed victory. Its principal error in 1970 had been to
divide its strength by presenting rival candidates for the right
wing *Partido Nacional and the center *Partido Demócrata Cristiano.
In fact, the March 1973 elections did significantly alter the
balance of power between Unidad Popular and the opposition.

With the *coup d'état of September 11, 1973, the Unidad
Popular and its constituent parties were outlawed, and many of
their members jailed, tortured, sent to *concentration camps, or
killed. Since then it has operated mainly in exile or underground,
each party within the coalition following its own course.
See: ALIANZA DEMOCRATICA; POLITICAL PARTIES.

UNIDAD PROLETARIA. A tabloid which became the organ of the
*Movimiento de Acción Popular Unitaria (MAPU). In 1975 and later
it has been published sporadically as an underground journal,
often calling on the forces of the left to unite in an armed struggle and overthrow the *military regime of President Augusto
*Pinochet Ugarte.

UNION, La. See: NEWSPAPERS.

UNION DE FEDERACIONES UNIVERSITARIAS DE CHILE (UFUCh).
Chile's United Federation of University Students was an important
student organization controlled in the 1960s and early 1970s by the

Christian Democrats (*Partido Demócrata Cristiano). Socialist and Communist students withdrew from UFUCh because they did not want unions from non-state (i.e. Catholic) universities admitted into membership. With the overthrow of President Salvador *Allende Gossens' government in September 1973, all universities suffered *intervencion by the *military regime, which abolished all student federations and depoliticized all educational institutions. See also: EDUCATION.

UNION DE TRABAJADORES DE CHILE (UTRACh). A Christian Democrat federation of trade unions, the Union of Chilean Workers, founded in 1968. See: TRADE UNIONS.

UNION DEMOCRATICA DE TRABAJADORES (UDT). One of the largest federations of *trade unions in Chile, founded in 1981 by the Group of Ten (*Grupo de los Diez), a Christian Democrat (*Partido Demócrata Cristiano) organization. It has a membership of 780,000.

UNION DEMOCRATICA INDEPENDIENTE. The Independent Democratic Union is a pro-government political party of the mid-1980s, led by Sergio Fernández Fernández (interior minister, 1978-82) and Jaime Guzmán.

UNION LIBERAL. A political combination of various parties of the right, including the *Partido Liberal, *Partido Liberal Democrático, *Partido Nacional and *Partido Democrático. It was formed in September 1919, when the other two coalitions of the right, the *Alianza Liberal and the *Coalición, dissolved. The *Partido Radical, which had formed part of the Alianza Liberal, refused to join the Unión Liberal. Just before the presidential election of 1920, the Unión Liberal joined the *Partido Conservador to form the *Unión Nacional.

UNION NACIONAL. (1). An alliance formed in 1920 through the merger of the *Unión Liberal with the *Partido Conservador, to oppose the candidate of a revived *Alianza Liberal (composed of the *Partido Radical, *Partido Liberal Aliancista and *Partido Democrático). The Unión put forward as its candidate Luis *Barros Borgoño. He lost to the Alianza's Arturo *Alessandri Palma, but the parliamentary elections of the following March gave the Unión Nacional a majority in the Senate. As a result, Alessandri was obliged to include two members of the Unión Nacional in his cabinet. The Unión Nacional played an active role in opposing the Alessandri government, and in 1925 it chose Ladislao Errázuriz Lazcano to run for President. When on January 25, 1925, Alessandri was recalled from his self-imposed exile in Italy to reassume the presidency, the Unión Nacional lost popular support and was dissolved.

(2). "Unión Nacional" has sometimes been used to refer to a

political party of the 1980s, the MOVIMIENTO DE UNIDAD NACIONAL, q.v.

UNION NACIONAL DE TRABAJADORES DE CHILE (UNTRACh). The National Union of Chilean workers was formed after General Augusto *Pinochet Ugarte seized power in September 1973. He immediately dissolved Chile's largest *trade union, the Central Unica de Trabajadores, and sponsored UNTRACh. But the new federation soon became critical of the regime's economic policies and demanded less curtailment of union rights.

UNION NACIONAL LABORISTA. Political party formed in 1958 to back the independent presidential candidacy of "el cura de Catapilco," Antonio ZAMORANO HERRERA, q.v. In the September 4 election, Zamorano obtained very few votes, and when his party failed to win any seats in *Congress in March 1959, the National Labor Union was dissolved.

UNION REBELDE COMUNISTA. See: COMMUNISM.

UNION REPUBLICANA (UR). An independent political party formed in 1932 soon after the fall of the first administration of Carlos *Ibáñez del Campo (1927-31). Most of the Republican Union's members were professional people, and the party's aims were the preservation of the democratic system in Chile and the introduction of universal *suffrage (women were not allowed to vote before 1934, and not in national elections until 1952). UR won no parliamentary seats, and in 1937 it merged with another group, *Acción Nacional, to form *Acción Republicana.

UNION REVOLUCIONARIA SOCIALISTA. A party formed in September 1932, shortly after Chile's twelve-day experiment with a socialist government known as the *República Socialista, by the union of Acción Revolucionaria Socialista and the Partido Socialista Unificado. The following April the Socialist Revolutionary Union became one of the constituent members of the new united Socialist Party (*Partido Socialista).

UNION SOCIAL REPUBLICANA DE ASALARIADOS DE CHILE (USRACh). A political party organized on October 4, 1925, as a left-wing response to the decision of all the established parties to endorse a single presidential candidacy, that of Emiliano *Figueroa Larraín. Its title, the Republican Social Union of Chilean Wage-earners, reflected its working-class membership. When Figueroa won the election, USRACh protested, alleging fraud, and immediately called a general strike (October 26) to demand his resignation. In the subsequent parliamentary elections the traditional parties campaigned as a block against USRACh, which embraced the Communists and Socialists allied to the Democrats. On April 7, 1927, Figueroa finally resigned, being succeeded by his interior minister, conservative army colonel Carlos *Ibáñez del Campo. The now general Ibáñez called a presidential election, which he won unopposed. When USRACh denounced him, this man of the sword declared the party illegal (1928) and dissolved it, persecuting many of its members as socialist or communist sympathizers.

UNION SOCIALISTA. A political party organized in November, 1937, and dissolved a few months later to form part of the political coalition of various right-wing parties, including the *Nacistas, known as the *Alianza Popular Libertadora. It supported the presidential candidature of Carlos *Ibáñez del Campo.

UNION SOCIALISTA POPULAR (USOPO). The Popular Socialist Union was a moderate party of the left that remained outside the *Unidad Popular coalition in the presidential election of September 4, 1970. It was dissolved after the fall of President Salvador *Allende Gossens on September 11, 1973.

UNITARY POPULAR ACTION. See: ACCION POPULAR UNITARIA.

UNITED KINGDOM, Relations with. The first English contact with Chile was when Sir Francis *Drake sailed through the *Strait of Magellan in 1570 to attack Spanish possessions along the Pacific coast. Other *pirates and privateers followed over the next hundred years or so. During the War of Jenkin's Ear (the War of the Austrian Succession, 1739-48), a British fleet under Lord *Anson established a base in the *Juan Fernández Islands. James Cook visited *Easter Island in 1774, gave his name to the western bay and left an account of his expedition written by his botanist. At the end of the 18th century *whaling and *seal hunting attracted British ships to Chilean waters. Philip Parker *King, assisted by Robert *Fitzroy in H.M.S. Beagle (see: DARWIN, Charles) carried out an important survey of the Chilean coast in 1828-34.

Britain had long sought trade with South America, at first by outright smuggling, and after 1713, under cover of trading in slaves (the Asiento de negros). In 1769 there were two Britons in La *Serena, and sixteen in all Chile in 1808 (Spain insisted on deporting all foreigners).

When France invaded Spain in 1808, replacing *Ferdinand VII with Napoleon Bonaparte's brother Joseph, the United Kingdom suddenly became Spain's ally. Using woolen goods, cotton and ironware, British merchants embarked on a more subtle conquest of Spanish America. After the wars of *independence, when Britain prevented the Holy Alliance from extending its intervention in support of Ferdinand VII's absolutist rule across the Atlantic, the British became the predominant economic brokers in most of Latin America. But the United Kingdom looked primarily to Mexico, the Caribbean and the River Plate region for its trade and investment, considering Chile too distant and too small for its oversea expansion. British influence in Chile was, nevertheless, considerable. The first authorized visit of a British merchant vessel was that of the brig Fly in 1811. Seven years later Scottish admiral Thomas *Cochrane accepted command of the infant Chilean *navy, which came to depend on British technology and training for its development. Chile's first foreign loan was obtained in 1822 by Antonio José de *Irisarri Alonso, Bernardo O'Higgins' representative in London: 1 million pounds at 6 percent interest, even though formal relations were not established between Britain and Chile until 1841. British investors were also instrumental in building Chile's *railways.

The British 1806 seizure of Buenos Aires and their reoccupation of the Falklands made Chileans (and other Latin Americans) apprehensive of British imperialist designs on their continent. O'Higgins sought to protect *Patagonia against such danger, but economic dependence on Britain was proving to be an even greater threat. In 1854 Chile signed a treaty of "friendship, commerce and navigation" with Great Britain, which prohibited discriminatory tariffs and guaranteed freedom of trade between the two nations. Between 1865 and 1875 Chile borrowed heavily from London banks, increasing her dependency. It was thus that the British became drawn into Chilean politics to protect their interests. Industrialization was just beginning, and many industries relied on the importation of raw materials. The pattern of Chilean development intensified its dependence on the largely British-controlled nitrate sector. In 1890 President José Manuel *Balmaceda Fernández tried to find an alternative to economic dependence on Britain and tried in particular to rescue the country's nitrate riches from foreign companies. This angered both the oligarchy and the British. The result was the *Civil War of 1891, in which Balmaceda was overthrown and the way opened to foreign exploitation of Chilean *nitrates and *copper.

From the fall of Balmaceda to the beginning of World War I in 1914, the British continued their dominance of Chile, selling the country 35 to 46 percent of its imports each year. British ships carried most of Chile's oversea trade, and her naval yards built most of Chile's warships. At this period, Chilean exports exceeded imports, and Britain was predominant at both ends of the trade. In the early 20th century there were some 10,000 immigrants from Great Britain in Chile, mostly working on the railroads, in *mining, shipping and banking.

After 1907 Chile began to expand its markets, attracting *foreign investment in copper and nitrates from other countries, especially the *United States, and by the outbreak of World War I Chile had become heavily indebted to the U.S. During the *Depression of the 1930s, many British merchant houses collapsed, and the economic predominance of the United Kingdom declined sharply. After World War II, the U.S. replaced the U.K. as Chile's chief trading partner, because Britain had to sell many of its investments to pay the cost of the war. Chile and other Latin American countries had resented the "economic imperialism" of the United Kingdom. Great Britain's fight against Hitler had won general admiration, and with the end of British economic dominance in Latin America the resentment virtually disappeared.

In 1962 Prince Phillip came to Chile to play polo. Six years later the British Royal family made a goodwill visit to Chile, clearly in the hope of promoting British exports. During the Salvador *Allende Gossens presidency (1970-73), U.K.-Chile relations were cordial but distant, and in 1975 the U.K. broke off diplomatic relations with Chile after the release from prison of a British physician, Sheila *Cassidy, who claimed she had been tortured. Amid considerable controversy over *human rights violations by the Augusto *Pinochet Ugarte government, a newly-elected Conservative government in Britain under Margaret Thatcher restored diplomatic relations with Chile in 1980. British military sales to Chile were resumed, and relations improved. It was even alleged that Chile gave covert help to the British in the 1982 Anglo-American war over the Falkland Islands.

See also: BRITISH INFLUENCE; FOREIGN RELATIONS; IMMIGRATION.

UNITED NATIONS (U.N.). Chile has been a member of the United Nations since its inception in 1945. Two Chileans have served as presidents of the U.N. General Assembly: José Maza (September 20-December 20, 1955) and Rudecindo Ortega (November 1-10, 1956). The most important U.N. organs in which Chile participates are: the U.N. Population Commission; the *Economic Commission for Latin America (ECLA); the Conference on Trade and Development (UNCTAD); Industrial Development Board of the U.N. Industrial Development Organization (UNIDO); the Commission on Human Rights; and the U.N. Development Program (UNDP). The seat of U.N. in Latin America is located in *Santiago de Chile.

Chile's special relationship with the U.N. came to an end with the overthrow of President Salvador *Allende Gossens in 1973. The new *military regime was antagonistic towards the U.N. and refused any review of its treatment of political prisoners or investigation of its alleged *concentration camps by the High Commission on Refugees and Human Rights. The government has also started a campaign against the United Nations, accusing it of harboring Communists and of being pro-Marxist.

UNITED STATES, Relations with. United States-Chile relations were cordial after Chile declared itself independent of Spain in 1818. The 1776 American Revolution had been an inspiration to Chile and to its political development, even down to the final form of the national flag. American influence on political theory was almost as important as that of *France in the cultural sphere or that of the *United Kingdom in economic matters. Many U.S. citizens played important roles in the formation of the Chilean nation. Outstanding among them were Joel Robert *Poinsett, first U.S. envoy to Chile and a close advisor of José Miguel *Carrera Verdugo; Mateo Arnoldo *Hoebel, responsible for Chile's first *newspaper; *railway pioneers William *Wheelwright and Henry *Meiggs; and businessman Pablo Délano, son in law of Jorge *Edwards Brown and a distant relative of Franklin Delano Roosevelt.

Chile and the U.S., had, however, little in common in way of trade, with the exception of American sealers and whalers who were active in Chilean waters (See: SEAL HUNTING; WHALING). But when the United States acquired California from Mexico in 1848, *Valparaíso became the most important port-of-call on the long passage from the North American east coast. Chile became for a while California's major oversea supplier of *wheat and other foodstuffs. The gold rush also attracted many Chileans to California.

In 1880 the U.S. tried to mediate in the War of the *Pacific, but the resulting Conferencia de *Arica was frustrated by both sides' intransigence over the future of *Antofagasta. This was the beginning of an American involvement in the boundary dispute between Chile and *Peru that lasted until the definitive Treaty of *Lima was concluded in 1929.

James G. Blaine, U.S. Secretary of State in 1881 and from 1889 to 1892, had wanted to intervene actively in the Pacific War. Shortly after the overthrow of President José Manuel *Balmaceda Fernández, Blaine was involved in a bitter dispute with Chile over the incident of the U.S.S. BALTIMORE, q.v.

In 1905 American firms purchased Chile's major *copper mines, and so acquired control over the bulk of the production of the mineral that by the 1930s replaced nitrates as the country's major export and foreign exchange earner. This caused resentment among Chileans who saw one super-power, the *United Kingdom, making way for another, the United States, in exploiting their nation's natural resources.

Despite these strained relations, Chileans generally looked up to the United States, considering it their favorite developed country. It could be said that Chile enjoyed better relations with the U.S. than it did with most of its neighbors. Chile, like so many other Latin American countries, came to accept military and other missions from the United States rather than, as previously, from Europe. Already by 1925 the *Kemmerer Mission had resulted in a major reform of Chilean finance. After World War II the U.S. became the predominant economic influence in Chile. Mutual interest in the defense of the Western Hemisphere fostered cooperation in military matters (see: ARMAMENTS, ARMED FORCES; ESCUELA MILITAR). This tradition of friendly relations was based on the mutually beneficial flow of technology and *foreign assistance from the U.S. and of copper from Chile. It lasted until 1970, when Chile elected a Socialist President, Salvador *Allende Gossens. The U.S. reaction to Allende's election was overtly cool. President Richard Nixon, for example, failed to send the customary congratulatory message to the President-elect. It also transpired that the *Central Intelligence Agency and the American multinational *I.T.T. had tried to interfere in the Chilean political process to thwart Allende's election from being confirmed by *Congress. Other manifestations of the strains between the two nations were Allende's nationalization of *banks and of large American-owned companies such as *Anaconda and *Kennecott (which, between them, owned 90 percent of Chile's copper), and the covert C.I.A. efforts to finance anti-government strikes (see: BOSSES' STRIKE) and the political opposition, hoping to induce the Chilean *armed forces to intervene.

The United States established official diplomatic contact with the Augusto *Pinochet Ugarte regime two weeks after the September 1973 *coup d'état that overthrew Allende. But the continued violation of *human rights in Chile led the U.S. Congress to impose sanctions against Pinochet and suspend the sale of military hardware. The accession of Jimmy Carter further strained relations as his new administration voted in international organizations to condemn Chile's human rights record. A particularly disturbing factor in the relations between the two countries was the Washington, D.C., assassination of Orlando *Letelier del Solar by the Chilean secret police, the *DINA. Chile's refusal to cooperate in the subsequent investigation by allowing the extradition of the Chileans involved was described as deplorable by the State Department. The poor state of U.S.-Chilean relations lasted until Ronald Reagan became president in 1981. Pointing to "encouraging signs" in the human rights picture, Reagan lifted the sanctions against Chile and invited the Chilean *navy to participate in joint exercises with the United States. But when Pinochet imprisoned leaders of the "loyal opposition" in 1983, even Reagan set some distance between the two governments. This, however, did not impair the improved state of bilateral relations. The embargo on weapon sales (see: ARMAMENTS) was lifted, and Chile became a preferred customer in renegotiating her close-to-$18,000-million foreign debt.

See also: FOREIGN RELATIONS.

UNIVERSIDAD AUSTRAL. Chile's Southern University is located in *Valdivia and was founded in 1954. After 19 years of autonomous service, it was subjected by the new *military regime to *intervención on September 11, 1973, as part of the *junta's vow to "extirpate the cancer of Marxism from Chile." When activities were partially resumed on September 17, a purge ensued in which the dean of the philosophy department and two members of the Spanish department were imprisoned. Many foreign professors and researchers were mistreated and jailed; others were asked to leave the country. This "cleansing" process was designed to eliminate all elements judged dangerous in the eyes of the military to the functioning of the university as they understood it.

See also: EDUCATION; UNIVERSITIES.

UNIVERSIDAD CATOLICA DE CHILE. The Catholic University of Chile was founded in *Santiago by the then *archbishop, Mariano *Casanova Casanova, on June 21, 1888. Its *law faculty was one of the first two faculties to begin classes in 1889, under rector Joaquín *Larraín Gandarillas. Over the next half-century, the Catholic University built up one of the finest reputations in Chilean institutions of higher learning. During the 1950s and 1960s the university enhanced its fine academic tradition, thanks to innovations in the curriculum brought about during the rectorship of Raúl, Cardinal *Silva Henríquez.

The imposition of military rule in Chile following the *coup d'état of September 11, 1973, led to *intervención in the UCCh as elsewhere in Chilean higher education. Faculty reductions were far fewer than those imposed on the *Universidad de Chile, but these affected the holders of a wide range of political opinion. While the first dismissals had been of teachers of leftist orientation, subsequent ones affected members of the centrist Christian Democrats (*Partido Demócrata Cristiano) and even independent conservatives who expressed disapproval of government involvement in the educational system. The latter groups had represented the bulk of the UCCh personnel. In terms of disciplines, the social sciences were hardest hit. Even the loud voice of the Roman Catholic *Church was not enough to prevent abuses. See also: EDUCATION; UNIVERSITIES.

UNIVERSIDAD CATOLICA DE VALPARAISO. The Catholic University of *Valparaíso was founded in 1928. Like its counterpart in *Santiago, the university was strong in *law, literature and the social sciences. When the military *coup d'état of September 11, 1973 put an end to university autonomy, drastic changes were introduced, particularly in the area of social studies. Four departments and institutes were eliminated; the Institute of Social Sciences, the School of Education, the School of Social Work and the Center of Studies of Vocational Training. All professors who had sympathized with Socialist President Salvador *Allende Gossens were dismissed, and more than thirty imprisoned, of whom one died during interrogation. Overnight the UCV was plunged into an academic witchunt; in this respect it was like any other university in Chile at the time. See also: EDUCATION; UNIVERSITIES.

UNIVERSIDAD DE CHILE. The University of Chile was founded on September 17, 1843, during the Presidency of Manuel *Bulnes Prieto. The renowned Venezuelan scholar Andrés *Bello López was its first rector. Prior to the *coup d'état of 1973, the UCh was regarded as an excellent center of higher learning, having made great strides in its departments of economics, engineering, and mathematics, and in the humanities. It was one of the few universities in South America that published several journals in various disciplines, and still produces an economic abstract for the Latin American countries.

After the *coup d'état of September 1973, the university suffered a systematic witchunt. All departments that had identified with the left were either closed or reorganized. Books were burned, professors were fired (some even imprisoned and tortured), and students who had identified with the Salvador *Allende Gossens regime were barred from enrolling. Thirty-six prosecutors worked closely with the new rector, Air Marshall César *Ruiz Danyau, to hear charges against faculty, staff and students and decide their fate. Although exact figures are hard to come by, at least 22 percent of the faculty were fired by 1975, about 2,000 altogether. This process continued in successive waves until well into 1976, when another 300 faculty members were relieved of their teaching assignments.

See: EDUCATION: UNIVERSITIES.

UNIVERSIDAD DE CONCEPCION. The University of *Concepción, founded in 1918 by Enrique Molina (and opened in 1919), was Chile's third university, and the first outside *Santiago. It was the university where the *Movimiento de Izquierda Revolucionario (MIR) was most active, and where there was most support for the *Unidad Popular government of 1970-73. As a result, Concepción suffered the brunt of the university repression that followed the *coup d'état of September 1973. Many administrators, professors and students lost their lives in the immediate aftermath; others were arrested and transferred to the *concentration camp on the nearby island of *Quiriquina. Students not already in their final year lost all credit for work done at the university. The military purge included the elimination of the institute of sociology, the school of journalism, the theater department and the university council (which had administered the university). Twelve students, picked by the military rector on the basis of their right-wing militancy, formed a committee to rule on applications for reregistration. Only 400 of the 2,400 students living on campus were readmitted, and only 11,000 altogether out of the pre-coup enrollment of 23,000. See: EDUCATION; UNIVERSITIES.

UNIVERSIDAD DE SAN FELIPE. Chile's colonial university and, at the end of the 18th century, the only one in the Americas south of Lima. Decreed in 1738 and named in honor of King *Philip V, it was not established until 1756 and only began functioning in 1758, not long before the banishment of the *Jesuits and closure of their colleges (1767) gave it added importance. Although its creation was the result of agitation by the lay *cabildo, its teaching staff were necessarily all churchmen, no other qualified teachers being available. During its 57-year active existence, it had 1,785 students, of whom 1,052 graduated. Of these, 299 (35 clergy, 244 laymen) obtained their doctorates. In 1813 the university became part of the *Instituto Nacional, although it was not formally abolished until 1839. When independent Chile set up the new *Universidad de Chile in 1843, the professors of the old university joined the faculty of the new one.

UNIVERSIDAD DE SANTIAGO. New name of the UNIVERSIDAD TECNICA DEL ESTADO, q.v.

UNIVERSIDAD DEL BIO-BIO. Located in *Concepción, the University of the Bío-Bío is one of Chile's newest institutions of higher learning; it was founded in 1981. With 174 professors and 2,671 students, it specializes in architecture, constructing and engineering.
See also: EDUCATION; UNIVERSITIES.

UNIVERSIDAD DEL NORTE. Founded in 1957, the University of the North has its main campus in *Antofagasta, but branch campuses have been set up in *Arica, Vallenar, and *Coquimbo. The post-1973 coup *intervención resulted in a total restructuring of the university, particularly in the areas of anthropology and sociology. The purge involved the jailing of dozens of professors and students, and the expulsion of 25 foreign instructors. University residences were ransacked, and several people high in the administration were shot by the authorities. See also: EDUCATION; UNIVERSITIES.

UNIVERSIDAD TECNICA DEL ESTADO. Founded in 1952, the State Technical University had its main campus in *Santiago, and was seen by the *military regime that came to power in September 1973 as a hotbed of leftist propaganda. On the day of the *coup d'état, the university was occupied by the *armed forces after a violent onslaught that left many dead and wounded (the attackers had used artillery). Professor Enrique Kirberg, the rector, was arrested, as was his wife. Everyone found inside the university was taken to the National Stadium. Victor *Jara, Chile's famous folk singer, was also taken prisoner and executed in front of hundreds in the stadium. The Technical University, like the *Universidad de Concepción, was then subjected to a violent process of "ideological purification." More than 60 of the faculty were dismissed, many of them killed or tortured. Evening and night courses were suppressed, and fewer than a third of the 15,000-strong student body were allowed to return to classes once the university was reopened. It has since been renamed the Universidad de Santiago.
See also: EDUCATION; UNIVERSITIES.

UNIVERSIDAD TECNICA FEDERICO SANTA MARIA. Located in Valparaíso, the Federico Santa María Technical University was founded in 1930. The post-1973 coup restructuring by the military included the cancellation of all student registrations and the abolition of the Social Science faculty. See also: EDUCATION; UNIVERSITIES.

UNIVERSITIES. Original Spanish policy was to set up universities in the viceregal capitals: the Universidad de San Marcos in Lima, *Peru, dates from 1551. These were supplemented during the 17th and 18th centuries by universities established as part of *Jesuit missions: in Chile the Universidad Pencopolitana in *Concepción functioned from 1724 until the Society's expulsion in 1767. Chile's first secular university was the UNIVERSIDAD DE SAN FELIPE (q.v.) of 1756, the forerunner of the national UNIVERSIDAD DE CHILE (q.v.) of 1843. The anticlericalism of Chile's *Partido Liberal administrations of the 1870s and 1880s led the *Church to create the independent UNIVERSIDAD CATOLICA DE CHILE (q.v.) in 1888. The first provincial university, the UNIVERSIDAD DE CONCEPTION (q.v.) opened in 1919. Nine years later another Church foundation, the UNIVERSIDAD CATOLICA DE VALPARAISO (q.v.) was set up in Chile's second city. Two years after that, in 1930, *Valparaíso acquired Chile's first technological university, the UNIVERSIDAD TECNICA SANTA MARIA (q.v.), something *Santiago would not emulate until the UNIVERSIDAD TECNICA DEL ESTADO (q.v.) was established there in 1952. The 1950s also saw the creation of the first universities in the extreme north and south of Chile: the UNIVERSIDAD AUSTRAL (q.v.) at *Valdivia in 1954, and the UNIVERSIDAD DEL NORTE (q.v.) at *Antofagasta in 1957.

In 1967-68, during the presidency of Eduardo *Frei Montalva, the Chilean university system underwent major reforms. As a result, students, faculty and administrative staff acquired the right to elect the rectors and university councils and were given a say in deciding which professors would be granted tenure and promotion, and who would be dismissed. These reforms expanded the responsibilities of faculty and students, but also helped politicize university life. A reaction came with the *coup d'état of September 1973, which instituted a *military regime in Chile. All civilian rectors were replaced by military delegate-rectors who took drastic steps to depoliticize university life. The previous guarantees of free expression and due process were eliminated, and distrust and intimidation became commonplace. By firing faculty and staff at will and by allowing only non-leftist students to enroll, the military began a "cleansing" process in a concerted effort to alter the structure and function of Chile's universities. (See: EDUCATION).

Since the coup, one new university has been created, the UNIVERSIDAD DEL BIO-BIO (q.v.) in 1981, giving Concepción its second university.

Enrollment in Chilean universities this century grew from 2,900 in 1911 to 6,200 in 1925, fell back to 4,900 in the *Depression year of 1930, but recovered to 6,400 in 1940; 11,000 in 1950; and 26,000 in 1960. Then a much faster growth took the total to 77,000 in 1970 and 147,000 in 1975. Since then, greater exclusiveness under the military regime has reduced it to 126,400 in 1979.

Besides their teaching and research role, Chilean universities have been important communicators. *Printing first came to Chile at the Universidad de San Felipe, and the universities remain important as book *publishers. They have been operators of radio stations--the physical destruction of the broadcasting facilities at the Universidad Técnica del Estado was one of the very first operations carried out by the insurgent military in the early morning of September 11, 1973--and all but one of Chile's five television channels are university owned and operated (see: TELECOMMUNICATIONS--D. Television).

UNIVERSITY OF CHILE. See: UNIVERSIDAD DE CHILE.

UNIVERSITY OF CONCEPCION. See: UNIVERSIDAD DE CONCEPCION.

UNIVERSITY OF SAINT PHILIP. See: UNIVERSIDAD DE SAN FELIPE.

UNIVERSITY OF SANTIAGO. See: UNIVERSIDAD DE SANTIAGO.

UNIVERSITY OF THE BIO-BIO. See: UNIVERSIDAD DEL BIO-BIO.

URANIUM. Geologists in 1982 found that Chile had considerable uranium reserves, much of them in association with *copper deposits at *Chuquicamata and *Exótica. Exploitation is under consideration by government officials and by foreign companies with the expertise to extract the ore. The Chilean government has been contemplating the construction of a nuclear power plant in order to lessen the country's dependence on imported *petroleum. See also: ENERGY AND POWER.

URMENTA GARCIA, José Tomás de (1808-1878). A wealthy philanthropist who administered many *mining enterprises and was important in developing Chile's *copper industry. He served as superintendant of *Santiago's first fire brigade (cuerpo de bomberos), which he established. He was elected to the Chamber of Deputies in 1846 and to the Senate in 1855. In 1871 he was the National Party (*Partido Nacional) presidential candidate, but lost to Federico *Errázuriz Zañartu, who was backed by the *Fusión Liberal-Conservadora.

URRIOLA BALBONTIN, Pedro Alcantara (1797-1851). Chilean patriot who fought at *Rancagua, and in 1816 joined Manuel *Rodríguez Erdoiza's guerrilla campaign against the Spanish in *Colchagua, but fell prisoner at Melipilla the following year. He served in Rodríguez's "Húsares de la muerte," but then retired to his farm. He resumed his military career in 1828, becoming lieutenant colonel in 1830. In 1831 he was promoted to colonel and appointed *intendant of Santiago. He held high command in the war with the *Peru-Bolivia Confederation in 1838-39, and was elected to the Chamber of Deputies on his return. During the political disturbances he led the so-called MUTINY OF URRIOLA (q.v.) against the government of Manuel *Bulnes Prieto and was killed in the fighting.

URRUTIA, Matilde (1913-1985). Widow of Pablo *Neruda. Matilde Urrutia studied voice at the conservatory of the *Universidad de Chile, was for a short time a professional singer, and met Neruda in 1946 at a symphony concert in the Parque Forestal, *Santiago. Six years later, Neruda left Delia del *Carril, with whom he had lived since 1934, and married Matilde. After the poet's death in 1973, Matilde gave a faithful account of how he spent his last hours, how he had been taken from their house by the military, and the difficulties he had experienced getting medical care. She bravely smuggled his memoirs, Confieso que he vivido (I confess to having lived) out of Chile, for publication. After one of their two homes had been ransacked, Matilde bravely decided to remain in Chile, retiring to their house in Isla Negra. She too was surrounded by many friends and began to manage Neruda's estate and to bring out her late husband's unpublished works. She died on January 5, 1985, after a long illness, without being able to see the end of military rule that she so much detested.

USOPO. See: UNION SOCIALISTA POPULAR.

USPALLATA PASS. A 14,500-ft. high pass through the *Andes on the Chilean-Argentine frontier at 32° 43'S, 69° 24'W, named from a small town of 500 inhabitants on the Argentine side. It is also known as La Cumbre Pass and as Bermejo Pass. On the main highway between *Santiago and *Mendoza, the pass is the shortest, widest and most direct route between central Chile and Buenos Aires. The original Indian trail provided the *conquistadores with access into fertile *Cuyo, but settlements there, cut off from the western side of the *cordillera from April to October, gradually came to look towards the River Plate rather than to Chile, a development eventually recognized in the separation of Cuyo from the captaincy general of Chile and its incorporation in the new Viceroyalty of the Plate in 1776. The route was in fact so hampered by winter snows as to be impassable even for horsemen. During the 1788-96 governorship of Ambrose *O'Higgins Ballenary, the trail was upgraded into a highway of sorts, the Camino de los Andes, later used by the vanguard of José de San Martín's liberating Ejército de los *Andes in 1817. From the mid-18th century the pass became the mail route to Argentina and Europe (see: POSTAL SERVICES).

Successful disarmament negotiations with Argentina were commemorated by the erection in 1904 of a 25-ft. statue, the *Christ of the Andes, at the summit of the pass. The Christ ceased, however, to be seen by most travelers after the 1910 completion of the *Transandine Railway, which tunnels through the pass at 10,500 ft. Most traffic nowadays goes by road, but the new highway also avoids the peak by the way of a two-and-one-half mile road tunnel.

USRACh. See: UNION SOCIAL REPUBLICANA DE ASALARIADOS DE CHILE.

- V -

VALDES SUBERCASEAUX, Gabriel (1919-). Lawyer and Christian Democrat (*Partido Demócrata Cristiano, PDC) leader. After graduating from the *Universidad Católica de Chile, Valdés became professor of economics there. During the Eduardo *Frei Montalva administration (1964-70), he was foreign minister. After Frei's death in 1982, Valdés succeeded him as PDC president and the military *junta's most outspoken critic. Almost from the moment the *armed forces took over power, the Augusto *Pinochet Ugarte government has been determined to deny the existence of "left-ist impurities" in Chilean society. The most serious charge that Valdés has leveled against the government is that the denial of *human rights is widespread and continuing, and that Chile has become a symbol of repression throughout the hemisphere.

On May Day, 1983, thousands of Chileans defied government threats and joined a mass protest against Pinochet (see: TRADE UNIONS). Other protests followed (four in a four-month period). The regime's harsh response left over 100 dead and many more wounded. In the *United States, the Reagan administration, which had long kept silent, giving the Pinochet government tacit support, condemned the violence and the arrest of 1,200 persons, including three prominent opposition leaders, Valdés among them. In face of mounting world protests, Pinochet decided to release Valdés and promised to talk with opposition leaders to see whether it might not be possible to hold elections before the 1989 date set by the *Constitution of 1980. The next year, 1984, however, Pinochet reversed himself, saying that Chile would not be ready for democracy before 1989, and possibly not even then. This led to further demonstrations. Besides calling for a quick return to democracy, Valdés had urged a revision of the government's economic policies, which had exacted a disproportionate social cost on poor families, whose real wages had plummeted while unemployment rates soared to 30 percent. (See: ECONOMY, The; EMPLOYMENT). In the violent protests that occurred on the eve of the 11th anniversary of the *coup, nine people were killed. Pinochet responded by reintroducing for six months the state of emergency that had ended in 1983. He accused ten opposition leaders, including Valdés and *Alianza Democrática president Mario SHARPE CARTE (q.v.), of trying to overthrow the regime, and threatened them with imprisonment. He then tried to reassure the nation that "the country was under control." In fact, by 1984 Chile was as divided and polarized as it had been under Socialist President Salvador *Allende Gossens. Pinochet's attitude toward his opposition, particularly his harsh repression of peaceful dissent, had sown division in a people used to more than 150 years of considerable freedom and of English-style respect for the loyal opposition. Valdés and other opposition leaders were momentarily silenced, but the regime's failure to promote democracy after eleven years in power cast doubts over its ability to remain in control much longer. Amid the noise of thousands beating on *pots and pans, which grew louder every day, Valdés predicted that Pinochet's days were numbered, although he recognized that his silencing of dissent was a factor in his ability to stay in power.

VALDES VERGARA, Enrique (1859-91). Lawyer brother of Francisco *Valdés Vergara. In January 1888 he founded El *Heraldo, a *Valparaíso newspaper which he made a major vehicle of the opposition to President José Manuel *Balmaceda Fernández. When the *Civil War of 1891 broke out, Valdés sailed to join the *congresista rebels in *Iquique, but was drowned in the sinking of the Blanco Encalada in *Caldera Bay.

VALDES VERGARA, Francisco (1854-1916). Chilean writer and politician. In 1877 he served in the Chilean legation in Bolivia, under Pedro Nolasco *Videla. When the War of the *Pacific broke out he was transferred to Panamá City as consul general there, and shortly afterwards made Chilean chargé d'affaires in Bogotá. Returning to Chile in 1881, he became editor of the *Santiago newspaper La época. From 1882 until 1884 he was interim governor of the newly acquired province of *Tarapacá. He had meanwhile entered the Chamber of Deputies, where he served on various economic commissions. In 1889 he became administrator of *customs in Valparaíso. In 1891 he succeeded his brother Enrique *Valdés Vergara as editor of El *Heraldo newspaper and was appointed finance minister. He sought the *Alianza Liberal nomination in the presidential election of 1901, but this was given instead to Germán *Riesco Errázuriz. On assuming office, Riesco made Valdés director of the Chilean customs service. From 1913 until his death Valdés served in the Senate.

VALDIVIA (city). Capital of the former province of Valdivia. The site, on the banks of the river of the same name, 18 km (11 miles) from the sea at 39° 46'S, 73° 15'W, was named by Gianbattista Pastene, a Genoese sailor sent to explore the southern coast in 1544 by Pedro de *Valdivia, who himself founded the city there in 1552. Destroyed by *earthquake in December 1575, it was rebuilt but destroyed by the *Araucanian Indians in 1599. It was then rebuilt and fortified, both against the Indians on land and *pirates at sea. In August 1643 it was taken by the Dutch pirate Hendrick Brouwer, who improved its defenses. When the Spanish returned in 1645 they completed Brouwer's work, and Valdivia became Spain's strongest military base in the Pacific. The destruction of its fortifications by Lord *Cochrane in February 1820 virtually ended Spanish power on the south Chilean mainland. After independence the place languished, having lost its usefulness, except as a place of exile for convicts (there was no overland connection with the rest of Chile). Development began with the arrival, from 1850 onwards, of German *immigration to *Llanquihue. Valdivia's population was still only 3,000 in 1865, but it grew to 15,229 by 1907; 30,000 by 1920; 50,000 by 1950; 97,000 by 1970; and 104,910 (est.) in 1986. The port is accessible by ships up to 4,000 tons.

VALDIVIA (province). Province of the new Region X, Los *Lagos. Valdivia was originally constituted a province in 1826, consisting of the departamentos of Valdivia, La Unión and Osorno. In 1861 it lost Osorno to the newly created province of *Llanquihue, leaving it with an area of 21,000 km^2 (8,100 square miles). The population has grown from 18,065 (without Osorno) in 1854 to 23,429 in 1865; 50,938 in 1885; 118,277 in 1907; 175,141 in 1920; 232,647 in 1952; 298,445 in 1971 (est.); 322,436 (est.) in 1982.

VALDIVIA (river). River of southern Chile, little more than the estuary of the rivers Cruces and Calle-Calle. Its mouth is the Bay of Corral.

VALDIVIA, Luis de (1560-1642). Spanish *Jesuit who came to Chile in 1593 with the first members of his order to be sent there. He served as rector of the Jesuit Colegio Máximo de San Miguel in *Santiago, one of the first high schools organized in Chile. He also prepared a grammar of the language spoken in the colony. He opposed the system of personalized service to which the Indians were subjected (see: ENCOMIENDA), believing that much of the difficulties with the *Araucanian Indians arose from the ill-treatment they received. His vigorous defense of them led to his being sent back to Spain, where he became noted as a general advisor to the Society of Jesus on Indian questions and acquired wide fame for his piety and learning.

VALDIVIA, Pedro de (1500-1553). Conqueror of Chile. Valdivia was born in La Serena in the province of Extremadura, Spain. He went to the New World, to Venezuela, in 1535, and two years later joined Francisco Pizarro's forces in Peru, helping him against Diego de *Almagro. He quickly won Pizarro's favor, becoming his maestro del campo (chief of staff). Despite Almagro's recent disaster in Chile, and the arrival of Pedro Sancho de la *Hoz with a royal patent to govern new southern conquests, Valdivia was determined to become the conqueror of Chile and got Pizarro to back him. Almagro's experience made it difficult to recruit men for a new expedition, but by 1540 Valdivia had managed to gather a force of 100. His march from Cuzco to central Chile revealed his courage and his leadership abilities in the face of mutinies, the difficulty of crossing the *Atacama desert and attacks from the hostile *Araucanian Indians, the toughest and most unyielding adversaries the Spaniards were to meet in the Americas.

In 1541 his expedition reached the *Mapocho valley, where on February 12 he founded the city of *Santiago. Six months later the Araucanians attacked and destroyed the city, killing some Spaniards and destroying nearly all their supplies. The settlers set about rebuilding while still surrounded by hostile Indians. In December 1547 Valdivia returned to Peru and came back with reinforcements, which raised the number of Spaniards in Chile to 500--and with the official title of governor. In 1549 La *Serena was founded, and the next year Valdivia set off to the south. *Concepción was founded in 1550, and *Valparaíso, *Imperial, *Valdivia, Villarica and Arauco in 1552. In December 1553, however, the Araucanians, under the command of *Lautaro, a former slave of Valdivia's, defeated the Spanish at the Battle of *Tucapel, killing Valdivia and most of his men.

VALDIVIANO FEDERAL, El (1821-1844). *Newspaper founded by José Miguel INFANTE ROJAS, q.v.

VALDIVIESO Y ZANARTU, Rafael Valentín (1804-1878). Chilean priest and politician. He studied at the *Instituto Nacional, receiving his law degree in 1825 and practicing law for eight years. He was elected to the Chamber of Deputies, serving from 1831 to 1840, and was ordained priest in 1834. A few years in the missions in northern and southern Chile established his reputation as a friend of the poor and an accomplished orator. In 1840 he became rector of the Instituto Nacional. In 1843 he published La revista católica (see: PERIODICAL PRESS) and became dean of the theological faculty of the newly created *Universidad de Chile. In 1848 he was consecrated *archbishop of Santiago, and as such was embroiled with the Manuel *Montt Torres government in the 1858 Cuestión del SACRISTAN, q.v. This reached the point of a sentence of exile on the distinguished prelate before accommodation was reached.

VALLE ALLIENDE, Jaime del (1931-   ). Foreign minister of Chile. Jaime del Valle became a law professor at the *Universidad Católica de Chile in 1957, dean of the law faculty in 1970 and vice-rector in 1974. From 1958-64 he was also a senior civil servant in the justice ministry and in 1962 went to the Dominican Republic as an *Organization of American States advisor on penal law and prisons. President Augusto *Pinochet Ugarte made him minister of justice on February 14, 1983, and on December 15, 1983, he succeeded Miguel Alex *Schweitzer Walter as minister of foreign affairs. The following November he signed the treaty with *Argentina that settled the long-standing *Beagle Channel dispute.

VALPARAISO (city). The second largest city of Chile, with a port
considered the "greatest commercial center" on the Pacific coast
of South America. Located at 35° 5'S, 71° 40'W, it is 116 miles
by *railway and 91 miles by road (the Pan-American *highway)
from *Santiago. Appropriately, the site was discovered from the
sea: the ship Santiaguillo reached it from El Callao, Peru, in
1536, calling it simply El Puerto. Valparaíso was originally the
name given to the nearby valley by Juan de Saavedra (one of
Diego de *Almagro's captains) after his birthplace in Spain.

Spanish colonial restrictions obliged Chilean trade to pass
through Panamá, so that, until independence, Valparaíso was only
frequented by coastal shipping. In 1810 its population was barely
5,000, and it was visited by just 14 ships. Eleven years later,
when it was made Chile's principal aduana (custom port), it had
15,000 inhabitants (3,000 of them foreign merchants), and was
visited by 111 ships. The development of *whaling in the 1830s
stimulated further growth, and by 1834 it had displaced Callao
as the first port of the Pacific. Manuel *Rengifo Cárdenas, as
finance minister (1831-51), fostered the port's development by
erecting large bonded warehouses. With the growth of British
trade with Puntarenas in Costa Rica, and then the California gold
rush of the late 1840s, Valparaíso grew rapidly, providing as
it did the first decent harbor for ships after they had made the
difficult passage round *Cape Horn. This traffic almost disappeared with the opening of the Panama Canal in 1914, but by then
Chile's own trade had long since grown sufficiently to sustain the
port's prosperity.

The city was raided by Sir Francis *Drake on December 5,
1578, bombarded by Casto *Méndez Núñez on March 31, 1866 (see:
VALPARAISO, Bombardment of), and has suffered a number of
serious *earthquakes, notably those of 1647, 1730, 1822, 1906
(the worst), 1965, 1971 and 1983. This, and the port's many
other similarities (topographic, climatic and commercial) with San
Francisco, California, has given Valparaíso the nickname of the
Chilean San Francisco.

Population reached 52,413 in 1854; 97,737 in 1875; 122,447 in
1895; 182,422 in 1920; 209,945 in 1940; 252,865 in 1960; and
266,876 (est.) in 1984. These figures do not include the suburbs,
notably *Viña del Mar. The whole "Gran Valparaíso" conurbation
had 841,020 inhabitants at the 1970 census, and an estimated
882,280 in 1978.

VALPARAISO (province). Province of north-central Chile, whose
capital is the city of that name. A law of 1819 had made the city
and port of Valparaíso a special gobierno (government) directly
dependent on the head of the Chilean state. The *Constitution
of 1833 made it a department of the province of *Santiago, but
in 1842 it was separated again, together with the department of
Casablanca, to form, with the addition of *Quillota department
from *Aconcagua province, the new province of Valparaíso. In

this century the administrative area of the province was extended
to include the Chilean oceanic dependencies of *Easter Island, the
*Juan Fernández Islands, *Sala y Gómez Island and the *San
Félix and San Ambrosio Islands, a total of 5,118 km² (1,976
square miles). In 1975 the old province became part of Region
V, *Acongacua, but at the same time the department of Valparaíso
(a subdivision of the province) was raised to the status of a
province within the new region.

The population of the former province was 116,043 in 1854;
178,523 in 1875; 220,756 in 1895; 281,385 in 1907; 320,398 in
1920; 425,065 in 1940; 732,372 (est.) in 1971; and 853,542 (est.)
in 1982. Its area contains 20 percent of Chilean industry, manufacturing refined sugar, textiles, varnishes, paints, pharmaceuticals and biochemical products.

VALPARAISO (region). The designations of the new regions (see:
REGIONS AND ADMINISTRATIVE RESTRUCTURING) are not yet
fixed in all cases. Region V is sometimes referred to as ACONCA-
GUA (q.v.), and sometimes as Valparaíso.

VALPARAISO, Bombardment of. Toward the end of the 1865-66 War
with *Spain, the enemy admiral Casto *Méndez Núñez received
orders to bombard the then undefended port of Valparaíso. As
in a similar situation at Rio de Janeiro in 1893, the British and
*United States governments, anxious to protect their own trade
and the lives and property of their own nationals, placed their
ships between the attacking fleet and the shore. Unlike his
Brazilian counterpart, the Spanish admiral called their bluff, and
they withdrew. The bombardment, on March 31, 1866, lasted
almost four hours, causing "immense" damage to the city. As
a result, coastal defense artillery was installed soon afterwards.

VALPARAISO CATHOLIC UNIVERSITY. See: UNIVERSIDAD CATO-
LICA DE VALPARAISO.

VANGUARDIA NACIONAL DEL PUEBLO (VNP). A political party of
the left founded in 1958 by the fusion of three groups of workers:
the Partido del Trabajo (Labor Party), the Alianza Nacional de
Trabajadores (National Workers' Alliance) and the Intransigencia
Radical Anti-imperialista (Anti-imperialist Radical Intransigent
group). Many of the members had belonged to the *Partido
Socialista de Chile (Socialist Party of Chile). In the parliamentary
elections of 1961, the VNP elected one candidate, Balthasar Castro,
to the Senate. Three years later the party joined the *Frente
de Acción Popular (FRAP) coalition, and backed Salvador *Allende
Gossens in the presidential elections of September 4, 1964. Unable to elect any of its candidates to *Congress, the Vanguardia
Nacional dissolved in 1966.

VANGUARDIA POPULAR SOCIALISTA (VPS). Political party of the

right founded in 1938 as a successor to the Nazi-inspired *Movimiento Nacional Socialista de Chile, with a doctrine based on nationalism and anti-imperialism. Like its predecessor, the VPS encountered strong opposition in Chile, and its history was marred by political incidents and street fights. Increasing disturbances convinced many of its members that it should dissolve. This was done in May 1941.
See also: NACISTAS.

VARA. Pre-metric unit of length (=0.836 meter). Two varas made a *braza. See: WEIGHTS AND MEASURES.

VARAS DE LA BARRA, Antonio (1817-1886). Lawyer who, together with President Manuel *Montt Torres founded the National Party (*Partido Nacional), also known as the Partido Montt-Varista. On graduation he became a teacher at the *Instituto Nacional, and in 1842 its rector. He founded the Caja de Crédito Hipotecario (Mortgage Bank) in 1855, remaining its director for 30 years. Elected to the Chamber of Deputies in 1842, he became minister of justice and *education and in 1851 interior minister in the administration of President Montt. In 1861 the National Party chose Varas as its presidential candidate, but he declined, persuading Montt and the party to support instead José Joaquín *Pérez Mascayano. He remained in the Chamber of Deputies, renowned for his oratorical skills until he entered the Senate in 1876. He held ministerial office again in the government of Aníbal *Pinto Garmendia (1876-81).

VASSALLO ROJAS, Carlos (1908-). A lawyer by profession, he dedicated most of his life to journalism, becoming in 1927 editor of El *Mercurio and *Ultimas noticias. In 1954 he was named minister of public health in the second administration (1952-58) of Carlos *Ibáñez del Campo. He has also been secretary to the minister of foreign affairs and Chilean delegate to UNESCO. He participated in the 10th General Assembly of the *United Nations as a member of the Chilean delegation.

VEGA URIBE, Daniel de la (b. 1892). Writer and poet. He has published more than 40 works, including the celebrated ¿El anticristo a la vista? (the coming of the anti-Christ?), 1972. He has written novels--notably Caín, Abel y una mujer (Cain, Abel and a woman), 1933, four volumes of memoirs, Confesiones imperdonables (unforgivable confessions), 1962-67, and has contributed regularly to the literary sections of *Ultimas noticias and El *Mercurio. Earlier in his career he was known for his plays, particularly the comedies El bordado inconcluso (unfinished embroidery), 1913, and Gente solitaria (solitary folk), 1931. He won the *Premio Nacional de Literatura in 1953 and the Annual Theater Award in 1962.

VEGAS DE SALDIAS, Las. Locality at 36° 44'S, 71° 52'W on the right bank of the Chillán river, near Pinto, in what became Nuble province, the site of Vicente *Benavides' last battle in the so-called "War to the Death" (*Guerra a muerte), October 9-10, 1821. Patriot forces led by Joaquín *Prieto Vial surprised the *realistas as they were fording the river and put them to flight, with the loss of 200 men, 300 horses and most of their supplies. Benavides, forced to become a fugitive, lost his authority over his troops and decided to return to Peru. He was captured in Colchagua province while on his way.

VEGAS DE TALCAHUANO, Las. Locality at 36° 44'S, 73° 4'W, just outside the city of *Talcahuano, and the site of a patriot victory in the so-called "War to the death" (*Guerra a muerte), on November 25, 1820. The Spanish commander Vicente *Benavides was besieging the city with 1,751 regular and 2,400 auxiliary troops when Ramón *Freire Serrano made a surprise sally with only 600 cavalry. He breached the *realista line and a rout ensued in which Benavides lost 180 dead, either killed in the fight and the pursuit, or shot on being captured.

VENEZUELA, Relations with. See: FOREIGN RELATIONS; PACTO ANDINO.

VERA Y PINTADO, Bernardo (1780-1827). Poet and Chilean patriot. Born in Mexico, he was brought up in Santa Fé (*Argentina) and so is generally referred to as an Argentine. Coming to Chile in 1799, he graduated in law at the *Universidad de San Felipe. At the outset of Chile's *independence struggle in 1810, the authorities accused him of subversion against Spain and he was ordered to Lima. By feigning illness he managed to stay in Chile until the formation of the *junta de gobierno de 1810, whereupon the Argentine government made him its representative in Chile. He became assistant editor of Chile's first newspaper, the *Aurora de Chile, in 1812. In July 1814 he became Chilean finance minister (secretario de estado en *hacienda), and in September that year, war minister. After the Patriot defeat at *Rancagua he escaped to *Mendoza. Returning with José de *San Martín's Ejército de los *Andes, he fought at *Chacabuco. He immediately became editor of the official Gaceta del supremo gobierno de Chile newspaper (February 26, 1817), and then of its successor, the Gaceta de Santiago de Chile (June 17, 1817). In 1819 Vera Pintado wrote the words of Chile's first *national anthem. In 1824 he was elected to *Congress as a deputy for *Linares. In 1826 he became a law professor at the *Instituto Nacional. His newspaper work did much to encourage literary expression in Chile.

VERGARA, Marta (b. 1898). Leader of the *Movimiento de emancipación de la mujer chilena (MEMCh) who wrote on the women's suffrage movement in England. Her autobiography (c.1962) appeared with the title Memorias de una mujer irreverente (an irreverent woman's memoirs). See also: WOMEN AND THE WOMEN'S MOVEMENT.

VERGARA DONOSO, José Francisco. As foreign minister, April-November 1902, signed the PACTOS DE MAYO (q.v.) with *Argentina.

VERGARA ECHEVEREZ, José Francisco (1833-1889). An engineer who made a large fortune as a subcontractor in the building of the *Santiago-*Valparaíso *railway and became an important Liberal (*Partido Liberal) politician. He participated in the War of the *Pacific in 1879, and a year later, as war minister, he organized the expedition to Peru which captured Lima. In 1881 he was interior minister in the administration of President Domingo *Santa María González. In 1886 he was chosen by the *Partido Nacional, the *Partido Radical and his own Liberal Party to be their presidential candidate. Unable to win the support of the Conservatives (*Partido Conservador), he withdrew. The Liberals then chose José Manuel *Balmaceda Fernández, who was elected.

VIAL CASTILLO, Javier (1934-). One of Chile's most prominent "conglomerateurs," who built a vast industrial and financial empire during the 1960s and 1970s, the GRUPO VIAL, q.v. He did spectacularly well from 1977 to 1981, only to encounter increasing legal and financial problems with the ungluing of the free market economic model at the end of 1981, which culminated in his arrest for fraud in 1983.

After graduating from the University of California with a degree in agronomy, Vial returned to Chile to work on his father's *latifundia. From 1956 to 1965 he was engaged in poultry breeding and marketing. From 1965 to 1973 he worked in *Santiago, where he rose from a directorship of the Banco Hipotecario de Chile (BHC) to the position of the bank's vice-president, and then its president. After the fall of Chile's socialist President Salvador *Allende Gossens (whom he had opposed) in 1973, he became president of the state *housing office, *CORVI, and Chilean strongman Augusto *Pinochet Ugarte named him director of ICARE (the Chilean Business Administration Institute). He also served on the executive committee of the National Agrarian Society. In 1976 he became president of the Latin American Federation of Banks (Federación Latinoamericana de Bancos--FELABAN). During this period he became identified with the "piranhas," a group of young entrepreneurs which included his partners Fernando *Larraín Peña and Manuel *Cruzat Infante: the name came from the voracity with which they purchased large blocks of stocks in 42 companies, plus a controlling interest in the BHC and 4.7 percent of the stock of the Banco de Chile, which gave Vial a seat on the bank's board of directors. In a short period of time, Vial's assets grew to encompass roughly 50 productive firms. Besides being the BHC president, he was also its greatest borrower.

Because of these "sweetheart loans," the BHC and other banks were accused of living "la dolce vita," i.e. lending excessively to their own subsidiaries and their own executives, regardless of the conflict of interest.

The result of this extreme laissez faire was that the grupos Vial and Cruzat-Larraín, became the dominant force in the *economy through their control of Chile's two largest private banks. But the banks became borrowers in turn, and they continued to borrow even when the size of their debt and worsening leverage indicated that they should slow down and consolidate. Much of this borrowing was from abroad. By 1983 the BHC owed over $1,000 million, of which 45 percent was due in "hard" currency. The Banco de Chile was the country's largest private holder of foreign loans: over $2,000 millions' worth. Of Chile's total $17,000 million foreign debt in 1983, the private sector owed about $10,500 million.

Ironically, the Pinochet government, which had espoused the doctrine that government should play the smallest possible role in the economy, found itself forced by foreign pressure into assuming responsibility for this private indebtedness (see: PUBLIC FINANCES). It had also to intervene directly, taking over the BHC, the Banco de Chile and seven other financial institutions that were in difficulty (see: BANKS, BANKING AND FINANCIAL INSTITUTIONS--B. The collapse of 1981-84). The performance of the Vial, Cruzat and Larraín conglomerates became dismal and was further weakened by successive devaluations of the *peso (see: EXCHANGE RATES). Given the high degree of interdependence between the groups, the government takeover was inevitable and caused several repercussions in the commercial sector. Meanwhile the BHC was dissolved and Vial was charged with embezzlement.

VIAL DEL RIO, Juan de Dios (1799-1850). Lawyer and Chilean patriot. Vial was deputy for *Talca in the first National *Congress in 1811, and was imprisoned during the *Reconquista Española. After *independence was won, he held various ministerial posts in the governments of Bernardo *O'Higgins and Ramón *Freire Serrano. From 1834 until his death he served in the Senate, being twice named president of that body (in 1839 and 1843).

VIAL SANTELICES, Agustín (1772-1838). Lawyer, member of the exaltados' party, and Chilean patriot. Deputy for *Valparaíso in the first National *Congress of 1811. During the next three years he served in various *junta governments, but was taken prisoner after the patriots' defeat at *Rancagua and exiled to the *Juan Fernández Islands. He returned after *Chacabuco, but was exiled for a year in 1820 by Bernardo *O'Higgins. O'Higgins recalled him in 1821 to appoint him acting finance minister (September 1821) and war minister (October 1821). Elected to the Chamber of Deputies in 1823, he originated the idea of selling

the *estanco monopolies to a private concessionary (see: SOCIE-
DAD PORTALES, CEA Y CIA). From 1831 until his death he sat
in the Senate, of which he was president in 1832.

VIAUX MARAMBIO, Roberto (1923-   ). A career *army officer involved in two attempts to overthrow Chilean governments. In
October 1969, after becoming general commanding the *Talca
garrison, led an abortive mutiny aimed at overthrowing the government of Christian Democrat (*Partido Demócrata Cristiano)
Eduardo *Frei Montalva. He was then asked to resign, but refused to do so. A year later, he and his father-in-law, Colonel
Raúl Igualt, were arrested in connection with the assassination of
army commander-in-chief René *Schneider Chereau in what had
been an attempt by right-wing officers to prevent the confirmation
of Socialist Salvador *Allende Gossens as President. During 1970
Viaux had received US$ 20,000 from the *United States *Central
Intelligence Agency, but seven days before he attempted to kid-
nap Schneider, the C.I.A. warned him that his coup attempt
had very little chance of success and would be "likely [to] damage any subsequent and more serious action." At the same time,
the agency's *Santiago office pledged its continued support for
Viaux in the future, letting word reach him that "the time will
come when you and your friends can do something. You still
have our support."
      The attempt went awry and the C.I.A., which had not wanted
Schneider to be killed, put some distance between itself and
Viaux, as did senior army officers, who wanted to organize a
coup with the united support of all the *armed forces. Nor,
after two abortive attempts, did the military trust Viaux. He
had tried both times to demonstrate that order had broken down
(thus paving the way for a military takeover) but had failed.
Subsequent efforts to stop Viaux succeeded, and finally, on September 11, 1973, a well coordinated coup involving all branches
of the armed forces was able to overthrow Allende without Viaux's
help.
      Before the 1973 *coup d'état, Viaux had been sentenced to
20 years' imprisonment. But President Augusto *Pinochet Ugarte
reduced the conviction from murder to lesser charges, and the
sentence from jail to banishment. General Viaux has since resided comfortably in Paraguay.
      See also: SCHNEIDER CHEREAU, René.

VICARIATE OF SOLIDARITY (Vicariato de Solidaridad). A creation
of Raúl Cardinal *Silva Henríquez to help the poor after the
*coup d'etat of September 11, 1973, which left many of them suf-
fering from economic hardship and political persecution. Parishes
served as sanctuaries and as soup kitchens, harboring those who
were in opposition to the *military regime of Augusto *Pinochet
Ugarte. By 1977, there were 127 community centers that worked

for the Vicariate of Solidarity, which, as an organization, had succeeded the ecumenical Committee of Cooperation for Peace (Comité de Cooperación para la Paz) in helping the poor (January, 1976). Within weeks of the coup an interdenominational committee was set up in Chile to aid refugees (CONAR), responsible for more than 5,000 of them safely going into exile. This was the antecedent to both the Comité de Cooperación para la Paz in Chile, and the Vicariato de Solidaridad. Besides feeding the hungry, the Vicariate became one of the last bastions of open opposition to the Pinochet regime over the issue of human rights. By the mid-1980s, the Vicariate had been warned on several occasions to "keep out of politics," although Church spokespersons pledged to keep on "protecting those who could not protect themselves," implying that the work of the Vicariate would continue so long as there was repression in the country.

VICUÑA GUIRRE, Pedro Félix (1805-1874). Liberal politician and journalist. Son of President Francisco Ramón *Vicuña Larraín and father of Benjamín *Vicuña Mackenna. Founded a number of liberal periodicals and newspapers, including El *Mercurio, and wrote for others, among them the *Valparaíso Gaceta del comercio. By the mid-1840s he was the effective leader of the populacheros (advanced liberals) and took part in the April 1851 *Mutiny of Urriola. When that failed he escaped to *Talcahuano, where he was largely responsible for instigating the southern rebellion in the *Civil War of 1851. He served in the Chamber of Deputies in 1831-34, 1843-46, and 1864-70, and in the Senate from 1870 until his death.

VICUÑA GUERRERO, Claudio (1833-1907). *Partido Liberal Democrati-co politician and President-elect during the *Civil War of 1891. He studied at the *Instituto Nacional, and then made his fortune in *agriculture, which permitted him to travel extensively in Europe in the late 1860s. He sat in *Congress as a deputy, 1873-79, and as a senator, 1879-91 and 1900-06. In October 1890 he became President José Manuel *Balmaceda Fernández's interior minister, and supported him loyally during the *congresista revolt. On July 22, 1891, he ran as Liberal candidate in the presidential election held by the *Balmacedista government and was elected. When Balmaceda's regime fell a month later he was driven into exile in Europe and his property was seized. He returned to Chile in 1895 and received a widespread ovation for his defense of Balmaceda. He joined the refounded *Partido Liberal Democrá-tico (representing the Balmacedista faction of the Liberals), giving it substantial financial support and being made its president in 1899. The previous year he had founded a newspaper in *Val-paraíso, La lealtad, to support his party's views. In 1900 he was offered the *Alianza Liberal's nomination as its presidential candidate, but withdrew in favor of Germán *Riesco Errázuriz as someone more likely to defeat the *Coalición candidate.

VICUÑA LARRAIN, Francisco Ramón (1788-1849). Chilean patriot who was briefly President of the Republic (1829-1830). A deputy to the Constituent Congress of 1811 and a senator in 1814, he also contributed to the patriot cause by organizing Chile's first musket manufactory. Accused of plotting against José Miguel *Carrera Verdugo, he was imprisoned and then exiled. He returned after the Chilean victory of *Chacabuco and was appointed by Bernardo *O'Higgins government delegate in northern Chile. Later in 1817 he became *regidor of the municipality of *Santiago. In 1823 he was elected deputy and held several ministerial offices including that of the interior and foreign affairs during 1825. The same year he acted briefly as Supreme Director of Chile during Ramón Freire Serrano's absence from Santiago. In 1828 he became vice-president of Chile, acting briefly as President when Francisco *Pinto Díaz fell ill. Pinto Díaz resigned shortly after his recovery, and Vicuña Larraín succeeded him. Great confusion ensued, and Vicuña fell from power when General Joaquín *Prieto Vial led a revolt against him. These events led to the *Civil War of 1829-30. Vicuña, who had been taken prisoner by the rebels, was released and retired into private life.

VICUÑA LARRAIN, Joaquín (17--?-1857). Member of a prominent *Coquimbo family, and founder in 1821 of the town of Vicuña on the River *Elqui, which bears the family name and gave him some fame. As a politician, he was obscured by his brother Francisco Ramón *Vicuña Larraín (President, 1829-30). In May 1829 Joaquín himself ran for President, came in fourth, but was nevertheless made vice-president by a *pipiolo-controlled *Congress, an act that directly precipitated the *Civil War of 1829-30. Joaquín fought in the war, and held minor military offices until his death. He was also sometime *intendant of Coquimbo.

VICUÑA LARRAIN, Manuel (1777-1843). First *archbishop of *Santiago. Of a distinguished Navarrese family, he was intimately connected to other wealthy Chilean families of the colonial period. Educated at the *Universidad de San Felipe, he was ordained in 1803. Thirty years later he was elevated to the bishopric of Santiago, and gained a reputation for administrative ability and eloquence. With his large inherited fortune he was able to undertake many works of charity. In 1840 he became primate of Chile on the elevation of Santiago to an archdiocese and the ecclesiastical separation of Chile from *Peru. Archbishop Vicuña, who was the elder brother of Francisco Ramón *Vicuña Larraín, also served as senator and counselor of state.

VICUÑA MACKENNA, Benjamín (1831-1886). Chilean historian, son of Pedro Felix Vicuña Aguirre and the latter's cousin Carmen, daughter of Juan *Mackenna O'Reilly and Josefa Vicuña Larraín de Mackenna. Benjamín Vicuña Mackenna was a lawyer by profession and a member of the *Sociedad de Igualdad. He participated in the *Civil War of 1851 and was taken prisoner, but somehow escaped and fled to California, spending the next few years traveling in the *United States and Mexico. From abroad he wrote many articles on the Chilean *independence struggle and the history of early Chile. These attracted the interest of Andrés *Bello López, gaining Vicuña Mackenna a reputation as historian and publicist. Returning to Chile in 1856, Vicuña Mackenna began writing for various newspapers and edited La Asamblea Constituente, in which he attacked Conservative President (1851-61) Manuel *Montt Torres. Vicuña Mackenna was again exiled in 1858 (see: CIVIL WAR OF 1859), but in 1863 he became editor of El *Mercurio of *Valparaíso and was elected deputy to *Congress. Two years later he served as a special envoy to the *United States, and in 1870 to Europe.

As a diplomat, he collected many historical documents on his trips, writing more than 100 volumes of history when he returned to Chile in 1872. He was the founder of the *Partido Democrático Liberal and was its presidential candidate for the 1876 election. He chose, however, not to run, despite his popularity, fearing civil conflict might result. He loyally supported, and reported on, Chile's cause in the War of the *Pacific, and his premature death left the citizenry of *Santiago in a state of shock and grief. Today one of the city's main streets is named after him, and his most enduring monument is the famous Santa Lucía Park, laid out during his 1872-75 tenure of the *intendencia of Santiago.

VIDAURRE GARRETON, José Antonio (1798-1837). Organizer of the *Quillota Mutiny which resulted in the death of Diego *Portales Palazuelos. He began his military career in 1813, attaining the rank of captain in just four years. He fought at *Talcahuano, *Cancha Rayada, *Maipu and in the *Chiloé campaign. During the period of *anarquía política (1826-30) he was involved in many intrigues. In 1829 he organized a batallion of infantry known as the Cazadores de Maipú, and his services at the Battle of *Lircay won him a commission as colonel. He organized the mutiny at Quillota in which Portales was seized and later shot. Vidaurre fled after the defeat at the mutiny but was captured four months later, in September 1837. His court martial accepted the allegation of Portales' assassin, Captain Santiago Florín, that he was obeying Vidaurre's orders. Vidaurre was sentenced to death and executed in the same plaza in which Portales had died.

VIDELA, Pedro Nolasco (1830-1879). Lawyer and diplomat. As Chilean minister in La Paz he was in charge of the negotiations over the Bolivian taxation of *nitrates in *Antofagasta, which led to the War of the *Pacific.

VIDELA VERGARA, Benjamín (1907-). A career *army officer who became a brigadier general in 1957. In the second administration of Carlos *Ibáñez del Campo (1952-58), he served as undersecretary of war (1953-55), minister of public works and communications

(1955) and later as defense minister and minister of the interior. In 1956 he became executive vice-president of *CORFO. In 1963 he became the first president of the *Partido Democracia Agrario Laborista.

VIEJA GUARDIA ("old guard"). A group formed after the suicide of President (1886-91) José Manuel *Balmaceda Fernández of followers who remained faithful to his liberal ideals.

VILLAGRA, Francisco de (1511-1563). Spanish *conquistador. He came to America in 1537 and may have fought with Francisco Pizarro against Diego de *Almagro. He accompanied Pedro de *Valdivia's Chilean expedition of 1540, becoming the first *regidor of *Santiago and holding other minor offices. He hoped to succeed Pedro de Valdivia after the latter's death in 1553, but García *Hurtado de Mendoza received the coveted appointment instead. In 1559 Villagra visited Neuquén and the Limay river, thus becoming the first explorer of the interior of *Patagonia. In 1561 he succeeded Hurtado de Mendoza as governor of Chile, dying in office two years later.

VILLAGRA, Pedro de (1508?-1577). Spanish governor of Chile, 1563-65. He accompanied his cousin *Francisco de Villagra to Chile in 1540, and was *regidor of *Santiago (1547) and governor of *Imperial (1555) before being named by his dying cousin to succeed him as governor. As such he appointed Chile's first bishop. A quarrel with other *conquistadores resulted in Villagra's being sent back to Lima for trial before the Real *Audiencia, which absolved him but did not reinstate him as governor.

VINA DEL MAR. Seaside resort: the Chilean Monte Carlo, attracting visitors from all the Southern Cone countries, yet, at the same time, an industrial suburb of *Valparaíso, with now more inhabitants (307,308 est. in 1984) than the port city itself. The factory area in the El Salto valley is conveniently hidden from the tourists' view. Viña del Mar owes its foundation and its name to Bartholomäus Blümlein ("Bartolomé Flores"), a companion of Pedro de *Valdivia, who planted a vineyard here.

VIVIENDA Y URBANISMO, Ministerio de. The Ministry of Housing and Urban Affairs was created by Statute no. 16391 on December 16, 1965. The ministry's main functions are to provide all Chileans with adequate housing under government-sponsored programs, and to supervise the cost of building materials throughout Chile. The most important of the ministry's departments is that of Urban and Rural Planning. The Housing Corporation (Corporación de la Vivienda, *CORVI) is under the direct control of the Ministry of Housing and Urban Affairs.

Housing ministers since the 1973 *coup d'état have been: Brigadier General Arturo Viveros Avila (September 1973); Rear

Admiral Arturo Troncoso Doroch (July 1974); Carlos Graniffo
(April 1975); Luis Edmundo Ruiz Undurraga (March 1977); General
Jaime Estrada Leigh (December 1978); General Roberto Guillard
Marinot (April 1982); Modesto *Collados Núñez (August 1983);
Miguel Poduje (April 1984). See also: HOUSING.

VOLCANOES. Chile has 55 active volcanoes, most of them in the
south. Throughout the years many eruptions have been registered. The most notable in the last two centuries include: Llaima
in Upper *Temuco, which occurred in 1835 and was recorded and
described by Charles *Darwin; Calbuco, in 1893, which produced
an hour-long rain of ash that plunged *Puerto Montt in total
darkness, with a lesser eruption occurring in 1917; Quisapu in
the high *Andes of *Talca, where in 1932 there was such a violent eruption that it was heard 150 miles away in Santiago, with
the volcano's ashes reaching as far east as Montevideo, Uruguay;
and Villarica, in 1948. See also: EARTHQUAKES.

VOZ, La. (1953-1969?). Subtitled "periódico cristiano." Originally
weekly, then monthly. See: NEWSPAPERS.

- W -

WAGES AND SALARIES. Chile has been historically a country with
a low-wage economy (see: ECONOMY, The; EMPLOYMENT). The
administration of Salvador *Allende Gossens (1970-73) sought to
depart from this tradition, but its policies were abruptly discontinued by the *armed forces' *coup d'état of September 1973.
After the collapse of the Chilean "economic miracle" induced by
the free market policies of the new regime, *inflation rose rapidly
from 1982 (see: EXCHANGE RATES). This undermined the living
standards of *obreros (manual workers) and *empleados (white
collar workers) alike. With inflation running at over 30 percent
a year, the middle income groups began to experience a pinch
for the first time since Augusto *Pinochet Ugarte came to power.
Salaries, like wages, declined in real terms by more than 20 percent per annum. Everywhere there were signs of how dramatically the quality of life was deteriorating, and the government's
economic policies were openly criticized. Outbursts of rioting
and growing street demonstrations indicated a decreasing tolerance
for belt-tightening by both the poor and the middle-income sectors.
Unemployment, at around 30 percent in most of the country and
rather worse in the capital, was another cause for concern. The
Instituto Nacional de Estadística (National Statistical Institute)
estimated that real wages fell 12.1 percent in the first ten months
of 1984.
　　See also: NATIONAL INCOME.

WALKER LARRAIN, Horacio (b. 1887). Lawyer and Conservative politician. Professor of international law at the *Universidad Católica de Chile, he became justice minister in 1932, and president
of the *Partido Conservador in 1933. In 1949 he led the formation of a splinter party, the PARTIDO CONSERVADOR SOCIAL
CRISTIANO, q.v.

WALKER MARTINEZ, Carlos (1842-1905). The son of an English
industrialist, Walker graduated in law at the *Universidad de Chile
in 1866. In 1867-68 he was secretary of the Chilean legation in
La Paz, and then traveled in Europe and the *United States. On
his return he joined the Sociedad de Amigos del País ("Society
of the friends of the country"), whose cause--opposition to
liberalism--he espoused for the rest of his life. He served in the
Chamber of Deputies, 1870-73, before returning to La Paz as
Chargé d'Affairs. As such he negotiated the treaty of 1874 (see:
BOLIVIA, Relations with). During 1874 he went to Europe again,
and then he held minor posts in the interior and foreign affairs
ministries. During the 1887 cholera epidemic in *Santiago, Walker
founded the Chilean Red Cross. In the *Civil War of 1891 he
supported the rebel *Congress against President José Manuel
*Balmaceda Fernández. After the congresista victory, Walker was
accused of instigating the looting of property and other reprisals
inflicted on Balmaceda's supporters. In 1894 he was elected
senator, and four years later he became interior minister in the
administration of Federico *Errázuriz Echaurren.

WALKER MARTINEZ, Joaquín (1853-1928). Conservative politician.
Cousin to Carlos *Walker Martínez and father of Horacio *Walker
Larraín. Mine owner and industrialist, he entered Congress in
1879. He played a prominent part on the rebel side in the *Civil
War of 1891, being minister of war and finance in the *junta de
gobierno de *Iquique.

WAR MINISTRY. See: DEFENSA NACIONAL, Ministerio de; GUERRA,
Ministerio de; GUERRA, Secretaria de; GUERRA Y AVIACION,
Ministerio de; GUERRA Y MARINA, Ministerio de.

WARS. A. External Conflicts. For Chilean involvement in Spain's
16th and 17th century wars, see: PIRATES AND PRIVATEERS.
For Chilean involvement in the War of the Austrian Succession,
see: ANSON, George. For Chilean involvement in the Napoleonic
Wars, see: FERDINAND VII; FRANCE, Relations with; UNITED
KINGDOM, Relations with. For the 1836-39 war against Andrés
de *Santa Cruz y Calahumada, see: PERU-BOLIVIA CONFEDERA-
TION, War with. Chile's subsequent foreign wars have been the
War of 1865-66 with SPAIN (q.v.), the War of the PACIFIC
(q.v.) and WORLD WAR II (q.v.).

B. Internal Conflicts. Since the time of the conquest, Chile has
been involved in: the Araucanian Wars (see: GUERRAS DE

ARAUCO), the Wars of INDEPENDENCE, q.v., the so-called War to the Death (see: GUERRA A MUERTE), the 1824-26 campaign to conquer CHILOE (q.v.); the CIVIL WAR OF 1829-30; the CIVIL WAR OF 1851; the CIVIL WAR OF 1859; the CIVIL WAR OF 1891.

WEIGHTS AND MEASURES. Chile officially adopted the metric system in 1843, only ten years later than its definitive adoption in France itself, and nearly thirty years before it became official in Spain. Unofficial use of the old Spanish measures (some of which have special Chilean variants) has however continued to some extent to the present. See also: ARROBA, BRAZA, CUADRA, LEAGUE, QUINTAL, TON, VARA.

The Gregorian Calendar was adopted in October 1583 (in English-speaking countries this did not happen until September 1757).

WHALING. Whaling in Chilean waters became important at the end of the 18th century when the country's offshore *Humboldt current was discovered to be a major whale migration route. By the early 1800s the southeast Pacific was attracting whalers from all over the world. By the 1840s the right and Pacific sperm populations had been decimated. The next boom in whaling in Chilean waters came at the turn of the century, after the invention of the explosive harpoon. The first permanent Antarctic whaling station was established in 1904, and soon the Blue Whale was almost extinct in the region. Overhunting and international conservation agreements have led to the virtual disappearance of Chile's whaling industry. The Caleta Molle factory at *Iquique closed in 1965; the Caleta Quintay at *Valparaíso closed in 1967; by 1974 only one remaining company, the Macaya Hermanos, was operating. Chile's whaling fleet fell from 17 vessels in 1964 to 3 in 1974. The 1971-72 season catch was 288 whales, 0.7 percent of the world total. In 1980-81 only 64 were taken, although this represented a larger proportion (2.2 percent) of a much reduced world total.

WHEAT. Of all the European customs the Spaniards took with them to the New World, none was so important, socially and economically, as a taste for wheaten bread. Few of the conquered lands, however, were suited for wheat cultivation. In Argentina, the pampas remained largely an Indian territory throughout the colonial period. It was not until several decades after independence that Argentina stopped importing wheat and grew her own, becoming one of the world's major producers. Chile was unique. Although in its central valley only a tenth of the agricultural land was used to grow food crops, the chief crop was, and still is, wheat. By the late 17th century Chile was self-sufficient and had already begun exporting wheat to Peru. Chile was also the only one of Spain's American colonies where wheat occupied more acres than

maize. By the mid-18th century Chile was producing annually
about 4,000 metric *tons, of which 1,800 were exported. With
the opening up of California a century later, Chile found herself
in the fortunate position of having the only wheat supply on the
whole Pacific coast (see also: AGRICULTURE). After the Cali-
fornians, and then later the Austrialians, began meeting their
own needs, Chilean wheat growers turned to Europe as a new
export market. Their exports peaked at nearly 5,000 tonnes a
year in the 1860s. As *mining production, especially of *nitrates
in northern Chile, began to contribute significantly to the *economy, wheat production stagnated. Soon Chile became a net importer of food: it was easier to use its new found wealth to
pay for food imports than to increase domestic production.

There were some attempts to change this policy in the altered
economic circumstances of more recent times, but these were
abandoned under the free-market policies of the post-1973 regime
of Augusto *Pinochet Ugarte. Between 1975 and 1980 the acreage
devoted to cereals in Chile fell from 2,394,720 (969,130 hectares)
to 1,332,259 (539,154 hectares). Of these, wheat declined the
most, from 1,723,695 (697,570 hectares) to 874,856 (354,049
hectares). Almost two thirds of Chile's food imports are wheat
or wheat flour (1,195,300 tonnes in 1973). This remains true
despite a considerable decline in consumption (from 2 million tonnes
in the mid 1970s to 1.5 million tonnes in the mid 1980s), because
the fall in acreage has been accompanied by a decline in yields
per acre as farmers have become increasingly unable to pay for
imported fertilizer.

The principal wheat growing areas today are *Araucania
(497,528 acres in 1980), *Bío-Bío (433,866 acres) and Los *Lagos
(249,814). But some wheat is grown in every region of the country, from *Tarapacá in the north to *Magallanes in the south.

WHEELWRIGHT, William (1798-1863). Transportation pioneer and
businessman. Born in Newburyport, Massachussets, he engaged
in South American trade early in life. In 1822 he was shipwrecked
off the coast of Buenos Aires, making his way by sea to Chile
two years later. He then traveled to Guayaquil, Ecuador, when
he occupied the post of *United States consul in 1829.

Encouraged by Chilean conservative statesman Diego *Portales
Palazuelos, Wheelwright established a passenger steamship line
in 1840, the Pacific Steam Navigation Company, to serve the west
coast of South America from *Valparaíso to Panamá (see: MER-
CHANT MARINE; POSTAL SERVICES). He was also responsible
for the development of Chilean *railways, *coal mines, telegraphs
and public utilities, using, for the most part, British capital.
In late 1852 he returned to Argentina to try to persuade the
government to build a *transandine railway to Chile, hoping to
make Buenos Aires the principal outlet for Chilean exports.
Turning once again to British capital, he opened the Argentine
Central Railway from Santa Fé to Córdoba, but ill health forced
his retirement to London, where he died.

WILLIAMS REBOLLEDO, Juan (1826-1910). Chilean admiral. Son of John Williams (a companion of Lord *Cochrane), Juan Williams Rebolledo was born in Curacaví in *Santiago province. He entered the naval school in 1844 and had a distinguished naval career, being responsible for many improvements in the Chilean *navy, particularly in strengthening its discipline and esprit de corps. He fought in the *Civil War of 1851 and commanded the Chilean fleet in the War with *Spain of 1865-67. He also explored the southern tip of Chile, venturing as far as *Antarctica. He was appointed commander-in-chief of the navy on the outbreak of the War of the *Pacific, but his health was failing, and although he took steps toward modernizing the fleet, he did not prosecute the war with the vigor he had shown in 1865, and on June 5, 1879, he resigned.

WINNIPEG, S.S. A ship that carried some 3,000 Spanish republican refugees to Chile at the end of the Spanish Civil War of 1936-39 (see: SPAIN, Relations with). The voyage was arranged by Chilean poet Pablo *Neruda, then Chilean consul in Paris, who had convinced President (1938-41) Pedro *Aguirre Cerda to give asylum to the refugees, many of whom were very young at the time; many still live in Chile today.

WOMEN AND THE WOMEN'S MOVEMENT. Already in the 19th century visitors were impressed by the unusual degree of freedom enjoyed by Chilean women, compared to the situation of women in other Hispanic countries. As early as 1877 women were granted admission to higher education in Chile, and within thirty years the country was boasting Latin America's first woman university professor. At a lower socioeconomic level, the labor market was much more open to women in Chile than in neighboring countries-- from clerical and secretarial positions to driving street cars. This originated when male workers were needed to fight in the War of the *Pacific and was perpetuated because of the shortage of men due to migration to the rich *nitrate fields of the north.
    Women's SUFFRAGE (q.v.) was nevertheless slow in arriving. It was advocated by Arturo *Alessandri Palma in his presidential campaign of 1920, but it was not granted in municipal elections until 1934, and not in national elections until 1949 (see: PARTIDO FEMENINO DE CHILE). The first opportunity Chilean women had to exercise this new right was in the presidential election of 1952. The necessary provision of extra polling booths was made in such a way as to segregate voters (and the published results) by sex, so allowing for interpretation of the voting along sexist lines.
    The women's movement became strong in Chile during the three-year presidency of Socialist Salvador *Allende Gossens (1970-73). Leaders of the movement included Moy de *Tohá, Elena Caffarena de Jiles, Marta *Vergara, Olga *Poblete de Espinosa and Angela Bachelet. They worked for such benefits as

equal pay for equal work, the provision of day-care centers,
divorce rights and the right to abortion. After Allende was
overthrown by the *armed forces, most women who had been active in the movement were regarded as revolutionaries and had
to go underground or into exile. Isabel *Allende Bussi, daughter
of the assassinated President, and her sister Beatriz *Allende
de Fernández left the country and became very active in exile.
Beatriz went to Cuba, while Isabel traveled through Europe,
Africa and Australia. Moy de Tohá, wife of Allende's minister
José de *Tohá González, traveled in North and South America,
speaking out about the achievements of the women's movement
under Allende and its subsequent repression under the *military
regime. Olga *Poblete de Espinosa and Elena Caffarena stayed
in Chile, continuing to organize women in defiance of government
repression. Angela Bachelet, widow of slain Air Force General
Alberto *Bachelet Martínez, experienced imprisonment and torture
before the efforts of *human rights organizations worldwide eventually secured her release. She now works for the *United
Nations Commission on Human Rights in Chile. La Baucatana, a
poet who sells her own poetry and drawings on the streets of
Santiago and whose verses appear regularly in La *Tercera de la
Hora, is the lyrical voice of the movement. Thousands of other
women have joined the movement in the 1980s, most of them
members of the Comité de Retorno, a committee organized to press
the government for the release of information about the desapare-
cidos (people who had disappeared, presumably killed or held in-
comunicado by the authorities).

After having operated mostly underground, the women's movement resurfaced in 1983, when more than 10,000 women met in
the Teatro Caupolicán to revive the historical MOVIMIENTO DE
EMANCIPACION DE LA MUJER CHILENA (q.v.). See: CAUPO-
LICANAZO.

The government of Augusto *Pinochet Ugarte admitted women
into the *armed forces for the first time in 1980. But Pinochet
discouraged the dissemination of information on birth control,
which had been a priority of the two previous administrations,
and he closed down the women's centers that had flourished under Allende.

But despite Pinochet's strong anti-feminist stand, the women's
movement was alive and well in Chile and highly visible in Santiago.
Thanks to an amnesty law of 1983, many women who had been
active in the movement were allowed to return from exile. Prominent among them was Moy de Tohá, who has become a rallying
point for the concerns of Chilean women. By 1984 women were
organized in dozens of movements throughout Chile and were once
again making information available on birth control to all those who
wanted it.

WORKS, Ministry of. See: OBRAS PUBLICAS, Ministerio de.

WORKS AND COMMUNICATIONS, Ministry of. See: OBRAS PUBLICAS Y VIAS DE COMUNICACIONES, Ministerio de.

WORKS AND PUBLIC HIGHWAYS, Ministry of. See: OBRAS Y VIAS PUBLICAS, Ministerio de.

WORKS, COMMERCE AND COMMUNICATIONS, Ministry of. See: OBRAS PUBLICAS, COMERCIO Y VIAS DE COMUNICACIONES, Ministerio de.

WORLD WAR II. Chile was neutral for most of the Second World War, although sympathetic to the Allied cause. It established diplomatic relations with the *U.S.S.R. (for the first time) on December 11, 1944, and signed the *United Nations pact on February 14, 1945. It did not, however, declare war until April 11, 1945, and then only on Japan.

- Y -

YAÑEZ PONCE DE LEON, Eliodoro (1860-1933). Lawyer and *Partido Liberal Doctrinario politician. Upon receiving his law degree in 1883 he became a relator in the appeal court in *Santiago. In 1894 he entered the Chamber of Deputies, becoming its vice-president the following year. From 1901 he was several times a cabinet minister, holding the foreign affairs portfolio in 1901 and that of the interior in 1917. He became a senator in 1924 and Chilean delegate to the League of Nations in 1925. Yáñez supported Carlos *Ibáñez del Campo, and in 1925 it seemed possible that Yáñez might run for President with Ibáñez's support. Instead, two years later, Ibáñez became President with Yáñez's support. But in June 1927 rumors circulated of a plot against the President led by infantry officers linked with Yáñez. This sufficed for Yáñez to be exiled to Paris and for his newspaper, La *Nación, to be taken over by the government. Yáñez returned after the fall of Ibáñez in 1931 and remained active in politics until his death.

YERBAS BUENAS. Village at 35° 45'S, 71° 34'W, seven *leagues south of the river *Maule, near the town of San Carlos in central Chile, the site of a battle fought on April 26-27, 1813. José Miguel *Carrera Verdugo ordered a night attack on an outlying detachment of the royalist army, but in the confusion the main body of the enemy was also engaged. Dawn revealed the small number of the patriot army, whereupon the Spanish commander, Antonio Pareja, attacked in force. The result was a disaster for the Chileans.

YRRARAZAVAL. Alternate spelling of the surname IRRARAZAVAL, q.v.

YUNGAY, Battle of. Fought at Yungay (9° 8'S, 77° 43'W) in a valley of northern Peru, January 20, 1839, against the *Peru-Bolivia Confederation. The Chileans, commanded by Manuel *Bulnes Prieto, routed the confederate army led by Andrés de *Santa Cruz. The victory put an end to the Confederation, and Bulnes returned to *Santiago a military hero. A district in the city was renamed Yungay in remembrance of the victorious troops, and the battle's anniversary was long observed as the Día del *Roto, the day of the ill-clad Chilean common soldier.

- Z -

Z PLAN. See: ZETA PLAN.

ZALDIVAR LARRAIN, Andrés (1936-). Lawyer and prominent member of the Christian Democrats (*Partido Demócrata Cristiano, PDC). During the 1964-70 presidency of Eduardo *Frei Montalva he served as undersecretary of the treasury and minister of the economy. From 1968 to 1970 he headed the Inter-American Development Bank, working closely with the *United States-sponsored Alliance for Progress. In the March 1973 parliamentary elections, when the PDC and its allies hoped for a majority large enough to permit the impeachment of President Salvador *Allende Gossens, Zalvidar was elected to the Senate. He supported the ousting of Allende in the *coup d'état of September 1973, but afterwards he became disenchanted with the economic policies of Augusto *Pinochet Ugarte and with the country's failure to return to democratic rule. He spoke out against the regime with the result that he was exiled in 1980 and spent three years in Spain. During that time he succeeded Mario Rumar as president of the World Union of Christian Democrats, uniting the PDC with similar political parties in Western Europe and in other Latin American countries. Taking advantage of a new amnesty law, Zaldivar returned to Chile in 1983. In a speech to his supporters at the airport, he vowed to continue to assist the anti-government forces seeking an end to military rule, declaring that "Chile will again be what it must be, a free country where no one is persecuted for his ideas."

ZAMORANO HERRERA, Antonio Raúl (1908-). A defrocked priest who ran in the 1958 presidential election. From his earliest years he followed the religious vocation and was ordained in 1932. He then became a professor in the seminary of *Iquique and also filled minor posts in the bishopric of Monsignor Labbé Márquez.

In 1940 he became the parish priest at Catapilco, a small village near the capital, hence his nickname, "El cura de Catapilco." He left the priesthood in 1956 to devote his life to social reform. He was elected to *Congress in 1957 as a FRAP (*Frente de Acción Popular) deputy for *Valparaíso, but a year later he organized his own political party, the *Unión Nacional Laborista, to support his presidential candidacy. Although he came last, with only 41,304 votes out of the total ballot of 1,235,552, his intervention probably cost FRAP candidate Salvador *Allende Gossens the election, since Zamorano's support exceeded the 33,500-vote plurality of winning candidate Jorge *Alessandri Rodríguez.

ZAÑARTU SANTA MARIA, Miguel José de (1786-1851). Chilean patriot and staunch supporter of Bernardo *O'Higgins. He participated in the uprisings of 1810, becoming judge advocate (auditor de guerra) of the patriot army of the south. Forced into exile after the Battle of *Rancagua, he returned in 1817 and became Secretario de Estado en Gobierno (foreign and interior minister) in the newly formed O'Higgins government. As such he was responsible, together with Manuel de *Salas Corvalán and Juan *Egaña Risco, with drawing up the text of Chile's Declaration of Independence (Declaración de *Independencia). He sat in *Congress, and received various diplomatic appointments to *Argentina and *Peru. Along with other *O'Higginistas, however, he was exiled by Ramón *Freire Serrano on October 8, 1825, and did not return until 1830. In 1831 he was named Chilean minister plenipotentiary to Peru by President (1830-31) Tomás *Ovalle Bezanilla, and was reelected to Congress in 1846.

ZAÑARTU ZAÑARTU, Aníbal (1847-1902). Acting President of Chile, May 1-September 18, 1901. Son of Miguel José de *Zañartu Santa María, he graduated in law in 1870, joined the Liberal *Club de la Reforma, being elected its secretary, and then, in association with his brother Manuel Aristides *Zañartu Zañartu, acquired *coal mining interests in Tomé (province of *Concepción). In 1880 he was appointed Chilean minister in Ecuador, and in 1884 was elected to *Congress as deputy for *San Fernando. In 1887 President José Manuel *Balmaceda Fernández made Zañartu interior minister, but dismissed him abruptly in July 1888. President Federico *Errázuriz Echaurren made him briefly interior minister again, September-November 1896, and yet again on May 1, 1901. As such he had to act immediately as vice-president in place of Echaurren, who had fallen ill and died on July 12. At the end of the presidential term, Zañartu handed over his powers to President-elect Germán *Riesco Errázuriz and retired in poor health to Tomé, where he died on February 1, 1902.

ZAÑARTU ZAÑARTU, Manuel Aristides (1840-1892). Lawyer, politician, journalist and philanthropist, with *coal mining interests in Tomé in association with his brother Aníbal *Zañartu Zañartu. He entered the Chamber of Deputies in 1885 and remained loyal to President José Manuel *Balmaceda Fernández during the *Civil War of 1891, becoming Balmaceda's interior minister in May 1891. He accompanied Balmaceda when the latter sought asylum in the Argentine embassy and then went into voluntary exile. On Zañartu's 1892 return to Chile he refounded the *Partido Liberal Democrático, becoming its president. In 1869 he had become editor of the *Concepción newspaper La Reforma. In 1892 he founded the Santiago daily La República.

ZEGERS HUNEEUS, Jorge. See: HUNEEUS ZEGERS, Jorge.

ZEGERS SAMANIEGO, Julio (1833-1918). Lawyer who represented the John Thomas North *nitrate interests in the National *Congress. He was appointed vice-rector of the *Instituto Nacional in 1858, qualified as a lawyer in 1860, and entered Congress as a *Partido Liberal deputy in 1876. Zegers became finance minister in 1878, and then in 1881 became lawyer to North's Compañía del Ferrocarril Salitrero de Tarapacá while still holding ministerial office. This connection with British nitrate interests made him a staunch opponent of President José Manuel *Balmaceda Fernández; it was Zegers who in July 1890 originated the claim that Congress might dismiss the President (see: CIVIL WAR OF 1891). After the war, the vehemence of his attacks on the defeated *Balmacedistas alienated even his fellow *congresistas.

ZENTENO DEL POZO Y SILVA, José Ignacio (1784-1847). A career *army officer who fought for Chilean *independence. He was a loyal supporter of Bernardo *O'Higgins and served the patriot government in 1813 as military secretary. After the battle of *Rancagua, Zenteno, like many other patriots, took refuge in *Mendoza. He became a close associate of General José de *San Martín, who made him his secretary. Returning with the Ejército de los *Andes, he fought at *Chacabuco as a lieutenant colonel. From 1817 to 1821 he served O'Higgins' government as secretario de estado en guerra (war minister), "the organizing genius of the new Chilean state." In 1821 he was made political governor of the gobierno of the port of *Valparaíso. Here he was primarily responsible for modernizing the Chilean *navy. In 1822 he was promoted to brigadier general, but the following year he was exiled to Peru by O'Higgins' successor, Ramón *Freire Serrano. Returning in 1826, he insisted on being tried by court martial, which acquitted him. He resumed his military career, becoming inspector general of the army in 1831, and entered Congress, where he was elected vice-president of the Chamber of Deputies. Interested in journalism, he founded El *Mercurio of Valparaíso and was its first editor.

ZETA PLAN. An alleged plot to impose a totalitarian Marxist government on Chile, which the *coup d'état of September 11, 1973, was supposed to have forestalled. Plan Zeta was to have been carried out on September 17, 1973, instigated and supported by Cuba, and would have put an end to Chile's democratic institutions. It called for the execution of 17,000 right-wing and moderate Chileans, including former President (1964-70) Eduardo *Frei Montalva, several senior military officers, Supreme Court justices, *trade union leaders, lawyers, businessmen, and other members of organizations opposed to Socialist President (1970-73) Salvador *Allende Gossens.

Details of the alleged plot were contained in a "white book" distributed by the *junta government. This "white book" was woefully deficient in documented evidence. A number of fragmentary documents had been badly put together, many undated, in no apparent logical sequence. Supposedly, they referred to procedures to assure the takeover of certain industrial districts in *Santiago and to establish guerrilla camps in unspecified rural or mountain areas. No indication was given as to how Plan Zeta had been discovered by the military; and no names or political groups were directly linked to the plan. All this cast serious doubt on the *armed forces' allegation that any such plan existed.

ZIG-ZAG, Empresa Editorial. Chilean magazine and book publisher, founded early in the 20th century as Universo. By the 1950s it had become Chile's leading trade book (i.e. non-schoolbook) publishing house, producing about a hundred titles a year, nearly half of them novels, and including translations of leading foreign writers. It was also one of the country's two major magazine conglomerates. In January 1971 a labor dispute led to an arbitration award of a 65 percent wage increase, an amount well above the current inflation rate. When this threatened the firm with bankruptcy, its workers demanded that the business be nationalized. As a result, the government took it over, renaming it the Empresa Editora Nacional Quimantú. Under a new manager, former *Partido Socialista de Chile deputy Alejandro Chelén Rojas, the firm at first concentrated on printing for third parties (including the Reader's Digest), but from 1972 it undertook a massive book publishing program of its own, both serious works and popular pamphlets such as the "Nosotros los chilenos" series. Producing each month as much as Zig-Zag had done in a year, Quimantú revolutionized the distribution and consumption of books in Chile. After the *coup d'état of September 1973, the name was changed again, to Editorial Gabriela Mistral. Under manager General Diego Barros Ortiz, the Gabriela Mistral imprint mixed traditional titles of Hispanic and Chilean culture with propaganda for the regime and its ideology, and the perceived demands of the market. Ortiz' successor, Juan Fernández Montalva (1977-81), concentrated once again on printing commissions from outside. But a state-owned publishing house was contrary to the Augusto *Pinochet Ugarte's economic philosophy, and in October 1982 the business was closed down and its assets sold off by public auction.

Zig-Zag, which had continued as a magazine publisher, is now back in book publishing.
    See also: PERIODICAL PRESS; PUBLISHERS AND PUBLISHING.

ZINC. Chile's zinc is mainly mined in Region XI, Aysén. Production had been falling in recent years: 5,053 metric *tons in 1976; 3,918 tonnes in 1977; 1,814 tonnes in 1978; 1,523 tonnes in 1981; but rebounded to 5,505 tonnes in 1982, and reached 19,000 tonnes in 1984.

ZUJOVIC, Edmundo Pérez. See: PEREZ ZUJOVIC, Edmundo.

BIBLIOGRAPHY

The bibliography has been divided according to the major topical entries found in the Historical Dictionary of Chile. In case of entries whose subject overlaps with other sections, the works entered have been asterisked to indicate that they also appear under other related headings. In arranging the bibliography it has seemed best to follow chronological order and to focus on the contemporary period. The aim of the author has been to suggest the principal sources and the most significant works covering the major topics. The reader should keep in mind that the following bibliography makes no attempt to be complete. It is only a lead from which the reader can branch out into any special field.

1. GENERAL BIBLIOGRAPHIES, HISTORIOGRAPHIES AND RESEARCH MATERIALS

Anrique Reyes, Nicolás, and A. Ignacio Silva. Ensayo de una biblio-grafía histórica i jeográfica de Chile. Santiago: Imprenta Bar-celona, 1902.

Aranguiz Donoso, Horacio, et al. Bibliografía histórica (1959-1967) Santiago: Instituto de Historia, Universidad Católica de Chile, 1970.

*Archivos de Don Bernardo O'Higgins. 27 vols. Santiago: Imprenta Universitaria, 1947-1973.

Barros Borgoño, Luis. Archivo Barros Arana. A través de una correspondencia. Santiago: Universidad de Chile, 1934.

_____. Archivo Barros Arana: Missión en el Plata, 1876-1878. Santiago: Universidad de Chile, 1936.

"Bibliografía chilena; selección de los libros y folletos ingresados a la Biblioteca Nacional por concepto de la ley de depósito legal." Mapocho. [Regular Feature]. Santiago: Biblioteca Nacional, Sección Chilena.

Blakemore, Harold. "The Chilean revolution of 1891 and its Historio-graphy," Hispanic American Historical Review, 45, August 1965, pp. 393-431.

Boletín de la Academia Chilena de la Historia. Santiago: Academia Chilena de la Historia, 1933- .

Castro García, María; Jean Gearing; and Margaret Gill. "Women and Migration--Latin American and the Caribbean: A Selective Annotated Bibliography, " no. 4. Gainesville, Florida: Center for Latin American Studies, University of Florida, February 1984.

Chiappa, Victor M. *Bibliografía de Don Diego Barros Arana. Temuco: Imprenta Alemán, 1907.

Chile, A Selected Bibliography in English. New York: Corporación de Fomento de la Producción (CORFO), 1964.

Clagett, Helen L. A Guide to the Law and Legal Literature of Chile. Library of Congress (Latin American Series), no. 28., Washington, DC: U.S. Library of Congress, 1947.

Colección de historiadores i de documentos relativos a la independencia de Chile. 40 vols. Santiago: Imprenta Cervantes, 1900-1970.

Collier, Simon. "The Historiography of the 'Portalian' Period (1830-1891) in Chile," Hispanic American Historical Review, 57, November 1977.

Cruchaga Ossa, Alberto, ed. Jurisprudencia de la cancillería chilena hasta 1865. Santiago: Imprenta Chile, 1935.

Diplomatic Correspondence of the United States Concerning the Independence of the Latin American Nations. 3 vols. Ed. William Manning. New York: Oxford University Press, 1925.

Feliú Cruz, Guillermo. "Andrés Bello y la historiografía chilena," Mapocho, no. 4, 1965, pp. 231-263.

_____. Andrés Bello y la redacción de los documentos oficiales del gobierno de Chile. Caracas: Biblioteca de los Tribunales, 1951.

_____. Historia de la fuentes de la bibliografía chilena. 4 vols. Santiago: Universidad Católica, 1966.

_____. Historia de las fuentes de la bibliografía chilena: Ensayo crítico. 3 vols. Santiago: Biblioteca Nacional, 1966-1968.

_____. Historiografía colonial de Chile. Santiago: Fondo José Toribio Medina, 1958.

Figueroa, Virgilio. *Diccionario histórico, biográfico y bibliográfico de Chile, 1800-1931. 5 vols. Santiago: La Ilustración, 1925-1931. Reprint. Nendeln, Liechtenstein: Kraus Reprint, 1974.

Griffin, Charles C. Latin America: A Guide to the Historical Literature. Austin: University of Texas Press, 1971.

Handbook of Latin American Studies. Vols 1-14. Cambridge, Massachusetts; vols. 15- , Gainesville, Florida, 1936- .

Hill, Roscoe R., ed. The National Archives of Latin America. Cambridge, MA, 1945.

Hilton, Ronald., ed. Handbook of Hispanic Source Materials and Research Organizations in the United States. 2nd ed. Stanford, CA: Stanford University Press, 1956.

Inter-American Review of Bibliography. Washington, DC: Department of Cultural Affairs, Pan American Union, January-March, 1951.

Jobet, Julio César. Literatura histórica chilena: Historiografía chilena. Santiago: Nascimento, 1949.

Laval, Ramón. Bibliografía de bibliografías chilenas. Santiago: Imprenta Universitaria, 1915.

Matas Anguita, Blanca. "Bibliografía de bibliografías chilenas, 1963-1971." 2 vols. Reuniones Bibliotecológicas, n. 23. Washington, DC: Pan American Union, 1973, II, pp. 313-324.

Medina, José Toribio. Bibliografía de la imprenta en Santiago de Chile desde sus orígenes hasta febrero de 1817. Santiago: Casa del autor, 1892. Additions and amplifications. Santiago: Universidad de Chile, 1939.

_____. Biblioteca hispano-chilena (1523-1817). 3 vols. Santiago: Impreso y grabado en casa del autor, 1897-1899.

Mesa, Rosa Quintero. Latin American Serial Documents: A Holdings List. Chile. vol. 7. Ann Arbor, MI: Xerox University Microfilms, 1973.

Montt, Luis. Bibliografía chilena; precedida de un bosquejo histórico sobre los primeros años de la prensa en el país. 3 vols. Santiago: Imprenta Universitaria, 1904-1921.

Neuremberg, Otto. A Guide to the Official Publications of the Other American Republics: IV. Chile. Library of Congress, Latin American Series, no. 17. Washington, DC: U.S. Library of Congress, 1947.

Nutt, Katherine Ferris. San Martín: One Hundred Years of Historiography. Hays, Kansas: Fort Hays State College, 1960.

Oppenheimer, Robert. Chile. Latin American Bibliographical Series no. 6. Los Angeles: California State University, 1976.

Pereira Salas, Eugenio. "Las tendencias actuales en la historiografía chilena," Revista Interamericana de bibliografía, 25, April-June, 1975, pp. 121-133.

Riesch, Mary and Harry Strharsky. Bibliographical Notes for Understanding the Military Coup in Chile. CoDoC Common Catalogue no. 1. Washington, DC: Cooperative in Documentation and Communication, 1974.

Ruiz Urbina, Antonio; Alejandro Zorba D.; and Luis Donoso Varela. Estratificación y mobilidad sociales en Chile: Fuentes bibliográficas (desde los orígenes históricos hasta 1960). Centro Latinoamericano de Investigaciones en Ciencias Sociales, Publicación no. 17. Rio de Janeiro: Gráfica Editora LIVRO, 1961.

Rybacek; Mlynkova; Jirina. "Chile Under Allende: A Bibliographical Survey." Rio de Janeiro: América Latina, no. 17, 1976, pp. 32-69.

Santiago de Chile. Biblioteca Nacional. Exposición bibliográfica sobre la Guerra del Pacífico (1879-1884). Santiago: Editorial Universitaria, 1961.

Sater, William. "A Survey of Recent Chilean Historiography, 1965-1976," Latin American Research Review, 14:2, 1979, pp. 55-88.

Sehlinger, Peter J. A Select Guide to Chilean Libraries and Archives. Bloomington: Latin American Studies Program, Indiana University, 1979.

Silva Castro, Raúl. "Los primeros años de la Biblioteca Nacional de Chile," Revista de Historia de América, no. 42, December, 1956.

Soto Cárdenas, Alejandro. Misiones chilenas en los archivos europeos. Mexico City; 1953.

Stein, Stanley J. "Latin American Historiography," Social Sciences Research on Latin America, edited by Charles Wagley, New York, 1964, pp. 88-124.

_____. "The Tasks Ahead for Latin American Historians," Hispanic American Historical Review, 41:4, November 1961, pp. 424-33.

Steward, Julian, ed. Handbook of South American Indians. 2 vols. Washington, DC, 1946-1948.

Thayer Ojeda, Tomás. "Los archivos históricos en 1913." Revista de biografía chilena y extranjera. Santiago, March, 1914.

_____. "La sección de manuscriptos de la Biblioteca Nacional de Chile," Hispanic American Historical Review, 4, February 1921, pp. 156-197.

Werlich, David P. Research Tools for Latin American Historians. New York: Garland Publishing, Inc., 1980.

Wilgus, A. Curtis. The Historiography of Latin America: A Guide to Historical Writing, 1500-1800. Metuchen, NJ: Scarecrow Press, 1975.

William, Lee H. The Allende Years; a union list of Chilean imprints, 1970-1973, in selected North American libraries, with supplemental holdings list of books published elsewhere for the same period by Chileans or about Chile or Chileans. Boston: G. K. Hall, 1977.

Woll, Allen L. *A Functional Past: The Uses of History in 19th Century Chile. Baton Rouge: Louisiana State University Press, 1982.

Woods, Richard D. Reference Materials on Latin America in English: The Humanities. Metuchen, NJ: Scarecrow Press, 1980.

2. BIOGRAPHIES

Alberdi, Juan Bautista. *Biografía del general don Manuel Bulnes, presidente de la República de Chile. Santiago: Imprenta Chilena, 1846.

Alemparte, Julio. Carrera y Freire. Santiago: Editorial Nascimento 1963.

Amunátegui, Miguel Luis, and Benjamín Vicuña Mackenna. La dictadura de O'Higgins. Madrid: Editorial América, 1853.

Amunátegui, Miguel Luis. Ensayos biográficos. 4 vols. Santiago: Imprenta Cervantes, 1893-1896.

*Archivo de Don Bernardo O'Higgins. 27 vols. Santiago: Imprenta Universitaria, 1947-1970.

Arteaga Alemparte, Domingo. Los constituyentes chilenos de 1870. 2 vols. Santiago: Biblioteca de escritores de Chile, 1910.

Cortés, Lía, and Jordi Fuentes. *Diccionario Político de Chile. Santiago: Editorial Orbe, 1967.

Díaz Valderrama, Francisco Javier. O'Higgins. Buenos Aires: Círculo Militar, 1946.

Diccionario biográfico de Chile. 5th ed. Santiago: Editorial La Salle, 1944.

Diccionario biográfico de Chile. 9th, 14th, 17th editions. Santiago: Editores Empresa Periodista de Chile, 1953-55; 1968-70; 1980-82 (respectively).

Edwards Vives, Alberto. La fronda aristocrática. 5th ed. Santiago: Editorial del Pacífico, 1959.

Encina, Francisco A. Portales, introducción a la historia de la época de Diego Portales. 2 vols. Santiago: Editorial Nascimento, 1934.

Eyzaguirre, Jaime. O'Higgins. 3rd ed. Santiago: Editorial Zig-Zag, 1950.

Figueroa, Pedro Pablo. Diccionario biográfico de estranjeros en Chile. Santiago: Imprenta Moderna, 1900.

Figueroa, Virgilio. *Diccionario Histórico y Biográfoco de Chile. 5 vols. Santiago: La Ilustración, 1925-31.

Larraín Bravo, Ricardo. Biografías sucintas de algunos próceres de Chile. Santiago: Editorial Nascimento, 1939.

Lastarria, José Victorino. Don Diego Portales. Santiago: Imprenta Cervantes, 1896.

Mitre, Bartolomé. Historia de San Martín y de la emancipación sud-americana. Santiago: Editorial Sudamericana, 1941.

Nabuco, Joaquín. Balmaceda. Santiago: Imprenta Universitaria, 1914.

Salas Edwards, Ricardo. Balmaceda y el parlamentarismo en Chile. 2 vols. Santiago: Imprenta Moderna, 1916.

Vergara Vicuña, Aguirre. Ibáñez, césar criollo. 2 vols. Santiago: La Ilustración, 1931.

Vicuña Mackenna, Benjamín. El ostracismo del general d. Bernardo O'Higgins. Santiago: in Obras completas de Vicuña Mackenna, 1886.

3. GENERAL WORKS

Aldunate Phillips, Arturo. Un Pueblo en busca de su destino. Santiago: Editorial Nascimento, 1947.

Allende, Salvador. *Chile's Road to Socialism. New York: Penguin Books, 1973.

Almanaque Mundial, 1983. New York: Editora Moderna, 1982. Annually.

America Latina: El pensamiento de la CEPAL. Santiago: Editorial Universitaria, 1969.

Ampuero, Raúl. *La izquierda en punto muerto. Santiago: Editorial Orbe, 1969.

Amunátegui y Solar, Domingo. *La democracia en Chile: Teatro político, 1810-1910. Santiago: Universidad de Chile, 1946.

Andreas, Carol. Nothing Is as It Should Be. Cambridge, MA: Schenkman Publishing Co., 1976.

Aranda, Sergio, et al. *Chile, hoy. Santiago: Siglo Veintiuno Editores, 1970.

Area Handbook for Chile. Washington, DC: U.S. Government Printing Office, 1969.

Bannon, John Francis, and Peter Masten Dunne. *Latin America: An Historical Survey. Milwaukee: Bruce Publishing, 1963.

Barros Arana, Diego. *Historia general de Chile. 16 vols. Santiago: Editorial Nascimento, 1941.

Bird, Junius B. Excavations in Northern Chile. New York: American Museum of Natural History, 1943.

Bowers, Claude. Chile Through Embassy Windows. New York: Simon and Schuster, 1958.

Bowman, Isaiah. Desert Trails of Atacama. New York: American Geographical Society, 1924.

Burr, Robert N. By Reason or Force. Berkeley: University of California Press, 1965.

Butland, Gilbert J. Chile: An Outline of Its Geography, Economics and Politics. London: Royal Institute of International Affairs, 1953.

_____. The Human Geography of Southern Chile. London: George Philip, 1957.

Carlson, Fred H. Geography of Latin America. New York: Praeger, 1936.

Carmagnani, Marcello. "Colonial Latin American Demography: Growth of Chilean Population, 1700-1830." Journal of Social History, vol. 1, no. 2, Winter 1967.

Castillo, Carmen. Un día de octubre en Santiago. Mexico: Biblioteca Era, 1982. (First edition in French, Un jour d'octobre à Santiago. Translated by Felipe Sarabia. Paris: Editions Stock, 1980.)

Chilcote, Ronald H. "The Press in Latin America, Spain, and Portugal." Hispanic American Report. Stanford, CA: Stanford University Press, August 1963.

*"Chile: Blood on the Peaceful Road." Latin American Perspectives, vol. 1, no. 2, Summer 1974.

Chonchól, Jacques, and Julio Silva. *El desarrollo de la nueva sociedad en América Latina. Santiago: Editorial Universitaria, 1969.

Daugherty, Charles H., ed. Chile: Election Factbook. Washington, DC: The Institute for Comparative Study of Political Systems, 1963.

Davies, Howell, ed. The South American Handbook. London: Trade and Travel Pub., 1965. Annually.

Demografía y asistencia social de 1966. Santiago: Dirección General de Estadística, 1969. Annually.

Edwards, Agustin. The Dawn: Being the History of the Birth and Consolidation of the Republic of Chile. Santiago: Editorial Nascimento, 1931.

Ellsworth, P. T. *Chile: An Economy in Transition. New York: Macmillan, 1945.

Evans, Les, ed. *Disaster in Chile: Allende's Strategy and Why It Failed. New York: Pathfinder Press, 1974.

Fergusson, Erna. *Chile. New York: Alfred Knopf, 1943.

Galdames, Luis. *A History of Chile, translated by Isaac Joslin Cox. Chapel Hill: University of North Carolina Press, 1941.

Gil, Federico. *The Political System of Chile. Boston: Houghton Mifflin, 1966.

Guía de Santiago. Santiago: Empresa Editora Zig-Zag, 1961.

Hilton, Ronald, ed. Handbook of Hispanic Source Materials and Research Organizations in the United States. 2nd ed. Stanford, CA: Stanford University Press, 1956.

_____, ed. The Movement Toward Latin American Unity. New York: Praeger, 1969.

_____. The Latin Americans. Philadelphia: J. B. Lippincott, 1973.

Historia del movimiento obrero. Santiago: Editorial POR, 1962.

Horowitz, Irving Louis, ed. The Rise and Fall of Project Camelot: Studies in the Relationship between Social Science and Practical Politics. Cambridge, MA: M.I.T. Press, 1967.

IDOC. *Chile: The Allende Years; The Coup; Under the Junta. New York: International North American Edition, no. 58, December 1973.

_____. *Chile: Under Military Rule. New York: International North American Edition, 1974.

Interpretación marxista de la historia de Chile. Santiago: Prensa Latinoamericana, 1972.

James, Herman G., and Percy A. Martin. The Republics of Latin America. New York: Harper Brothers, 1963.

James, Preston. Latin America. 3rd ed. New York: The Odyssey Press, 1959.

Johnson, Dale, ed. *The Chilean Road to Socialism. California: Anchor Press, 1973.

Joxe, Alain. *Las fuerzas armadas en el sistema político de Chile. Santiago: Editorial Universitaria, 1970.

Kinsbrunner, Jay. *Chile: A Historical Interpretation. New York: Harper Torchbooks, 1973.

Lavell, Carr B. Population Growth and the Development of South America. Washington, DC: George Washington University Press, 1959.

Loveman, Brian. *Chile. New York: Oxford University Press, 1979.

MacDonald, Austin F. Latin American Politics and Government. New York: Thomas Crowell, 1954.

Magdoff, Harry. The Age of Imperialism. New York: Monthly Review Press, 1969.

Mallory, Walter H. Political Handbook and Atlas of the World, 1964. New York: Harper and Row, 1964.

McBride, G. M. *Chile, Land and Society. Milwaukee: Bruce Publishing Company, 1971 (1936).

Merril, Andrea T., ed. *Chile: A Country Study. Area Handbook Series. Washington, DC: U.S. Government Printing Office, 1982.

Mitrani, Barbara, and Francisco José Moreno. Conflict and Violence in Latin American Politics: A Book of Readings. New York: Thomas Crowell, 1971.

Moreno, Francisco José. Legitimacy and Stability in Latin America. New York: New York University Press, 1969.

Morris, James O. Elites, Intellectuals and Consensus: A Study of the Social Question and the Industrial Relations System in Chile. Ithaca, NY: Cornell University Press, 1966.

NACLA. New Chile. North American Congress on Latin America, 1973.

O'Brien, Phillip, ed. *Allende's Chile. New York: Praeger, 1976.

Osborn, Frederick. Population: An International Dilemma. New York: Population Council, 1958.

Pendle, George. The Land and People of Chile. New York: Barnes and Noble, 1963.

Petras, J., and Z. Zetlin, eds. Latin America: Reform or Revolution? Greenwich, CT: Fawcett Press, 1966.

Pike, Frederick. *Chile and the United States, 1880-1962. Notre Dame, IN: University of Notre Dame Press, 1963.

Pinochet de la Barra, O. La Antártica chilena. Santiago: Editorial del Pacífico, 1948.

Pinto, Anfbal. Chile, hoy. Mexico City: Siglo Veintiuno Editores, 1970.

Pinto Lagarrigue, Fernando. *La masonería: su influencia en Chile. Santiago: Editorial Orbe, 1966.

Ramírez Necochea, Hernán. *Balmaceda y la contrarrevolución de 1891. Santiago: Editorial Austral, 1965.

Sachs, Moshe Y., ed. Worldmark Encyclopedia of the Nations. (Vol: Americas). New York: Harper and Row, 1963.

Silvert, K. H. *Chile, Yesterday and Today. New York: Holt, Rinehart and Winston, 1965.

_____. The Conflict Society: Reaction and Revolution in Latin America. New Orleans: Hauser Press, 1961.

Solberg, Carl. "Immigration and Urban Social Problems in Argentina and Chile 1890-1914," The Hispanic American Historical Review, May 1968. Durham, NC: Duke University Press, pp. 215-233.

Steinberg, H. S., ed. The Statesman Yearbook 1964-65. London: Macmillan and Company, 1964. Annually.

Subercaseaux Vicuña, Benjamin. *Chile, a Geographic Extravaganza. Translated by Angel Flores. New York: Macmillan, 1943.

Subversion in Chile: A Case Study of U.S. Corporate Intrigue in the Third World. England: Bertrand Russell Peace Foundation, 1972.

Uribe Arce, Armando. *The Blackbook of American Intervention in Chile. Translated by Jonathan Casart. Boston: Beacon Press, 1975.

Veliz, Claudio, ed. Obstacles to Change in Latin America. London: Oxford University Press, 1965.

White, Judy, ed. *Chile's Days of Terror. New York: Pathfinder Press, 1974.

Wilgus, A. Curtis, ed. *Argentina, Brazil and Chile since Independence. Washington, DC: George Washington University Press, 1935.

Wilgus, A. Curtis, and Raul d'Eça. Latin American History. New York: Barnes and Noble, 1969.

Wingeate Pike, David, ed. *Latin America in Nixon's Second Term. Paris: American College in Paris Publication, 1982.

Zañartu, S., and J. J. Kennedy, eds. *The Overall Development of Chile. Notre Dame, IN: The University of Notre Dame Press, 1969.

4. HISTORY

Ahumada Corvalán, Jorge. La crisis integral de Chile. Santiago: Editorial Universitaria, 1966.

Ahumada Moreno, Pascual. Guerra del Pacífico. 8 vols. Valparaíso (and Paris): Solar, 1884-1891.

Alberdi, Juan Bautista. *Biografía del general don Manuel Bulnes,

_____ presidente de la República de Chile. Santiago: Imprenta Chilena, 1846.

Alessandri, Arturo. Recuerdos de gobierno. 3 vols. Santiago: Editorial Nascimento, 1967.

Almeyda Arroyo, E. Biografía de Chile. Santiago: Editorial Zamorano y Caperán, 1943.

Amunátegui, Miguel Luis. Camilo Henríquez. Santiago: Imprenta Nacional, 1888.

_____. "El templo de la compañía de Jesús en Santiago de Chile." Revista de Santiago, May 15, 1872.

_____. La encíclica del Papa Leon XII contra la independencia de América. Santiago: Imprenta J. Núñez, 1874.

_____. Los precursores de la independencia de Chile. 3 vols. Santiago: Imprenta Barcelona, 1870-1872.

Amunátegui y Solar, Domingo. Archivo epistolar de Don Miguel Luis Amunátegui. 2 vols. Santiago: Universidad de Chile, 1942.

_____. El instituto nacional bajo los rectorados de Don Manuel Montt, Don Francisco Puente i Don Antonio Varas, 1835-1845. Santiago: Imprenta Nacional, 1891.

_____. Historia de Chile. Santiago: Editorial Nascimento, 1933.

_____. Historia social de Chile. Santiago: Editorial Nascimento, 1932.

_____. La sociedad chilena del siglo XVIII: mayorazgos y títulos de Castilla. 3 vols. Santiago: Imprenta Barcelona, 1903-1904.

Angell, Alan. *"Counter-revolution in Chile." Current History, vol. 66, January 1974, pp. 6-9.

Arellano, José P. "Las políticas sociales en Chile: breve revisión histórica. Revista Interamericana de Planificación, vol. 17, no. 68. Mexico, D.F.: December 1983, pp. 132-50.

Azcoaga, Juan. El horizonte chileno. Buenos Aires: Cuenca Ediciones, 1973.

Bader, Thomas. "Early Positivistic Thought and Ideological Conflict in Chile." The Americas, no. 26, February 1970, pp. 375-393.

Bagú, Sergio. Economía de la sociedad colonial. Buenos Aires: El Ateneo, 1949.

_____. Estructura social de la colonia. Buenos Aires; El Ateneo: 1952.

Bañados Espinosa, J. Balmaceda: su gobierno y la revolución de 1891. Paris: Garnier Frères, 1894.

Bannon, John Francis, S. J. and Peter Masten Dunne. *Latin America: An Historical Survey. Milwaukee: The Bruce Publishing Co., 1963.

Barbier, Jacques. "Elite and Cadres in Bourbon Chile." Hispanic American Historial Review, August 1972.

Barros Arana, Diego. *Historia jeneral de Chile. 16 vols. Santiago: R. Jover, 1902.

_____. Obras completas. 16 vols. Santiago: Imprenta Cervantes, 1905-1906.

Barros Borgoño, Luis. Archivo Barros Arana. A través de una correspondencia. Santiago: Universidad de Chile, 1934.

_____. Archivo Barros Arana: Misión en el Plata. Santiago: Universidad de Chile, 1936.

Bello, Andrés. Obras completas. 16 vols. Santiago: Pedro G. Ramírez, 1884.

Bernascina, Mario. Derecho municipal chileno. 3 vols. Santiago: Editorial Jurídica de Chile, 1952.

Bilbao, Jon, and William A. Douglass. Amerikanauk, Basques in the New World. Reno: University of Nevada Press, 1975.

Bravo Kendrick, Anibal. La revolución de 1891. Santiago: Imprenta Cultura, 1946.

Camejo, Peter. Allende's Chile: Is It Going Socialist? New York: Pathfinder Press, 1971.

Campos Harriet, Fernando. Historia constitucional de Chile. Santiago: Editorial Jurídica de Chile, 1956.

Carrasco, D. Adolfo. Descubrimiento y conquista de Chile. Madrid: Establecimiento Tipográfico "Sucesores de Rivadeneyra," 1892.

Castedo, Leopoldo, and Francisco Encina. Historia de Chile. Santiago: Editorial Universitaria, 1969.

Chiappa, Victor M. *Bibliografía de Don Diego Barros Arana. Temuco: Imprenta Alemán, 1907.

Clissold, Stephen. Bernardo O'Higgins and the Independence of Chile. New York: Praeger, 1969.

Collier, Simon. Ideas and Politics of Chilean Independence. Cambridge, England: Cambridge University Press, 1967.

_____. "The Historiography of the Portalian Period 1830-1891 in Chile." Hispanic American Historical Review, November 1977.

Constitución Política de la República de Chile. Chilean Government Publications. Santiago: Decreto Ley 3465, 1980.

Cruchaga Ossa, Alberto. Estudios de historia diplomática chilena. Santiago: Editorial Andrés Bello, 1962.

Dinges, John, and Saul Landau. Assassination on Embassy Row. New York: Pantheon Books, 1980.

Donoso, Ricardo. *Alessandri, agitador y demoledor: cincuenta años de historia política de Chile, 2 vols. Mexico: Fondo de Cultura Económica, 1952, 1954.

_____. *Desarrollo político y social de Chile desde la Constitución de 1833. Santiago: Imprenta Universitaria, 1942.

_____. Hombres e ideas de antaño y hogaño. Santiago: Ercilla, 1937.

_____. *Historia de las ideas políticas en Chile. Mexico: Fondo de Cultura Económica, 1946.

Doussinague, José M. Pedro de Valdivia. Madrid: Espasa-Calpe, 1963.

Eberhardt, Enrique. Historia de Santiago de Chile. Santiago: Editorial Gutemberg, 1916.

Encina, Francisco Antonio. História de Chile desde la prehistoria hasta 1891. vols. 1-20. Santiago: Editorial Nascimento, 1952.

_____. La literatura histórica chilena y el concepto actual de la historia. Santiago: Editorial Nascimento, 1935.

_____. Resumen de la historia de Chile. Santiago: Editorial Zig-Zag, 1954.

Eyzaguirre, Jaime. Breve historia de la fronteras de Chile. Santiago: Editorial Universitaria, 1968.

_____. Ideario y ruta de la independencia chilena. Santiago: Imprenta Universitaria, 1972.

Feliú Cruz, Guillermo. Barros Arana, historiador. 5 vols. Santiago: Ediciones AUCh, 1959.

_____. La abolición de la esclavitud en Chile. Santiago: Editorial Latinoamericana, 1942.

_____. Un esquema de la evolución social en Chile en el Siglo XIX. Santiago: Editorial Nascimento, 1941.

Fergusson, Erna. *Chile. New York: Alfred A. Knopf, 1943.

Figueroa, Virgilio. *Diccionario Histórico y Biográfico de Chile. 5 vols. Santiago: La Ilustración, 1925-31.

Fuenzalida Grandón, Alejandro. La evolución social de Chile, 1541-1810. Santiago: Imprenta Barcelona, 1906.

Galdames, Luis. *A History of Chile, translated by Isaac Joslin Cox. Chapel Hill: University of North Carolina Press.

Gil, Federico; Ricardo Lagos; and Henry Landsberger, eds. Chile, 1970-1973. Madrid: Editorial Tecnos, 1977.

Hale, Charles A. "The Reconstruction of Nineteenth Century Politics in Spanish America: A Case for the History of Ideas." Latin American Research Review, vol. 8, 1973, pp. 53-73.

Hanisch Espíndola, Walter, S. J. "Tres dimensiones del pensamiento de Bello: religión, filosofía, historia." Historia, vol. 4, 1965, pp. 8-190.

Heise González, Julio. 150 años de evolución institucional. Santiago: Editorial Andrés Bello, 1960.

Herring, Hubert. A History of Latin America from the Beginnings to the Present. New York: Alfred A. Knopf, 1961.

Hervey, Maurice. Dark Days in Chile. London: Macmillan Co., 1891-92.

Hilton, Ronald. La América Latina de ayer y de hoy. New York: Holt, Rinehart and Winston, 1970.

Inostrosa Jorge. Hidalgos del mar. 2nd edition. Santiago: Editora Zig-Zag, 1959.

Izquierdo F., Gonzalo. Un estudio de las ideologías chilenas. Santiago: Centro de Estudios Socioeconómicos, 1968.

James, Herman G., and Percy A. Martin. The Republics of Latin America. New York: Harper Brothers, 1963.

Johnson, John J. Pioneer telegraphy in Chile, 1852-1876. Stanford, CA: Stanford University Press, 1948.

Kiernan, V. G. "Foreign Interest in the War of the Pacific." Hispanic American Historical Review, vol. 35, 1955.

Kinsbruner, Jay. *Chile: A Historical Interpretation. New York: Harper and Row, 1973.

Korth, Eugene H., S. J. Spanish Policy in Colonial Chile. Stanford, CA: Stanford University Press, 1968.

Lastarria, José Victorino. Obras completas. 15 vols. Santiago: Imprenta Barcelona, 1909.

Letelier, Valentín. La evolución de la historia. 2 vols. Santiago: Imprenta Cervantes, 1900.

López, Vicente Fidel. Manual de la historia de Chile. Valparaíso: El Mercurio, 1845.

Machuca, Francisco A. Las cuatro campañas de la Guerra del Pacífico. 4 vols. Valparaíso: Imprenta Victoria, 1926.

Markham, Sir Clements R. The War Between Peru and Chile: 1879-1882. London: Sampson Low, Marston, Searle and Rivington, 1882.

Mellon, Stanley. The Political Uses of History. Stanford, CA: Stanford University Press, 1958.

Méndez García de la Huerta, Alejandro. La guerra a muerte. Santiago: Editorial Nascimento, 1964.

Meza Villalobos, Nestor. La actividad política del reino de Chile entre 1806 y 1810. Santiago: Universidad de Chile, 1958.

Millar, Walterio. Historia de Chile. Santiago: Editora Zig-Zag, 1959.

Millington, Herbert. American Diplomacy and the War of the Pacific. New York: Columbia University Press, 1948.

Nef, Jorge. "The Politics of Repression: The Social Pathology of the Chilean Military." Latin American Perspectives, vol. 1, no. 2, Summer 1974, pp. 58-77.

North, Lisa. Civil-Military Relations in Argentina, Chile and Peru. Berkeley: University of California Press, 1966.

Olavarría Bravo, Arturo. Chile entre dos Alessandri. 2 vols. Santiago: Editorial Nascimento, 1962-65.

Ovalle, Alonso A. Histórica relación del reino de Chile. Santiago: Editorial Universitaria, 1969.

Pérez Rosales, Vicente. Ensayo sobre Chile. Santiago: El Ferrocarril, 1859.

Pike, Frederick B. *Chile and the United States, 1880-1962. Notre Dame: Notre Dame University Press, 1963.

Pinto Lagarrigue, Fernando. *La masonería: su influencia en Chile. Santiago: Editorial Orbe, 1966.

Ramírez Necochea, Hernán. *Balmaceda y la contrarrevolución de 1981. Santiago: Editorial Universitaria, 1969.

_____. *Historia del imperialismo en Chile. Berkeley: University of California Press, 1969.

Republica de Chile. "Constitución política y reglamiento del senado." Santiago: Imprenta Universo, 1954.

Romano, Ruggiero. Una economía colonial: Chile en el siglo XVIII. Buenos Aires: Editorial Universitaria, 1965.

Ross, Augustín Edwards. Reseña histórica sobre el comercio de Chile en la era colonial. Santiago: Imprenta Cervantes, 1894.

Sater, William F. Chile and the War of the Pacific. Lincoln: University of Nebraska Press, 1986.

Sears, J. and B. W. Wells. The Chilean Revolution of 1891. Washington, D.C.: U.S. Government Printing Office, Office of Naval Intelligence, 1893.

Simon, W. M. European Positivism in the Nineteenth Century. Ithaca: Cornell University Press, 1963.

Sotomayor Valdés, Ramón. Historia de Chile durante los cuarenta años transcurridos desde 1831 hasta 1871. 2 vols. Santiago: (published in the newspaper La estrella de Chile) 1875-1876.

Subercaseaux Vicuña, Benjamín. *Chile, a Geographic Extravanganza. Translated by Angel Flores. New York: Macmillan, 1943.

_____. Crónicas de centenario; la colonia-la patria vieja. Santiago: Sociedad Imprenta y Litografía Universo, 1910.

"Terror in Chile," New York Review of Books, May 30, 1974.

Valdés Vergara, Francisco. Historia de Chile. Santiago: Litografía Universo, 1923.

Vicuña Mackenna, Benjamín. Introducción a los diez años de la administración Montt, Don Diego Portales. 2 vols. Valparaíso: Imprenta Mercurio, 1863.

Vives, Alberto Edwards. El gobierno de Don Manuel Montt: 1851-1861. Santiago: Editorial Nascimento, 1932.

Wilgus, A. Curtis, ed. *Argentina, Brazil and Chile Since Independence. Washington, DC: George Washington University Press, 1935.

Woll, Allen L. *A Functional Past: The Uses of History in 19th Century Chile. Baton Rouge: Louisiana State University Press, 1982.

Zegers, Cristian A. Aníbal Pinto: Historia política de su gobierno. Santiago: Editorial Universitaria, 1969.

Foreign Relations

Amunátegui, Miguel Luis. La cuestión de límites entre Chile i Bolivia. Santiago: Imprenta Nacional, 1863.

_____. La cuestión de límites entre Chile i la República Argentina. 3 vols. Santiago: Imprenta Nacional, 1879-1881.

_____. Títulos de la República de Chile a la soberanía i dominio de la estremidad austral del continente americano. Santiago: Imprenta Nacional, 1855.

Bianchi Gundian, Manuel. Chile and Great Britain. London: Organ, 1944.

Chile and the United Naitons. New York: Permanent Mission of Chile to the United Nations, 1967.

"Chile's Foreign Policy." The New York Times. January 25, 1971, p. 73.

Dennis, William J. Tacna and Arica. An Account of the Chile-Peru Boundary Dispute. New Haven, CT: Yale University Press, 1931.

Encina, Francisco A. Las relaciones entre Chile y Bolivia, 1841-1963. Santiago: Editorial Nascimento, 1963.

_____. La cuestión de límites entre Chile y la Argentina desde la independencia hasta el tratado de 1881. Santiago: Editorial Nascimento, 1959.

Evans, H. C. Chile and Its Relations with the United States. Durham, NC: Duke University Press, 1927.

Labarca Goddard, Eduardo. *Chile invadido. Santiago: Empresa Editorial Austral, 1968.

McBride, G. M. *Chile, Land and Society. Milwaukee: Bruce Pub. Co., 1971 (1936).

Petras, James, and Morris Morley. The United States and Chile: Imperialism and the Overthrow of the Allende Government. New York: Monthly Review Press, 1975.

Pike, Frederick B. *Chile and the United States 1880-1962. Notre Dame, IN: University of Notre Dame Press, 1963.

Prokhorov, A. M., ed. "Soviet-Chilean Agreements," in The Great Soviet Encyclopedia. New York: Macmillan Education Corporation, 1973.

Ríos Gallardo, Conrado. Chile y Peru: Los pactos de 1929. Santiago: Editorial Nascimento, 1959.

Roett, Riordan. *"Democracy and Debt in South America." Foreign Affairs: America and the World, vol. 62, no. 3, 1984.

The United States and Chile During the Allende Years, 1970-1973. "Hearings Before the Subcommittee of Inter-American Affairs." Washington, DC: U.S. Government Printing Office, 1975.

Uribe Arce, Armando. *The Blackbook of American Intervention in Chile. Translated by Jonathan Casart. Boston: Beacon Press, 1975.

5. ECONOMY

Ahumada, Jorge. En vez de la miseria. Santiago: Editorial del Pacífico, 1958.

*Anuario de los paises del ALALC. Buenos Aires: Instituto Publicaciones y Estadísticas S.S., 1968 (3rd edition).

Arellano, José Pablo. "De la liberalización: el mercado de capitales en Chile 1974-83." Estudios Cieplán, Corporación de Investigaciones Económicas para Latinoamérica, no. 11. Santiago de Chile: December 1983, pp. 5-49.

Ayres, R. "Economic Stagnation and the Emergence of the Political Ideology of Chilean Underdevelopment." World Politics, vol. 25, October 1972.

Baird, Jane. "The Rise and Fall of Javier Vial." Institutional Investor, August 1983, pp. 82-90.

Baklanoff, Eric N. "Copper in Chile: The Expropriation of a Partially Nationalized Industry." University of Texas at Austin. Institute of Latin American Studies. Technical Papers Series, no. 38. 1983, Austin: pp. 1-15.

Banco Central de Chile. "Consideraciones sobre las consecuencias de las modificaciones cambiarias." Centro de Estudios Monetarios Latino-Americanos, Boletín. no. 29. Mexico, D.F.: July/August 1983, pp. 169-174.

Barrera, Manuel, and Teresita Selame. "La política de capacitación ocupacional del gobierno militar chileno." Revista Latino-americana de Estudios Educativos. no. 12. Mexico, D.F., Mexico: Fall 1982, pp. 11-36.

"Basic Aspects of the Economic and Financial Policies of the Chilean Government." The New York Times, January 25, 1971, p. 73ff.

Bergquist, Charles W. "Exports, Labor, and the Left: An Essay on Twentieth-Century Chilean History." Woodrow Wilson International Center for Scholars, Latin American Program. Working Papers, no. 97. Washington, DC: 1981, pp. 1-61.

Bitar, Sergio. "Monetarism and Ultraliberalism, 1973-80." International Journal of Politics. no. 12. Armonk, NY, Winter, 1981-83, pp. 10-47.

Bohan, Mervin L., and Morton Pomeranz. Investment in Chile. Washington, DC: Department of Commerce, 1960.

Branes Ballesteros, Raúl. "Chile: la nueva constitución económica; los modelos constitucionales neoliberales." Comercio Exterior, no. 32. Mexico, D.F., Mexico: January 1982, pp. 36-42.

Briones, Guillermo. "Segmentación y heterogeneidad educativa en mercados laborales urbanos; el caso del gran Santiago: 1976-1980." Revista Latinoamericana de Estudios Educativos, no. 12. Mexico, D.F., Mexico: 4th Quarter, pp. 11-18.

Briones, Rodriso K. "Chilean Malaise." Challenge. no. 27. Armonk, NY, March/April 1984, pp. 57-60.

Caldemartori, José. La economía chilena: un enfoque marxista. Santiago: Editorial Universitaria, 1968.

"Capitalism Under Stress." Euromoney. London: October 1983, pp. 64-73.

Carey, Jorge. "Chile's Foreign Exchange Programme." International Financial Law Review. London, September 1983, pp. 16-17.

"Chile: An Economist's Predictions." Latin America Newsletter (Weekly Report). WR-84-23, June 15, 1984, p. 7.

"Chile Asks Creditors to Allow It to Delay Some Debt Payments." Wall Street Journal, November 3, 1983, p. 29ff., 34.

"Chile Copper Nationalization Looms as Bill Nears Passage." The Denver Post, May 3, 1971, p. 18.

Chile Economic Report, no. 144. New York, Corporación de Fomento de la Produccion (CORFO), July 1983.

_____, no. 146. New York: Corporación de Fomento de la Producción (CORFO), September 1983, Monthly.

"Chile; Goodbye Chicago?" Banker, no. 133. London, U.K., February 1983, pp. 69-70.

"Chile: How the Rich Get Poorer, and the Poor, Poorer Still." Latin America Regional Reports (Southern Cone). June 29, 1984, p. 2. 1984. Weekly.

Chile Hoy. Centro de Estudios Socio-Economicos, Mexico: Siglo Veintiuno Editores, 1970.

"Chile 1980 Economic Profile." New York: Corporación de Fomento de la Producción (CORFO), prepared with the Central Bank of Chile and the National Planning Office (ODEPLAN), 1980.

"Chile: No Devaluation." Latin American Week, no. 13. Lima, Peru, May 14, 1982, pp. 1-2.

"Chile Today." International Journal of Politics. no. 12. Armonk, NY, Winter 1982-83, pp. 1-90.

"Chile: Where Major New Copper Output Can Materialize Fast." Engineering and Mining Journal, no. 180. New York, November, 1979, p. 68.

"Chilean Inflation, Unemployment." Wall Street Journal, December 6, 1983, p. 18.

"Chile's Creditor Banks Commit 90% of Loan to Cover 1984 Needs." Wall Street Journal. May 10, 1984, p. 35.

"Chile's Economy: A Bleak Picture for 1984." Latin America Newsletter (Weekly Report), WR-84-20, May 25, 1984, pp. 10-11.

Chonchól, Jacques, and Julio Silva. *El desarrollo de la nueva sociedad en América Latina. Santiago: Editorial Universitaria, S.A., 1969.

Coeymans, Juan Eduardo. "Determinantes de la migración rural-urbana en Chile según origen y destino." Cuadernos de Economía, no. 20. Santiago, Chile, April 1983, pp. 43-64.

Cohen, Alvin: Economic Change in Chile, 1929-1959. Gainesville: University of Florida Press, 1960.

Congdon, T. G. "Apertura Policies in the Cone of Latin America." World Economy, no. 5. Oxford, U.K.: September 1982, pp. 133-47.

Congdon, Tim. "What Happened to the Chilean Economic Miracle?" Economic Affairs, no. 4. London: January 1984, pp. 29-31.

"Copper Conflict Deepens." Mining Journal. no. 302. London: February 17, 1984, pp. 101-03.

Corbo, Vittorio. "Desarrollos macroeconómicos recientes en la economía chilena." Cuadernos de Economía. Santiago, Chile: April 1983, 20:5-20.

_____. "Desequilibrio de stocks, shocks monetarios y la estabilidad de la demanda por dinero en Chile." Cuadernos de Economía, no. 19. Santiago, Chile: December 1982, pp. 305-23.

Corbo, Vittorio, and Morton Stelcner. "Earnings Determination and Labour Markets; Gran Santiago, Chile--1978." Journal of Development Economics, no. 12. Amsterdam, Netherlands, February/April 1983, pp. 251-66.

Corbo, Vittorio, and Mary Pollack. "Fuentes del cambio en la estructura económica chilena: 1960-1979." Estudios de Economía, no. 18. Santiago, Chile: First Semester, 1982, pp. 55-96.

Cortázar, René. "Chile: resultados distributivos 1973-82." Desarrollo Económico, no. 23. Buenos Aires: October/December 1983, pp. 369-94.

Cruzat, Magdalena. "No a los extremos." Ercilla. Santiago: May 2, 1984.

De Onís, Juan. "Pinochet Fires Chile's Economic Planners." Los Angeles Times, April 3, 1984, p. 4.

De Vylder, Stefan. *Allende's Chile. Cambridge, England: The Cambridge University Press, 1976.

Dooley, Michael, and William Helkie. "Analysis of External Debt Positions of Eight Developing Countries Through 1900." U.S. Board of Governors of the Federal Reserve System. International Finance Division. International Finance Discussion Papers, no. 227. Washington, DC: August 1983, pp. 1-17.

Douglas, Hernán Cortés. "Políticas de estabilización en Chile: inflación, desempleo y depresión 1975-1982. Cuadernos de Economía, no. 20. Santiago: August 1983, pp. 149-75.

The Economist. London: 1983. Weekly.

Edwards, Sebastián. "Deuda externa, ahorro doméstico y credimiento económico en Chile; una perspectiva de largo plazo: 1982-1990." Estudios Internacionales. Santiago, Chile, July/September 1982, pp. 260-75.

"El cobre." Polémica. Santiago: May 1969, No. 5.

*"El fraude de la 'nacionalización pactada.'" Punto Final, No. 83, July 15, 1969, pp. 8-9.

"El tema central América Latina ante la recesión." Pensamiento Iberoamericano. no. 4. Madrid: July/December 1983, pp. 1-185.

Ellsworth, P. T. *Chile, An Economy in Transition. New York: The Macmillan Co., 1945.

Endesa. Santiago: Corporación de Fomento de la Producción, (CORFO) 1948, Annually.

Ensayo crítico del desarrollo económico-social de Chile. Santiago: Editorial Latinoamericana, 1965.

Estadística Chilena. Santiago: Dirección General de Estadística. Monthly 1960-70.

_____. Santiago: Dirección General de Estadística. Monthly, 1970-1980.

Estevez, Jaime. "Chile: derrumbe del neoliberalismo." Economía de América Latina. Mexico, D.F.: September 1983, no. 10.

"External Payments Considerations to the Fore." Quarterly Economic Review of Chile. London: February 28, 1964, pp. 3-6.

Felix, David. "Chile," in Economic Development. New York: Harper, 1961.

Ffrench-Davis, Ricardo. "Chile: monetarismo y recesión: elementos para una estrategia externa. Pensamiento Iberoamericano, no. 4. Madrid: July/December 1983, pp. 171-80.

_____. "El experimento monetarista en Chile: una síntesis crítica." Estudios Cieplán, Corporación de Investigaciones Económicas Para Latinoamérica, no. 9. Santiago de Chile, Chile, December 1982, pp. 5-40.

_____. "El experimento monetarista en Chile: una síntesis crítica." Desarrollo Económico, no. 23. Buenos Aires, July/September 1983, pp. 163-96.

_____. "Monetarist Experiment in Chile: A Critical Survey." World Development, no. 11. Oxford, November 1983, pp. 905-26.

_____. "Relaciones financieras externas y su efecto en la economía latinoamericana, 1983." Mexico, Fondo de Cultura Económica, 1983.

Flórez-Valderrama, Carmen Elisa. "Técnicas de poblaciones noestables para el análisis de mortalidad adulta: el caso de Chile." Desarrollo y Sociedad, no. 11. Bogota, May 1983, pp. 45-74.

Fortín, Carlos. "Failure of Repressive Monetarism. Chile, 1973-83." Third World Quarterly, no. 6. London, April 1984, pp. 310-26.

Foxley, Alejandro. "La economía chilena: algunos temas del futuro." Estudios Cieplán, Corporación de Investigaciones Económicas Para Latinoamérica, no. 6. Santiago de Chile, December 1981, pp. 177-88.

García H., Alvaro and John Wells. "Chile: A Laboratory for Failed Experiments in Capitalist Political Economy." Cambridge Journal of Economics, no. 7. London, September/December 1983, pp. 287-304.

Gedicks, A. "The Nationalization of Copper in Chile." Review of Radical Political Economics, vol. 5, Fall 1973.

"Goodbye Chicago?" The Banker. London: Financial Times Business Publishing Ltd., February 1983, pp. 69-70.

Griffith-Jones, Stephany. "A Chilean Perspective." IDS Bulletin, no. 14. Institute of Development Studies at the University of Sussex (Brighton), January 1983, pp. 50-54.

Gunder Frank, Andre. Latin America: Underdevelopment of Revolution. New York: Monthly Review Press, 1969.

_____. "The Underdevelopment Policy of the United Nations in Latin America." NACLA Newsletter, Vol. III, No. 8, December 1969, pp. 1-10.

Gutiérrez Urrutia, Mario. "Ahorro y crecimiento económico en Chile: una visión del proceso desde 1960 a 1981 y proyecciones de mediano plazo." Banco Central de Chile. Serie de Estudios Economicos, no. 18. Santiago, February 1983, pp. 1-67.

Hastings, Nicholas. "Chile Asks Banks for $1 Billion in New Lending." Wall Street Journal, February 15, 1984, p. 34.

Herrera, Felipe. América Latina intégrate. 2nd edition. Buenos Aires: Editorial Losada, 1967.

Hirschman, Albert O. (ed.). Latin American Issues: Essays and Comments. New York: Twentieth Century Fund, 1961.

_____. *Journeys Toward Progress. New York: Twentieth Century Fund, 1963.

Hojman, David E. "Income Distribution and Market Policies: Survival and Renewal of Middle Income Groups in Chile." Inter-American Economic Affairs, vol. 36, no. 2, pp. 43-63.

Hurtado-Beca, Cristina. "Chile, 1973-1981: Desarticulación y reestructuración autoritaria del movimiento sindical." Boletín de Estudios Latino-Americanos y Del Caribe, no. 31. Amsterdam, Netherlands: December 1981, pp. 91-117.

Inter-American Economic Affairs, no. 36. Washington, DC.: Autumn, 1982, pp. 43-64.

_____. "Wages, Unemployment and Expectations in Developing Countries: The Labour Market and the Augmented Phillips Curve for Chile." Journal of Economic Studies, vol. 10, no. 1. Bradford, 1982, pp. 3-16.

"IMF; Chile's Flexible Friend." Economist, no. 287. London, U.K.: May 14, 1983, pp. 86-91.

"IMF Visit to Chile." The New York Times. May 14, 1984, p. 28.

Jarvis, Lovell S. "¿Cuál ha sido la tasa real de crecimiento en los años recientes? Una nota acerca de las cifras de producción de la agricultura chilena en el período 1975-1979." Estudios Cieplán Corporación de Investigaciones Económicas Para Latinoamérica, no. 6. Santiago de Chile, December 1981, pp. 85-116.

Johnson, Dale. *"Special Report: The Two Forces Battling for the Presidency Contrast Their Programs." South Pacific Mail. Santiago, September 3, 1964, p. 10ff.

Kaffman, Luis. "Monetarists Carry the Can in Chile as Pinochet's

Problems Mount." The Third World Magazine, no. 25. London, November 1982, pp. 64-65.

Kaletsky, Anatole. "Chile's Economic Experiment: The Model That Didn't Travel." Financial Times. Frankfurt and London, March 9, 1983, p. 14.

La economía de Chile en el período 1940-1956. Santiago: Instituto de Economía, 1963.

Labarca Goddard, Eduardo. *Chile invadido. Santiago: Empresa Editoria Austral, 1968.

Labor in Chile. U.S. Department of Labor, Bureau of Labor Statistics. Washington, DC: Agency for International Development, 1962.

Labra, Pedro. "Estilos de desarrollo y la práctica de la planificación urbano-regional en América Latina: el caso de Chile 1964-1980." Revista Interamericana de Planificación, no. 16. Mexico, D.F., International: June 1982, pp. 38-53.

Lagos A., Ricardo. La concentración del poder económico. Santiago: Editorial del Pacífico, 1965.

Lagos, Ricardo, and Victor E. Tokman. "Monetarismo global, empleo y estratificación social." Trimestre Económico, no. 50. Mexico, D.F., July/September 1983, pp. 1437-73.

_____. "Monetarism, Employment and Social Stratification." World Development, no. 12. Oxford, January 1984, pp. 43-65.

"Latin America in Crisis: Common Themes and Diverse Experiences." Amex Bank Review, no. 4, London, April 25, pp. 2-6.

"Latin America; The Trembling Earth." Economist, no. 287, London, May 7, 1983, pp. 21-26.

"Latin American Crisis: 1, Mexico; 2, Brazil; 3, Chile." International Currency Review, no. 15. London, May 1983, pp. 19-56.

Maani, Sholeh. "La duración del desempleo y el salario de reserva de varones desempleados: el caso chileno." Cuadernos de Economía. no. 20. Santiago de Chile, April 1983, pp. 101-11.

_____. "El desempleo en Chile: una estimación de la probabilidad de empleo para varones." Cuadernos de Economía, no. 20. Santiago de Chile, p. 229.

Mamalakis, Markos J. The Growth and Structure of the Chilean Economy: From Independence to Allende. New Haven, CT: The Yale University Press, 1976.

Mamalakis, Marcos, and Clark Reynolds, eds. Essays on the Chilean Economy. Homewood, IL: Richard Irwin Press, 1965.

"The Mining Sector." Quarterly Economic Review of Chile. London, February 28, 1964, pp. 9-11.

Monteón, Michael. *Chile in the Nitrate Era. Madison: University of Wisconsin Press, 1945.

Montero Jaramillo, Felipe. Política chilena del cobre y sociedades mineras mixtas. Santiago: Editorial Universitaria, 1969.

Mujica A., Rodrigo. "Análisis de la demanda y predicción del consumo de hidrocarburos en Chile: 1980-2000." Cuadernos de Economía, no. 19. Santiago, December 1982, pp. 357-76.

Nef, J. "Revolution That Never Was: Perspectives on Democracy, Socialism, and Reaction in Chile; A Review Essay." Latin American Reserach Review, vol. 18, no. 1. Albuquerque, NM, 1983, pp. 228-45.

Niering, Frank E., Jr. "Chile: New Terms Set for Exploration." Petroleum Economist, no. 49. London, June 1982, pp. 227-28.

"On the Cross of Politics." Quarterly Economic Review of Chile. London, February 28, 1964, pp. 1-3.

Panorama Económico. Santiago: No. 242, March 1969.

_____. No. 244, May 1969.

_____. No. 245, June 1969.

_____. No. 246, July 1969.

_____. No. 247, August 1969.

_____. No. 248, September 1969.

Paredes, Ricardo. "Diferencias de ingreso entre hombres y mujeres en el gran Santiago: 1969 y 1981." Estudios de Economía, no. 18, Santiago: 1982, pp. 97-121.

Parkin, Vincent. "Economic Liberalism in Chile, 1973-82: A Model for Growth and Development or a Recipe for Stagnation and Impoverishment?" Cambridge Journal of Economics, no. 7. London, June 1983, pp. 101-24.

Pedraza-Bailey, Silvia. "Allende's Chile: Political Economy and Political Socialization." Studies in Comparative International

Development, no. 17. New Brunswick, NJ, Summer 1982, pp. 36-59.

Política, Economía, Cultura. Santiago, July 4, 1969.

Porras P., Ivan. "Algunas consideraciones acerca de tasas de interés internacionales." Banco Central de Chile. Serie de Estudios Económicos, no. 13. Santiago, April 1982, pp. 1-27.

Raczynski, Dagmar, and César Oyarzo. ¿Por qué cae la tasa de mortalidad infantil en Chile?" Estudios Cieplán, Corporación de Investigaciones Económicas Para Latinoamérica, no. 6. Santiago de Chile, December 1981, pp. 45-84.

Ramírez Necochea, Hernán. *Historia del imperialismo en Chile. Santiago: Empresa Editora Austral, 1960.

Rivera Urrutia, Eugenio. "Crisis económica, política de estabilización y nueva hegemonía; el caso chileno." Revista Centroamericana de Economía, no. 3. Tegucigalpa, Honduras, May/August 1982, pp. 87-123.

Robinson, Alan. "Chile Turns Its Banks into Debt Collectors." Euromoney. London, February 1983, pp. 59-67.

Rosenkranz, Hernán. "Actitudes norteamericanas hacia la junta militar chilena: continuidad y cambio, 1973-1978." Foro Internacional, no. 22. Mexico, D.F., July/September, 1981, pp. 70-89.

Rosett, Claudia. "Looking Back on Chile: 1973-1984." National Review, June 1, 1984, p. 25.

Rozas, Patricio. "La crisis actual del sistema financiero chileno." Economía de America Latina, no. 10. Mexico, D.F., September 1983, pp. 117-26.

Sánchez Martínez, Hilda, Crisis y política económica, una perspectiva instrumental (1978-1982). Mexico: Economía de América Latina, CIDE, 1984.

Sanders, Thomas G. "Chile's Economic Crisis and Its Implications for Political Change." Universities Field Staff International Reports, South America, no. 4. Hanover, NH, 1983, pp. 1-12.

Schwank, Lucy. "Unintended Lessons from the 'Chicago Boys.'" Wall Street Journal, December 23, 1983, p. 9.

Sesaris, Lake. "What the Chicago Boys Did to Chile." Mother Jones, January 1984, p. 31.

Skarmeta M., Claudio. "Economías de escala en la banca comercial chilena." Centro de Estudios Monetarios Latino-Americanos, Boletín, no. 28. Mexico, D.F., November/December 1982, pp. 302-12.

Subercaseaux Vicuña, Benjamín. Monetary and Banking Policy of Chile. Oxford: Clarenden Press, 1922.

Thompson, John K. "Chile's Experiment with Free Markets." Bankers Magazine. no. 166. Boston: November/December 1983, pp. 10-17.

Torres Aguirre, Manuel. "Evolución de la actividad textil; período: 1969-1980." Banco Central de Chile. Serie de Estudios Económicos, no. 9. Santiago, December 1981, pp. 1-80.

Torres R., Cecilia. "Evolución de la política arancelaria: período 1973-1981." Banco Central de Chile. Serie de Estudios Económicos, no. 16. Santiago, Chile: September 1982, pp. 1-57.

Toso C., Roberto. "El tipo de cambio fijo en Chile: la experiencia en el período 1979-1982." Monetaria, no. 6. Mexico, D.F., July/September 1983, pp. 315-30.

"Two Top Economic Aides Are Dismissed in Chile." The New York Times, April 3, 1984, p. 7.

Vega, Hector. "L'Economie du Populisme: Le Chili des Annés 60." Civilisations, vol. 31, no. 1A4. Brussels, 1981, pp. 247-314.

Vergara B., Pedro Pablo, and José Miguel Yrarrazaval E. "Medición des desarrollo financiero chileno (1975-1980)." Banco Central de Chile. Serie de Estudios Económicos, no. 17. Santiago, November 1982, pp. 1-55.

Welsh, Ellen. "Yes, Imports Are Restricted but These Nations Are Still Buying." American Import-Export Management, May 1984, p. 30.

White, C. Langdon, and Ronald H. Chilcote. "Chile's New Iron and Steel Industry." Economic Geography, Vol. 37, No. 3, July 1962.

Willmore, Larry. "Energy Demand in Chilean Manufacturing." Cepal Review, no. 18. Santiago de Chile, December 1982, pp. 131-37.

Yuravlivker, David E. "Crawling Peg and the Variability of the Real Exchange Rate." Economics Letters, vol. 9, no. 2. Amsterdam, 1982, pp. 185-90.

Zañartu, S. and J. J. Kennedy, *The Overall Development of Chile. Notre Dame, IN: The University of Notre Dame Press, 1969.

Agrarian Reform

Agricultura e industrias agropecuarias, Año agrícola, 1965-66--Comercio exterior de 1968--Comercio interior y comunicaciones de 1966--Finanzas, bancos, y cajas sociales de 1967--Industrias de 1967--Minería de 1966. Santiago: Dirección General de Estadística, 1969-70.

Barria, Jorge. Trayectoria y estructura del movimiento sindical chileno, 1946-1962. Santiago: Instituto de Organización y Administración del departamento de relaciones laborales, 1963.

Coeymans, Juan Eduardo. "Determinantes de la migración rural-urbana en Chile según origen y destino." Cuadernos de Economía, no. 20. Santiago: April 1983, pp. 43-64.

Corvalán, Luis. Cosas nuevas en el campo. Santiago: Imprenta Lautaro, 1960.

Klein, Emilio. "Problemas metodológicos de una encuesta rural en Chile y estructura del empleo." Cuadernos de Economía, no. 20. Santiago, December 1983, pp. 345-61. With English summary.

Smith, T. Lynn, ed. Agrarian Reform in Latin America. New York: Alfred A. Knopf, 1965.

Swift, J. Agrarian Reform in Chile. Lexington, MA: D.C. Heath, 1971.

Tierra y libertad por la reforma agraria. Santiago: Acción Sindical Chilena, 1961.

Urzua, Raúl. La demanda campesina. Santiago: Editorial Universitaria, S.A., 1969.

6. POLITICS

"A Third Warning for Pinochet." Time, July 25, 1983, p. 9.

Alexander, R. "Socialism's Uncertain Future." New Politics, vol. 9, Fall 1971.

Allende, Salvador. *Chile's Road to Socialism. New York: Penguin Books, 1973.

Ampuero, Raúl. *La izquierda en punto muerto. Santiago: Editorial Orbe, 1969.

Amunáteguy y Solar, Domingo. *La demoncracia en Chile: Teatro Político, 1810-1910. Santiago: Universidad de Chile, 1946.

Anderson, Jack. "The Chilean Caper, ITT and Watergate." The Washington Post, March 9, 1973, p. 18.

Andreas, Carol. "The Chilean Woman: Reform, Reaction, and Resistance." Latin American Perspectives, vol. 4, no. 4, Fall 1977.

Angell, Alan. *"Counter-Revolution in Chile." Current History, vol. 66, January 1974, pp. 6-9.

_____. "Chile One Year After the Coup." Current History, vol. 68, no. 401, January 1975, p. 13 and ff.

Aranda, Sergio, et al. *Chile, hoy. Santiago: Siglo Veintiuno Editores, 1970.

"Argentina's Example." Christian Science Monitor. vol. 76. December 16, 1983, p. 17.

Barrera, Manuel. Los partidos políticos chilenos: trayectoria y organización. Santiago: Universidad de Chile, 1966.

Barros Grez, Daniel. Pipiolos i pelucones; tradiciones de ahora cuarenta años. Santiago: Imprenta Franklin, 1876.

Bernstein, Dennis, and Connie Blitt. "Chile, Then and Now." Progressive, vol. 48. April 1984, p. 14.

Birns, Laurence. "The Death of Chile." New York Review of Books, vol. 20, no. 17, November 1, 1973, pp. 32-34.

"Bishops Oppose Censorship." Rocky Mountain News, June 25, 1983, p. 30.

Bizzarro, Salvatore. "Chile." In Encyclopedia of Developing Nations. New York: McGraw-Hill Book Company, 1982.

_____. "Chile Under the Jackboot." Current History, vol. 70, no. 413, February 1976, pp. 57-60, ff. 81.

_____. "Rigidity and Restraint in Chile." Current History, vol. 74, no. 434, February 1978, pp. 66-69, ff. 83.

_____. "The Struggle for Power in Chile." Leviathan, vol. 1, no. 4, April 1973, pp. 15-16.

Bizzarro, Salvatore, and Peter Blasenheim. "Collapse of Allende Regime Signifies Death of Democratic Rule in Chile." The Catalyst, vol. 5, no. 3, September 21, 1973, p. 1.

Blakemore, H. British Nitrates and Chilean Politics, 1886-1896. London: Athlone Press, 1974.

"Bomb Derails Subway in Chile, Injuring 22." The New York Times, April 30, 1984.

Bonilla, Frank, and Myron Glaser, eds. Student Politics in Chile. New York: Basic Books, 1970.

Bowers, Claude G. *Chile Through Embassy Windows 1936-1953. New York: Simon and Schuster, 1958.

Briones, Alvaro. "Chile: El dictador solitario." Le Monde Diplomatique (in Spanish), No. 62, February 1984.

Burnett, B. G. Political Groups in Chile. Austin: University of Texas Press, 1970.

Cáceres C., Leonardo. "La elección parlamentaria de marzo." Mensaje, Vol. XVIII, no. 177, March-April, 1969, pp. 68-70.

Carey, Barbara. "Chile: Popular Unrest Is Growing, but So Is Repression." Canadian Dimension, vol. 18, Mar. 84, p. 35.

Castro, Fidel. Fidel in Chile. New York: International Publishers, 1972.

Chaparro, P., and J. Prothro. "Public Opinion and the Movement of the Chilean Government to the Left 1952-1972." Journal of Politics, vol. 36, January 1974.

"Chile abre comercio con Cuba." El Mercurio (International Edition). Santiago: February 16-22, 1970, p. 1.

"Chile: Blaming It All on Pinochet--An Interview with General Leigh." Latin American Regional Reports (Southern Cone), RS-84-07, September 7, 1984, p. 2.

*"Chile: Blood on the Peaceful Road." Latin American Perspectives, vol. 1, no. 2, Summer 1974.

"Chile Imposes Curfew as Rallies Draw Near." The New York Times, March 27, 1984, p. 2, ff. 7.

"Chile: Mandate for Allende." Time, April 19, 1971, pp. 24-25.

"Chile: One Carrot, Many Sticks." Time, August 22, 1983, p. 38.

"Chile Plays Dumb in Assassination Probe." The Gazette Telegraph, March 13, 1978, p. 11.

"Chile Protestors Build Toward General Strike; Pinochet Scornful of Foes but Appears Unable to Deter Them Without Repressive Measures." Los Angeles Times, March 30, 1984, p. 5.

"Chile: Right-wing Hopes and Projects." Latin American Newsletter (Weekly Report), WR-84-07, February 17, 1984, p. 9.

"Chile: Scandal Surrounds the President." Latin America Newsletter (Weekly Report), WR-87-14, May 4, 1984, p. 3.

"Chile: Terror Under the Junta." Time, June 16, 1975, p. 14.

"Chile: The Last Best Hope." Look, New York, June 2, 1964, pp. 80ff.

"Chile: The Political Labyrinth." Latin America Review of Books, no. 1, 1973.

"Chilean Workers Call for More Democracy." The Denver Post, June 26, 1983, p. 15.

"Chileans Pressing for Democracy Open the Door to Rightists." The New York Times, April 15, 1984, p. 8.

Chonchól, Jacques, and Julio Silva. *El desarrollo de la nueva sociedad en América Latina. Santiago: Editorial Universitaria, S.A., 1969.

Clarke, Kate. Reality and Prospects of Popular Unity. New York: Lawrence and Wishart, 1973.

Cleaves, Peter. Bureaucratic Politics and Administration in Chile. Berkeley: University of California Press, 1974.

"Consecuencias políticas del paro de la CUT." El Mercurio (International Edition). Santiago, July 6-12, 1970, p. 5.

Constitución política de la República de Chile. Santiago: Editorial Nascimento, 1925.

"Constitución política y reglamento del senato." República de Chile. Santiago: Imprenta Universo, 1954.

Cooper, Marc. "Pinochet, Your Days Are Numbered." Mother Jones, vol. 9. January 1984, p. 28.

Cortés, Lía, and Jordi Fuentes. *Diccionario político de Chile (1810-1966). Santiago: Editorial Orbe, 1967.

Crummett, María de los Angeles. "El Poder Femenino: The Mobilization of Women against Socialism in Chile." Latin American Perspectives, vol. 4, no. 4, Fall 1977.

Cruz-Coke, Ricardo. Geografía electoral de Chile. Santiago: Editorial del Pacífico, 1952.

568 / BIBLIOGRAPHY

Debray, Regis. Conversación con Allende. Mexico City: Siglo XXI editores, 1971.

_____. The Chilean Revolution: Conversations with Allende. New York: Vintage, 1971.

De Onís, Juan. "Argentina's Trials Disturb Military Neighbors." Los Angeles Times, January 29, 1984, p. 3.

Diehl, Jackson. "Chile Puts Troops in Streets; 5 Killed in Renewed Protests." Washington Post, March 28, 1984, p. 16.

_____. "Chile's Pinochet Veers Between Crackdowns and Conciliation." Washington Post, April 13, 1984, p. 25.

_____. "Chile's Political Crisis Reaches a Stalemate." Washington Post, December 15, 1983, p. 1.

_____. "Pressure on Pinochet Said to Increase as 6 Die in Demonstrations in Chile." Washington Post, October 15, 1983, p. 19.

_____. "Renascent Communists Upset Pinochet but Also His Opponents." Washington Post, April 14, 1984, p. 19.

_____. "U.S. Stand on Liberalization Irks Chilean Regime." Washington Post, November 24, 1983, p. 38.

Donoso, Ricardo. *Alessandri, agitador y demoledor. 2 vols. Mexico: Fondo de Cultura Económica, 1954.

_____. Barros Arana, educador, historiador y hombre político. Santiago: Imprenta Universitaria, 1931.

_____. *Desarrollo político y social de Chile. Santiago: Imprenta Universitaria, 1942.

_____. *Historia de las ideas políticas en Chile. Mexico: Fondo de Cultura Económica, 1946.

Edwards Vives, Alberto, and Eduardo Frei Montalva. Historia de los partidos políticos chilenos. Santiago: Editorial del Pacifico, 1949.

*"El fraude de la 'nacionalización pactada.'" Punto Final, no. 83, July 15, 1969, pp. 8–9.

Evans, Les, ed. *Disaster in Chile: Allende's Strategy and Why it Failed. New York: Pathfinder Press, 1974.

"Evidence Growing on Torture in Chile." The New York Times, October 19, 1975, p. 3.

Feinberg, Richard E. The Triumph of Allende. New York: Mentor, 1972.

Foxley, Alejandro. "Algunas condiciones para una democratización estable: el caso de Chile." Estudios Cieplán, Corporación de Investigaciones Económicas para Latinoamérica, no. 9. Santiago de Chile, December 1982, pp. 139-69.

Francis, M., and H. Vera Godoy. "Chile: Christian Democracy to Marxism." Review of Politics, vol. 33, 1971.

Garreton M., Manuel Antonio. "Institucionalización y oposición en el régimen autoritario chileno." Washington, DC: Wilson Center Working Paper no. 59.

Gil, Federico. *The Political System of Chile. Boston: Houghton Mifflin, 1966.

Goldenberg, Mauricio. ¿Después de Frei, Quién? Santiago: Editorial Orbe, 1966.

Gómez, R. A. Government and Politics in Latin America. New York: Random House, 1964.

Goodsell, James Nelson. "Chile's Military Gives Civilians an Inch-- But They Want a Mile: Centrist Political Parties, Banding Together for Strength, Say Pinochet Liberalizations and 1990 Vote Are Not Enough." Christian Science Monitor, October 11, 1983, p. 16.

_____. "Feisty Chilean Tries to Hasten End of Junta; Back from Exile, Zaldivar Chips Rust off Civilian Politics." Christian Science Monitor, October 4, 1983, p. 16.

Guilesasti Tagle, Sergio. Partidos políticos chilenos. Santiago: Editorial Nascimento, 1964.

Halperin, E. *Nationalism and Communism in Chile. Cambridge, MA: M.I.T. Press, 1965.

Hanke, Lewis. Modern Latin America: Continent in Ferment. Princeton, NJ: Van Nostrand, 1959.

Hersh, Seymour M. The Price of Power (Kissinger, Nixon and Chile). New York: Summit Books, 1983.

Hispanic American Report. Stanford, CA: Stanford University Press, Vol. XVII, No. 6, August 1964.

_____. Vol. XVII, No. 7, September 1964.

_____. Vol. XVII, No. 8, October 1964.

_____. Vol. XVII, No. 9, November 1964.

Holden, D. "Allende and the Myth Makers." Encounter, January 1974.

Hormazábal, Manuel. Chile: una patria mutilada. Santiago: Editorial del Pacífico, 1969.

Horne, Alistair. Small Earthquake in Chile. New York: Macmillan, 1972.

IDOC. *Chile: The Allende Years, The Coup, Under the Junta. New York: International North American Edition, no. 58, December 1973.

————. *Chile: Under Military Rule. New York: International North American Edition, 1974.

Iglesias, Augusto. Alessandri, una etapa de la democracia en América. Santiago: Editorial Andrés Bello, 1960.

"Inscrita la candidatura presidencial de Allende." El Mercurio (International Edition). Santiago, February 9-15, 1970, p. 1.

"Interview: Rodolfo Seguel." Newsweek, August 15, 1983, p. 56.

"J. Chonchól propone un pacto revolucionario con partidos y organizaciones laborales." El Mercurio (International Edition). Santiago, September 29-October 5, 1969, p. 5.

Jobet, Julio. El socialismo chileno. Santiago: Prensa Latinoamericana, 1965.

*Johnson, Dale. *"Special Report: The Two Forces Battling for the Presidency Contrast Their Programs." South Pacific Mail. Santiago: September 3, 1964, pp. 10ff.

————, ed. *The Chilean Road to Socialism. California: Anchor Press, 1973.

Johnson, Tim. "Chile's Pinochet Keeps Firm Grip on Power, Despite Riots." Christian Science Monitor, September 11, 1984, p. 11, ff. 16.

Joxe, Alain. *Las fuerzas armadas en el sistema político de Chile. Santiago: Editorial Universitaria, 1970.

Kandell, Jonathan. "Chile's Military Chiefs Abolish Nation's Largest Labour Group." The New York Times, September 26, 1973, p. 7.

Kinzer, Stephen. "Again Allende's Name Brings Cheers in Chile." The New York Times, September 22, 1983, p. 8 ff.

Kirkwood, Julieta. "Women and Politics in Chile." International Social Science Journal, vol. 35. no. 4. Paris: 1983, pp. 625-37.

Labarca Goddard, Eduardo. Chile al rojo. Santiago: Impresora Horizonte, 1971.

"Law and Order in Chile." The New York Times Magazine, April 13, 1975, p. 83.

Lechner, Norbert. La democracia en Chile. Buenos Aires: Ediciones Signos, 1970.

Loveman, Brian. *Chile. New York: Oxford University Press, 1979.

Maira Aguirre, Luis. "De la chilenización a la nacionalización pactada." Mensaje, vol. XVIII, no. 181, August 1969, pp. 334-344.

Marcus, Elliot A. "Pinochet's Failure to Reunite Chile." The Christian Science Monitor, September 16, 1983, p. 22.

Martin, Everett G. "Chilean Center Loses Hope as Communist Threat Consolidates Anti-communists Around Pinochet." Wall Street Journal, October 11, 1983, p. 60.

_____. "Chilean Protests May Force a Loosening of Austerity Policies, Not Military Rule." Wall Street Journal, September 27, 1983, p. 30 ff., 39.

_____. "Democracy Spreads in South America." Wall Street Journal, p. 26 ff., 30.

Mattelart, Armand; Carmen Castillo; and Leonardo Castillo. La ideología de la dominación de una sociedad dependiente. Buenos Aires: Ediciones Signes, 1970.

Mejido, Manuel. Esto pasó en Chile. 4th edition. Mexico: Editorial Extemporáneos, 1981.

Merril, Andrea T., ed. *Chile: A Country Study. Area Handbook Series. Washington, DC: U.S. Government Printing Office, 1982.

Molina, Sergio. El proceso de cambio en Chile. Santiago: Editorial Universitaria, 1972.

Montalbano, William D. "Protest, Charges Trouble Chilean Leader." Los Angeles Times, May 12, 1984, p. 3.

Moreno, Francisco José. Legitimacy and Stability in Latin America: A Study of Chilean Political Culture. New York: New York University Press, 1969.

NACLA. Chile: The Story Behind the Coup. North American Congress on Latin America (Latin America and Empire Report), October 1973.

Nelson, Anne. "Chileans Relive a Dark Decade in a Struggle Toward Catharsis." Los Angeles Times, vol. 102. October 2, 1983, p. 2.

Nelson Goodsell, James. "Chilean Demonstrators Step Up Attack." The Christian Science Monitor, September 16, 1983, p. 3.

_____. "Chile's Top Diplomat Lambastes United States Press Reports on Human Rights." The Christian Science Monitor, September 19, 1983, p. 6.

_____. "Chile's Top Officers Push Reform in Bid to Save Military Rule." The Christian Science Monitor, September 12, 1983, p. 4.

_____. El Niño Behind Them, Chile's Fishermen Revel in Shrimp." The Christian Science Monitor, September 27, 1983, p. 2.

Núñez, Carlos. Chile: ¿La última opción electoral? Santiago: Ediciones Prensa Latinoamericana, 1970.

O'Brien, P., and J. Roddick. "Chile: Too Close for Comfort." Latin America Review of Books, no. 2, 1974.

O'Brien, Phillip, ed. *Allende's Chile. New York: Praeger, 1976.

Olavarría Bravo, Arturo. Chile bajo la democracia cristiana. 6 vols. Santiago: Editorial Nascimiento, 1965-70.

"Olvídense de elecciones y trabajen más." La Segunda, September 12, 1975, p. 3.

Palacios, Jorge. Chile: An Attempt at "Historic Compromise." The Real Story of the Allende Years. Chicago: Banner Press, 1979.

"Partidos de izquierda mantienen sus posiciones." El Mercurio (International Edition). Santiago: December 29, 1969-January 4, 1970, p. 1.

"Partidos de la 'Unidad Popular' dieron a conocer programa básico." El Mercurio (International Edition). Santiago: December 22-28, 1969, p. 4.

Paulsen, Fernando. "Chilean Cabinet Shakeup Signals Policy Changes." Wall Street Journal, April 3, 1984, p. 34ff, 36.

Petras, James. "Achievements of the Allende Government." New Politics, vol. 9, Fall 1971.

_____ . Politics and Social Forces in Chilean Development. Berkeley: University of California Press, 1969.

"Pinochet Declares War of Unemployment." The Mexico City News, August 18, 1983, p. 8.

"Pinochet Hints of Civilian Role in Chile Politics; But as Protests Continue, He Doesn't Put Forth Specific Changes in Constitution." Wall Street Journal, September 12, 1983, p. 33ff., 37.

"Pinochet Says Chile Regime Is a 'Developing Democracy.'" The New York Times, November 12, 1983, p. 4.

"PN reconocerá la primera mayoría." El Mercurio (International Edition). Santiago: August 24-30, 1970, p. 6.

"Quest for Pinochet Successor." Latin American Regional Reports (Southern Cone), RS-83-05, July 1, 1983, pp. 1-2.

"Rage and Repression in Santiago." Newsweek, August 22, 1983, p. 35.

Ramírez Necochea, Hernán. *Balmaceda y la contrarrevolución de 1891. Santiago: Editorial Universitaria, 1969.

_____ . *Historia del imperialismo en Chile. Berkeley: University of California Press, 1969.

_____ . Origen y formación del Partido Comunista de Chile. Santiago: Editoria Austral, 1965.

Ranstead, Donald D. "Chile Turns Left." Commonweal. New York: September 4, 1964, pp. 594-96.

Recabarren Serrano, Luis Emilio. Obras escogidas. Santiago: Editorial Recabarren, 1965.

Rodríguez Bravo, Joaquín. Balmaceda y el conflicto entre el congreso y el ejectutivo. Santiago: Imprenta Gutenberg, 1921.

Roett, Riordan. *"Democracy and Debt in South America." Foreign Affairs: America and the World, vol. 62, no. 3, 1984.

"Santiago's Mean Streets." Newsweek, September 19, 1983, pp. 57-58.

Schumacher, Edward. "Chile's Leader, Belittling Foes, Vows to Stay On." The New York Times, August 8, 1984, p. 1ff., 4.

_____ . "Claudio Arrau Returns to Chile Triumphantly." The New York Times, May 14, 1984, p. 20ff.

_____. "Wave of Bombings in Chile Spurs Fear of Radical Violence." The New York Times, May 20, 1984, p. 1.

Sergeyev, F. Chile, CIA, Big Business. Moscow: Progress Publishers, 1981.

Sethi, Patricia J. "Destiny Save Me the Job." Newsweek, March 19, 1984, p. 67.

Silvert, K. H. *Chile, Yesterday and Today. New York: Holt, Rinehart and Winston, 1965.

"Slaughterhouse in Santiago." Newsweek, October 8, 1973, p. 54.

Spooner, Mary Helen. "A New Season of Discontent." Macleans, April 9, 1984, p. 22.

Steenland, K. "Two Years of Popular Unity in Chile." New Left Review, no. 78, March–April 1973.

Stevenson, John Reese. The Chilean Popular Front. Philadelphia: University of Pennsylvania Press, 1942; London: Oxford University Press, 1942.

Talbot, David. "And Now They Are Doves (Robert McNamara, McGeorge Bundy, William Colby)." Mother Jones, May 1984, p. 26.

"The Andes: A Nationalist Surge." Time, July 26, 1971, p. 38.

"The Chilean Military Government Extends Its Emergency Powers." The Wall Street Journal, September 11, 1984, p. 1.

The Chilean Presidential Election of September 4, 1964. Washington, DC: Institute for the Comparative Study of Political Systems, 1965.

"Torture in Chile: Doctors Who Make Pain." Newsweek, August 1, 1983, p. 27.

Turner, Jorge. "La Izquierda en las elecciones chilenas." Sucesos para todos. Mexico City, April 18, 1970, pp. 20–23.

Urzúa, Valenzuela, Germán. Los partidos políticos chilenos. Santiago: Editorial Jurídica de Chile, 1968.

Valenzuela, Arturo. "Chile's Political Instability." Current History, vol. 83, no. 490, February 1984, pp. 68–72, ff. 88.

_____. "The Scope of the Chilean Party System." Comparative Politics, vol. 4, January 1972.

Valenzuela, Arturo and J. Samuel Valenzuela. Chile: Politics and Society. New Brunswick, NJ: Transaction Books, 1976.

_____. "Party Opposition Under the Chilean Authoritarian Regime." Working Papers no. 125, Latin American Program. Washington, DC: The Wilson Center, 1983.

Veliz, C. "The Chilean Experiment." Parliamentary Affairs, vol. 49, Summer 1971.

Vicuña Mackenna, Benjamín. La guerra del pacífico. Santiago: Editorial West, 1969.

Vitale, Luis. ¿Y después del 4, qué? Santiago: Prensa Latinoamericana, 1970.

White, Judy, ed. *Chile's Days of Terror. New York: Pathfinder Press, 1974.

Whitehead, L. "The Socialist Experiment in Chile." Parliamentary Affairs, vol. 25, Summer 1972.

"Why Chile's Secret Police Killed Orlando Letelier." The Village Voice, October 4, 1976, pp. 11-12.

Wingeate Pike, David. *Latin America in Nixon's Second Term. Paris: American College in Paris Publications, 1982.

Young, Peter. "Allende: A Special Kind of Marxist." Life, New York, July 16, 1971, pp. 38-40.

Zammit, J. Ann, ed. *The Chilean Road to Socialism. Institute of Development Studies. Brighton: University of Sussex, 1973.

Zeitlin, Maurice. "Chilean Revolution: The Bullet or the Ballot." Ramparts, April 1971.

_____. "The Social Determinant of Political Democracy in Chile," in James Petras and Maurice Zetlin, *Latin America: Reform or Revolution. New York: Fawcett World Library, 1968.

7. CHURCH

Alonso, Isidoro; Renato Poblete; and Ginés Garriso. La iglesia en Chile: estructuras eclesiásticas. Madrid: Espasa-Calpe, 1961.

Araneda Bravo, Fiedl. El Arzobispo Errázuriz y la evolución política y social de Chile. Santiago: Editorial Jurídica de Chile, 1956.

Barros Borgoño, Luis. La misión del vicario apostólico don Juan Muzi, notas para la historia de Chile. Santiago: Imprenta de "La Epoca," 1883.

"Cardinal Cautions About Socialism." Latinamerica Press, November 30, 1973.

Cassidy, Sheila. Audacity to Believe. Cleveland, OH: William Collins and World Publishing Co., 1978.

"Chile: Turbulent Priests Upset the Government." Latin America Regional Reports (Southern Cone), RS 82-04, March 9, 1984, pp. 6-7. Weekly.

"Christian Socialism Praised." Latinamerica Press, Lima, April 19, 1973.

Coleman, William J. Latin American Catholicism: A Self Evaluation. New York: Maryknoll Publications, 1958.

Comblin, Jose. "The Church's Ministry of Promoting Human Rights." Maryknoll, September 1976, pp. 3-8.

Considine, John J., ed. The Church in the New Latin America. Notre Dame, IN: University of Notre Dame Press, 1964.

Crawford, William R. A Century of Latin-American Thought. Cambridge, MA: Harvard University Press, 1961.

Diehl, Jackson. "A Tent City Puts Challenge to Pinochet; Squatters Seeking Land Are Aided by Church." Washington Post, November 20, 1983, p. 17.

Domínguez, Oscar. El campesinado chileno y la acción católica rural. Fribourg: FERES, 1961.

Donoso Loero, Teresa. Los Cristianos por el Socialismo en Chile. Santiago: Editorial Vaitea, 1973.

"Elogió Pinochet la visita del Papa a México porque impugnó a los métodos marxistas en América Latina." Santiago: Latinamerica Press, April 19, 1973.

Eyzaguirre, José Ignacio Victor. Historia eclesiástica, política, i literaria de Chile. Valparaíso: Comercio, 1850.

Flusche, Dela M. "City Councilmen and the Church in Seventeenth Century Chile." Records of the American Catholic Historical Records of Philadelphia, vol. 81, no. 3, 1970.

Frasca, Tim. National Catholic Reporter, vol. 30. March 30, 1984, p. 24.

Galilea, Segundo. "El Pueblo y el estado: cruz pastoral." Mensaje, April 1977, pp. 131-35.

Gheerbrant, Alain. The Rebel Church. Lonson: Penguin Books, 1974.

Krischke, Paulo J. The Church and Politics in Latin America. Toronto: Latin American Research Units Studies, 1977, pp. 62-92.

Lernoux, Penny. Cry of the People. Garden City, NY: Doubleday, 1980.

_____. "Latin America's Insurgent Church." The Nation, May 22, 1976, pp. 618-25.

Lernoux, Penny, and Mark Winiarski. "CIA Ordered to Survey Latin American Church." National Catholic Reporter, February 16, 1979.

McAfee Brown, Robert. "Reflections on 'Liberation Theology.'" Religion in Life, 1974.

Mecham, J. L. Church and State in Latin America. Chapel Hill: The University of North Carolina Press, 1966.

Pike, Frederick B. The Conflict between Church and State in Latin America. New York: Knopf, 1964.

Poblete, Renato. La iglesia en Chile. Fribourg: FERES, 1962.

Rashke, Richard. "Chile Connection: White House, Church, CIA." National Catholic Reporter, July 1977.

Read, William R.; Victor M. Monterroso; and Harmon A. Johnson. Latin American Church Growth. Grand Rapids, MI: Eerdmans, 1969.

Sanders, Thomas G., and Brian H. Smith. "The Chilean Catholic Church During the Allende and Pinochet Regimes." AUFS West Coast South American Series, no. 22, New York, 1975.

Scharper, Philip. "A Theology of Liberation." World Parish, January 1973.

Schmitt, Karl M. The Roman Catholic Church in Latin America. New York: Knopf, 1972.

Turner, Frederick C. Catholicism and Political Development in Latin America. Chapel Hill: University of North Carolina Press, 1971.

Woll, Allen L. *A Functional Past: The Uses of History in 19th Century Chile. Baton Rouge: Louisiana State University Press, 1982.

8. EDUCATION

Alfonso A., José. La Sociedad de instrucción primaria de Santiago de Chile. Santiago: Casa nacional del niño, 1937.

Alvarez, Oscar. "Aspectos sociológicos del problema educacional en Chile." Revista Mexicana de Sociología, vol. 20, no. 3, 1958.

Amunátegui, Miguel Luis. Estudios sobre instrucción pública. 3 vols. Santiago: Impresa Nacional, 1897-98.

Amunátegui, Miguel Luis, and Gregorio Victor Amunátegui. De la instrucción primaria en Chile, lo que es, lo que debería ser. Santiago: Imprenta de Ferrocarril, 1856.

Barrera, Manuel J. "Trayectoria del movimiento de reforma universitaria en Chile." Journal of Latin American Studies, no. 10, 1968.

Blitz, Rudolph C. "Some Observations on the Chilean Economic System and its Relation to Economic Growth." Education and Economic Development. Chicago: Aldine Publishing Co., 1965.

Campos Harriet, Fernando. 150 años de desarrollo educacional: 1810-1960. Santiago: Editorial Andrés Bello, 1960.

Cortés Pinto, Raúl. Bibliografía anotada de educación superior. Valparaíso: Universidad Técnica del estado Federico Santa María, 1967.

Gill, Clark C. Education and Social Change in Chile. Washington, DC: U.S. Government Printing Office, 1966.

Jaksic, Ivan. "Philosophy and University Reform at the University of Chile: 1842-1973." Latin American Research Review. vol. 29, no. 1, Albuquerque, NM, 1984, pp. 57-86.

Jobet, Julio César. Doctrina y praxis de los educadores representativos. Santiago: Editorial Andrés Bello, 1970.

Labarca Hubertson, Amanda. Historia de la enseñanza en Chile. Santiago: Impresa Universitaria, 1939.

Ministerio de Educación Pública. "Algunos antecedentes para el planteamiento integral de la educación chilena." Santiago: Chilean Government Printing, 1964.

_____. "Bases generales para el planteamiento de la educación chilena." Santiago: Chilean Government Printing, 1961.

_____. Sarmiento, Director de la escuela normal. Santiago: Imprenta Universitaria, 1942.

Stuardo Ortiz, Carlos. El Liceo de Chile. Santiago: Imprenta Universitaria, 1950.

Woll, Allen L. "For God and Country: Historical Textbooks and the Secularization of Chilean Society: 1840-1890." Journal of Latin American Studies, vol. 7, no. 1, May 1975, pp. 23-43.

Yaeger, Gertrude Matyoka. "Barros Arana, Vicuña Mackenna, Amunátegui: The Historian as National Educator." Journal of Inter-American Studies, no. 19, May 1977, pp. 173-200.

9. LITERATURE

Alegría, Fernando. Las fronteras del realismo. Santiago: Zig-Zag, 1962.

_____. Literatura chilena del siglo XX. Santiago: Zig-Zag, 1962.

_____. Walt Whitman en Hispanoamérica. Mexico: Colección Studium-5, 1954.

Alonso, Dámaso. Poesía y estilo de Pablo Neruda. Buenos Aires: Editorial Sudamericana, 1940.

Anderson Imbert, Enrique, and Eugenio Florit. Literatura hispanoamericana. New York: Holt, Rinehart and Winston, 1960.

Bizzarro, Salvatore. Pablo Neruda/All Poets the Poet. Metuchen, NJ: Scarecrow Press, 1979.

Blackwell, Alice Stone. Some Spanish American Poets. New York: Columbia University Press, 1929.

Dala, Doris, ed. Selected Poems of Gabriela Mistral. Translated by Doris Dana. Washington, DC: Johns Hopkins Press, 1971.

Delano, Luis Enrique, and Edmundo Palacios, eds. Antología de la poesía social de Chile. Santiago: Editora Austral, 1962.

Dölz Henry, Inés. Los romances tradicionales chilenos. Santiago: Editorial Nascimento, 1976.

Durán Cerda, Julio. Panorama del teatro chileno, 1842-1959. Santiago: Editorial del Pacífico, 1959.

Escudero, Alfonso M., O.S.A. Apuntes sobre el teatro en Chile. Santiago: Universidad Catolica de Chile, 1967.

_____. "Fuentes para el conocimiento de Neruda." Mapocho, vol. 2, no. 3, Santiago, 1964.

Gómez-Gil, Orlando. Historia crítica de la literatura hispano-americana. New York: Holt, Rinehart and Winston, 1968.

Henríquez Ureña, Pedro. Las corrientes literarias en Hispano-américa. Mexico: Fondo de Cultura Económica, 1949.

Hespelt, E. Herman, ed. An Introduction to Spanish American Literature. New York: Appleton, Century, Crofts, Inc., 1946.

Leal, Luis, and Frank Dauster. Literatura de Hispanoamérica. New York: Harcourt, Brace and World, 1970.

Loveluck, Juan, ed. El cuento chileno, 1864-1920. Buenos Aires: Editorial Universitaria, 1964.

Macías, Sergio, ed. Los poetas chilenos luchan contra el fascismo. Berlin, RDA: Comité Chile Antifascista, 1977.

Melfi, Domingo. Estudios de literatura chilena. Santiago: Editorial Nascimento, 1938.

Montes, Hugo, and Julio Orlandi. Historia de la literatura chilena. Santiago: Editorial del Pacífico, 1955.

Pierce, Frank, ed. Histories of Araucana (by Alonso de Ercilla y Zúñiga). Translated by George Carew. England: Manchester University Press, 1964.

Pinilla, Norberto. Panorama y significación del movimiento literario de 1842. Santiago: Universidad de Chile, 1942.

Rodríguez Monegal, Emir. Latin American Literature. 2 vols. New York: Alfred A. Knopf, 1977.

Rojas, Manuel. Historia breve de la literature chilena. Santiago: Editorial Zig-Zag, 1964.

Schwartzmann, Félix. El sentimiento de lo humano en América. Santiago: Universidad de Chile, 1953.

Silva Castro, Raúl. Antología de cuentistas chilenos. Santiago: Editorial Zig-Zag, 1957.

_____. Don Andrés Bello. Santiago: Andres Bello, 1965.

_____. El modernismo y otros ensayos literarios. Santiago: Editorial Nascimento, 1965.

_____. Eusebio Lillo, 1826-1910. Santiago: Andres Bello, 1964.

_____. "Lastarria, nuestro primer cuentista." Atenea, no. 90, 1948, pp. 20-26.

_____. Panorama literario de Chile. Santiago: Universidad de Chile, 1961.

_____. Prensa y periodismo en Chile, 1812-1956. Santiago: Universidad de Chile, 1958.

Torres Ríoseco, Arturo. Ensayo de bibliografía de la literatura chilena. Cambridge, MA: Harvard University Press, 1935.

_____. The Epic of Latin American Literature. Berkeley: The University of California Press, 1942.

Vega, Miguel Angel. Literatura chilena de la conquista y de la colonia. Santiago: Editorial Nascimento, 1954.

Vilches, Roberto. "Las revistas literarias chilenas del siglo XIX." Revista Chilena de Historia y Geografía, no. 91, 1942, pp. 325-355.

Zamudio, José. La novela histórica de Chile. Santiago: Ediciones Flor Nacional, 1949.

Travel Literature

Baxley, Henry Willis. What I Saw on the West Coast of South and North America. New York: D. Appleton, 1865.

Boyd, R. Nelson. Chile: Sketches of Chile and the Chileans, 1879-1880. London: W. H. Allen, 1881.

Brackenridge, Henry M. A Voyage to South America (1817-1818). 2 vols. Baltimore: John Toy, 1819.

Caldeleugh, Alexander. Travels in South America During the Year 1819, 1820, 1821. London: John Murray, 1825.

Carvallo y Goyeneche, Vicente. "Descripción histórico-geográfica del reino de Chile." Colección de Historiadores, no. 10, Santiago: Librería del Mercurio, 1879.

Cleveland, Richard J. A Narrative of Voyages and Commercial Enterprises. 2 vols. Cambridge, MA: Harvard University Press, 1842.

Cochrane Dundonald, Thomas. Narrative of Services in the Liberation of Chile, Peru and Brazil from Spanish and Portuguese Domination. 2 vols. London: John Ridgeway, 1859.

Darwin, Charles. The Voyage of the Beagle. Garden City, NY: Doubleday, 1962.

Findlay, George Alexander. A Directory for the Navigation of the South Pacific Ocean. London: R. H. Laurie, 1863.

Graham, Maria. Journal of a Residence in Chile During the Year of 1822. London: John Murray, 1824.

Haenke, Thaddeus Peregrinus. Descripción del reyno de Chile. Santiago: Editorial Nascimento, 1942.

Haigh, Samuel. Sketches of Buenos Ayres and Chile. London: J. Carpenter, 1829.

Hunter, Daniel J. [pseudonym used by Benjamín Vicuña Mackenna]. A Sketch of Chile. New York: S. Hallett, 1866.

Johnston, Samuel Burr. Cartas escritas durante una residencia de tres años en Chile. Translated by José Toribio Medina. Madrid: R. A. Curtis, 1917.

Lafond de Lurcy, Gabriel. Viaje a Chile. Santiago: Editorial Universitaria, 1970.

Merwin, Mrs. C. B. Three Years in Chile. New York: Follett and Foster, 1863.

Miers, John. Travels in Chile and La Plata. 2 vols. London: Craddock & Joy, 1826.

Ocaña, Fray Diego de. "Relación de viaje a Chile: año de 1600." Anales de la Universidad de Chile, no. 120, 1960.

Ruschenberger, William S. W. Three Years in the Pacific: 1831-1834. Philadelphia: Carey, Lea and Blanchard, 1834.

Russell, W. H. A Visit to Chile and the Nitrate Fields of Tarapaca. London: J. S. Virtue, 1890.

Sarmiento, Domingo F. Chile: descripciones-viajes-episodios-costumbres. Buenos Aires: Hurd & Houghton, 1961.

Schmidtmeyer, Peter. Travels into Chile over the Andes in the Years 1820-1821. London: Longman, Hurst, Reese, Horme, Brown and Green, 1824.

Stevenson, William Bennet. A Historical and Descriptive Narrative of Twenty Years Residence in South America. 3 vols. London: Hurst, Robinson, Edinburgh, Constable & Oliver and Boyd, 1825.

Sutcliffe, Thomas. Sixteen Years in Chile and Peru by the Retired Governor of Juan Fernández. London: Fisher, 1841.